Fatal Love

Fatal Love

Spousal Killers, Law, and Punishment in the Late Colonial Spanish Atlantic

Victor M. Uribe-Uran

STANFORD UNIVERSITY PRESS

STANFORD, CALIFORNIA

Stanford University Press
Stanford, California

Printed and bound by CPI Group (UK) Ltd, Croydon, CR0 4YY

Library of Congress Cataloging-in-Publication Data

Uribe-Uran, Victor, author.

Fatal love : spousal killers, law, and punishment in the late colonial Spanish Atlantic / Victor M. Uribe-Uran.

pages cm

Includes bibliographical references and index.

ISBN 978-0-8047-9463-3 (cloth : alk. paper) — ISBN 978-0-8047-9631-6 (electronic)

1. Uxoricide—Mexico—History. 2. Uxoricide—Spain—History. 3. Uxoricide—Colombia—History. 4. Mariticide—Mexico—History. 5. Mariticide—Spain—History. 6. Mariticide—Colombia—History. 7. Criminal justice, Administration of—Mexico—History. 8. Criminal justice, Administration of—Spain—History. 9. Criminal justice, Administration of—Colombia—History. I. Title.

HV6542.U75 2015

364.152'3—dc23

2015027412

Typeset by Newgen in 10/12 Sabon

This book is dedicated to Valerie, Ana Luna, Antonia, and Sebastian, hoping that one day they will live in a world where family violence is at last unacceptable.

Contents

Illustrations

MAPS

FIGURES

TABLES

Preface

> **Interviewer:** There are symbols in your poetry which recur, and they always take the form of the sea, of fish, of birds . . .
>
> **Neruda:** I don't believe in symbols. They are simply material things. The sea, fish, birds exist for me in a material way. I take them into account, as I have to take daylight into account. The fact that some themes stand out in my poetry—are always appearing—is a matter of material presence.
>
> **Interviewer:** What do the dove and guitar signify?
>
> **Neruda:** The dove signifies the dove and the guitar signifies a musical instrument called the guitar.
>
> —Pablo Neruda, "The Art of Poetry, No. 14."[1]

I believe in straightforward narratives where, much as in Neruda's poems, a dove is a dove and a guitar is a guitar.[2] I try to stay away from jargon and complex abstractions as much as I can. I also think that historians and social scientists should document profusely and, if at all possible, quantify the problems they address—even if only modestly, as is the case here. Abundant empirical information is something I treasure, as is providing a clear sense of how representative, if at all, the available evidence is of the larger universe to which it belongs. I could even be blamed for applying the larger share of my creative energy to documenting and analyzing more than to theorizing. For this reason, I spent several years amassing as large a data set as possible on spousal killings, gathered in archives and libraries in several countries (more than a dozen repositories in Spain alone, half a dozen in Mexico, three in Colombia, and a few in the United States). These records have allowed me to develop detailed case studies and tentatively measure a variety of similar (chronological, demographic, ethnic, gender, occupational, situational, material, motivational) categories or circumstances, cross-referencing particular information about each case with the rest for comparative purposes.

Indeed, comparative analysis is the second methodological principle for the development of this narrative. Comparison makes it possible to highlight possible cultural or context-specific idiosyncrasies (high rates of pardon for Indians in Mexico, elevated frequency of adulterous affairs in Spain, greater-than-expected participation of women in domestic crimes in Colombia) and commonalities, including the root causes of domestic tensions, the impact of alcohol, judicial procedures, the gathering and handling of evidence, sentencing, the administration of punishment, and pardons. Comparing two colonial societies (New Spain and New Granada) with each other and with their imperial core (Spain) allows us to see that, rather than a mosaic of eccentric regional realities, common social, legal, and judicial features characterized the Spanish Atlantic. In particular, a Spanish Atlantic common institutional frame and culture of criminal law, and ample access to justice, united the European and American portions of the Spanish empire in intriguing ways.

A third element present in this narrative is the multidimensional nature of social life and change. The examination of an extreme expression of domestic violence at a critical moment of political and legal transition (to independence, in the case of Mexico and Colombia, and to a constitutional monarchy, in the case of Spain) offers valuable glimpses into more than just the history of judicial and legal procedures and norms: It speaks to social and cultural patterns and changes as well. Gender, ethnic relations, and the culture of honor form a central aspect of the narrative. The behavior, motivations, cultural perceptions, and legal treatment of male and female criminals differed considerably. Similarly, Indians and blacks took an active part in the murders under study and received different judicial treatment than did whites. Furthermore, in Spain and elsewhere, many murders involved a particular understanding of the culture of honor. However, yet another key dimension of Atlantic legal culture and history surfaces as the story unfolds: the process of the de facto humanization (which others prefer to call "civilization") of Spanish Atlantic criminal law over the course of the eighteenth century but, actually, centuries earlier too. This may be one of the book's most valuable and unexpected findings overall, one taking shape precisely from intense documentation without preconceived models, in particular those positing that the most dramatic changes in history happen brusquely as a consequence of revolutions.

A developmental or long-term approach to historical change is therefore an additional emphasis of this book. It is common knowledge that the Enlightenment changed society's understanding of many aspects of political and social life, including the treatment of crime and punishment. Michel Foucault wrote one of the best-known studies of this transition, which posits that in France the punishment of bodies shifted to the punishment and disciplining of minds. A move away from visible, spectacular, and painful forms of execution and toward a preference for confinement was characteristic of this moment in time. The penitentiary, in particular, appears in Foucault's narrative as a point of rupture whereby the presence of royal power would no longer be experienced through sporadic displays of public pain but rather through less visible means of permanent vigilance and restrictions on freedom. The significance of the penitentiary project typical of that period was its ability to replicate itself elsewhere (especially in mental hospitals and schools) as time went on, to the point of becoming emblematic of the "normalization" characteristic of this version of modernity.[3]

Foucault's work has been the subject of criticism over time, thanks in particular to the outstanding research by Dutch historian Pieter Spierenburg. Spierenburg's detailed study of the history of executions in the Netherlands (especially Amsterdam), with additional comparative evidence from Germany, France, and England, reveals a more nuanced and empirically verifiable picture of the "rise to prominence, continued functioning and ultimate disappearance" of public executions in Europe.[4] Unlike Foucault's, Spierenburg's study is based on systematic evidence from archival sources, which revealed that the transition between systems of punishment was less clear-cut and swift than the French thinker believed. Instead, Spierenburg argues that the process was "developmental" and that the "infliction of pain and the public character of punishment" did not disappear overnight but "slowly retreated in a long, drawn-out process over several centuries."[5] Even though some forms of physical punishment, including mutilation, were on the decline as far back as the early seventeenth century, public executions continued until the 1860s. The panorama was definitely more complex than Foucault had assumed. Spierenburg went on to claim that changes in the mode of repression reflected changes in "sensibilities."[6] Following the work of Norbert Elias, the Dutch historian suggested a process of "conscience formation" made up of two elements: restraints on the infliction of injury and the transition of several aspects of life from the private to the public arena. An additional contributing factor was the process of state formation on a grand scale. The existence of a network of states sped rejection of public executions.[7]

This book's Atlantic narrative is consistent with Spierenburg's long-term developmental model. In spite of their belief that despicable crimes such as spousal murder deserved *vindicta pública* (public vengeance) and that their punishment should instill fear in the population, Spanish Atlantic state officials, the Catholic Church, and laypeople were clearly troubled by the suffering of criminals and convicts. Over time, in addition to royally sanctioned avenues toward reduced punishment (sanctuary, individual and collective pardons, sentence reductions), silent changes in practice limited pain as much as possible, making a veritable mockery out of a number of ancient judicial practices (torture, hanging, burning, mutilation, etc.). These changes were well under way even before liberal legislation (1808–1830s) did away with the old norms. While the Age of Revolution undeniably brought about constitutional and legal restrictions on punishment, along with due process requirements and other liberal restraints, at the local and regional levels many restrictions on inflicting pain were already in effect. They had become by accretion a normal component of humanized or civilized justice and punishment in the late colonial Spanish Atlantic. This trend went unnoticed in Francisco Tomás y Valiente's otherwise outstanding work on the criminal law of absolutist Spain.[8]

However, Tomás y Valiente did notice the significance of the passage from private revenge (*venganza privada*) to the monopolization of this right for the king (*ius puniendi*), underscoring the role of criminal law in the imposition of royal authority and preservation of the "social order." He also appreciated the fact that criminal law reflected the features of a hierarchical (*estamental*) and unequal society, a point addressed in this work as well.[9] Tomás y Valiente touched on a number of other critical issues discussed in the following pages (judicial torture, royal pardons, practical criminal law manuals, punishment), but he argued that the ultimate triumph of enlightened thought would occur only after the fall of the ancien régime ("*el triunfo de la razón tardó en producirse. En los problemas penales las reformas importantes, desde luego basadas en las ideas de la ilustración, se implantarían después de la caída del Antiguo Régimen.*").[10] Although reforms under Napoleonic rule and the Cortes of Cádiz officially did away with such harsh practices and penalties as judicial torture, flogging, dragging, hanging, and mutilation, the cases of spousal murder examined in this book reveal that the de facto humanization of criminal law began much earlier.

Map P.1. New Spain (colonial Mexico), eighteenth century

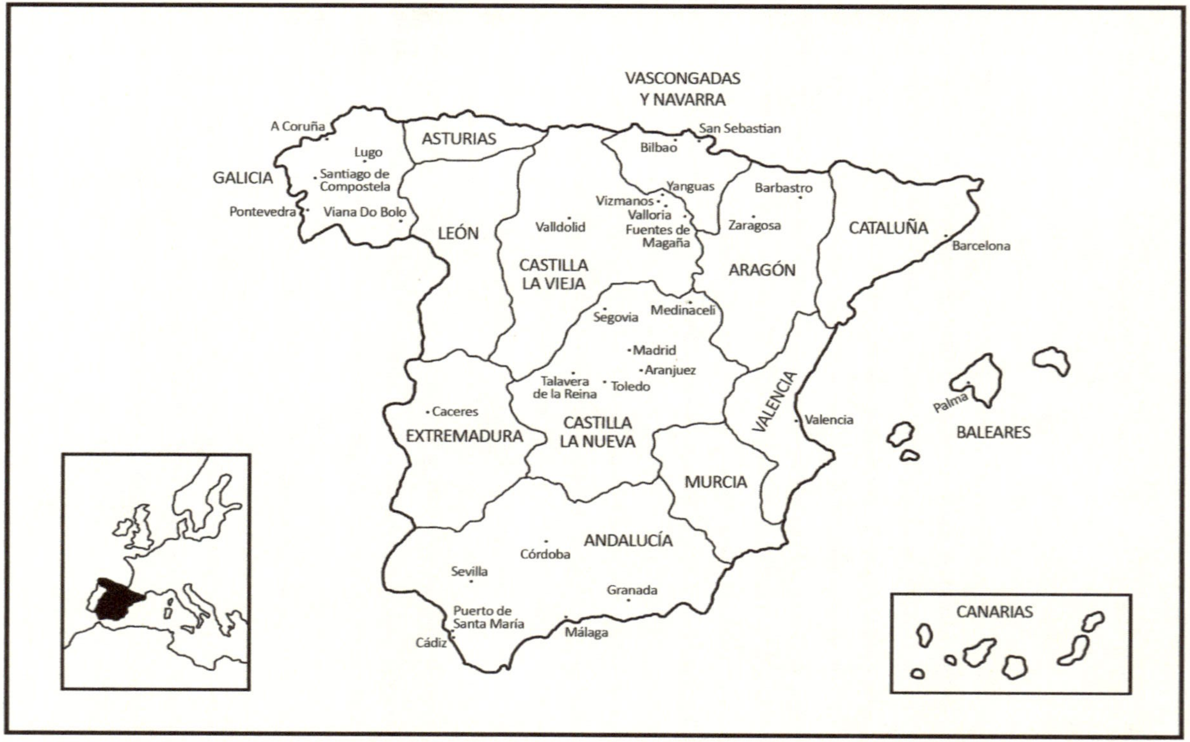

Map P.2. Spain, historical regions

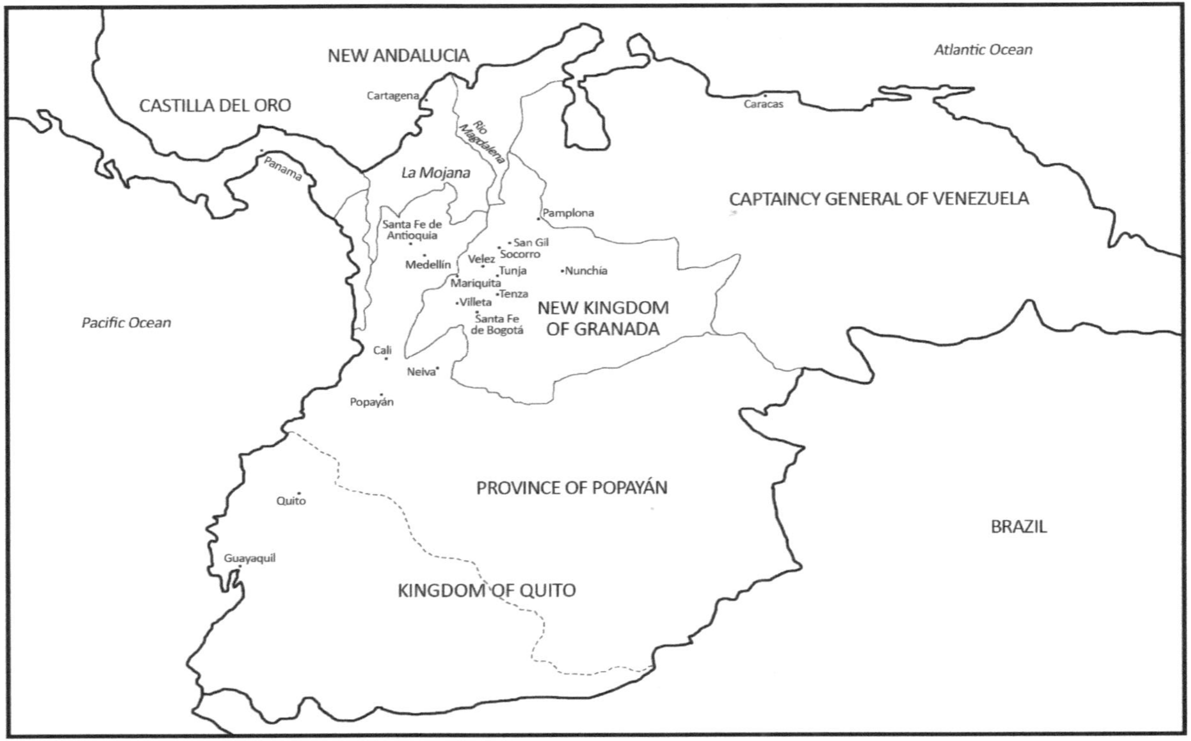

Map P.3. New Granada (colonial Colombia), eighteenth century

Acknowledgments

Because of various professional, logistical, and personal reasons, this book has taken many more years to write than I would have wished. In fact, I could have used even more time to finish it. Like most academic studies, this one could have continued to be polished ad infinitum, and undoubtedly there are many more meaningful things to be said about the more than 200 spousal killings it is based on and their social, cultural, and legal ramifications. However, it was finally time to wrap up; if it were not to turn into an unbearable professional or psychological burden, this project had to come to an end.

My main concern is that in the "rush" to finish and provide a historical interpretation conversant with current academic trends and debates I not neglect the human dimension. I would like to convey at least in part the deep human meaning and tragedy behind the dozens of spousal murder stories dealt with here, remote though they are in time. I especially do not want to overlook the terrible pain and sorrow that many of these eighteenth- and early nineteenth-century couples and individuals experienced as a result of the violence they inflicted on one another. Their family and personal lives were shattered when one of them died at the hands of the other or on the scaffold. Many other men and women lost their freedom, their property, their public dignity, or their right to live alongside their relatives, friends, and children.

I am lucky to have by my side a loving family, whose most immediate members are my dear sister Olga Lucia, my wife, Valerie, and my children, Ana Luna, Antonia, and Sebastian. I thank them for their company and care, without which I would not have managed to finish this book. The project has taken me away from them physically and psychologically more than I would have wished. I am grateful for their understanding and patience. Valerie has carried more of the family load than may be fair, exemplifying subtly and overtly the heavy burden that patriarchal relations can impose on modern wives, too. I apologize for it.

I would like to thank my colleagues in the Department of History at Florida International University, in particular Bianca Premo, Noble David Cook, Aurora Morcillo, Darden Pyron, and Mark Szuchman, and my colleague, friend, and fellow legal historian Matthew Mirow, from the FIU College of Law, for reading and critiquing some chapters. George Reid Andrews, Alexandra Parma Cook, Susan Kellogg, Tomás Mantecón, Jaime Rodriguez, and Pieter Spierenburg also provided valuable comments. Their suggestions and criticisms were truly inspiring, as were those of Professors Ann Twinam and Eric Van Young, who critiqued the manuscript line by line in a most judicious and helpful way. That I was stubborn enough not to always accept their suggestions could explain why this book is not much better than it is. I take full responsibility for this. I am grateful too for the research and publications of many historians, in particular Tommaso Astarita, Benoit Garnot, Tomás Mantecón, Pieter Spierenburg, and William Taylor, whose works are a hard act to follow and whose findings on spousal and other murders and related methodological lessons have served as beacons to my own research.

For their financial support, I thank the National Endowment for the Humanities and Florida International University's College of Arts and Sciences, under the wonderfully supportive Deans Kenneth Furton and Michael Heithaus. I also thank the College of Law's founding Dean Leonard Strickman and incumbent Dean Alex Acosta. Several cohorts of graduate students in the FIU doctoral program in Atlantic civilization pushed me to learn more about crime and punishment and the Atlantic itself, among whom Mary Antelo, Veronica Hale, Sven Kube, Micah Oelze, Roberto Pacheco, Angelo Santa Lucia, and Rene Silva merit particular mention. Over the years I also benefited from the research assistance of Alicia Florián, Orián Jiménez, Luis Alejandro Palacio, Martha L. Pinzón, Carolina Zumaglini, and, most recently, my dear cousin, Santiago Uribe Sánchez, a wandering and inspirational poet, always attentive to my many needs and requests. I acknowledge and thank my dear friends Alisa Newman and Elisabeth O'Kane-Lipartito for their valuable assistance with copy editing, insightful questions, and gentle but effective criticism. I also thank Pedro Botta and Vanessa Reyes for their help with maps and tables, respectively. I thank the numerous staffers of the various archives and libraries I visited over the years. It goes without saying that the mistakes and lapses of judgment that remain, in spite of all of this help, are mine and mine alone.

Excerpts of this book while it was in progress appeared chronologically in the following journals: "Colonial *Baracunatanas* and Their Nasty Men: Spousal Homicides and the Law in New Granada, 1750–1810," *Journal of Social History* 35.1 (2001): 43–72; "Innocent Infants or

Abusive Patriarchs? Spousal Homicides, the Punishment of Indians and the Law in Colonial Mexico, 1740s–1820s," *Journal of Latin American Studies* 38.4 (2006): 793–828; "'*Iglesia me llamo*': Church Asylum and the Law in Spain and Colonial Spanish America," *Comparative Studies in Society and History* 49.1 (2007): 446–472. I thank the editors and publishers of the above publications for their permission to reprint.

Introduction

In the distant mission outpost of San Antonio in northern Mexico, a man named Bentura, his brother, Primo, and Primo's lover, Eulalia, all Indian *neofitos* (persons newly baptized into the Catholic faith), plotted the murder of Eulalia's husband, Juan Californio. One night in December 1800, while the victim was sleeping, the men tied a rope around Juan's neck. One of them sat on his body while the other pulled on the rope and the woman, grabbing her husband by the legs, pulled in the opposite direction. After Juan suffocated, Eulalia ran to the mission and reported that her husband had choked while chewing tobacco. The mission's priests soon noticed that the death had not been an accident and reported the crime to the authorities in charge of the nearest *presidio*—a military station in remote frontier areas—in Monterrey.

Eulalia had complained to the mission priests that her husband was abusing her, but they seem to have concentrated instead on stopping her extramarital affair with Primo. Not long before the fatal incident, the priests had flogged her lover (*le dieron muchos azotes*) and cut off Eulalia's hair (*le tumbaron el pelo*). The two lovers seemed determined to be together. Because filing for divorce was a difficult bet that would not even allow them to be legally united, just in concubinage and subject to harassment from Church and civil officials, they saw that their only chance to become a couple was to get rid of Juan Californio.

With the criminal investigation in process, Eulalia promptly sought sanctuary (*asilo*) in the mission's church. After the trial, the two brothers were eventually sentenced to death and were publicly executed on December 31, 1801, making them among the few Indian defendants in our case sets who actually received the death penalty. Even rarer was that a firing squad rather than hanging or garroting was the means of execution. Thanks in part to the fact that she had been granted religious asylum, Eulalia's life was spared, and after consulting with the ecclesiastical authorities the court sentenced her to six years of correctional confinement in an institution (*recogimiento*) at an undetermined location.[1]

SIGNIFICANCE: GENDER VIOLENCE; ETHNIC RELATIONS; AND THE CULTURE OF HONOR, LAW, JUSTICE, AND CRIME

Given their intimate connection with individual longings (for companionship, love, and sex) and hurtful feelings and actions (jealousy, deception, betrayal, and violence), stories of spousal murder in the current study such as the one involving Eulalia and her companions have intrinsic human and literary fascination. They are full of drama and tragedy, featuring extramarital affairs; bossy, domineering, and absurdly abusive husbands; independent, outgoing, and challenging wives; men and women lying under judicial oath; bloody crime scenes and cunning attempts by culprits to hide corpses; daring escapes from jail; and highly symbolic punishments and pardons. The various tales of love gone wrong behind the hundreds of cases found in judicial archives in regions on both sides of the Atlantic (and elsewhere) can be morbidly intriguing and tragically entertaining, even colorful.[2] But there is more to them than amusement, theater, or tragedy.

For historians, spousal murders are significant for what they reveal about social and family history, in particular the hidden history of day-to-day gender relations, conflicts, crimes, and punishments. In some instances, such as Spanish American colonial societies, the records of murder trials also reveal a great deal about ethnic relations and understandings of "the other," especially the treatment of subaltern criminal subjects, individuals such as Juan, Eulalia, Bentura, and Primo. In those societies and also in metropolitan settings—in this case, Spain—stories of intimate homicides shed light on family history, gender roles, relations, and tensions while illuminating social hierarchies and the cultural values or worldviews (*mentalités*) allegedly guiding social behavior—in particular, overt royal and ecclesiastical paternalism, domestic patriarchy, and overall conceptions of honor.

The academic significance broadens when the research includes a focus on the legal and judicial dimensions of the crimes. The legal norms and doctrines concerning crimes associated with spouses and lovers (homicide, battery, adultery, concubinage, abandonment of one's family), criminal procedures (the phases and mechanics of criminal investigations and trials), legal justifications for and the mechanics of detaining defendants and confiscating their assets, legal understandings of what constituted sufficient evidence of criminal wrongdoing, and—most important—reasons for and varieties of acquittal, pardon, or punishment all speak directly to issues of justice. These considerations reflect conceptions about and the practical operation of justice in particular societies, in our case those under Spain's old aristocratic and absolutist monarchical order (*ancien régime*), where its administration was one of the king's basic attributes and functions, and a key source of royal legitimacy.[3] Law and justice were also central to the development of royal hegemony or, in other words, social control largely dependent upon voluntary compliance.[4] Let us briefly examine some of these aspects of family life, gender, ethnicity, culture, justice, and law, and their relationship to spousal violence and crime.

Family, Marriage, and Violence

This book examines the phenomenon of spousal murder, a crime known at the time as "parricide," a broader category involving not just spouses but also parents and other relatives.[5] It focuses on the late colonial Spanish Atlantic.[6] Addressed in it are incidents occurring in New Spain (colonial Mexico), New Granada (colonial Colombia), and Spain from the 1740s to the 1820s. Besides providing snapshots of several specific cases, the book also looks at broader trends evident in the more than 200 cases consulted. It considers not only the social features of the murders, but also the legal discourses and judicial practices guiding the historical treatment of spousal murders. As noted above, subtexts involving gender, ethnicity, and honor underlay the ways in which the law punished and prosecuted intimate aggressions.

Looking at intimate aggression allows one to explore a critical dimension of family history. As Lawrence Stone explained years ago, along with family studies focusing on demographic aspects (age at marriage, nuptiality patterns, fertility) and on the size and composition of households, studies of human relationships (sentiments, affect, mutual expectations, attitudes toward sexuality, morality, honor and shame, choice of marriage partners, marital unhappiness, illicit love, betrayal, breakdowns) are essential for a fuller historical understanding of marriage and the family.[7] This had already been made obvious, or would soon be confirmed, by the fine works of a host of French, American, and Latin American historians, including authors such as Philippe Ariés, Georges Duby, Jean Louis Flandrin, François Lebrun, Silvia Arrom, Richard Boyer, Ramón Gutiérrez, Asunción Lavrín, Patricia Seed, Susan Socolow, Ann Twinam, Carmen Castañeda, Guiomar Dueñas, Pilar Gonzalbo Aizpuru, Maria Emma Mannarelli, María Beatriz Nizza da Silva, Sergio Ortega, Pablo Rodríguez, and Ronaldo Vainfas.[8]

The Latin Americanists, in particular, addressed not only the fact that, as numerous incidents of adultery examined in this work confirm, colonial sexuality expressed itself widely through channels other than marriage, but also that marriages at the time were quite different from modern ones. They were not just highly ritualistic religious sacraments and virtually unbreakable legal bonds but also complex economic, social, and cultural pacts. Although the subject has resulted in heated historiographical debate, it is fair to say that in colonial times marriage was not the result of extensive and free courtships, nor was it generally informed primarily by sexual attraction or personal emotions, including affection or romantic love. It corresponded instead to institutional considerations, both religious and secular, of the most appropriate ways to ensure social/sexual order and control, and to familial, parental, or personal considerations of the social or economic value of a specific spouse.

The value placed on one's spouse was not mainly, if at all, to ensure fulfilling and supportive intimate relations within marriage, but rather to promote familial or personal interests through one or a combination of factors, including access to honorable and socially acceptable mates, convenient partnerships between already-formed families, avenues for upward economic and/or social mobility, attractive dowries, and community harmony, continuity, and stability. After marriage, domestic life could sooner or later become tedious, emotionally and sexually unfulfilling, and generally unbearable. As we shall learn, this is why many spousal disputes could occur over even trivial matters. Of course, a number of other factors (drinking, child rearing, material stress, jealousy, misunderstandings over rights and obligations) also intervened to trigger aggressions, even extreme ones.

Even if by some standards murder may have been rare in the late colonial Spanish Atlantic, spousal murder was not that unusual within the world of homicide. Hundreds of people stood trial for spousal murder in this region during this period. The prosecution of their crimes offers a unique vantage point for understanding the intersection between, on the one hand, cultural practices such as patriarchal authority, honor, and ethnicity and, on the other, the functioning of the Crown, the Church, the law, and justice.[9]

Public Women: The Long and Conflictive History of Gender

As shall soon become clear, in the Spanish American world—from the colonial period to the present—women have been the regular victims of physical, psychological, and sexual abuse by intimate partners. In turn, women have not infrequently inflicted violence on their intimate partners.

Spousal murder, the ultimate form of domestic violence regardless of gender, thus sheds light on the mutual character of domestic aggression and the dynamic and multilayered background and escalation of day-to-day gender disputes and tensions.

Based on past and present records, and in light of the academic research this book builds on, it seems safe to argue that spousal murders are not random and deviant outbursts of aggression but rather systematic gender disputes over autonomy and obedience, deference, sex, money, domestic chores, relations with children and relatives, a mate's drinking, and general clashes over men's and women's understandings of reciprocal marital rights and duties.[10] The triggering factors have typically included gender-based conflicts derived from alleged disobedience on the part of women; their response to verbal attacks by male partners; failure to prepare and serve meals correctly or punctually; alleged dereliction of household or child care duties; impertinent questions or comments about drinking, money, or relations with other women; unjustified absence from the domestic space; refusal to have sexual intercourse; and suspicions or actual instances of infidelity. Men and women alike also lashed out physically against one another for the freedom to leave the marriage and be with a lover instead.[11] All of these factors have most definitely operated in a socially built misogynist and patriarchal milieu. However, patriarchy did not mean that women lacked any rights, were under absolute subordination, were unable to physically or legally defend themselves, or were not actually the primary attackers.

Women as well as men were the perpetrators of domestic violence, even spousal murder. In New Spain and New Granada, women were three to five times more likely to kill their husbands than to murder anyone else. The research for this book even suggests that women rather than men committed most murders in Spain related to extramarital affairs. On many occasions, these acts were not in self-defense. Motives ranged from a response to male aggression against the female perpetrator or other members of the household to a wife's desire to leave her husband for a lover. As was the case with men, a variety of random circumstances, including drinking and accidents, also contributed. More important, counter to what previous works have argued, and in line with copious findings by other historians, this study finds that spousal murders committed by women cannot be explained by women's supposed confinement to the domestic sphere (within which they were thus allegedly compelled to choose their victims).[12] This book will confirm that, if anything, significant numbers of women who killed their husbands did so precisely because of extra-domestic behavior and public encounters. It therefore joins the historiography that has extensively documented female participation in the Spanish and Spanish American public realm.

As recent works have demonstrated, in their daily lives women came into regular contact with outsiders, broke away from the isolation imposed on them by their domestic duties, and became active participants in all kinds of public activities and affairs.[13] Although patriarchs generally ruled the household, ordinary women, whether single, married, or widowed, participated in a range of economic activities, from textile manufacturing and raising and selling livestock, fruit, and vegetables to domestic service, cooking, laundering, street vending, food and beverage preparation, and peddling, to mention but a few.[14] These activities, along with regular attendance at church, parties (*fandangos*), and visits to the homes of neighbors and relatives, plus a number of other late eighteenth-century celebrations and leisure activities (festivals, comedies and theater, traveling, bullfights), afforded women the opportunity to engage in social (and sexual) exchanges.

Public engagements tended to annoy husbands and put a strain on marriages. The situation was even more frequent in humble rather than elite households, given poor women's dependence on the income derived from extra-domestic chores. Culturally, these women's virtue was not as tied to seclusion as was that of women from influential families. This does not mean that women from elite families did not engage in activities outside the household or attack their husbands. Still, we ought to keep in mind that the largest portion of metropolitan and colonial society (perhaps more than 80 percent) comprised low-income groups, which consequently committed the majority of the crimes under consideration. In Spanish America, these sectors predominantly consisted of people of color.

Ethnic Relations: Colonial Paternalism Versus Domestic Patriarchy

Many clashes between men and women involved nonwhite couples and individuals living in a colonial context where the color of their skin may have represented a social and legal disadvantage. In addition to providing a look into gender relations and tensions, the study of spousal murders is also helpful for making sense of ethnic relations and conflicts in a colonial society. When royal legislation and justice officials handled homicide cases committed by Indians, blacks, and *castas* (mestizos, mulattoes, and other half-bloods), their actions reflected cultural values and biases, as well as tensions between the dominant white sectors ruling the Spanish empire and ethnic "others." Specifically, they embodied the latent contradiction between royal "clemency" and "terror": the tension between the king's paternalism toward subjects considered socially and culturally inferior or weak, and the need for royal justice to respond appropriately to abhorrent domestic crimes (while at the same time upholding "natural" patriarchal rights and privileges).[15]

Some scholars have argued that the monarch had to administer justice without weakening the patriarchal prerogatives accruing to the male heads of households in his realm, whatever their ethnicity, including the right to discipline wives, a legally and socially sanctioned privilege of marriage.[16] The solution was for the king to show leniency. This is why, in these scholars' opinion, such a considerable gap existed between written law (e.g., the death penalty for those who committed atrocious murders) and actual practice (in particular, the great leniency the law showed toward Indians, regarded as "miserable" subjects in need of special legal protection).[17]

This work argues instead that royal paternalism and a subaltern husband's patriarchy were complementary. This was true not because of the leniency typical of Spanish law in general and the law of the Indies (*derecho indiano*) in particular, which made it possible for the king to dispense justice while upholding the patriarchal prerogatives of nonwhites; in fact, the leniency shown toward Indian patriarchs and others stemmed from long-standing doctrines and practices in Western law and jurisprudence that did not necessarily reflect gender or ethnic biases but instead obeyed religious and charitable concern for a variety of defenseless peoples (*miserabiles personae*). In practice, enforcement of the law did not always favor the victims of crime, whether female, Indian, or otherwise; sometimes, it just favored the "weak" or criminals in general. Furthermore, many of the crimes accorded such leniency were not, as has been alleged, actions committed to safeguard values sacred to the dominant culture. This was the case, for instance, of crimes linked to a defense of honor.

Honor: A Dominant Cultural Value?

For decades, and perhaps longer, historical and cultural texts have presented honor (*honra,* in early modern Spain) as a dominant value of Spanish and, more generally, Mediterranean culture.[18] By extension, the Spanish colonies and other premodern societies fit a similar mold.[19] The reputations of families and individuals—in other words, the respect they enjoyed in the eyes of the larger community and the monarchy—were a function of both social condition (legitimate birth, white blood, distinguished social rank, and Old Catholic religious background) and honorable/virtuous behavior. The standards for such behavior varied according to gender. Society expected women to observe chastity and sexual virtue, values that were generally associated with or accompanied seclusion, the preservation of virginity, and public decorum.[20] For men, honorable behavior was tied to public service, the ability to command others, strict control over their households, bravery, and manliness in general.[21] Therefore, males betrayed by their spouses were expected to take justice into their own hands. After all, they had legal authority to kill the adulteress and her lover to prevent further damage to the husband's honor.[22]

Many of the cases under examination here break significantly with the pattern of the betrayed husband/spousal killer portrayed in honor-centered stories and narratives from the time of Golden Age Spanish comedies onward.[23] In many of the incidents involving adulteresses, in fact, particularly in Spain, the women were the culprits rather than the victims. Cuckolded husbands were not necessarily prominent among spousal murderers, and these criminals did not seem to be particularly concerned with rarefied notions of honor. If anything, the opposite was true. How the law—and the many litigants and judicial actors who contributed to forge the law—dealt with such crimes shall be of interest to readers, for in many of the cases the legal practices, discourses, and outcomes were most peculiar.

Bringing Back In the History of Law and Justice

Legal and judicial discourses on such matters as a king's prerogative to forgive his subjects, a husband's right to "correct" his wife, or a criminal's right not to suffer any bodily pain if given sanctuary at a Catholic church, assisted in structuring particular "worlds" (colonial, patriarchal, and Catholic, for instance).[24] These discourses played an essential role in sociopolitical relations and were central to the exertion of political power and the implementation of social domination and control—understood here both at the macro (state) and micro (familial) levels.[25] They were also critical to the historical repression of social deviance.

Many scholars now agree that the law was and is multidimensional and contested, and that it was far from being historically irrelevant in Spain and Spanish America. Therefore, studying the legal doctrines and practices of the time is a valuable approach to understanding ideologies, values, cultures, attitudes, social mores, and day-to-day social exchanges.[26] Consensus on this point is relatively recent, however, and some disagreement remains regarding various historical features of law and justice.

The older generation of studies focusing on the law and justice of Spain and colonial Spanish America, including works by such authors as Rafael Altamira, José María Ots Capdequí, Alfonso García Gallo, Ricardo Levene, and Silvio Zavala, understood the law to be mainly the doctrines and institutions that developed from royal statutes compiled at various times (e.g., the thirteenth-century *Siete Partidas,* the *Ordenamiento de Alcalá* [1348], the *Leyes del Toro* [1505], the *Leyes Nuevas* [1542], the *Nueva Recopilación de Castilla* [1567], the *Recopilación de Indias* [1681], and the *Novisima Recopilación* [1805]). Insightful works by those scholars generally paid greater attention to state-produced formal legal texts and institutions than to practices and implementation.[27] More-innovative scholars, in particular Portuguese jurist and historian Antonio Manuel Hespanha, focused instead on the discursive dimensions of the law and the significance of long-standing "textual traditions" that contributed to forge "canonical" truths with impact on daily life.[28] For him, as for us, the law matters not as an abstract institution but as a tight, living web of discourses that are part of and shape social reality.

Later generations of historians became more attentive to the social and economic structures, interests, and conflicts behind juridical texts, principles, and actions. Some, including Fernando de Trazegnies, Herman L. Bennett, Susan Kellogg, Sergio Serulnikov, Steve Stern, and Malick Ghachem, proposed an instrumental view of the law as a tool or a "space" molded or taken advantage of by different social groups—dominant and subaltern alike—intent on promoting particular interests and agendas. They understood the law to be an arena of conflict, acculturation, and accommodation characterized by zero-sum confrontations and eventual winners and losers.[29] Some, Ann Twinam and Tanja Christiansen included, even held that justice mattered more than the law and reflected the relative strength or weakness (social and rhetorical) of those presenting disputes before magistrates.[30]

Other historians, among them Woodrow Borah, Charles R. Cutter, and, more recently, Brian P. Owensby, looked at the law as an intrinsically benevolent mechanism for attaining justice and the protection of subaltern groups, especially Indian communities, which actively engaged it.[31] While noting its centrality for colonial rule, Bianca Premo also highlighted the protectionist nature of law in some areas of family relations.[32] At least one among this younger generation of scholars, Tamar Herzog, has proposed the revisionist idea that the law did not exist in abstract but only at the moment of its application, making it one and the same as justice. In this view, justice was, in turn, not a top-down command but instead a communal or collective enterprise based much more on social and theological rules and interests than on civil legal norms or principles.[33]

This work adopts an eclectic perspective, embracing discrete aspects of several of these various streams of thought, none of which is generally exclusive of the other. As older generations of legal historians claimed, laws, formal though they were, mattered, even in the abstract, for they acted as means for the organization of colonial institutions and administrative routines and served as sources of royal legitimacy. As Premo has put it, Spanish colonialism was highly legalistic.[34] Laws provided state officials and the community points of reference concerning appropriate behavior and procedure, whether or not they were actually observed. I also endorse the views of scholars who have gone so far to regard laws not just as important texts or discourses, but also as "realities" and "social facts" with "a life and an evolutionary logic of their own."[35] In this view, written laws are social realities and day-to-day conceptual forces that help to further shape other social and cultural relations. However, many rules for organization, behavior, and procedure were not written but customary.[36] In addition, they were not pure "legal" texts, if such a thing has ever existed, but were instead, as Herzog holds, a blend of theological and social rules and everyday vernacular meanings.[37] This does not mean that they lacked any separate existence or significance aside from justice, just that the ultimate meaning ascribed to them in judicial cases, and the particular manner of their application, was not apparent, univocal, or undisputed.

As Christiansen, De Trazegnies, Ghachem, Hespanha, Kellogg, Premo, Stern, Serulnikov, Twinam, and others claim, laws were subject to contestation, for the law is a social discourse or grammar in need of interpretation and susceptible, perhaps more clearly and legitimately than any other discourse, to rhetorical arguments and counterarguments, claims, and counterclaims. That the disputes were sometimes resolved in favor of, say, members of indigenous communities was at least in part a result of the fact that, as Borah, Cutter, and Owensby argue, legal texts and justice officials may have been inclined to paternalism and the protection of indigenous communities in response to the emphasis in Roman and canon law on sheltering needy people (*miserabiles personae*). This is not meant to detract from the agency of the natives who learned how to use the legal system and did so regularly and effectively, sometimes combined with physical threats.[38] As Serulnikov notes, the courts sometimes found in favor of indigenous people to avoid the threat of communal violence.[39]

At other times, too, outcomes favorable to particular social groups or individuals resulted from ethical, religious, pseudoscientific, or "jurisprudential" views, even ones derived from long-standing canon law principles whose significance was established decades ago in the remarkable work of Harold Berman.[40] However inconsistent, they owed their existence to doctrinal views on a variety of issues, from the nature of evidence to the understanding of causal relations between human actions and death. Of course, outcomes could be the direct result of the words and actions of the various participants, for, as Owensby demonstrates insightfully, the law was a "complex, open-ended interplay between recognized legal principles and the words and actions of all who took part in legal proceedings." "Legal meaning" was thus not solely about written laws or communal understandings, but was also at least in part the result of the interaction of "complainants, witnesses, advocates, interpreters, notaries and judges."[41]

In sum, laws, legal texts, principles, traditions, doctrines, particular conceptions of justice, and judicial procedures were factors in the way that familial relations unfolded and also shaped the way that litigants and authorities addressed domestic violence in both the colonies and the metropolis during the period of this study. Patriarchal customs, ethnic hierarchies, colonial interests, and other dominant cultural values informed and infused these factors, but they cannot by themselves account for the dynamics of family life or the judicial system's handling of battery and spousal murder. To make better sense of gender, ethnic, and other social relations and conflicts linked to spousal murders, we must bring legal history back in alongside historical sociology and social history.

Therefore, this book discusses gender, familial, ethnic, and cultural relations and practices as well as the meaning of law, legal culture, and royal justice in shaping daily life and responding to crime. It relies not only on actual criminal records but also on an array of legal texts and manuals that were widely referred to by litigants (for an example, see Figure I.1) and sometimes cited by contemporary justice officials. Through both practical instructions for litigants, justice officials, and the public in general, and the forging of routine, such manuals eased access to justice and undoubtedly assisted the Spanish monarchy in establishing colonial control ("hegemony") in its realm, both at home and overseas. This book also looks at the legal doctrines, customs, and traditions embedded in judicial procedures that appear to have been more or less standardized with the support of ancient, medieval, and more-recent texts and practical manuals that helped legitimate recourse to justice and legal mechanisms, creating "a certain habit (*habitus*) toward obedience."[42]

Beyond the gender, ethnic, economic, and cultural biases that it represented and enforced, the law, along with the complex set of principles and practices incorporated in it over time, constituted a creative, living, and relatively autonomous force.[43] This can be appreciated in the late colonial period probably more clearly than ever before. At that time, canon law had turned marriage into a routine ("natural") affair. Also, perhaps

PROSPERI
FARINACII
IVRISCONSVLTI
ROMANI,

OLIM IN VRBE CAVSARVM CRIMINALIVM FAMOSISSIMI Aduocati, postmodum in eadem Vrbe in Tribunali Illustrissimi Domini Auditoris Cameræ in Criminalibus semel atque iterum Locumtenentis; deinceps verò tempore Clementis Octaui Pontificis Maximi in sacra eius Consulta integerrimi Consultoris; & nunc Sanctissimi Domini nostri Pauli Papæ Quinti, & eius Cameræ Apostolicæ Procuratoris fiscalis generalis, &c.

PRAXIS, ET THEORICÆ
CRIMINALIS,
Pars Tertia,

De { Reo confesso, & conuicto. / Pœnis temperandis. }
De { Varijs & diuersis quæstionibus. / Varijs ac diuersis criminibus. }

[illegible] in ea tractatarum versa pagina exhibet.

Pluribus eiusdem Auctoris Additionibus, quæ in prima editione non aderant, his notis [ ] in textu, hac verò † in margine indicatis, illustrata.

[illegible] principalium quæstionum, sed etiam [illegible] locupletissimo.

LVGDVNI,
Sumptibus Horatij Cardon.
[illegible]

Figure I.1. *Prosperi Farinacii,* Praxis, et Theoricae Criminales *(Lugduni: Sumptibus Iacobi Cardon & Petri Cauellat, 1621 [1612]).*

by virtue of "repetition" over centuries and the rise of practical manuals (*prácticas criminales*), local justice officials and appeals courts alike appear to have agreed on basic mechanisms that royal law prescribed to address spousal conflicts and investigate related criminal behavior, secure the defendants and their property, push forward criminal proceedings, interrogate witnesses, evaluate evidence, confer pardons, grant special protections, and apply penalties.

By the close of the eighteenth century, marriage and criminal trials both in the metropolis and overseas followed a well-established "routine" and were virtually "formulaic," adhering to "centuries-old standards of Spanish judicial procedure."[44] While far from completely systematic, rational, or always consistent, judicial procedure and the law, written and customary, were nevertheless an actual force and a vivid reality at the social level. In the process of its application, different social segments struggled (by legitimate and illegitimate means) to shape or mold them to their respective advantage. Justice was the end product.

After the consolidation of the Spanish monarchy in the fifteenth century, royal justice became a critical manifestation of the monarch's presence among even his most distant and humble subjects. Apart perhaps from tax collection and military functions, the main day-to-day manifestation of royal power was the handling and adjudication of judicial disputes throughout the realm. This role gained further importance given the litigious nature of metropolitan and colonial society.[45] Litigation over all sorts of material and cultural interests was common from early on in the colonial period. Individuals and communities from every social background, from glamorous noble families to ragged Indians and blacks, *pardos,* and mulattos, went to court to contest land ownership and boundaries; property claims; civil, commercial, and ecclesiastical contracts (including marriage); bureaucratic and ecclesiastical appointments; labor rights; autonomy and freedom; and many other issues.[46] The adjudication of these disputes, for better or worse, was an expression of the king's (and the Church's) power and, more important, embodied the monarch's (and God's) paternal concern for the happiness, peace, and stability of his realm, not to mention decency, morality, and other Catholic standards. This included not only civil and ecclesiastical litigation, but also judicial punishment of crime.

Crime in the Late Colonial Spanish Atlantic

A good portion of the judicial cases before the monarchy's local justice officials and appeals courts concerned a wide assortment of crimes, mainly assaults against property, life, physical and sexual integrity, public order, royal finances, and individual honor.[47] Homicides were, of course, one of the most serious of these violations. The subject has received little study in Spain, however,[48] and even in colonial Spanish America, few works have followed the pioneering volume written three decades ago by William B. Taylor (one of these an important essay by Taylor himself).[49] Even fewer studies address crimes with gender, ethnic, and cultural implications, such as the spousal murders examined here.[50] Several related aspects remain unclear as well. For instance, the question of whether late colonial Spanish Atlantic society was more murderous than other parts of the world in this or other eras is difficult to answer with a definitive "yes" or "no." Complex answers to this query unfold throughout this and other chapters.

As recent works on New Spain, New Granada, Ecuador, Brazil, Peru, and the Río de la Plata region make clear, crime was a serious problem in late colonial Spanish America.[51] Available statistics do not allow us to assess accurately the social and economic impact of crime, but they do show that colonial officials and courts regularly heard cases of homicide, assault and battery, robbery, rape, adultery and concubinage, incest, infanticide, sodomy, prostitution, slander, and a host of offenses against "order and tranquility." Tentative data presented throughout this study suggest that a majority of these crimes, probably one-quarter to one-third of the total, were property-related offenses, muggings and thefts in particular. Another one-quarter to one-third were violent crimes, including cases of homicide and bodily injury. From one-quarter to one-fifth were family- and sex-related offenses, including adultery, incest, concubinage, *estupro* (sex extracted under the promise of marriage), and rape. The remainder was a mixed bag comprising drunkenness, gambling, vagrancy, and numerous cases of *injuria* (defamation) and *desacato* (disobedience of royal officials).[52]

Many criminal acts, of course, went unreported or found settlement by extrajudicial means. Historians and other social scientists have coined specific concepts ("infrajustice," "extrajustice," "dark figures") to characterize this large universe of undercounted criminal behaviors.[53] Therefore, any general statistics offered here are meant to serve as a mere approximation to be approached with great caution. In the particular case of homicide, however, the "dark figure" should be relatively small. Rape, adultery, or battery may not have been reported and thefts could remain hidden, but violent death most likely sooner or later came to light and entered the judicial records.[54] Probably only a few murders committed through drowning or poisoning could go unnoticed, passing as natural deaths.[55] Furthermore, Spanish law did not require victims to file charges but compelled judicial officials to investigate "public" (serious) crimes such as murder but not necessarily other "nonpublic" crimes, an issue we shall come back to in Chapter 1. The records for homicides are thus more comprehensive than those available for other crimes in colonial societies.[56]

In the last half of the eighteenth century, records are available for several hundred homicides in New Spain and New Granada (Table I.1). Although municipal authorities in New Spain described murder as a common fact of daily life, the truth is that murders did not occur that frequently. They probably happened at an average rate—quite modest by today's standards—of five to ten per year in central urban areas within each viceroyalty, a figure close to that of some European cities around the same time. During a 35-year interval in central Mexico, the authorities recorded about 2.45 homicides per 100,000 people.[57] In Antioquia, a northwest province of New Granada, the number was almost the same—5.33 per 100,000 people over an interval of 69 years.[58]

Spain seems to have had great variations in the murder rate. Data for Madrid in the period 1700–1766, for instance, show 728 homicides. In the early decades there were about 20.8 per year, equivalent to 17 per 100,000 people. By the middle of the century the number had declined to about 9 per year—that is, 6 per 100,000 people.[59] Data for the regions of Galicia and Granada reflect regional disparities in the 300+ murders prosecuted in the late eighteenth and early nineteenth centuries. In Galicia, in the northwest corner of the Iberian Peninsula, a sample suggests an annual average of more than two dozen murders, whereas in Granada, in the south of Spain, the rate appears to have been closer to three dozen, and much higher per capita.[60] Data for rural Cantabria, in northern Spain, indicate an annual average of only 4.1 murders. More-general but fragmentary statistics available for the mid-1780s suggest that homicides all over Spain could have represented an average of about 20 percent of all crimes, but it is difficult to estimate the annual rate or proportion relative to population.[61]

No accurate information exists for how many of the total homicides in most Spanish American colonies involved spouses. Some research indicates that in central Mexico in the period from 1780 to 1815, approximately 25 percent of homicides targeted spouses, sex partners, or rivals.[62] The inclusion of the last two categories makes the data hard to compare to the cases under study, which focus exclusively on legally married spouses.[63] In New Granada, spousal killings amounted to as much as one-quarter of total homicides reported in and around Santa Fé de Antioquia, capital of a key mining province, a peculiarly high proportion.[64] Representative data from the central and northeastern provinces of Santa Fé de Bogotá, Tunja, and Pamplona suggest that such crimes

TABLE 1.1. *Violent crimes in select Spanish provinces and Spanish American colonial regions*

Place	Homicides/ assaults	Population	Absolute index per 100,000 population	Annual index per 100,000 population
1780–1815				
New Spain				
Central Mexico				
(Mexico and Hidalgo)	344	140,000[a]	2.45	(0.07)
Mixteca Alta (Teposcula)	100	—	—	—
1750–1810s				
New Granada[b]	893	792,468[c]	1.12	(0.018)
Santa Fe	193	91,147	2.12	(0.035)
Antioquia[d]	247	46,366[e]	5.33	(0.08)
Tunja (province)	126	236,429	0.53	(0.008)
Pamplona[f]	123	34,118	3.61	(0.06)
1780s–1810s				
Spain				
Madrid (1751–1766)	126[g]	121,038[h]	1.05	(0.07)
Galicia[i]	332	1,340,000[j]	0.24	(0.02)
Granada[k]	375	1,804,000[j]	0.207	(0.034)
Cantabria[l]	167	160,169[m]	1.04	(0.026)

SOURCES: AGN, Colonia, Juicios Criminales, Indice; Taylor, *Drinking, Homicide, and Rebellion,* 75; Haslip-Viera, *Crime and Punishment,* chapter 3; Lozano Armendares, *La criminalidad en la ciudad de México,* 43; AGN, Colombia, Indice Criminales; Angel Alloza, *La vara quebrada de la justicia* (Madrid: Catarata, 2000), 130–131; ARCG, Libro de Providencias Definitivas, 1799–1815, libro 324; ARG, Indice Topográfico Cronológico, sección 7, serie causas, I—años 1762–1835; Tomás Mantecón, *La muerte de Antonia Isabel Sánchez* (Alcala de Henares: Centro de Estudios Cervantinos, 1998), 35; Ramón Lanza, *La población y el crecimiento económico de Cantabria en el Antiguo Régimen* (Ediciones Madrid: UNAM–Universidad de Cantabria, 1991), 101; David Ringrose, *Madrid and the Spanish Economy, 1560–1850* (Berkeley: University of California Press, 1983).

[a]Early nineteenth-century population of Mexico City.

[b]Judging by research on Antioquia, regional data are significantly more comprehensive. When available, they were added to the general data used here. See, for instance, Patiño, *Criminalidad, ley penal y estructura social,* 257, 534. Misleading partial figures (e.g., 160 homicides, 72 injury cases) for the entire viceroyalty, based upon a sample of more than 500 cases, are offered in Gabriel de Domínguez, "Delito y sociedad," 337; McFarlane, *Colombia Before Independence,* 353.

[c]1778–1780 population of New Granada.

[d]Data for 1750–1819 from regional archives used by Patiño, *Criminalidad, ley penal y estructura social,* 257, 534.

[e]1778–1780 population of Antioquia.

[f]Including Girón.

[g]Sample for the period 1751–1766.

[h]Population data for 1769.

[i]Sample for the period 1803–1815.

[j]Population figures for 1787. The figure for Granada corresponds to the entire region of Andalusia.

[k]Sample for the period 1799–1805.

[l]Rural portion, period between 1790 and 1830.

[m]Data for the year 1787.

constituted from 8 percent to 16 percent of all homicides. Additional fragmentary evidence shows that spousal killings constituted from one-twentieth to one-fifth of all homicides in other provinces.[65] Throughout New Granada, spousal murders represented approximately 11.4 percent of all homicides, a proportion close to some late nineteenth-century United States measurements.[66]

Spousal homicide in the Spanish region of Granada represented about 3.6 percent of all homicides for the period for which data are available. In Cantabria during the seventeenth and eighteenth centuries, an estimated one spousal murder was committed annually.[67] Figures in Galicia and Cantabria are about the same.[68] Though tentative, this statistical information gives us a general idea that spousal homicides in the Atlantic could have represented between a low of 3 percent and a high of 25 percent of all murders, far from a negligible component of all homicides during the period under study. It also appears that, proportionally, spousal murder was far more frequent in Spanish America than in Spain, or at least was prosecuted more frequently. The relative significance of homicide in general and spousal murder in particular, regardless of their frequency, is easier to understand when one looks at a very meaningful period in the history of the Atlantic.

PERIOD, METHODOLOGY, AND OUTLINE

The Time of Private "Corporate Patriarchy" and Enlightened Punishment

The second half of the eighteenth century and the first decades of the nineteenth, the temporal focus of this study, were a time of scientific awakening, enlightened reform, intense social upheaval, and revolutionary change. Part of the larger "Age of Democratic Revolution" (ca. 1750–1850),[69] this era witnessed major economic, social, political, and military changes inside the Spanish monarchy, known collectively as the Bourbon Reforms. For instance, the Bourbons passed laws tightening up state monopolies and increasing taxes, making indispensable the consent of parents for white couples of a certain age to marry, easing the whitening of *castas,* restricting family networks in the bureaucracy and the purchase of certain state appointments, and strengthening citizen militias.[70] Ultimately, in part because this reform program was far from smooth, coherent, rational, and successful, the era also witnessed the end of Spain's rule over most of its American colonies, including both Mexico and Colombia. More important from the standpoint of domestic violence, these years corresponded to the development of a particular type of patriarchal control that some scholars have called "corporate patriarchy," whereby mature Spanish colonial societies "divided along the lines of estate, race and gender" tried to strengthen patriarchal privilege.[71] This meant, among other things, that the boundaries between "private" and "public" were being redrawn.

The colonial project in Spanish America involved either a relative confusion of the "public" and the "private" or a view of these notions that was ideologically and practically quite different from the one embraced in other regions and times.[72] Still, despite selective interventions by the colonial state in a number of family-related activities (the enforcement of marriage promises, the policing of concubinage and restrictions on inheritance, the investigation of paternity), based on the idea that fathers and husbands had ample and undisputed legal authority over their households, the laws and society of the time generally regarded domestic disputes as "private" affairs. Such conflicts did not normally trigger forceful state interventions, for they were not regarded as grave ("public") issues or matters pertaining to "international human rights" or "public health," as they are viewed today.[73] Victims were generally left to fend for themselves.

As this book will establish, however, women were far from physically constrained and disabled, or legally defenseless.[74] They played active public roles and not infrequently resorted to violence of their own. Moreover, as the spousal murders in our case studies illustrate, not all family conflicts were actually private. Spousal murders, whether committed by women or by men, were not run-of-the-mill domestic conflicts. Deaths automatically triggered the intervention of royal justice, whatever the wishes of those affected. In that sense, such homicides were "public" crimes worthy of prosecution under any circumstance.[75] Corporate patriarchy was not absolute, not just because of the actual day-to-day practices that made it fluid and contested but also, at least in part, because of some legal provisions.

Furthermore, looking at spousal murders as the colonial period drew to a close in Spanish America will provide us a window into the way that much larger social and political changes and tensions in the metropolis and the colonies may have affected, and possibly strained, patriarchy and families in general, even if just in indirect ways.[76] Did enlightened reformism alter the way that justice officials approached such cases, making them more sensitive, for example, to the pleas and needs of victims? Did the concern of officials over the suffering of criminals in general, spousal murderers included, experience any transformation? More broadly, did patterns of punishment in general change over time?

For Michel Foucault, the second half of the eighteenth century saw a momentous transition in the understanding and practice of punishment.

It was the transition from punishment as ceremony, spectacle, and "the art of pain" to punishment as the "abstract certainty" of retribution and an "economy of suspended rights." Accordingly, public executions began to disappear in France and England, followed soon thereafter by branding[77] and torture.[78] Did this enlightened trend apply to Spain and its colonies? Colonial law prescribed that spousal murderers face one of the most symbolic and spectacular forms of punishment ever invented: *encubamiento,* a technique borrowed from ancient Rome in which culprits were placed alive inside a leather bag (*cuba* or *cuia*, from the Latin *cuieus*) with a monkey, a rooster, a snake, and a dog. Once the bag was tightly sealed, the criminals—not being worthy of burial because of the particularly despicable nature of their crime—were dumped in the nearest ocean or river along with their animal companions. The procedure was designed not only to ensure a horrible death but also to erase all material traces of their existence. Examining whether, when, and how this astonishing form of punishment was performed allows us to track what, if any, changes occurred in Spain and its domains as a result of the liberal trends taking place in neighboring societies. By looking at the metropolis and two colonial regions, which shared relatively similar government, religious, and legal institutions; parallel views and practices concerning gender, marriage, and family relations; equivalent approaches to ethnic and other social relations and hierarchies; comparable general conceptions of honor; and analogous day-to-day cultural practices, including pomp, drinking, and religiosity; it is possible to propose further comparisons. For instance, it is feasible to compare and contrast punishment trends across the Atlantic and to illustrate what this work argues was their de facto humanization (or "civilization") over the course of the eighteenth century and even earlier. Comparison also sheds light on a larger number of issues.

Comparison and Case Selection

While social history's discrete descriptions of ordinary lives and material conditions are central to this study, comparison and contrast are also critical. The narrative is enriched by experiences in Spain, late colonial Mexico, and late colonial Colombia. Why compare and contrast (and how)? Why concentrate on these three areas in particular?

Many years ago, historians and historical sociologists taught us the value of the comparative method, whether for validating broad social theories, proposing mid-level generalizations with analytical value, or interpreting the idiosyncratic nature of historical change in various socio-geographical areas. Comparative history also leads to the formulation of better and more-challenging research questions and more-precise and persuasive findings.[79] This work attempts to interpret idiosyncratic realities, highlighting the particularities of the crimes within each of the three regions (Chapters 2, 4, and 6), but also proposes overarching analytical generalizations based on descriptive quantitative and some qualitative findings. The same set of variables informs the tables used in all three case studies.

The tables offer mainly descriptive statistics such as frequencies or general tendencies and simple cross-tabulations of data. The charts sum up not only the main basic characteristics (number of incidents, distribution by time intervals, geographical origin) of the set of cases used as evidence for each chapter but also essential sociological features of the crimes themselves, including circumstances of time, place, method, demographics of victims and culprits, motives, punishment, and so forth. As the same categories and format appeared across the three regional case studies, it is possible to draw some general inferences about both the reliability and comprehensiveness of the study's evidence and also about the substance of the crimes that it addresses.

The tables are also helpful for comparative purposes, as I attempt to demonstrate from the outset. For instance, Chapters 2, 4, and 6 provide tables focusing on distinct regions, but where patterns from one of these regions appear relevant, they will be brought up in early tables, even before the respective geographical area is fully introduced. The tables allow the tracking of various patterns in a more efficient or economical way, making it less necessary, I believe, to spend pages dealing "thickly" with such issues as the place or time of crimes, a certain weapon, or a particular motive. Instead, I opted for a more sociological treatment of these various aspects. When examples are used, they are meant to illustrate, as vividly and clearly as possible, general situations of domestic violence, enlivening and driving the historical narrative and sociological discussion through snapshots of individual cases of aggression and murder.

Besides bearing in mind the common features highlighted above, the choice of the three cases under study stems from various other considerations. When it comes to Spanish America, colonial Mexico is always a sound research choice, if only by virtue of being the cradle of one of the most important indigenous cultures of the Americas, the Aztecs. It represented the oldest and, by the eighteenth century, most productive of the viceroyalties that Spain established in the Americas. It has also been at the center of significant revolutionary processes, making it the focus of some of the most prolific and innovative historical research. Mexican historiography is at the vanguard of the historical literature on Latin

America, including the most abundant and valuable research on the history of crime, law, gender, and culture in general, which are this book's main concerns.[80]

Colonial Colombia, in contrast, was not the center of a large native empire comparable to the Aztecs and thus developed a society largely made up of racially mixed groups. It became a viceroyalty in the early eighteenth century, two centuries after Mexico, and has remained relatively more marginal in the historiography. This makes it a good choice for comparisons and contrasts with both the most strategic and mature of the colonies and the imperial core.

Finally, scholars of Latin American culture, slavery, social life, and independence have enriched their research findings by placing them in a larger Atlantic framework.[81] Under the influence of these academics, many historians—including me—have become increasingly aware of the need to link the history of the region with developments in the metropolis to which it was so closely tied during the colonial period (1490s–1820s). Studying two American portions of the Spanish monarchy alongside events unfolding in Spain itself extends to the history of crime and the law the benefits of the ambitious Atlantic approach that we have learned so much from in recent years.[82]

Nature, Breadth, and Validity of Evidence

This book relies on criminal records. Similar to other judicial sources, the information they provide is incomplete; likely distorted by the intervention of scribes, interrogators, and lawyers; full of biases; and even plainly untruthful as it was meant to advance the interests of accusers, defendants or Crown officials, all moved to a larger or lesser extent by ulterior motives. Still, trial transcripts are rich in general data for a comparative study like this that pays perhaps greater attention to the social, sociological, and material circumstances of crime and punishment and its overall legal treatment than to ethnographic nuances and thick description.[83] Even if one takes with a grain of salt specific versions about, say, offensive words or drinking preceding one's crime or other particular motives behind one's aggression, the composite picture drawn from dozens of cases sheds fairly reliable light on aspects such as weapons, places, and so forth. More important, the legal records are also reliable concerning justice officials' general approach to criminal procedures, punishment, and pardon, as well as the Crown's and the Church's approach to forgiveness and pain, all critical to our narrative.

The criminal records in question were mostly those found in *reales chancillerías* or *reales audiencias*, the appeals courts of the colonial period, which were not just judicial bodies but also key elements of government. *Audiencias* in the Spanish New World were initially conceived as judicial tribunals to deal with civil and criminal matters but over time became almost separate realms with extensive administrative, political, and military functions. Each colonial viceroyalty had at least one of these courts in the capital city, sometimes two or even three, located in other important urban centers. Spain had many more, a total of eleven during the period covered in this study. A few of the judicial files in all of these courts were complete and contained hundreds of pages of procedures, witness depositions, requests from both prosecutors and defense attorneys, property inventories, and the like. Many more were partial files whose outcome is unknown. Several others were yet more fragmentary and limited to petitions for pardon (*indulto*) accompanied by vague descriptions of the crime and generally cursory decisions by justice officials.[84] Taken together, this variety of records yielded a substantial composite picture of the world of domestic aggression.

In any case, using *audiencia* archives rather than local records turned out to be a better way to obtain as large a group of cases as possible, for the law required that final decisions in incidents of homicide tried at the local level be confirmed with the nearest *audiencia*. Therefore, copies (*testimonios*) of local records were sent to and generally saved in each of the main *audiencia* capitals. In Spanish America, I consulted all of the relevant criminal cases available in the two main appeals courts belonging to the territory that later became Mexico: Mexico City's Audiencia de la Nueva España and Guadalajara's Audiencia de Nueva Galicia. To make up for possible gaps, I consulted other regional and local archives as well: the Judicial Archives of Puebla and Oaxaca, the regional archive of the state of Zacatecas, and the city archive of Veracruz. A few other murder cases came from the early nineteenth-century *Diario de México* and secondary sources for Valladolid (today Morelia) and Patzcuaro, Michoacán. As was the case elsewhere, these supplementary sources yielded a small percentage of cases when compared to those found in the Mexico City and Guadalajara *audiencia* archives; therefore, it seems safe to assume that further exploration of additional archives in other important local and regional centers, such as Yucatán, would produce relatively minor changes in a group now consisting of 87 incidents occurring between 1747 and 1821.[85] In colonial Colombia, evidence comes from all of the extant Audiencia de Santafé criminal records housed in Colombia's central historical archive, the Archivo General de la Nación in Bogotá. Supplemented by partial information from *fondos criminales* in Antioquia's Archivo Histórico (Medellín) and the Archivo Central del Cauca

(Popayan), these provide fragmentary evidence of at least 54 spousal murders in the viceroyalty between 1754 and 1812.

In Spain I relied on all of the cases that could be found in six of the eleven courts that existed at the end of the eighteenth century: Valladolid, Sevilla, Galicia, Granada, Extremadura, and Valencia. The law required local judicial authorities to consult these courts in cases of homicide tried within their respective jurisdictions, and I examined the entire set of records available as a result of such consultations and related appeals. This exercise yielded a total of 65 cases occurring between 1753 and 1823. The records were sparse in part because many criminal files were destroyed over time during officially authorized "expurgations" of crowded archives.[86] Because of this and other factors, in fact, the entire criminal records of three other *audiencias*—in Mallorca, Oviedo, and Zaragoza—have disappeared.[87] I also consulted the criminal records available in the Archivo General de Simancas, the Córdoba and Segovia provincial archives, and, in Madrid, the national archival records of the *Alcaldes de Casa y Corte,* officials charged with investigating crimes in the kingdom's capital and its environs. The Archivo General del Palacio also furnished valuable information on royal pardons, an important legal institution and tradition. Finally, I obtained supplementary secondary information about the region of Cantabria and the city of Cádiz.

Altogether, these various archives yielded a data set of 206 cases. As I will explain while going over each of the three partial case sets in the early chapters of this book, it is safe to say that the study's aggregate of cases represent no less than 10 percent (Spain) and possibly as much as 34–35 percent (New Granada and New Spain) of the spousal murders that occurred during late colonial times. They could be construed as a random set that excludes only cases unsystematically lost over the years as a result of the indiscriminate destruction of documents because of fires, fungi, humidity, or pests, or the authorized or unauthorized sale or disposal of bundles of paper from archives to clear needed space. The set presents great variance and is well suited for tentative statistical inferences. In any case, statistical analysis of sociologically meaningful data (for instance, demographics, alcohol consumption, timing, place, weapons, methods, and motives) is perhaps secondary to this study's findings concerning larger patterns involving culture, justice, punishment, and the law. Other kinds of qualitative data assist in this respect.

In addition to criminal proceedings found in judicial archives, I relied on a large array of legal texts and manuals widely used by litigants and sometimes cited by contemporary justice officials. Altogether, judicial proceedings and legal materials provide a comprehensive picture of the world of spousal murderers. They also speak to the meaning of law and legal culture and to the operation of royal justice.

Chapter-by-Chapter Outline

This study contains two overlapping components. The first, which those interested in legal history will find more engaging and may decide to read first or exclusively, looks at the various judicial and legal aspects (laws and procedures, rules of evidence, mitigating circumstances, pardons, and punishments) that came into play in the resolution of spousal murder cases (Chapters 1, 3, 5, 7, and 8). The other, appealing to those interested in social history (the daily life of "ordinary" people) and historical sociology (understanding and formulation of broad social trends through comparison and contrast of historical, even quantitative, data), presents three case studies, each based on dozens of murders. In those chapters (2, 4, and 6), social and sociological aspects take precedence over legal issues. Rather than grouping together and presenting chapters on legal materials and case studies apart from one another, I decided to intersperse them, hoping that readers going through the sequence shall notice the organic nature of historical processes and, hopefully, the text as well.

Chapter 1 looks at ecclesiastical and civil laws pertaining to marriage and marriage-related conflicts and crimes in Spain and the colonies, and judicial procedures concerning trials for murders and other public crimes. Chapter 3 delves into secular (royal) forgiveness, mechanisms whereby royal law reduced or excused punishment altogether. These included preferential treatment because of one's condition as a "wretched person" (*miserabilis persona*), drinking, a lapse of time between aggression and actual death, royal pardons, and jail visitations. Chapter 5 shifts attention to the role of the Church in ameliorating punishment, including sanctuary, Good Friday pardons, and ecclesiastical assistance during and after execution. Chapter 7 examines punishment and pays particular attention to death sentences and incarceration. The book's final section, Chapter 8, concerns a point of historical inflection, the transition to the "modern" world. After a discussion of the developmental (long-term) changes in punishment, it considers the consequences of constitutionalism and independence for the prosecution of spousal murder and related crimes. It examines, in particular, formal legal changes concerning due criminal process and notions of the appropriate punishment for domestic crimes under "modern" liberal constitutions and criminal codes.

The book's social history chapters tell the stories of specific crimes in Mexico, Spain, and Colombia, respectively. Here again, I decided not to group together and separate colonial cases from the metropolitan experience, hoping to capture and suggest instead the Atlantic's fluid nature, even its unity in diversity. The incidents in each of these chapters sometimes reappear later in the text, making the regional studies progressively more comparative and multi-layered. Chapter 2 focuses on 87 cases of spousal murder in late colonial Mexico. In addition to shedding light on circumstances and motives, the discussion centers on the ethnic dimensions of the crimes, largely committed by members of the indigenous community. Chapter 4 examines 65 murders committed by Spanish wives and husbands. Given the saliency of murders committed by unfaithful wives, this chapter explores the culture of honor and the extent to which it could be considered central to explaining the events under consideration. Chapter 6 examines 54 cases of spousal murder in late colonial Colombia. Similar to the discussion on Mexico, this chapter addresses the circumstances and motives of the crimes. Rather than concentrating on their ethnic aspects, however, it highlights the gender dimension. This is important in light of the fact that women committed a considerable portion of the New Granada murders, a peculiarity that the chapter seeks to explain. Finally, before adding some concluding comments on domestic violence in the contemporary world, it may be useful to place the phenomenon in its historical context, interpersonal violence in general.

Interpersonal Violence

Interpersonal violence has been the subject of more systematic historical inquiry in the United States and Europe than anywhere else in the world. Most recently, we have seen the production of comprehensive historical surveys and social scientific analyses addressing both regions. The most important of these studies pose such questions as why adult homicide rates in the United States are so high or examine patterns in the character, incidence, social meaning, and cultural context of murder in Europe from the Middle Ages to the present.[88]

Randolph Roth's massive study found that peacetime murder rates in the British American colonies ranged from 100 to 500 annually per 100,000 adults. The murder rate in the United States today is 10 to 50 times lower, a product of "political stability" and "increasing solidarity among subjects."[89] In a recent book summarizing the available scholarship on the long-term evolution of murder (and other forms of interpersonal violence) in Europe from medieval to recent times, Pieter Spierenburg concludes that in the old continent, murder and other forms of interpersonal violence decreased considerably from the 1450s to the 2000s, from 35 to less than five per 100,000 inhabitants annually.[90] This decline was in part a result of what Norbert Elias refers to as the "civilizing process": the monopolization of force by the state, the reduction of inter-state conflicts, stronger social integration, and increased individual self-restraint.[91]

Domestic homicides seem to have followed a relatively different trend. The dramatic decline in the homicide rate in the United States did not extend to homicides involving lovers, spouses, and other relatives. From the seventeenth through the nineteenth centuries, Roth found, family and intimate homicide rates varied very little, operating in response to forces unrelated to those driving homicides among unrelated adults.[92] In Europe, too, despite a general decline in the murder rate, domestic violence seems to have actually increased in relative significance. Intimate homicides accounted from 5 to 10 percent of all murders in the seventeenth century, and from 30 to 50 percent in the nineteenth and twentieth centuries.[93] Scholars have attributed the relative rise in the significance of domestic violence, unaccounted for by Elias's model—which limits itself to forms of male public violence in wars—to factors such as the reluctance of the state to interfere in "private conflicts," social tolerance, prevailing honor codes, and legal discourses.[94]

As this book establishes, domestic homicides were common in the late colonial Spanish Atlantic as well. Although long-term quantitative information on interpersonal violence is still fragmentary, such homicides are likely to have followed trends similar to those observed in the United States and Europe. They are disturbingly common even today.

Domestic Violence: Enduring and Widespread

Unfortunately, domestic violence is a very old social phenomenon. Evidence exists of the problem since antiquity.[95] The crime persists to this day in all parts of the world. The United Nations Population Fund considers gender-based, including domestic, violence to be perhaps the "most widespread and socially tolerated of human rights violations" in the world today.[96] Latin American societies have had their fair share of it, but they are by no means alone. For example, recent studies show that husbands or boyfriends killed 40–70 percent of female murder victims in Australia, Canada, Israel, South Africa, and the United States.[97] In the early 1980s, an estimated 17 percent of all homicides in the United States occurred within the family, half of them between husband and wife.[98] An annual average of about 3,000 intimate-partner homicides were recorded in this country from 1970 to 2000. The most recent estimates indicate that intimate partners kill approximately 1,800 adults in the United States every year.[99]

In 1993, responding to the murder of 28 women (and six of their children) at the hands of husbands or boyfriends, Massachusetts Governor William Weld declared a state of emergency. One of his successors, Governor Deval Patrick, took a similar step in June 2008, citing the tripling of domestic violence homicides in the previous two years.[100] However, homicides pale in number when compared to the staggering incidence of domestic battery. Incidents of abuse by intimate partners occur in the tens of thousands annually not just in the United States but in numerous, perhaps all, countries of the world, a situation it would be fair to call, as the World Health Organization did not long ago, a true planetary public health emergency.[101]

This study of two overseas regions of the late colonial Spanish Atlantic and the Spanish peninsula itself helps illustrate the historical manifestations of one of the most extreme forms of intimate violence, spousal murder. The cultural and legal practices surrounding the hundreds of cases of spousal murder prosecuted in Spain and its overseas colonies may help us understand the historical intersection of domestic violence, private and state/Church patriarchy, and the law. The cases in this book show the closely intertwined nature of the authority of household, state, and Church, reflecting larger ethnic, gender, and other cultural hierarchies in ways more complex than, and even counterintuitive to, traditional assumptions.

CHAPTER ONE

Access to Justice

Domestic Violence, Laws, and Procedures

Marriage and crimes involving family and/or sexuality have long been the focus of special moral and religious concern and legal regulation. In deeply Catholic Spain and its American territories, both the Catholic Church and civil Crown authorities actively intervened to police these spheres and participated in the discussion, enactment, and enforcement of religious and secular laws to address them. They were also instrumental in granting access to justice to the various parties and all that it entailed: monitoring and accompaniment, spiritual and otherwise, as well as protection, forgiveness, and punishment.[1]

The Church understood marriage to be a sacred act, subject—from beginning to end—to its jurisdiction and regulation under the ecclesiastical legal system referred to as canon law. Ecclesiastical authorities viewed crimes of different types, including domestic injuries and homicides, as well as other offenses against family principles and sexual standards (e.g., *estupro,* sex generally extracted under false pretenses such as the promise of marriage; adultery; concubinage; bigamy; and incest), as sinful acts, violations of divine precepts and commandments, and punishable by God and the Church. At the same time, these and various other crimes, including even homicides and robberies, sometimes prompted benign Church intervention through paternalistic and charitable mechanisms such as mediation among quarreling parties, requests for leniency, and the type of asylum granted to Eulalia, the spousal killer mentioned in this book's introduction. The Church also accompanied and administered last rites to those sentenced to death, and religious brotherhoods proactively intervened to humanize their punishment. The Spanish Crown, in turn, enacted various parallel bodies of legislation touching on marriage, crime, and punishment both at home and in its overseas colonies, providing reprieve, pushing forward investigations and trials, and enforcing and monitoring punishment.[2]

Following is a comprehensive discussion of some of the legal dimensions of marital disputes, including the substantive applicable laws and, especially, the procedures followed to try crimes against spouses. I list the substantive laws to provide some context for future discussions but pay particular attention to criminal procedures that reflect the judicial routines on which state domination was, at least in part, founded. In general, and in spite of the claim that Spanish justice was to a large extent discretionary, legal procedures like the ones discussed here tended to be somewhat formulaic and without apparent social biases. Bias on the part of justice officials with regard to gender and other social factors (ethnicity and social rank) will become clearer in subsequent chapters. The main finding in this particular section, apart from the long-standing and habitual nature of judicial procedures, is that canon and civil law went hand in hand and were both central to the regulation of marriage and the resolution of domestic conflicts. More important, unlike other family disputes considered to be private matters, the law treated spousal murders not as a private matter but rather as an issue of grave public interest subject to automatic prosecution. As future chapters will demonstrate, however, multiple expedients were available to minimize both the gravity of the offense and its punishment.

CANON LAW: MARRIAGE AND MARITAL CONFLICTS

The period of this study included two separate bodies of legislation touching on marriage and family/sexuality relations and conflicts. The first, secular in nature, was royal or "civil" law, enacted by the Crown and examined later in this chapter. The other, canon law, was made up of the orders, rules, and commentaries—variously referred to as bulls or briefs, edicts, decrees, letters, sanctions, constitutions, and laws—issued by the Church, that is, by popes, councils (meetings of the high clergy, especially archbishops and bishops, of an ecclesiastical province), diocesan synods (meetings of the priests and clerics of a diocese, presided over by their bishop), archbishops, and bishops. The most important collections of ecclesiastical regulations (the *Decretum* of Gratian, *Decretals* of Gregory IX, and Boniface VIII's *Sextus or Liber Sextus Decretalium*) were compiled in the twelfth and thirteenth centuries. The Council of Trent (1545–1563) introduced major additions and reforms touching particularly on aspects of marriage. Similar other ecumenical councils (meetings of the bishops of the world, presided over by the pope), provincial councils, and diocesan synods produced various other relevant additions to and binding commentaries on canon law.[3]

Spain and its American domains commonly observed and enforced all of the laws and regulations made or adopted by ecclesiastical authorities, and lawyers and priests studied them avidly. Law schools and ecclesiastical seminaries in the Iberian Peninsula and Spanish America systematically taught canon law.[4] The Crown's authorities and its subjects recognized its legitimacy and were generally willing to uphold and follow its precepts. With the Crown's acquiescence, and following the mandates of the Council of Trent, the Church maintained registries (of births, baptisms, marriages, and deaths), authorities, and institutions—not only missions, parish priests, bishops, and archbishops but also ecclesiastical courts of justice. As early as the fifteenth century, the Church also established the tribunals of the Inquisition, which, along with ecclesiastical judges, kept track of and policed the observance of canon law and other religious precepts throughout the kingdom. All of these organs enforced legal prescriptions on marriage and other aspects of Christian life.

In the words of a standard legal manual, marriage was a spiritual and legal bond, joining a man and a woman together for life. As a prosecutor in one of the murders in this book referenced, St. Paul considered it to represent the union between the divine and human nature.[5] In contrast to later Protestant views of marriage as a worldly institution, the Catholic Church's approach was founded on the late medieval notion of the marital union as one of the Seven Sacraments of Evangelical Law instituted by Jesus Christ, equivalent in significance to baptism, confirmation, the Holy Eucharist, orders, extreme unction, and confession.[6] All of these sacraments were under the exclusive jurisdiction of the Church, which regulated the various conditions and formalities of their attainment.

For instance, the Church established the minimum legal age for marriage (fourteen for males, twelve for females) and required the mutual free consent of the parties contracting marriage; required both parties to have been previously admitted into the Church through baptism; and precluded any impediments (e.g., consanguinity, affinity, a valid previous marriage, the killing of one's former spouse) to an intended marriage, prescribing the need for banns (public announcement of the names of the contracting parties in church during Mass by their own parish priest on three consecutive Holy Days) to learn if any such impediments existed. One of the main objectives of marriage was procreation, and husband and wife had the obligation to be faithful to each other and to live together at all times, for the Church considered marriage as absolutely indissoluble. More important, canon law also stressed patriarchal authority as the guiding principle of social life, marriage, and family relations.

This fundamental "truth," allegedly based on divine will as expressed in biblical precepts, legitimated the differential treatment afforded to men and women, most evident, for example, in the inconsistent approach to battery.[7]

Nevertheless, canon law was by nature controversial and malleable. Jurists offered diverse and at times conflicting interpretations of its prescriptions regarding marriage and heatedly debated the Crown's authority to modify them and supervise the clergy in charge of enforcing them.[8] Over time, some exceptions (*privilegios* and *dispensas*) to the general requirements for entering into marriage became possible. These were especially common in the case of the subaltern ethnic groups (blacks and Indians) that fell under the domination of Europeans during the fifteenth century. The exceptions were intended to aid unions blessed by the Church among "primitive" cultures.[9] However, some principles allowed for no exceptions.

For instance, patriarchal authority and indissolubility were absolute rules for everyone entering into Catholic marriage, irrespective of social origin or cultural affiliation. The Church regarded husbands such as Juan Californio, the victim of the story in the introduction, as heads of family, dominant over wives, children, and others in the household. The Church also encouraged and ordered husband and wife to remain together for life, in good times and bad, "in sickness and in health." Members of the clergy, especially parish priests and confessors, received instructions to mediate to heal marital disagreements and reunite couples in distress. The repressive interventions of the San Antonio missionaries in 1800 against Eulalia's extramarital affair were in line with these precepts. So was the intervention of a priest (*vicario*) who ordered the confinement (*depósito*) of María Ignacia, an indigenous woman, for her own protection after she complained that a powerful local chief had raped her in the central Mexican mining town of Zacualpan around 1794, turning her subsequent marriage to another man in the community a living hell.[10] Conflictive marriages like those of Eulalia and of María were not at all uncommon, and many faced separation.

Although it did not happen in our opening story, ecclesiastical judges frequently reviewed incidents of "divorce" in colonial times.[11] Divorce was in practice a generic expression used at the time to refer to, on the one hand, petitions for annulment (divorce *quoad vinculum*), after which either spouse could usually marry someone else, and, on the other, requests for physical separation (divorce *quoad thorum et cohabitationem* or *quoad thorum et mensam*), also known as "bed and table" divorce, which did not free spouses to enter into a new marriage but did at least legitimate living apart.[12] The first type of divorce does not concern us much here, for it was based upon the demonstration that some essential requisite for a valid marriage (free will, legal age, absence of kinship, no valid previous marriage, baptism, etc.) had been lacking and was generally not related to domestic conflicts and violence. Only one exceptional instance is relevant to this work: marriage to someone guilty of having killed his or her former spouse.

Under canon law, the crime of *conyugicidio* (spousal homicide) constituted a "diriment impediment"—that is, an obstacle rendering a marriage between the aggressor and his or her lover and/or accomplice void. A person who murdered a spouse to marry another partner was expressly forbidden to contract marriage with this individual if the two had cooperated in the murder for the purpose of this marriage or if the pair had committed adultery and the murder was intended for the sole purpose of their contracting marriage.[13] This is precisely what Antonio León, a Colombian Indian, did in 1807. He beat his wife, María Isidora Cano, to death while traveling on a deserted road and then claimed that she had died after falling off a horse. He also falsified the date of her death: On the death certificate that he submitted to the ecclesiastical authorities to marry his lover, Luz Miranda, a few days after the murder, he claimed that María Isidora had died four years earlier. The priest celebrating the new marriage became suspicious, and the crime was eventually uncovered.[14] In many other instances in both colonial Colombia and Mexico and late Bourbon Spain, people killed their spouses to be free to marry their lovers, but the case just mentioned is the only one where evidence of a subsequent marriage between accomplices is readily available. Such marriages fell under the rules of divorce *quoad vinculum* and were null and void under canon law.

In contrast to the limited significance of *quoad vinculum* divorce to this study, the second type of divorce, physical separation, relates both directly and indirectly to the dynamics of spousal murder. Such separations involved domestic disputes of different types, some of which culminated in homicide. For instance, *sevicia* (battery) constituted a justifiable cause for physical separation from one's spouse and could help prevent more tragic results. Adultery and drinking, activities frequently linked to spousal homicides, could also lead to *quod thorum et mensam* divorce.[15]

According to contemporary legal and religious manuals that reflect the gender ideology and inequalities of the period, wives could file for ecclesiastical divorce only in cases of "cruel and atrocious battery" (*malos tratamientos graves y atroces*). Both civil and canon law considered it permissible for a husband to practice "discreet and moderate" or "reasonable" punishment, but they did not provide a clear definition of these open-ended expressions. The provision allowed men such as Mariano

Rafael Mendoza, who killed his wife in Mexico in 1815, to claim that they had merely been trying to "correct" an unruly spouse and make her "change her ways" (*enmendar*).[16] Furthermore, for light battery to be a sufficient cause for divorce under canon law it had to be "chronic" (*cotidiano*) and without any "just cause," both vague conditions.[17] This is why, even during criminal investigations for murdering their wives, husbands such as Manuel Llerena or Hermenegildo Peña unashamedly admitted having punched their wives several times before. Llerena, awaiting sentence in a Madrid jail for the killing of his wife, Isabel Aloset, in 1780, explained that she was insolent and, although he tried to be patient, he had to punch her from time to time.[18] Peña mentioned beating his wife "just" about five times and "lightly" over several years of marriage because of "issues" typical among couples.[19] José Chavez, tried in 1813 for the killing of his wife, María Gertrudis, in the jurisdiction of Guadalajara, Mexico, also asserted that he never imagined his recent beating could have killed his wife, for in the past when he hit her, she merely fainted.[20]

Limited though the possibilities for divorce may have been, evidence exists of 300 divorce petitions filed with Mexico City's ecclesiastical judge (*Provisor Eclesiastico*) in the eighteenth century. A telling number, 94 (31.3 percent of the total), were based on *malos tratos* inflicted by husbands against their wives. Interestingly enough, these cases represented only three-quarters of the battery-related divorce suits; the remaining quarter involved 31 husbands (10.3 percent of the total) who reported being verbally and physically abused by their wives.[21] An average of just a little more than one abuse-related petition for divorce per year seems rather insignificant for as densely populated a region as central Mexico.[22] This figure most likely does not reflect the true magnitude of domestic conflicts but merely some of its extreme manifestations. Divorce may have been a way to preempt further abuse, even murder, although in at least some instances divorce suits and complaints over abuse accomplished just the opposite, triggering spousal homicide. This was the tragic result for two Mexican women killed by their husbands in 1760 and 1791, respectively, after they sued for divorce on the grounds of battery. The same thing happened to Anastasia Martin in Segovia, Spain, late in 1801. She sued her husband, Matias Piu, a thirty-eight-year-old innkeeper (*bodegonero*), for battery and abuse, and he stabbed her to death in retribution.[23]

Unlike battery, which tended to be mainly a male offense, adultery had a broader meaning under canon law. Royal law considered adultery a crime only when committed by females, but under canon law either spouse could cite it as a reason for ecclesiastical divorce.[24] In the eyes of the Church, such behavior was a mortal sin irrespective of gender. Furthermore, from early on canon law opposed private vengeance (murder) against adulterous spouses, for it viewed adultery not as an offense against male honor but as a gender-neutral, individual sin that violated marital obligations. The behavior revealed the existence of lies, lust, infidelity, and a violation of a spouse's exclusive sexual power over his or her partner's body, part of the conjugal or marital debt (*débito*) that included the obligation to give one's spouse sex on demand.[25] Mexico City's archbishopric recorded forty-two of these allegations in the eighteenth century; wives filed twenty-three of them, and husbands filed the other nineteen. The men in question seemed to be searching for a solution rather more peaceful than the one favored by long-standing codes of honor sanctioned into royal law—that is, the legitimate killing of wives caught having intercourse with their lovers, an issue this book addresses later. Archival records of adultery-related complaints reveal a low average number of annual petitions (0.4), but at least some instances were being tried. This almost never happened with drinking, another common form of misconduct.

Drinking was admissible grounds for divorce only if it was habitual and represented a "grave danger" to the wife. Divorce requests were rarely, if ever, based upon this sole motive. More likely, they resulted from the drinker's inability to provide for his family and/or problems with vagrancy.[26]

Therefore, divorce was a potential remedy under canon law for some serious marital tensions and disputes. In practice, however, the provision was neither widely available to the majority of people nor a popular means for resolving family feuds.[27] Mediation by relatives, neighbors, priests, and civil authorities to discourage breakups, lack of money, insufficient access to legal advice, geographical obstacles, fear, or a combination of all of these circumstances made many spouses, especially modest Indian and peasant women like Eulalia, generally unwilling or unable to sue for divorce. They were more likely to use de facto remedies, including abandoning their spouses.

Despite ecclesiastical admonishments and *censura* (mainly excommunication) of spouses who separated informally, civil provisions ordering the reunification of estranged couples, and even criminal sanctions, abandonment was a fairly common recourse in late colonial Colombia, late colonial Mexico, and Spain.[28] In some instances, recurrent abandonment, followed by unification mandated by ecclesiastical or civil authorities or achieved under family mediation and persuasion, resulted in escalating tensions, even murder. In mid-eighteenth-century Oaxaca, for example, an Indian named Diego Andrés killed his wife, María Esteban, in exasperation over her habit of returning to her father's home for days or weeks every time they fought.[29] Similarly, Simpliciano Vega stabbed his wife to death in central New Granada in 1766 in the wake of recurrent fights that prompted the woman to seek shelter at her father's house.[30]

More accessible and inexpensive than divorce was the option of denouncing one's spouse as a criminal to *justicias mayores* or local magistrates (*alcaldes* and *corregidores*).[31] Except in cases in which religious asylum—the canon law institution invoked by Eulalia—was an issue, many crimes were neither regulated by canon law nor investigated by ecclesiastical authorities, falling instead under the Crown's own body of secular laws and judges. These, as will be shown below, were a multilayered and complex series of rules, compilations, and authorities of diverse origin and scattered regional coverage or jurisdiction. Much like canon law, they generally upheld patriarchal authority and made manifest and "natural" other contemporary social biases and hierarchies.

ROYAL LAW AND *DERECHO INDIANO*

At the time the Spanish monarchy took possession of the New World, Spain's preeminent legal system was the *Ordenamiento de Alcalá* (1348), a legal statute that originated in the central region of Castile. Issued by the king of Castile and his *cortes* (a representative assembly akin to a parliament), it mainly addressed property, criminal, and procedural issues. As opposed to the judge-made law that would become dominant in England and its "common law" colonies years later, statutory laws like this one—generally divided into thematic books, titles, chapters, and individual laws—went on to characterize the legal ("civil law") system of Spain and its possessions, as well as the rest of continental Europe. Although the role of judges was not at the time strictly limited to the mechanical application of such statutes to individual cases—there were many gaps in the legislation, and the statutes and legal experts accorded considerable discretion to justice officials—the weight of increasingly detailed law compilations in continental Europe became substantial, reaching its climax with the systematic early nineteenth-century Napoleonic Codes. When addressing marriage, these legal texts for the most part endorsed and paraphrased canon law provisions.

Beneath the *Ordenamiento de Alcalá* were so-called local *fueros* or municipal charters, especially the *Fuero Real* found in many Spanish cities, to which one could resort if no specific royal law applied. The *Fuero Real* (1255) was a group of laws that touched on the Catholic faith, the king and his bureaucracy, lawsuits, marriages, inheritance, and crime. Compilations of feudal customs and usages were in place as *fueros* in various individual kingdoms within Iberia, for instance Aragón and Valencia.[32] In the absence of royal law, as well as a municipal or regional *fuero,* jurists could consult *Las Siete Partidas,* a renowned legal text originally issued in the thirteenth century (1251–1265) and based on Roman, canon, and feudal law. Credit for its enactment went to King Alfonso X of Castile, who was unable to enforce it at the time, however, because of resistance by the nobility. This monumental and comprehensive body of laws dedicated to all kinds of civil, criminal, procedural, and administrative issues became enforceable only in the fifteenth century and only when royal laws or *fueros* did not cover a particular issue. It nevertheless remained influential for centuries, and until the end of the colonial period, litigants, justice officials, and jurists cited it frequently.

Las Siete Partidas reflects a basic fact of Spanish life, the institutionalization and naturalization of social rank. It included several articles indicative of the intensely hierarchical character of Iberian society, displayed from early on and projected over at least the following six centuries. One article, for instance, established that "hidalguia is nobility that men acquire through lineage, and this is why those who have a right to it must be careful not to damage it . . . by marrying a hijodalgo [male] with a commoner or a commoner with a hijadalgo [female]. But for the most part men gain hidalguia through their fathers' honor, for even if their mother is a commoner and the father a hijodalgo, the son they give birth to could be counted as a hijodalgo, but not as a noble, but if such son is born from a hijadalgo and a commoner, they are not entitled that he be counted as a hijodalgo."[33] The combination of status and gender prejudice is notable in this and other contemporary statutes. It also appears in the doctrinal commentaries that justified such legal distinctions and equivalent precepts establishing them as logical renderings of "natural" and "civil" differences among people.

As this standard legal manual edited numerous times in the late eighteenth and early nineteenth centuries explained, "natural" differences were threefold: first, between unborn and already born human beings; second, between men and women; and third, between minors and adults. "Civil" differences, those derived not from nature but from "men's will," were said to include the distinction between natives of these kingdoms (*naturales de estos Reynos*) and foreigners; nobles and plebeians; laypeople and members of the clergy; and, last, freemen and slaves.[34] Notice that the distinction between married and unmarried people was not listed among the "civil" classifications but appeared instead as a separate category under "family status" (*estado de familia*).[35] Furthermore, the reality of civil or social distinctions was still more intriguing than suggested, for we know that in the colonies significant differences (many viewed as "natural") also applied to, for instance, the legal treatment of Indians, castes, and whites, respectively, none of whom, unlike slaves, were included in the standard legal divisions. In any case, *Las Siete Partidas* safeguarded marriage, which, much like procedural routines and institutionalized social hierarchies, was central to social order and control.

For instance, several laws in the seventh *partida* dealt with marriage-related criminal behaviors, including adultery. They made clear that this conduct harmed only married men and the female culprit's close kin; therefore, only these men (the woman's husband, father, brothers, and uncles) could denounce it because only they suffered "damage" (*daño*) and "dishonor" (*deshonrra* [*sic*]).[36] As a result, a husband had the right to kill the man he found in bed with his wife. However, unlike the woman's father, who could kill both lovers, the husband could not kill her but had to let judges handle the matter. Justice officials would flog the offender and lock her in a convent for no less than two years, even for life. In addition, she would lose her wedding tokens (*arras*) and dowry, which would revert to the husband.[37] We will come back to the regulation of adultery in Spanish legislation later.

Another section of the same *Siete Partidas* code dealt with the murder of close kin (offspring, grandchildren, parents, grandparents, parents-in-law, children-in-law, siblings, and spouses), establishing that, as according to "ancient Emperors and sages," the culprits should be flogged publicly and then killed. The killing was to be done by *encubamiento,* which I shall discuss in Chapter 7.[38]

The sixteenth century brought two new bodies of legal statutes: the *Leyes de Toro* (1505), a brief text dealing mostly with inheritance, entails, and family issues; and the comprehensive *Recopilación de Leyes de estos Reynos*, also known as *Nueva Recopilación de Castilla* (1567). The *Nueva Recopilación* went through several more editions, most of which added laws issued before their respective dates of publication (1569, 1581, 1592, 1598, 1640, 1723, 1725, 1745, 1773, 1775, and 1777). The result added up to three thick volumes.

Finally, early in the nineteenth century, King Charles IV enacted a new collection of laws, the 1805 *Novisima Recopilación de Leyes de España,* to supersede all previous laws that proved contradictory; otherwise, old statutes remained in place. Like the *Siete Partidas,* most of these massive and overlapping *recopilaciones* (compilations) dealt with a wide range of issues: administrative regulations concerning the Church and Crown bureaucracies, fiscal provisions, rules about the jurisdiction of ecclesiastical authorities vis-à-vis royal authorities, and civil laws and procedures. They also contained criminal laws and procedures for such offenses as adultery, general injuries, and homicides.[39] For instance, an entire section (libro XII, tit. XXVIII) transcribed all laws relating to adultery.[40]

Because the Indies, as Spanish America became known, belonged to the Crown of Castile, the Castilian legal system also applied to this New World. In addition, a specialized separate body of law for these overseas territories, later known as *derecho indiano,* gradually took shape through the sixteenth and seventeenth centuries. At first it was made up of general Crown statutes for governing the new territories and prescribing the proper treatment of its inhabitants (see, for example, the *Leyes Nuevas* of 1542). A constant flow of royal regulations (*reales provisiones, reales cédulas,* and *pragmáticas*) reached the colonies as well. Through these individual prescriptions and orders, the king or his *Consejo de Indias*—an advisory board for governing the Americas—appointed royal officials and instructed them on issues such as Indian labor, land use, mining, taxes, ceremonials, and precedence.[41] *Derecho indiano* was in any case another institutional source of social distinction, and it was produced not just in Spain but in overseas territories as well.

The highest authorities in the Americas, especially viceroys and *audiencias,* issued hundreds of casuistic local orders, regulations, and legal commentaries variously known as *decretos, bandos, despachos, mandamientos, ordenanzas de gobierno,* and *autos acordados*. Over time, in addition to a number of bulky collections of these norms, the main corpus of *derecho indiano* became the compilation of laws known as the *Recopilación de Indias* (1681), which took precedence in the colonies over general laws on the same subjects. Following the typical structure of the Spanish legal compilations (i.e., thematic books divided into titles and laws), the *Recopilación de Indias* encompassed various volumes dedicated to issues relevant to colonial affairs, such as mining, grants of Indian labor (*encomiendas*), and the lawful treatment of "wretched" Indians. The juridical condition of miserable Indians, another manifestation of hierarchies instituted by this variety of Spanish law, is discussed separately in Chapter 3 of this study. The *Recopilación* also contained at least one title on crime and punishment.[42]

This intricate system of ecclesiastical and secular laws on marriage and family/sexual crimes in the Iberian Peninsula and Spanish America was made still more complex by the fact that the law, its interpreters, and actual social interactions in the metropolis and overseas did not construe the various members of society as equal. The legal system was founded on social inequality and privilege.[43] By design it aimed to treat a few "extraordinarily" or gently, whereas others faced "ordinary" or even harsher treatment than the bulk of the population.

The laws enacted in the peninsula—even ancient ones such as *Las Siete Partidas*—and/or the provisions contained in the *Recopilación de Indias* served as guides for local justice officials and courts of justice (the Spanish *chancillerías*, the Spanish and American *audiencias*, Madrid's *Sala de Alcaldes de Casa y Corte*, and the *Consejo de Indias*) in investigating and resolving marital disputes and domestic crimes. Well into the late eighteenth and early nineteenth centuries, in the peninsula and all over the colonies, litigants, lawyers, prosecutors, and judges cited those provisions and supported their views with a number of popular legal treatises, some of which I discuss below (see Figure 1.1).

To understand the laws' provisions and their practical applications, we must first review procedural matters and classifications. Related issues, including the legal treatment of specific social groups such as women, Indians, and nobles; the handling of drunken criminals and asylum seekers; and forms of punishment and royal pardons will be covered in the following chapters.

JUDGES, PUBLIC CRIMES, CRIMINAL PROCEDURES, AND EVIDENCE

For a long time, unpaid local magistrates (*alcaldes mayores, alcaldes ordinarios,* or *alcaldes pedaneos*) elected by prominent local residents (*vecinos*) were in charge of administering justice in small villages and some cities in Spain and its domains. In larger cities, justice was generally in the hands of *corregidores,* appointed officials paid by the Crown (see Figure 4.1). In Spain these tended to be trained attorneys. This was only occasionally the case in the colonies.

In rather exceptional instances, local justice was also in the hands of the directors of large royal factories. A case in point is the Real Fábrica de Paños de Guadalajara, Spain, in operation since 1719 and significant enough to entrust its director (royal superintendent) with the *fuero* to investigate and try criminal cases involving the company's many employees. This occurred in December 1799 when one of the *fabrica*'s smelters, Andres Corral, murdered his wife, Juliana Nogues, also an employee.[44]

In remote outposts such as Spanish America's presidios, military governors or commanders could stand in as judges, as happened in the incident that opened the introduction. In some exceptional instances, subordinate officers actually started the investigation. For instance, in a 1796 case involving the killing of a woman named Rebeca by her fellow Chumash Indian husband, Silverio, a corporal (*cabo de escolta*) present in

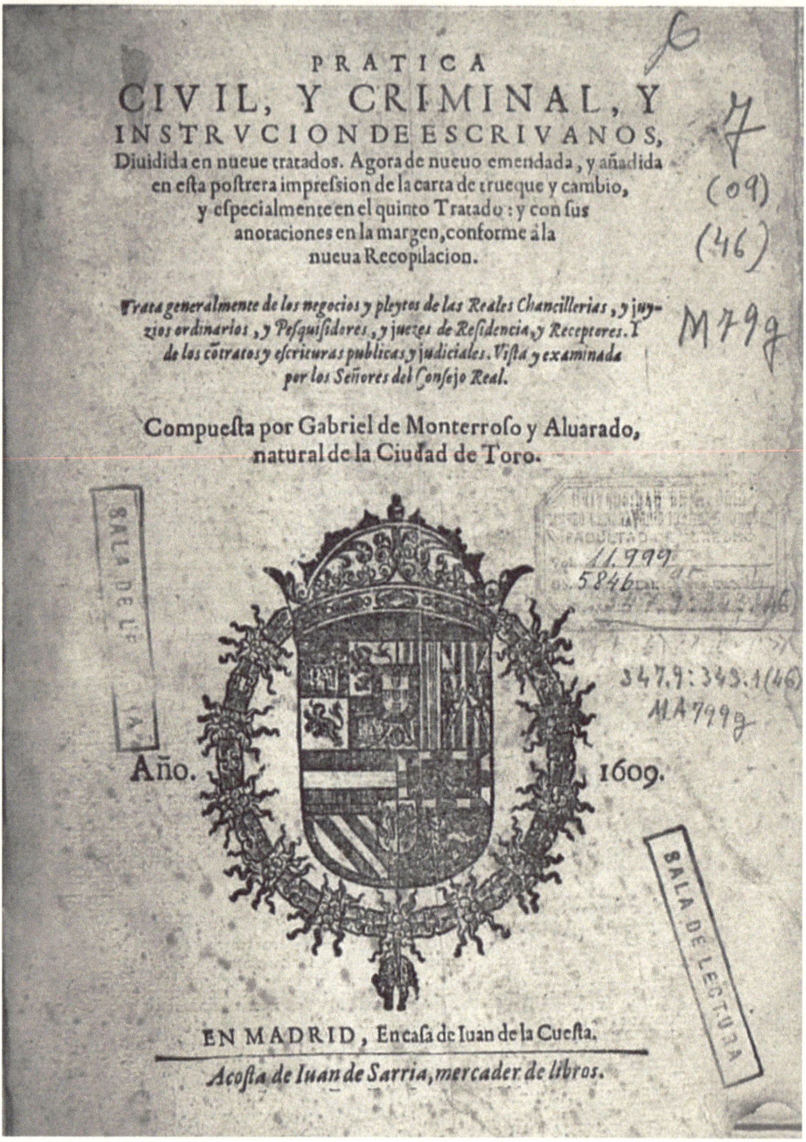

Figure 1.1. Gabriel Monterroso y Alvarado, Practica Civil y Criminal & Instrucción de Escribanos dividida en nueve tratados: Agora de nuevo enmendada y añadida, en esta postrera impresión *(Madrid: En Casa de Juan de la Cuesta, 1609 [1591]).*

the Catholic mission of San Luis where the incident occurred opened the case and took the defendant's and witnesses' depositions until the lieutenant from the nearby Santa Barbara Presidio took over four months later. Curiously enough, the corporal was a neophyte from the culprit's native community and served later as an interpreter during the judicial proceedings.[45]

A fair number of these various all-male justice officials, especially most *alcaldes* and many *corregidores,* were untrained in the law. To make up for this weakness they had access to practical legal manuals with detailed instructions on how to handle cases. A wide variety of doctrinal books commenting on legal issues had circulated since the sixteenth century, the most quoted of which were perhaps the ones in Latin by sixteenth-century jurists Diego de Covarrubias y Leyva (1512–1577), Antonio Gomez (1501–1562/1572), and Gregorio López (1496–1560).[46] Soon thereafter, manuals of a more practical type started to circulate. Some were in Latin and, like the doctrinal texts, accessible only to university-trained priests and lawyers (see Figure I.1). Several manuals in Spanish were soon published as well, however.[47] The most popular was a down-to-earth guide for county mayors or *corregidores* by royal bureaucrat Jerónimo Castillo de Bobadilla (1546/47–1605), extensively used and quoted in both the peninsula and the colonies for centuries (see Figure 4.1).[48]

By the late eighteenth century, numerous step-by-step manuals were available. Typically titled "*práctica*" or "*instrucción manual,*" they addressed all kinds of civil, criminal, and ecclesiastical subjects, even specialized matters, and were intended for "lawyers, prosecutors, lay judges and local magistrates, scribes, consultants," and so forth (see Figures I.1, 3.2, 4.1, 5.1, and 6.1). Some of them went through several editions, a testimony to their popularity and wide readership.[49] They could be found in many colonial libraries; in the collections of bureaucrats, priests, magistrates, lawyers, institutions, universities, and convents; and even indigenous communities (*reducciones*).[50]

In addition to using the manuals prior to making significant decisions, particularly sentencing, lay judges had to consult an *asesor letrado* (lawyer), whose advice they normally followed. Still, in some remote areas, such as New Mexico (then a part of northern New Spain), the lack of *alcaldes,* scribes, *asesores,* or any other people with minimal legal knowledge posed an obstacle to filing cases. Community leaders in Taos, New Mexico, cited this problem to explain the lack of progress in the case of Indian Juan Domingo Romero, who killed his wife in 1804.[51]

In cases involving homicide or other major crimes subject to corporal punishment, local authorities had to refer the final sentences to the nearest royal *audiencia.* Colonial Mexico had one (*Real Audiencia de la*

Nueva Galicia) in the city of Guadalajara and another in Mexico City (*Real Audiencia de México*). Mexico City also had a special court, the *Tribunal de la Acordada,* established in the early eighteenth century to fight banditry, theft, and the contraband trade in liquor. In place for an entire century (1719–1818), it also dealt with cases of physical violence, sometimes even spousal murders, three of which this research uncovered.[52] In colonial Colombia, the only *audiencia* available was located in Santafé de Bogotá, and there were no other high courts like the ones available in Mexico or Spain.

During the sixteenth and seventeenth centuries, Spain's main *audiencias* were in the Canary Islands (Palma), Galicia (La Coruña), and Seville. From the eighteenth century on, the Crown established new ones in Aragon (Zaragoza), Asturias (Oviedo), Catalonia (Barcelona), Extremadura (Cáceres), Mallorca (Palma de Mallorca), and Valencia. In Spain's two most traditional and important judicial districts (Valladolid and Granada), consultation was with the *real chancillería,* a multi-judge tribunal staffed by the most prominent judges in the kingdom. Madrid, the monarchy's capital, also had a special section within the *Consejo de Castilla*, the *Sala de Alcaldes de Casa y Corte* (Magistrates of the King's Court). Among other things, it heard appeals of criminal cases tried in its jurisdiction and those decided by its individual members in the first instance, and it reviewed all cases that incurred the death penalty.[53] Finally, the Crown's *Consejo de Indias,* based in the Spanish city of Seville, intervened to solve conflicts between major authorities in the Indies (*audiencias* and viceroys in particular) concerning the handling of specific criminal cases. It also settled similar disputes between the ecclesiastical and secular (civil or military) authorities, especially cases involving church asylum.[54] All of these high courts intervened mainly at the end of the criminal proceedings. Up until then, local magistrates were the ones in charge.

Local justice officials undertook the investigation of spousal murders, drawing on information from defendants, injured parties, relatives, neighbors, and other witnesses. Children reported many cases, as they often were, unfortunately, the main witnesses to spousal murder and abuse inside the home. Because of their legal status, the value of their testimony was controversial.

As previous research has amply documented, minors both in the metropolis and overseas enjoyed protected status under Spanish law. Some of the protections were inherited from medieval law, but others appear to have developed overseas as part of the colonial legal system.[55] According to a leading practical legal manual of the time, children had to be at least fourteen to testify in civil cases, and be twenty in criminal cases.[56] Furthermore, a child's testimony did not have full legal value and merely constituted a "presumption" or clue.[57] On paper, children who were related by blood up to the fourth degree to one of the parties were prohibited from testifying in cases involving relatives.[58] This category clearly included sons and daughters, but these prescriptions were subject to interpretation and not always observed.

In the case of spousal murders, children's involvement sometimes included assistance in hiding and disposing of the corpse of their father or mother, but was usually limited to denouncing and/or testifying to aggression committed by one of their parents against the other. Contrary to statutes and doctrinal opinions, legal protections seem not to have hindered minors' appearances in court. In consideration of the "public" nature of spousal murder, it did not matter who reported the crime, even if a minor was the one who raised the alarm. One prosecutor explained that "otherwise incapable witnesses . . . must be deemed sufficient and competent" and that "hidden crimes may be discovered through children."[59] Once justice officials became aware of a murder, by any means whatsoever, they had the obligation to investigate. Therefore, the authorities stepped in after the two young daughters of Vicente Cano and Francisca Ramirez reported (*dieron voces*) that their father had hanged their mother in Tizapán el Alto (Guadalajara).[60] Similarly, in April 1803 a little girl from an Indian family went directly, without the need for adult mediation, to ask the justice officials of San Juan de Teotihuacan (northeast of Mexico City) to come immediately to her modest home, where her father, a local peon and cowboy, had stabbed and killed her mother during an argument over his drinking *pulque*.[61] The authorities reacted immediately, and the crime was prosecuted without legal challenge.

Children actively reported such crimes in Iberia, too. Seven-year-old Manuela Vicenta Escudero, along with a teenage servant girl, saw her father dispose of her mother's corpse after he killed her at their home in Spain in 1771.[62] Manuela Vicenta's testimony became the key instrument in the prosecution and sentencing of her father. She even testified without the participation of a tutor, and her testimony was never systematically challenged.[63] The defense tried to argue that, under law, the girl could not be considered an able witness even in less serious matters than criminal proceedings for homicide.[64] The prosecution retorted that although it was true that a child's testimony was not sufficient to condemn anybody, it was acceptable as a basis for further inquiries, particularly in the event of grave, lèse-majesté (*lesa majestad divina o humana*) offenses. It was also perfectly valid for the investigation of secret and clandestine cases (*delitos clandestinos y secretos*) that occurred at odd hours or in remote locations (deserts, forests, mountains) and were thus difficult to prove without the testimony of children, servants, and other generally unqualified individuals, typically those of lower social standing.[65] Spanish legal codes of old, such as the *Siete Partidas,* attributed more value to the testimony of nobles (*hijosdalgo*), patrons, and freemen than they did to that of commoners, servants, and serfs.[66] The same was true in *derecho indiano* for the testimony of Indians.

In Spanish America the testimony of Indians generally had less weight than the testimony of whites. As early as 1629, colonial jurist and legal author Solórzano y Pereira summarized the standard legal practice in Peru and other regions concerning Indian testimony, as mandated by Viceroy Francisco de Toledo: "In grave cases when it is indispensable to examine [Indian] witnesses, the testimony of no less than six such witnesses must be gathered either simultaneously or individually so that they depose about what they know; but even if they concur in their declarations, such testimony must not be given more credit or value than that of a single able [white] witness."[67]

According to legal historian Charles Cutter, though, in practice indigenous subjects were "routinely" viewed as qualified witnesses, especially in borderland areas such as northern New Spain.[68] This also seems to have been the case in many of our examples, but instances occurred even in the late colonial period when Spanish law (*derecho patrio*) rejected Indian testimony unless six indigenous witnesses agreed in their declaration. This is why some experienced lawyers, including sixty-year-old Nazario Peimbert, who served as an advisor to a local magistrate in a spousal murder case tried between 1819 and 1821 in northern Mexico, continued to claim that Indian testimony was "weak" and should not be trusted.[69] Notwithstanding these reservations, local magistrates proceeded expeditiously even in response to notification and testimony by children and Indians.

Except for a few instances involving evidence of negligent delays, these officials appear to have acted promptly, starting the investigation within hours and concluding it within a few months, two years at most. In the majority of cases tried in New Granada, for example, with or without a guilty plea the investigation and sentencing were generally completed within one to two years of the crime.[70] Even so, and as will be seen, cases that took just four months from beginning to end, such as the main incident in this book's chapter on Spain, prompted complaints and the removal of justice officials considered negligent in the handling of such grave matters.

Spousal murders, and indeed all homicides, were understood to be "public" crimes. Unlike *delitos privados*—for instance, *daños* (property damage), *injurias* (slander), and adultery—homicides and other public crimes (e.g., robbery, brigandage, sedition, and contraband) did not require a particular victim to file charges (*querella*). Anyone, *cualquiera del pueblo,* could bring such offenses to the authorities' attention. Local justice officials could investigate these crimes upon receiving notice (*denuncia*) or a formal accusation. Even if accusations or notices were withdrawn, the officials had to prosecute the cases automatically (*de oficio*) to satisfy the need for "public vengeance" (*vindicta pública*), an expression repeated frequently throughout the trials.[71]

Having received notice of the crime, the officials in charge of administering local justice summoned a public scribe (*escribano público*) or, if none was available, acted directly (*como juez receptor* or *por receptoria*) in the presence of witnesses who could corroborate the proceedings. For this purpose, justice officials sometimes forcefully enlisted (*de sopetón y a todo vigor*) witnesses if they did not wish to volunteer. For instance, this happened around 1802 to a surprised young man (*mozo*) ordered to accompany the lay judge investigating a spousal murder in northern Colombia to the scene of the crime.[72]

The justice official immediately issued a ruling (*auto de oficio* or *cabeza de proceso*) to begin the investigation, starting by summoning medical experts to examine the corpse. Before the examination, it was typical for the officials in charge to call out the victim's name three times. This was the procedure followed in the case of Antonio Salas, killed by his wife and her lover in Colima, western Mexico, in 1812.[73] Upon receiving no answer, the officials pronounced him dead.

According to the law, two local physicians (*médicos*), two surgeons (*cirujanos*), or one of each had to participate in the examination and testify about the results. This, as well as the retention of any objects related to the crime (weapons, suspicious substances, bloody objects or garments), was indispensable for obtaining what was known as full proof (*plena prueba*) of the body of the crime (*cuerpo del delito*).[74] In theory, and only in exceptional circumstances such as remote locations lacking medical doctors or surgeons, was the testimony of a single medical expert sufficient. In practice, however, most of the cases discussed in this book saw the intervention of only one medical expert. This appears to have been standard practice even in midsize urban centers where several physicians or surgeons were likely available. In yet more extraordinary cases where licensed medical experts were unavailable, local healers (*curanderos*), midwives, or even laypeople (*prácticos*) could be asked to examine corpses to help determine the approximate nature of the injuries and the probable cause of death. In the northeastern Colombian jurisdiction of Cucuta, for instance, in the absence of a surgeon the local judge designated two "intelligent neighbors" to inspect the corpse of

Maria Natividad, a black slave whose husband and fellow slave, Agustin Peralta, stoned to death at a local farm in 1803.[75] In general, however, evidence of intervention by *prácticos* in our cases is limited, probably because their testimony was likely to be challenged later.[76]

Furthermore, whenever medical or equivalent examinations were omitted, the defense was eager to argue insufficient proof to indicate the possible cause of death. A solicitor used this excuse in the case of Maria Dolores, an indigenous woman murdered in the central Mexican town of Atlitalaquia, in 1805. Because of the dearth (*inopia*) of physicians in this locale, a proper examination of the woman's corpse was not performed. As a result, the solicitor argued, the husband should be released or his punishment considerably reduced.[77]

In those early or "summary" stages (*informaciones sumarias* or *sumario*) of the criminal investigation, it was standard practice for local magistrates to ask at least two other people, sometimes more, to accompany medical personnel—the scribe (if there was one) and the local judge to the scene of the crime and/or location of the corpse. They were later asked to testify about what they saw.[78] This strengthened the medical evidence with regard to the body and the circumstances of the crime, contributing, along with the medical testimony, to obtaining full proof that a murder had been committed.

If the corpse had been buried before being examined by expert medical witnesses, or a previous medical examination was found to be defective, local justice officials occasionally ordered bodies to be exhumed.[79] Ecclesiastical authorities, usually the local priest, had to approve the procedure, as they did in the case of Tomas Rojo, exhumed two weeks after his burial in the jurisdiction of Valladolid, Spain, around 1787.[80] The civil authorities suspected foul play by his wife. If a priest was not immediately available, exhumations could proceed without authorization. This occurred in 1802 in Magangué, northern Colombia, where officials charged the wife of Matias Ostia and her lover of killing him and burying the body to hide their crime.[81] In this and similar cases, officials in charge of the investigation issued orders for the priest to rebury the corpse after the necessary medical review was complete.

Justice officials also had to find and seize the murder weapon as promptly as possible and to ascertain whether it was a prohibited one, in which case the eventual punishment could be more severe. The list of prohibited weapons generally included firearms and a range of spades, swords, and knives, even ones used in cooking.[82] In other instances, justice personnel confiscated suspicious substances that may have been used as poison, among the most common of which was, at least in Iberia, the mercury-based compound *soliman*.[83]

In some cases the investigating officials were actually able to talk to the injured victims prior to their deaths and learn the circumstances of the crime firsthand. In 1815, for example, a Mexican indigenous woman named María Estefana described to the judge how her husband hit her over the head with a small bench after she came home late one night. She died of her injuries about a month later at a local hospital in Guadalajara. There were no other witnesses to the crime.[84] Similarly, before her death a few weeks later, Maria Paula Garcia told the local magistrate that her drunken husband, José Manuel, struck her on the head with a machete after they argued at a neighbor's party in 1819. Maria Paula even said that she forgave him. Several witnesses declared that the two had argued after José Manuel flirted with other women.[85]

In most instances, of course, the officials had only a corpse to examine. They thus began by hearing the statements of relatives, witnesses, neighbors, and/or acquaintances, whether directly or with assistance of a third party. In the colonies, translators sometimes had to assist in interviewing native witnesses who did not speak Spanish. On a few occasions, although this was rather exceptional, the judge went on to interrogate the defendants directly to obtain their preliminary testimony (*declaración preparatoria*) or confession.[86] That interrogation, especially in cases involving spouses who killed with the assistance of their lovers, usually included several questions aimed at establishing whether or not the murder had been premeditated.

When defendants went into hiding, justice officials issued three public summons asking them to present themselves. If they did not appear, they were declared to be in "contumacy" (*rebeldía* or *contumacia*) and tried in absentia. This sometimes occurred years after the crime, as was the case with Antonio Ureña, whose *contumacía* was declared in 1815, three years after authorities failed to apprehend him for killing his lover's husband with her assistance in a western Mexican town.[87]

When suspects were available, the authorities issued an order (*orden o mandamiento de prender*) to imprison them in the local jail, frequently along with suspected accomplices or their children, considered potential accomplices who were prone to lie to protect the surviving parent. The suspects were kept in different jails or separate areas of the same one to avoid any communication or exchange of information. In smaller population centers where adequate jails or resources could not support inmates, officials transferred detainees to the closest city. This happened regularly in small Indian towns such as Santa Isabel, in northern Mexico, whose criminals were sent to Chihuahua jails for trial.[88] The same happened when proactive friends or relatives (*apasionados*) threatened to free the culprit from a local jail, as in the case of Gregorio Moreno, tried for killing his lover's husband in Valladolid, Spain, in 1813.[89] In the colonies the transfer sometimes took place at the expense of the entire community, which the local viceroy held responsible for the cost of transportation.[90]

In most instances the authorities preemptively seized the defendant's and any accomplices' property, placing it under the care or deposit of a third party.[91] The seizure (*embargo preventivo* or *secuestro*) covered all material possessions, ranging from animals, crops, and agricultural and other tools to furniture, clothing, and cooking utensils. When available, land and houses were also included. All property had to be carefully inventoried, and some of it could be sold to pay for the partial costs (*costas*) of the ongoing investigation or the custody and maintenance of the defendant in jail. In many instances, as in the case of Manuel Davila, tried in Galicia for the violent murder of his wife and sentenced in 1816 to spend ten years in an overseas *presidio,* the properties were liquidated at the end of the trial to support the defendant and any dependent relatives, in this case a son.[92] Lawyers, justice officials, scribes, and expert witnesses—medical experts, in particular—were all eager to obtain compensation for their services and also, we can presume, to ensure the sufficient and extended *secuestro* of property or the continuing detention of those charged until they paid. For instance, in a case in which the value of confiscated assets was not sufficient to cover judicial costs, the stepsons of Josefa Ruiz—allegedly killed in 1781 by her husband, Melchor Hernández, in Soria, northern Spain—remained under detention even after they had been acquitted.[93]

Disputes over the administration of confiscated property and the alleged seizure of goods not belonging to the defendant were common and could turn bitter. Allegations of corruption or mismanagement on the part of the designated administrator were also common. This occurred in the case of an indigenous woman, Ana Victoriana, tried in 1796 for killing her husband, Salvador, in Xochimilco, central Mexico. An allegedly incompetent and corrupt administrator (*depositario*) mismanaged her property, and upon her acquittal, she was left almost destitute.[94] Ordinarily, even when evidence of the defendant's responsibility was not compelling, the officials in charge did not lift the *secuestro* until the very end of the investigation. In addition, even in cases when they were ultimately acquitted, defendants were often ordered to pay the full costs of the judicial proceedings. This happened not only to Ana Victoriana but also to Josefa Muñóz, who was acquitted in 1788 for allegedly killing her husband in Valladolid, Spain, one year earlier.[95] Arbitrary criminal proceedings, regardless of their final outcome, could result in the ruin of modest individuals and families. Not only could the costs of prolonged judicial investigations be considerable, but while they lasted, a defendant's lands often remained idle and livestock and crops consumed or damaged by those in charge of their custody.[96]

The preliminary evidence gleaned from early inquiries (examination of corpses, witness testimony, confessions) was generally collected without the defendant's full participation and thus was not on its own sufficient to resolve the case. The next step was for a judge to order that the case enter into the discovery phase (*probanzas*). This decision (*auto de pruebas o probanzas,* sometimes also called *auto de culpa y cargo*) moved the criminal trial into a new stage called a plenary proceeding (*procedimiento plenario*), which lasted nine days in the case of private offenses and fifteen days for public crimes like the ones under consideration here. However, magistrates could extend the term to more than eighty days, which they regularly did.[97]

During this stage, the authorities designated a prosecutor (*promotor fiscal*). This could be a layperson whom an attorney (*persona de ciencia y conciencia*), typically paid with part of the assets confiscated, assisted.[98] The defendant, in turn, had the right to an advocate (*defensor*), who was normally a lay member of the community (*vecino*), and a curator (*curador*) if required by law. *Curadores* were required for minors (females between the ages of twelve and fourteen, males ages fourteen to twenty-five) and all Indian defendants, such as the Tarahumara native Maria Getrudis, tried in Guadalajara for killing her husband, Mariano, in 1806. As was typical, her court-designated curator's efforts to get her sentence reduced highlighted her "weak gender" and "natural imbecility."[99]

In the plenary stage the defendant faced at least one more interrogation (*confesion con cargo*) and thereafter received full notification of all major procedures about to take place. To ensure the legal admissibility of evidence, observance of all of the required legal formalities—in particular, cursory confirmation (*ratificación*) by defendants and witnesses of their previous testimony, and notifications (*traslados*) to the various parties—was critical.[100] During this stage, witnesses sometimes had to confront one another or the defendant (*careados*), and it was common for justice officials, even lay ones, to interrogate the various parties aggressively, admonishing them (*reconvención*) about any apparent contradictions in their testimony.[101] A typical expression directed toward witnesses or the defendant was that they were testifying with "little shame and fear for God and justice, incurring perjury and hiding the truth" (*poco pudor y temor de Dios y de la justicia, perjurándose y faltando a la verdad*). For instance, this is how justice officials confronted Maria Espitia when, despite abundant evidence she had repeatedly struck her husband with a machete, she claimed ignorance of the reason for her imprisonment in 1802.[102]

This phase ended, at least in theory, when the term expired or all necessary procedures concluded. The local judge would then issue an order to make public all proofs (*publicación de probanzas o de testigos*), giving the parties (*defensor* and *promotor fiscal*) six days to submit closing argument or final allegations (*alegato de bien probado* or *escrito de buena prueba*) against or supporting each defendant. The main purpose of such allegations was to sum up incriminating evidence and highlight aggravating circumstances or, alternatively, propose justifications for the defendant's behavior and bring extenuating circumstances (*excepciones*) to the attention of the judge. Another possibility for the defense was to challenge (*tachar*) the available proofs, demonstrating that some of the evidence lacked validity or veracity.

After this last phase, in some exceptional cases or for lack of full proof, the defendant could in theory be subject to judicial torture if the judge so ordered (*sentencia interlocutoria de tormento*). Even a child's testimony was sufficient for ordering the judicial torture of suspects to extract a confession.[103] Although the law made clear that children under the age of fourteen could not be subjected to judicial torture themselves, some prosecutors claimed that the practice could not be entirely ruled out even in cases of very young children if they witnessed a crime that was difficult to prove otherwise.[104] In any case, as we shall see elsewhere, by the late eighteenth century torture represented almost exclusively a threat to force last-minute confessions.

Barring delays (such as the need to threaten defendants or witnesses with torture, or actually inflict it), the case could be finalized and a definitive sentence issued.[105] Prior to a final decision, however, the file went for consultation to a lawyer (*asesor letrado*), who normally had to issue an opinion (*dictamen*) as to whether the case had been handled properly or presented some procedural mistakes (*nulidades*).[106] This lawyer had the opportunity to suggest a resolution or punishment, if applicable, and the local judge then made a final decision (*sentencia*), usually endorsing the *letrado*'s recommendations. This was ordinarily a cursory statement, without substantial reasoning or much justification. In 1768 the king actually prohibited judges from explaining their sentences.[107] According to a contemporary practical manual, sentences should not address possible motives or justifications lest the verdict elicit doubts.[108]

The sentence ultimately mandated either the defendant's release or punishment, typically following the *asesor letrado*'s recommendation. In such cases the expectation was that the judge would rely on full proof (*plena prueba*) of the facts, which generally consisted of the testimony of two credible adult witnesses (*dos testigos mayores de toda excepción*) who concurred in all details. Alternatively, a combination of various forms of evidence could lead to full proof—for instance, a single adult witness and several compelling clues (*indicios* or *presunciones*), or a plurality of clues.[109] In any case, sentences rarely if ever went over the mathematics of evidence or otherwise justified the punishment imposed. In cases of homicide the law required the records to be sent to the nearest *audiencia* or *chancillería* for consultation.[110] Once the consultation was finished, the costs of the process could be assessed and charged, and the sentence executed.[111]

The standard procedure just described could become more protracted and cumbersome when, as was not uncommon, a defendant claimed the right to church asylum (*asilo sagrado*). In such cases, royal justice officials had to wait for ecclesiastical judges to conclude a parallel special procedure (*causa de inmunidad*) prescribed by canon law to ascertain whether or not the claimant was entitled to church protection. These procedures could be lengthy and frequently resulted in clashes between ecclesiastical and civilian authorities. Technically, such clashes had to be resolved through special appeals (*recursos extraordinarios de fuerza*) to the *reales audiencias* and *chancillerías*. These were mechanisms to hear cases in which ecclesiastical judges were accused of having overstepped their bounds in granting protection to a particular defendant. Even in instances when civil authorities received authorization to extract a defendant from a sacred place, typically a church, they had to provide a formal oath (*caución juratoria*) ensuring that the defendant would be spared any corporal punishment.[112] Subsequent chapters of this book offer numerous instances of this practice.

CONCLUSION

In the late colonial Spanish Atlantic, legal institutions such as marriage, and the formal judicial procedures in place to solve disputes and crimes involving them, were vital means to strengthen social cohesion and control. For centuries, ecclesiastical and criminal justice unquestionably contributed to strengthen the social bond and ensured a fair degree of predictability in ecclesiastical and state interventions to address family conflicts, criminal and otherwise. To a greater or lesser extent, all of the parties with an interest in resolving conflictive situations (victims, defendants, witnesses, representatives, relatives, priests, state agents, the community) knew that, despite a fair amount of social mediation (infrajustice) and judicial discretion in place, there were standard norms and procedures, and a range of law enforcement and judicial authorities, with legitimacy and power to step in, conduct investigations, and implement "public vengeance" to redress any possible wrongs. Under this system, access to justice was vital to hegemonic rule on the part of both ecclesiastical and royal power.

Both canon law and civil law, and their related jurisdictions, had much to say about marriage and family conflicts. They set the framework for couples to enter into lifelong unions and provided traditional rules for dealing with many of the circumstances that spouses encountered during their married life. These ranged from the direction of the household and formation and administration of the family's patrimony to the resolution of marital disagreements and conflicts. Ecclesiastical divorce was one of the exceptional means that canon law made available to deal with serious breaches of the peace between spouses. Canon law also imposed special restrictions on spouses who inflicted violence against their life partners—in particular, prohibitions against marrying their accomplices in spousal murders. It was the Crown's system of law, however, rather than canon law, that addressed most criminal behavior.

Under the Crown's (civil) law, the prosecution of spousal and other murders was a public obligation. Justice officials had to investigate such crimes even in the absence of a private complaint. The different phases of related criminal proceedings and the evaluation of testimonies and other evidence followed long-standing routines and criteria prescribed in myriad legal statutes and summed up in multiple practical manuals. These manuals, some of which dated back to the sixteenth century, served as useful guides for civil and canon law professors, justice officials, attorneys, scribes, procurators, and others, even the parties to the crime (*profesores de entrambos derechos, y fueros, y jueces, abogados, escribanos y procuradores, litigantes y otras personas*).[113]

Justice unfolded as the result of the intervention of multiple voices and parties, but legal procedures and rules of evidence were more or less fixed and technical. In all but a few instances, most notably exemptions from the application of judicial torture as a method to obtain evidence of hard-to-document crimes, social hierarchies do not seem to have played a role during the formalities observed in trial proceedings. The social tensions behind legal rules and procedures will be much more evident in future chapters, which examine the way that the law differentiated between legal subjects in consideration of their ethnicity, gender, and social status. For instance, the next chapter offers a detailed discussion of spousal murders in colonial Mexico and considers the biases surrounding the treatment of native peoples.

CHAPTER TWO

Innocent Infants?

Indians and Domestic Violence in Colonial Mexico

On a Monday morning in early October 1775, Lorenzo Macapa, the son of an Indian leader (*capitan*) and hacienda owner, knocked his wife to the ground and proceeded to kick her several times in the lower back and stomach. The couple was returning from the local Catholic mission of Nuestra Señora del Rosario Viñadaco near New Spain's Presidio de Loreto, a Spanish military outpost in the remote region of Baja California (see Figure 2.1).[1] Along with them marched another group of Indian *neófitos*. The husband was angry and jealous because, a few days before, his wife had gone hunting with a *gentil* (a non-Christian), the brother of another Indian captain named Quilipaqua.

At the Catholic mission, three days before their fateful departure, Lorenzo beat his wife for the first time. Later, as they left the mission and were walking home, he ordered her to carry a pot containing *mescal*, a distilled alcoholic beverage made from agave. She refused, for the pot was heavy and she was pregnant, and asked him to leave her alone. Her refusal and reluctance to walk beside him further enraged Lorenzo. After pushing her down and kicking her brutally, he left his wife behind and walked on to catch up with the rest of the group. The woman stood up and managed to walk a little more, but shortly thereafter had to stop by the side of the road and lie down under a tree. When two native women and a man approached and asked her if she was in pain, she complained that she was pregnant and that her husband's kicks had most likely killed her unborn baby. As for her, she said she would not endure three more days. Still lying in the same spot, holding her stomach and in terrible pain, the woman died on the afternoon of the following day.

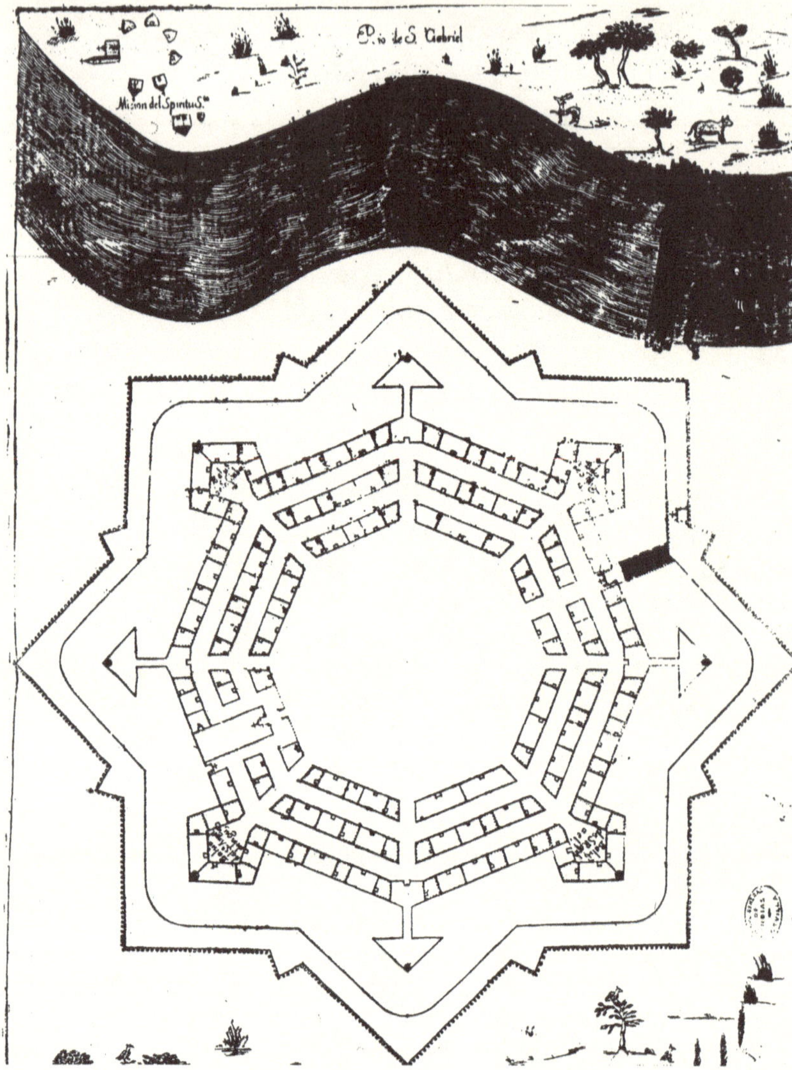

Figure 2.1. Presidio de N. S. de Loreto. AGI, Seville, MP-Mexico, 116bis, rollo 8.

The region's Spanish governor undertook the investigation of the incident. Under Spanish legislation, the death of Lorenzo's wife was considered a possible homicide, a crime that could be punishable by death.[2] Two of the mission's Franciscan priests, Fray Manuel Pérez and Fray Francisco Calisteo, sent letters asking for leniency. They argued that in spite of his alleged crime, Lorenzo Macapa had been helpful in the "*reducción de una crecida rancheria*," the taming and conversion of a large Indian community of which his father, Agustín Macapa, was the leader. Captains like him enjoyed continuing authority in New Spain's frontier areas, where the power of Indian rulers had not declined as it had in Mexico's central valley. They helped mobilize resources and peoples, thus contributing actively to the conversion process. The elder Macapa, seeking clemency for his son, not only made gifts to the soldiers who captured him but also brought twenty-four other Indians to the mission for conversion and expressed his willingness to help Christianize the rest of the Indians in the community. The rate of conversion was indeed quite high around the time of the incident, thanks to Captain Macapa's active support.[3]

A year later, the viceroyalty's prosecutor argued that the fact that Lorenzo was the son of a captain and, along with his father, had cooperated in the conversion of other Indians, as well as his obvious *rusticidad* (primitive condition), were sufficient reasons to order his release with merely a reprimand. The prosecutor also pointed to legal errors in the prosecution of the case. However, he did not mention that the entire criminal procedure could be declared null and void because the accused was not represented by a curator (*curador ad litem*), as the law mandated in criminal cases where the defendant was a "minor"—a category that included all Amerindians under Spanish law. He did criticize, though, the investigators' failure to order a medical examination of the victim's corpse to ascertain if she was indeed pregnant and whether her husband's kicks were the real cause of her death. Some of the prosecutor's views concurred with the petitions of the mission priests and were accepted by New Spain's highest court (*audiencia*), which ordered Lorenzo Macapa's immediate release in October 1776.[4]

By no means unique, the incident involving Macapa and his wife reflects the complex interaction of patriarchy and paternalism during the colonial period. In response to a native's brutal aggression against his wife, the clergy and the royal authorities opted for benevolence. The outcome of the case suggests that the Crown's self-interested "compassion" and condescension could carry the day over other concerns, such as a native woman's right to life and physical well-being or the safety of spouses and women in general. In other words, the role of Indian chiefs on New Spain's northern frontier as strategic power brokers and, more generally, the public representation of Indians as naive infants in need of legal protection took precedence over appropriate responses to the behavior of violently domineering patriarchs ready to suppress any sign of spousal insubordination, disobedience, or disloyalty, whether real or imaginary. Although the law often treated Spanish and mestizo aggressors benignly, it accorded natives—influential ones even more so—particular forgiveness, both to further the higher interests of spreading Christianity and imposing the Spanish colonial order and because Indians in general were assumed not to know any better.

Like Lorenzo, a sizable portion of New Spain's defendants managed to walk away from heinous crimes with little more than a slap on the wrist. However, the issue of punishment was generally not just a function of political expediency or paternalism, but rather the result of a dynamic combination of ethnic relations, royal munificence, and, in particular, legislation and legal culture, which sanctioned a "politics of difference"[5] based on the notion of "miserable people" (*miserabiles personae*)—a category that included those considered to be vulnerable or weak because of a variety of reasons (gender, civil status, family situation, health, age). In the New World, the law added Indians to this peculiar list.[6]

Differential punishment for people in this broad group derived from a complex combination of sociocultural factors and legal doctrines and traditions. We shall come back to this point and establish that *miserabilis persona* was not a dismissive colonial concept; rather, it was a longstanding Roman legal notion that underwent several transformations over the centuries and was embraced by canon law as a mechanism for the Church to claim "jurisdiction" in cases that would normally be handled by the Crown. Over time, it came to be implemented in the Americas as a paternalistic device to shelter natives involved in legal proceedings, as if they could be compared to other people "whom nature moves us to pity" and were considered "weak" under canon law.[7] This conceptual transformation corresponds well to Harold Berman's findings that as time went on, the law in Western societies ended up assuming a variety of meanings, even seemingly contradictory ones. It could be, for instance, a means of social control and oppression, while also serving as an expression of morality or a means to protect against arbitrary rule or, in our case, harsh punishment. The explanation, at least in part, is that legal institutions carry over into the future meanings derived from earlier periods of history when they may have originated under very different circumstances and to pursue other ends.[8]

However, lenient treatment of natives did not mean that criminal law was of no consequence in their cases. Written laws such as the ones punishing homicide were not simply dead letters. Therefore, I do not believe that the judicial treatment of those spousal murderers reflected a gap between the law (the death penalty for spousal murderers, for example) and practice (forgiveness for the majority of Indians charged with this crime).[9] Written laws and legal doctrines concerning aspects such as the treatment of *miserabiles personae,* the evaluation of evidence, the existence or lack of criminal intent, the attribution of responsibility, the defendant's capacity to discern right from wrong, the law's understanding of the causal connection between aggression and death, the universal right to be eligible for royal and ecclesiastical clemency—all of these carried considerable weight and closely informed highly discretionary judicial practices.[10] Although embedded in enduring cultural traditions of sovereign rule, even the king's leniency derived from deeply entrenched legal principles.[11] Several chapters of this study address these various aspects in some depth. For now, our attention will focus on other social features, including patriarchy, ethnicity, and gender.

The claim that the application of royal justice against abusive spouses clashed with a basic societal principle, a husband's authority over his household, is as doubtful as the alleged insignificance of the law.[12] Royal leniency was not really the way to resolve the long-standing dilemma between the king's strict paternal rule and fathers' patriarchy in the home.[13] As suggested long ago by Silvia Arrom, and established more recently by Bianca Premo, royal paternalism and the patriarchal behavior of individual royal subjects were complementary, not contradictory.[14] Furthermore, though it certainly contributed to strengthen the Crown's legitimacy and was also a means to appease his Christian soul, the king's clemency was a legal tradition not necessarily driven by ulterior motives.

In sum, law did not always favor political pragmatism over juridical doctrine, nor was leniency toward spousal murderers merely the result of patriarchal and paternalistic royal custom.[15] Laws and legal doctrines of various kinds mattered greatly and made it quite possible for kings to be patriarchs on their thrones and fathers to be patriarchs in their homes at the same time. Legal norms and principles were by no means irrelevant.

Under the law, for instance, being Indian or committing a crime while drunk—both characteristics of many of the defendants in the records—were mitigating circumstances and could lead to acquittal. Royal graces, an important mechanism that played a significant role in easing the situation of domestic and other criminals, required clear legal justifications and also the observance of strict legal procedures. These legal facts suggest, at least in part, that the possible contradiction between the public representation of Indians in criminal law as defenseless minors, on the one hand, and, on the other, their private behavior as heavy-handed patriarchs enjoying special protections under canon and civil law was more apparent than real.[16]

After summarizing the material, demographic, and institutional setting, this chapter examines several additional examples of domestic battery and homicide in Mexico. It addresses preliminarily the interaction among ethnic relations, legal culture (long-standing legal principles and practices), and royal rituals in explaining the standards of justice applied to Indians and other defendants. For now, the discussion touches mainly on issues relating to the social history of crime, including the social profile of criminals, the setting, the social context, and motives driving criminal behavior.[17]

William Taylor's pioneering studies of homicide in three different regions of colonial Mexico during roughly the same period is invaluable as a methodological guide and comparison, as is Mexican historian Juan J. Pescador's preliminary but insightful analysis of a much smaller set of cases in central Mexico from around the same years.[18] I also cite additional comparative inferences from a previous case study of spousal murders in another Spanish American colony, New Granada, that will be discussed in Chapter 6.[19] The discussion draws as well on observations that quarrels between men and women in colonial Mexico and elsewhere did not derive from diffuse social tensions or the frustrations of marginal or "deviant" subjects, but instead had more or less obvious gender roots. The chapter shares Steve Stern's conclusion that the gender roots in question were related to disputes over "patriarchal pacts" between subaltern men and women—in other words, male–female contestation over the character and boundaries of reciprocal rights and obligations.[20] It also concurs with Susan Kellogg's views on the relative decline in the status of Indian women as a result of the imposition of Spanish legal culture. However, this does not mean that indigenous women were incapable of employing legal and judicial means to promote their interests or to act before the law with full capacity. As we shall see, they did so on a regular basis.[21]

COLONIAL NEW SPAIN: THE INSTITUTIONAL, ECONOMIC, AND SOCIAL SETTING

In the late eighteenth century, the Spanish empire continued to administer its American colonies by dividing them into kingdom-like units known as viceroyalties, of which there were four at the time: from north to south, New Spain, New Granada, Peru, and Río de la Plata. The largest and most economically significant was the viceroyalty of New Spain, created soon after the conquest of the Aztec Empire in the early sixteenth century. It encompassed an enormous territory stretching all the way from California to Panama—fourteen times the size of Spain and considerably larger than the recently founded United States of America. This extensive viceroyalty included smaller territorial units presided over by high courts of justice with extensive administrative, political, and even military functions known as *audiencias*. As explained earlier, colonial Mexico had two main *audiencias:* the Audiencia of New Spain, in Mexico City, and the Audiencia of New Galicia, in Guadalajara, both dating back to the sixteenth century.[22] In the late eighteenth century (1780s), to improve policing and taxation, the Spanish Crown divided its viceroyalties and *audiencias* into *intendencias,* state-like centers of financial and military administration supervised by the viceroy but presided over by a semi-independent official. These administrative divisions varied in population but were all mostly rural.

Although it contained large urban centers, including Mexico City, the most densely inhabited city in North America with a total population more than twice the size of Philadelphia's and more than three times that of New York,[23] colonial Mexico was predominantly a rural society. It was dotted with little peasant and mining towns, small Indian communities and villages, and remote mission outposts such as Lorenzo Macapa's Nuestra Señora del Rosario Viñadaco. The territory also included vast unpopulated plains and mountainous areas.

Population centers were scattered throughout this rough terrain, which Cortez had compared to a "crumpled sheet of paper," and were poorly connected to one another. To reach distant and even neighboring areas required long treks on foot or, sometimes, exhausting trips by mule or, less commonly, horseback, nearly always along narrow mule paths passing through steep ranges or the extended valleys in between. On the best routes—of which there were not many—elite travelers could occasionally outfit themselves with *forlones,* coaches with four wheels, two seats, and one or two horses. A few carriages were available to the well-to-do for circulation within larger urban centers such as Mexico City, Puebla, Guanajuato, and Guadalajara.[24] Water transport was infrequent, however, for in this mostly semiarid land rivers and streams were predominantly non-navigable.

In spite of the dry climate, the colony produced abundant maize, wheat, sugarcane, tobacco, cacao, barley, maguey and other agaves, cotton, vegetables, and fruit. Agricultural production was scattered among large self-sufficient estates, haciendas, middle-sized farms, and small peasant plots. Livestock raising was also central, supplying horses, mules, donkeys, and oxen for the transportation of people and cargo; the plowing of fields and the operation of mines and sugar mills (*trapiches*); meat and milk; wool for textile miles (*obrajes*); tallow, potash, and fat for soap making and candle making; and hides for tanneries. Mining, especially of the rich silver deposits in central and northern Mexico (Guanajuato, Pachuca, and Zacatecas), was a key activity for both the Spanish Crown and local elites, as were long-distance and retail trade.

Like the rest of the Spanish colonies, Mexico was a deeply hierarchical society, segregated along economic and, primarily, racial lines. The plebeian sectors, representing up to 80 percent of the colony's entire population, were not only poor but also generally nonwhite. Although phenotype or skin color was sometimes ambiguous and malleable, and economic or even cultural incorporation into superior groups was possible, black slaves and free blacks were generally on the lowest step of the social ladder, followed upward by mulattoes (born of whites and blacks), *coyotes* (African and indigenous mix), Indians, *mestizos* (born of whites and Indians), and *castizos* (*mestizo* and Spanish mix). Poor whites were considered socially superior to other poor people with darker skin. Spaniards, also called *gachupines,* were at the very top of the social scale, followed by their white, American-born descendants, known as *criollos* or Creoles. *Gachupines* and *criollos* dominated the wealthy classes; the few wealthy *mestizos* or Indians were generally looked down upon and kept segregated, although as time went on they gained greater social acceptance.

Finally, dress was an important social marker too. People in all of these social groups dressed not only on a level with their wealth but also their physiognomy. People at the top wore shoes and clothing made up of fine woolens, silk, and other imported fabrics with lace, silver, and gold adornment, jewels, scarves, and tissues. Ordinary Indians went barefoot or in sandals, and their clothes were made of coarse, locally woven cotton. Half-bloods and poor whites endeavored to dress as Spaniards of fortune, but many had to content themselves with local attire.

This work focuses mainly on the rural and urban poor, who also happen to have been the most active participants in the domestic disputes and crimes in our case set. Most of colonial Mexico's poor were Indians, a group that constituted between 42 percent and 88 percent of the population, depending on the area (see Table 2.1). New Spain's Indian

TABLE 2.1. *Indian population of some colonial Mexican intendancies, 1810s*

Intendancy	Population	Indian population	Percentage of Indians
Mexico	1,600,000	1,000,000	62.5
Puebla	800,000	600,000	75
Oaxaca	600,000	530,000	88.3
Guadalajara	485,000[a]	—	—
Michoacán	400,000	170,000	42.5
Veracruz	190,000	140,000	73.6
Tlaxcala	90,000	65,000	72.2

SOURCES: Taylor, *Drinking, Homicide, and Rebellion,* 26; Humboldt, *Ensayo politico sobre el reino de la Nueva España,* 2: 13–14.

[a]Population in 1793 according to Humboldt.

communities were quite diverse, some not yet fully integrated into Spanish society and sometimes openly rebellious.

The Tarahumara peoples of Chihuahua, in northwestern Mexico, barely had contact with the Spaniards well into the late eighteenth century, and then mainly through Catholic missionaries. In the far north, in what is today New Mexico, were the Pueblo Indians, sedentary groups who coexisted peacefully with the Spaniards, also through the intermediation of Catholic missions. Peoples of Coahuiltecan and Karankawa origin inhabited Texas, living by hunting and gathering and moving regularly in pursuit of their livelihood. Both New Mexico and Texas, and also the northern region of Sonora, were also home to other groups that whites called barbarian or brave Indians, *indios bravos* or *indios barbaros*, because of their raids on Spanish settlements. These included Chichimec-related communities, among them Apaches (or Lipanes), Mayo, Mecos, Opata, Seri, and Yaqui, some of whom had a reputation as warriors who jealously guarded their independence from Spaniards and were the main inhabitants of Sonora. Bloody Yaqui and Mayo revolts had occurred in this region in 1740, and as late as the early 1780s, General Commander Joseph de Galvez reported difficulty pacifying native groups not only in Texas and New Mexico, but also in Coahuila and New Vizcaya (the modern northern states of Chihuahua and Durango).[25] Only missionaries, especially the Jesuits and, later, the Franciscans and Dominicans, seem to have been able to establish mutually beneficial relations with some of these communities, including central and southern California's Chumash and Baja California's Ñapika and Cochimí peoples, the group to which Lorenzo Macapa belonged.

However, the densest Indian communities were in the viceroyalty's central and southern regions. Nahuatl-speaking peoples and their Hispanicized relatives represented a large percentage of the population in the Valley of Mexico. In the Puebla area, two-thirds of the population consisted of Tlaxcalans, and in Oaxaca, several Indian communities spoke local Mixtec and Zapotec dialects. Central Mexico also featured a range of other linguistic groups, including Mazahuas, Otomis, and Tarascans (Puerépechas). The south was home to another series of cultures. Maya-speaking groups inhabited Yucatan, and Chiapas contained a large variety of ethnicities, including the Cho´l, Kanjobal, Mam, Mayas Lacandones, Tojolabal, Tzeltal, Tzotzil, and Zoques,. Numerous other communities (Acaxes, Aibinos, Capaxes, Coanos, Nebomes, Nures, Tagues, Tebacas, Tepehuanes, Vitzuritas, Xiximies, Zayahuecos, etc.) were scattered across the rest of the colonial Mexican landscape and contributed to the formation of strong and distinct regional cultures and economies. By the late eighteenth century, many of these culturally and linguistically diverse native peoples, even the many Hispanicized ones, were impoverished peasants who performed manual and low-status activities. Before discussing this aspect, though, a few words are in order first about family structures and patterns.

Around this time, nuclear families were as frequent as extended ones. Such households could be based upon informal unions, but marriage, encouraged by the Crown, was common among not only the white segment of the population but also among *castas* (mixed-race groups), and the natives.[26] Although these patterns changed over time and from region to region, in the 1790s female Indians usually married between the ages of sixteen and twenty, earlier than either *casta* or Spanish women. Nuptial rates in the late colonial period were as high as 70–85 percent for women over the age of fifteen in several regions of Mexico. Average household size in regions such as Oaxaca varied between three to five persons, with elite families tending to be slightly larger than more modest ones. Among the latter it was common for several families to share the same house. For instance, fully half of households in Oaxaca in the 1770s featured anywhere from two to four families living together.[27] Like space, other material conditions were challenging.

Peasants tended to live in small adobe or reed houses, shacks, or huts with dirt floors and thatched roofs, located on plots frequently bordered by maguey or cactus. They sometimes had a separate kitchen area and one or, at most, two other rooms where the family lived without much privacy and in crowded conditions, often sleeping on thin straw mats (*petates*) or the floor. As inventories in criminal cases suggest, such families owned very few clothes, a blanket or two, some clay pots and dishes, a stone for grinding corn (*metate*), a clay dish for cooking tortillas (*tecale* or *tecomal*), a knife, a leather urn or wooden chest (*petaca* and *huacal*) to store "valuables" (clothes in particular), a leather and maguey rope band for carrying loads on one's back (*mecapal*), and some farm implements, most likely a hatchet or a pike. Occasionally, families may have owned a mule or horse along with a saddle, harness, spurs, and a leather or henequen whip or cord (*mecate*).

Urban dwellers did not fare better. The poorest city dwellers rented small rooms (*cuartos*) in run-down tenements or *casas de vecindad*. Others rented houses in poor condition or in total disrepair, even lacking doors or windows. Several families often shared small rental homes. Plebeians, especially in important urban centers such as Mexico City, rarely owned their own homes. Like rural dwellers, the city's poor possessed little personal property, mostly a few clothes, kitchen utensils (*trastos*), a portable stove (*brasero*), some blankets, a woven straw mat, a hammock, and a coffer or chest. Only a small number of middling people owned a house and a few more clothes, and even some paintings, metal tools, little silver boxes, and a donkey or two (see Appendix 1).

Some of the poorest rural Mexicans were unemployed, landless, or worked for others. In general, the poor, whether Indians or not, drew their sustenance from the land. Some worked on other people's haciendas, ranches, and farms or in sugar-processing mills (*trapiches*) as peons (*gañanes*) or cowboys (*vaqueros*). Others worked or put their animals to pasture in communally owned lands, while the better off had their own small plots (*milpas*), where they grew principally maize, beans, and chili peppers or raised chickens, a couple of pigs, or even a few sheep, goats, or cows. Many combined agricultural or livestock-related activities with weaving, pot making, or the selling of foodstuffs or *pulque*, a fermented drink ("heaven's water") made from the juice of the maguey plant, consumed widely and avidly and dispensed to neighbors and passersby from the doorways of many peasant households.

By the late eighteenth century, whole Indian communities had abandoned farming and become more or less full-time muleteers (*arrieros*), potters, basket weavers, or hired hands on private estates, in mines (*reales de minas*), or on public works projects. In small towns and cities alike, poorly dressed, barefoot Indians begged for alms or worked as servants, wet nurses, nannies, or cooks. Many sold food and sweets in streets and plazas as well as vegetables, herbs, fruits, and spices in small public markets (*tianguis*). Men worked in construction as brick makers, carriers or porters (*tamemes*), street sweepers or trash collectors. Some found work in cigar factories (*cigarreros*), candle- and soap-making workshops and tanneries, and textile workshops (*obrajes*), or served as assistants in butcher shops (*tocinerias*). Still others found manual employment in the many Catholic churches, convents, or monasteries around.

Cities and towns also attracted poor artisans from other racial backgrounds, particularly mulatto and *mestizo* pot makers, shoe makers, carpenters, bakers, leather workers, blacksmiths, tailors, and seamstresses. Others worked as coach drivers, itinerant peddlers, or common soldiers, occupations that, like farming and mining, also drew poor whites. Finally, on occasion, both in the countryside and urban areas, common people made a living as petty thieves, robbers (*ganzueros*), and bandits. Some with no resources to draw on spent long periods of time living in Catholic churches and cemeteries as refugees (*retraidos*).

In addition to their struggle to find work and make a living, commoners devoted significant portions of their time to three other main activities: praying, smoking, and drinking. Deeply devout Mexicans could practice the first of these occupations in the colony's many Catholic churches and shrines; in cemeteries, where All Souls' Day (*Dia de los*

Muertos) drew entire families for night-long vigils; and in modest and colorful home altars or chapels in virtually every household, where the most widely revered icon was the dark Virgin of Guadalupe. Smoking, a traditional pre-Columbian practice, was encouraged by the presence of cigar factories, including a huge one in Mexico City. Finally, consumption of a range of alcoholic beverages (*chinguirito*, *tepache*, *mescal*, *mistela*, *tesquino*) and wine, but especially *pulque*, was widespread not only at home (jugs were available for purchase from itinerant peddlers, nearby haciendas and farms, or the doorways of neighboring peasant homes) but also in public taverns (*pulquerias* and *vinaterias*). Drinking was also common at processions and festivals, home parties (*fandangos*), bullfights, and cockfights.[28] Unfortunately, as we shall see, it was also a frequent component of domestic disputes in colonial households.

SPOUSAL CONFLICTS AND PROLONGED BATTERING

Physical clashes between spouses were commonplace through the many years of this study and seemed present in virtually every Mexican region. The list of cases would fill hundreds of pages, but a few random snapshots illustrate the circumstances and protagonists. In most cases the victims themselves, their parents, or their offspring reported the crimes. For instance, in 1763, María Josefa del Castillo, a *mestiza*, denounced her husband, Manuel Antonio Ortíz, to the local authorities in the central Mexican city of Puebla, claiming that her life was at risk as a result of his constant verbal and physical abuse. He was a leather worker, and according to María Josefa, he had slashed her face with a knife. On other occasions, he smashed her head with rocks and beat her for no apparent reason except the fact that he was habitually drunk. His abusive behavior had won him several stints in jail, but his mistreatments had not ceased, and she lived in constant fear.[29]

In late 1775, Josefa Teodora, assisted by her father, Indian *cacique* (leader) Juan de Dios Tlatic, told the authorities in Xochimilco, central Mexico, that for the three years of her marriage her husband, Santiago Antonio, had constantly battered her and their little daughter. He had threatened Josefa with a pocketknife and had punched and even stoned her and her father. Santiago conceded that he punched his wife occasionally but claimed it was because of disagreements with his intrusive father-in-law and to stop Josefa from drinking *pulque*. She insisted that the sole reason for the terrible life (*mala vida*) her husband had given her was his abusive temper.[30]

According to the 1803 testimony of a nine-year-old Indian girl named María Josefa, her father, thirty-year-old cowboy Lazaro Antonio, often beat her mother ("*le daba mala vida, le reñia mucho y le daba de golpes*") while the child and her older brother took the family's sheep to pasture somewhere near the town of San Juan de Teotihuacan, northeast of the Valley of Mexico. On several occasions, the children had to call in the neighbors to pacify their father, who had been jailed at least twice and received several lashes from the local Indian governor.[31]

In Llerena, a little mining community north of Zacatecas, to cite just one more example, Maria Guadalupe Rodarte asked the local authorities to arrest her husband, white farmer and miner Vicente Arroyo. She alleged various abuses during the last eight years of their fifteen-year marriage. Most recently, in late 1817 her husband had beaten her for complaining to her father-in-law about Vicente's two-day absence from the house and expressing distress over his habitual drinking.[32]

Despite the evidence of the role of alcohol in fueling many examples of domestic violence in colonial Mexico and elsewhere in the Americas, recent studies find more-complex reasons for disputes pitting lower-class men and women against their spouses or partners. Many of these reasons involved differences in male and female perceptions of their mutual privileges and responsibilities in the relationship. Couples fought over economic issues, child rearing and discipline, relationships with in-laws, physical mobility, and alleged misbehavior ranging from temper tantrums and jealousy to extramarital affairs, alleged dereliction of domestic tasks, "disobedience," and "insolence." Some fights began as verbal disputes but escalated into outbursts of physical violence.[33]

As several of the examples above show, domestic abuse could be severe and continue for a long time, even years. Cultural and institutional, especially legal, reasons helped account for the persistence of the problem. Probably the most significant cultural reason why individuals withstood a spouse's physical abuse was the religious conception of marriage and the Catholic Church's approach to marital disputes. Under the influence of Christianity, patriarchy was the guiding principle of family and other relationships in colonial Mexico. For instance, religious doctrine held that whenever there was reasonable cause, and as a means to obtain a wife's obedience and make her amend her faults, husbands had a legal right to punish and even strike their wives "in moderation." When women experienced marital troubles, the Church advised them to use kind words to appease their husbands, to pray, and, in extreme cases, to appeal to their husband's confessor or other priests. Clergy called in to mediate domestic disputes were instructed to preserve the sanctity of marriage by reconciling couples.[34] All of these "solutions" favored prolonging marriages, regardless of how dysfunctional they might have been.

Only as a last resort were families advised to request civil protection. Even in these cases, however, wives faced institutional factors that contributed to the extension of abusive marital relations. The law was quite casual in addressing cases of *malos tratos* or *sevicia* (battery). The criminal legislation of the time did not deal specifically or in any detail with the problem. Beyond acknowledging that it was "unfortunately quite frequent" (*demasiado frecuente, por desgracia*), contemporary legal manuals did not discuss battery, except in passing.[35] In general, this conduct was not subject to automatic prosecution; rather, it was considered a *delito privado* (private crime) and as such required the injured party to file charges. For the conduct to result in automatic prosecution it had to cause "serious injuries," "severe bleeding," or "public outrage."[36] However, it did constitute a justifiable cause for *quod thorum et mensam* (bed and table) divorce—that is, physical separation from one's spouse—and, as Chapter 1 suggests, it was the motive most commonly invoked by Mexican wives who petitioned for divorce.[37]

Even in cases in which husbands physically abused their wives, the expectation was that state officials would make every effort possible to reconcile the parties.[38] Couples of modest means were not likely to sue for divorce or bodily separation, considering that such petitions generally required the services of a lawyer, payments in excess of 50 pesos (about half of the annual income of an ordinary peasant), and access to ecclesiastical courts (*provisoratos eclesiásticos*) in important urban centers—Mexico City, Puebla, Valladolid, or Guadalajara.[39] In such families it was more common for a spouse, in many instances after abandoning the household, to file a complaint before the local authorities for spousal abuse or *malos tratos*. Such complaints were relatively frequent, but their efficacy is open to question. In many cases in which the authorities used corrective measures (whipping, fines, payment of security bonds, short terms in a local jail, admonishments, and threats of more severe chastisement) to stop the battery, such as the example of Lázaro Antonio narrated below, the result was often an infuriated, abusive spouse, sometimes enraged to the point of murder.

STORIES OF SPOUSAL MURDER

A few stories from different time periods and places should suffice to give an initial overview of the circumstances characterizing typical cases of spousal homicide, their defendants, and their victims in colonial

Mexico. These cases, presented in chronological sequence, are meant to highlight some dominant features of the individuals involved, such as the fact that most of the offenders were male and Indian; common factors behind the crimes, including female disobedience, male jealousy, and alcohol consumption; and the benign punishments such crimes generally received.

In Villalta, Oaxaca, in late March 1747 (during the Catholic Holy Week), fifty-three-year-old Indian Diego Andrés, a leader (*cacique principal*) in his hometown of Tonaquia, turned himself in to the authorities for killing his *mestizo* wife, María Estevan, by beating her on the head with a hatchet handle. The couple had been married for less than a year. It seems that the marriage had been arranged between the bride's father, a poor man who later declared himself to be financially unable to travel to Antequera de Oaxaca to hire a lawyer to prosecute the case, and the Indian *cacique* groom, a widower. Having likely married against her will, and being younger and whiter than her husband, María Estevan seems to have refused to comply with her expected duties as a wife. She would not cook for her husband, called him "Indian, old, savage and *acolitado*"—in what seems to have been a pejorative reference to Diego Andrés's occupation as a *ministro de capilla*, or assistant at the church—talked back to him constantly using foul language, and on various occasions went to stay at her father's house for days at a time before reluctantly returning to resume married life with her husband.

On at least one occasion, Diego Andrés lost his patience, got drunk, and beat his wife, threatening her with a machete. For the most part, however, he claimed to have indulged her and tried to persuade her that it was too late for regrets: They were married for good, and there was no turning back. He reminded the woman that it was not appropriate for her to disrespect him, lest people gossip, for "even Indians know how to distinguish right from wrong."[40] He also urged her to go and see the local priest for advice. The last of their fights resulted from María Estevan's obstinate refusal to dress appropriately for church on Holy Thursday. Diego Andrés's mother and sister were present but could not understand the reasons behind the fight, for husband and wife spoke to each other in Spanish, a language that the two Indian women did not understand. Even though there was circumstantial evidence that María Estevan was pregnant at the time of her death and that at least some of her wounds were caused not by the wooden handle of the hatchet but by a sharp object such as a knife (or perhaps the hatchet blade itself)—evidence which would have aggravated the crime—Diego Andrés received a sentence of just ten years' banishment from his hometown and service in a local church. He did not have to spend any time at all in jail.

Incidents involving drunken natives annoyed by their wives' insolence abound. For instance, in Santiago de Tepetape, central Mexico, on a Saturday afternoon in late April 1803, thirty-year-old Lázaro Antonio, a tribute-paying Indian (*indio tributario*), stabbed his Indian wife, María Josefa, to death. They had been married for more than eleven years and had three children: a boy, who was probably eleven or twelve; a younger daughter, nine-year-old Manuela; and a baby girl. They lived on their own farm, where they had a patch of corn, a few hens, some sheep and pigs, two donkeys, and four oxen. Besides the income from the farm, Lázaro Antonio also earned money working as a cowboy on a nearby hacienda. On the day of the incident, he had returned from his duties at the hacienda with some corn, a silver peso, and a small leather bag containing *medio real* of *pulque*, all of which he proudly presented to his wife.

After some rough times during which the husband had been jailed for allegedly keeping a concubine and regularly mistreating his wife, the couple appeared to be getting along better. The extramarital affair had concluded a couple years before, after the concubine was banished from the town and Lázaro Antonio received several lashes from the Indian governor. Upon his release from jail, he had hanged his wife from a tree, beaten her badly, and forced her to promise that she would never again denounce him to the authorities. Once he set her loose, however, the woman, probably with the support and encouragement of her siblings and parents, who lived nearby, told local officials what her husband had done and said that the only way she would go back to live with him was if he were required to provide a security bond. The man managed to convince an uncle to serve as his *fiador*, or bondsman, and the couple resumed living together. Even after the *fiador* died and Lázaro Antonio felt more at ease to misbehave and beat María Josefa, husband and wife stayed together and added a third child to their family.

On the afternoon of the murder, the two were drinking *pulque* while their older son was out tending to the sheep and pigs, and little Manuela and the baby were around the house. It seems that the couple started to fight after the *pulque* was finished and the man insisted on getting more. María Josefa refused and asked him to give her some money he had hidden under his belt. Perhaps to defend herself from her husband's aggression, she allegedly lifted her hand, threatening to give him a *guanton* (punch). Grabbing her by the hair, the offended husband dragged her out of the house. As the fight escalated, little Manuela ran to call for help. By the time that relatives arrived, Lázaro Antonio had already used the knife he kept to cut maguey to stab María Josefa in the chest.

The relatives summoned the local Indian authorities, who found María Josefa's corpse lying in the front yard. They restrained Lázaro Antonio and took him along with the corpse to the justice official of San Juan Teotihuacan, where a lengthy trial commenced. The woman's siblings pressed charges but because of lack of money were forced to give up. The trial dragged on until May 1806, when Lázaro Antonio was sentenced to six years in a *presidio* working on a public road (*el camino de Perote*). He could deduct the three years he had already spent in jail. The judge rejected a plea for acquittal from the Indian's curator, who argued that the violent act had been an appropriate response to the woman's insubordination and her violation of Saint Agustin's dictum that "though Adam sinned, women must always be subordinated to men."[41] Nonetheless, this was a light sentence. After apologizing for the long delay in the resolution of the case, the judge based his decision on the mitigating circumstance that the man committed the crime while drunk.

Upon subsequent review of this decision in December 1808, the *audiencia* did not even need to resort to the assertion of Mexico's *Procurador de Indios* that the man had reacted understandably to the threat to his honor when his wife attempted to slap him.[42] Instead, the *audiencia* simply declared that the crime was covered by a royal pardon enacted back in 1803 and ordered Lázaro Antonio's immediate release. The judges rejected the prosecutor's observation that *parricidas* (a generic term applied at the time to killers of close relatives) could not enjoy royal graces.[43]

Leniency seems to have been the norm as our final case, involving another inebriated native, illustrates. It is from Guadalajara, where Juan José de los Reyes Sánchez, a thirty-year-old Indian weaver in a textile workshop (*obrajero*), fatally injured his wife, thirty-year-old Indian María Estefana Lara, by smashing her over the head with a wooden chair. On the night in question, early in October 1815, the husband had returned home drunk after an evening with friends. He fell asleep upon his arrival, but he woke up shortly afterward and became angry at not finding his wife in the house (a common source of family disputes).[44] When she returned, explaining that she had merely gone outside to defecate by the side of their corn patch, Juan José began to scold her, complaining that she had left the house unprotected and at the mercy of thieves. She responded that she was not his servant nor was she being paid to watch over him as he slept, and told him to "shut up." Later, probably to mitigate his unjustified aggression, the man would add that she had also called him a cuckold (*cabrón* and *alcahuete*) and had scratched his face. These could all be construed as major offenses against manliness and honor.[45] After her husband struck her with the chair, María Estefana went to the local hospital, where doctors said her head wounds did not appear to be serious. However, she soon developed a high fever and was transferred to "Medicine," a special section of the hospital for the treatment of serious cases. She died there a couple of weeks later. The local authorities seemed to have concluded that her death was unrelated to the blow from her husband, as was customary in cases when a lapse of several days separated time of death from the original aggression. Ultimately, Juan José was sentenced to just six months working on the boats in a nearby lake.

PATTERNS IN OTHER SPOUSAL KILLINGS IN NEW SPAIN

The cases just described belong to a larger group of all the spousal murder files found in the criminal archives of Mexico's two highest courts of justice in the colonial period, in Mexico City and Guadalajara, respectively.[46] The majority of cases available in the archives consulted date to the first two decades of the nineteenth century. Only a handful of cases are available for the period between 1740 and 1790, or the 1820s (see Table 2.2). The irregular character of this distribution is certainly a function of record keeping and suggests the incomplete and fragmentary nature of the evidence available. Assuming that it is fair to consider as a normal pattern the higher number of cases from, say, 1800 to 1820 (identical in each decade), a crude extrapolation of these figures (disregarding the impact of demographic growth on the crime rate over time) would mean that an average of at least twenty-eight cases could have occurred in each of the decades for which information is missing. This generous

TABLE 2.2. *Distribution of spousal homicides in New Spain, 1747–1821, by ten-year intervals*

Years	Number	Percentage[a]
1741–1750	1	1.15
1751–1760	4	4.6
1761–1770	4	4.6
1771–1780	6	6.9
1781–1790	5	5.7
1791–1800	11	12.64
1801–1810	28	32.1
1811–1820	28	32.1
1821	1	1.15
Total	87	

SOURCES: AGN, Mexico City, Acordada, Californias, Criminales, General de Parte, Presidios y Cárceles, and Provincias Internas; AJO; AANG, Criminales; AJP; Archivo Provincial de Zacatecas; Municipal Archive of Veracruz; *Diario de México* 176, March 25, 1806, 334–336; 1646, April 4, 1810, 373–374; Marín Tello, "Justicia penal y orden social en Michoacán," 217–218; Castro Gutiérrez, "Condición femenina y violencia," 6.

[a]Percentages do not necessarily total 100 because of rounding.

estimate would imply that the universe of possible cases between the 1740s and the 1820s might have approached 252 cases across Mexico.

The group of cases analyzed here may therefore constitute approximately 34.5 percent of the total incidents, sufficient to suggest some general trends. It is also large enough to formulate tentative answers to sociological questions relatively similar to the ones posed in William Taylor's classic and unique study about, for example, the physical and temporal circumstances of the crimes; the social identity of defendants and victims; and their motivations, legal treatment, and punishment. Although Taylor completed his research decades ago, these remain basic aspects for anybody interested in the historical sociology of crime.

The eighty-seven incidents in the sample occurred all over the viceroyalty, although a majority took place in rural parts of central Mexico—including Puebla de los Ángeles, towns and mining camps in the region later named Hidalgo (40), and in the regions of Guadalajara (12) and Oaxaca (14). Very few of them occurred in large cities or in peripheral areas such as Chihuahua, Colima, Sombrerete (Zacatecas), or San Luis Potosí; faraway missions and *presidios* (Presidio de Loreto's Nuestra Señora del Rosario Viñadaco Mission, San Antonio's Mission, Presidio de Monterrey's San Luis Obispo Mission, Presidio de San Diego's San Juan Capistrano Mission); or remote provinces such as Nuevo Santander (modern Tamaulipas) and Baja California.[47]

The murders seem to have occurred randomly throughout the day, with a few more at night than in the morning or afternoon (see Table 2.3). If we compare them to the figures for all kinds of homicides,

TABLE 2.3. *Distribution of spousal and other homicides in New Spain, 1747–1821, by time of day*

	Spousal murders		General homicides					
	Mexico		Central Mexico[a]		Mixteca Alta[b]		Jalisco[c]	
Time of day	Number	Percentage	Number	Percentage	Number	Percentage	Number	Percentage
Morning	11	26.8	11	11	6	11	7	8.5
Afternoon	14	34.1	36	35	12	21	21	25.6
Evening	16	39	55	54	38	68	54	65.9
Unknown	46	52.8 (of total)						

SOURCES: AGN, Mexico City, Acordada, Californias, Criminales, General de Parte, Presidios y Cárceles, and Provincias Internas; AJO; AANG, Criminales; AJP; Archivo Provincial de Zacatecas; Municipal Archive of Veracruz; *Diario de México* 176, March 25, 1806, 334–336; 1646, April 4, 1810, 373–374; Taylor, *Drinking, Homicide, and Rebellion*, 77, 98; idem, "Amigos de sombrero," 86.

[a]These cases are concentrated in the 1790–1810 period.

[b]These cases correspond to the periods 1600–1630, 1730–1740, and 1780–1790.

[c]These cases correspond to the 1784–1820 period.

however, what could be a significant contrast emerges: In proportion, more than twice as many spousal homicides than general homicides were committed in the morning. Unlike homicides that required outside contact and were most likely to occur at other times of the day, domestic disputes could and did begin early, even before men and women began their day's work. And while a good portion of general homicides occurred on Sundays—time during which people socialized in churches, markets, and taverns—the distribution of spousal murders throughout the week seems relatively even, with only a few more statistically insignificant instances happening on Sundays and Thursdays (see Table 2.4).

Distribution throughout the year also seems random, except for the fact that a larger number of these crimes took place in the month of October, a circumstance yet to be explained but that could involve the harvest cycle and stresses associated with the end of the consuming year (see Table 2.5). With regard to day and time, this sample does not share many similarities with Taylor's findings, in which homicides occurred mostly after normal working hours (after work in the fields ended in the evening, on Sundays, and before and after June and July, peak periods of agricultural labor).[48] However, the couples in our set of cases did not need to make an effort to find one another at certain days, months, or times. Living together, they found time to quarrel at any time, day, or month of the year.

As is to be expected, most crimes happened within the spouses' community and at home. A few occurred at the homes of friends or neighbors, sometimes while the victim was seeking shelter after a major aggression. A minority took place in open public places, such as streets and roads, or

TABLE 2.4. *Distribution of spousal and other homicides in New Spain, 1747–1821, by day of the week*

	Spousal murders		General homicides					
	Mexico		Central Mexico		Mixteca Alta		Jalisco	
Day of the week	Number	Percentage	Number	Percentage	Number	Percentage	Number	Percentage
Sunday	6	17.1	44	51	21	44	31	29.8
Monday	5	14.2	11	13	9	19	15	14.4
Tuesday	5	14.2	7	8	4	8	10	9.6
Wednesday	3	8.6	3	3	—	—	10	9.6
Thursday	6	17.1	8	9	4	8	12	11.5
Friday	5	14.2	4	5	4	8	11	10.6
Saturday	5	14.2	10	11	6	13	15	14.4
Undetermined	52	59.7						

SOURCES: AGN, Mexico City, Acordada, Californias, Criminales, General de Parte, Presidios y Cárceles, and Provincias Internas; AJO; AANG, Criminales; AJP; Archivo Provincial de Zacatecas; Municipal Archive of Veracruz; *Diario de México* 176, March 25, 1806, 334–336; 1646, April 4, 1810, 373–374; Taylor, *Drinking, Homicide, and Rebellion*, 78; idem, "Amigos de sombrero," 86.

TABLE 2.5. *Distribution of spousal and other homicides in New Spain, 1747–1821, by month*

	Spousal murders		General homicides					
	Mexico		Central Mexico		Mixteca Alta		Jalisco	
Month	Number	Percentage	Number	Percentage	Number	Percentage	Number	Percentage
January	4	8.2	13	7	11	10	9	8.3
February	5	10.2	18	10	6	5	9	8.3
March	4	8.2	15	9	8	7	7	6.4
April	5	10.2	14	8	14	13	9	8.3
May	4	8.2	10	6	17	15	5	4.6
June	3	6.1	8	5	3	3	6	5.5
July	2	4.1	12	7	5	5	7	6.4
August	4	8.2	13	8	13	12	15	13.8
September	2	4.1	13	8	12	11	6	5.5
October	8	16.3	19	11	5	5	13	11.9
November	3	6.1	21	12	7	6	9	8.3
December	5	10.2	19	11	10	9	14	12.8
Undetermined	38	43.6						

SOURCES: AGN, Mexico City, Acordada, Californias, Criminales, General de Parte, Presidios y Cárceles, and Provincias Internas; AJO; AANG, Criminales; AJP; Archivo Provincial de Zacatecas; Municipal Archive of Veracruz; *Diario de México* 176, March 25, 1806, 334–336; 1646, April 4, 1810, 373–374; Taylor, *Drinking, Homicide, and Rebellion*, 78; idem, "Amigos de sombrero," 87.

more or less "hidden" locations such as forests, rivers, and ditches, both in and outside of the couple's community (see Table 2.6). For what are probably obvious reasons, this distribution contrasts significantly with the general homicides examined by Taylor. Twice as many spousal homicides than general homicides occurred at home, not a single one seems to have happened near a *pulquería* or tavern, and far fewer occurred outside of the victim's home community.[49]

Going beyond the setting and looking into the circumstances of the homicidal act, one finds rich information, particularly about methods and choice of weapons (see Table 2.7). Many of the murderers used knives (24, or 35.2 percent of the cases for which information is available). Several other cases involved stabbing with undetermined weapons or other sharp objects, such as machetes, pikes, or spears. This was also the case in colonial Colombia and, as we shall observe later, in Spain.[50] Knives (*belduques*), though forbidden as weapons, were common instruments in cooking and farming, which also required the use of machetes and other sharp objects. Therefore, the choice of weapon is in keeping with the circumstances of material life and labor at the time. Other cases involved rocks (8, or 11.7 percent), including the stones ordinarily used for cooking (*metlapil*). Clubs, fists, and kicks were also common, as were hanging and poison. A minority of the cases involved lashes, aggression

TABLE 2.6. *Location of spousal homicides in New Spain, 1747–1821*

	Number	Percentage
Within the community		
At couple's home	27	50.9
At a friend's or neighbor's home	3	5.7
On the street	3	5.7
On a road	4	7.5
By a river, creek, or ditch	4	7.5
In a forest	2	3.8
Total	**43**	**85**
Outside the community		
Near a mission	4	7.5
On a street or road	3	5.7
Undetermined	1	1.9
Total	**8**	**15**
Undetermined	34	39

SOURCES: AGN, Mexico City, Acordada, Californias, Criminales, General de Parte, Presidios y Cárceles, and Provincias Internas; AJO; AANG, Criminales; AJP; Archivo Provincial de Zacatecas; Municipal Archive of Veracruz; *Diario de México* 176, March 25, 1806, 334–336; 1646, April 4, 1810, 373–374; Taylor, *Drinking, Homicide, and Rebellion*, 77, 98; idem, "Amigos de sombrero," 86.

TABLE 2.7. *Distribution of spousal homicides in New Spain, 1741–1821, by method/weapon, compared to other homicides*

	Spousal murders		Homicides in general[a]					
	Mexico		Central Mexico		Mixteca Alta		Jalisco	
Method/weapon	Number	Percentage	Number	Percentage	Number	Percentage	Number	Percentage
Stabbings	24	35.2	91	48	29	37	51	41.1
Rocks	8	11.7	32	17	14	18	15	12.1
Machete/spears/ pikes	6	8.8	8	4	5	6	21	16.9
Fists, kicking	6	8.8	19	10	10	13	5	4
Clubs	7	10.3	17	9	12	15	19	15.3
Hanging	5	7.3	1	0.5	—	—	3	2.4
Poison	4	5.9	2	1	1	1	2	1.6
Whip	3	4.4	2	1	2	3	1	0.8
Cooking utensils	2	2.9	—	—	—	—	—	—
Furniture	1	1.5	—	—	—	—	—	—
Firearms	1	1.5	6	3	2	3	1	0.8
Other	1	1.5	12	6.3	4	5	3	2.4
Undetermined	19	21.8						

SOURCES: AGN, Mexico City, Acordada, Californias, Criminales, General de Parte, Presidios y Cárceles, and Provincias Internas; AJO; AANG, Criminales; AJP; Archivo Provincial de Zacatecas; Municipal Archive of Veracruz; *Diario de México* 176, March 25, 1806, 334–336; 1646, April 4, 1810, 373–374; Taylor, *Drinking, Homicide, and Rebellion*, 81; idem, "Amigos de sombrero," 89.

[a]These columns represent 190 homicides in Central Mexico, 79 in Oaxaca, and 124 in Jalisco.

with cooking utensils or furniture, or a combination of the methods cited above. The killers used firearms—in one case, a rifle or *carabina*—only rarely.

In general, these findings coincide with Taylor's conclusion that stabbing and beating were the murder methods in colonial Mexico. However, hanging and poison, rare in Taylor's larger sample, are relatively striking in our set of cases. The latter method probably points to the fact that poison could be more easily administered in a household setting—especially at mealtimes, either gradually or in large doses. This is confirmed by the fact that, as illustrated in several cases addressed below, in all instances in which poison intervened, women—the household members typically charged with food preparation—were the killers. More important, the use of poison suggests the premeditated nature of the crime.[51]

As for the occupation of the offenders, most cases involved manual workers belonging to the humble classes who constituted the bulk of the population (more than 80 percent) in this and other viceroyalties.[52] Journeymen and farmers were a majority among defendants whose occupations are known. Eleven defendants described themselves as farmers (*hortelanos* or *labradores*), eleven more as peons (*gañanes*) or cowboys ("*campistas*"). Second in importance were artisans. Among the accused were a pot maker, a boot maker, a carpenter, and a leather worker (one of the *gañanes* also claimed to have been a baker). Also in the sample were two tavern keepers, two construction workers, a bricklayer, and a brick maker. Finally, the defendants included an assortment of dependent and independent workers, including a *pulque* collector (*tlachiquero*), a weaver in a textile workshop (*obrajero*), a miner, and so forth (see Table 2.8). These manual occupations were more or less typical of criminals in other places in Spanish America during the colonial period as well as in other areas of the world at different times.[53] Workers from the lower classes were a majority among domestic criminals; no crimes implicated members of the elite.

As various works corroborate, the authorities would have made every effort to keep elite crimes, even serious ones, from coming to public attention and ending up in court. In a 1771 report to his successor, Viceroy Marques de Croix stated this much.[54] However, Silva Arrom lists various divorce cases among elite couples in which wives alleged that their husbands were cruel and abused them physically, perhaps a minor scandal given the likelihood of these distinguished husbands to justify their actions as part of marriage's male prerogatives.[55] Nonetheless, crime of most kinds, except perhaps defamation, was most prevalent among the nonelite groups.[56] The frustration resulting from oppressive living conditions, lack of education, and limited possibilities for upward mobility

TABLE 2.8. *Distribution of spousal homicides in New Spain, 1747–1821, by defendant's occupation*

Occupation	Number	Percentage
Farmers	11	22
Gañanes (peons)/cowboys	11	22
Artisans	8	16
Construction workers	2	4
Wood cutter/*maderero*	2	4
Tavern keeper	2	4
Arriero (mule pack driver)	2	4
Indian governor	1	2
Caporal in *cofradía*	1	2
Church assistant	1	2
Mayordomo (winemaker)	1	2
Tlachiquero (*pulque* collector)	1	2
Tax collector	1	2
Sugar *trapiche* worker	1	2
Viajero (itinerant peddler)	1	2
Coach driver	1	2
Miner	1	2
Obrajero	1	2
Unemployed (former soldier)	1	2
Unknown	37	42.5

SOURCES: AGN, Mexico City, Acordada, Californias, Criminales, General de Parte, Presidios y Cárceles, and Provincias Internas; AJO; AANG, Criminales; AJP; Archivo Provincial de Zacatecas; Municipal Archive of Veracruz; *Diario de México* 176, March 25, 1806, 334–336; 1646, April 4, 1810, 373–374; Taylor, *Drinking, Homicide, and Rebellion*, 77, 98; idem, "Amigos de sombrero," 86.

made these groups perhaps more likely to reject social norms. Drinking, fighting, vandalism, and assorted criminal behaviors were in any case common forms of release for some of them.[57] However, this does not mean that domestic violence was merely an expression of generic social tensions and economic frustrations, but rather a response to the specific dynamics of male–female relations.[58] This issue will be discussed further when we examine the motives that defendants cited for their behavior.

The majority of the criminals (33, or 75 percent of the total) whose age and gender are known were men between the ages of twenty-one and thirty-five. Women committed far fewer of the crimes (19, or 22 percent), as did people over age forty (11 percent) (see Tables 2.9 and 2.10). The age distribution corresponds to findings for late colonial New Granada and is consistent with other available information on crime in late colonial Mexico and eighteenth-century Spain. In most societies to this day, people between the ages of sixteen and thirty-nine have the highest criminal potential.[59]

However, the findings on gender depart considerably from the data for colonial Colombia, presented in Chapter 6. There, women appear to have

TABLE 2.9. *Distribution of spousal homicides in New Spain, 1747–1821, by defendant's age*

Age group	Number	Percentage
16–20	2	4.5
21–25	11	25
26–30	16	36.3
31–35	6	13.6
36–40	4	9
41–45	2	4.5
46–50	1	2.3
51–55	1	2.3
61–75	1	2.3
Unknown	43	49.4
Total	87	

SOURCES: AGN, Mexico City, Acordada, Californias, Criminales, General de Parte, Presidios y Cárceles, and Provincias Internas; AJO; AANG, Criminales; AJP; Archivo Provincial de Zacatecas; Municipal Archive of Veracruz; *Diario de México* 176, March 25, 1806, 334–336; 1646, April 4, 1810, 373–374; Taylor, *Drinking, Homicide, and Rebellion*, 77, 98; idem, "Amigos de sombrero," 86.

TABLE 2.10. *Distribution of spousal and other homicides in New Spain, by defendant's gender*

	Spousal murders		General homicides					
	Mexico		Central Mexico		Mixteca Alta		Jalisco[a]	
Gender	Number	Percentage	Number	Percentage	Number	Percentage	Number	Percentage
Males	68	78	230	96	93	99	177	97.2
Females	19	22	10	4	1	1	5	2.8
Total	87							

SOURCES: AGN, Mexico City, Acordada, Californias, Criminales, General de Parte, Presidios y Cárceles, and Provincias Internas; AJO; AANG, Criminales; AJP; Archivo Provincial de Zacatecas; Municipal Archive of Veracruz; *Diario de México* 176, March 25, 1806, 334–336; 1646, April 4, 1810, 373–374; Taylor, *Drinking, Homicide, and Rebellion*, 84; idem, "Amigos de sombrero," 90.

[a]Figures for Jalisco combine homicides and armed assaults.

committed around 38.8 percent of spousal murders, a much larger share than in Mexico.[60] Unless one considers this a random situation and/or a function of record keeping, further research is necessary to explain this intriguing contrast. It could possibly be caused by factors linked to the largely mixed-race (*mestizo*) background, seemingly assertive personalities, and greater economic independence of the Colombian women who killed their husbands when compared with their Mexican counterparts, mainly dependent Indians intent on absconding with their lovers. Even so, Mexican women's participation in spousal murder appears to have been considerably higher than in the general homicides that Taylor recorded in his seminal studies of Central Mexico, Mixteca Alta, and Central Jalisco.[61] Whereas women committed between 1 percent and 4 percent of all the homicides he examined, they committed 22 percent of the spousal homicides under study, an indication that women were at least five times more likely to kill their husbands than any other person. This pattern was about the same in New Granada, suggesting that the conclusion that the numerous spousal homicides committed by colonial Colombian women reflected conflicts resulting from their freedom to participate in public activities (outings, parties, markets, festivals, and celebrations) might also be pertinent in the case of Mexico.[62]

Women's intense involvement in public activities is confirmed by Arrom's research demonstrating late-colonial women's active participation in production, commerce, and service activities, all of which required public exchanges; and by Maria Espejo-Ponce Hunt and Matthew Restall, who find late eighteenth-century women actively working in cities and the countryside in all kinds of activities and also acting as "owners, vendors, and purchasers."[63] It is clear from these studies that colonial women had regular contact with the outside social and economic world.[64] As we will discuss below, for example, the largest portion of the spousal murders committed by women in Mexico resulted from the wife's desire to run away with a lover. This circumstance, despite insufficient information about the way extramarital affairs began, confirms that female contact with outsiders, though certainly not the institutional norm, was not at all unusual.

A majority (67.6 percent) of the Mexican defendants whose ethnicity is known were Indians, and only a small number were "*de color quebrado*," or mixed-race (4.2 percent) (see Table 2.11). This constitutes a departure from the Colombian pattern, where mixed-race individuals and Indians had roughly equal rates of spousal homicide.[65] Even if, for the sake of argument, we assume that all of those whose ethnic background is unknown were *mestizo* (19, or 21.8 percent of the total), which most certainly was not the case, Indians would still constitute the largest single group among spousal killers in New Spain. In both Colombia and Mexico, Indians were responsible for between one-half and two-thirds of all spousal murders.[66] Whites' participation offers some minor contrasts, as they represented a lower percentage of criminals in New Spain (16 percent) than in New Granada (25.9 percent).[67] Relative to the ethnic distribution of Mexico's population in the late eighteenth century, the participation of the different ethnic groups seems a bit disproportional. Indians accounted for more homicides than their share of the population in contrast to whites and mixed-race sectors. What prompted them to kill?

TABLE 2.11. *Distribution of spousal homicides in New Spain, 1747–1821, by defendant's ethnicity*

Ethnicity	Number	Percentage	Percentage of known race	Ethnic group as a percentage of population
Indian	48	55.2	67.6	51.7
White	14	16	19.7	22.6
Mulatto	6	6.9	8.5	25.4
Mestizo	3	3.4	4.2	
Black	—	—		0.12
Unknown	16	18.4		
Total	87			

SOURCES: AGN, Mexico City, Acordada, Californias, Criminales, General de Parte, Presidios y Cárceles, and Provincias Internas; AJO; AANG, Criminales; AJP; Archivo Provincial de Zacatecas; Municipal Archive of Veracruz; *Diario de México* 176, March 25, 1806, 334–336; 1646, April 4, 1810, 373–374; Taylor, *Drinking, Homicide, and Rebellion*, 77, 98; idem, "Amigos de sombrero," 86; Humboldt, *Ensayo político sobre el reino de la Nueva España*, 210.

The triggering factors, immediate causes, and circumstances of the murders varied widely. Recent publications on the history of gender in general, and gender conflicts in particular, have shown that family disputes mirror individual and collective perceptions of class, ethnic, and gender hierarchies.[68] In keeping with a growing segment of literature intersecting the history of crime, gender, and sexuality, the conjugal homicides examined here appear to be linked to particular social understandings of marriage duties, sexual virtue, and women's status and identity on the part of both subaltern subjects and the colonial state.[69] Like other equivalent gender-related crimes, they thus contribute to show, as Laura Gowing puts it, the "workings of sex, gender and honor in language, law, and popular practice."[70]

Several of the crimes under consideration, perhaps even the one narrated at the beginning of this chapter, were "love" crimes, what in the nineteenth century would be dubbed "crimes of passion." Some of the recent historiography downplays this circumstance, preferring to highlight disputes over domestic duties such as housekeeping, cooking, and child rearing.[71] In fact, a large portion (44 percent, or 26 of a total of 61 cases for which there is information) were linked to jealousy, infidelity, or a desire to turn extramarital affairs into permanent relations.

Contrary to the belief that the only way to preserve their manliness and honor was to physically attack their unfaithful wives, some men actually showed restraint, preferring to denounce their wives to the authorities or have them locked (*recogidas*) in a convent. For instance, this was the case of an *audiencia* scribe whose wife had a scandalous extramarital affair with one of the Guadalajara Audiencia judges (*oidores*) around 1751.[72] However, this was not the general pattern, and in fact the men who committed most of the crimes in our case set were motivated by jealousy and infidelity. Whether as a convenient strategy to mitigate their responsibility or in response to imaginary or real betrayals, they alleged that it was their prerogative to punish their wives, a behavior considered "honorable" in Iberian culture.[73] For instance, Iberian law gave men the right to kill adulterous spouses caught *in fraganti,* requiring only that they kill both wife and lover to free themselves from any murder charges.[74]

Women, on the other hand, committed the largest number of crimes meant to turn extramarital affairs into permanent relations (7 of 8, or 87.5 percent). Furthermore, these crimes constitute 50 percent of all spousal homicides by wives for which we have information on motives. Three of these cases involved poison and were clearly premeditated. In Xochimilco in February 1790, for example, thirty-five-year-old Indian Josefa María gave her drunken husband poisoned *aguardiente* so she could marry her *amacio* (lover), thirty-year-old Indian widower Matías Salvador.[75] In the central Mexican town of Zumpahuacan, thirty-year-old Indian Lorenza Juliana wanted to be free of her husband, Pascual Bernardo, so she could move in with her *amacio,* Pedro Gregorio. One October day in 1799, she slipped poison into the *atole,* a corn-based beverage that she served Pascual for breakfast.[76] And in Nueva Galicia, thirty-five-year-old Indian María Antonia Corona poisoned her blind husband, José Román, and ran away with her lover, Mariano Casillas, in October 1819.[77] In two other instances, Indian women violently killed their husbands (by hanging and with a machete, respectively) with the assistance of their lovers.[78] Another Indian woman, thirty-year-old María Alejandra, paid a third party to do the job.[79] While these incidents are vastly outnumbered by instances of male violence, they suggest that female adultery triggered a substantial portion of the crimes that wives performed. These women must have been deeply unsatisfied with their family life—so much so that they were willing to kill to be rid of their husbands.

Second in importance to crimes of passion were homicides resulting from a spouse's alleged disobedience or insolence, which constituted eighteen (30.4 percent) of the cases for which we have some information. Not surprisingly, husbands committed all of these crimes. Four more cases that may be linked to the insolence/disobedience category involved disagreements over disciplining children, elevating the total number of disputes linked to these motives to 37.2 percent. In almost two-thirds of these incidents, the victims were women seeking to protect children from excessive punishment. Two other related crimes seem to have been committed by women whose husbands beat them, which is to say that they constituted acts of self-defense.

Some of the many cases the records generically present as resulting from "insolence" or "disobedience" corroborate the hypothesis that quarrels between men and women in colonial Mexico and elsewhere derived from constant disputes over the boundaries of gender rights and obligations, sexual and otherwise.[80] Our evidence suggests that conjugal homicides were a representative element of gender-rooted social conflicts involving such disputes. In many cases, men who killed their wives complained that the women had disobeyed their orders; failed to perform their domestic duties, especially cooking; answered back when scolded; or complained about their mate's irresponsible, abusive, or lustful behavior.[81] Defense attorneys bolstered the men's arguments, claiming that their clients had to cope with women who were "bad tempered" (*de genio aspero y recio*) or predisposed to aggression (*mal sazonada y peor dispuesta*) and unwilling to observe the respectful attitude (*buenos oficios*) required before one's husband.[82] Patriarchy, partly understood as a male claim to superior status and power over female comportment, sexuality, reproductive roles, and labor, was unquestionably a factor triggering aggression.[83]

Several of the cases cited above illustrate this dynamic: Diego Andrés, who killed his wife for disobeying his orders to change her dress for church; Lázaro Antonio, who stabbed his wife, Josefa, for refusing to let him buy *pulque;* and José de los Santos Reyes, the Indian *obrajero* who dealt his wife a fatal blow to the head for her insolence. Similar cases abound: Simón Antonio Retama, an Indian *gañan* who stabbed his wife, Petra María, to death for not being there to serve him dinner when he returned home from work one night in May 1795 in Pachuca; Indian Anastasio Pérez, who stoned his wife, María Dolores, to death for speaking to him insolently in the town of Atitalaquia, central Mexico, in 1805; José Marcelino, an Indian *gañan* in Cuernavaca, who stoned his wife to death on a Thursday morning in 1806 after she threatened to tell his father and the local Indian governor about his habitual drinking; José Gerbasio Chávez, a *mestizo* cowboy in Guadalajara who beat his wife, María Gertrudiz, to death one night in August 1813 for refusing to serve him dinner and scolding him for failing to bring firewood; and Mariano Rafael Mendoza, an Indian weaver in his sixties or early seventies in the town of Tulancingo, central Mexico, who killed his much younger wife, María Antonieta Josefa, in 1815 with a large animal bone for refusing to follow his orders to stop sewing some pants.[84] Patriarchy seems to have been at work in all of these cases.

Other recent research on family relations in late colonial and early postcolonial New Spain indicates that tensions between spouses increased when the "balance of reciprocal duties and obligations was upset as well as the hierarchy of marriage."[85] For instance, this occurred when husbands could not fulfill their duties as heads of the family, when wives earned more than their spouses, or when fathers-in-law rather than husbands supported the couple. One-half of the cases of *malos tratos* (abuse) compiled in a study by Sonya Lipsett-Rivera include complaints by women that their husbands did not give them enough money to feed and clothe themselves and their children, making it necessary for the extended family to lend support.[86] Although most of the cases under study here do not explicitly mention these factors, the insolence/disobedience-related killings confirm Lipsett-Rivera's observation of male complaints about wives who abandoned their domestic duties. Such transgressions required at least moderate correction and punishment, the men argued, which could escalate into fights, injuries, and even death.[87]

In third place after passion and alleged female disobedience or insolence, drinking was a key circumstance behind spousal killings. By itself, drinking seems to have triggered just four (6.8 percent) otherwise inexplicable homicides, but combined with some of the reasons mentioned above, especially a spouse's insolence, it accounted for a total of twenty-six (44 percent) of the crimes. Several authors have already established the shortcomings of defendants' pleas that drinking, alone or combined with other factors, precipitated their crimes. Criminal husbands used alcohol as an excuse and exculpatory factor.[88] Nonetheless, drinking was far from irrelevant and was linked to between 13 percent and 60 percent of spousal and other homicides in Mexico, depending on the region (see Tables 2.12 and 3.1). A husband's aggression toward his wife may have derived primarily from suspicions of infidelity or challenges to his patriarchal authority, but in several of the cases under study, alcohol consumption prior to the crime seems to have constituted, at the very least, a catalyst for violence. Subsequent chapters of this book will devote fuller discussion to the legal treatment of drinking as a precipitating factor in spousal homicides.

Finally, an additional two crimes resulted from the defendants' insanity, and two others were the product of random circumstances, including an accident caused by a drunken husband.[89]

Elsewhere I will elaborate further on the relatively mild legal treatment of indigenous spousal killers and address the possible interaction among ethnic relations, legal culture, and royal rituals in explaining the standards of justice applied to Indians and others.[90] The punishment that all of these murderers actually received will also be discussed separately.[91]

TABLE 2.12. *Motives cited by offenders in spousal homicides in New Spain, 1747–1821*

	Total cases		Cases with male defendant		Cases with female defendant	
Motives	Number[a]	Percentage	Number	Percentage	Number	Percentage
Drinking (combined with other motives)	26	44	20	76.9	6	23.1
Drinking (as "exclusive" motive)	4	6.8	4	100	—	—
Jealousy	13	22	11	84.6	2	15.3
Desire to be with one's lover	8	13.6	1	12.5	7	87.5
Infidelity	5	8.5	4	80	1	20
Insolence	9	15.2	9	100	—	—
Disobedience	9	15.2	9	100	—	—
Disagreement over child rearing	4	6.8	3	75	1	25
Self-defense	2	3.4	—	—	2	100
Insanity	2	3.4	2	100	—	—
Other	2	3.4	2	100	—	—
Undetermined	28	32.2	22	78.6	6	21.4

SOURCES: AGN, Mexico City, Acordada, Californias, Criminales, General de Parte, Presidios y Cárceles, and Provincias Internas; AJO; AANG, Criminales; AJP; Archivo Provincial de Zacatecas; Municipal Archive of Veracruz; *Diario de México* 176, March 25, 1806, 334–336; 1646, April 4, 1810, 373–374; Taylor, *Drinking, Homicide, and Rebellion*, 84; idem, "Amigos de sombrero," 90.

[a]Total is more than 87, for some drinking-related cases are cross-listed in at least one other category. Cross-listing of cases in more than one category is also the reason that the total exceeds 100%.

CONCLUSION

Domestic violence was a frequent occurrence among the humble classes in the Spanish Atlantic and in the particular case of New Spain involved numerous members of native communities. Confrontations between spouses occasionally resulted in homicide, committed for the most part by Indian males between the ages of twenty-one and thirty-five, a majority of them peasants, farmers, or artisans. In numerous instances the defendants had ingested alcohol. The most common motivations were jealousy, allegations of extramarital affairs and female infidelity, and insolence or disobedience. In other cases, unfaithful wives killed their husbands to run away with lovers, a circumstance discussed further in this book's Colombian and Spanish case studies.

The dynamic interaction of not only gender, but also ethnicity and legal culture, contributes to explain the relatively benevolent treatment of Indian defendants tried for spousal murder in New Spain and elsewhere. As we shall see, a high percentage of the cases for which evidence of sentencing patterns is available ended in blanket pardons, mainly benefiting male aggressors. In general, the legislation not only discriminated against women, but based on a paternalistic logic, it also required Indian aggressors (predominantly male) to be treated kindly because of their "miserable" condition as brutish, uncivilized, and incompetent "minors." These issues will be discussed more fully later in this book, as will the Spanish Crown's practice of celebrating special occasions with generous amnesties.

Publicly, besides falling into the longstanding Western legal category of weak peoples (*miserabiles personae*), Amerindians fit Spanish conceptions of brutes, barbarians, and perpetual drunkards. They were understood to be vulnerable and inferior people, even "minors," in need of constant help to become civilized. In private, however, Indian men behaved like any other adult males of the time, patriarchs in control of their households, ready to assert their dominant male roles through violent means and other abusive methods whenever necessary. Interestingly enough, when it came to violent spousal conflicts, the public and private spheres complemented each other: By granting them favorable legal treatment and generally protecting them from harsh punishments, the state legitimated Indian males' abusiveness and reinforced their patriarchal conduct. The same favorable legal treatment extended to some Indian women, but they were a minority among criminals and, especially when their crimes were linked to extramarital affairs, found little sympathy among male colonial officials. In these cases, as we shall see, the judges were not inclined to show leniency to either female defendants or their male lovers.

Susan Kellogg has argued that in the civil realm, the status of native women declined considerably by the seventeenth century as their legal identity became intertwined with that of their husbands. Another factor was the breakdown of social institutions in which women held power and authority. Indian women could no longer serve as legal guardians of minor children in lawsuits, and they seem to have participated much less than before in property transactions.[92] Although considered controversial in the civil realm, this thesis may prove valid for the criminal one.[93] The treatment of Indian males who killed their spouses could illustrate the decline in the status of Indian women as a result of the imposition of Spanish legal culture, this time in the criminal sphere. That culture generally favored Indian wife killers, even more so if they were drunk. The following chapter will discuss this phenomenon, pointing out that while blanket pardons benefited spousal killers of all kinds, the fact that a majority of the killers happened to be Indian males meant that royal graces indirectly reinforced Indian patriarchy as well.

CHAPTER THREE

The King's Forgiveness

Earthly Intercessions and Legal Culture

Although this study shall later show that punishment could be overt and severe, for a fair number of spousal murderers the road leading to it was full of detours and exits, reflecting the rather baroque landscape of the dominant legal culture. Marked by the Crown's (and Church's) use of clemency or "love" to instill obedience and loyalty in their subjects, such culture was not, however, entirely pragmatic.[1] It was founded upon a series of doctrinal principles to lighten (or increase) punishment, dating back to Roman times and sprinkled with tenets of canon and feudal law. This legal system featured abundant opportunities for reduced sentences or acquittals owing to a variety of circumstances, among them drinking, insanity (*furia*), rage and blind passion, or the victim's delayed death. As we shall see in the sections that follow, general royal pardons (*indultos*) could decrease or eliminate punishment completely for many criminals. Punishment could also be reduced in consideration of the culprit's "wretched" condition. These factors, central to the period's legal culture, account for the apparent gap between the expectation of the death penalty for spousal murderers according to formal legislation and the rather benign treatment that many of them actually received.[2]

The following pages consider legal treatments of inebriation, insanity, elapsed time between an assault and the victim's death, and indigenous ethnicity, as well as the impact of royal pardons. The discussion confirms that legal doctrines and culture contributed greatly to exempt criminals from the full theoretical consequences of violent acts against spouses. In the process they strengthened the legitimacy of royal justice and the monarchy.

DRINKING, INSANITY, AND OTHER MITIGATING FACTORS

In early 1796, after walking to Xochimilco, central Mexico, to attend Mass on the Catholic holiday of Jesus Christ's Incarnation, an Indian couple from the neighboring town of Xochitepec stopped by a notary's home to sign a document certifying the final purchase of a house. Then they decided to celebrate; as early as ten in the morning, the pair went drinking at the *pulquería* owned by Don Manuel de Arana, a Spaniard they appear to have known well. When the moon rose that evening (*al saltar la luna*), the husband, thirty-five-year-old Indian tribute collector Juan del Carmen Espiricueta, woke up by the side of a road near his hometown. He immediately went searching for his wife, Dominga María, and found her on the road not far away, where she had passed out from drink. Juan del Carmen carried her home, later saying that while she couldn't speak, she was still breathing. Upon arriving home around four in the morning, he placed the woman's body on the floor. At sunrise, the couple's eldest son called in a healer (*curandera*), who pronounced her dead.

Juan del Carmen alleged that he couldn't remember anything that had happened after leaving the *pulquería* with his wife, for they were so drunk that he was "unable to reason" (*la suma embriaguez . . . le privó del uso de razón*). He also claimed that the couple had lived peacefully, had not fought, and his wife had probably fallen and injured herself. However, her corpse showed signs of violence, and justice officials suspected the man, who promptly ran away. Although he tried to resist arrest, he was soon apprehended. With the assistance of an interpreter, for he did not speak Spanish, he was eventually sent to trial. His curator and advocate claimed that when the incident occurred, Juan del Carmen and his wife were "out of their minds" (*fuera de si*) and "entirely deprived of their senses" (*privados enteramente de sus sentidos*). By 1799, the defendant had escaped from jail and was in hiding. Years later, the case remained unresolved.[3]

Juan del Carmen's claim of drunkenness and his advocate's assertion that the man was out of his senses at the time of the crime were common defenses in cases involving Indians. As historian William B. Taylor has established, next to jealousy and a husband's prerogative to discipline his wife, "the cause of violent crime most frequently pleaded by peasant offenders in central Mexico was alcohol."[4] Taylor's pioneering work on the history of drinking in colonial Mexico revealed changes in patterns of alcohol consumption by Mexico's native peoples from the pre-Colombian period to the eighteenth century. Although Taylor rejects Spanish claims that Indians were constantly inebriated, he establishes that alcohol consumption did in fact increase after the conquest. This spike undoubtedly owed something to the fact that, for the first time, alcohol production became a major commercial activity. For example, the sale of *pulque* burgeoned in areas close to Mexico City.

Contemporary observers and officials took worried note of this increased alcohol consumption. Colonial chroniclers, local priests, and administrators regularly complained about widespread Indian drinking and bemoaned its associated evils (lack of church attendance, abandonment of domestic responsibilities, violence). In the early 1720s, a royal prosecutor tellingly claimed:

> As San Agustin says, drunkenness is "the mother of all crimes, subject, root, and cause of all faults and vices, perturbation of the brain, subversion of the senses, a storm for the tongue, a tempest for the body, sinking of chastity, waste of time, voluntary insanity, ignominious disease, clumsiness of customs, dishonor of life, infamy against honesty, corruption of the soul, soft devil, hard poison, due to which men commit innumerable sins and become themselves all sin."[5]

Official measures regulating taverns or controlling the use of additives in *pulque,* though ineffectual, attempted to limit public intoxication or at least diminish its negative effects. However, moral concerns soon gave way to regulations designed to bring in revenue: the licensing and taxing of liquor sales, and bans on the production of illegal beverages and the clandestine trade in legal drink.[6] It seems fair to say that benign attitudes toward alcohol-related crimes were consistent with a rather self-interested and ultimately permissive official attitude toward drinking.

Despite their statements to the contrary, the elite and the Crown actually promoted drinking. Michael Scardaville and others have demonstrated that Mexican aristocrats owned maguey plantations and *pulquerías,* giving them a vested interest in the protection and expansion of the *pulque* trade.[7] Research by Mexican scholar Pedro Viqueira Albán suggests that the Spanish Crown also had a stake in promoting the sale and consumption of *pulque* and other alcoholic beverages from which the colonial state derived substantial profits.[8] The Crown's inability to police this business effectively, in spite of its alleged preoccupation with drunkenness and the dissolution it caused, was likely a direct result of its financial dependence on the revenue from alcohol.[9] The Catholic Church was no different.

Although years earlier it had bemoaned the use of alcohol, in the mid-eighteenth century the Mexican clergy was claiming that the sale of *pulque* was not a sin (*la venta del pulque no es pecaminosa*). Ranking members of the clergy even argued with local hacienda owners who complained about the tithes they paid on the agave juice used in *pulque* production.[10] In New Granada, Cartagena's Jesuit order, represented by father Pedro Ignacio Altamirano, was involved in legal disputes that reached the Consejo de Indias concerning the newly established royal monopoly on the *aguardiente* trade. The priests and their *hacendado* allies depended on the revenue from molasses and sugar cane liquor they had sold freely until recently.[11] One could argue that, knowingly or not, the Spanish Crown and, to a certain extent, the Church, pushed alcohol on the Indian population to profit from the taxes charged at every step of its production up to its consumption in government-licensed venues. Research also indicates that Indians arrested for drunkenness constituted a vital pool of laborers for public works projects.[12] In any case, when defendants in spousal homicide cases alleged the influence of alcohol, they could reasonably expect to receive more favorable treatment.

In New Spain, almost one-half of spousal homicide cases for which there is sufficient evidence involved the use of alcohol (26, or 44.1 percent). If one considers the total number of cases, in several of which evidence is limited, the percentage of alcohol consumption is around one-third (29.9 percent) (see Table 3.1).[13] The first figure is slightly lower than Taylor's findings for some regions of Mexico, where he established a strong link between alcohol and peasant homicide in general: almost 60 percent in Central Mexico and over 50 percent in Jalisco.[14] Even judging by the lower estimate, however, alcohol consumption was

TABLE 3.1. *Alcohol's role in spousal and other homicides in New Spain, 1747–1821*

Spousal homicide			General homicide		
Total	Alcohol-related (number)	Alcohol-related (percentage)	Total	Alcohol-related (number)	Alcohol-related (percentage)
87[a]	26	29.9	103[b]	13	12.6
59[c]	26	44.1	240[d]	143	59.6
			80[e]	41	51.3

SOURCES: AGN, Mexico City, Acordada, Californias, Criminales, General de Parte, Presidios y Cárceles, and Provincias Internas; AJO; AANG, Criminales; AJP; Archivo Provincial de Zacatecas; Municipal Archive of Veracruz; *Diario de México* 176, March 25, 1806, 334–336; 1646, April 4, 1810, 373–374; Marín Tello, "Justicia penal y orden social en Michoacán," 217–218; Castro Gutiérrez, "Condición femenina y violencia," 6; Taylor, *Drinking, Homicide, and Rebellion*, 95; idem, "Amigos de sombrero," 79.

[a]All cases, even ones in which evidence is limited.

[b]Figure for Mixteca Alta.

[c]Only cases for which there is sufficient evidence to judge.

[d]Figure for Central Mexico.

[e]Figure for Central Jalisco.

more prevalent in the Mexican incidents than in all cases taking place in Colombia or Spain, in which about 33 percent and 10 percent of the defendants seem to have been intoxicated (although evidence is limited in some of these cases).[15] Considering just the cases for which there is sufficient evidence, Colombia rises to the top with more than half (52.9 percent) of spousal murder defendants having used alcohol prior to their crimes, whereas Spain continues to be the lowest, with just 20 percent (see Table 3.2).

Of course, as Taylor himself has demonstrated, the fact that one or both of the parties had been drinking does not imply a causal relation between alcohol consumption and homicide.[16] Steve Stern has also argued persuasively that alcohol was not so much a cause of domestic violence as it was a "discursive strategy" for the accused.[17] Violent criminals in the colonies and Spain, conscious of the legal advantages it entailed, alleged that drinking caused them loss of memory, rage, anger, confusion, and lack of self-control.

As Taylor notes, colonial courts accepted intoxication as a "mitigating consideration while sentencing the offender."[18] How could this be so if Spanish state officials and priests decried the problem of drinking among the natives and the Crown was taking legal measures to curb consumption of intoxicants?[19] Long-standing legal doctrines and culture seem to hold the clue to the apparent contradiction between official views on alcohol and the benign treatment of drunken criminals.

Roman and canon law considered the mental state of offenders a mitigating circumstance that could diminish criminal responsibility. Canon law teacher Rolandus, who taught at the famous university of Bologna during the twelfth century (ca. 1150), argued that in determining the punishment to be imposed for extramarital offenses, judges should consider the offender's sobriety or lack thereof.[20] Renowned Spanish jurist Antonio Gómez (1501–1562/72), in a monumental study of civil and criminal

TABLE 3.2. *Alcohol's role in spousal homicides in New Granada and Spain, 1750–1824*

		Alcohol-related		Males		Females	
Place	Total	Number	Percentage	Number	Percentage	Number	Percentage
New Granada	54[a]	18	33.3	13	72.2	5	27.8
	34[b]	18	52.9				
Spain	65[a]	6	9.2	5	83	1	17
	30[b]	6	20				

SOURCES: AGN, Colombia, Colonia, Juicios Criminales; AGN, Madrid; Audiencia Archives.
[a]Total cases.
[b]Cases for which there is clear evidence.

law cited through the end of colonial times, quoted various Roman authors to stress that individuals who committed a crime while drunk could be considered to have acted with lesser criminal intent than others (*quia ebrietas tollit dolum in delicto*) and were eligible for lesser punishment (*non aute poena ordinaria, sed mitiori poena*).[21]

Taking a similar approach, sixteenth-century author and magistrate Diego Covarrubias Leiva (1512–1577) of the Chancillería de Granada stressed with regard to homicide that *quia ebrius furioso similis est*: that those who committed crimes while drunk could be regarded as mad or insane. While they were not exempt from punishment, he argued, they should be subject to an "extraordinary" (meaning reduced) rather than "ordinary" penalty.[22] Influential Roman criminologist and politician Prospero Farinacci (1554–1618) shared this view. In his multivolume theoretical and practical manual on criminal law (see Figure I.1), he asserted that along with such factors as lack of criminal intent, ignorance, rage, minor age, and insanity, drunkenness was an extenuating circumstance in determining punishment. Judges should therefore disregard the law's ordinary punishment for the crime and apply a reduced one of their choice (*castigo arbitrario*).[23]

As early as the medieval *Siete Partidas*, Spanish legislation explicitly considered drinking to be a factor in "ameliorating" punishment.[24] As a popular law manual put it, drinking constituted a legal "exception," a legal excuse or factor justifying behavior and limiting responsibility.[25] It served to demonstrate that the defendant's mind was not healthy when the crime was committed, as if the person had been uncontrollably furious or insane. As magistrate and legal writer Francisco Elizondo elaborated, "Drunks are prone to lust, adultery, corruption, constant family feuds, homicides, and other evils."[26] This afforded them a convenient excuse.

The records consulted for this work, especially the Mexican ones, confirm this defense strategy. Some defense attorneys placed great emphasis on the numerous drunken Indians to be seen along the public roads, some lying by the wayside and unable to walk. All advocates, whether defense lawyers, curators, or officials in charge of promoting the interests of the natives (*procuradores de Indios*), found this image useful not only in requesting exoneration of the "minor" they represented but also, occasionally, as a way to blame victims for their own deaths. For example, Juan del Carmen's defense lawyer argued that if Dominga María were lying drunk in the road, she could have been injured and killed accidentally.[27] Legal strategies aside, the records typically contain evidence that in both colonial Colombia and Mexico the drinking of alcoholic beverages—*chicha*, *guarapo*, *pulque*, *aguardiente*, *tepache*, *chinguirito*, *tesquino*, or wine—preceded many crimes. Those who committed crimes under the influence benefited from laws, legal opinions, and legally effective defense strategies and arguments entitling them to "arbitrary" or "extraordinary" punishment. Not only was their punishment likely to be reduced; evidence suggests that drinking also made them more likely to benefit from general and individualized pardons.

In a few exceptional cases, defendants were sentenced to death in spite of evidence of drinking. The only Mexican case we are aware of involved José Thomas Medina, nicknamed "El Congo," a mulatto coach driver from Puebla de los Ángeles who stabbed his wife, a washerwoman, in their home one night in November 1780. Despite a lack of witnesses, the defendant's record of habitual drinking and domestic disputes suggested that the murder was the culmination of a pattern of behavior. After the crime, he took refuge in a local church but, rather than seek asylum, left to join a mulatto militia battalion (*Tercio de Milicianos Pardos*). Because his whereabouts were for some time unknown, he was tried in absentia and sentenced to death. The verdict ordered that he be transported on a beast of burden and paraded through the streets, with a town crier announcing the nature of his crime. Hanging would then follow, with his body exhibited on the gallows until the local governor ordered it cut down. The main reason that this case did not receive an "extraordinary" or reduced sentence was the defendant's contumacy and, though this was not made explicit, the fact that his drinking was not random but habitual. Without question, his ethnicity was also a negative factor: He was one of three mulattoes on a list of just six defendants who received death sentences in late colonial New Spain.[28]

A similar case involved a black Colombian slave, Agustín Peralta, who killed his wife on a Monday afternoon in 1803. He too was drunk and, like "El Congo," went into hiding and was tried in absentia. Despite evidence he had been drinking, because his crime was deemed premeditated or *alevoso*, he was sentenced to lashes followed by hanging.[29]

Two other cases mirror this pattern. In one of them, thirty-one-year-old weaver María del Carmen Martínez from the town of Simacota, in northeastern Colombia, stabbed her husband, Pedro Aguilar, on a Sunday night in August 1805. According to the accused, her husband systematically mistreated her, and one witness testified that hours before committing the crime María del Carmen had told a group of other women what she intended to do. This was likely construed as a sign of premeditation, and despite evidence that she drank alcohol prior to the crime, María del Carmen was sentenced to death and denied the pardon she requested from the local judge.[30]

The second case occurred in 1814 in the town of Susa, in the center of the viceroyalty. In this incident, white farmer Juan Ignacio Moya was hanged by his son, Nicolás, who acted with the complicity and encouragement of his sister, Concepción, and his mother, Francisca Casallas. The motive for the murder was to stop Juan Ignacio from denouncing thefts that his family had committed. Even though Nicolás and his sister were both drunk on corn beer (*chicha*), the local magistrate sentenced them and their mother to death by hanging. In 1819 the Bogotá Audiencia, normally more lenient and inclined to stick to technical rules of evidence during its review of cases, confirmed the sentence without acknowledging the customary treatment of drinking as an extenuating circumstance. The reasons for this omission are unclear, but the malicious nature of the crime and the fact that this was a time of intense internal revolutionary conflict could have contributed to the *audiencia*'s heavy-handed approach.[31]

In general, however, lenient treatment of drunkards was most definitely the norm, even in Spain. According to legal author Francisco Elizondo (see Figure 5.1), who served for many years as a prosecutor in Spain's Real Chancillería de Granada in the late eighteenth century, it was rare for defense attorneys in the most serious homicide cases tried in the Peninsula not to argue that their clients had been drunk or insane, or both. They were certain that this was a valid legal excuse.[32]

However, in Spain, as well, the courts did not always accept alcohol as an extenuating factor. An example is thirty-seven-year-old muleteer and grain trader Melchor Martin Alonso, who stabbed and killed his wife, Josefa Raga, in June 1772 after she refused to leave a Madrid *aguardientería* (tavern) and come home with him. Melchor got several witnesses to testify to his good character but well-known intolerance for alcohol. The day that he stabbed his wife he had drunk both wine and aguardiente. Despite his apparent inebriation, the Alcaldes de Casa y Corte sentenced him to death in 1773. He begged for the king's leniency on Good Friday and expected his sentenced to be commuted to life in prison, but there is no record of this happening.[33]

More typically, the lives of drunken defendants were spared. For instance, soldier Francisco Gil received a long prison term from a military court after killing his lover's husband with her apparent complicity. The crime occurred in 1821 inside a tavern in Santiago de Compostela, Galicia, where the aggressor had been drinking. In this case his inebriation probably worked in his favor.[34] As already noted, this was not a capricious judicial practice but rather a long-standing legal doctrine, along with the idea of insanity (*furia*) and, to a lesser extent, rage as exculpatory circumstances.

Insanity, Rage, and Blind Passion

Prevailing law considered people who were mentally ill, deaf, or mute to lack judgment and therefore be incapable of acting with criminal intent (*dolo*).[35] The available records contain few relevant cases: two in Mexico and another two in Spain. One of the incidents occurred in the mining town of Pachuca, in central Mexico, where forty-year-old Juan Manuel Méndez, a white potmaker (*alfarero*), fatally struck his wife, Felipa Palacios, on the head with a rock. The circumstances of the aggression were inexplicable; no fight or argument seemed to have preceded the attack, but as she lay dying, Felipa declared that in recent weeks her husband had presented episodes of madness (*furor* or *furia*) and was taking medication. The prosecutor requested the expert testimony of a medical doctor, and the only one available, a local priest, certified that the man seemed to have been afflicted by "a rush of insanity and nostalgia" (*ascención de locura y nostalgia*). Ultimately, the authorities pardoned Juan Manuel and sent him to a hospital for treatment.[36]

Another case took place in Puebla de Bollon, Galicia, in 1815. A local man, Javier Macia, stabbed his wife, Amara Rodríguez, fifty times with a pair of scissors. He was originally sentenced to serve a ten-year presidio sentence in Africa, but even the local prosecutor was convinced that the man was insane and asked the local *audiencia* to overturn the sentence. Eventually, the Real Audiencia de Galicia complied and released Javier into the custody of his closest relative, with the proviso that he be medicated and cared for by medical doctors.[37] In the other two available instances, the defendants were acquitted and referred to mental institutions.[38] In general, people proven to be insane could be punished only if prosecutors could demonstrate that at the moment of their crime they were experiencing a lucid interval, something difficult to prove and for which evidence in the many cases researched is absolutely lacking.[39]

More complex were cases of individuals who, though sane, claimed to have been in a state of temporary rage (*fuerte frenesi, ira,* or *coraje*) at the moment they killed their spouses. This was the case of Tomás de Villanueva, a black slave in colonial Colombia. During his criminal trial in 1791, Tomás argued that he had killed his wife, Isidora Murillo, with a machete because he was "swept away" or "blinded" by rage (*arrebatado* or *ciego de cólera*). As a result, he said, he had been out of his senses (*destituido de todo conocimiento*) and unable to discern the circumstances of his crime (*no reparó en las circunstancias*), in particular the fact that he was using a machete rather than a club as he first allegedly thought. His rage, the man and his defender claimed, was triggered by his wife's supposedly disrespectful comments concerning Tomás's right to boss around children who were not his but had instead been fathered by the woman's lovers.[40] Like Tomás, some of the other self-described *ciegos de cólera* were men who believed their wives or lovers to have betrayed them, a circumstance that made them unable to pause (*atender a nada*) or think clearly (*reflexionar*).[41]

In other cases the culprits claimed to have had their judgment addled by "excessive love." In Chapter 4, which deals with spousal murder in Spain, I shall have the opportunity to observe cases such as that of Blas Ballesteros, a young man who in 1784 helped his lover, Jesusa, kill her husband under the influence of the "rage and craziness produced by excessive love" (*furor y demencia que produce un excesivo amor*).[42] Carpenter Juan Antonio Rudino, who strangled his shepherdess wife, María Alberta Allende, in Banos de Cunta, Galicia, in May 1803, also argued that he was "blinded by passion" (*ciegamente apasionado*) for his lover, Josefa. As proof of his insanity, he admitted that even though he was already married, he had become formally engaged to Josefa.[43] The blinding passion of love was also to blame in the case of Dominga Espitia, who, along with her lover, was tried in Colombia in 1803 for killing her husband, Nicolás Ostia, in the northern region of Magangué. The two killers were "madly" in love and claimed not to have had a clear sense of the gravity of their offense.[44]

These claims may sound spurious, but culprits and their lawyers crafted convenient narratives to make the case that the killers had been unable to act in a rational and sane manner. Like the drunk or the mentally insane, the defense argued, their punishment should not be severe or "ordinary," but rather minor (*menor*) and random (*arbitrario*) and left up to the judge's discretion. However, the legislation and legal doctrine of the time were not as conclusive in cases involving passion as in those featuring drunkenness or mental impairment. Highly regarded experts in criminal law such as Farinacci included rage (*iracundia*) among the factors extenuating punishment,[45] but others argued that, rather than mitigating circumstances, rage and rancor (*ira, encono o rencor*) should serve as clues that the accused had indeed committed the crime.[46] A "sudden and unexpected outburst of passion" became an exculpatory circumstance only in some postcolonial criminal codes, in particular the Colombian one of 1837 (Art. 120). For the most part, though, effective excuses based on sophisticated views of conditions impacting an individual's psyche would have to await the development of positivist criminology and psychology in the last quarter of the nineteenth century. Not until then did concepts such as "rage and intense pain" (*ira e intenso dolor*) become valid pseudoscientific excuses in criminal defenses for spousal murder and related crimes.[47] But while limited scientific understanding of the workings of the human mind barred impassioned criminals from availing themselves of some scientifically credible and legally valid excuses, the same ignorance afforded others valid justifications for murdering their spouses in the late colonial Spanish Atlantic.

Prolonged Deaths

In cases in which victims of violence died days after the original aggression, the medical science of the time raised serious doubts about the real cause of death. This excuse was even more powerful when, as often occurred, it was combined with drinking. In Teposcolula, Oaxaca, for instance, forty-year-old Indian José Mejía hit his wife, María Aniceta, with a rock. They were having a minor argument while returning home with the woman's mother after selling corn in a nearby town early one afternoon in 1818. The three were completely drunk, for after the sale they had met one of the couple's *compadres* for lunch and drunk quite a bit of the local *tepache,* a fermented pineapple-based beverage. But the main legal defense wasn't so much drunkenness as the fact that María Aniceta didn't die until a few days following the aggression. In fact, as her husband and mother testified, after she was injured María Aniceta stood up and walked home by herself. She was later taken to a local healer and returned home with a headache but said that she was fine (*buena*). Soon after the attack, José, who was so drunk he could hardly stand, was dragged off to jail by two constables. The next day, having recovered his sobriety, he was flogged, a typical punishment for Indians who committed crimes resulting in minor injuries (*lesiones*). However, María Aniceta's condition continued to deteriorate, and a couple of days later, after receiving last rites, she died. Upon examining the corpse, the local *cirujano* (surgeon) stated that her skull was fractured and that he had no doubt her death was a result of her head injury. The defendant's curator disagreed, arguing that her death was not caused "necessarily and immediately" by the injury from the rock but rather from a lack of adequate medical care. If she had not lived in a town so far away from a big city and had had access to scientifically based medical assistance, if she had followed an appropriate diet and not done what "barbarian Indians" customarily did—that is, attempt to "cure themselves through rustic and wild medicines"—she could very well have survived, the curator maintained. Responding to the judge's petition, another physician from the city of Oaxaca who had not even examined the corpse nonetheless expressed some doubts about the earlier medical testimony. Even with good care, head injuries were dangerous, he acknowledged, but Indians, especially in remote locations like the one where the case had occurred, tended to rely on herbal medicines that could worsen their condition. Combined with a bad diet, this probably contributed to the woman's death, he concluded. Faced with this contradictory medical testimony, the *audiencia* sentenced the man to just one year of public works in Oaxaca.[48]

Other cases revealed the widespread popular belief that an injured person exposed to the moon would worsen. If the person died, this exposure (*alunamiento*) was attributed more significance than the original injuries themselves. A purported example of such a case was Pedro Pacateque, an Indian from the central Colombian town of Soraca, whose wife, Ana María Yanquen, died after a vicious beating in December 1802. Husband and wife were returning home one afternoon after attending Mass in the nearby town of Ramiriqui. Both were drunk on corn beer (*chicha*) and, for unknown reasons, started to quarrel. Pedro beat his wife severely, biting her nose, and kicking and punching her repeatedly all over her body. Finally, he grabbed her by the hair and dragged and pushed her to the ground several times. The woman later testified that when, with great difficulty, she managed to make it home, her husband was in bed. Afraid to wake him, she stayed outside and fell asleep. She couldn't say whether the moon had worsened her condition (*le haría mal*), but the local midwife who examined her the next day noticed that her belly and one of her legs were considerably swollen. Three of her ribs were broken, her belly was as hard as a rock, and she was running a fever. By late January her condition had not improved in spite of the assistance of the local healer, and she died in early February. Several witnesses testified that her death happened probably not so much a result of her husband's beating but rather because she had slept outside under the full moon and did not follow the right diet upon receiving medication. The man's curator presented a similar argument. The judge's legal advisor asked for an "extraordinary" punishment of two-year labor service in consideration of the fact that, even though the husband's assault was likely to have contributed to her death, the woman's medical care was probably inappropriate. Although the Bogotá Audiencia eventually doubled this punishment, the *protector de Indios* filed motions stressing that the lower classes (*la plebe*) frequently punched and kicked their women and hit them with stones and clubs, but the women rarely died. Therefore, it was unreasonable to believe that, without some intervening circumstances, a mere beating could have caused the victim's death so many days later. Besides, the *protector de Indios* continued, just days after the attack the victim had attended Mass and slept outside in the moonlight again, a fatal decision.[49]

In other cases, exposure to the sun rather than the moon was blamed for fatalities.[50] A combination of weak witness testimony, faulty medical evidence, and a belief system inclined to attribute deaths occurring several days after an attack to circumstances other than the aggression itself often led justice officials to reduce a defendant's punishment. In doing so, they did not necessarily act capriciously or simply out of a belief in folk medicine but followed doctrines of legal evidence that excused not only deaths committed "without any criminal intent" or "in legitimate defense of one's life," but also those produced "not from injuries but from fault or negligence in curing these."[51] Clearly, such doctrines were applied rather casually, for the legal manuals also required that, as far as possible, more than one physician should certify whether or not the injuries were fatal and the medical cure suitable. These provisions were not followed in at least one of the two cases cited and in several more in our case set. When in doubt, as in the other case cited, the law presumed that a death following an injury was caused by it and placed upon the defendant the burden of proving otherwise. Presumption of guilt was even stronger when it could be demonstrated that the victim had been in ill health from the time of the injury to the time of death.[52] These legal doctrines appear to have been disregarded in the cases cited, an indication that local judges sometimes paid more attention to the law's general orientation than to the strict technical requirements of legal evidence and/or the complex circumstances of specific cases. This apparent gap would be filled in the 1820s and 1830s, when new criminal codes established precise time limits between aggression and death to determine when an attacker could be charged with murder or merely personal injury.

INDIANS AND THE LAW

Yet a more powerful circumstance lay behind the lenient treatment of some culprits: their ethnicity. The intricate system of ecclesiastical and secular laws on marriage and family/sexual crimes in the Iberian Peninsula and Spanish America, discussed at the outset of this book, was made yet more complex by the fact that the law, its interpreters, and actual social interactions in the metropolis and overseas did not view the various members of society as equal. Some were believed to be ethnically and culturally superior, civilized, and rational, while others were subaltern, uncivilized, and irrational; some were regarded as public actors and heads of households (*pater familias*), and others as subordinate domestic actors. Some were treated as adults, and others as minors; some addressed as noble and thus socially superior, and others as commoners and inferior; some were seen as sheltered by their privileged ecclesiastical or military occupations, and others viewed and treated as ordinary civilians. In sum, the body of laws, made up of diverse and at times mutually contradictory statutes, institutionalized social difference and thus, in the process, forever guided and shaped actual social interaction. By design these laws treated a few "extraordinarily" or gently and others "ordinarily" or even more harshly than the rest of the people.

To be sure, the category of "ordinary" people was not monolithic—historical realities rarely are—but had room for some notable exceptions or qualifications. For instance, the law required that "wretched" native peoples (*miserabiles personae*), despite (or rather, because of) their low status and as a way to compensate for their "natural" or "civil" weaknesses, be treated with particular consideration, leniency, and "equity." In many cases, indigenous defendants capitalized on their limited status and deployed it strategically to their advantage.

Of course, Spanish legal manuals did not address the treatment of indigenous peoples until the development of *derecho indiano* after the conquest of the New World. The law's approach to indigenous peoples was complex and at times more inconsistent than any of the other forms of social discrimination examined in this book.[53] As we have already seen, Spaniards viewed natives as brutish and uncivilized, but because of that deserving of particular kindness. As William Taylor notes, the most common expression for referring to native inhabitants in documents of the time was *miserables* (wretched). This term appears from the sixteenth century onward in colonial laws, religious and legal manuals, and commentaries by local priests and magistrates.[54] However, it referred not to Indians' lack of material wealth but rather to their need for legal protection and sympathy because of their natural state as unfortunate, ignorant innocents.

This legal expression had a long history tracing back to the legal concept of *miserabilis persona* found in Roman and, later, medieval canon law. It was first used in Emperor Constantine's protections for widows and orphans in AD 334 and later in the medieval Church's attempt to carve out legal jurisdiction in the thirteenth century over the same types of cases.[55] Eventually, it became a rather vague or open-ended canon law concept whose exact meaning was to be determined on a case-by-case basis. In fact, canon law jurisprudence eventually considered not only women and children but also wards of the state, the insane, lepers, pilgrims traveling to holy sites, and a loosely defined group of the wretched or disadvantaged (the elderly, widows, the weak or chronically infirm, and arguably even possibly parents and the "desperately in love") as needy persons deserving pity and special treatment. The Church felt a special responsibility to demonstrate solicitude and minister to their needs, and attempted to wrest away from temporal courts the handling of cases in which injury or violence threatened any of these *miserabiles*.[56]

By the second half of the sixteenth century, when the expression started to be used in the New World, it continued to imply a special juridical and social status but had undergone an intriguing transformation, adding native peoples to the list of all those whose particularly frail status or living conditions had made them deserving of mercy over centuries.[57] The law and legal thinkers now instructed both secular and ecclesiastical judges to feel sorry for such weak peoples and to use discretion in granting them exceptional treatment and protection. This was meant to correct or balance the disparity in power between them and other, more-fortunate members of society who could possibly abuse, exploit, and fool them easily.[58] The idea, as historian Maria-Elena Martínez rightly asserts, was to "lessen the possibility that the native people would be the victims of fraud, violence and other types of abuses," thus placing them in a "particularly strong paternalistic relationship with the Spanish state and the Church."[59]

Renowned seventeenth-century legal author and magistrate Juan de Solórzano y Pereyra supported the inclusion of Indians among the kingdom's *miserabiles personae*. They were fragile beings, he argued, comparable to "minors and women," lacking in free will and unable to govern their own behavior, making it necessary for others to "orient, govern and assist them."[60] The legal treatment of Indians generally reflected this type of paternalistic attitude. Courts appointed guardians to accompany them during trials and special officials to hear their complaints and try their cases; gave them more direct access to protective administrative decrees, judicial hearings, and proceedings in their favor; reduced or waived legal costs; and extended other implicit protections, even lesser punishments and generous pardons.[61]

All of the Indian defendants and witnesses in this study were considered legally incompetent to stand trial on their own and were addressed in the trial documents as "minors" (*menores*).[62] However, their treatment differed from that of "absolute" minors—defendants under the age of twelve (females) or fourteen (males), and other individuals, such as the mentally ill, lacking the legal capacity to stand trial or conduct other legal transactions independently. These all required a *tutor*, usually their father, to act on their behalf. Indians, along with young people between the ages of twelve and twenty-five, were assigned a curator (*curador ad litem*) to assist them. These court-appointed officials were usually white neighbors (*vecinos*), mostly merchants, landowners, or even local tax or postal administrators, and were required to be present at all of the "minor's" judicial proceedings. Otherwise, proceedings were null and void, as a legal advisor warned would be the case if Tarahumara Indian defendant Maria Gertrudis were not appointed a curator to represent her in the trial for killing her husband, Mariano, in the northern Mexican town of San Francisco Javier Satevó in 1806.[63]

In many cases, the court simultaneously appointed *curadores* to serve as the defendant's advocate or *defensor*. Because curators tended to be laymen, even illiterate, they had the burden of procuring adequate legal representation for the Indian defendant in the form of a trained attorney they paid to assist them during trial.[64] Because of the expense of paying for legal counsel, curators sometimes—as in a spousal murder trial in Colima, Mexico, in 1818—refused the appointment.[65]

To overcome any language barriers, natives also had the right to use the services of a court-appointed interpreter. In the cases in this book, most of the natives appear to have been conversant in the Spanish language. Defendants required such assistance more often in far-away *presidios* (see Figures 2.1 and 3.1) or other remote regions such as the mission of San Luis Obispo, California, where a Chumash Indian named Silverio used an interpreter to defend himself against charges that he killed his wife, Rebeca, in 1796. (The authorities accused him of killing his wife to run away with his lover; he claimed that a bear had attacked her in a nearby forest.)[66]

Besides *curadores,* defenders, and translators, other officers and even entire courts were established over the years to assist the natives. In consideration of their allegedly fragile nature, Indians enjoyed a special protective system in addition to the usual safeguards for legal minors under the colonial legal code. As early as the 1530s, a special state official, the *protector de Indios*, was charged with representing their interests in all legal proceedings in New Spain. Modeled after Roman law's *defensor civitates*, the same institution soon extended to other colonial regions.[67] Most instances under study here did not involve a *protector* but instead *procuradores de Indios,* called in to act as solicitors upon a magistrate's request.[68] A General Indian Court (*Juzgado General de Indios*) started to function in New Spain in the 1590s to try all suits involving Indians. The court's overriding obligation in the two centuries of its operation (1592–1820) was to protect and defend the indigenous population, simplifying legal procedures and reducing legal costs.[69] Finally, the indigenous population was also removed and exempted from the jurisdiction of the Holy Inquisition. Their religious and moral conduct came instead under the control of the special Office of the Provisor of Indians (*provisorato de indios*) and related vicar generals.[70]

Over time, the natives were also able to use special injunctive administrative actions (*amparos*) as a first resort to protect their rights. As Brian Owensby has established, starting in the late sixteenth century the natives filed thousands of *amparo* petitions to prevent or redress individual or collective damages. Some were to protect crops from trespass or other threats to native lands; several more involved tribute payments or labor abuses. Such petitions became prevalent, and the Indians thoroughly came to "internalize the idiom and idea of amparo,"[71] but this tool did not apply to domestic disputes. Indians were in theory also exempt from paying legal fees, including those owed to notaries and court officers under Church jurisdiction.[72]

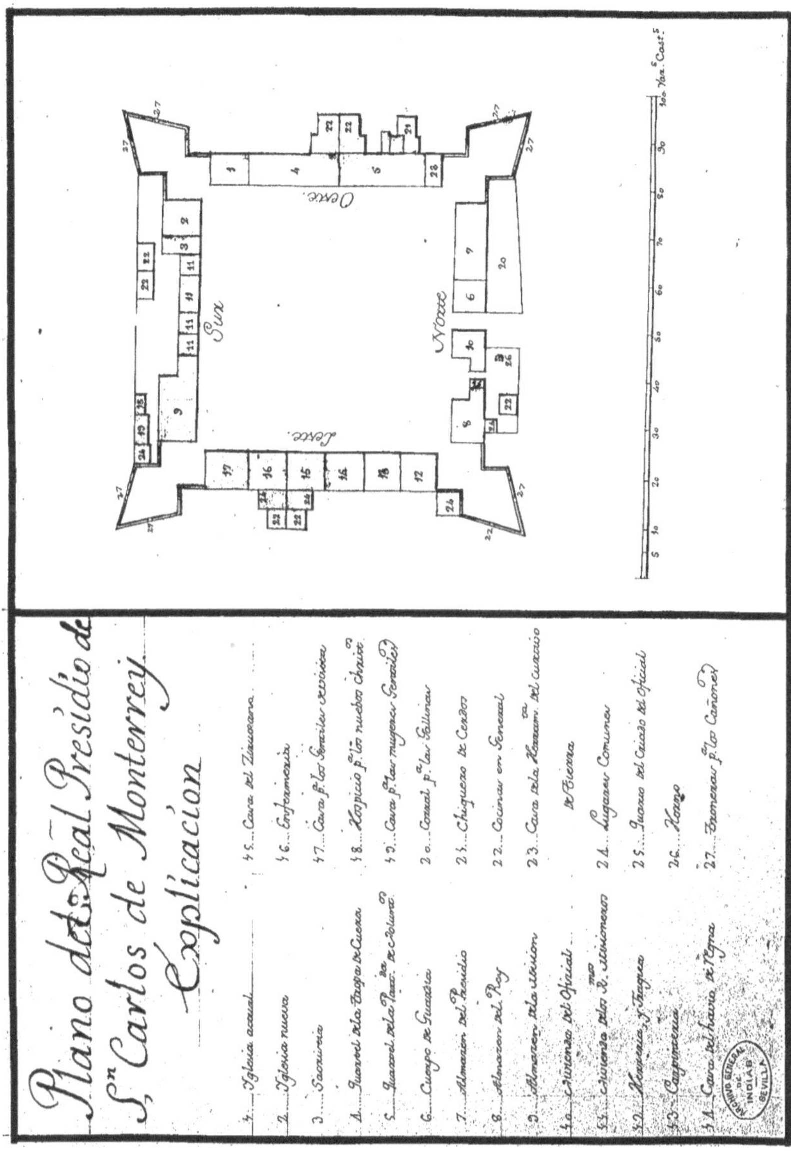

Figure 3.1. Plano del Real Presidio de San Carlos de Monterrey. AGI, Seville. MP-Mexico, 269, ter. rollo 7.

Evidence of legislation enacted by the Spanish Crown suggests other legal mechanisms designed to protect Indians. In a *Real Cédula* issued on June 17, 1682, for example, the viceroys and *audiencias* of New Spain received orders to accept all appeals or legal recourses in cases with Indian defendants.[73] According to an undated *auto acordado* (edict from a royal court, in this case the Consejo de Indias, acting as a collective body or in *acuerdo*) cited in a 1796 case, Indians were also exempt from confiscation of their property, a customary penalty in criminal cases against other defendants. This ruling was not always observed in the spousal murder cases for which we have evidence;[74] in one example in Chapter 1, confiscation left an Indian family in total ruin. Finally, Indians could not be sentenced to the galleys, banished beyond the district of their provincial capital, or forced to pay high fines.[75] Our cases do not contradict these provisions.

Despite some gaps, judicial practice seems to have been as lenient as the written law. Curators and defenders in criminal trials often cited the supposedly vengeful, conflictive, stupid, irrational, uncivilized, or barbarian character of the natives as an exculpatory factor. The fiscal *del crimen* of the Mexican *audiencia* declared in one case that "because of Indians' stupidity, they deserve to have all their actions be excused" (*la estupides del Indio merece disculpa en todas sus acciones*).[76]

Another *curador* in a 1795 case argued that natives accused of killing their wives should be treated with leniency because "his kind is Indian, and these unhappy creatures lack solid principles, full reason, and do not have sufficient education, as a result of which they think and act clumsily. . . ."[77] Similar evidence in other cases alludes to the belief that Indians were "always drunk," "rustic and childlike," "ignorant and drawn to the jungle," "barbarous and insincere," "of little understanding," "of little capacity," "always at war with one another," "deprived of complete reason, "stupid," and "vengeful and brutal."[78]

Some of these reasons were mixed in with misogynist remarks typical of the period. In one case the defendant's *curador* argued that even the best Indians are always "at war with their neighbors, their relatives and their women no matter how much they love them, whence comes the abuse of Indian women who don't believe their husbands love them if they do not batter them. . . ."[79] In another instance a defendant presented an Indian woman who had stoned her husband to death in the town of La Joya, northern Mexico, as "pusillanimous," as all women were alleged to be, even more so if they were Indians. It was "well known" (*notorio*), he claimed, that Indians have little spirit (*encogimiento y cortedad de animo*).[80] In a case in which an Indian was charged with hanging his wife, for example, the defendant's advocate argued that the woman had actually killed herself to take revenge on her husband. His reasoning? Indian women were known to be vengeful:

> [M]any have done so [commit suicide], and this is quite plausible in this case due to the vengeful character of natives: how many times does not it happen that Indian women, just for the pleasure of seeing their husbands punished, take their own skin off, damage their own face and cause themselves other harm to give more credibility to their complaints. There isn't anything more common and in this case it is not difficult to believe that, knowing the harm her death would cause her husband, Cayetana Justa wished to take revenge this way [by killing herself] for her husband's lashes.[81]

He went on to say that Indian women were sexually "easy" and that it was understandable for their husbands to suspect them of infidelity and to punish them accordingly.[82]

Indians themselves made strategic use of these stereotypes and claimed that their criminal acts should be excused because they were the result of their condition (*calidad*) as natives, which caused them to act ignorantly. This was especially more so the case if they suffered from the additional "weakness" of being female. Maria Concisión, from the village of Tecoman, used this defense, invoking her ignorance and the "weakness of her sex and her Indian condition" (*la debilidad de su sexo y la calidad de India*), after killing her husband, Felipe Cruz, in 1817 with the complicity of her mulatto lover.[83] In many cases, judges tended to agree.

As late as 1805, some sentences systematically referred to legal provisions calling for criminal cases against Indians to be conducted "with paternal love" (*con amor paternal*). Under this logic, officials were expected to approach the question of physical punishment for Indians out of a sense of fatherly duty rather than as severe judges (*oficio de padres [más que] de jueces severos*). After all, Indians had "little capacity" and if possible must be pardoned, given reverence (*venia*), and treated as "privileged" defendants.[84] Such leniency, owing at least in part to the defendants' condition as Indians, was behind the sentence of ten years of banishment accorded to Captain Diego Andrés, who killed his wife with a club in Oaxaca in 1747; the pardon of Lorenzo Macapa, who kicked his pregnant wife to death near a California mission in 1776; the two-year exile of José Tomás Mendoza after he stoned his wife to death in central Mexico in 1805; and the pardon the ordinarily severe Acordada judges granted Bernardino Antonio, a resident of Actopan, who fatally beat his wife in 1808 after they argued about the best way to discipline a child who had forgotten to feed the pigs.[85] Several of these pardons were not necessarily a function of ethnicity alone but also constituted an expression of another significant factor contributing to ameliorate the condition of spousal murderers—namely, the king's prerogative to forgive them irrespective of the severity of their actions.

PARDONS, ROYAL CELEBRATIONS, AND THE LAW

As Michel Foucault insightfully argued, body-centered punishment spectacles were vehicles for revealing the sovereign's presence. However, Foucault was careful enough not to miss another important point: The king's majesty and authority were made manifest not only through repressive and punitive acts such as the ones he described in gruesome detail, but also through munificent acts of kindness and forgiveness. As the French author put it, "the sovereign was present at the execution not only as the power exacting the vengeance of the law, but as the power that could suspend both law and vengeance."[86] The sovereign longed to be thanked and "loved," an end he pursued through regular shows of paternal magnanimity and generosity toward his subjects, even despicable criminals (see Figure 3.2).[87] In addition to using fear to make apparent his existence, therefore, the Spanish monarch also relied on gratitude to consolidate his hegemonic power. Criminals knew their punishment could be reduced and held the "hope of [royal] intervention."[88]

Royal pardons of various types were a significant and practical manifestation of the king's presence in every corner of the realm. General blank amnesties (*indultos generales*) and individual pardons (*indultos particulares*) were a traditional way for the Crown to commemorate and celebrate special occasions in the life of the royal family, as well as civic and military events. Other pardons based on theological considerations, such as the *perdones de viernes santo* (to be discussed separately), also symbolized the king's ability to deliver mercy, only this time as a messenger of God's forgiveness. For now, I shall address general pardons (*indultos generales*) founded on predominantly secular motives. Such pardons were a long-standing tradition; unlike other exceptional royal attributes, such as the king's "healing touch" (which, as Marc Bloch has ably demonstrated, strengthened the power of the French and English kings, raising them to mystical status in the Middle Ages before fading away over the centuries[89]), the king's capacity to forgive criminals endured.[90] In the Spanish Atlantic, it remained an essential royal attribute well into the nineteenth century.[91]

Legal writers presented merciful treatment, including pardons, as a right of sovereign majesty (*derecho mayestático*) or a "most precious jewel decorating the monarch's crown" (*una de las más preciosas regalias que adorna la corona de los soberanos*), a privilege that "monarchs could

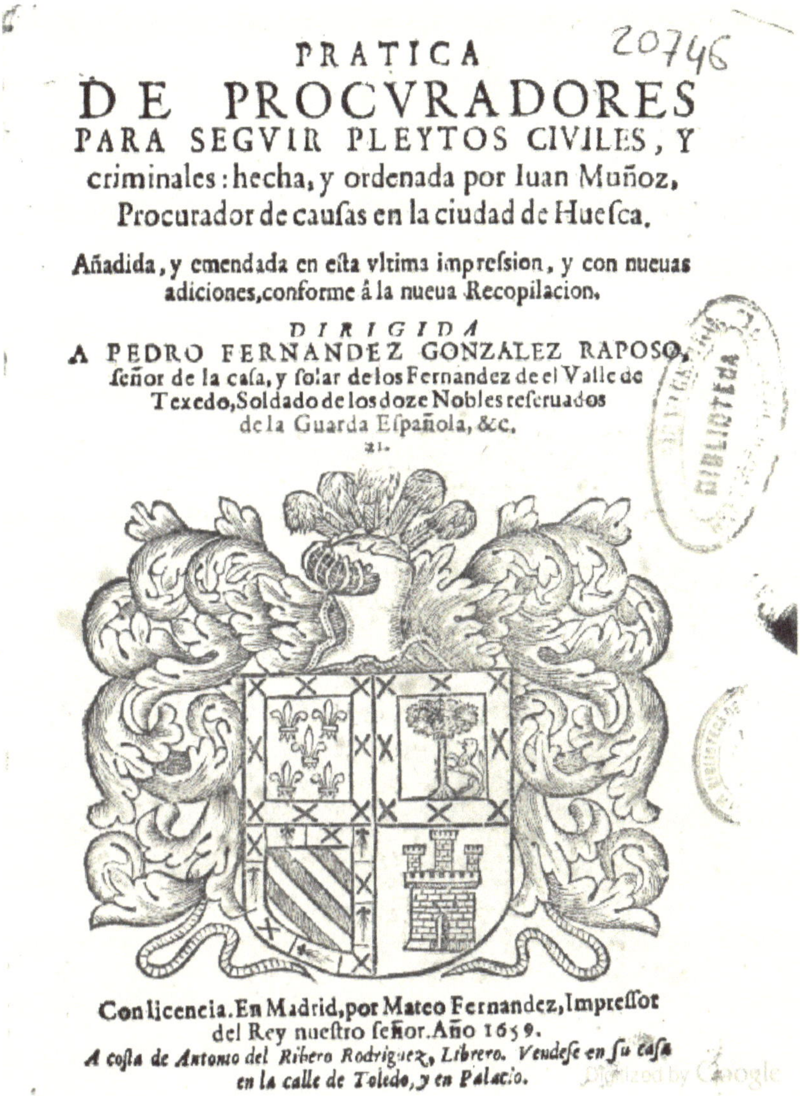
PRATICA
DE PROCVRADORES
PARA SEGVIR PLEYTOS CIVILES, Y
criminales: hecha, y ordenada por Iuan Muñoz,
Procurador de cauſas en la ciudad de Hueſca.

Añadida, y emendada en eſta vltima impreſsion, y con nueuas
adiciones, conforme à la nueua Recopilacion.

DIRIGIDA
A PEDRO FERNANDEZ GONZALEZ RAPOSO,
ſeñor de la caſa, y ſolar de los Fernandez de el Valle de
Texedo, Soldado de los doze Nobles reſeruados
de la Guarda Eſpañola, &c.

Con licencia. En Madrid, por Mateo Fernandez, Impreſſor
del Rey nueſtro ſeñor. Año 1659.
*A coſta de Antonio del Ribero Rodriguez, Librero. Vendeſe en ſu caſa
en la calle de Toledo, y en Palacio.*

Figure 3.2. Juan Muñoz, Práctica de procuradores para seguir pleitos civiles y criminales *(Madrid: Mateo Fernandez, Impresor del Rey, 1659).*

never lose nor any ordinary human being ever acquire."[92] Its application reminded all subjects of the king's power while making apparent his magnanimity. These secular acts of royal munificence were surrounded by as much pomp and circumstance as were public executions and punishments. No matter how physically distant the throne might have been, royal pardons symbolically demonstrated the king's paternal presence throughout his kingdom and amid all his peoples, including the realm's least-pleasing subjects. In this regard, pardons served a function similar to the sumptuous parade of the king's portrait and the pageantry that accompanied viceroys sent to represent the king's presence and sovereignty over his colonies.[93] More importantly, rather than the exception, these generous gestures seem to have occurred on a regular basis.

Indultos Generales

The monarch issued general pardons to thank God and to mark special occasions in the lives of the kingdom and the royal family. One such occasion was the ascent of a new monarch to the throne, an opportunity to display the new king's sovereign capacity for mercy. These types of *indultos* occurred in 1746, 1760, 1788, and 1808, soon after Bourbon monarchs Ferdinand VI (1746–1759), Charles III (1759–1788), Charles IV (1788–1808), and Ferdinand VII (1808–1833) became kings of Spain.[94] Each of these pardons was typically preceded by lavish ceremonies, both in the metropolis and the colonies.

The first *indulto general* in the period covered by this study followed the coronation of Ferdinand VI. To mark his ascent to the throne, a royal *cédula* ordered every city council in the realm to swear allegiance (*acto de jura*) to the new sovereign, with public displays of collective joy to celebrate the glorious occasion. In observance of the royal mandate, the city of Guadalajara in New Spain staged a colorful celebration. The members of the city council, joined by other influential locals (*muchos caballeros de la más distinguida nobleza de esta corte*), rode solemnly on horseback to the residence of the provincial governor and captain general, where he awaited them along with the members of the *audiencia*. The city councilors dismounted, entered the governor's palace, and announced that they would escort and lead him, the *audiencia* judges, and other royal officials to the first platform designated for the ceremony, installed within the *audiencia* building. The group first staged a procession around the city's main square, then entered the *audiencia* building and occupied its designated seats. There followed a ritual during which first the governor, and then the rest of the participants, including some of the city's artisans and representatives of several Indian communities, expressed Nueva Galicia's (Guadalajara's) allegiance to the king and celebrated the joyous occasion with gun salutes, coin throwing, and cries of jubilation, described as follows by a contemporary royal scribe:

> [T]he governor and Captain General . . . having passed the banner to his hands, and the royal guard being asked for silence, the illustrious President gave an

address saying New Galicia, New Galicia, New Galicia, for our lord Ferdinand the Sixth, king of Castile and Leon and the Indies, whom may God happily save! Everyone replied Amen, Amen, Amen!, and Hurray, Hurray, Hurray!, which was echoed by all of those present, a collective cry of all the groups lined up in the central square, including distinguished merchants, tailors, and natives from the three Indian towns of Saint Joseph, Saint Sebastian and Saint John of Mixcalzingo: both the Alférez Real Mayor and his godfather, the Alcalde Ordinario, threw silver coins. All of the city churches tolled their bells and a while later, the Royal Guard and Alférez Real Mayor asked all for their attention, and grabbing the banner in his hands the latter said in a loud voice: Guadalajara, Guadalajara, Guadalajara, for Ferdinand the Sixth, our king and natural lord. May God save him for many years. Hurray, Hurray! Everyone repeated the same, and once more there was arrow and coin throwing, bell tolling and gun shots. [95]

There followed a solemn parade (*paseo*) through the city's main streets, with stops at other platforms installed in places symbolic of the city's various ecclesiastical and bureaucratic powers. One especially lavish (*sumptuosisimo*) stop was the bishop's palace, followed by the city council building and the customs house. A similar ceremony took place at each location. The celebrations lasted all day and finished at midnight. The city's buildings were decorated and illuminated for the occasion "with big candles placed in balconies, windows, and doors, and many lit oil lamps placed in rooftops and streets . . ." (*con hachas en balcones, ventanas, puertas y candiles en las azoteas y en las calles muchísimas luminarias*), and the central square featured live music and a fireworks show paid for by the wax producers guild (*cereros*). People of all social conditions (*así principal como plebeya*) participated actively in the festivities. Parades, a special Mass, music, floats, arrow throwing, and all kinds of parties continued the next day (*al día siguiente hubo nuevos desfiles y misa, música, carrozas, lanzamiento de flechas al aire, y fiestas de toda clase*).[96] These ceremonies were representative of many others held elsewhere on similar occasions.[97]

Criminals were as thrilled as royal officials, the clergy, merchants, artisans, and the rest of the people, even indigenous communities, when a new king came to the throne. They knew that pardons were imminent. Such was the case of José Pioquinto and Máximo Antonio, the lover and husband, respectively, of María de la Concepción, an Indian woman. José Pioquinto, a sixteen-year-old Indian orphan, worked as a *gañan* (day laborer) and lodged in the married couple's home in Coyoacán, in Central Mexico. He and María de la Concepción, who was thirty, had been having an affair for the past two months. They had had sexual encounters near the edge of the forest, in an animal shed behind the house, in the kitchen, and, most recently, in the main room of the house. On this Monday afternoon in late December 1806, Máximo Antonio arrived home unexpectedly and found María de la Concepción combing the boy's hair. Already made suspicious by his wife's failure to appear at work that day, he proceeded to attack the two lovers. One at a time, he grabbed each of them by the hair and smashed their heads with a rock. The woman's head injuries were severe, and she died shortly afterward. José Pioquinto survived the man's assault but was jailed for adultery. Several witnesses testified about his illicit relationship with María de la Concepción, and indeed the lovers confessed to their affair shortly before she died. Less than two years later, however, both the boy and his would-be killer were released from jail under the royal pardon (*comprehendidos en la gracia de indulto*) issued in 1808 to celebrate King Ferdinand VII's ascension to the Spanish throne.[98]

Coronations were relatively rare occasions. The majority of general pardons accompanied the celebration of events significant to the royal family. For instance, King Charles III issued half a dozen *indultos generales* to share his joy over the birth of a prince or princess and other royal *infantes*, including his grandchildren. In 1771 the king declared that God having granted the monarchy the joyous delivery of a royal infant (Carlos Clemente, son of Prince Charles and his wife, María Luisa), it was only right to forgive all prisoners in Madrid and other parts of the kingdom (*habiendo debido a la Divina Providencia el importante beneficio y consuelo para esta Monarquía del felíz y dichoso parto de la Princesa, mi muy cara y amada nuera, dando a luz un infante: vengo en conceder indulto general a todos los presos que se hallasen en las cárceles de Madrid, y demás del Reyno*). In 1775, 1777, 1779, and 1780, the king granted further pardons to celebrate the births of his grandchildren Carlota Joaquina, María Luisa, María Amalia, and Carlos Domingo Eusebio.[99] In 1783 he was even happier because his daughter-in-law had given birth to healthy twin boys, Charles and Philip: "*dos robustos Infantes, a quienes se han puesto los nombres de Carlos y Felipe.*" To celebrate, he granted general amnesty to prisoners in Madrid and elsewhere.[100] Ferdinand VII issued a similar *indulto* in September 1817 to celebrate the birth of his first child with María Isabel de Borbón, an *infanta* of Portugal's House of Braganza.[101]

Royal weddings were an additional opportunity for the king to express his largesse, as was the case in 1765, when the Prince of Asturias married María Luisa, Princess of Parma, or in 1795, when King Charles IV (1788–1808) celebrated the weddings of his beloved daughters: "*las Serenísimas Infantas Doña María Amalia, y Doña María Luisa, mis amadas hijas.*" Charles IV issued another *indulto* in 1803 to mark the prince's recent wedding, "*con motivo del matrimonio del Príncipe Ntro Señor con la Serenísima Sra Da María Amalia princesa de Nápoles.*"[102] His successor, Ferdinand VII, granted still another in September 1816 to celebrate his own marriage and that of royal infante Charles: "*los venturosos enlaces de S.M (Ferdinand VII) y del Srmo. señor infante Don Carlos.*"[103]

Military and political events were a further motive for rejoicing and issuing pardons. The 1795 *indulto*, in addition to celebrating the princesses' weddings, marked the signing of a peace agreement with France (*el ajuste de Paz con los Franceses*).[104] The inauguration of *cortes generales* was also customarily commemorated with an *indulto*.[105] During Ferdinand VII's captivity under Napoleon, for instance, the newly established regency council (*Consejo de Regencia*) and the parliament (*Cortes Generales*), following in the footsteps of various kings before them, enacted pardons to celebrate the parliament's installation in 1810 (*el feliz acontecimiento de su instalación*) and the promulgation of the monarchy's first constitution (*el plausible día de la publicación de la Constitución Política de la Monarquía*) in 1812.[106] Ferdinand VII issued another in 1820 to celebrate, albeit reluctantly, the reenactment of the Cádiz constitution following a liberal revolt at home.[107]

Criminals Take Advantage

The king's largesse did not go unheeded. Amid the general rejoicing, criminals took as much advantage as they could of royal *indultos*. To the chagrin of royal authorities, they seem to have abused this privilege as much as religious sanctuary, an institution discussed further in Chapter 5. Although there are no explicit records of spousal murderers doing so, the behavior of other criminals makes it fair to presume at least a few did as well. Would-be criminals and those in hiding appear to have become skilled at taking advantage of pardons they knew were forthcoming, especially when a royal birth was near.

Balthasar de Arregui, who seems to have been a high-ranking justice or ecclesiastical official from the northeastern Spanish city of Zaragoza, complained about this problem in a document addressed to the king in early January 1779. In addition to bemoaning the abuse of sanctuary, the author expressed concern over the growing number of homicides, which he estimated at thirty-three in 1777 and forty in 1778. According to him, the homicide rate actually increased before expected *indultos* (*tiene observado que en las cercanías a los indultos menudean estos [homicidios] y otros delitos*), such as the one likely to be granted upon the birth of a child to King Charles IV and his wife, María Luisa. (The infant, María Amelia, was born on January 10, 1779.) Knowing that the birth was imminent, Arregui warned, criminals would indulge their habits freely, for they knew their crimes would be soon forgiven, as they had seen happen to others (*la esperanza de indultos anima a las gentes a perpetrar maldades con la de que decretados aquellos quedan indemnizados como lo han visto en otros*). He concluded by suggesting that his majesty use other means to express his gratitude to God.[108]

Other problems were associated with general *indultos*. In addition to the potential for a spike in crime, chaos could result from the release of numerous prisoners all at once. On December 31, 1783, for example, Charles III had asked his council to advise him how best to narrow and limit royal pardons. He voiced concern over the disorder and negative consequences of releasing too many criminals, which typically ensued after mass pardons (*los desórdenes y malas consecuencias que han solido nacer de la libertad de mucho número de delincuentes*), and requested assistance in averting this potential situation.[109] In fact, all *indultos* were subject to strict legal limitations, but this was not nor probably ever would be sufficient to contain abuses.

Legal Characteristics and Doctrine

Indultos were more than just cultural traditions allowing monarchs and other rulers to commemorate special occasions by displaying their religious fervor, power, and munificence. They constituted a major legal institution as well. One of the main legal treatises on the subject made clear that while the prerogative to grant pardons was an expression of the king's mercy, it could not be regarded as an absolute royal attribute. Neither was it an arbitrary custom; rather, the royal privilege to pardon criminals always required a legal justification (*justa causa*)—in other words, a permissible occasion, such as commemorations of the death or birth of Jesus Christ, coronations, royal weddings, victories over tyrants, and the opening of *cortes generales*.[110]

Furthermore, every one of the graces mentioned above took the form of a royal decree (*royal cédula*) with the consultation and monitoring of the king's legal advisors in the royal council and chamber (*Consejo y Cámara*). Their legal opinions specified the timing and geographical scope of the pardon, the conditions for it to be granted, and the list of crimes excluded from the benefit.[111] For instance, some decrees applied only to criminals in Madrid jails, while some extended these graces to the rest of the kingdom. As a rule, the grace covered only those crimes committed before the decree's publication, not subsequently (*crímenes futuros*). Decrees usually restricted pardons for military desertion and excluded money forging, smuggling, sodomy, blasphemy, arson, dueling, and the killing of priests. Also ineligible were state fiscal officials accused of fraud or bribery (*cohecho*) and individuals who committed crimes against the monarchy or God (*crímenes de lesa Magestad, Divina o humana*).[112]

The main exclusion affecting spousal murderers concerned homicides committed with *alevosia* (treachery)—that is, with the victim in a particularly disadvantageous position. Two other conditions could also rule out pardon: not receiving the forgiveness of the victim's family and fugitive status (*reos que estén fugitivos, ausentes y rebeldes*). Royal decrees were not always explicit about these exclusions, but widely accepted doctrinal and legal principles established them.[113]

The most common exception that legal authors examined was the need for criminals to receive the forgiveness of the deceased's closest kin, especially parents and brothers ("*perdón de la parte agraviada*" or "*que los agraviados remitan sus ofensas*").[114] This was indispensable for receiving the king's own forgiveness, for it was understood that the king would never want his clemency to cause harm to a third party or curtail the public's right to revenge (*que de esta gracia resulte perjuicio a tercero, ni a la vindicta pública*).[115] To ensure eligibility for pardons, prisoners became skilled at producing "letters of remission" formalized by public notaries.[116]

Even criminals in hiding did not find themselves entirely excluded from pardon. The authorities sometimes issued a deadline—usually one to two years—for them to appear before justice officials if they wished to be eligible for *indulto*. The king and his advisors favored cases in which the criminal appeared directly at one of the superior courts, the *chancillerías* or *audiencias*.[117] As they were exceptional graces, pardons could not be finalized by local justice officials but required the ultimate intervention of the highest tribunals in the land.

Another common procedural requirement was for the nearest *chancillería* or *audiencia* to review the petition for *indulto* and the criminal proceedings as a whole. In part thanks to this demand, historians have access to records that would otherwise be difficult or impossible to find in local archives. Finally, the law also prescribed that criminals whose pardon was confirmed by a high court should be considered free from corporal and pecuniary punishment (*penas pecuniarias*) and from any penalty against their good social standing (*penas infamatorias*). The remission of *penas pecuniarias* and *penas infamatorias* did not cover those whose final sentences had already been issued. In these cases, *indultos* freed the beneficiaries only from corporal punishment. They could recover neither the property nor the good name (*fama*) they had lost as a result of their crime.[118] As stringent as some of the conditions mentioned above might seem, in practice the many royal *indultos* during the period of this study reached and benefited a fair number of defendants accused of killing their spouses.

Indultos *for Spousal Murderers*

General pardons occurred frequently. In addition to the numerous individual Good Friday pardons delivered over the years (about twenty annually and discussed later), the monarchy issued no fewer than nineteen general *indultos* covering hundreds of prisoners during the period considered in this work. Four marked the enthronement of kings, eight celebrated royal births (six of them under King Charles III alone), four commemorated royal weddings, and three more culminated politico-military occasions. There may even have been more *indultos* for which we have no record.

Spousal murderers were among the many criminals who could unquestionably rejoice in the monarch's largesse. As mentioned in a previous chapter, one-quarter of the spousal murderers in the sample for New Spain (23) received pardons of one kind or another.[119] Spousal killers in late Bourbon Spain (6) and colonial Colombia (3) received a few additional pardons. This geographical disparity is hard to explain. The majority of the beneficiaries were men: 26, compared to 6 women. Close to half were Indians (15), followed by whites (11). *Mestizos* were a minority of those pardoned (2 or, if we add those of undetermined ethnicity, a total of 6). Finally, two-thirds of the pardons in our case set occurred in the first two decades of the nineteenth century, likely a function of uneven evidence and an indication that the list may have included numerous others (see Table 3.3).

As the fragmentary statistics suggest, Spanish kings granted royal pardons with relative generosity for the crimes under examination. Sometimes as many as three spousal murderers were pardoned in the single years of 1806, 1815, and 1819, respectively. This generosity is a little surprising if one notes that royal pardons excluded particularly "atrocious" crimes, a category that generally included all parricides.[120] The refusal of the grace to several spousal murderers in our group was usually because the culprits were in hiding or the victim's family refused to forgive them.[121] As in the case of sanctuary, however, the number of beneficiaries was by no means trivial.

VISITAS DE CÁRCEL

As if pardons did not suffice, jailed inmates had an additional opportunity for royal mercy via the on-site decisions of *audiencia* judges during visits to local prisons. Like general pardons, regular jail visits were a venerated legal institution in the Spanish Atlantic. They afforded officials at the local level the opportunity to extend charity to prisoners on behalf

TABLE 3.3. *Spousal murderers pardoned, by date, gender, and ethnicity: Mexico, Colombia, and Spain, 1750s–1820s*

Crime's date	Defendant's gender	Defendant's ethnicity	Place of crime	Alcohol-related
1754	Female	—	Ibague, Col.	
1761	Male	White	Madrid, Spain	Yes
1776	Male	Indian	Presidio Loreto, Mex.	
1782	Male	White	Madrid, Spain	
1793	Male	White	Aranjuez, Spain	
1797	Male	Indian	Presidio San Diego, Mex.	
1802	Male	—	La Mesa, Col.	
1803	Female	—	Valladolid, Mex.	
1803	Male	Indian	Teotihuacan, Mex.	Yes
1805	Female	White	Villarobledo (Granada), Spain	
1806	Male	Indian	Cuernavaca, Mex.	Yes
1806	Male	Indian	Coyoacan, Mex.	
1806	Male	Indian	Mexico City, Mex.	Yes
1807	Male	White	Pachuca, Mex.	
1807	Male	Indian	Calimaya, Mex.	Yes
1808	Male	White	Pachuca, Mex.	Yes
1808	Male	Mestizo	Cuernavaca, Mex.	Yes
1808	Male	Indian	Siachoque, Col.	Yes
1813	Male	White	St. Maria Lagos, Mex.	Yes
1813	Male	Mestizo	St. Isabel, Mex.	
1814	Female	White	Sombrerete, Mex.	
1815	Male	White	Soria, Spain	
1815	Male	Indian	Tulancingo, Mex.	Yes
1815	Male	Indian	Actopan, Mex.	
1816	Male	White	Galicia, Spain	
1818	Male	—	Nombre Dios, Mex.	Yes
1819	Female	Indian	Colotlan, Mex	Yes
1819	Male	Indian	Guadalajara, Mex.	Yes
1819	Female	Indian	San Pedro, Mex.	
1820	Male	Indian?	Colima, Mex.	
1820	Male	White	Mexico City, Mex.	
1821	Male	Indian?	Tulancingo, Mex	

SOURCES: AGN, Mexico, Criminales, vol. 22, case 16; vol. 33/113, cases 2/2; vol. 50, case 16; vol. 108, case 10; vol. 116b, case 16; vol. 119, case 8; vol. 137, case 6/7; vol. 530; vol. 46, case 3; vol. 8, fols. 301–357; vol. 44, case 12; vol. 64, case 3; AGN, Mexico, Californias, vol. 72; Archivo Real Audiencia Nueva Galicia, Guadalajara, vol. 18, 8-308; vol. 21, 7-345; vol. 60, 3-965; v. 67, 4-1092; vol. 57, 12-925; vol. 58, 24-2420; vol. 59, 4-951; vol. 157, 23-2389; AGN, Colombia, Criminal, Colonia, vol. 179, fols. 408–435; vols. 25/108, fols. 504–517/914–960; vol. 2, fols. 748–751; ARCV, caja 204, case 2; ARG, legajo 131, no. 40; AHN, Madrid, Sala Alcaldes Casa y Corte, fol. 97.

of the king. As a contemporary legal manual put it, they constituted "another means through which the King dispenses clemency, because in his glorious name justice ministers gave freedom to those who deserve to enjoy it."[122]

Audiencia justices had the obligation to dedicate part of their time and efforts to oversee the condition of prisons in the capital of their judicial districts. They visited and inspected the local jail sometimes as often as once a week and met with interested inmates. In Madrid, two members of the king's Consejo and the several Alcaldes de Sala y Corte were charged with making such visits. The most junior members of the council made supplementary visits on Mondays and Thursdays.[123] The visits did not occur in a random fashion but followed a certain protocol.

Legal manuals summarized the main purpose of the visits and provided officials and legal experts guidance on how to proceed. In the late seventeenth century, for example, López de Cuellar specified that the officials visiting the Madrid prisons on Saturday afternoons should verify the wardens' and jailers' treatment of the inmates; whether or not attorneys, scribes, and *procuradores* dispatched the cases with due diligence; whether inmates gambled, staking their own clothes or alms; whether the prohibition on women, even wives of inmates, in male prisons was being upheld; whether or not the doctor in charge was tending to the inmates' wounds and illnesses; whether the prison chapel had all of the sacred ornaments required to celebrate Mass on a regular basis; and whether the local mayors performed nightly patrols and ensured the prison's safety. Once they had verified the various issues listed, the officials made a visual inspection of the cells and heard any complaints or requests, including petitions for release.[124]

This is how María Antonia Gómez, who was in the female jail (*galera*) for killing her husband, Fernando Andujar, managed to gain her freedom in March 1805. The Audiencia and Chancillería of Granada had sentenced her to an unspecified prison term. She had already spent several years in jail and petitioned the inspectors to look into her situation. Upon review of her case, they waived the remainder of her sentence under a "pardon granted during a jail visitation" (*indulto dispensado durante la visita de cárceles*).[125] But jail visitations could result not just in the forgiveness of an individual sentence but also in collective reductions of the punishment of almost all of those housed in a certain prison.

In some instances, during these "general visits of prisoners" (*visita general de presos*), Indian procurators and pro-bono defenders (*defensores de pobres*) proactively seized the opportunity to request a general reduction of the punishment for all inmates. Evidence shows that such reductions were actually decreed, and rather generously so. In late colonial Mexico City, for instance, the royal authorities decided that all of the inmates in the jails recently visited, who had not received any other benefit in the past, would have one-third of their entire sentences commuted.[126] This arbitrary show of magnanimity must have benefited at least a handful of spousal murderers. More important, it confirmed the importance that clemency always had for the operation of justice: the feeling that the king was always present amid his people, thus strengthening the monarchy's (and the Church's) legitimacy and hegemonic rule.

CONCLUSION

In the late colonial Spanish Atlantic, royal justice officials administered public vengeance to spousal murderers and other criminals in accordance with long-standing legal procedures and customs, sometimes dating back to ancient Roman times. As subsequent chapters will illustrate, the proceedings included the threat of judicial torture and punishments ranging from fines and expropriation to death by hanging or the *garrote* and the supplementary *encubamiento,* as well as intermediate penalties such as banishment, confinement (*recogimiento*, *presidio*, *prisión*), and forced labor. However, criminals also enjoyed increasingly more moderate or humanitarian treatment and ample opportunities to seek mitigation. Some of the moderation may have resulted, as Foucault argued, from a new political economy of punishment linked to enlightened reactions to the severity of body-centered, public, and painful chastisement. In other cases the changes had deeper roots and a much longer lineage.

Although the law discriminated against or in favor of criminals from particular ethnic, age, gender, and status groups, making their judicial situation more or less complicated than that of others involved in similar crimes, it also afforded all defendants an interesting series of opportunities to mitigate punishment or, if possible, get away with murder. Such opportunities were almost intrinsic to the logic of criminal law from immemorial times and to legal and scientific understandings of what various notions central to the judicial process, such as sanity, criminal intent, and treachery, actually meant.

More important, behind the diverse outcomes of criminal cases—fines, banishment, lashes, *recogimiento,* jail, hard labor, the galleys, the death penalty, reduced sentences, pardons, and acquittals—lay fascinating reasoning, symbolism, and ritual revealing the cultural universe and ancestry of Spanish society, law, and justice. Various paradoxes were also apparent. For example, the widespread use of alcohol became the object of social scorn and diatribe at the same time as it represented a popular source of income for individuals and institutions, including the Catholic Church and the Crown. For defendants, alcohol could be the catalyst leading to fatal aggression, but it was also an ideal exculpatory factor. Similarly, an attack of blinding rage could be a valid clue that one had indeed committed the crime under investigation, but it was also a reason to claim forgiveness. A victim's long agony was proof of an attack, but when combined with lunar cycles, exposure to the sun, and folk remedies, it could diminish or rule out any responsibility on the part of the attacker. Finally, the king's absolute power, allowing him to suspend punishment for culprits who had committed a major crime, became a source of empowerment for delinquents who avidly took advantage of the dozens of opportunities to escape the death penalty or jail. As the study of Spain will show, royal intervention benefited still other defendants by at least ensuring a less painful and more honorable execution.

The following chapter presents findings from another detailed case study, the Spanish metropolis itself. These findings confirm the importance of royal interventions in ameliorating the punishment facing some spousal murderers. However, even more significant is the discovery of numerous murders committed by wives determined to run away with their lovers, a circumstance that challenges long-standing assumptions about the way honor operated in the Spanish Atlantic.

CHAPTER FOUR

Honor and Punishment in Late Eighteenth-Century Spain

As with the case study of Mexico presented before, this chapter on Spain also starts with the story of an individual crime to probe various aspects of the social history of spousal murders. One such aspect is the phenomenon of women who killed their spouses to be free to start a new life with their lovers. As the examples in this chapter make clear, unfaithful females were not always the primary victims of spousal murder; frequently, they were the aggressors. This fact has revisionist historiographical implications, especially concerning the honor codes that, according to Spanish Golden Age stereotypes, prescribed that men murder wives or other female relatives who disgraced their or their family's reputations.

In the first incident we will examine, a wife's infidelity culminates in the murder of her husband. Judging by this and other similar cases, the strategy of avenging male honor by murdering dishonorable females and their lovers was, in practice, rare. Contrary to conventional wisdom, husbands who killed their wives and male lovers to avenge their personal and familial honor were not the norm. In fact, wives were often the ones committing the crimes, assisted by their lovers. Although a few adulterous husbands certainly followed through with such crimes, wives were more apt to kill their husbands to end their marriages and be free to do as they pleased. The examples below provide a glimpse into Spanish mores, the justice system, crimes and criminals, and means of punishment.

The issue of punishment, a revealing aspect of the overall discussion, is addressed in more detail later in the book. The discussion in this chapter makes some general points about punishment and social hierarchy—in particular, the fact that criminals of even the lesser nobility continued to receive differential treatment during trial and sentencing in symbolic and other ways—for example, exemption from judicial torture and from having one's hands tied; exemption from being forced to ride a pack animal or be dragged through the streets, as were ordinary criminals or those in the colonies; opportunity of being given a quicker death and/or permission to decorate one's scaffold. Nobles were by no means spared major punishment, however, even long terms of forced labor and the death penalty.

On December 9, 1797, a rainy Sunday night in the village of Aranjuez near Madrid, a wealthy cloth (*lienzos*) merchant by the name of Francisco del Castillo was stabbed at his home while recovering in bed from an ailment. He received a total of eleven wounds, including three in the chest and two in the lower abdomen, and died immediately. The murderer, who covered his face with a mask that the defenseless victim unsuccessfully struggled to remove, turned out to be his wife's lover, twenty-four-year-old Santiago San Juan, a law intern on his way to becoming an independent practicing attorney. San Juan, a native of Barbastro in the northeastern region of Aragón, received ample assistance and encouragement from the victim's wife, thirty-two-year-old María Vicenta Mendieta, not only his lover but also, apparently, a distant relative.

María Vicenta and her merchant husband, who seems to have been much older than she was, had been married for ten years. She was quite unhappy, claiming he was bad tempered and abusive. Witnesses confirmed that the man indeed had a difficult character but also said he was a generous husband, allowing her to go out regularly and even accept visits from San Juan, despite his disapproval of the closeness of their relationship and the threat it represented to his social standing. María Vicenta, a native of Santander, Cantabria, was the only child of a distinguished family. Her father, Pedro Agustín de Mendieta, was district magistrate (*alcalde mayor*) of the Puerto de Santa María, a cozy port city near Cádiz. In 1789 he also won a prestigious post as subordinate judge for criminal cases (*alcalde del crimen*) in one of the kingdom's high courts of appeal, Granada's Royal Chancillería and Audiencia.[1] Not only María Vicenta's honor but also that of her illustrious family was at stake as a result of her indiscretions.

In his important work on the history of interpersonal violence in Europe from medieval times to the twentieth century, Dutch historian Pieter Spierenburg establishes that in the Old Continent "female honor . . . played a role in almost every act of violence that involved one or more women," who remained a minority among criminals. He also reminds us that, whereas in the eighteenth century a man's honor was tied to physical courage, bravery, manliness, readiness for violence, defense of his land and family, and, one might add, distinguished service to the king, a woman's honor was instead closely linked to her marital fidelity, general passivity, discretion, and even silence. Rumors of any kind, especially that a woman was not a virgin (*doncella*) and engaged in acts of sexual impropriety and/or sorcery, were disastrous to her reputation and that of her household.[2] A married woman's prestige suffered further damage if, along with her adulterous comportment, she rebelled against the husband she was expected to "love, honor, and obey."[3] Therefore, the murder of a husband with an adulterous wife's active assistance and participation, especially if premeditated, was a truly heinous conduct in ancien régime Spain. People in general and justice officials in particular did not sympathize with acts of this sort or with their dishonorable protagonists.[4]

Juan Meléndez Valdés (1754–1817), for example, a distinguished and enlightened poet, academic, and jurist, and a Royal Prosecutor before the *Alcaldes de Casa y Corte,* was scandalized by the case of María Vicenta Mendieta. The place of the crime, Aranjuez, was within the jurisdiction of the *Alcaldes de Casa y Corte,* an influential section of the Royal Government Council (*Consejo Real y Supremo de su Magestad*),[5] in part a tribunal of justice similar to the royal *audiencias* or appeals courts. Titled nobles and former or future secretaries of state—the Count of Floridablanca, for example—often staffed or presided over it. The institution was in charge, among other things, of investigating and trying major crimes in the court and five leagues around ("*la Corte de Madrid y su rastro*"); advising the king on the commutation of punishment or forgiveness of criminals on Good Friday, a long-standing royal practice addressed in Chapter 5; and assisting the king in the design of new criminal policies.[6] Influential prosecutors appeared before the tribunal and voiced their opinions, sometimes published later as forensic speeches or reports.[7] Prosecutor Meléndez Valdés's views on this spousal murder were, as can be expected, essentially patriarchal and deeply religious. He found the act of the unfaithful pair to be a loathsome assault on a respectable *pater familiae.* In the prosecutor's opinion, it was tantamount to the killing of other highly regarded patriarchs—even the king himself, a bishop, a judge, a father, or a brother. For Meléndez Valdés, the crime in question had ended the life of not only a betrayed husband but also a distinguished, loyal, and knowledgeable tradesman, an honorable public figure who, he claimed, was scheduled to represent the Spanish king in international trading ventures before the Court of London. He also deplored the murder as an attack on Catholicism and a desecration of the holy sacrament of matrimony:

> It is an horror, an execration, an insult to Christianity, that a woman through a bloody and vicious hand had committed such an act against the law of Jesus Christ who instituted the Sacrament of Marriage, a great feat according to Saint

Paul as a result of the excellence of its meaning, none other than the union between divine and human nature. It is the greatest homicide not only because it includes in itself all others, as has been established, but also because with it natural reason is offended, conjugal love trampled on, without respect towards God, without honor for the sacrament, and thus tarnished the church, and filled with scandal and horror the entire republic.[8]

Especially in a world ruled by males, María Vicenta's was an *enorme* (most serious crime). In the prosecutor's words, "the voice of the people, the stones in the town's streets, and the sacred walls of the unfortunate merchant's home and studio" (*la voz del pueblo, las piedras de sus calles, y las sagradas paredes de la casa y gabinete mismo del desgraciado Castillo*) cry for the punishment of such crime, committed unfortunately by a woman of high society ("*de clase y circunstancias*").[9] María Vicenta's honor had been gravely compromised, beginning with her extramarital affair with her accomplice. Several of the household servants knew of their liaison and, to his deep chagrin, even the husband himself suspected it. Her unfaithfulness, followed by her participation in the murder, only added to her shame.[10]

For a liberal mind such as royal prosecutor Meléndez Valdés, however, all defendants in criminal cases deserved humane treatment and guarantees. He and other progressive jurists in Spain and elsewhere embraced a relatively modern concept at the time: respect for the physical integrity of suspects and the avoidance of physical pain. For instance, Meléndez Valdés would have found judicial torture unacceptable for ascertaining the facts of the crime, no matter how heinous, for he deemed torture inhumane as well as ineffective. Besides, in his opinion, it was outmoded or in "*desuso*" by the late eighteenth century.[11] Although the two defendants complained of having suffered physical abuse (*apremios*),[12] judicial torture does not appear to have been practiced in their case. The death penalty was another matter.

Like other criminal reformers opposed to torture, including the better-known Manuel de Lardizabal y Uribe, Meléndez Valdés supported the death penalty.[13] The only caveat that these and other reformers had was their rejection of hanging in favor of the more effective, thus "humane," garrote (strangulation with an iron collar affixed to a post and tightened with a screw) to avoid a "prolonged and cruel death full of torments."[14] Otherwise, in their view, certain criminals deserved to die. In this case, in light of the lovers' elevated social condition, which made their behavior even more shocking, Meléndez Valdés requested no mercy for them and demanded that they be publicly executed, ideally in the street facing the house where the crime had occurred. Nevertheless, he accepted that they be granted certain benefits while they were being led to their execution and during the act itself in deference to their social position. Before attempting to explain this, however, we need a fuller sense of the extramarital affair and murder.

Several people, including the family's servants, eventually testified to the spouses' frequent quarrels, even a recent incident during which the wife had badly scratched her husband's cheeks with her fingernails. On this occasion she spoke dismissively toward him and asked the servants, who intervened to stop the fighting, to leave her alone because she was more than capable of "finishing off her husband" on her own ("*la dejasen, que ella era bastante para acabar con su marido*"). The servants also mentioned the dishonorable love affair between the defendants, manifested by María Vicenta's secret gifts of clothes, money, and even a bed for the young man; her habit of sneaking out of the house at odd hours, apparently to join him; and San Juan's daily visits to the woman's home, in spite of the merchant's dislike and suspicions. This was all certain to elicit mockery of a cuckolded husband ignorant of his unfortunate fate. A "*cabrón*" was the pejorative adjective attached to such men: Unlike rams, which defend their females, goats (*cabros*) do not have a sense of propriety and let them mate freely with others in the pack.[15]

Most recently, an acquaintance had spotted the lovers at a local park. They also seem to have spent some time at San Juan's new place of residence, a rented room in a home whose *posadera* or concierge declared that the pair used fake names (Joaquina Santos and Eugenio Izquiero), likely in an effort to conceal their romantic liaison. In another instance, about two months before the crime, San Juan had tricked María Vicenta's husband into believing he was taking a trip to Valencia, and the merchant even assisted him with money. The reality is that he stayed in Aranjuez and took advantage of his time to see María Vicenta, whose husband had liberally granted her the freedom to go to the theatre twice a week and leave the house regularly. The servants also reported at least one party at the house during one of the husband's absences, following which the lovers spent the night together and San Juan's sister stayed over with an infantry officer. The women's daring behavior contradicted dominant honor codes but, as we shall later see, was not that unusual at all.

On the night of the crime, María Vicenta made certain that a male servant and a close friend of her husband's were out of the house before opening one of the blinds to signal San Juan that it was time to come in. She had previously given him a key to the house and had also cut the string that activated the doorbell so that the servants would not notice that an intruder had entered. As the crime was being committed, in spite of her husband's desperate cries of "María Vicenta! María Vicenta!" she kept the servants distracted and away from the room where the tragedy was unfolding. Minutes later, she experienced a fainting spell, apparently a ruse to aid the culprit's escape from the scene of the crime. To make the murder appear to be a common burglary gone wrong, San Juan stole some gold coins from a chest near where the victim lay. Unaware of the magnitude of the crime, the servants who sounded the alarm initially raised a cry of "thieves! . . . thieves!" but the soldiers who responded immediately from a nearby regiment could not catch San Juan. Only after the interception of a coded letter María Vicenta sent her anxious lover a few days later via a servant did the authorities apprehend the murderer and uncover the lovers' sinister plot.

After a trial requiring the replacement of the original local judge, who was accused of dragging his feet in the investigation, the two were sentenced to death, albeit by garrote rather than hanging in recognition of their family's honorable condition (*por el honor de la familia*).[16] Although it would soon be applied to all "citizens" irrespective of social status, in the 1790s this faster method of execution, whereby an iron collar strangled or broke the victim's neck, was generally reserved for nobles.[17]

For the defendants, the decision to carry out their execution by this expedient means was a relief and indicative that their family background still mattered, as did their occupation. Belonging to "hidalgo" families and being actively involved in decent or nonmechanical trades (*empleo no bajo*) would earn them a more dignified death.[18] A good family name and tradition of royal service on the part of the woman's father, and San Juan's dedication to the noble legal occupation—along with his lack of a criminal record and the fact that he was "blinded by love" at a vulnerable young age—appear to have worked in their favor.

The prosecutor nevertheless asked for their execution to be followed by the severing and public exhibition of their right hands, concluding with the *encubamiento* of the two corpses. This corresponded to standing legal prescriptions. In fact, the law codes (*Siete Partidas*, ley 12, tit. 8, partida 7) actually prescribed that such crimes be punished with public flogging as well as *encubamiento*,[19] the old Roman punishment.[20]

The couple asked for further leniency and until the very last minute petitioned the king to overturn the death sentence. María Vicenta argued that her husband was vicious, while San Juan claimed that love had "blinded his reason" at a young age. Their excuses were to no avail. In the end, María Vicenta had to content herself with permission to display her family's honorable condition by decorating her gallows with the mourning symbols (*lutos*) reserved for people of distinction, as well as the privilege of having her corpse surrounded by candles (*blandones*). These two concessions needed express authorization by the *Alcaldes de Casa y Corte,* who ruled them an entitlement for even lesser nobles (*hidalgos*).[21]

Around noon on Monday, April 23, 1798, less than four months after the crime, the authorities transported the two lovers to a public square in Madrid with their hands untied, on mules covered with black cloth, accompanied by a crier, several priests, and a select group of justice officials. This contrasted greatly with the treatment of ordinary criminals, especially those in colonial territories, who typically had their hands tied and were dragged through the streets by unadorned pack animals. Unlike ordinary criminals, María Vicenta and her lover were spared flogging as well. Fearing unruly crowds during the execution, the local authorities provided a contingent of sixty soldiers and three officers in addition to those typically assigned to keep the peace. After the execution, the defendants' corpses remained at the gallows until nighttime, when the executioner received authorization to remove them and hand them over to the Catholic Peace and Charity Brotherhood, which would take care of the burial. The records contain no actual evidence of the severing of the prisoners' hands or their *encubamiento*.[22]

The case of María Vicenta and her lover reveals a number of intriguing characteristics of spousal murders committed in Spain around the same time. These do not concern ethnic relations and discrimination, as in the case of the colonial Mexican murders examined earlier, but rather patterns of female contestation, as stressed later in the study of colonial Colombia. Most striking is the female identity of many protagonists and the apparently "dishonorable" circumstances surrounding their crimes. This seems consistent with recent narratives about the significant power and agency that the era's Spanish women displayed, contradicting traditional historiographical views of the role of honor and shame in Spanish society.[23] Like the protagonist of this story, many other Spanish women did not observe the prescribed honor codes and sexual norms calling for purity and restraint, nor was it the norm for macho Spanish males to kill their dishonorable spouses. In many instances they merely denounced the women to the authorities or were killed before being able to do so. To better understand these cases, some background information, especially concerning the political, social, and economic context, is in order.

THE SETTING

In the late eighteenth century, the Spanish monarchy was still a somewhat disjointed assortment of kingdoms, principalities, manors (*señorios*), and overseas colonial territories. As an assemblage of multiple political communities, it was also a collection of diverse regional ecologies, economies, societies, and cultures. Despite the Bourbon court's attempts to curtail them, there remained in place a large array of legal *fueros:* the special immunities, rights, or exceptions granted to kingdoms, principalities, and towns on a wide variety of economic, fiscal, legal, and other matters. *Fueros* also covered particular entities, most prominently the clergy and the military. Individuals, nobles in particular but also workers in royal factories, fell under them in intriguing ways as well.[24]

An equally complex ecological, economic, social, cultural, and legal diversity characterized the various individual kingdoms, subkingdoms, and principalities (e.g., Asturias, Aragon, Cantabria, Castile and Leon, Catalonia, Galicia, Navarre, Valencia). The Kingdom of Castile alone had twenty-two provinces that contained 75 percent of the peninsula's entire population. These provinces included the originally separate Kingdom of Galicia, which not only presented linguistic differences relative to the rest of Castile but also comprised four disparate provinces (A Coruña, Lugo, Ourense, and Pontevedra), each with its own idiosyncrasies. Spain's 1787 and 1797 censuses referred to as many as forty demographic subdivisions, including *reynos, principados,* and *provincias.* "Historical" reasons caused further regional variations. By focusing on historical commonalities, loosely defined as they may have been, scholars have identified at least fourteen "historical regions" in Spain in the second half of the eighteenth century (see Map P.2).[25] To manage such a diverse array of settings and circumstances, Spain came to be administratively divided into thirty-three provinces.[26] Starting mainly around 1749, these were grouped into civil sub-divisions called *intendencias,* of which about two dozen existed by the 1790s.[27] At the local level, justice was in the hands of local magistrates, whether *alcaldes ordinarios* or the higher-up *corregidores* (see Figure 4.1). In exceptional circumstances, as in the case of a couple working at a royal textile factory, a *fuero* determined that the case be tried directly by the plant manager or director (*superintendente*).[28] Higher in the judicial ranks were the district appeals courts, or *reales audiencias* and *reales chancillerías*, numbering as many as eleven in the late eighteenth century. Consultation with these courts was mandatory in cases of homicides even in the most remote locations within their jurisdiction.[29]

According to the famous 1752 *Catastro de Ensenada,*[30] the combined population of Spain's kingdoms, provinces, *intendencias,* villages, and smaller localities (*lugares*) was 9.4 million. This was equivalent to around twice the population of late eighteenth-century New Spain and about ten times that of New Granada.[31] More or less similar results appeared in three other censuses in the decades following: 1768 (census of Aranda), 1786–1787 (census of Floridablanca), and 1797 (census of

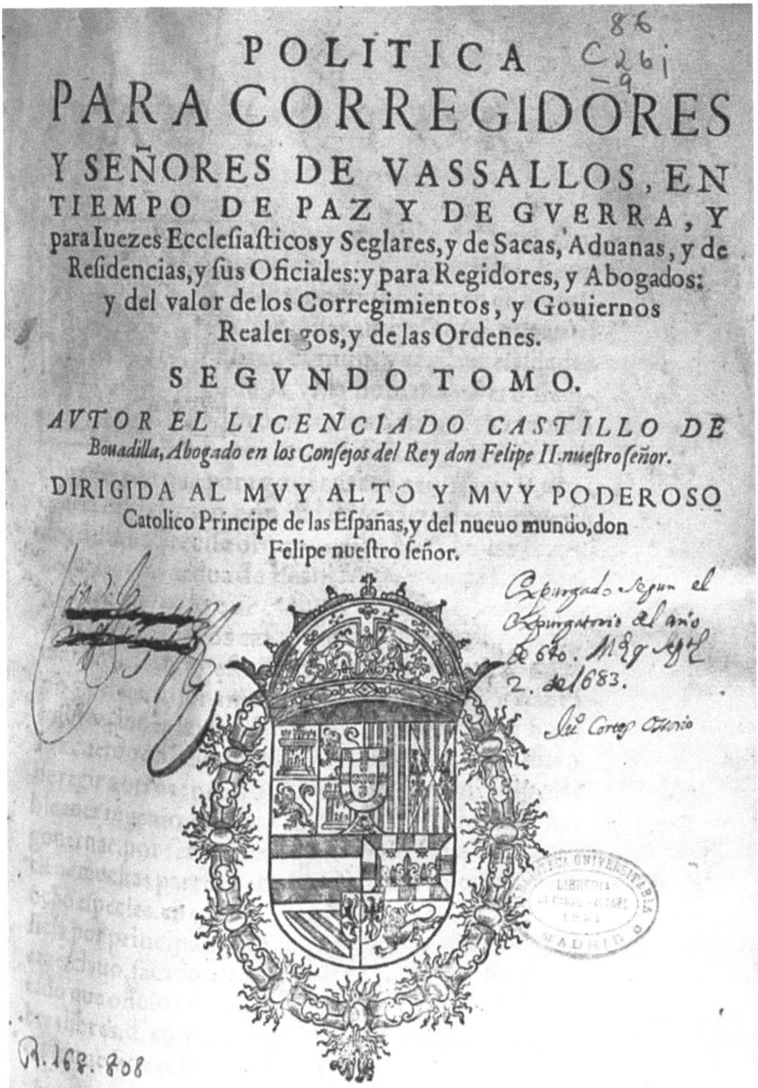

POLITICA
PARA CORREGIDORES
Y SEÑORES DE VASSALLOS, EN
TIEMPO DE PAZ Y DE GVERRA, Y
para Iuezes Eccleſiaſticos y Seglares, y de Sacas, Aduanas, y de
Reſidencias, y ſus Oficiales: y para Regidores, y Abogados:
y del valor de los Corregimientos, y Gouiernos
Realengos, y de las Ordenes.
SEGVNDO TOMO.
AVTOR EL LICENCIADO CASTILLO DE
Bouadilla, Abogado en los Conſejos del Rey don Felipe II. nueſtro ſeñor.
DIRIGIDA AL MVY ALTO Y MVY PODEROSO
Catolico Principe de las Eſpañas, y del nueuo mundo, don
Felipe nueſtro ſeñor.

Con priuilegio, En Madrid, Por Luis Sanchez:
Año M.D.XCVII.

Figure 4.1. Jerónimo Castillo de Bobadilla, Política para corregidores y señores de vasallos en tiempos de paz y de guerra *(Madrid: Por Luis Sánchez, 1597).*

TABLE 4.1. *Growth and distribution of the population of Spain in fourteen historical regions, 1787–1797*

Region	1787[a]	Percentage	1797[a]	Percentage
Andalusia	1,804	17.6	1,904	18.2
Aragon	614	6.0	657	6.3
Asturias	346	3.4	364	3.5
Balearics	176	1.7	187	1.8
Canaries	167	1.6	174	1.6
Castilla la Nueva	1,122	10.9	1,170	11.2
Castilla la Vieja	1,213	11.8	1,256	12.0
Catalonia	802	7.8	859	8.2
Extremadura	412	4.0	429	4.1
Galicia	1,340	13.1	1,143	10.9
Leon	620	6.0	619	5.9
Murcia	332	3.2	383	3.6
Valencia	792	7.7	825	7.9
Vascongadas y Navarra	529	5.2	505	4.8

SOURCE: Adapted from Massimo Livi Bacci, "Fertility and Nuptiality: Changes in Spain from the Late 18th to the Early Twentieth Century, Part 2," *Population Studies* 22.2 (1968): 211–234, esp. 211.

[a]Numbers in thousands.

Godoy-Larruga), which placed the total population at 9.3 million, 10.4 million, and 10.5 million, respectively (see Table 4.1).[32]

The Spanish population lived unevenly distributed in an assortment of large and densely populated urban centers. In the mid-eighteenth century, these included Madrid, with 142,000 inhabitants, and a range of cities averaging around 100,000 inhabitants each, among them Barcelona, Seville, Valencia, and Granada. Next appeared medium-size cities including Cádiz, Málaga, and Zaragoza, each with around 50,000 inhabitants; various smaller cities of about 10,000 people, such as Bilbao and San Sebastián; and places with just 3,000 to 5,000 inhabitants, such as Soria and a host of others. In addition, of course, many small rural villages, *lugares* or *sitios* (small settlements), with sometimes just a few dozen people dotted the country.

At least three generations of Spaniards inhabited cities and the remaining population centers. More than one-third of the late eighteenth-century population was under the age of sixteen, and another third was between the ages of sixteen and forty (see Table 4.2). Only about one-quarter of Spaniards were over forty, the general life expectancy being just about twenty-seven years at the time.[33]

There are no official statistics on births, deaths, and marriages prior to 1857, but some calculations have been attempted for the late eighteenth century (see Table 4.3). They indicate, for instance, that more than half of females age sixteen to fifty were married.

TABLE 4.2. *Population of Spain by age and sex: 1768, 1787, and 1797 censuses*[a]

	Males			Females		
Age	1768	1787	1797	1768	1787	1797
0–7	842,383	957,048	997,433	823,616	915,464	968,265
7–16	845,468	931,747	895,906	801,299	883,233	851,159
16–25	678,515	802,531	764,283	698,393	829,456	832,207
25–40	996,004	1,103,131	1,113,113	1,056,979	1,131,981	1,181,068
40–50	588,043	601,067	649,838	605,984	621,240	663,433
50–60	583,223	713,648	434,232	640,092	777,604	449,648
60+			365,544			374,165
Total	**4,533,636**	**5,109,172**	**5,220,349**	**4,626,363**	**5,158,978**	**5,319,945**
			Percentage			
0–7	18.6	18.7	19.1	17.8	17.7	18.2
7–16	18.6	18.2	17.2	17.3	17.1	16.0
16–25	15.0	15.7	14.6	15.1	16.1	15.6
25–40	21.9	21.6	21.3	22.8	21.9	22.2
40–50	13.0	11.8	12.4	13.1	12.1	12.5
50–60	12.9	14.0	8.3	13.9	15.1	8.5
60+			7.0			7.0
Total	100.0	100.0	100.0	100.0	100.0	100.0

SOURCE: Massimo Livi Bacci, "Fertility and Nuptiality: Changes in Spain from the Late 18th to the Early Twentieth Century, Part 2," *Population Studies* 22.1 (1968): 83–102, esp. 93. Copyright © Population Investigation Committee, reprinted by permission of Taylor & Francis Ltd, www.tandfonline.com, on behalf of the Population Investigation Committee.

[a]The data shown in this table do not include a section of the population—individuals belonging to regular and secular religious orders, inmates in hospitals, prisons, etc.—living in institutions. This segment of the population accounted for 148.9, 140.6, and 66.2 thousand individuals, respectively, in 1768, 1787, and 1797.

Commensurate with Spain's regional and demographic diversity, its economy was made up of a number of isolated and mostly self-sufficient local markets, separated from one another as a result of internal taxes, bad roads, poor transportation, and a weak demand for industrial raw materials, except for wood and wool. There was for the most part little possibility for travel across provinces by cart or boat.[34] For example, travel by cart from Madrid, in central Spain, to Cádiz, in the far south, became possible only in 1785, with new routes added in 1800. Only Aragon and Castile began construction of canals, and until the nineteenth century none of them had been actually completed. The little internal commerce that there was relied on horses and mules for the transportation of people, foodstuffs, and other commodities. Still, in exceptional urban centers such as Madrid, the movement of foodstuffs and other commodities could take a rather frantic pace. Over a two-week period in the early 1780s, for instance, more than 10,000 carts, pushcarts, and covered wagons (*carretas, carros y galeras*) came through the city's

TABLE 4.3. *Spain's married females in the fertile age group, 1787–1797*

Region	1787 percentage[a]	1797 percentage[a]
Andalusia	56.9	55.8
Aragon	64.3	67.2
Asturias	55.8	56.4
Balearics	58.4	51.2
Canaries	48.2	48.6
Castilla la Nueva	63.2	59.9
Castilla la Vieja	62.1	60.5
Catalonia	58.8	54.6
Extremadura	67.3	65.4
Galicia	52.4	48.3
Leon	61.0	58.8
Murcia	63.0	55.7
Valencia	65.1	65.1
Vascongadas y Navarra	55.3	54.5

SOURCE: Adapted from Massimo Livi Bacci, "Fertility and Nuptiality: Changes in Spain from the Late 18th to the Early Twentieth Century, Part 2," *Population Studies* 22.2 (1968): 211–234, esp. 216.

[a]Married females 16 to 50 years per 100 females in the same age group.

gates hauling goods of all kinds, mostly agricultural products and other comestibles.[35]

Agriculture, a key economic activity all over the kingdom, revolved mainly around the production of wheat and other grains, oranges and olives, and vegetables, mostly for domestic consumption. Vineyards and wine production were also significant economic ventures on an industrial scale.[36] Raising livestock was another important activity, and in the winter months thousands of sheep migrated to pasture in public grasslands in the more temperate south, Extremadura in particular.[37]

Limited manufacturing also took place at the time, mostly in the form of small hat- and silk-making and processing workshops, and occasionally some larger royal manufacturing enterprises.[38] The latter included the Real Fábrica de Tabacos de Sevilla, in operation since 1758 with hundreds of workers. However, the main industrial sector in Spain at the time was textile manufacturing, mostly in the northeastern principality of Catalonia. Other centers included the Castilla-La Mancha region, especially the huge Real Fábrica de Paños de Guadalajara, in operation since 1719 and significant enough to entrust its director (Royal Superintendent) with the *fuero* to investigate and try criminal cases involving the company's many employees.[39]

Despite historical discrimination against Gypsies, Jews, and Muslims and notwithstanding the importance of "purity of blood" (*limpieza de sangre*) since late medieval times, rather than being divided into castes or racially segregated groups, as was the case in Spanish America at the time, Spanish society mainly featured *estamentos* (social estates).[40] The highest on the social ladder, the clergy and the nobility, constituted around 2 and 4 percent to 7 percent of the total population, respectively, with significant variations over the years and across regions. These two privileged segments of Spanish society monopolized vast tracts of land and received preferential treatment (*fueros*) even in court, for ancien régime societies lacked the modern republican sense of equality before the law. The close to 90 percent of the kingdom's total population that made up the third *estamento,* the *estado llano* (common people), generally lacked any such privileges. In all of these estates, occupation mattered greatly.

Late eighteenth-century records list a variety of occupational groups. A minority of the population was made up of professionals who worked mainly in urban settings, including many of the 36,000 state employees (*empleados a sueldo del rey*), around 22,000 priests (*curas* and *tenientes de cura*), close to 10,000 scribes (*escribanos*), and around 6,000 lawyers. The Floridablanca census also lists around 78,000 military officers and soldiers, 51,000 students, 40,000 manufacturers (*fabricantes*), and 35,000 merchants, including 14,000 silk producers and traders. Finally, 57,000 sheep owners and wool traders were also identifiable. As suggested above, however, the bulk of the population belonged to the humble classes, the *estado llano.* Most of these people worked in the countryside, in subsistence agriculture or pastoral activities, a large contingent of them as shepherds, farmhands, landless peasants, artisans, journeymen, tenants, or domestic servants. For example, servants numbered more than 280,000. One million farmhands (*labradores*) and close to another million journeymen (*jornaleros*) each represented about 10 percent of the kingdom's total population. Alongside these groups, one can identify around 270,000 artisans, among them 33,000 tailors, 31,000 carpenters, and 12,000 blacksmiths, as well as 200,000 nonagrarian workers, half of whom worked in the textile industry and at least one-quarter in construction.[41]

Although deeply diverse and fragmented, Spain was bound together through the king, his court, and a semiprofessional royal bureaucracy and military. Similar civil and ecclesiastical institutions, administrative and judicial, at the provincial and even local levels (i.e., *alcaldes ordinarios, corregidores, ayuntamientos* and *regidores, parrocos, obispos, audiencias* or *chancillerias*) also contributed to some semblance of homogeneity and unity. So did a range of deep-rooted cultural values, beliefs, and practices shared by the bulk of society. These included, among others, great appreciation for pomp and ceremony; the observance of patriarchal mores;

a deep-seated religiosity and belief in Catholicism; fondness for wine, festivals, and diversions; and a high regard for social status, virtue, and, most of all, honor.[42] In fact, for a long time historians and other scholars have viewed the "passion of honor" as a true "national trait" and considered it to be the "one passion capable of defining the conduct of the Spanish people."[43] The concept is closely related to, among other central themes, family life and sexuality, and could logically be considered not only a force binding people together but also, conversely, a major source of social stress, conflict, and crime.

CRIME, CONFLICT, AND THE FAMILY

Catholic marriage was one of the formal foundations of Spanish society. A religious sacrament, marriage, as I noted, constituted an indissoluble and exclusive bond, closely regulated by ecclesiastical (canon) and civil law. Divorce and remarriage were practically impossible; bigamy constituted a serious crime; and sexual relations and births out of wedlock, albeit common, were illegitimate and subject to punishment. Marriage itself thus became, at least in theory, a means for the maintenance of social order, the policing of social comportment and equality, and the promotion of dominant cultural (and also material) interests.[44] Combating crimes against it was, logically, another key mechanism to accomplish these objectives.

According to statistics on crime in Madrid and its environs (at the *corte y su rastro*), the fifteen-year period between 1751 and 1766 saw approximately 382 murders; 1,440 cases of injury; 645 incidents of "*malos tratos,*" mainly battery; 1,681 cases of theft and 451 other crimes against property (money forgery, fraud, smuggling); 531 cases of slander, defamation, or threat; and about 1,590 sex-related offenses (concubinage, adultery, *estupro,* illicit relations, etc.).[45] As is clear from these data and two random case sets gathered for this study, a local one and a regional one, most crimes in late eighteenth-century and early nineteenth-century Spain concerned, in approximate order of magnitude, physical integrity (injuries, homicides, and battery) and property. A variety of other criminal conducts followed, with slander a common offense in such an honor-centered culture. Sexual crimes were also widespread.

For example, a fifty-year sample for the city of Segovia and surrounding areas lists 359 crimes. A majority of these, more than one-quarter, were bodily injuries (see Table 4.4). Thefts came next, representing close to another quarter, followed by slander, homicides, an assortment of sexual crimes (*estupro*, rape, sodomy, concubinage, and other illicit sexual liaisons) and battery, all of which added up to an additional quarter.

TABLE 4.4. *Sample of crimes tried by local justice officials in Segovia, 1750–1800*

Type of crime	Number	Percentage
Injuries	94	26.0
Robbery/theft	82	22.8
Slander	37	10.3
Homicide	22	6.1
Sex-related	15	4.2
Battery	10	2.8
Others	99	27.6
Total	**359**	

SOURCE: Inventario Criminal de Oficio, Archivo Provincial de Segovia, caja 1383.

Various other forms of misconduct (fights, "*excesos*," vagrancy, carrying of illegal weapons, threats, etc.) accounted for the rest.

A random six-year sample of the cases listed in Granada, one of the various *real audiencia* archives, presents a much larger percentage of homicides. This can be explained by the fact that the appeals court had to review all murders occurring in its district, which was not the case for lesser crimes or the ones addressed by local justice officials in places like Segovia. Homicide was therefore the leading category of crime in the Granada sample, followed by bodily injury (see Table 4.5). Together with domestic battery and fights, they amounted to about one-third of total crimes. Next on the list came robbery and theft, representing about

TABLE 4.5. *Sample of crimes tried by the Real Audiencia and Chancillería of Granada, August 1799–August 1805*

Type of crime	Number	Percentage
Homicide	192	16.6
Injury	183	15.8
Robbery	150	13.0
Theft	147	12.7
Slander	60	5.2
Carrying of weapons	48	4.1
Abuse of authority (*excesos*)	41	3.5
Illicit liaison with a woman	36	3.1
Estupro	24	2.1
Escape from jail	24	2.1
Fights	23	2.0
Domestic battery	22	2.0
Others	207	17.9
Total	**1,157**	

SOURCE: Archivo de la Real Chancillería de Granada, Libro de Providencias Definitivas, 1799–1815, libro 324.

one-quarter of criminal conducts, with the last quarter composed of the remainder: slander, the illegal carrying of weapons, abuse of authority, jail breaks, an assortment of *tratos ilicitos con mujeres* (illicit sexual liaisons), and sex extracted under false pretenses (*estupros*). Other regions present similar trends.[46]

Many of the injury and homicide cases involved married couples. In Granada, domestic battery accounted for close to 2 percent of all criminal offenses but was responsible for nearly 12 percent of all bodily injuries. Spousal homicides represented, in turn, about 3.6 percent of all homicides in this six-year sample from the Granada region. In seventeenth- and eighteenth-century Cantabria, on Spain's northern coast, domestic violence represented about 4 percent of all criminal cases and 15 percent of crimes involving physical aggression. One authoritative scholar estimates that about fifteen cases of battery per 100,000 inhabitants occurred each year, along with one spousal murder.[47] To take an additional example, a total of 332 violent murders occurred in Galicia, in northern Spain, during the thirteen-year period from 1803 to 1815. The same period saw about ten spousal murders (almost one per year, as in Cantabria), equivalent to around 3 percent of all homicides, a figure close to the 3.6 percent mentioned for Granada.[48] Therefore, the research for this study captures what appears to be a fragment of the spousal murders over time in various Spanish regions.

We know that colonial Mexico, a region with nearly half the population of eighteenth-century Spain, could have experienced more than 200 spousal murders in an eighty-year interval. Colonial Colombia, which had one-tenth the population of Spanish Iberia, could have had more than 100 spousal homicides in the same lapse. Therefore, the cases of spousal murder available for various Spanish regions may be considerably underrepresented. Even in the worst possible scenario, however—if the spousal murder rate in Spain were in proportion to its population approximately similar to colonial Mexico or colonial Colombia—the information at our disposal would amount to about 10 percent of all spousal murders actually occurring in the peninsula during the interval of time under consideration. Compared to the sources we have relied on for colonial Mexico and colonial Colombia, therefore, the evidence available to document the characteristics of spousal murders in Spain during the period from 1750 to 1820 may be thus somewhat narrower, but it is more than sufficient to allow for some provisional conclusions on a variety of issues.

Because of purging or accidental destruction over the years, archives in Spain record fewer spousal murder cases than do colonial archives. A search of the most relevant provincial archives across Spain yielded

TABLE 4.6. *Distribution of spousal homicides in seven Spanish regions, 1750–1824, by ten-year intervals*

Years	Number	Percentage
1750–1759	1	1.5
1760–1760	8	12.3
1770–1779	3	4.6
1780–1789	10	15.4
1790–1799	11	16.9
1800–1809	16	24.6
1810–1819	12	18.5
1820–1824	4	6.1
Total	**65**	

SOURCES: ARCV, Pleitos Criminales and Sala de Vizcaya; AHN, Madrid, Consejos Suprimidos; ARG; AGI; ARGC, Libro de Providencias Definitivas; AHPCo; AHPC; AGS, Gracia y Justicia; Tomás A. Mantecón, *La muerte de Antonia Isabel Sánchez*, 84; Arturo Morgado, *Derecho de asilo y delincuencia en la diócesis de Cádiz*, 124; "Acusación Fiscal contra Marcelo J . . ., reo confeso de parricidio por la muerte violenta dada a su muger María G . . . pronunciada el día 23 de Abril de 1798 en la sala segunda de Alcaldes de Casa y Corte," in Meléndez Valdés, *Discursos Forenses*, 46–70.

only sixty-five cases, distributed irregularly across time and space, some of which are incomplete and fragmentary (see Table 4.6). The number of cases seems to have increased since the 1780s, all the way until the unstable 1810s, with a significant number in the decade between 1800 and 1809.[49] However, this distribution over time cannot be other than a function of irregular record keeping.

The geographic distribution of the data is partial as well. In all likelihood, several additional relevant cases could have been found in the archives of the few remaining *audiencias* not consulted for this study.[50] Even if each of these archives contained the same number of cases as those with the largest available set (twenty-five for Madrid), a very unlikely situation, we would be missing at most about seventy-five additional extant cases. Therefore, the case set compiled for this study probably represents nearly half, likely more, of all extant information available in *audiencia* or *chancillería* archives for Spain in its entirety.

Relative to their share of the Iberian population, we have perhaps a disproportionate number of crimes from Castile and Leon, here represented by the cities of Madrid and Valladolid, and the region of Galicia. Valencia is underrepresented, as is Andalusia (see Table 4.7). We are also missing information for key places such as Aragón, the Canary Islands, Catalonia, the Basque country, and Navarre. Although the data used here includes the universe of cases available in most *audiencia* districts that have any relevant records, this regional distribution is unquestionably a

TABLE 4.7. *Distribution of spousal homicides in Spain by region, 1750–1824*

Region	Number	Percentage	Percentage of total population
Andalusia	10	15.4	17.5
Cantabria	2	3.1	3.3[a]
Extremadura	3	4.6	4
Galicia	14	21.5	13
Madrid	25	38.5	28.7
Valladolid	10	15.4	
Valencia	1	1.5	7.7
Total	**66**		

SOURCES: ARCV, Pleitos Criminales and Sala de Vizcaya; AHN, Madrid, Consejos Suprimidos; ARG; AGI; ARCG, Libro de Providencias Definitivas; AHPCo; AHPC; AGS, Gracia y Justicia; Tomás A. Mantecón, *La muerte de Antonia Isabel Sánchez,* 84; Arturo Morgado, *Derecho de asilo y delincuencia en la diócesis de Cádiz,* 124; "Acusación Fiscal contra Marcelo J . . ., reo confeso de parricidio por la muerte violenta dada a su muger María G . . . pronunciada el día 23 de Abril de 1798 en la sala segunda de Alcaldes de Casa y Corte," in Meléndez Valdés, *Discursos Forenses*, 46–70; Massimo Livi Bacci, "Fertility and Nuptiality: Changes in Spain from the Late 18th to the Early Twentieth Century, Part 2," 211–234, esp. 211.

[a]Overall population for Asturias is the one found in available charts.

function of the lopsided nature of our case set. Still, historical evidence is rarely complete. Until additional data are brought forward, those we have reveal some valuable, even if tentative, patterns worth mentioning concerning regional distribution, circumstances, motives, participants, and other factors.

Although data concerning time of day are available for only 41.5 percent of the cases in our set, they reveal a trend: A fair number of spousal murders occurred at night (see Table 4.8). This is true of 59.2 percent

TABLE 4.8. *Distribution of spousal homicides by time of day*

	Spain		Colonial Colombia		Colonial Mexico	
Time of day	Number	Percentage	Number	Percentage	Number	Percentage
Morning	7	25.9	4	11.4	11	26.8
Afternoon	4	14.8	7	20.0	14	34.1
Evening	16	59.2	24	68.6	16	39.0
Unknown	38	58.5	19	35.1	46	52.9
Total	**65**		**54**		**87**	

SOURCES: Sources: ARCV, Pleitos Criminales and Sala de Vizcaya; AHN, Madrid, Consejos Suprimidos; ARG; AGI; ARCG, Libro de Providencias Definitivas; AHPCo; AHPC; AGS, Gracia y Justicia; Tomás A. Mantecón, *La muerte de Antonia Isabel Sánchez,* 84; Arturo Morgado, *Derecho de asilo y delincuencia en la diócesis de Cádiz,* 124; "Acusación Fiscal contra Marcelo J . . ., reo confeso de parricidio por la muerte violenta dada a su muger María G . . . pronunciada el día 23 de Abril de 1798 en la sala segunda de Alcaldes de Casa y Corte," in Meléndez Valdés, *Discursos Forenses*, 46–70; Taylor, *Drinking, Homicide, and Rebellion*, 78; idem, "Amigos de sombrero," 86.

of the incidents in the Spanish peninsula for which there is information, compared to 68.6 percent in colonial Colombia and 39 percent in colonial Mexico. Indeed, notwithstanding my comments on morning crimes in the Mexico chapter, homicides in general tended to occur at night, probably out of a logical belief that darkness would make it easier for culprits to hide corpses and reduced the number of witnesses.

No clear trends are discernible regarding the day of the week when the Spanish crimes occurred (see Table 4.9). This was also the case in colonial Mexico. Colonial Colombia showed a slightly larger proportion of crimes occurring from Friday to Sunday, but this finding is far from conclusive. Spousal murders in Spain and elsewhere seem to have occurred randomly throughout the week. The same can be said about the months during which these homicides happened. No clear pattern stands out in this regard in any of the three regions considered in this book (see Table 4.10).

As for the places where the crimes took place, similar to what we observed in both colonial Colombia and colonial Mexico, the large majority of crimes in Spain occurred within the community, mostly at the couple's home (see Table 4.11). Virtually no crime for which there is information occurred outside of the community.

In keeping with the pattern observed thus far in the Spanish American regions, most of the Spanish murders whose method is known involved the use of knives or similar objects (*navajas* or pocketknives and scissors). A handful occurred as a result of punching, kicking, or strangling, and a very few made use of cooking utensils, farm tools, firearms, hanging, or poison (see Table 4.12). In contrast to the colonies, however, none of the

TABLE 4.9. *Distribution of spousal homicides by day of the week*

	Spain		Colonial Colombia		Colonial Mexico	
Day of the week	Number	Percentage	Number	Percentage	Number	Percentage
Sunday	3	9.4	6	27.2	6	17.1
Monday	4	12.5	2	9.1	5	14.2
Tuesday	5	15.6	1	4.5	5	14.2
Wednesday	7	21.9	2	9.1	3	8.6
Thursday	5	15.6	1	4.5	6	17.1
Friday	2	6.2	4	18.2	5	14.3
Saturday	6	18.7	6	27.3	5	14.3
Undetermined	33	50.8	32	59.2	52	59.8
Total	**65**		**54**		**87**	

SOURCES: ARCV, Pleitos Criminales and Sala de Vizcaya; AHN, Madrid, Consejos Suprimidos; ARG; AGI; ARCG, Libro de Providencias Definitivas; AHPCo; AHPC; AGS, Gracia y Justicia; Tomás A. Mantecón, *La muerte de Antonia Isabel Sánchez*, 84; Arturo Morgado, *Derecho de asilo y delincuencia en la diócesis de Cádiz*, 124; "Acusación Fiscal contra Marcelo J . . ., reo confeso de parricidio por la muerte violenta dada a su muger María G . . . pronunciada el día 23 de Abril de 1798 en la sala segunda de Alcaldes de Casa y Corte," in Meléndez Valdés, *Discursos Forenses*, 46–70.

TABLE 4.10. *Distribution of spousal homicides by month*

Month	Spain		Colonial Colombia		Colonial Mexico	
	Number	Percentage	Number	Percentage	Number	Percentage
January	1	2.9	2	5.3	4	8.2
February	2	5.9	1	2.6	5	10.2
March	1	2.9	1	2.6	4	8.2
April	2	5.9	—	—	5	10.2
May	3	8.8	1	2.6	4	8.2
June	5	14.7	6	15.7	3	6.1
July	2	5.9	7	16.2	2	4.1
August	5	14.7	7	18.4	4	8.2
September	4	11.8	2	5.3	2	4.1
October	3	8.8	3	7.9	8	16.3
November	4	11.8	3	7.9	3	6.1
December	2	5.9	5	13.2	5	10.2
Undetermined	31		16	29.6	38	43.7
Total	**65**		**54**		**87**	

SOURCES: ARCV, Pleitos Criminales and Sala de Vizcaya; AHN, Madrid, Consejos Suprimidos; ARG; AGI; ARCG, Libro de Providencias Definitivas; AHPCo; AHPC; AGS, Gracia y Justicia; Tomás A. Mantecón, *La muerte de Antonia Isabel Sánchez,* 84; Arturo Morgado, *Derecho de asilo y delincuencia en la diócesis de Cádiz,* 124; "Acusación Fiscal contra Marcelo J . . ., reo confeso de parricidio por la muerte violenta dada a su muger María G . . . pronunciada el día 23 de Abril de 1798 en la sala segunda de Alcaldes de Casa y Corte," in Meléndez Valdés, *Discursos Forenses,* 46–70.

TABLE 4.11. *Location of spousal homicides in late Bourbon Spain*

	Number	Percentage
Within the community		
At couple's home	22	68.7
At in-law's home	2	6
At a tavern	2	6
Near a house	1	3
On a road	2	6
By a river, creek, or ditch	1	3
In a forest	1	3
In an undetermined public place	1	3
At a friend's or neighbor's home	—	
In the street	—	
Subtotal	32	**49.2**
Outside the community		
On a road	—	
In a forest	—	
By a creek	—	
Subtotal	0	
Undetermined subtotal	33	50.8
Total	65	

SOURCES: ARCV, Pleitos Criminales and Sala de Vizcaya; AHN, Madrid, Consejos Suprimidos; ARG; AGI; ARCG, Libro de Providencias Definitivas; AHPCo; AHPC; AGS, Gracia y Justicia; Tomás A. Mantecón, *La muerte de Antonia Isabel Sánchez,* 84; Arturo Morgado, *Derecho de asilo y delincuencia en la diócesis de Cádiz,* 124; "Acusación Fiscal contra Marcelo J . . ., reo confeso de parricidio por la muerte violenta dada a su muger María G . . . pronunciada el día 23 de Abril de 1798 en la sala segunda de Alcaldes de Casa y Corte," in Meléndez Valdés, *Discursos Forenses*, 46–70.

TABLE 4.12. *Distribution of spousal homicides in Spain by method/weapon*

	Number	Percentage
Stabbings	17	45.9
Fists, kicking	4	10.8
Strangling	3	8.1
Hatchet	2	7.4
Cooking utensils	2	5.4
Farm tools	2	5.4
Firearms	2	5.4
Hanging	2	5.4
Machete/spear/pike	1	2.7
Poison	1	2.7
Furniture	1	2.7
Whip	—	—
Rocks	—	—
Clubs	—	—
Undetermined	28	43
Total	**65**	

SOURCES: ARCV, Pleitos Criminales and Sala de Vizcaya; AHN, Madrid, Consejos Suprimidos; ARG; AGI; ARCG, Libro de Providencias Definitivas; AHPCo; AHPC; AGS, Gracia y Justicia; Tomás A. Mantecón, *La muerte de Antonia Isabel Sánchez*, 84; Arturo Morgado, *Derecho de asilo y delincuencia en la diócesis de Cádiz*, 124; "Acusación Fiscal contra Marcelo J . . ., reo confeso de parricidio por la muerte violenta dada a su muger María G . . . pronunciada el día 23 de Abril de 1798 en la sala segunda de Alcaldes de Casa y Corte," in Meléndez Valdés, *Discursos Forenses*, 46–70.

Spanish crimes involved the use of crude weapons such as rocks or clubs, which were employed in 17 to 22 percent of the Colombian and Mexican cases, respectively.

Of the twenty-five cases for which the occupation of defendants is known, the majority were farmers and manual workers (see Table 4.13). As in the colonies, therefore, the bulk of criminals came from Spain's humble sector (*estado llano*), which accounted for the majority of the Spanish population. However, the cases this chapter describes in detail reveal that peninsular elites fell prey to domestic violence as well, including both battery and murder. Three crimes seem to have involved members of the upper classes, two of whom were hacienda owners; the other, in the case described at the opening of this chapter, was a law intern whose lover and accomplice was a housewife from a distinguished family. Additional evidence available in the historical records confirms the involvement of elites in crimes of domestic violence.[51] Many of the aggressors in this and other social groups were rather young.

TABLE 4.13. *Distribution of spousal homicides in Spain by defendant's occupation*

Occupation	Number	Percentage
Farmer (*labrador*)	7	28
Hacienda owner	2	8
Coach driver	1	4
Mule driver (*arriero*)	1	4
Shepherd	1	4
Dancer	1	4
Foundry master	1	4
Carpenter	1	4
Construction master	1	4
Construction official	1	4
Journeyman	1	4
Housewife	1	4
Law intern	1	4
Storekeeper	1	4
Goat keeper	1	4
Potato salesman	1	4
Servant	1	4
Soldier	1	4
Undetermined	40	61.5
Total	**65**	

SOURCES: ARCV, Pleitos Criminales and Sala de Vizcaya; AHN, Madrid, Consejos Suprimidos; ARG; AGI; ARCG, Libro de Providencias Definitivas; AHPCo; AHPC; AGS, Gracia y Justicia; Tomás A. Mantecón, *La muerte de Antonia Isabel Sánchez,* 84; Arturo Morgado, *Derecho de asilo y delincuencia en la diócesis de Cádiz,* 124; "Acusación Fiscal contra Marcelo J . . ., reo confeso de parricidio por la muerte violenta dada a su muger María G . . . pronunciada el día 23 de Abril de 1798 en la sala segunda de Alcaldes de Casa y Corte," in Meléndez Valdés, *Discursos Forenses,* 46–70.

The age distribution of the few cases (33.8 percent) for which data are available is also in keeping with what we have learned about murderers in Spanish America and what is known about most societies to this day: Most of the culprits (77.2 percent), including the ones in our opening case, were younger adults between the ages of sixteen and forty (see Table 4.14). Most of these were males.

As far as gender is concerned, the majority of the Spanish defendants were male, as was the case in colonial Colombia and colonial Mexico, but Spain seems to be right in the middle. Whereas in Colombia women committed almost half (four of every ten) of spousal murders, a remarkable trend to be discussed later in this book, females appear to have committed about one-third of the crimes in the peninsula (see Table 4.15). Still, as I will argue later, the nature of some of their crimes was disproportionately meaningful because of the intriguing motives behind them.

TABLE 4.14. *Distribution of spousal homicides in Spain by defendant's age*

Age group	Number	Percentage
16–20	1	4.5
21–25	3	13.6
26–30	4	18.2
31–35	5	22.7
36–40	4	18.2
41–45	1	4.5
46–50	2	9.1
51–55	1	4.5
56–60	1	4.5
61–75	—	—
Unknown	48	68.6
Total	70[a]	

SOURCES: ARCV, Pleitos Criminales and Sala de Vizcaya; AHN, Madrid, Consejos Suprimidos; ARG; AGI; ARCG, Libro de Providencias Definitivas; AHPCo; AHPC; AGS, Gracia y Justicia; Tomás A. Mantecón, *La muerte de Antonia Isabel Sánchez,* 84; Arturo Morgado, *Derecho de asilo y delincuencia en la diócesis de Cádiz,* 124; "Acusación Fiscal contra Marcelo J . . ., reo confeso de parricidio por la muerte violenta dada a su muger María G . . . pronunciada el día 23 de Abril de 1798 en la sala segunda de Alcaldes de Casa y Corte," in Meléndez Valdés, *Discursos Forenses*, 46–70.

[a]Includes five accomplices.

TABLE 4.15. *Distribution of spousal homicides in Spain and overseas by defendant's gender*

	Spain		Colonial Colombia		Colonial Mexico	
	Number	Percentage	Number	Percentage	Number	Percentage
Males	45	69.2	33	61.1	68	78.2
Females	20	30.8	21	38.8	19	22.0

SOURCES: ARCV, Pleitos Criminales and Sala de Vizcaya; AHN, Madrid, Consejos Suprimidos; ARG; AGI; ARCG, Libro de Providencias Definitivas; AHPCo; AHPC; AGS, Gracia y Justicia; Tomás A. Mantecón, *La muerte de Antonia Isabel Sánchez,* 84; Arturo Morgado, *Derecho de asilo y delincuencia en la diócesis de Cádiz,* 124; "Acusación Fiscal contra Marcelo J . . ., reo confeso de parricidio por la muerte violenta dada a su muger María G . . . pronunciada el día 23 de Abril de 1798 en la sala segunda de Alcaldes de Casa y Corte," in Meléndez Valdés, *Discursos Forenses,* 46–70.

Concerning triggering factors and/or motive, drinking (52.9 percent and 44 percent respectively in Colombia and Mexico) carried much more weight in the colonies than seems to have been the case in Spain (20 percent) (see Table 4.16). Perhaps alcoholic beverages were consumed more widely in the colonies or had a higher alcohol content. Further variation is found in another important regard: In the Spanish American cases,

TABLE 4.16. *Motives cited by offenders in spousal homicides in Spain, 1750–1824*

Motives	Total cases		Cases with male defendant		Cases with female defendant	
	Number[a]	Percentage	Number	Percentage	Number	Percentage
Drinking (combind with other motives)	6	20	5	83.3	1	16.7
Drinking (as "exclusive" motive)	—	—	—	—	—	—
Desire to be with one's lover	10	33.3	3	30	7	70
Infidelity	2	6.6	2	100	—	—
Insolence	1	3.3	1	100	—	—
Disobedience	4	13.3	4	100	—	—
Chronic aggression	4	13.3	3	100	—	—
Self-defense	—	—	—	—	—	—
Insanity	2	6.6	2	100	—	—
Other	4	13.3	3	75	1	25
Undetermined	35	53.9				

SOURCES: ARCV, Pleitos Criminales and Sala de Vizcaya; AHN, Madrid, Consejos Suprimidos; ARG; AGI; ARCG, Libro de Providencias Definitivas; AHPCo; AHPC; AGS, Gracia y Justicia; Tomás A. Mantecón, *La muerte de Antonia Isabel Sánchez,* 84; Arturo Morgado, *Derecho de asilo y delincuencia en la diócesis de Cádiz,* 124; "Acusación Fiscal contra Marcelo J . . ., reo confeso de parricidio por la muerte violenta dada a su muger María G . . . pronunciada el día 23 de Abril de 1798 en la sala segunda de Alcaldes de Casa y Corte," in Meléndez Valdés, *Discursos Forenses,* 46–70.

[a]The total adds up to more than 65, reflecting the fact that drinking is often cited along with other motives.

alleged insolence and disobedience on the part of the victims were more important factors (20–31 percent) than they were in Spain (16.6 percent). This may hint at the fact that assertiveness on the part of Spanish women was more socially acceptable and thus husbands generally did not use it as a valid excuse. Another contrast and remarkable trend worth highlighting in the Spanish case set is that, leaving aside the added motive of drinking, in close to half of cases (40 percent) for which information is available the crimes were the result of infidelity or the desire to be with one's lover. This is a larger proportion than in colonial Colombia (24.9 percent) and colonial Mexico (22.1 percent).

Given the small numbers of cases in this study and the possibility of considerable variation if new data come to light, we will turn away from quantitative factors at the moment to examine a series of examples useful for making sense, in particular, of the significant phenomenon of extramarital liaisons in Spain at this time. These examples are especially important because of what they reveal with regard to gender and the weight of "honor" in this society. Only in a very small number of them was an unfaithful wife killed by her husband.

SPOUSAL MURDERS: PASSION, BETRAYAL, AND DISHONOR

As discussed above and illustrated at the outset of this chapter, many of the domestic crimes in Spain at this time seem to have involved extramarital affairs on the part of culprits, not victims. Cases of battery due to this circumstance were widespread, and husbands, the main culprits in illegal liaisons, were unquestionably the main aggressors. An example is the case of Margarita de Soto in the northern Galician village of St. Pedro, who in late 1794 accused her husband, Baltasar Villafañe, of severe physical abuse. Baltasar, she said, was having an affair with the wife of the overseer of a nearby estate and over the past five months had assaulted Margarita on several occasions, at least once publicly outside of the local church. Another time, in front of their servants, he stuffed her mouth with cow excrement; threw her to the floor; kicked her in the face, knocking out one of her teeth; and called her a witch and a whore. He even tried to break one of her hands and could have killed her if those around had not intervened. More than once, Margarita sought shelter at her father's home in fear for her life. She also complained of being unable to support herself because her husband had taken sole charge of the several properties her mother had bequeathed her.[52]

In the *lugar* of Puente Valga in St. Miguel parish, also in Galicia, Domingo Antonio Pineiro nearly killed his twenty-two-year-old wife, Antonia Agudin, shortly after the couple went to bed one night in February 1802. According to Antonia's recollection, she and her mother-in-law were spinning some wool, but Domingo ordered her to go to bed, and she obeyed. She awoke when she felt a rope around her neck and discovered that her husband was trying to strangle her. She struggled and tried to call out to her father-in-law, who also lived in the house, but Domingo pulled the rope tighter and tighter until she fell unconscious. When she came back to her senses in the early morning hours, her in-laws and her own mother, who lived nearby, were trying to assist her. Domingo was nowhere to be found. It seems that prior to the incident the man had spent at least one month away from home, in the Kingdom of Portugal. Upon returning, in spite of the fact that Antonia was in her fifth month of pregnancy, he treated her coldly and without much consideration. He does not seem to have mistreated her previously during their three-year marriage, but he was now a changed person, and for reasons she did not understand, perhaps involvement with another woman, he appeared to want to be rid of her.[53]

The Real Audiencia of Extremadura in Cáceres, in southwestern Spain, also heard numerous cases of domestic battery in which extramarital affairs seemed directly tied to men's abuse of their wives.[54] In southeastern Valencia, too, there is evidence of numerous instances of extramarital affairs, referred to in the archives as a man's "frequent entry and exit into and out of the home of women whose identity is not revealed due to their [married] condition" (*frecuentes entradas y salidas a casa de mujeres que por su estado [casado] se calla*).[55] Some of these situations gave rise to domestic disputes.[56]

The Real Chancillería of Valladolid heard similar cases. In 1814, in the town of Fuentes de Magaña, province of Soria, a local surgeon, forty-year-old Manuel Sánchez, was charged with attempting to poison his wife, María González. Manuel was having an affair with a thirty-two-year-old widow named Juana Fernández, a servant in a local household. Apparently, Manuel's extramarital escapades were the source of many disputes among the couple, at least one of which had sent María to bed incapacitated. Following one such incident, Manuel stole a mercury-based compound (*solimán*) from the local pharmacy and mixed it with medicine a local doctor had prescribed. After taking the concoction, María became afflicted with "melancholy, anxiety" and violent vomiting spells. She was lucky to receive prompt treatment from two local doctors, who by all accounts saved her life. The Valladolid high court in charge of the case reversed the one-year presidio term imposed by the local *alcalde ordinario* who had processed the incident. The court determined instead that the time the surgeon had spent in jail, close to a year, was sufficient punishment for the physical abuse and attempted murder of his wife.[57]

Other wives and husbands were not as fortunate as María González and died at the hands of their spouses. An example is another case involving a noble person, similar to the scenario that opens this chapter. It is especially revealing for its implications involving a number of legal issues important to this work, specifically torture, sanctuary, the intervention of child witnesses, and humanitarian concerns regarding the severity of punishment.

Early on a Saturday morning in 1771, passersby discovered Isabel García Romero dead inside a fountain in Vizmanos, a tiny northeastern rural community. Near the body was a jar that suggested that Isabel had stopped at the fountain to collect water. However, certain clues, including the body's placement and condition—the fact that her stomach was not swollen and that she did not expel water through her mouth or nostrils—led the local authorities to suspect that she was not the victim of accidental drowning but instead had been murdered, with her body placed in the fountain after death. Further evidence were the body's red and swollen neck, purple lips, and crushed upper vertebrae. Eventually, the authorities apprehended Isabel's husband, thirty-five-year-old landowner

Juan Francisco Escudero García, widely known in town as "*el hidalgo*" because of his condition as a lesser nobleman, and charged him with the murder.

The investigation determined that Juan Francisco and Isabel had fought constantly. On several occasions, Isabel chose to spend the night at an aunt's nearby home to protect herself from her husband's beatings. Once she even refused to return home, and her husband likewise refused to take her in. The couple resumed their life together only through the intervention of Juan García, Isabel's brother, a priest in the nearby town of Valloria. *El hidalgo* claimed they fought because Isabel liked to drink wine and acted crazy when she had too much, but the real cause was his affair with the local priest's maid, a twenty-eight-year-old widow named Teresa Ballesteros. At least a few people in the little town probably knew about their liaison.

In the late eighteenth century, Vizmanos was home to a total of just over fifty families, most of whom were engaged in growing wheat and barley and raising sheep. Day-to-day social interaction mostly concerned work routines and contacts related to these occupations. In the little village, fifty-seven *labradores* (small farmers) and several wool dealers handled these trades and exchanges. The village was also home to one carpenter, two bricklayers, one locksmith, one blacksmith, one *botero*,[58] one veterinarian (*albeitar*), and eleven wool weavers and their apprentices. Social contact also occurred at the local church, St. Pedro Apostol, where residents attended Mass and prayed the rosary on a daily basis. The community housed a tavern, a butcher shop, and a small dry goods store. There was no bakery, another typical social space in many rural towns; instead, a local woman baked the town's bread daily and retailed it to her neighbors. Finally, the municipality of Yanguas, to which Vizmanos belonged, had at least two more churches, Santa María and San Miguel; two mills; and the little hospital of Villa Vieja.[59] The small Cidacos River ran through it, providing a source of water and also entertainment for locals during the summer months.[60] The winter, though, was probably gloomier. Isabel was killed then.

As it turned out, the murder took place in the kitchen of the couple's home at midnight the day before the body surfaced in the town's fountain. Two children were the unfortunate witnesses: seven-year-old Manuela Vicenta, one of the couple's two daughters, and fourteen-year-old Isabela Vicenta, a maid who had been working in the Escudero household for just a few weeks and spent nights at the house, sharing a bed with the little girl. From her room on the second floor, little Manuela heard her mother beg her father to let her live a little longer (*dejame vivir una hora más*). He refused and said that that even if the Devil took him, he must kill her right then and there. The child declared that next she heard her sobbing mother recite the Lord's Prayer (*Padrenuestro*). Peering from a window above the front door, Manuela allegedly also witnessed her father and two women—who could have been Isabela Vicenta's mother, Francisca Martínez del Prado, and Teresa Ballesteros, *el hidalgo*'s lover—carrying Manuela's mother's corpse from the house. After reaching the fountain, located about twenty yards from the house, they parted company and went their separate ways. Afterward, Manuela testified, she went to bed crying, but her father noticed that she was awake. He suspected that she might have been peeping through the window and allegedly threatened that if she ever said anything (*si parlas*), he would kill her, too!

The maid testified that her mistress had been at the local church praying the rosary that night when her husband asked her to come home to prepare some food for a trip he was taking the next day. She heard the couple arguing, as they did frequently. While eavesdropping to hear what was going on in the kitchen, she was able to press her eye to a small hole in the door and see Escudero hoist his wife's corpse over his shoulder and carry it to the front door. The next day he left early, traveling by mule to the city of Soria at daybreak to purchase a few items for the household and neighbors. Upon returning late in the afternoon the same Saturday his wife's corpse was found, he was placed under arrest. Escudero denied involvement in the murder, claiming to have left his wife in good health prior to his departure. He continued his denials throughout the legal proceedings that followed.

Although his noble condition prevented Escudero from being subjected to judicial torture (*tormento*), the authorities, led by the prosecutor, still threatened him with it in an attempt to make him confess, which he never did. After about one year in the local jail, Escudero escaped with the assistance of the maid, Isabela, and her mother, Francisca Martínez. Both women had also been placed under detention but were able to walk freely about the jail. They managed to steal the female warden's keys to the lock that kept Escudero chained to the wall, but he still had manacles (*grillos*) around his feet and was unable to run very far. He sought sanctuary at the nearby San Pedro Church, which afforded him protection from bodily harm or the death penalty.

Thanks to the church's mercy and delays in the trial, allegedly because of the assistance of influential friends or relatives (*sujetos calificados*), Escudero's life was spared, and he was sentenced to ten years in one of the African *presidios*—a harsh penalty nonetheless.[61] His lover, Teresa Ballesteros, who gave birth to his son in jail, faced six years of confinement in a *casa de recogidas*[62] to be designated by the judges of the Real

Audiencia and Chancillería in Valladolid, where the case had gone on appeal. The maid's mother, Francisca Martínez, received the same punishment, not an unusual outcome for women criminals. The maid herself, who was believed to have lied about important details in the case and assisted in her master's escape, was sentenced initially to banishment from the village for four years, but considering the time she had spent in jail, the judges later reversed this sentence with the admonishment that she observe the sacred duty to tell the truth.[63]

The Escudero case is extraordinary in many regards, not so much for its motives but because of the aggressor's gender. Infidelity was a common trigger of domestic aggression, but the protagonists of lethal violence in such situations were predominantly wives, not husbands.

RAGE AND CRAZINESS PRODUCED BY "EXCESSIVE LOVE": HONOR UPSIDE DOWN

As in the case described at the beginning of this chapter and the one just detailed, extramarital affairs were a factor in numerous spousal murders in Spain over the seven decades covered by our case set. Of the entire number of cases available, including the ones for which we lack detailed information on motives, 18.4 percent (12 of 65) were related to adultery, a significant portion of the total. The proportion is even larger when we focus exclusively on cases for which more complete information on motives is available. Excluding drinking as an added factor, in 33.3 percent of all spousal murders for which information on motives is known, the defendant's desire to be permanently with his or her lover was the dominant factor, with females accounting for most defendants (7 of 10). Conversely, just 6.6 percent of murderers—a total of only two!—all of them husbands, cited the victim's infidelity as the motivating factor behind the killing. In sum, in instances involving extramarital relations, the infidelity of the culprit, not the victim, was the driving force behind the murder. Further, among unfaithful spouses, women accounted for the majority of spousal killers, usually with their lovers' assistance.

For instance, in the village of Ajalvir near Madrid, twenty-two-year-old Blas Ballesteros helped his lover, Jesusa Oñoro, who was "over the age of 15," kill her husband, Alonso López, one night in December 1784. Blas hit the sleeping victim several times on the head with a hoe, and Jesusa then strangled him with a rope. The murder scene, even the walls, was covered with blood, and the two culprits cleaned it with a towel as best as they could. They then visited nearby neighbors to play cards, returning to the house at midnight to attempt to dispose of the corpse. They loaded Alonso's body on a mule and headed toward the road to Madrid, in the process leaving bloodstains on a mat and in the dirt near the entrance to the house. Jesusa went back home shortly afterward, probably to finish cleaning the evidence, but her lover stayed with the mule to transport the corpse as far away as possible. After dumping the body by the side of the road, he returned home to sleep with the woman. In a subsequent request for clemency, Blas pleaded for his life to be spared because he was young and afflicted by the "rage and craziness produced by excessive love" (*furor y demencia que produce un excesivo amor*).[64] The judges were unmoved by his request and sentenced the culprits to death by hanging.

With the exception of the perhaps more modest social background of some of the protagonists, several other cases in the historical record were similar to the one in Aranjuez described earlier and the Ajalvir crime just mentioned. In all of them, women who wanted to run away with their lovers were the aggressors or instigators. At La Mina in the town of Talavera de la Reina, Valladolid, in August 1801, for example, thirty-two-year-old laundress Antonia Velasco allegedly strangled her husband, Joaquín Martín, whom she had already unsuccessfully tried to poison. Antonia was having an affair with Ventura Palomo, a journeyman who worked on a nearby farm, whose clothes she laundered on a regular basis. Although evidence of Palomo's complicity in the crime was weak and he justified his frequent visits to the woman's house by the need to drop off or collect his laundry, a search found him to be in possession of a small amount of the poisonous compound *solimán*. This, coupled with circumstantial evidence of Antonia's previous attempt to poison her husband and the extramarital love affair, was sufficient for the two to be tried and condemned. The woman received a death sentence and the man four years in an African presidio, a sentence that was later commuted to eight years of service in the army.[65]

Several other examples illustrate a similar pattern. In the town of Medinaceli, northeast of Madrid, thirty-three-year-old María Lario and her lover, twenty-seven-year-old journeyman Gregorio Moreno, were accused of having killed the woman's husband, wool weaver Vicente Anguita. The crime occurred one night in early November 1813 while the victim was in bed with his wife. According to the widow, Moreno, an old acquaintance of her husband's, committed the murder with a hatchet. Moreno admitted he killed the wool weaver but said he did it with a rifle, and not in the house but on a nearby farm where Anguita was allegedly trying to steal a goat. Regardless of the precise circumstances, it later emerged that the lovers, with the assistance of Moreno's sister and brother-in-law, transported the man's corpse on a donkey late at night and dumped it in a faraway location. Judges ultimately sentenced Moreno to death by hanging and the woman to be confined for life in an undetermined institution, most likely a *casa de recogidas*.[66]

In Santiago de Compostela, Galicia, authorities charged Rosa Llamas with the murder of her husband, Manuel López, in 1821. Rosa's lover, Francisco Gil, a soldier with the Aragon Volunteer Forces, had stabbed López to death in a local tavern. The woman was present, and though her specific involvement in the murder is unclear, she tried to escape. Members of their community seem to have known about Rosa and Francisco's romantic liaison, which had allegedly caused "great scandal in the neighborhood," and the two were sentenced to eight years of imprisonment.[67]

Finally, in June 1824, in Rivero de Alba near Santiago de Compostela, wine merchant Roque Jacinto de Alba died by poisoning at his in-laws' home. The culprit turned out to have been his wife, María del Carmen Feijoo, who desired not only her freedom but also the merchant's money so she could run away with an unidentified lover. The outcome of the case is unknown.[68]

The six cases mentioned thus far, involving people from all Spanish regions and social backgrounds, are among a total of ten murders linked to adultery in our case set. In none of them was the culprit a macho Spanish male who, dishonored by his spouse's infidelity, lashed out and murdered her.[69] Instead, the perpetrators were wives and their lovers, acting contrary to the dominant honor code, in an attempt to be rid of inconvenient husbands.

Discarding the honor–shame paradigm may not be necessary to explain all of these "anomalous" cases, however.[70] Several decades ago, French cultural historians Bartolomé Bennassar and Marceline Defourneaux had already noted contradictions in the historical record concerning the behavior of Spanish women and men both in and out of wedlock. Some documents, they argued, spoke to women's virtue, virginity, and conjugal fidelity, while others highlighted their coquettish, hypocritical, libertine, and faithless nature. Evidence for men was also contradictory, ranging from their depiction as ready to settle amorous rivalries and infidelity with the knife to their portrayal as liberal and free from jealousy.[71] Bennassar tried to provide a historical explanation for these contradictions, though he remained cautious about the impressionistic nature of his evidence. Starting in the seventeenth century, he noted, "adultery seems to have become much more frequent and marriage to have been often mocked."[72] He also claimed that in the seventeenth and eighteenth centuries, "seduction, adultery, concubinage, and the complacent acquiescence of husbands or parents, became ever more common."[73]

It is not possible to support or refute the change alleged by Bennassar with the evidence collected for this volume, but a recent historical study of Yébenes, a town twenty-five miles south of Toledo, largely agreed that the killing of wives suspected of adultery was widespread during the Golden Age.[74] Things may have changed later, toward the seventeenth century, as Bennassar claimed. The records consulted for this book reveal that in late eighteenth-century Spain, extramarital love affairs were a relatively common occurrence. In several instances, husbands involved in liaisons out of wedlock became aggressive with their spouses, but instances of murder seem limited. Thanks to the prevailing patriarchal mindset and context, men probably did not need to get rid of their wives to continue their illicit romances. Even when wives were the ones responsible for adultery, husbands did not always react violently. Often, men contented themselves with a formal complaint to the authorities.[75] While some cases culminated in the killing of one's adulterous spouse, a far more common scenario, contrary to the norm in Golden Age novels and plays, was for an adulterous spouse to commit murder to be free to run away with his or her lover.[76] Moreover, in a majority of cases the culprits were married women who acted with the complicity of their lovers. Sexual attachment and seemingly passionate love as well, not to mention patriarchy's social exigencies, unquestionably influenced these women's behavior much more than adherence to codes of honor.

Bennassar rightly claimed that matters of love clearly troubled and interested "the whole [Spanish] population in the highest degree."[77] Citing abundant evidence, the author also stressed the significance of the closely related notion of honor. In his and other accounts, this idea was central to Spanish culture.[78] The exaltation of honor among people from all social backgrounds, from humble peasants and artisans to powerful noblemen, endured "down to the end of the nineteenth century and even through the civil war." He and several other authors defined honor as a form of pride whose meaning, much like that of *casta* status, was situational. Further, it was not static but evolved considerably over time. It originally derived mainly from heroic acts and courage. Later, it took the form of keeping one's promises or upholding moral responsibility. Subsequently, it assumed the shape of social or public reputation, including appropriate ancestry—in particular, "purity of blood" or old Catholic lineage. It also came to be associated with the ability to abstain from mechanical or manual activities. Ultimately, the notion of honor was linked to shame (*pundonor*). Whereas for men shame took the general form of social prejudice and pride, for women it was understood to reside mainly in virginity or, for married women, fidelity.[79]

As Bennassar told us long ago, and Spierenburg has confirmed recently, even if "honor was [not] responsible for all or even for the majority of the acts of violence" in Spain for centuries, it "certainly encouraged them." The incidents allegedly included "cases of 'honorable men' who became murderers as a result of brawls or because they killed their wives" as "vengeance for besmirched honor."[80] However, it seems evident that a fair number of spousal murders in our case set did not occur because a cuckolded husband had to avenge his besmirched honor. As historian Allyson Poska has established, the dominant honor–shame paradigm in actuality may have worked in ways more complex than expected based on literary archetypes.[81] But this does not mean that we should completely discard the idea. Bennassar himself claimed several decades ago that the wide diffusion of honor among all social groups did not imply that "this ideal of seigneurial [chivalric and aristocratic] origin was unanimously accepted, that it was not combatted, more or less explicitly rejected, and even ridiculed."[82] In sum, in his opinion, as in the recent evidence presented by Poska and in this study, anti-honor was also pervasive in historical reality.

The cases of extramarital female passions run amok presented here unquestionably speak vividly of anti-honor at work.[83] They belie our expectations and run counter to agreement among some academics about the way that honor functioned in daily life in eighteenth-century Spain and, perhaps, other European societies. Practically all of these randomly selected cases involve women who were having extramarital relationships and were not killed as a result. In fact, in only two instances (less than 17 percent of the entire adultery-related group of cases), did enraged husbands murder unfaithful wives.[84] In our case set, the wife was ultimately more than twice as likely to be the killer as was the husband. In other words, women and men both engaged in extramarital relations, but the latter were more likely to fall victim to murder as a result than were their wives. To redress such wrongs, the Spanish judicial system devised exemplary punishments. Like the ideal of honor, however, these evolved considerably over time and were often quite different in theory than in practice.

CONCLUSION

Spain witnessed dozens of spousal murders in the late eighteenth and early nineteenth centuries. Although far from conclusive, the evidence from a case set of sixty-five such murders across the peninsula's territory yields suggestive findings concerning crime and domestic violence in Iberia. Most of the crimes occurred at night, with knives, and involved mostly commoners, and many derived from extramarital affairs on the part of the defendants and their accomplices. Even though in absolute numbers men committed the bulk of the murders, women were also capable of murderous and violent behavior. In fact, in most of the crimes stemming from adulterous liaisons, which represented the largest category of spousal murders, the culprits were female.

Contrary to Spanish Golden Age and other widespread stereotypes, most spousal killings were not committed by men being cuckolded by their wives. Furthermore, as the circumstances of the crimes reflect, most spousal murders, far from representing a defense of the defendant's honor, involved actions that contradicted any notion of honorable behavior. The crimes and the defendants' motivations violated the vows of Catholic sacraments, resulted from sexual liaisons between sometimes socially unequal partners, involved brutal attacks against defenseless victims in the sanctity of their own homes, and profited from the victim's trust and the cover of night. None of these circumstances spoke to Spanish society's alleged obsession with male honor and female virtue. Instead, the records present us with deeply dishonorable men (scheming, deceitful, traitorous, and cowardly) and women who were as far from virtuous as possible.

When it came to law and justice, in both Spain and its overseas territories, nonwhites, women, commoners, and colonial subjects in general could expect to get the short end of the stick. Social hierarchies mattered a great deal in these societies, and equality under the law was by no means one of the rules of the legal game in the Spanish ancien régime. This liberal and modern idea would take some time to materialize. In the meantime, social mores upheld inequality as a perfectly reasonable and justifiable, even natural, state of affairs. However, the treatment afforded Spanish spousal murderers somewhat contradicts this expectation. *Hidalgos* frequently met death sentences or faced harsh presidio terms, and, as the next chapter will establish, commoners were likely to be pardoned. Furthermore, as established later while discussing punishments across the three regions, all peninsular Spanish subjects received harsher treatment than their peers overseas.

The disjuncture between expectations and reality can be explained at least in part by the fact that legal proceedings and judicial outcomes did not merely reflect cultural values and social norms, but also followed dynamics determined to a greater or lesser extent by the logic of legal rules, principles, customs, judicial doctrines, and culture. The following chapter explores other paradoxes inherent to the judicial system, such as the status of churches as semipermanent refuges for offenders against the sacrament of marriage and the earthly logic behind pardons inspired by Catholic faith.

CHAPTER FIVE

God's Forgiveness

Heavenly Intercessions

The close historical connection between the Catholic Church and the Crown, or ecclesiastical and secular power, and between their theological and politico–juridical discourses and practices, including canon and royal (civil) law, can be traced back to the Middle Ages. Thereafter, and since at least early modern times, this connection came to be at the core of the structure and functioning of, among other institutions, the deeply Catholic Spanish monarchy, both at home and overseas. A long-standing subject of academic attention for scholars of the West's political, legal, and intellectual history, this virtually hybrid situation entailed mutual borrowing of concepts, ceremonials, symbols, and practical tools to control and rule over the populace effectively and "legitimately," which is to say hegemonically.[1] It also involved a fair amount of competition and dispute over jurisdiction and precedence.

Both Church and Crown conceived of justice as a strategic mechanism to enforce their commands. Justice was not only a way to instill fear and respect but also, just as important, to draw subjects' recognition, loyalty, and gratitude. Both institutions seemed determined to show their judicial might and prevail over the other in the handling of specific legal disputes. To prevail meant either to claim full control over judicial resolution of certain quarrels or to be in a position to affect the outcome of those handled by the other's courts. As we have already seen, the Catholic Church came to monopolize the investigation and resolution of many disputes concerning marriage (separation and nullification) as well as some sexual or marriage-related violations of Catholic orthodoxy (bigamy, incest, and, in some places, sodomy).[2] Over the centuries, the Church also institutionalized a major mechanism to intervene in many criminal trials to ensure the reduction of the defendant's sentence, no matter the gravity of the offense being punished. This mechanism applied even to crimes threatening family life, which seems paradoxical, for as we know the Church was quite concerned with protecting marriage.

The Catholic Church intervened proactively in marital disputes to ensure as much as possible that couples and families remained together, to see that a spouse at fault received appropriate reprisal, and, only in the most extreme cases, to sanction dissolution of the union, as discussed earlier and illustrated elsewhere in this work. Curiously, in fulfillment of its charitable mission, the Church also provided protection for criminals, even those who had committed heinous offenses against the sanctity of marriage. The Church granted sanctuary (*asilo*) in churches and other sacred places to most criminals seeking it, including spouse killers. Further, since Catholic dogma actually emphasized the pardon of all sinners by God and his representatives on earth, the Church sheltered criminals with as much conviction and determination as it displayed in the prosecution of heretics! In the process, it left a visible mark of the considerable power that the clergy wielded vis-à-vis the monarchy. The ecclesiastical arm, as much as secular law, played an active function in the criminal process, showing support for and compassion toward defendants and—why not?—openly claiming credit for it.

The king, therefore, was not alone in staging displays of self-serving benevolence and altruism such as the ones discussed in Chapter 3. Neither did he, in issuing judicial decisions, always rely on entirely secular motives or justifications. In fact, in several instances, as when he granted forgiveness to criminals during Holy Week, he acted as a faithful servant of God, as God's proxy and to imitate the almighty's infinite clemency while simultaneously invoking it, in exchange, for himself and his family.

In the eyes of the populace, expressions of ecclesiastical or royal munificence founded upon religious considerations were part and parcel, source and symbol, of not only the presence and power but also the very legitimacy of the two main institutions binding together late colonial Spanish Atlantic societies. Unquestionably, this contributed to solidify each institution's separate and joint hegemony over and acceptance by all social groups, both subaltern and dominant alike. But while the hegemonic royal and ecclesiastical powers often complemented and reinforced each other in showing benevolence toward criminals, the king and the Church—and their respective courts and bodies of law (civil and canon)—sometimes entered into heated competition and intense doctrinal, jurisdictional, and political disputes over the prerogative to grant mercy, a sign of tangible power and influence in the daily lives of the peoples they ruled. This tug of war reflected the constant tension between the secular and spiritual realms that accompanied the colonial project from its inception until its collapse centuries later. Criminals seemed aware of, at times passively benefited from, and on many other occasions proactively took full advantage of this intriguing dynamic.

This chapter discusses three of the central spiritual expressions of ecclesiastical forgiveness toward spousal murderers and other criminals. The discussion begins with the examination of sanctuary (*asilo*), the refuge accorded to criminals in Catholic churches and cemeteries, typically soon after they committed their crimes. It continues with individual Good Friday pardons (*perdones de Viernes Santo*), some of which occurred during the course of the judicial process or after it had ended, granted as they sometimes were even to those already convicted, including murderers, spousal and otherwise. *Asilo,* an understudied practice, will be discussed in more detail than pardons, some of which (general ones, in particular) have already been addressed in this book and are the subject of various specialized monographs.[3] In both instances, the discussion addresses the legal processes and principles underlying these benevolent traditions. Neither institution was truly arbitrary, nor did they derive from the unlimited power of the Church or the sovereign. Instead, both were informed by long-standing legal doctrines and practices, and followed specific courses of legal action. As in the case of criminal procedures in general, formalities and routine were of the essence. The chapter ends with a brief account of additional religious efforts to assist condemned inmates or spare their corpses punitive rituals considered contrary to Catholic sensitivity.

SANCTUARY (*ASILO*) AND THE LAW

Several of the individuals whose crimes are the subject of this book pursued the recourse of *asilo*. For instance, Chapter 1 describes how Eulalia, an Indian woman who lived near the remote Mission of San Antonio in northern Mexico, sought refuge in the mission church in late 1800 after local justice officials began to suspect her and two male accomplices—one of whom was her lover—of killing her husband. Across the Atlantic three decades earlier, Juan Francisco Escudero García, a landowner and nobleman in the tiny village of Vizmanos in northern Spain, whose crime is mentioned in the previous chapter, applied for *asilo* at San Pedro Church after escaping from jail in mid-1772, almost a year after strangling his wife to pursue an extramarital affair. The next chapter includes references to white dressmaker María de la Luz Castro of Vélez, a small town in northeastern New Granada, who fled to church one afternoon in 1792 after stabbing her allegedly abusive husband, José Manuel de Luengas, so she could run away with her lover.

As can be seen from these examples, defendants across ethnic and class lines—a poor Indian woman, a wealthy Spanish nobleman, and a middling female artisan—in the colonies as well as the metropolis resorted to ecclesiastical asylum. They all seemed well aware that taking refuge in a church would improve their lot during trial and sentencing. In all, more than 11 percent of the defendants in the cases that this study examines chose this option. Several more, among them former soldier Hermenegildo Peña, tried in Chihuahua, Mexico, for killing his wife, María Josefa, in 1817, planned to seek asylum but did not manage to reach sanctuary in time.[4]

A venerable legal tradition and a widely known defense, *asilo* nevertheless sparked heated doctrinal, procedural, jurisdictional, and political controversy.[5] Let us keep in mind that even long-standing legal routines are not exempt from contestation, interpretation, and rhetorical give and take. This is more so the case when two proud and powerful entities clash in an effort to prevail over each other and thus secure or strengthen respect, recognition, and allegiance, in this case by criminals or victims, their families, and the many local people who became aware of the newsworthy events surrounding their confrontation. We will begin with some general comments about the nature and origins of the practice and move next to the legal doctrine supporting *asilo* and other related matters.

General Background

"Church is my name" ("*Iglesia me llamo*") was a phrase uttered over and over again by criminals during judicial interrogations throughout the Iberian kingdoms that ultimately became Spain, and in the Spanish American colonies.[6] Even after committing heinous crimes, these outlaws sought and received shelter at local churches, where they were known as *retraídos*.[7] Once they had received *asilo,* criminals felt entitled to withhold information from justice officials. An example is mulatto saddle maker Diego Joseph Bolaños, who hid in the bell tower of the Teposcolula Church in Oaxaca, Mexico, in the mid-eighteenth century after killing his wife, Maria Ponce, because she didn't make him dinner that night. When justice officials went to capture him, his initial statement was "*Iglesia me llamo,*" and he answered all subsequent questions with the simple response "the Church knows it" ("*la iglesia lo sabe*").[8]

Criminals like Bolaños were confident that it would not be easy to remove them from the church for punishment. Indeed, groups of wrongdoers even turned churchyards, churches, cloisters, and adjoining cemeteries into permanent residences. They were alleged to move freely in and out of church buildings under cover of night and to bring friends, lovers, and liquor in for enjoyment. Their presence terrorized neighbors and passersby, inconveniencing priests and parishioners alike. Despite the controversy, Church and Crown generally upheld the institution. All parties knew that asylum included the promise that criminals, even if proven guilty, would not be sentenced to death or severe corporal punishment (*poena aflicitiva corporis*).[9] It was not clear whether the credit for this corresponded to Heaven or Earth, but the practice was an old one.

In an attempt to establish supremacy for their respective institutions, clerical and *regalista* (royalist) authors argued about whether sanctuary was a "gift from God" or a secular custom.[10] The debate continued well into the nineteenth century and was never resolved.[11] However, it is clear that religious asylum in Christian temples had been an important defense for criminals from the early days of Christendom. Constantine (ca. AD 274–337) recognized sanctuary, as did Theodosius (AD 346–395) and other fourth-century Roman emperors.[12] Asylum was introduced into regions of what later became France and England by no later than the sixth century AD.[13] It appeared in laws enacted in some Iberian kingdoms as early as 610 and became the subject of regulation by Church councils in, among other places, Toledo in 633, 638, and 681.[14] The Byzantine Empire witnessed a debate during the eleventh century over the expansion of asylum to those who killed deliberately, which suggests that the practice was established much earlier in Byzantium for other types of crimes.[15] In any case, by the thirteenth century religious asylum had clearly become a central institution in canon law, the "universal" law of the Catholic Church. Some of the first canon law compilations addressed it, particularly Pope Innocent III's *Compilatio quarta,* issued in 1216, and Gregory IX's Decretals of 1234, one chapter of which (Cap. 9 and feq. de Immunit. Ecclef.) dealt with asylum under the heading of immunity (*immunitate ecclesiae*). By this time, it was already clear that without ecclesiastical authorization, civil justice officials could not remove criminals who found shelter in a Catholic church. Only a few crimes were excluded from the privilege, usually brigandage or banditry and murders committed in a church or cemetery.

The institution of sanctuary was part of not only religious but also civil law from as early as the seventh century and is found in several local *fueros* (municipal charters with privileges) from the ninth century.[16] Seventh-century Germanic law accepted asylum, in particular the Visigoth *Liber Judiciorum* (Book of the Judges), which came to be known in the Spanish kingdoms as the *Fuero Juzgo* after its Spanish translation and adoption in 1254 by King Alfonso X.[17] Later, not only the *Fuero Juzgo* (1254) but also the *Fuero Real* (1255), *Siete Partidas* (1251–1265), and *Ordenanzas Reales de Castilla* (also known as *Ordenamiento Real or Ordenamiento de Montalvo,* 1484), contained provisions protecting murderers, thieves, debtors, and other criminals who sought refuge in Catholic churches and related places. For instance, the *Fuero Real* provided that breaking into a church or cemetery to extract a refugee constituted sacrilege. It legitimated giving shelter to criminals, except for publicly known robbers; vandals who took advantage of the cover of night to destroy vineyards, trees, and property markers (*mojones de heredades*); and anyone who committed murder inside a church or cemetery.[18]

The *Siete Partidas,* in turn, established that debtors and other "wrongdoers" could not be expelled from churches where they had sought refuge, nor could they be killed or subjected to bodily chastisement (*dalle pena en el cuerpo ninguna*). Anyone who wished to extract them from their shelter had to provide a *caución* (security bond) supported by a bondsman or, if unable to do so, swear an oath under God that, once extracted, the culprit would not suffer any bodily harm (*mal ninguno en el cuerpo*). For example, Silverio, a member of the Chumash indigenous tribe, agreed to leave the San Luis Mission church where he had sought refuge in 1796 after killing his wife only upon being assured in writing by a local priest that ecclesiastical immunity would protect him.[19] The same benefit applied to serfs who ran away from their masters and entered churches.

The *Siete Partidas* excluded from the benefit of asylum traitors, rapists of virgins, forgers, and royal tax evaders, exceptions that suggest the particular gravity attributed to these offenses at the time.[20] In turn, the *Ordenanzas Reales de Castilla* made special reference to the need to limit the liberal practice of granting asylum to adulterous women, robbers, perfidious murderers, and others flocking to the locality of Valdezcaray, east of Burgos in northern Spain. Over time, perhaps because it was a manor (*señorío*) and therefore subject to seigniorial as opposed to royal justice, this area had become a center for all sorts of Spanish criminals seeking shelter.[21] In an indication of how widespread the practice of sanctuary had become, the institution is featured in Spanish literature from the 1550s through the seventeenth century. Though literary narratives may not be an accurate reflection of reality, in general they make it clear that Church asylum was a well-known recourse in cities across the kingdom, including Madrid, Toledo, and, most prominently, the southern city of Seville, which was the mercantile and bureaucratic hub and port of entry to and from the American colonies.[22]

The *Nueva Recopilación,* issued in 1567 and revised and edited various times thereafter through the late eighteenth century, also contained several provisions about ecclesiastical immunity that were strikingly similar to those of the *Fuero Real.*[23] Throughout the seventeenth and eighteenth centuries, this legislation applied to numerous asylum cases in Iberia. In the region of Cádiz alone, more than 785 people, including spousal murderers, claimed asylum during that time.[24]

In Spain's overseas possessions, asylum occurred from the moment that Europeans arrived in the new territories. One of the earliest chroniclers of the conquest, Gonzalo Fernández de Oviedo (1478–1557), author of the monumental *Historia general y natural de las Indias*, published in Seville between 1535 and 1537, gives examples of New World asylum in the 1520s.[25] By 1569, King Phillip II had already issued provisions asking that ecclesiastical immunity be preserved in the colonies and that justice officials refrain from breaking into churches and extracting criminals sheltered within.[26] This order unquestionably benefited Basque transvestite Catalina de Erauso (1585–1650), an extraordinary figure in the colonial era, who because of her escape to the New World, military deeds in it, and autobiography, gained notoriety as "*la Monja Alférez*" ("the Lieutenant Nun"). In the first half of the seventeenth century, she was under asylum at least half a dozen times.[27] Dozens more asylum requests occurred in New Mexico starting in the 1680s.[28]

Even though the law admonished monasteries in Spanish America not to give shelter to criminals whose offenses were excluded from immunity or to impede the removal of those criminals by royal justice officials, the 1681 *Recopilación de las Indias* fully recognized the institution of ecclesiastical asylum. It ordered viceroys, governors, *audiencias,* and justice officials in general to respect canon law, the decisions of diocesan synods, and ecclesiastical pronouncements in cases tried by ecclesiastical courts. It warned them not to introduce any innovations, even when dealing with atrocious crimes.[29] This is why, despite early warnings by the late eighteenth-century monasteries—or *mongerios,* as the natives preferred to call them—the clergy actually became protective of, among others, spousal murderers, in particular neophyte Indians living in the missions in places such as San Antonio, San Luis Obispo, and San Juan Capistrano, in northern Mexico.[30] By this time, sufficient doctrine had accumulated to back up their actions.

Legal Doctrine

Virtually every treatise on criminal law from the sixteenth through the eighteenth century gave detailed attention to Church asylum. Renowned legal experts Antonio Gómez (1501–1562/1572), Diego de Covarrubias y Leyva (1523–1577), Jerónimo Castillo de Bobadilla (1546/47–1605), and Juan de Hevia Bolaños (1570–1623) all discussed sanctuary in important treatises or commentaries on Castilian law. In the process they contributed to unifying doctrine and establishing a routine for the handling of cases.

Much in the manner of the *Fuero Real,* Gómez explained, religious immunity did not cover public thieves, vandals who destroyed crops at night, offenders who committed crimes inside churches, and those guilty of treacherous homicides. To this list he added prisoners who escaped from jail and sought sanctuary inside a church, which happened in several of the spousal murder incidents discussed here, including the ones involving Spanish *hidalgo* Escudero García (see Chapter 4) and his compatriot Maria Lario, mentioned below. Covarrubias also reviewed in detail the list of excluded crimes and advised that while immunity cases were being discussed, justice officials should follow the French model of extracting criminals from churches and locking them up in jail to prevent ecclesiastical authorities from transferring them to another location.[31] This seems to have been a frequent occurrence. For instance, in 1816, three years after her crime, judicial authorities removed Maria Lario, an accomplice in the seemingly premeditated murder of her husband, Vicente Anguita, from the Iglesia Colegial in Medinaceli, Spain, where she had sought refuge upon escaping from the house where she was under confinement. Such extractions ordinarily required ecclesiastical permission, which in this case, perhaps because of her previous escape, seems to have been omitted.[32] Castillo de Bobadilla, a former *corregidor* who belonged to the Royal Council and was *fiscal* (Crown attorney) of the Real Chancillería of Valladolid, warned that justice officials who wanted to extract criminals from the churches where they sought refuge needed ecclesiastical authorization, even when the crimes in question were excluded from immunity. He advised secular judges with the necessary authorization to proceed discreetly and with extreme caution and deference (see Figure 4.1).[33]

Hevia Bolaños's widely used *Curia Philippica* (1602) provided the most liberal interpretation of the institution. Any church could offer asylum, he argued, even unconsecrated ones that did not celebrate Mass or had been demolished for renovation. He extended the concept to include cloisters, dormitories, refectories, gardens, hospitals, monasteries, and cemeteries (*claustros, dormitorios, refectorios, huertas, hospitales, monasterios y cementerios*). Even criminals who had been excommunicated or subjected to other forms of religious censure (*suspensos* and *entredichos*) were eligible for the benefit for all crimes except those on the list of traditional exclusions. Finally, he decreed, the beneficiaries of sanctuary could not be deprived of food, nor would guards be permitted to surround the church.[34]

Acknowledging sanctuary's centrality for the handling of criminal proceedings, several seventeenth-century works of jurisprudence continued to elaborate on this institution.[35] Discussing the history of asylum to highlight what he considered to be its secular origins, royalist author Fernando González de Socueba gave a much narrower interpretation of its scope in 1766 than the one proposed by Hevia Bolaños. According to González de Socueba, asylum was originally intended to protect debtors, accidental murderers, and petty criminals. He lamented that over the years it had become a widespread practice and celebrated its restriction in England, Germany, Italy, and Portugal.[36] Other authors were much more flexible.

In the sixth edition (1796) of his popular manual on criminal and civil law, Spanish jurist and magistrate Francisco Elizondo explained that religious asylum had to be granted not only to those who entered a church but also to those who approached its doors, touched its walls, or entered the adjacent homes of priests if the church was closed (see Figure 5.1). This is why, for instance, after stabbing his wife to death in 1772, Melchor Martin Alonso felt entitled to sanctuary upon reaching a shed (*cobertizo de teja*) adjacent to a Franciscan monastery and its church in the city of Madrid. Eventually, the authorities had to obtain permission from the ecclesiastical jurisdiction to legalize his transfer to a jail.[37] In the same vein as Hevia Bolaños, albeit with a few more restrictions, Elizondo also agreed that criminals could seek asylum at remote *ermitas* [*sic*], pilgrimage altars, chapels, and rural churches as long as Mass was more or less regularly celebrated within. He also proposed resolutions to regular controversies between ecclesiastical and secular authorities, and stressed that judges who violated ecclesiastical immunity risked excommunication.[38]

The contradictions among jurists such as González de Socueba and Elizondo mirrored even more intense disputes over the institution of *asilo,* particularly in the eighteenth century. During that time, ecclesiastical and royal officials alike concurred in trying to reform the privilege. This was in large part the result of controversial practices in the New World.[39]

Conflicts over Asylum

Asylum-related conflicts between Church and Crown, perhaps more regular, protracted, and notorious than any other conflict involving both institutions, persisted well into the late colonial period, The eighteenth century became undoubtedly the most intense period of discussing and revising asylum rules and practices, especially in the New World. Moreover, the quarrels had a clear impact not only at the imperial level but also at the local one, where they touched both the upper echelons of society and the masses.

The disputes mainly concerned the crimes covered by asylum and the exact procedure in cases involving religious immunity—in particular, how to extract criminals from churches and transfer them to royal prisons while they were being tried. Related arguments concerned the excommunication of royal officials accused of forcibly removing people from sanctuary. Documented cases speak of the attitudes and tribulations of those involved in these disputes, especially the clergy, royal officials, and the criminals themselves. Archival records show that the clergy, confident of the Church's privileges, frequently refused to cooperate with royal officials trying to extract asylum seekers, even when the offenders' crimes were officially excluded from the sanctuary benefit. This category included state officials accused of malfeasance and spousal murderers.[40] Some of the disputes resulted in the excommunication of royal functionaries or the indefinite suspension of Mass (*entredichos*) for entire localities.[41]

Confrontations between Crown and clergy in these cases frequently reached the point of requiring the intervention of the highest authorities in the New World, the royal *audiencias*, as well as the Council of the Indies in Spain. The historical records are full of such cases.[42] The clergy sheltered murderers, thieves, abusive spouses, and people engaged in illicit sexual affairs even if such protection resulted in clashes with civil or military authorities, as in the case of several culprits who were soldiers.[43]

Ecclesiatical–military cooperation did sometimes occur. In 1758, after numerous incidents involving soldiers under Church asylum, the naval commander of Havana, Lieutenant General Francisco Caxigal de la Vega, and that city's bishop reached a *concordia* (agreement) for the prompt extraction of military personnel from local churches.[44] Church and royal officials in Mexico City and Guadalajara reached similar agreements. Generally, however, royal authorities became impatient with the Church's zealous stance on asylum and could not persuade the clergy to be more flexible or careful in determining which crimes were covered by the privilege. The records suggest that the clergy was willing to shelter criminals whose offenses were clearly excluded from sanctuary (bandits, royal officials undergoing *residencias*, people who had committed crimes inside cemeteries or churches, and escaped prisoners, as well as spousal murderers) and spared no resource, human or divine, to do so.[45]

At least a few of the criminals whose cases generated disputes were spousal killers. Like other criminals, spousal murderers turned to the Church to avoid receiving harsh (or any!) punishment. For instance, in December 1686, Isabel de Tejeda sought refuge in a nearby *ermita* after savagely killing her husband, Manuel Espinoza, in Mazapil, a mining town (*real de minas*) in northern Mexico.[46] More than eight decades later, within the period of our interest, in 1774, Pedro Martín availed himself of the same recourse, seeking refuge in a Guadalajara church after killing his wife.[47] Numerous cases certainly occurred between these two and subsequent to the latter.

As Table 5.1 shows, twenty-four defendants—more than 11 percent of the total cited in this work—received ecclesiastical immunity after killing their spouses. Eleven of the cases occurred in Spain, eleven more in Mexico, and just two in Colombia, where, for reasons that are unclear, the criminals did not seem to have invoked this mechanism as often. Half of the incidents took place in the 1760s and 1790s, and the rest are more or less evenly scattered over the rest of the period. Given the fragmentary and uneven nature of the records, more unrecorded instances were likely.

TABLE 5.1. *Spousal murder cases involving church asylum by date and punishment applied: Colombia, Mexico, and Spain, 1750s–1810s*

Year of crime	Defendant's gender	Defendant's ethnicity	Place of crime	Final sentence
1753	Male	Mulatto	Teposcolula, Mexico	Unknown
1755	Male	Indian	Teposcolula, Mexico	Unknown
1761	Male	White	Madrid, Spain	Royal pardon
1762	Female	Mestiza?	Somondoco, Colombia	Unknown
1763	Male	White	El Alamo, Spain	Unknown
1763	Male	White	Madrid, Spain	Unknown
1764	Female	White	Madrid, Spain	Unknown
1764	Male/Female	White	Madrid, Spain	Unknown
1769	Male	White	Mexico City, Mexico	Unknown
1774	Male	Unknown	Guadalajara, Mexico	Unknown
1771	Male	White	Yanguas, Spain	10-year presidio sentence
1772	Male	White	Madrid, Spain	Unknown
1780	Male	White	Tarifa, Spain	Unknown
1791	Male	White	Ozumba, Mexico	Unknown
1792	Female	White	Pamplona, Colombia	Unknown
1793	Male	White	Aranjuez, Spain	Royal pardon
1796	Male	Indian	Monterrey Mission, Mexico	8-year service
1797	Male	Indian	San Diego Mission, Mexico	4-year labor
1799	Male	White	Guadalajara, Spain	Unknown
1800	Female	Indian	Nueva Galicia Mission, Mexico	6-year service
1804	Male	White	Mexico City, Mexico	Death: *garrote*
1807	Male	White	Pachuca, Mexico	Royal pardon
1813	Female	White	Medinaceli, Spain	Death: *garrote*
1816	Male	Indian	Cuernavaca, Mexico	8-year prison sentence

SOURCES: AGN, Mexico, Criminales, vol. 2, 2, fols. 31–69; vol. 33, 2, fols. 43–63; vol. 113, 2, fols. 51–52; vol. 203, 11, fols. 433–439; vol. 203, 2, fols. 440–446; AGN, Mexico, Californias, vol. 65, cases 6 and 8; AJO, vols. 31 and 32, cases 937 and 951; F. Sedano, *Noticias de México,* 3: 93; *Diario de México* 116, March 25, 1806, 334–336; AGN, Colombia, Criminal, Colonia, vols. 43, fols. 996–1000; vol. 44, fols. 1–262; vol. 95, fols. 380–499; AGI, Guadalajara, 402; ARCV, Spain, box 270, case 2; box 245, case 2; AGN, Madrid, Sala Alcaldes Casa y Corte, libro 1390, fols. 74–76; legajo 9742, fol. 97; AGS, Gracia y Justicia, legajos 804, 808, 874; ADC, legajo 1841, exp. 3.

Of the spousal murderers seeking asylum, the majority (18) were male and white (15), compared to about one-quarter who were female (6) and nonwhite (5 Indians, 1 mulatto, and 1 mestizo). In close to half of the cases the outcome is unknown, but it is clear that in the vast majority of cases for which evidence is more complete, culprits ended up with four- to ten-year prison sentences. Only a handful (two) received the death penalty, an unusual outcome given that the purpose of asylum was to save the criminal's life. These exceptional cases will be discussed later. First, we will detail apparent abuses of the privilege that would prompt calls for reform.

A Privilege Abused

In some cases at least, the beneficiaries of *asilo* clearly abused the refuge they were granted and became a real public menace. Rather than devoting themselves to prayer and contemplation, many criminals under sanctuary seem to have had other occupations in mind, at various points bringing state officials (and some bishops) to the verge of desperation. Picaresque novels suggest some of this behavior; the legal record confirms it.[48] In Havana, criminals drank and brawled inside holy places and were alleged to have assaulted passersby. This was the main reason for the 1758 agreement between the bishop of Havana and the local governor to extract criminals from the city's churches and transfer them to the presidio in St. Augustine, Florida.[49]

The authorities received similar complaints in late colonial Mexico. Upon completing his term, Viceroy Carlos Francisco de Croix (1766–1771) left his successor an account of the difficulties he had faced during his tenure. He lamented the many criminals sheltered in the city's churches and reported that some of them ventured out from their refuge to commit further crimes. They switched sanctuaries almost at will. ("*Había muchos reos, que con insolencia salían de ellos [refugios] de día y de noche a cometer robos y muertes, y se volvían a dichos refugios, mudándose de uno a otro.*") He boasted of unspecified reforms,[50] but judging by subsequent events, these had limited effect. During the same decade, a *fiscal* of the *audiencia* accused the *retraídos* in Mexico City's holy places of committing bloody crimes inside churches and cemeteries, and abandoning their sanctuaries to commit assault, murder, or theft in the city streets. The fiscal attributed this behavior partly to their "evil inclinations and extreme poverty" (*mala inclinación o suma pobreza*).[51]

In some cases, criminals seem to have been simply annoyed by the authorities' attempts to restrict the comfortable lifestyle they had created in their safe havens. For example, two *retraídos* in the Santa Catalina parish cemetery in Mexico City fought with a representative of the Tribunal de la Acordada, the parish priest, and some of his assistants. This episode occurred shortly after the authorities separated the city's male and female *retraídos* and transferred them to separate shelters. The delegation had come looking for two "tramps" (*mujercillas*) the criminals had smuggled into the sanctuary.[52] The men went after the officials, killing the one from the Acordada. They injured two of his assistants and even came close to beating up the vicar. A few months later, another group of *retraídos* in the San Miguel parish church hurled stones at guards patrolling the neighborhood. They injured one, spurring the others to shoot and kill one of the criminals. Yet another example comes from Guadalajara in 1778, when the clergy transferred to another church murder suspect María Potenciana, a mulatta and the only female among a large group of asylum seekers in the cathedral. She refused to stay there and kept returning to the original sanctuary until the authorities charged her with causing constant "scandals" and remanded her to the city jail.[53] All of these cases show outlaws seeking to preserve a modicum of autonomy and thumb their noses at the authorities.

Time was on their side. The Crown resented the fact that criminals could stay in the churches for years at a time while their cases idled. Canon law proceedings in matters of asylum (*trámite de los artículos de inmunidad*) were notoriously slow. For example, in the late seventeenth century an ecclesiastical judge in the mining center of Mazapil, in northern Mexico, ruled that a woman accused of complicity in the murder of her husband could not be covered by asylum sixteen months after leaving her place of sanctuary. By this time the woman had died, and, the record states, the local chief justice, who had been excommunicated for his role in the case, continued to live in spiritual agony.[54] Perhaps hyperbolically, an official report addressed to one of the king's closest advisors, Joseph Miguel de Gálvez, in August 1779 noted that in the recent past some cases of refugees and fugitives had lasted up to twenty years without resolution![55] The norm was probably shorter, as in the case of Ignacia de Ontiveros, who sought refuge in the Guadalajara cathedral to avoid going to jail for an illicit affair with a married treasury official. She lived there for more than eighteen months, even giving birth inside.[56] A list of prisoners housed in the same cathedral includes people whose cases had been pending for more than two years. Apparently, they remained in the holy place the entire time.[57]

Over the long periods that spousal murderers and other accused criminals spent in Catholic sanctuaries, ecclesiastical authorities could lose track of who had done what. The clergy could not even be sure whether all of the church dwellers had committed a crime or whether they were just *ociosos y bagamundos* (idle vagrants) posing as criminals to receive free food and shelter.[58] The Church's internal procedures in cases involving sanctuary were lengthy, as were related judicial disputes between Church and Crown, especially the so-called *recursos de fuerza* (equivalent to an appeal to royal tribunals against ecclesiastical judges' decisions).[59] The ecclesiastical authorities appeared anxious to prevail at any cost and were committed to litigate cases for as long as it took: years, if necessary.

Apart from any possible material incentive, besting the Crown, especially in cases involving powerful members of society, had symbolic value for Church authorities. It ratified the magnanimity and humanitarian character that the Catholic Church strove to project and, more important, demonstrated that the clergy was as powerful as high-ranking state officials. For example, the ecclesiastical authorities could invoke the frightening sanction of excommunication to block the government's actions. Church victories also served to illustrate that divine justice was mightier than human justice. In the minds of zealous clergy, these benefits seem to have justified possible overindulgence of wrongdoers.

As a result of protracted legal procedures, sanctuaries often became overcrowded, a problem that concerned everyone. One of the best examples comes from Guadalajara, colonial Mexico's second-largest urban center. In February 1778, no fewer than eighteen *retraídos* were living in the city's cathedral. The group was a peculiar mix, an interesting sample of local society and the criminal universe. All but one were male, and they included representatives of all ethnic and racial categories: at least four "Spaniards" (that is, whites), three *coyotes* (offspring of a mestizo and an Indian), two mulattos, one *pardo* (brown or mulatto), one Indian, one foreigner (French), and six others whose ethnicity was not revealed but who can be assumed to have been mestizos.[60] Seven were accused of homicide, two of theft, and two others of illicit affairs with married women. One was a debtor. The others' crimes, possibly including spousal murders, were not specified, in one case because the individual perhaps was not a criminal at all but, as he himself put it, was in the sanctuary because *le conviene* (it was convenient for him). Conditions in Mexico City were similar; on a visit to the capital, *fiscal* Diego Acosta, one of Guadalajara's Crown attorneys, learned that the authorities had recently extracted many criminals from the city's overcrowded churches and cathedral.

Until early 1778, large groups of men and women reportedly lived together in Mexico City's churches and cemeteries for extended periods, bringing boyfriends, girlfriends, and prostitutes in for nights of partying, drinking, and card games. The authorities blamed these gatherings for the criminals' recidivist inclinations. As the Mexico City *fiscal* put it, if a single person has evil inclinations, "what could be expected from a group of crooks? What do they think about and plan, what lessons do they teach each other, and how much do they egg each other on?"[61] Capital officials tackled this critical situation by segregating males and females into separate sanctuaries. They transferred offenders who did not qualify for asylum to local jails until their cases were decided and expelled from sanctuary those whose cases did not have sufficient merit, debtors in particular.[62]

Encouraged by the news, *fiscal* Acosta requested a similar procedure for Guadalajara. To this end, he compiled reports from ecclesiastical authorities and local justice officials about ongoing asylum cases and the people currently living in local churches. The historical records contain references to similar efforts to control asylum in colonial Buenos Aires, Chile, Colombia, Guatemala, Panama, Peru, and the Philippines.[63] It is no wonder that efforts at reforming the privilege became intense, led by the Church itself as a probable reaction against recurrent scandals.

Attempts at Reform

Problems connected to asylum—the excommunication of officials and the suspension of Mass for entire localities, prolonged proceedings, overcrowding, and scandalous behavior—persisted despite several papal bulls and briefs (*breves*) and around half a dozen royal *cédulas* (decrees) enacted in the eighteenth century to regulate and moderate the practice. Four different popes during that period issued canonical decrees that addressed various aspects of the issue. Some of these measures excluded from asylum all cases of voluntary homicide, forgery of ecclesiastical documents, and counterfeiting. Several limited the number of churches where criminals could seek refuge, excluding rural churches and hermitages (*ermitas*) as well as the exterior walls of church buildings, most priests' residences, private chapels, and bell towers detached from a church. Others agreed to allow one or, at most, two churches in each major urban center to offer shelter to criminals.[64]

The Holy See (*Santa Sede*) and the Spanish Crown eventually signed a *concordato* (covenant) on the issue of sanctuary on September 26, 1737. Several of its provisions confirmed that any crime on public roads involving death or bodily mutilation would be excluded from asylum, as would conspiracy against the Crown. The *concordato* ruled out the possibility of ecclesiastical immunity in rural churches and *ermitas* and also rejected "cold church" asylum (*asilo en iglesias frias*), the term used to describe false claims by criminals that they had been removed unjustly from a church. This seemed to be a common maneuver.[65]

Even after the *concordato,* the Crown enacted royal decrees to clarify and expedite the procedure for secular judges to extract criminals from their places of asylum (*sagrados*). The various royal orders stipulated that to extract criminals as promptly as possible, secular judges should observe the requirement to offer a guarantee or promise that the individuals removed from religious asylum would not be "offended" (*caución juratoria de no ofender*)—in other words, not be subject to the death penalty or any corporal punishment. The decrees also specified the legal recourses that justice officials could invoke to protest and contain abuses (*fuerzas*) by ecclesiastical authorities.[66] In addition to such general rules, local authorities issued ad hoc measures to resolve critical situations, such as the one in Mexico City in early 1778. Similar measures were later adopted everywhere in the Spanish realms.[67] There is some evidence that at least in some remote locations, for instance, the Mission of San Juan Capistrano in Southern California, routine procedures existed by then for the extraction of criminals under sanctuary. As late as 1797, spousal murderers such as recent convert Aurelio Jujuvit were asked to leave the church with a written assurance by a member of the clergy that their sanctuary, no matter how brief, would carry weight (*defender mucho*).[68]

In November 1800 the Crown issued a *cédula* extending the Mexican policy on asylum to all of its domains. All of the American possessions after 1787 had implemented the policy and reemphasized it in an additional 1797 royal decree, but over time the orders fell into disuse. The *cédula* was a reminder that extraction of criminals from churches be prompt and followed by a timely criminal investigation, with any jurisdictional controversies between ecclesiastical and secular judges decided swiftly under a procedure spelled out in great detail. The royal decree also upheld the long-standing policy on punishment: Sentences for criminals extracted from asylum could not exceed ten years of presidio, labor, public service, or *destierro* (banishment).[69]

In practice, this limit was not observed in at least a few spousal murder cases. For example, records show that José María Jaso, a tailor whose March 1806 execution in Mexico City for the murder of his wife is recounted in detail elsewhere in this book, sought refuge in a local church after his crime. Perhaps due to the heinous circumstances of the murder—multiple stab wounds preceded by savage punches and kicks while the young (seventeen-year-old!) victim was on the ground—the ecclesiastical authorities handed him swiftly over to royal justice officials (*aunque el reo tomó asilo, fue consignado lisa y llanamente por la jurisdicción eclesiástica*). After trial, he was garroted and his body consigned to *encubamiento*.[70] Something comparable happened in the case of Maria Lario and her lover, Gregorio Moreno, tried in Medinaceli, Spain, for the killing of Maria's husband, Vicente Anguita, in 1814. Despite claiming the right to sanctuary, both culprits were sentenced to death. In their case, a number of aggravating factors—the murder was premeditated, the pair sought sanctuary after escaping from their places of confinement, and, subsequent to their petition for asylum, they broke out of jail again and had to be tried in absentia—may have limited the court's mercy.[71]

In March 1807 the king issued yet another *cédula* to aid the eviction of criminals from sacred places. It required secular judges to give oral rather than written notification to priests before the imminent extraction of criminals from churches. While maintaining the promise to respect the criminal's life and physical integrity (*de no ofenderle su vida y sus miembros*), this measure was aimed at expediting removal and preventing escape.[72] All of the various reforms did not keep legal experts from continuing to issue recommendations about the troublesome but popular institution.

Additional Legal Doctrine

After several late eighteenth-century and early nineteenth-century reforms, legal manuals continued to address the controversial institution of sanctuary. Joseph Marcos Gutiérrez, Juan Alvarez Posadilla, Miguel Cayetano Sanz, and Francisco Elizondo were among the best-known authors and magistrates to address the topic in their widely read texts on criminal law and procedures. Commenting in 1789 on the classical work of sixteenth-century jurist Antonio Gómez, Gutiérrez listed the crimes that the contemporary canon and royal law excluded from asylum.[73] Alvarez Posadilla, a *fiscal* in one of Spain's *audiencias* in the early nineteenth century, included the list in his treatise on criminal law, along with detailed procedures for extracting criminals from sacred places. He endorsed the late eighteenth-century papal bulls designating only one or two churches in a village as sanctuaries.[74]

For Cayetano Sanz, a legal writer and *relator del crimen* in Spain's Chancillería de Valladolid, the most controversial issue was whether secular judges needed ecclesiastical authorization to extract criminals whose crimes were excluded from asylum. Basing his opinion on the most recent papal bulls and numerous classical legal authors, he contended that ecclesiastical orders were indispensable in all cases.[75]

Elizondo, the Chancillería de Granada *fiscal,* took a narrower approach. In the sixth edition of his legal manual (see Figure 5.1), he declared that only the vicar general of a bishopric could authorize a royal justice official to extract criminals. In addition, the judge was required to offer a guarantee (*caución*) that the asylum seeker's life and physical integrity would be protected. Should the ecclesiastical authorities, upon reviewing the case, conclude that the accused had a valid claim to asylum, the person would be immediately restored to the church designated

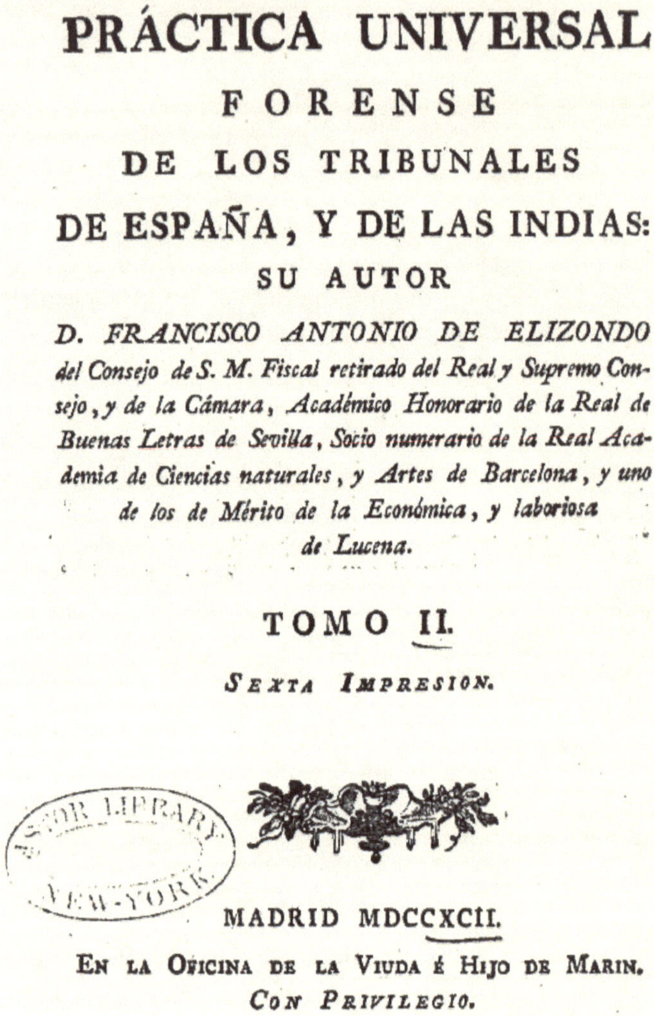

PRÁCTICA UNIVERSAL
FORENSE
DE LOS TRIBUNALES
DE ESPAÑA, Y DE LAS INDIAS:
SU AUTOR
D. FRANCISCO ANTONIO DE ELIZONDO
del Consejo de S. M. Fiscal retirado del Real y Supremo Consejo, y de la Cámara, Académico Honorario de la Real de Buenas Letras de Sevilla, Socio numerario de la Real Academia de Ciencias naturales, y Artes de Barcelona, y uno de los de Mérito de la Económica, y laboriosa de Lucena.

TOMO II.
Sexta Impresion.

MADRID MDCCXCII.
En la Oficina de la Viuda é Hijo de Marin.
Con Privilegio.

Figure 5.1. Francisco Antonio de Elizondo y Alvarez, Practica universal forense de los tribunales de España y de las Indias, *6ª impresion (Madrid: En la Oficina de la Viuda e Hijo de Marin, 1792 [1770]).*

by the vicar's order (*carta de restitución*). If secular judges disagreed with the ecclesiastical decision, they could present a petition (*recurso de fuerza*) to the nearest royal *audiencia* or *chancillería* arguing that the criminal was excluded from asylum rights and therefore should remain in a secular jail. Justice officials who refused to obey ecclesiastical orders risked excommunication. Elizondo suggested that they could ask higher courts to protect or absolve them and their villages from this punishment or other forms of religious censure (*censura*), such as a ban on celebrating Mass.[76]

Overall, the institution of asylum does not appear to have changed dramatically over more than a century. Legal reforms notwithstanding, the procedures that Elizondo and others discussed continued to be formalistic and protracted. Disputes between justice officials and clergy over asylum persisted and were intense and acrimonious. Meanwhile, individual culprits—including some spousal murderers among them, whose crimes were technically excluded from asylum—could do as they pleased: run away, sabotage the investigation, or simply fade into oblivion, confident that they would not receive the death penalty or other form of bodily punishment. A few, like spousal murderer Pedro Ormeña, whose case is discussed below, even went on to benefit from a blank royal pardon on Good Friday, another long-standing tradition supported by Catholic doctrines.

PERDONES DE VIERNES SANTO

Royal forgiveness of criminals operated at two levels, secular and spiritual. Unlike secular general pardons (*indultos generales*), which were comprehensive graces benefiting a large number of criminals to commemorate royal feasts or civic occasions, Good Friday pardons benefited specific individuals for a mainly religious reason. Issued during the Catholic Holy Week since at least the thirteenth century, perhaps even earlier, these individual pardons were traditionally granted by Spanish monarchs to honor and imitate God and implore his clemency.

According to some legal authors, these pardons could be granted on Easter Sunday. However, the available evidence suggests that in practice they commemorated another of the week's most solemn days, Good Friday, which thus became known as the day of forgiveness (*el dia de indulgencias*).[77] The medieval *Siete Partidas* addressed this kind of pardon, stating that they were bestowed for "love of our Lord Jesus Christ, as is done on Good Friday. . . ."[78] At the 1447 Cortes de Valladolid, King John II stated that he would grant individual royal pardons annually with the assistance of his ecclesiastical confessor, who would present him with a detailed list of the ones requested so that he could choose no more than twenty every Good Friday (*el viernes santo de la crúz*).[79] Apparently, the king did not always observe this limit and, in the seventeenth century at least, awarded as many as forty in a single year.[80]

Regardless of the exact number granted, the graces were in any case known as "annual pardons of the Good Friday of the Cross" (*indulto anual del Viernes Santo de la Crúz,* or *perdones de Viernes Santo* for short). This was the day when "Jesus Christ died to redeem humanity and save those who crucified him" ("*porque en tal día . . . Nuestro Señor Jesucristo recibió muerte y Pasión por salvar el linaje humano y perdonar su muerte a los que le crucificaron*").[81] Just as Christ forgave his executioners, for centuries Spanish kings honored the Christian duty to forgive wrongdoers, especially murderers. Of the more than 1,300 pardons of all kinds granted in Iberia in 1474 to 1499, the period for which comprehensive statistics are available, about one-third (407, or 31 percent) took place on a Good Friday. Like other pardons, even general ones, most of the beneficiaries were accused or already convicted of murder.[82] Statistics are also available for the seventeenth century but seem inconsistent. Some researchers report 581 pardons of a similar kind between 1618 and 1652.[83] According to others, between 1623 and 1699 the king awarded about 434 more Good Friday pardons. [84] Comprehensive statistics for the following centuries are unavailable, but considering their continuing use in the 1700s, one can presume that the king issued several hundred more.

By the late eighteenth century, traditional practice called for choosing two accused murderers from among the prisoners in Madrid's *cárcel de corte* (royal jail) and one from the capital of each *chancillería* or *audiencia.*[85] No evidence exists of an equivalent practice to benefit criminals in overseas territories, however. Lest it lose some of its mystical appeal, such an essential royal prerogative was probably not entrusted to viceroys, powerful though they were in the colonies. Difficulties with logistics and timing may have also preempted the king from trying to confer the reprieve to faraway subjects across the Atlantic. Good Friday pardons remained a metropolitan grace.

Every year, two weeks before Holy Friday, the members of the judicial section of the Consejo Real or Consejo de Castilla (*gracia y justicia*), the king's closest advisory board for judicial matters, requested abstracts of a select group of homicide cases pending before Madrid's Alcaldes de Casa y Corte and those up for trial before the various peninsular *audiencias* and *chancillerías.*[86] In general, the cases could not include ones in which relatives demanded punishment, murders for hire, or killings committed during muggings or under undignified circumstances. Such offenses demanded appropriate public retaliation (*vindicta pública*).[87] After evaluating the eligible cases, which generally included a petition by the offender or one of his close relatives as well as an abstract prepared by staffers, the Consejo made a confidential (*reservada*) recommendation to the king so that he could decide among the criminals listed as he pleased (*lo que sea de su real agrado*).[88]

Among the cases the king selected was that of Antonio Martínez, a twenty-eight-year-old coachman who killed his considerably older wife, sixty-four-year-old Francisca Vásquez. The couple allegedly drank and fought on a regular basis until one October day in 1761, when Martínez hit his wife over the head with a stew pot (*puchero* or *cazuela*). The king considered Martínez deserving of divine and royal mercy and awarded him pardon, apparently in view of the fact that the crime was not treacherous, the man was drunk, and the woman allegedly died from medical complications rather than as a direct result of the blow.[89]

Another beneficiary of a Good Friday pardon was Manuel Llerena, a forty-year-old potato salesman who killed his wife, Isabel Aloset, in October 1780 in Madrid. The two quarreled after Llerena returned home drunk. Aloset had been embarrassed earlier that day when the owner of a donkey the couple had bought at the public market came by their home demanding payment. Upon seeing her husband return home, drunk, still without money for the animal, Aloset exploded and accused him of being "deceitful, a thief, unworthy, Indian-face, drunk, liar" (*pícaro, ladrón, indigno, arrastrado, cara de indio, borracho, engañamundos*). This was not the couple's first fight; according to testimony from neighbors and acquaintances, they drank and argued constantly, and Llerena had already been jailed twice for injuring his wife. The night of their last argument, annoyed by her complaints and the fact she had not prepared any food for dinner, he hit Aloset brutally over the head with a shovel and a winnowing fork. She died three weeks later. On Holy Friday, the king commuted Llerena's sentence to banishment for a period of four years.[90]

Pedro Ormeña, a twenty-eight-year-old construction worker (*oficial de albañil*), killed his wife, María Jiménez, after an argument over his refusal to give her his week's wages. The woman accused him of being irresponsible with her and their two little daughters, deceitful (*picaro*), promiscuous, and a drunk. They came to blows, and Ormeña punched and kicked her in the back, stomach, and face. The subsequent autopsy found catastrophic damage to Jiménez's lungs and stomach. Ormeña sought sanctuary in a local church, but ultimately it was the king who saved him, on God's behalf of course. A Good Friday pardon spared Ormeña punishment for the crime, which had occurred in the *real sitio de Aranjuez* on August 18, 1793.[91]

By forgiving murderers such as Martínez, Llerena, and Ormeña, the king acted both mercifully and out of self-interest for his and his family's spiritual well-being. The monarch hoped not only to imitate Christ's compassion but also to gain divine favor. His expectation was that God would extend his life, protect his kingdom, and secure forgiveness for his parents' souls and his own (*alargar mis días y ensalzar mi Estado y corona real y perdonar las almas de los Sres. Reyes mis progenitores y la mía cuando de esta vida partiese*).[92]

The king and his advisors had demanding standards, and the few pardons granted each year were by no means easy to obtain. The archives contain evidence of perhaps as many rejections as cases accepted for pardon. One of the losers was thirty-two-year-old coachman Agustín Suárez, found guilty of murdering his brother-in-law, Matheo Hoyos, whom he discovered menacing his sister, twenty-six-year-old Antonia, with a pocketknife. The crime occurred inside the couple's tavern home one night in May 1764. Originally, Agustín was sentenced to death by hanging, and Antonia, deemed an accomplice, was banished for six years. In 1765, however, the king's advisors recommended that Agustín's sentence be commuted to six years of confinement and Antonia's erased altogether. But when Holy Week arrived, the king denied the pardon without offering an explanation (*no viene en ello y se continúa la causa*).[93] The same seems to have occurred in the case against Melchor Martín Alonso, whose crime is mentioned in Chapter 1. The king's final determination is unknown, but as Holy Week 1773 approached, one of the monarch's closest advisors, the Count of Aranda, recommended against the pardon.[94]

Having lost their precious Holy Week opportunity, these and other wrongdoers could still hope to benefit from the general pardons discussed previously. After they had exhausted their appeals, however, they had to withstand the severity of the king's punishment, relying for consolation on the Church and its religious brotherhoods.

ACCOMPANYING AND ALLEVIATING DEATH AND ITS AFTERMATH

When all else failed, criminals could still count on the company of the Catholic Church and religious organizations to ease the moral agony they experienced prior to their execution. Even after executions, ecclesiastical and charitable intervention protected Catholic sensitivities by ensuring appropriate burial and preventing desecration of the corpse or unnecessary exposure of remains or body parts. This is all part of what Pieter Spierenburg and others have termed the sacralization of executions, an important transformation put in place in European societies around the seventeenth century, perhaps earlier.[95]

Since at least the mid-sixteenth century, prisoners sentenced to death had the right to receive communion prior to their execution. Pope Pius V had ordered so in 1568, and King Philip II soon issued a royal decree (*pragmatica*) accepting the Church's mandate. This seems to have been the origin of having chapels (*capillas*) inside of prisons, a practice for which evidence exists as early as 1569.[96] In these areas, those sentenced to death received last rites and spiritual accompaniment during the three days prior to their death. Between 1578 and 1616, a single Jesuit priest, father Pedro de León, spiritually assisted more than 300 people sentenced to death and eventually executed in Spain.[97] More than 100 inmates in Mexico City also received the sacraments and underwent spiritual exercises in 1806 alone.[98] It is fair to presume that this was common practice throughout the centuries all over the empire.

We know for a fact, for instance, that prior to his execution in 1806 for killing his wife, Jose María Jaso spent three days in *capilla*, the special area of Mexico City's royal jail especially designated for inmates sentenced to death. A chaplain, Father Manuel Ramirez, visited and assisted him regularly, allowing him to receive communion. The morning of the execution, the priest heard his religious confession, administered Jaso the last rites, and asked God to protect his soul. He then helped him dress in a special gown. Prior to being blindfolded, Jaso had the opportunity to kneel and pray briefly before a crucifix of the Christ of Mercy (*Cristo de la Misericordia*), brought by knights (*caballeros*) of a local religious brotherhood (*Archicofradia*) to the jail especially for this purpose. A procession then led Jaso to the gallows.

Several members of the religious brotherhood accompanied the procession, and to ease his physical discomfort, lifted up the mat where the prisoner had been placed as a horse (to whose tail the mat was tied) pulled and dragged it along. Monks carrying lanterns also joined. At the scaffold itself, a priest stayed with Jaso during his last moments, remaining at his side until the execution was completed. As the corpse dangled from the rope, the priest presided over some additional prayers (*sermon* or *platica*). Once Jaso was cut down, the charitable knights removed his gown, wrapped his corpse in a sheet (*mortaja*), placed it in a coffin, and accompanied the priest during the Catholic burial service. Several Masses, paid for by a local nobleman, were held over the following days to ask God to have mercy on the soul of the deceased. We know all this thanks to an exceptionally detailed journalistic account of a ritual that must have taken place numerous times in the Spanish Atlantic from the sixteenth to the nineteenth century with minor variations.[99]

In Spain and Colombia, for instance, Agustinian monks, Franciscan friars, and members of various religious brotherhoods accompanied the processions of other spousal murderers to the gallows. Examples include Chapter 4's Maria Vicenta Mendieta and Santiago San Juan, executed in 1798, and Chapter 7's Juliana Zambrano and Francisco Robles, executed in 1773. In these and other cases, priests intervened to spiritually assist the condemned as they approached death.[100] Charitable brotherhoods and priests were also instrumental in securing the burial of spousal murderers. Under law, these criminals were not deserving of a Christian burial. In practice, however, these proscriptions softened over time. Even after *encubamiento,* the corpses of spousal murderers were not consigned permanently to the water but were instead buried properly, with full observance of Catholic rites. Religious intervention continued after death with Catholic Masses such as those held for Jaso and charitable requests for exemption from postmortem burning or lengthy exposure of corpses and remains.

During the period under study, religious brotherhoods petitioned the judicial authorities to refrain from burning the corpses of recently executed criminals or demanded that the display at least be shortened. In the petitioners' opinion, there was no need for fire to consume the corpse entirely.[101] Similarly, Catholic brotherhoods filed requests during the second half of the eighteenth century asking that the limbs and other remains of recently executed criminals be collected as promptly as possible for immediate burial.[102] We shall return to this issue in the following chapter.

CONCLUSION

Over many centuries, magnanimity founded on religious considerations became a significant mechanism for ameliorating the situation of criminals across Spain's territories. Mercy of this kind exemplified an important dimension of hegemonic ecclesiastical and secular power, and was used and appreciated by those who committed serious offenses. Even spousal murderers, despicable criminals in the eyes of both Church and Crown, were eligible for and benefited from ecclesiastical and royal graces.

In the act of granting forgiveness, both religious and secular representatives made their authority tangible and vital. Through religious sanctuary, the Catholic Church made its presence felt in many criminal trials. Defendants who reached sacred ground could count on the Church's protection of their life and physical integrity. According to the data sets for this study, more than one in ten criminals took advantage of religious sanctuary. In all such instances, criminal hearings included the participation of ecclesiastical judges, whose consent was required to transfer asylum seekers from churches and other sacred spaces to royal jails. Ecclesiastical judges could demand assurance that even after their transfer elsewhere, the criminals would be returned to sacred terrain upon request. More important, under no circumstances could those covered by sanctuary be sentenced to death or suffer any bodily injury. Both ecclesiastical and royal legislation backed this prohibition.

Virtually all legal experts writing on criminal procedures, even the most conservative authors, provided guidance for justice officials who handled such cases. Despite frequent disagreement between ecclesiastical and secular power, and among different legal authors, general formulas and routines were developed to address cases where Church asylum became an issue. These long-standing mechanisms were widely known and generally upheld, if only because of the risk of incurring religious sanctions (excommunication and exclusion from Catholic Mass, in particular).

The Spanish king and his justice officials were not only respectful of graces awarded by the Catholic Church for fear of divine retribution but also proactively sought to imitate God's mercy themselves. They expected that such mercy would be a source of gratitude and continuing loyalty on the part of their subjects but, more important, that it would earn them divine protection and forgiveness. Especially during Holy Week, they acted as Christ's proxies in displaying their own generosity of spirit toward criminals. They awarded a select number of pardons to those charged or convicted of homicide, including spousal murder. Like sanctuary, Good Friday pardons acquired formal rituals, along with the intervention of the king's closest legal advisors.

Finally, executions became sacralized very early on. Priests, monks, and members of religious brotherhoods played an active role during the last days of inmates awaiting execution. They closely accompanied the condemned, prayed for their souls, and assisted in their burial. They also intervened to stop the burning of corpses and to make sure that neither corpses nor body parts remained on display and unburied for too long.

The following chapter presents the third and final case study, late colonial New Granada. Like previous portions of this book, this section confirms the fact that, contrary to stereotypes, the lives of women were not circumscribed to the household and their behavior was far from passive. In examining the social history of several dozen murders, this discussion reveals that women's active public life could bring them into intense conflicts with their husbands, sometimes culminating in murder.

CHAPTER SIX

Dangerous Women

Gender, Ethnicity, and "Domestic" Disputes in New Granada

One night in late December 1802, a young, mixed-race woman by the name of Dominga Josefa Espitia was enjoying herself at a raucous *bunde* party in the company of her husband, Matías Ostia.[1] Her lover, thirty-two-year-old miner Nicolás A. Rua, also attended the party, held at a rural home near one of several rivers in the Mojana area of northern Colombia. Dominga and Nicolás had been having an affair for about four months.[2] At some point in the evening, for reasons that are not apparent but may have involved the woman's flirtation with Nicolás, Matías dragged his wife out of the celebration. Noticing this, and fearing for her safety, Nicolás followed the couple at a distance. Dominga later testified that after walking through a nearby banana plantation, her husband grabbed her by the shirt and, with no explanation (*sin más antecedente ni pleito*), began hitting her on the head with a machete. She received three blows, including one over the right eyebrow, and fell to the ground as a result. Nicolás then jumped in and attacked Matías with another machete, severing both of his arms (*bajado los brazos de un machetazo*).

Dominga and her lover differed in their accounts as to what happened next. She claimed that Nicolás continued to hit her husband with the machete, killing him in the process. Nicolás, in turn, testified that he stepped back after striking the first blows and that it was Dominga who, with her husband's own machete, ended his life. In any case, they worked together to drag Matías's corpse to the edge of the plantation, and while Dominga sat and waited, Nicolás dug a grave, in which they buried him. According to Dominga, they agreed that she would return to the party to have her wounds treated and would claim that her husband had fled after attacking her. Nicolás would wait for her in the plantation. However, Nicolás said that he was the one who returned to the party and that Dominga waited for him near a farm, where he later rejoined her. Captured the day after the killing, the pair denied having planned or intended to commit the murder, although they admitted that they had talked on occasion about the possibility of running away together. Dominga also claimed that her husband had mistreated her (*le daba mala vida*), and that is why she found a lover.

After a three-year trial, the Bogotá Audiencia sentenced Nicolás to ten years of hard labor in Cartagena and the confiscation of one-half of his possessions. Apart from a death sentence or life in prison, applied in all but a few cases, this typically was the harshest possible punishment. Dominga was sentenced to work without a salary for six years in "pious public works" (*obras pías*) in Cartagena. She was ordered to dress at all times in a dark gown made of coarse cotton to symbolize the gravity of her crime.[3] This was not the harshest possible punishment, but it was not mild either and carried with it a mark of infamy.

As with this case, many of the crimes detailed in this chapter, set this time in late colonial New Granada (Colombia), show women participating in public activities and celebrations, engaging in extramarital relations, and clashing with their spouses over this behavior. This finding confirms abundant historical research over the past two decades showing that, far from being secluded in their homes, women in colonial Spanish America had active lives in the streets, markets, temples, and other places where they interacted with a variety of people. This afforded them the opportunity for encounters, romantic and otherwise, that sometimes led to intense disputes and fatal confrontations with their spouses.

These disputes could hardly be characterized as strictly "domestic" or pertaining to the "household." In fact, many fights and murders involving spouses were precisely over extra-domestic engagements, suggesting that we may need to reconsider the nature of patriarchy. In late colonial New Granada, at least, men could hardly claim to monopolize control of their wives' destinies, daily routines, labor, and sexuality, and attempts on their part to do so did not go unchallenged. Before we address these issues, however, some background is needed about this region's institutional, economic, and social setting.

COLONIAL NEW GRANADA: THE INSTITUTIONAL, ECONOMIC, AND SOCIAL SETTING

Given the absence of powerful Indian empires like the Aztec or the Inca, New Granada did not witness epic conquests and remained a marginal colonial outpost of the Spanish monarchy for many decades. Nevertheless, in the century after the conquest of Mexico and Peru, many of New Granada's native communities experienced dramatic demographic decline because of violence, overwork, and disease. The economy also decayed. Despite the development of a mining rush in several regions during the sixteenth century, gold mining faltered in the seventeenth century, and the economic mainstay became agriculture. A rudimentary textile- and hat-manufacturing sector also emerged, especially in central regions such as Tunja and the northeastern provinces of San Gil and Socorro. Trade, both legal and illegal, seems to have been important as well, but information about this activity is limited.

The government and bureaucracy also remained weak. Unlike the viceroyalties of New Spain and Peru, established shortly after the Spanish conquest of the Aztec and Inca empires in the 1520s and 1540s, respectively, one of the highest authorities in New Granada for centuries was the high court (*audiencia*). Founded in the mid-1500s, its seat was in Bogotá, from where it oversaw legal and judicial matters and the region's civil government. New Granada did not become a viceroyalty until the eighteenth century. Peru was the only viceroyalty in South America up to that time. It extended from present-day Panama all the way to Argentina, and by the eighteenth century it had become increasingly difficult to administer. The vastness of its territory; the great distance from the capital, Lima, to northern South America, including the major port of Cartagena de Indias; and frequent clashes between the local authorities in Santa Fé de Bogotá and their counterparts in Quito and Panama convinced the Crown to create a new viceroyalty to help with administrative matters in the area.

Revenue collection, a major concern for the financially embattled Spanish Empire, also benefited from tighter supervision and policing of economic activities in some portions of the Andean colony, such as the northwestern gold-mining provinces of Antioquia and Mariquita, and the vast agricultural and livestock-raising estates of Bogotá, Tunja, and Popayán. In addition to financial concerns, military considerations, particularly the heightened colonial rivalry between European powers in the Caribbean, also dictated the convenience of keeping a closer watch on affairs in strategic places such as Cartagena de Indias and Portobelo, the port of entry into Panama and the most expedient gateway to Spanish South America. In the 1730s, therefore, King Phillip V, the first Bourbon monarch to rule Spain (1700–1746), sanctioned the permanent establishment of the new Viceroyalty of New Granada by carving out the northernmost territories of the Viceroyalty of Peru, including present-day Colombia, Panama, Ecuador, and parts of Venezuela.

Like Bogotá, Panama and Quito had each had an *audiencia* since the sixteenth century. The 1730s reform eliminated the Panama *audiencia,* however. The other two remained in place to deal with civil and criminal matters and government affairs, and the entire region encompassing the three territories was officially upgraded to the superior legal status of viceroyalty. Northern South America thus became a sort of separate semi-kingdom comparable, at least formally, to New Spain and trimmed-down Peru.

The monarchy implemented other economic and military reforms in New Granada during the 1770s and 1780s: stricter tax collection, an expanded army with improved leadership and organization, a system of disciplined militia, and new territorial changes.[4] Unlike colonial Mexico and Peru, however, New Granada was spared an additional wave of administrative reforms later in the century: the introduction of *intendencias,* a new system devised by another Spanish Bourbon, Charles III (1759–1788), to ensure even closer financial and military supervision at the provincial level. Tax riots in the early 1780s, led by whites and joined by large numbers of mestizos, undoubtedly contributed to delay this innovation in colonial Colombia. As it turned out, *intendencias* would never materialize in the portion of the Spanish Empire represented by New Granada.[5]

Despite differences in its administrative configuration and institutional history, colonial Colombia was much like colonial Mexico in other respects, especially the difficulty of its terrain and the predominance of rural life. The harshness of the territory resulted mostly from the fact that it was traversed by three steep mountain ranges (*cordilleras*) running north to south. These mountains, while contributing to create a diverse climate and rich ecosystem, made communications and transportation a challenge. New Granada had even fewer roads than Mexico, and those that did exist were mostly no more than hard paths worn down by mule hooves. Trips between towns meant long journeys by foot or arduous treks on mule or horseback along narrow mountain trails that were almost impassable during the prolonged rainy season. The teams of peons (*cargueros*) carrying bulky or heavy objects that could not be loaded on mules faced an even greater challenge.

The Magdalena River, running in a northerly direction, connected a good portion of the tropical territory, although only parts of it were navigable. Given the lack of bridges, hanging seat-like structures (*taravitas*), manually operated by pulling ropes, were in place to assist travelers across the river, especially at high points above passes. Not only was this system somewhat frightening; it was also cumbersome, requiring the unloading, changing, and reloading of mules from pass to pass.

The aboveground riverine passes also required the transfer of people and merchandise into canoes or pole boats operated by rowers (*bogas*), who could be unreliable and unruly. The tropical climate was a further challenge. Temperatures in the tropics vary not according to the season but with altitude. Colombia's hot lowlands were disease-ridden, and most people thus avoided them, preferring to settle in the cooler highlands.

All of these geographical and demographic features, combined with a lack of engineering know-how and absence of sufficient investment in the little transportation infrastructure there, contributed to divide the territory into relatively disjointed subregions. These were made up of clusters of dispersed peasant settlements (*caserios*), little parishes (*parroquias*), midsize towns or villages (*villas*), and small and "big" cities (*ciudades*). These clusters led to the development of distinct and more or less self-contained regional economies, most of which were primarily devoted to agriculture and livestock on extensive haciendas, communally owned lands (*resguardos*) belonging to Indians, and a large number of small peasant plots.

Like Mexico's, the eighteenth-century economy of New Granada relied primarily on agriculture and stock raising, but it presented some distinct features. For instance, neither corn nor chili peppers had the overwhelming economic and social significance that they did in Mexico. There were no *maguey* fields in the northern Andes, and so no *pulque*. Instead, potato fields and potato-based foodstuffs, negligible in Mexico, were central elements of the diet and economy in colonial Colombia. More important, New Granada's economy overall was not only fragmented but also much less dynamic than the economy of colonial Mexico. Even though Mexico was by no means an industrially developed economy, industrial establishments were even fewer and smaller in colonial Colombia, limited to small craft or cottage industries in some central and northern areas mostly dedicated to producing coarse cotton cloth (*lienzos ordinarios* and *lienzos caseros*) spun or woven by hand.

Unlike Mexico and central Peru, where mining had long been a key means of enrichment for the white elites and a critical source of revenue for the Spanish Empire and the colonial state, New Granada had only recently turned again to mining, and the most-affluent deposits were not large silver veins but shallow gold mines. Nevertheless, besides emeralds, by the late colonial period the only significant export coming out of the territory was gold, except for short-lived exports of small quantities of quinine (*quina*), cotton, and dyewood. Most other agrarian goods (rice, tobacco, wheat, sugar cane, cacao, plantains, fruits, and vegetables), as well as livestock and related products, wool in particular, were for local consumption, frequently within the dispersed and isolated regional economic pockets where they originated. A few products circulated between regions. For instance, gold-mining Antioquia, in the northwest, received livestock and textiles from the southern and northern parts of the viceroyalty. Cotton from Socorro and Indian-woven woolens sold everywhere, along with wheat from Bogotá and Tunja, and cacao from the southern region of Neiva and northwestern Cúcuta. However, even this modest "national" market weakened and contracted over the course of the eighteenth century because of external pressures—in particular, increased imports of British flour and cloth. The size of the internal market was in any case limited, as the population of the entire viceroyalty was just around one million people—less than one-quarter than that of colonial Mexico and less than one-tenth than that of Spain.

New Granada's major urban centers paled in comparison to Madrid or Mexico City and even smaller Mexican cities such as Puebla or Guanajuato. The largest and most important city in the viceroyalty, Santafé de Bogotá, had less than 20,000 inhabitants in 1778 and had barely reached 25,000 by 1810, less than one-seventh the population of Madrid and not even one-sixth the size of Mexico City. Most other "big" cities did not even reach the 15,000-person mark in the late eighteenth century, making them much smaller than any of the top five urban centers of colonial Mexico.[6]

In another major demographic contrast to colonial Mexico, ethnic miscegenation was extensive in Colombia. The largest sector of the population, almost one-half, was not Indian but rather mixed-race—*zambos*, mulattoes, and, especially, mestizos.[7] Second in number were white Spaniards and Creoles, who represented about a quarter of the viceroyalty's population. Indians came in third, and last in numerical importance were black slaves (see Table 6.1). These demographics gave rise to major economic contrasts between the two regions regarding, for instance, access to a labor force or the collection of Indian tribute. It should not be surprising, then, that the nature and treatment of marital conflicts in New Granada also differed significantly from the predominantly Indian disputes of colonial Mexico.

Before going on to analyze spousal conflicts in more detail, we must first underline some additional dominant features of New Granada's late colonial society. Like the rest of Spanish America, New Granada was a deeply hierarchical society in which the long-standing caste system imposed by Spain tended to segregate Indians from whites, blacks from Indians, and these from other racial groups. This regime, the preconquest location of Indian communities, and the specific destinations of blacks coming through the slave market of Cartagena de Indias created racially diverse pockets of population throughout the viceroyalty. The

TABLE 6.1. *Comparative ethnic distribution of population in late colonial Mexico and Colombia*

	Ethnic group as a percentage of total population	
Ethnicity	Colombia, 1778–1781	Mexico, 1814
Mestizos, Mulattoes, *Zambos*	49.2[a]	25.4[a]
Whites	25.3	22.6
Indians	18.8	51.7
Blacks	6.2[b]	—

SOURCES: "Padrón general del Virreinato del Nuevo Reino de Granada, 1778–1781," in José Manuel Pérez Ayala, *Antonio Caballero y Góngora;* "Memoria sobre la población de la Nueva España, México, 1814," cited by Humboldt, *Ensayo político sobre el reino de la Nueva España,* 2: 287.

[a]Includes also free blacks.

[b]Refers only to black slaves.

descendants of the Muiscas—a community from the most significant Indian culture of New Granada, the Chibcha—clustered in the viceroyalty's central plains, especially the areas neighboring Bogotá and Tunja. Here they subsisted modestly on potatoes and corn, using as their main intoxicant fermented corn beer called *chicha*. Other native peoples, the Caribs, Arawaks, and Taironas, resided in the far north near the Caribbean, as did the Wayuu communities that occupied the northernmost portion of the territory, the dry lands of the Guajira peninsula. The southern highlands around Popayán also contained a more or less dense Indian population, the Paez and Guambiano peoples. Even farther to the south, near the border with Ecuador, were the Pastos. Numerous other cultures, among them the Emberas, Ingas, Kankuamos, Pijaos, Zenues, and Wiwas, were scattered throughout the highlands and in lowland areas.

Black slaves were plentiful in Antioquia and Popayán, where they had been brought to mine placer deposits of gold in rivers, as well as in the Pacific lowlands (Buenaventura and Chocó) and other larger deposits in Mariquita, northwest of Bogotá. They also worked on sugarcane haciendas along the Caribbean coastal plains, around Cartagena and neighboring Santa Marta. Smaller numbers of African-descended slaves were scattered throughout the entire territory mostly as domestic servants, wet nurses, craftsmen, porters, rowers (*bogas*), and peons on haciendas and in sugar mills. White Europeans and Creoles were dominant in all urban centers. The most-prestigious white and Creole families, especially in larger cities such as Cartagena, Bogotá, Tunja, Medellín, Antioquia City, and Popayán, were made up of landowners, merchants, priests, lawyers, military officers, public officials, and mine owners. Excluded from higher education, female members of the elite had to choose, at least in theory, between the convent and the household. It was not possible for them to join the professions, the bureaucracy, or the army. To be sure, some of them, especially widows, ran farms and businesses. Those further down the social ladder were also active in street and market vending, crafts, textile production, and some service activities (laundering other people's clothes and serving as wet nurses and domestic servants).

This sketch of a society spatially and culturally divided along neat economic and racial lines is misleading, however. As noted above, miscegenation was more extensive here than perhaps anywhere else in the Americas. Large numbers of mulattoes and mestizos were everywhere, negotiating their coexistence with wealthy and poor whites alike and, at times, mixing still further with whites, Indians, and, to a lesser extent, blacks. The sheer force of mestizo numbers alone turned New Granada into a more fluid society. The growing mestizo population was not just a demographic and social reality but also an important economic and cultural presence. Some of its members had gained considerable wealth over the years, and mestizos in general had a reputation for being particularly assertive and unruly. The behavior of some mestizo women, who, unlike Mexican Indian women, appear to have committed a fair number of spousal killings, would seem to confirm this stereotype.

Although they varied according to race, social status, and geographical location, average households in key urban centers such as Tunja, Cartagena, Medellín, and Cali were small nuclear families, two-thirds of them with five members or less. Only a minority (5 to 30 percent) of homes housed groups of as many as ten people. These included the few individual nuclear families with more children than the average three found in most homes; extended households made up of a variety of relatives, including grandparents, aunts and uncles, cousins and in-laws; and, finally, houses inhabited by more than one family unit, normally a single principal family and one or more unrelated units crowded into rental rooms (*gente de los cuartos*).

Most of New Granada's poor, counting those in urban centers, lived in adobe houses (*bohios* or *ranchos*) with thatched roofs, dirt floors, a single room, a kitchen area usually located toward the home's backyard, and a small garden patch. Only some black slaves or Indian servants resided in their masters' more ample homes, in humble quarters, of course. They helped their white or mestizo masters with domestic tasks or ran errands at commercial establishments such as general stores (*tiendas*), dry goods stores (*pulperias*), bakeries, or mills (*molinos*).

Like Mexico's poor, colonial Colombia's lower classes lacked material comforts. Most of them owned no more than a hammock or wooden bed (*cuja* or *barbacoa*) without a mattress or pillows, a couple of chairs, a rustic table, and a Catholic cross. They would also have had a few clay pots, jars, and plates; gourds to serve liquids; wooden spoons; and maybe one kitchen knife. The few garments available to the common people were one or two dresses or pairs of pants and a shirt, all made of coarse cotton. Some peasants wore leather or henequen sandals (*alpargatas*), but most walked barefoot. In the cooler highlands, poncho-like cloaks called *ruanas* made of thick wool were also common, and in many places people wore straw hats, woolen ones being more expensive or simply unavailable.

Daily routines involved praying in the morning (*primera oración*) and at night (*oración de la tarde*), starting and tending fires, cooking and eating at least three daily meals (*desayuno*, *comida,* and *cena*), and working in the fields or at home. Such labor was common not only for women in charge of running households, preparing meals, and raising children, but also for most artisans, male and female alike. Hat makers (*sombrereros*), pot makers (*alfareros*), shoe makers (*zapateros*), weavers (*tejedores*), carpenters, and others tended to have their workshops in corners of their own little homes, where they worked assisted by wives, children, or other relatives. To supplement their meager income, a few households also retailed alcoholic drinks, in particular corn beer (*chicha*) or sugarcane-based *aguardiente*. Church attendance and trips to market, activities that sometimes implied long journeys, were common on weekends. As in colonial Mexico, processions and festivals, parties (*fandangos* and *bundes*), bullfights, and cockfights were favorite pastimes, as was visiting taverns (*chicherias*).[8] Inevitably, some of these routine activities and entertainments became a source of tensions, verbal disputes, and even physical clashes between spouses, as in the case opening this chapter.

SPOUSAL CONFLICTS AND PROLONGED BATTERING

Couples in New Granada, like their counterparts in colonial Mexico and elsewhere, engaged in frequent disputes. Numerous couples became estranged as a result of such tensions, including cases in which men ran off with lovers, went on long business trips and established permanent residence elsewhere, were banished from their hometowns, or were jailed for criminal behavior. Census data from the late colonial period make it clear that separations, whether de facto or legally authorized, were a common phenomenon.[9]

Spousal battery was one of the main reasons for breaking up a marriage or filing for divorce.[10] In 1801, for instance, forty-year-old farmer

José Ignacio Vargas, a habitual drunkard, faced accusations of having sexually abused several local women, including his young stepdaughter, in the parish of Nunchia, near the city of San José de Pore in eastern Colombia. He came before the local judicial authorities for beating and trying to murder his wife, María Gucio, by pushing her against some rocks. This last incident led to the confiscation of several of his livestock and a protracted investigation intended to separate the couple.[11]

In the Socorro region in northwestern New Granada, twenty-eight-year-old tailor Laurián Regueros seems to have abused his wife, Rosalía Vásquez, verbally and physically throughout their conflictive marriage. One day in 1808 or 1809, he hit her repeatedly with a club, hurled a big rock at her chest, and tried to make her drink poisoned liquor. On other occasions he clubbed, punched, and kicked her badly enough to send her to bed for three weeks, and burned one of her arms while she was ironing clothes to earn the household some extra income. She kept on forgiving him, at least in part because he knelt and swore before a crucifix that he would never hurt her again. Finally, in 1822 he stabbed her twice in the back, claiming that she had been unfaithful—a common justification for husbands in such incidents. This time she decided that separation was the only alternative.[12]

Because of cultural, religious, and institutional factors similar to those observed in Mexico (patriarchal mentality; advice and intervention from family members, the clergy, or legal authorities; legal indifference), some marriages endured despite frequent fights and extreme abuse. In another of many cases available in the historical archives, Pedro José Rodríguez, a white, twenty-seven-year-old blacksmith, regularly battered his wife, María Ignacia Cristancho, on one occasion cracking her skull and bruising her face. In 1806 he even stabbed his mother-in-law with a knife when she tried to keep him from violently dragging María Ignacia out of the house. At his trial, however, María Ignacia and her family withdrew the accusation and asked that he be released from jail, declaring that they had forgiven him so that the couple could peacefully resume the "sacrament of marriage."[13]

The same occurred in the criminal case against Luciano Rivera, a forty-year-old farmer accused by his wife, Juana Ramírez, of trying to kill her one night in February 1806. Accusing her of an extramarital affair, Luciano undressed her, tied her hands, and hanged her from the ceiling. While she was dangling, he beat her repeatedly with a sword, bruising her entire body. After he fell asleep, one of her children helped Juana free herself, and she ran to the local priest for help. She was placed on "deposit" at a local home to protect her from any additional abuse, but Luciano hunted her down and took her to another city. When he was eventually jailed in the little town of Villeta, northwest of Bogotá, Juana complained that she had wanted the priest only to admonish him to treat her better and reunite them "in peace so that each could go on taking care of their duties." She claimed to have left the safe house voluntarily and insisted that she did not want to be separated from her husband, requesting his immediate release from jail.[14]

Women like Rosalía, María Ignacia, and Juana were probably afraid to be left alone, for in many instances they and their children depended upon their husbands for economic support, protection against other men, and a place to live. They were also under pressure from their relatives and religious authorities to preserve family unions. In many other cases, the women were simply afraid of the possible physical or social consequences of denouncing their spouses, took pity on their "poor" husbands, or, as in the case of Rosalia, trusted their promises to cease any further abuse. This naiveté sometimes came at a high price. However, there were cases in which women struck first, and not always in self-defense. Battery was but one in a complex set of circumstances preceding the murder of one's spouse.

STORIES OF SPOUSAL MURDER

As the following examples illustrate, at least a portion of the spousal murders committed in late colonial Colombia involved chronically abused women who killed their victims in self-defense.[15] Several of them were white or mixed-race (mestizo or mulatto) and had a more or less active public life related to their trades as artisans or retailers. However, the relative frequency with which women in late colonial Colombia killed their husbands reflects not only desperation on the part of long-abused wives but also verbal disputes over matters of honor or alleged female disobedience. More important is the saliency of spousal tensions of other types, in particular those resulting from active female involvement in extramarital affairs and other extra-domestic or public activities against their husbands' wishes. Some of these women received help from lovers or paid a third person to get rid of their husbands. The examples also involve the consumption of alcohol by both parties. Reference in several of the cases to the harsh nature of the punishment imposed also serves as a striking contrast with the case of Mexico.

María Eugenia Quintero, a fifty-year-old mestizo weaver from the eastern region of Socorro, stabbed her husband, Salvador Rugeles, to death one afternoon in June 1781. María Eugenia was allegedly busy preparing lunch and had a knife ready to cut some plantains and cassava but instead turned it against her husband—in self-defense, she claimed. Salvador had a bad temper and had frequently mistreated her during their marriage. On the fatal afternoon, Salvador was resting; he became angry and tried to hit María Eugenia when she disturbed him by retrieving the vegetables from under the bed, where they were stored. After her crime, the woman fled to a nearby town, but constables promptly apprehended her. The authorities seem to have doubted her claim of self-defense and sentenced her to a harsh ten-year term in the local jail. Of course, it could be true that, rather than responding to a specific aggression, María Eugenia was tired of her husband's general abuse and plotted to kill him while he was sleeping, a homicide considered particularly heinous because of the victim's inability to defend himself.[16]

A woman's unwillingness to put up with any sign of abuse, even bad jokes, is evident in other cases. In the parish of Tenza, in central Colombia, thirty-year-old laundress and corn beer (*chicha*) retailer Albina Arias killed her husband, Agustín de Angarita, by hitting him in the stomach with a *machete* handle, causing him to fall and injure his head. Although several witnesses declared that the couple frequently argued and fought, the tragic results of their last altercation seem to have owed more to drinking and accidental circumstances that were, in any case, clearly linked to the social exchanges that Albina enjoyed with her customers. The crime occurred on a Friday night in May 1790 at their home in the presence of relatives visiting for a drink and a chat. The couple, who had two young sons, had been drinking the *chicha* they sold to supplement the family's income. They had an argument when Agustín implied, maybe in jest or because he was drunk, that most of their customers came to the house not just for the *chicha* but also to sleep with his wife, who that night would have to sleep with him instead. Albina was insulted and retaliated by striking him. After he died, her sister and brother-in-law and a would-be customer dragged the corpse away from the house in the middle of the night and suspended it from a tree near the local church, hoping that the death would be considered a suicide. One of the participants recounted the story to a relative, who denounced the crime to the authorities. Unfortunately, the case is incomplete, and we do not know much about the punishment that the hot-tempered laundress received.[17]

Resistance to a husband's unwelcome orders or to his sexual escapades was another typical trigger. In Medellin one night in July 1800, weaver and pot maker Cecilia Heredia, a forty-year-old mulatto, stabbed her husband, Ignacio Torres, four times, killing him. The couple had argued after Ignacio urged his wife to evict an elderly woman she was sheltering. This was only one issue causing friction in the household. The couple also argued often about Ignacio's extramarital affairs, and on at least one occasion Cecilia had defended herself with a knife. On the night of the crime, when Ignacio knocked Cecilia to the floor, she grabbed his *ruana* (poncho) and once more pulled a knife from a leather bag. This time, however, she did not just threaten him but actually stabbed him to death. She then gathered together a few belongings and ran away. Once captured, she pled self-defense. Although spared a death sentence, she received a ten-year jail term, quite a harsh punishment. Like other female inmates, she was required to perform domestic chores in the prison kitchen and laundry.[18]

Finally, female defiance with drinking as a catalyst is evident in the case of another weaver, thirty-eight-year-old María Dolores García, probably white or mestizo. She stabbed her elderly husband, seventy-year-old Juan José Rueda, on a Sunday night in August 1802 at their home in San Gil, in northeastern Colombia. Husband and wife were drunk on *chicha,* and they argued when Juan José ordered María Dolores not to go into a certain room of the house. She insisted defiantly that she would go where she pleased, and her husband responded by beating her with a club that they kept to scare the pigs away. Both because she was drunk and allegedly acted in self-defense, María Dolores did not receive a death sentence, nor was she punished as harshly as the women in the rest of the stories just narrated: Her original sentence of six years of labor in either the local *carcel de divorcio* or the hospital was reduced to four years upon appeal.[19] Like the other sentences, however, it was far from lenient. Given the life expectancy and sanitary conditions of the time, some of them might have been tantamount to a life sentence. In fact, they contrast sharply with the light punishment that, as described earlier, male Mexican Indians who committed similar crimes received. It is hard not to attribute this contrast to at least some degree of gender bias. Following is a detailed sociological analysis of the larger New Granada case set to which all these examples belong.

HOMICIDES: TIME, PLACE, AND CIRCUMSTANCE

The available records are irregular, and, as is usual with historical evidence, it is fair to presume them incomplete. Judging by the uneven distribution of these cases by decade (see Table 6.2), for instance, it is fair to assume that many other incidents may be missing from the case set. Information is more abundant for the last years of the period because of undetermined factors that probably involved better reporting or record keeping at that time.[20]

TABLE 6.2. *Spousal homicides in New Granada, 1754–1812, by decade*

Years	Number	Percentage
1750–1759	4	7.4
1760–1769	5	9.2
1770–1779	3	5.5
1780–1789	5	9.2
1790–1799	12	22.2
1800–1809	23	42.5
1810–1812	2	3.7
Total	54	

SOURCES: AGN, Colombia, Colonia, Juicios Criminales; Sosa Abella, *Labradores, tejedores y ladrones*, 60, 146–147; Patiño, *Criminalidad, ley penal y estructura social en la provincia de Antioquia*, 376, 516; Gloria Luna Rivillas, "Documentos para el estudio de la criminalidad sexual en la provincia y gobernación de Antioquia (Siglos 17 y 18)" (history thesis, Universidad Nacional de Colombia, Medellín, 1988, 554–564).

In absolute terms, the case set of murders at hand comprises a limited number of incidents. Based on the trend in the years 1800–1809, however, the decade with the greatest number of incidents, and assuming for the sake of argument that at least a similar number of spousal murders could have occurred in each of the other decades under study, the case set still easily represents around one-third (33.5 percent) of spousal murders in the viceroyalty at the time. It therefore offers an approximation of reality and a legitimate starting point for a discussion of general features of this form of criminality in late colonial New Granada. With some qualifications, the evidence may even be representative of patterns in other regions of colonial Spanish America.

Most of the extant cases occurred in the rural areas of Santa Fé/Mariquita and Tunja/Pamplona, the viceroyalty's central and northeastern provinces and two of its most densely populated regions (see Table 6.3).[21] Tunja/Pamplona alone accounted for 48.1 percent of total crimes, a disproportionately high figure relative to these regions' share of New Granada's population (34.1 percent) and total crime (32.5 percent).[22] Surprisingly few cases (just three!) are reported in the Cartagena area, in northwestern New Granada. Cartagena was the second-most-densely populated province and the viceroyalty's main port, and it accounted for 8.6 percent of all crimes in the viceroyalty. There are no records at all of cases from important and relatively densely populated areas such as the gold-mining region of Popayán, in southern New Granada, and the prosperous southern valley of the Cauca River.[23] Information on circumstances is equally limited.

TABLE 6.3. *Spousal homicides in New Granada, 1756–1812, by region*

Province	Number	Percentage of total spousal murders	Percentage of total New Granada population[a]
Antioquia	5	9.2	5.8
Cartagena	3	5.5	14.9
Neiva	1	1.8	3.3
Los Llanos	4	7.4	2.6
Santa Fe/Mariquita	12	22.2	18
Tunja/Pamplona	26	48.1	34.1
Other	3	5.5	—
Total	54		

SOURCES: AGN, Colombia, Colonia, Juicios Criminales, Indios y Mestizos, Negros y Esclavos; Sosa Abella, *Labradores, tejedores y ladrones,* 60, 146–147; McFarlane, *Colombia Before Independence,* 353–363; Patiño, *Criminalidad, ley penal y estructura social en la provincia de Antioquia,* 376, 516; Luna Rivillas, "Documentos para el estudio de la criminalidad sexual en la provincia y gobernación de Antioquia," 554–564.

[a]Data from 1778–1780 census.

Unlike colonial Mexico, where a majority of spousal homicides seem to have occurred randomly throughout the day, with a few more incidents at night, Table 4.8 (see Chapter 4) indicates that, similar to Spain, in colonial Colombia most such crimes, more than two-thirds, occurred at night. Similarly, distribution by day of the week was relatively arbitrary in colonial Mexico and Spain, whereas in colonial Colombia crimes appear to have occurred mostly from Friday to Sunday (see Table 4.9). As in the previous case, however, the lack of sufficient information about a fair number of cases makes it impossible to draw any firm conclusions about the reasons why or whether or not these patterns are even reliable.

More data are available about the months during which spousal murders occurred. In colonial Colombia and in Spain, a majority (50.3 percent and 47.1 percent) occurred from June to August and June to September, respectively, whereas in Mexico there was no clear trend, except for the seemingly random fact that a slightly larger number occurred in October, as shown in Table 4.10. These circumstances are yet to be explained but could be linked to stress related to the end of the agrarian cycle.

As in Mexico and Spain, an overwhelming majority of spousal homicides in colonial Colombia occurred within the community—in particular, at the couple's home, as Table 6.4 suggests. Indeed, fewer of these crimes occurred outside of the community in Colombia than in Mexico. This may be a random circumstance or perhaps was indicative that a much smaller society with fewer urban centers, as Colombia was, offered less incentives and opportunities for couples to travel long distances from their homes. Criminal methods and weapons differed only slightly.

TABLE 6.4. *Location of spousal homicides in Colombia and Mexico, 1740s–1820s*

	Colonial Colombia		Colonial Mexico	
	Number	Percentage	Number	Percentage
Within the community				
At couple's home	31	72.1	27	52.9
At a friend's or neighbor's home	1	2.3	3	5.9
In the street	2	4.6	3	5.9
On a road	1	2.3	4	7.8
By a river, creek, or ditch	2	4.6	4	7.8
In a forest	2	4.6	2	3.9
At patron's or master's hacienda	1	2.3	—	—
In a field	1	2.3	—	—
Unknown location	1	2.3	—	—
Total	**42**	**97.4**	**43**	**84.2**
Outside the community				
On a road	—	—	3	5.9
In a forest	1	2.3	4	7.8
Unknown location	—	—	1	2.0
Total	**1**	**2.3**	8	**15.7**
Undetermined	10	18.5	34	39

SOURCES: AGN, Colombia, Colonia, Juicios Criminales; Sosa Abella, *Labradores, tejedores y ladrones*, 60, 146–147; Patiño, *Criminalidad, ley penal y estructura social en la provincia de Antioquia*, 376, 516; Luna Rivillas, "Documentos para el estudio de la criminalidad sexual en la provincia y gobernación de Antioquia (Siglos 17 y 18)" (history thesis, Universidad Nacional de Colombia, Medellín, 1988), 554–564; AGN, Mexico City, Acordada, Californias, Criminales, General de Parte, Presidios y Cárceles, and Provincias Internas; AJO; AANG, Guadalajara, Casos Criminales; AJP; Archivo Provincial de Zacatecas; Municipal Archive of Veracruz; Taylor, *Drinking, Homicide, and Rebellion*, 77, 98.

The killers, as Table 6.5 illustrates, resorted to all types of methods and weapons, particularly stabbings, beatings, and machetes. Machetes and knives were women's weapons of choice, whereas men used these as well as their fists and feet. Aggressors used clubs and rocks only on occasion. In a few instances, men engaged in exceedingly cruel behavior, such as throwing burning coal on the victim's face or, in one case, damaging the victim's internal reproductive organs with their bare hands.[24] Poison, a subtle and handy method, seems to have been used much less often than in colonial Mexico (5.9 percent), appearing in just one of the cases under consideration (2.4 percent), as also happened in Spain (Table 4.12). It was probably employed in a few other instances that went unrecorded; deaths that showed strong evidence of violence were more likely to be investigated, but murder by poison may have gone undetected. This may also have occurred in some cases of drowning.[25]

Spousal murderers were for the most part long-term residents of the communities where they committed their crimes. The available data suggest relatively little long-distance internal migration; a good portion of

TABLE 6.5. *Spousal homicides in New Granada, 1750–1812, by method/weapon*

Methods/weapons	Number	Percentage
Stabbings	16	39
Fists, kicking	8	19.5
Machetes	5	12.1
Hanging	3[a]	7.3
Clubs	4	9.7
Rocks	3	7.3
Poison	1	2.4
Other	1[b]	2.4
Undetermined	13	24
Total	54	

SOURCES: AGN, Colombia, Colonia, Juicios Criminales; Sosa Abella, *Labradores, tejedores y ladrones*, 60, 146–147; Patiño, *Criminalidad, ley penal y estructura social en la provincia de Antioquia*, 376; Luna Rivillas, "Documentos para el estudio de la criminalidad sexual en la provincia y gobernación de Antioquia," 554–564.

[a]At least in one instance combined with punches.

[b]Throwing burning coal on victim's face.

the defendants whose place of birth is listed in the records seem to have been natives of the places where the crimes occurred, or else they had been born in nearby villages.[26] So were many of the witnesses interviewed.

In terms of occupation, as in a majority of the cases of Spain and Mexico, New Granada's spousal murderers were modest manual workers from all walks of life (see Table 6.6). The defendants included hat makers, pot makers, tailors, journeymen, farmers, miners, weavers, laundresses, cooks, *bogas* (boat rowers), *trasquiladores* (shearers), retailers, and the unemployed. Almost one-third of those whose occupation is known were farmers and day laborers, a finding consistent with the overall agrarian character of New Granada's economy, which featured a combination—depending upon the region—of large landholdings, small farms, and subsistence peasant agriculture.[27]

An especially large number of female spousal murderers were weavers (almost one-third of total female offenders). Most of them came from white or mestizo communities in the central and northeastern regions of Tunja, Socorro, and San Gil, centers for weaving cotton and woolen cloth. These communities led revolts against the Bourbon tax reforms in 1780–1781, a tumultuous period in New Granada's history. Humble Socorro women such as Manuela Beltran, who seems to have been from a petty merchant and cigar-making family, instigated the crowd with cries of "long live the king and death to bad government." Another remarkable woman from this region, Antonia Santos Plata, was an active member of

TABLE 6.6. *Spousal homicides in New Granada, 1750–1812, by defendant's occupation*

Occupation	Number	Percentage
Farmer	9[a]	25
Weaver	8[b]	22.2
Day laborer	3[b]	8.3
Housewife	3	8.3
Shoemaker	2	5.5
Chicha retailer	1[b]	2.7
Laundress	1	2.7
Carpenter (slave)	1	2.7
Hat maker	1[b]	2.7
Miner	1	2.7
Pot maker	1[a]	2.7
Salt retailer	1	2.7
Boat rower	1	2.7
Tailor	1	2.7
Dressmaker	1	2.7
Shearer	1[b]	2.7
Undetermined	20	35.7
Total	**56**[c]	

SOURCES: AGN, Colombia, Colonia, Criminales; Sosa Abella, *Labradores, tejedores y ladrones*, 60, 146–147; Patiño, *Criminalidad, ley penal y estructura social en la provincia de Antioquia*, 376; Luna Rivillas, "Documentos para el estudio de la criminalidad sexual en la provincia y gobernación de Antioquia," 554–564.

[a]One to four combined this activity with weaving; all of these are included in the total count just once.

[b]At least one in each row combined this activity with farming.

[c]Table includes accomplices in two of the murders.

the Socorro guerrilla forces during the Independence era, exemplifying the assertiveness of northeastern Colombian women from the middle and lower social classes. Women from these social groups committed several of the spousal murders in our case set.

Unlike the findings for the Spanish cases, elites are not represented at all in the New Granada spousal murders. We should not necessarily construe this as a defect of the case set. As in the chapter on Mexico, we can assume that the authorities would have made every effort to keep elite crimes from coming to public attention and ending up in court. In addition, poor people constituted the overwhelming majority of the population in this and other colonial regions.

Many of the individuals implicated in spousal murder cases, as Table 6.7 shows, were quite young, at least by today's standards. Some of the couples were newlyweds in their twenties and thirties (close to one-third of the defendants). Most spouses in New Granada fell into the 26–30 and 36–40 age range, which in part explains this finding.[28] It also corresponds to similar findings for late colonial Mexico and Spain.

TABLE 6.7. *Spousal homicides in New Granada, 1750–1812, by defendant's age*

Age	Number	Percentage
15–19	2	5.4
20–25	8[a]	21.6
26–30	8	21.6
31–35	2	5.4
36–40	9	24.3
41–45	—	—
46–50	5	13.5
51–55	1	2.7
56–60	1	2.7
61–65	—	—
66–70	1	2.7
Over 70	—	—
Undetermined	20	35.1
Total	57	

SOURCES: AGN, Colombia, Colonia, Juicios Criminales; Sosa Abella, *Labradores, tejedores y ladrones,* 60, 146–147; Patiño, *Criminalidad, ley penal y estructura social en la provincia de Antioquia,* 376; Luna Rivillas, "Documentos para el estudio de la criminalidad sexual en la provincia y gobernación de Antioquia," 554–564.

[a]Includes three accomplices.

In most societies to this day, young adults between the ages of 16 and 39 are the age group most prone to commit crimes.[29] However, eight of the New Granada spousal homicide cases—more than one-fifth of the total (21.6 percent of those whose age is known)—involved couples who had lived together for more than thirty years, meaning that the assassins and victims were at least in their late forties and fifties. This figure also mirrors late colonial Mexico, where the same age groups were involved in 10 to 17 percent of all crimes.[30]

The ethnic background of spousal murderers across regions differed slightly. For New Granada, we know the ethnic background of half of the accused. They appear to represent a cross-section of the viceroyalty's ethnic groups, especially Indians and mestizos. Only a handful appear to have been "pure" whites, and very few had black ancestry.[31] According to the available data on Indian spousal homicides, incorporated into Table 6.8, indigenous people were responsible for almost one-third of spousal murders for which we know the defendant's ethnic identity, and perhaps even more.[32] If these numbers are accurate, New Granada's Indians, like those of colonial Mexico, committed many more spousal murders (33.3 percent) proportionally than their overall share of the population (18.8 percent).

Conversely, given late colonial New Granada's demographics (see Table 6.1), mestizos appear to have committed few such crimes relative to

TABLE 6.8. *Spousal homicides in New Granada, 1750–1812, by defendant's ethnicity*

Ethnicity	Number	Percentage of defendants of known race	Ethnic group as a percentage of population
Whites	7	25.9	25.3
Indians	9	33.3	18.8
Mestizos	6	22.2	
Mulattoes	2[a]	7.4	49.2
Zambos	1	3.7	
Blacks	2	7.4	6.2[b]
Undetermined	27	50	
Total	54		

SOURCES: AGN, Colombia, Colonia, Juicios Criminales; Sosa Abella, *Labradores, tejedores y ladrones,* 60, 146–147; Patiño, *Criminalidad, ley penal y estructura social en la provincia de Antioquia,* 376; Luna Rivillas, "Documentos para el estudio de la criminalidad sexual en la provincia y gobernación de Antioquia," 554–564; "Padrón general del Virreinato del Nuevo Reino de Granada," in José Manuel Pérez Ayala, *Antonio Caballero y Góngora.*

[a]One was an accomplice in a crime committed by his lover, a white woman.

[b]Refers to black slaves.

their share of the population. The records frequently omit ethnic descriptions of individuals other than blacks and Indians, however, which makes it likely that many of the twenty-seven murderers of undetermined ethnic background (see Table 6.8) were in fact mestizos or other light-skinned, mixed-race individuals, including mulattoes. Even though the number of crimes committed by blacks is proportionate to their share of the viceroyalty's population, the case set probably also underrepresents black slaves, nearly 6.2 percent of New Granada's inhabitants. Most slaves (35.4 percent) resided in Cartagena and Popayán, regions for which evidence of spousal murders is scant. The same underrepresentation extends to people of African ancestry in general. Our case group includes only two mulattoes and one *zambo*, a person of mixed Indian/African ancestry.[33]

CONDITIONS AND MOTIVES

One-third of the defendants, several of them women, were drunk when they murdered their victims (see Table 6.9). This figure probably includes Albina Arias, who, as described above, killed her husband, Agustín de Angarita, by hitting him in the stomach with a *machete* handle.[34] Thirty-one-year-old weaver María del Carmen Martínez was also drunk when she committed her crime. After ingesting some alcohol (*había bebido*), she stabbed her husband, Pedro, who was drunk as well, after he allegedly made undetermined accusations "against her honor" and began beating her, as he did regularly.[35] María Dolores García, thirty-eight,

TABLE 6.9. *Motives cited by offenders in spousal homicides in colonial Colombia, 1750–1812*

Motives	Total cases		Cases with male defendant		Cases with female defendant	
	Number[a]	Percentage	Number	Percentage	Number	Percentage
Drinking (combined with other motives)	18	30	13	72.2	5	27.8
Drinking (as "exclusive" motive)	1	1.6	—	—	1	100
Jealousy	3	5	2	66.6	1	33.3
Desire to be with one's lover	10	16.6	4	40	6	60
Infidelity	5	8.3	4	80	1	20
Insolence	6	10	6	100	—	—
Disobedience	6	10	6	100	—	—
Self-defense	4	6.6	—	—	4	100
Dispute over in-laws	2	3.3	2	100	—	—
Constant unexplained fights	4	6.6	3	75	1	25
Other	1	1.6	—	—	1	100
Undetermined	12	16.6				
Total	72[a]					

SOURCES: AGN, Colombia, Colonia, Criminales; Sosa Abella, *Labradores, tejedores y ladrones,* 60, 146–147; Patiño, *Criminalidad, ley penal y estructura social en la provincia de Antioquia,* 376; Luna Rivillas, "Documentos para el estudio de la criminalidad sexual en la provincia y gobernación de Antioquia," 554–564.

[a]Total is more than 54, for some drinking-related cases are cross-listed in at least one other category.

also a weaver, is a similar case. She killed her seventy-year-old husband, Juan, after he accused her of being disobedient and beat her with a club. Both spouses had been drinking *chicha* all day long.[36] Fifty-seven-year-old farmer and weaver Juan F. Ortíz also drank *chicha* prior to beating and killing his wife, Silvestra, who disobeyed his order not to go to a *fandango* (fiesta).[37] *Zambo* boat rower Tomás A. Sierra got drunk on distilled sugarcane liquor (*aguardiente*) and *guarapo,* a fermented cane- or fruit-based liquor, before killing his wife, Eduarda, one night in 1799.[38] Drinking was a factor in eighteen, or one-third, of fifty-four cases of spousal murder in New Granada, confirming its role as a precursor to violent crime and, according to legal doctrine, as an ideal excuse as well (see Figure 6.1).[39] By itself, however, drinking is not enough to explain many of the cases in our sample.

Several murders listed in Table 6.9 under the categories of self-defense, "insolence," and "disobedience" were the culmination of long patterns of battery and abuse, a situation typical of other urban settings and historical periods.[40] Domestic abuse (*malos tratos*) was one of the leading categories of violent crime in late colonial New Granada. More than

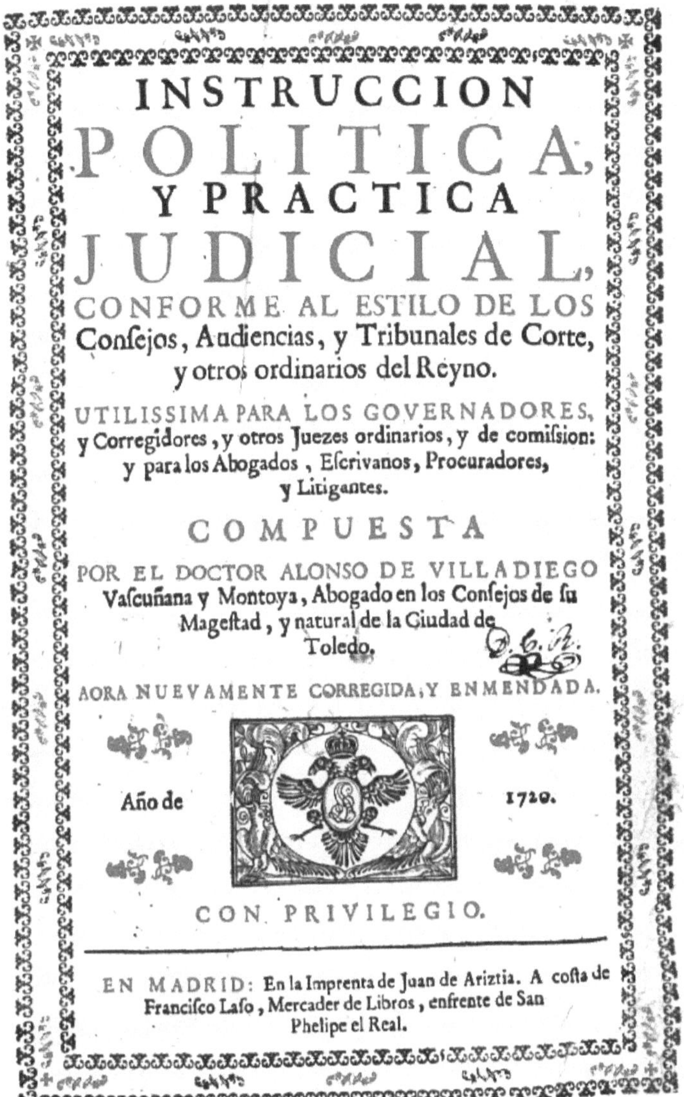

INSTRUCCION
POLITICA,
Y PRACTICA
JUDICIAL,
CONFORME AL ESTILO DE LOS
Confejos, Audiencias, y Tribunales de Corte,
y otros ordinarios del Reyno.

UTILISSIMA PARA LOS GOVERNADORES,
y Corregidores, y otros Juezes ordinarios, y de comifsion:
y para los Abogados, Efcrivanos, Procuradores,
y Litigantes.

COMPUESTA
POR EL DOCTOR ALONSO DE VILLADIEGO
Vafcuñana y Montoya, Abogado en los Confejos de fu
Mageftad, y natural de la Ciudad de
Toledo.

AORA NUEVAMENTE CORREGIDA, Y ENMENDADA.

Año de 1720.

CON PRIVILEGIO.

EN MADRID: En la Imprenta de Juan de Ariztia. A cofta de
Francifco Lafo, Mercader de Libros, enfrente de San
Phelipe el Real.

Figure 6.1. Alonso de Villadiego Vascuñana, Instrucción Política y Práctica Judicial *(Madrid: Imprenta de Juan de Ariztia, 1720 [1641]).*

21 percent of all assaults reported in the viceroyalty in the late colonial period were cases of wife beating (58 cases in a sample of 275 crimes).[41] *Malos tratos* were also prevalent in other Spanish American regions and cities, such as Río de la Plata (especially Buenos Aires), the central valley of Costa Rica, Peru, and presumably elsewhere.[42]

For instance, Eugenio J. Verdugo, who killed his wife, María, by beating her and throwing burning coal in her face, was portrayed by several witnesses as a habitual wife abuser, a cruel person (*sevicioso*) feared by his neighbors and even by his own parents.[43] Thirty-six-year-old mestizo day laborer and *chicha* retailer Francisco Díaz had a similar reputation. Prior to killing his wife, María, by hurling a large stone in her face, he often beat her for allegedly drinking too much, "provoking" him (she called him a *verdugo,* or oppressor), and uttering shameful remarks against him (*le decia desverguenzas*) and calling him "cunt face" (*cara de concha*).[44] Fifty-year-old mestizo retailer Hilario Cepeda was known to have battered his wife regularly, hitting her with his fists and even with iron bars and a whip before killing her in 1799.[45] On several occasions before he finally beat her to death one night in 1806, Lorenzo de Ospina battered his wife severely, threw her in a river, and attempted to stab her.[46] Fifty-seven-year-old Indian Juan Francisco Ortíz also mistreated (*maltrataba*) his wife regularly without any apparent reason (although he alleged that she talked back using foul language and did not work hard enough). One day, he beat her severely enough to injure her reproductive organs, causing her death.[47]

As all of these cases show, murder was sometimes the culmination of a pattern of protracted abuse. Even though, in certain instances, battery seems to have been habitual or its reasons are hard to ascertain, in various others it was clearly related to an abusive husband accusing his wife of provocative, disrespectful, or insolent behavior. This included, in particular, insults—even more so if they included foul language or sexual connotations—and refusal to work as hard as husbands considered appropriate. Men expected their wives to prepare and serve meals, wash clothes, look after children and livestock, and, in some cases, produce goods for sale to supplement the family's income. Any failure on their part in these and related chores could unleash a confrontation and, in some cases, physical assault.

Some cases cite only circumstantial evidence of previous battery but suggest that husbands felt entitled to "correct" unruly wives. Several instances of vicious behavior show men asserting their patriarchal prerogative by means of physical abuse. Society and the law had a high tolerance for such behavior. The lawyer for one female victim accepted that husbands could chastise (*castigar*) their insubordinate spouses, although he qualified that punishment should be in moderation and "corrective."[48] No wonder, then, that a main excuse husbands used to justify beating and even killing their partners was a wife's disobedience, insolence, or rebellious attitude.

As we have seen, one drunken defendant killed his wife because she went to a *fandango* against his wishes,[49] while another murderer claimed that his wife answered him back using foul language.[50] In another case, forty-six-year-old Martín Blanco stabbed his wife, Juana, in the back because she disobeyed his orders not to leave the house while he was away on business. Not only was she out of the house on the morning when her husband came home, but also, when she returned later in the day, she was in the company of a woman her husband disapproved of for having a love affair with a married man. Martín construed this to mean that his wife was also "taking the wrong steps" (*malos pasos*)—that is, betraying him.[51] Twenty-one-year-old day laborer Vicente Gómez made deadly use of his fists against his wife, Francisca, because she returned home from Mass without waiting for him as he had commanded. He was already furious because she had gone to church against his wishes.[52] In another case, farmer Emigdio Pabón, who began to feel ill while visiting neighbors with his wife, asked her to stay a little longer with him, but she went home instead. He then followed her, arguing along the way that he was the boss (*el que manda*). When she replied that he could go and boss his own pants (*mandara en sus calzones*), he stabbed her to death.[53] When Eduarda A. Garzón's husband, Tomás, returned home after a prolonged absence, she refused to allow him into the house and told him to go and "spend the winter where he had spent the summer." Tomás, who was drunk and annoyed by his wife's apparent infidelity (after a long absence he came back home and found her pregnant), did not like this irreverent treatment and stabbed her in the chest.[54] These and other cases make it clear that a hint of insolence could put some women at risk of their lives.

Women were not defenseless, though. A significant portion of spousal murders, one-third of those committed by women, occurred as a defensive response to abusive behavior. In fact, as Table 6.9 indicates, several women in our case set—four out of twenty—including the one in the case with which this chapter begins, were responding to repeated abuse by their husbands. This abominable behavior caused ample female resistance, which in several instances took the form of murder. We have already mentioned two female defendants (weavers María Dolores García and María del Carmen Martínez) who killed their oppressive husbands, one to escape a beating for going into a forbidden area of the house and the other to avenge remarks "against her honor."[55] A similar case is that of Cecilia Heredia, who, as discussed above, stabbed her husband,

Ignacio Torres, who had knocked her to the floor and beaten her repeatedly. This was not the first time he had beaten her ("*le daba cuero*"), and on at least one other occasion she pulled a knife to defend herself.[56] Mestizo weaver María E. Quintero twice stabbed her husband, Salvador, complaining that she was tired of being treated "with cruelty." Witnesses confirmed that he beat her constantly.[57] Marcela Metauten, a 39–40-year-old *mestiza*, beat her husband, Ramón, to death with a stick as he slept. For reasons that the records do not explain, Ramón had mistreated her since shortly after they were married.[58]

Beatings and abuse such as the acts described above were, in turn, related to the everyday domestic disputes that some authors describe as the "contested boundaries of gender rights and obligation."[59] Late colonial women regularly challenged patriarchal domination and tried to assert their "rights," sometimes obstinately, contentiously, or disobediently (e.g., resisting verbal deference by speaking up forcefully and aggressively, displaying an "insolent" physical mobility by abandoning husbands and/or coming or going at will, and challenging drunken, spendthrift, and unfaithful men). Threatened patriarchs struck back with a harshness that, at least in their minds, was "justifiable."

Yet another motivation was jealousy or the desire, mostly on the part of males, to avenge alleged infidelity. One ought to keep in mind that husbands accused of killing their wives may have used infidelity as an excuse to elicit judges' sympathy. All-male, honor-obsessed state officials were inclined to be lenient in such cases, backed by laws that, as explained earlier in this book, justified crimes against unfaithful wives.[60] Several of the cases under study involved supposedly unfaithful victims, such as "disobedient" Juana, stabbed by her husband on suspicion of being in *malos pasos*.[61] After tying his Indian wife, Rosalia, down by the throat and hands and beating her to death with his fists, Jacinto González argued that she was having an affair (*amancebada*) with Francisco Bernal, a white neighbor. At the time of her death, Rosalia was pregnant; the baby also died.[62] In a similar case, twenty-eight-year-old farmer Luis Marcelino González hit his wife, María Teresa, eight times with a machete on different parts of her body, including the head, throat, and hands. He killed both her and the baby she was expecting. Luis's excuse was that he felt *verguenza* (shame) at finding her one night with another man.[63] Juan Francisco Soler, a twenty-five-year-old weaver, also claimed that he was blinded by *impaciencia y colera* (impatience and rage) when he caught his wife, Manuela, having *actos ilicitos* (sexual acts) with a man in their marriage bed. The lover fled the house in a rush, leaving his pants behind, and Juan Francisco proceeded to beat Manuela to death.[64] Upon returning from an eight-month absence, drunken boat rower Tomás A. Sierra found his wife, Eduarda, in her sixth month of pregnancy. Declaring his honor and *estimación* destroyed (*mancillado*), he struck her with a machete, killing her and the baby in her womb.[65] In most of these instances the women were pregnant, further infuriating husbands who believed that their wives were engaged in extramarital affairs. In addition, despite questions raised earlier about the true weight of "honor" in Iberian societies, all of these cases show aggrieved husbands responding violently but "appropriately"—"honorably," they would say—to their wives' adultery, whether alleged or real.[66] No wonder then that Iberian history and literature are full of stories of such crimes, possibly an approximation of social reality.[67]

Husbands who were having extramarital affairs also tended to batter their wives. In several instances, men killed their wives so they could run away with or marry their lovers. To marry his concubine, María, thirty-year-old Antonio Cano, who had long ago abandoned his wife, Isidora, allegedly took his estranged spouse to a deserted place and poisoned her. A little later he forged the date on the death certificate to make it look older and submitted it to a nearby parish as proof that he was free to remarry, which he in fact did. The priest suspected him of wrongdoing, and he was eventually apprehended and tried.[68] In an even more sordid case, Salvador León used a machete to kill his wife, Manuela, and his stepson. He was enraged at the fact that Manuela had punished her twenty-year-old daughter María, Salvador's stepdaughter, after learning that the two had been having incestuous relations for over a year. Salvador subsequently ran away with the frightened girl.[69]

Men did not always manage to have their way, however. In several instances, women were the ones who fought and eventually killed their husbands over the men's extramarital affairs. Both María del Carmen Martínez and Cecilia Heredia, whose cases are discussed above, killed their husbands after major brawls over their infidelities.[70] Unfaithful women were also prominent on the list of killers. Almost one-third of the total female killers whose motives are known were wives who killed their husbands to run away with their lovers. Long-abused women sometimes engaged in extramarital affairs as a release. Later, sometimes with the active help of their lovers, they did away with their husbands. A typical case was that of Dominga Espitia, cited at the beginning of the chapter, who enlisted her lover, Nicolás, to help kill her husband, Matías.[71] The records contain several more such cases. In the town of Velez, in 1792, nineteen-year-old dressmaker María de la Luz Castro stabbed to death her husband, José, alleging long-standing battering on his part. More important, she also confessed that she wanted to be with her lover.[72] In 1798, twenty-five-year-old María de la Cruz, a resident of Nocaima, northwest of Santafé de Bogota, also helped her mulatto lover, twenty-seven-year-old Juan Agustín, kill her husband, José, with a knife. José, she alleged, beat her (*le daba*) regularly.[73]

Other women may have had extramarital affairs and tried to do away with their husbands in less justifiable circumstances, but the evidence available for such cases is scant. A few stand out—for example, thirty-year-old Catarina Bermúdez, who made a living baking bread, making soap, sewing, and brewing *chicha* in the town of Somondoco, Tunja. On a Saturday morning in July 1762, she killed her husband, Pablo de Vergara, with the assistance of her lover. The two, who planned to elope, beat up the man and drowned him in a nearby river. Evidence of domestic abuse preceding this murder is unclear.[74] The same is true in the case of thirty-year-old María Gertrudiz Vanegas, a white weaver whose lover paid an assassin to get rid of the woman's husband, Miguel Pérez, in Socorro's main square one Saturday night in 1797.[75] Although in absolute terms, therefore, men committed the majority of the crimes under study, the large number of women who murdered their husbands is striking and worth discussing further.

DEFENDANTS AND GENDER

As we have already noted, men committed about two-thirds of spousal murders and women more than the remaining one-third in our case set (see Table 6.10). The same general pattern characterizes criminals in other areas of the New World during the same period. In at least two other Spanish American regions, and as well in Brazil during the late colonial years, men were more likely to participate in all manner of criminal misconduct, especially violent acts. In late colonial Río de la Plata, for instance, women committed less than 9 percent of the violent crimes under investigation.[76] Men were arrested for more than 72 percent of crimes committed in colonial Mexico during the mid-1790s, with women accounting for 27 percent.[77] In some Brazilian regions, women were

TABLE 6.10. *General homicides in New Granada, 1756–1808, by defendant's gender*

Gender	Number	Percentage
Men	332	88.7
Women	30	8
Undetermined	12	3.2
Total	**374**	

SOURCE: AGN, Colonia, Criminales.

detained for as few as 4 percent of all criminal offenses in 1780–1833.[78] The same was true of New Granada, where men committed 91.3 percent of all crimes reported in the 1750–1810 period.[79]

If we consider the involvement of men and women in all types of homicide listed in Table 6.10, the intriguingly high proportion of female involvement in spousal murders in colonial Colombia becomes especially apparent. Around the world, women typically seem to have committed about one in ten murders in the late 1700s to early 1800s. In some regions of eighteenth-century England, for instance, just 13 percent of all murders and manslaughters were blamed on women.[80] In a random sample for 1800–1812 in Mexico City, women were found liable for two of twenty-five general homicides, or 8 percent of the total.[81] The figure was about the same in New Granada, according to a comprehensive index of late colonial trials.[82] When it came to killing spouses, however, New Granada's women committed more than one-third (38.8 percent) of all murders, as indicated in Table 6.11. In other words, women were more than four times more likely to commit spousal murder than any other type of homicide, a much higher proportion than in either Spain or Mexico (see Table 4.15 in Chapter 4). In Spain they were defendants in about twenty cases (about 30 percent of the case set), and in Mexico they were defendants in nineteen cases out of eighty-seven (22 percent). This would mean that women in colonial New Granada were almost twice as likely to kill their husbands as were their Mexican peers.

As far back as medieval times, court documentation indicates that women were more likely to perpetrate violent crimes against family members than against other persons.[83] The findings for colonial Spanish America are compatible with evidence for late sixteenth-century and seventeenth-century England, which shows that females involved in homicide were more likely (42 percent as opposed to 7 percent) to kill members of their own household—relatives and servants included—than victims outside of the family.[84] Finally, this conclusion is in keeping

TABLE 6.11. *Spousal homicides in New Granada, 1750–1812, by defendant's gender*

Gender	Number	Percentage
Men	33	61.1
Women	21	38.8
Total	54	

SOURCES: AGN, Colonia, Criminales; Sosa Abella, *Labradores, tejedores y ladrones*, 60, 146–147; Patiño, *Criminalidad, ley penal y estructura social en la provincia de Antioquia*, 376; Luna Rivillas, "Documentos para el estudio de la criminalidad sexual en la provincia y gobernación de Antioquia," 554–564.

with modern studies of homicide, which demonstrate that a majority (51.9 percent) of females who kill target family members.[85] However, this research has focused mainly on "family" or "domestic" homicides, which include crimes against offspring, relatives, servants, and even apprentices, a category much broader than the spousal murder cases examined here. In some samples, husbands represented as few as one-third of the victims. The evidence in this chapter is more precise concerning Spanish America's spousal murders in late colonial times than any previous academic findings.[86]

Still more interesting is the prevalent academic explanation for the pattern of heavy female involvement in domestic crimes. According to this theory, because a woman's place was firmly in the home, it was only logical that she would restrict her criminal activities to the domestic sphere.[87] On the surface this makes sense. A woman would more likely quarrel and accumulate grievances with the people with whom she had daily contact, husbands and children in particular. She would also more likely strike (or be struck) in the space where she was normally expected to circulate: the home. However, quite a few of our female assassins and victims appear to have led active "public" lives and interacted on a daily basis with a wide variety of people. A few of the female defendants were *chicha* retailers who were in regular contact with neighbors, local customers, and travelers. This was also true of weavers, a majority among our female criminals, who by the very nature of their activity entered into regular contact with sheep raisers, wool retailers, and market vendors. In addition, some of the women involved in the crimes under discussion quarreled with their husbands over their attendance at *fiestas* or *fandangos* and at Mass or visits to neighbors and friends, activities that gave them the opportunity to socialize with diverse groups of men and women.

To be sure, many of the women committed their crimes or were murdered inside their homes. However, this is not because they were absolutely restricted to this space but because, having reached out and displayed irreverent character and behavior (talking back, walking away, being coquettish during parties, going to forbidden places, and seeing forbidden people), they provoked their husbands' domineering character, jealousy, and rage. The husbands, sensing that their patriarchal prerogatives were spinning out of control, resorted to abuse. Some of them killed their wives, or, if the women were lucky, they killed their husbands first. Contrary to other studies of "domestic crimes," therefore, this study argues that female spousal murderers and victims transcended domestic spaces and relations, placing themselves more at risk of clashing with their spouses.[88]

In making sense of the larger number of homicides committed by women in New Granada than in Mexico, ethnicity may be a factor as well (see Table 6.12). None of colonial Colombia's female killers appear

TABLE 6.12. *Female spousal killers in colonial Colombia and colonial Mexico by ethnicity, 1740s–1820s*

	Colonial Colombia			Colonial Mexico		
Ethnicity	Number	Percentage	Ethnic group as a percentage of population	Number	Percentage	Ethnic group as a percentage of population
White	5	62.5	26.9	1	6.2	22.6[a] / 17.9[b]
Mestizo	2	25	46.4 (Mestizo and Mulatto combined)	1	6.2	25.4[a] / } 21.8[b] (Mestizo and Mulatto combined)
Mulatto	1	12.5		3	18.7	13.3[a] /
Indian	—	—	19.7	11	68.7	51.7[a] / 60[b]
Black	—	—	7.6	—	—	0.12[a] / —[b]
Unknown	13	61.9		3	15.8	
Total	**21**			**19**		

SOURCES: AGN, Mexico City: Acordada, Californias, Criminales, General de Parte, Presidios y Cárceles, and Provincias Internas; AJO; AANG, Guadalajara, Casos Criminales; AJP; Archivo Provincial de Zacatecas; Municipal Archive of Veracruz; AGN, Colombia, Colonia, Juicios Criminales; "Padrón general del Virreinato del Nuevo Reino de Granada, 1776," in José Manuel Pérez Ayala, *Antonio Caballero y Góngora.*

[a]Data from Alejandro Humboldt, *Ensayo político sobre el reino de la Nueva España,* 210.

[b]Data from "Memoria sobre la población de la Nueva España, México, 1814," cited by Humboldt, *Ensayo político sobre el reino de la Nueva España,* 2: 287.

to have been Indian. Instead, a majority (7 or 87.5 percent) of those whose race is known were whites and *mestizas*. If we add to this category some of the female killers of unknown race (13), white and mixed-race women appear to have been responsible for an overwhelming majority of female spousal murders, representing a much larger proportion of these crimes than their ethnic group's share of the region's population. The decision to include women of unspecified race in the white/mixed-race category is justified by the fact that they were almost certainly non-Indians, for otherwise a curator would have represented them at trial, which the records indicate was not the case. In Mexico, conversely, the majority of female spousal killers were Indians, in proportion with their share of the region's population. Although the evidence is fragmentary, it is fair to speculate that, free from the constraints of communal life and hierarchy, colonial Colombia's numerous white and mestizo women seem to have been more rebellious and assertive than the region's minority native women. In Mexico, where natives were a majority of the population, the trend appears to have been more or less the opposite.

AFTERMATH

Once the murders had been committed, a good part of those responsible in New Granada and elsewhere remained at the scene of the crime, usually their home, with the corpse or alongside their dying partners.[89]

Others ran away and managed to evade justice for a while, even several years.[90] Still other defendants buried their victims to hide the crime or dumped the corpse in a river or creek in order to fake drowning or leave no trace.[91] Even considering that we are studying cases in which offenders underwent prosecution, it is fair to say that hiding the crime appears to have been difficult. A body was not easy to conceal for long without eliciting suspicions. Neighbors, friends, or relatives were certain to notice and gossip about prolonged absences and possibly report them to local priests or justice officials. Unless a death could be attributed to accidental drowning or disguised as a disease-related incident, an explanation would be needed. Confessions were therefore common, but many offenders stubbornly denied their crime, coming up with remarkably creative lies.

Several of the accused confessed their acts shortly afterward and showed remorse; others denied their crimes by attributing their spouse's death to natural causes, especially prior illnesses (menstruation-related conditions included), food poisoning, accidents, and even witchcraft. Eugenio Verdugo tried to blame the death of his badly beaten wife on *tavardillo* (typhus), a disease from which she allegedly suffered.[92] Francisco A. León argued that his poisoned wife died of a stomach ailment, as did day laborer Vicente Gómez, who also claimed that his wife had menstruation-related colic, got wet while crossing a creek, and became even sicker from eating prunes [93] Forty-six-year-old white farmer and hat maker Martín Ruíz claimed that his wife died not from stab wounds but due to a *maleficio* (a spell that damaged her liver).[94]

Except when secular or divine interventions, and/or attenuating circumstances such as those discussed in previous chapters reduced their punishment, these and other individuals ended up facing severe consequences for their crimes, even death. The next chapter discusses these various forms of punishment in detail.

CONCLUSION

Trials of spousal killers reveal intriguing aspects of everyday life among colonial Spanish America's rural poor. For example, criminal records unveil a world of infrequent internal migration, efforts by peasant families to combine diverse economic activities (retailing, farming, day labor, washing clothes) to make a living, and active socializing among relatives and neighbors, including regular drinking and party going. The records are even more revealing of the dynamics of gender relations among the lower classes. Colonial Spanish American societies displayed high levels of aggression and violence between spouses. Although women appear to have been the predominant victims, the records suggest that, far from playing a passive role, women could be defiant and ready to attack their male counterparts.[95] Women reacted to domestic abuse in a variety of ways: talking back, abandoning husbands or leaving them behind, refusing to submit to restrictions on their physical mobility, engaging in extramarital affairs, defending themselves from aggression with knives and sticks, and, in extreme circumstances, killing their husbands. It is true that in a region of around 800,000 people, only twenty-one women appear to have killed their husbands over a period of sixty years. It is also true that women were more likely themselves to be the victims of spousal murder. However, women who killed their husbands represented a sizable majority of female murderers.

The fact that women were more likely to kill relatives and spouses than other victims did not result, in any case, from their restriction to the domestic sphere. In fact, such crimes seem to have been caused by the exact opposite situation—the escalation of marital tensions when women transcended the circumscribed space of the household and displayed an "insolent" tendency to be with relatives, friends, market people, village party goers, and even lovers. One could go as far as to argue that the circumstances surrounding spousal murders committed by women call into question the "domestic" nature and character of the female sphere in colonial Spanish American and other societies.

As the historiography has demonstrated over the past two decades, it would be a mistake to assume that the female sphere in colonial Latin American societies was a space of mundane domesticity and seclusion where women dedicated themselves exclusively to providing for the needs of their households, which could include parents, husbands, offspring, or siblings. It is also a mistake to imagine that this sphere always contrasted with the male world, which was—arguably—authoritative, productive, active, and public. Females were not exclusively relegated to performing menial domestic activities and related chores (cooking, cleaning, sewing, nurturing, child care) geared to satisfying the private needs (material, emotional, or sexual) of family members. All women, housewives in particular, were not truly removed from the world outside of the home, nor were their external connections limited mainly to church attendance and local market activities.[96] Even their crimes transcended their home and tended to be extra-domestic.

The character and circumstances of some spousal homicides reveal this sharp public/domestic dichotomy to be not only an organizing fiction of social life but an academic fiction as well.[97] The world of the home was in reality closely linked to the world of the street, not only because of churches and marketplaces, which were indeed important public spaces for female contact with the larger society, but also because of the active character of social life in *chicherías, pulquerias*, theaters, bullfights, parties and popular festivals, and the homes of neighbors, friends, and relatives.[98] The tensions emerging from women's ordinary day-to-day interactions in all of these public arenas regularly unleashed marital conflicts.[99] This was yet more so given that women's active public life appeared, to husbands in particular, as a sign of impropriety and insolence and a challenge to dominant patriarchal norms. Nonetheless, women who were "insolent" in public do not seem to have really been so exceptional; otherwise, it would be difficult to understand the frequency with which females faced marital disputes or killed their husbands to protect their physical integrity and safeguard what they seemed to consider their prerogative to enjoy unrestricted and richer lives. Ultimately, patriarchal norms could be and were enforced by male colonial officials and a male-biased legislative structure that brought order and sense back to the sometimes turbulent and irreverent lives of women and men.

Evidence of gender bias on the part of officers rendering judicial decisions in cases involving spousal murderers is still inconclusive. As we shall see in the following chapter, preliminary findings suggest that New Granada's judicial authorities displayed more leniency toward men found guilty of killing their spouses than they did toward women under the same circumstances. This bias becomes clearer in a consideration of the legal structure. As a reflection of the dominant male Hispanic culture, formal laws from the sixteenth century to the early nineteenth century were skewed on behalf of men. These laws may have served as a reminder that the period's patriarchal frame of mind viewed female domesticity and obedience as sacred and worth preserving and/or restoring. Like the colonial state officials in charge of enforcing the law, however, women could also choose to obey patriarchal mandates and laws only halfway (*a medias*). The next chapter discusses the various punishments resulting from women's transgressions and from those of their spouses.

CHAPTER SEVEN

The Many Shades of Pain and Punishment in the Spanish Atlantic

Despite what we have learned about the significance of royal and ecclesiastical magnanimity and how it may have contributed to hegemonic rule, coercion remained an essential component of royal and ecclesiastical power in the late colonial Spanish Atlantic. The investigation and punishment of murder and other crimes in the Spanish ancien régime were, after all, supposed to be essentially a matter of "public vengeance" (*vindicta pública*), an expression that justice officials and prosecutors often invoked during criminal investigations and trials. As it did under other absolutist monarchs, and much along the lines described in Michel Foucault's classic work *Discipline and Punish,* the justice meted out by the Spanish king and his colonial officials could take the form of extraordinary physical and moral suffering.[1] The potential for bodily suffering existed even in the early phases of trial proceedings. Torture was a possibility, at least in theory, for obtaining information from reluctant defendants and witnesses. In addition to compassion and forgiveness, whether based on secular or religious considerations, royal justice thus included collective retribution, applied in public and painful ways. Perhaps nothing illustrates this better than the intriguing punishment known as *encubamiento*. This chapter includes descriptions of several such executions.

Sentences for *parricidas* could include not only the death penalty but also other forms of painful punishment, ranging from flogging to hard labor and service in the galleys. To underscore the offenders' public shame, infamy, and loss of honor, the enforcement of death and other sentences was often surrounded by considerable display, including loud broadcasting of the crime and sentence by the town crier and the culprit's obligation to wear emblematic garments during and after imposition of the penalty.

The language used in judicial proceedings of the time makes it clear that royal justice and penalties were intentionally designed to scare (*escarmentar*) both defendants and potential criminals through an open show of the serious consequences facing convicted offenders. In addition to *encubamiento*, the town crier, and symbolic dress, these rituals included tying criminals to a donkey or horse and dragging them through a town's central streets, leaving bodies hanging from scaffolds or in garrotting chairs for hours at a time for people to see, and publicly exhibiting the body parts of drawn-and-quartered criminals on pikes or in special iron cages. All of these practices, along with others such as *recogimiento* (confinement in special institutions for "deviant" women) and harsh jail terms in unhealthy prisons or presidios, in some cases even for life, continued well into the early nineteenth century. This fact raises the question of whether the transition that Foucault suggested took place in France and elsewhere in the late eighteenth century—from the public and physically painful chastisement of bodies, punishment as the "vengeance of the sovereign" or "punishment as spectacle," to the private repression of minds, "punishment as the defense of society" or punishment as discipline, a hidden component of the penal process—occurred in the Spanish Atlantic at that time as well.[2]

This chapter begins by addressing judicial torture. It continues with a discussion of the main corporal punishment prescribed for the crime of spousal murder: death by *encubamiento*. Finally, it provides a comparative analysis of the penalties delivered for dozens of cases of spousal murder in each of the three regions under study. One of the main points to emerge from this discussion is that both the torture of witnesses and defendants and death by *encubamiento* had a great deal more to do with appearances than reality. Over time, because of growing concerns about the need for humane treatment, physical punishment often became more ceremonial than real. In this sense, and because harshness did materialize occasionally, it was an ideal complement to a monarch's forgiveness. In other words, if royal and ecclesiastical power rested on hegemony, they also required a select and symbolic dosage of force, however diminished with time.

THE FADING AWAY OF JUDICIAL TORTURE

Historically, the Spanish and other European monarchies had embraced the use of torture (*tormento*) since around the thirteenth century, not exactly because of an irrational and insatiable thirst for retribution but especially in pursuit of sufficient proof to punish wrongdoers under the demanding standards of the Roman canon legal system of evidence.[3] Notwithstanding abundant doctrinal comments about its proper and justifiable use, and despite judicial orders that it be applied in the late colonial period, torture was actually already much less common at the time than ever before. Humanitarian and legal concerns led to its slow demise.

A 1789 judicial manual upheld judicial torture as a fully just and rational measure to uncover crimes that could otherwise remain unpunished.[4] The judicial records are full of examples similar to the 1771 case in Chapter 4, in which the prosecutor ordered officials to torture Spanish nobleman Juan Francisco Escudero to secure a confession that he strangled and murdered his wife in the northwest community of Vizmanos. The Bogotá Audiencia heard a similar request in 1786 concerning a Panamanian man, Francisco Saldaña, accused of killing his lover's husband, Manuel Pastoriza, while he slept. Pastoriza's wife appeared to be an accomplice, but she refused to admit her involvement, spurring the judge to decree that Saldaña be subjected to judicial torture to ascertain the whole truth.[5] Another case from New Granada involved the strangling of José Ignacio de la Parra in Tunja in 1793 as he slept. The suspects were his wife, Rosalía Alvarez, and her lover, eighteen-year-old Francisco Daza. The youth fled, and the woman escaped from jail but was recaptured a few years after the crime. By 1799, she had still refused to confess her participation in the murder or incriminate Daza. Lacking sufficient evidence (*plena prueba*) against both defendants, the local magistrate, at the suggestion of the lawyer (*asesor letrado*) assisting him in the case, decreed that the woman be tortured. The Bogotá Audiencia had to make a final ruling on the magistrate's order after the woman's defense filed an appeal.[6]

Following the ancient medieval code known as *Las Siete Partidas*, Spain's ancien régime considered torture a legally admissible means to establish the truth in some criminal investigations. Even though the practice seems to have waned over the years and, like the death penalty, became the target of criticism by enlightened thinkers and reformers,[7] some prosecutors continued to request it well into the late eighteenth century. A typical argument was that torture was an effective means for discovering crimes because of its ability to terrify criminals into confessing their deeds. Justice officials cited it as an important deterrent, a key means to preserve social peace, and an effective mechanism to find out the truth in accordance with custom, reason, and even Church precepts. In the words of a prosecutor, the world could not remain in peace without the fear caused by torture ("*[E]l mundo no se puede mantener en paz sin el temor del tormento . . .*").[8] Although some authors were critical, several legal treatises continued to dedicate special sections to this practice (see Figures 3.2, 5.1, and 6.1).[9] Commenting liberally on the laws still available on the subject, they offered detailed explanations of the formalities, circumstances, and evidence required for a judge to issue the order (*sentencia interlocutoria de tormento*) to torture a defendant or a witness, as well as instructions for administering it and evaluating any evidence gleaned as a result.

According to legal experts, judicial torture was admissible only in the case of serious crimes punishable by death or other "corporal" punishment, lest the means of obtaining evidence turn out to be more severe than the final punishment itself. In such cases, the order to torture could occur only after the judge had decreed the disclosure of evidence through a *publicación de probanzas o de testigos*. To justify the order, the judge had to establish that while full proofs of the crime were lacking, sufficient partial evidence (*semiplena prueba*) or even serious circumstantial clues (*indicios bastantes* or *urgentisimos*) pointed to the defendant's guilt. The judicial order decreeing it could be appealed, but once confirmed it had to be implemented immediately in the manner prescribed. The order indicated the specific type of torture to be administered, which generally did not include older methods such as "boiling water or cold irons."[10]

The main form of torture still in use during the late eighteenth century was *agua y cordeles* (water and ropes). The subject was placed on a torture table (*potro*) with arms and legs tied to ropes that the executioner (*verdugo*) could gradually tighten and/or harden by applying water. The judge determined the duration and intensity of the procedure and, if no evidence was obtained the first time, had the authority to order it repeated once more. For it to be legally admissible, the subject had to corroborate any evidence obtained this way the following day without torture and in a different location.[11]

Normally, torture could be applied again just once, in cases where the available evidence justifying its application was "very grave and compelling" (*muy grave y urgente*) or if the criminal confessed to the crime during the first torture session but refused to confirm his or her testimony subsequently. Only in exceptional cases, when subjects confessed to the crime under torture twice but failed to ratify their confession afterward, was it possible to apply the method a third time.[12]

Evidence indicates that, though it was already rare, torture continued to be sparsely practiced in Spain in the late 1760s and early 1770s.[13] Similarly, remember that during the investigation of their crime in 1798, *hidalga* María Vicenta Mendieta and her lover claimed to have been subjected to torture. The justice officials insisted, perhaps euphemistically, that interrogators simply used pressure (*apremios*) and added that both defendants had reiterated their confessions on three separate days and in different locales with no coercion of any kind.[14] Cases like these might have been the exception rather than the rule; despite repeated requests by prosecutors and detailed guides in legal manuals, torture was hardly ever used formally by the late eighteenth century as anything but a threat.[15] In every one of the cases mentioned above, for example, torture was ordered but appears not to have ever been carried out.

We already know that in the 1770s the Spanish *hidalgo* Escudero was spared torture, allegedly because of his noble condition. In a 1786 spousal homicide, the Panamanian governor who tried the case expressed concern to the Bogotá Audiencia that the region lacked the instruments required to apply torture and voiced his scruples regarding the proposed method, suggesting that it was uncommon there and probably elsewhere, as well. In addition to these arguments, the overtly racist governor also complained that the executioner, a black man, was inexplicably clumsy (*inexplicablemente torpe*). In a 1793 murder the Bogotá Audiencia rejected the Tunja judge's authorization for torture to be used as a means of uncovering more conclusive proof. To show that it was far from lenient, however, it opted to send the woman (Rosalía Alvarez) to jail for eight years based upon the available circumstantial evidence.

Torture became less common as more and more critics condemned the practice and questioned its utility. Although torture was allegedly not a punishment in itself but rather a means to obtain evidence, some denounced it as cruel and, in some cases, even more severe than the final punishment that most spousal murderers received. Despite the fact that some supporters in Spain, most notably the Madrid lawyers' guild,[16] defended it into the late eighteenth century, Montesquieu, Voltaire, and other enlightened European authors had already published tracts against the practice. Perhaps the best-known such work was *On Crimes and Punishments* (1764) by the Italian aristocrat Cesare Bonesana, Marquis of Beccaria, who considered torture a "cruel," "senseless," "ridiculous," and "savage" test of truth.[17]

Critics in eighteenth-century Spain included librarian and jurist Alfonso María de Acevedo (1736–1774),[18] former judge and statesman Gaspar Melchor de Jovellanos (1744–1811),[19] prosecutor and literary figure Juan Meléndez Valdez (1754–1817),[20] law professor Juan Pablo Forner (1756–1797),[21] and anticlerical diplomat Manuel de Roda y Arrieta (1708–1782),[22] to mention but a few. Members of the St. Barbara Legal Academy also spoke against it by the 1780s.[23] However, the most prominent criticism came from Mexican intellectual, penologist, and magistrate Manuel de Lardizábal y Uribe (1744–1820), *alcalde del crimen* in the Granada Audiencia. In his 1782 *Discurso sobre las penas,* Lardizábal echoed the criticisms of Beccaria and others, deriding torture as punishment disguised as a means of interrogation. Rejecting one by one the pro-torture writings of Spanish clergyman Pedro de Castro, Lardizábal ridiculed it as a fallible and useless mechanism.[24] These opinions, and changes in the European law of evidence that lowered the standards of proof for serious crimes, unquestionably contributed to the decline of the practice other than as a ruse.[25] Another institution that also evolved and declined considerably over time was the death penalty.

VINDICTA PÚBLICA, DEATH BY *ENCUBAMIENTO*, AND OTHER HARSH PUNISHMENTS

Leaving aside mechanisms of social self-regulation and discipline ("infra-justice"), which undoubtedly played a significant role in the containment of social conflict,[26] the main response to criminal malfeasance in the late colonial Spanish Atlantic was mostly public royal justice. In spite of many loopholes, such justice could be a deeply vengeful enterprise. Virtually all criminal proceedings, without exception, routinely referred to the need for criminals to receive effective public vengeance, or *vindicta pública*. The Spanish monarchy proudly upheld this practice as a symbol of its advanced legal civilization, implying as it did a general rejection of the notion of private retaliation (*vindicta privada*).[27] The right of cuckolded husbands to kill their wives and lovers served as a reminder that some remnants of private vengeance remained embedded in the legislation, but as exceptions meant to safeguard the culturally superior value of male and family honor.[28] For the most part, justice was a matter of process-bound and formally administered collective/public retribution rather than arbitrarily imposed private and individual revenge.

And retribution it was: Criminal justice was definitely not understood as leading to modern liberal goals such as preemption, correction, or rehabilitation, but was rather a means of atonement designed to instill fear in criminals (*escarmentar al delincuente*) and "general terror" among the rest of the population (*terror en los demás miembros de un estado*).[29] As the *Siete Partidas* put it, the primary objective of punishment was to scare criminals and "to make sure that all of those who saw or heard about it, keep it as an example and warning and refrain from committing any wrong for fear of it. . . ."[30] For example, criminals sentenced to public whipping commonly received their punishment on market days to ensure a large audience and more "fruitful" deterrence ("*ser más probable . . . el fruto del escarmiento*").[31] Such punishment was viewed as naked payback, Foucault's "vengeance of the sovereign," and justice officials avidly sought opportunities to institute it. As late as the nineteenth century, outspoken observers appreciated the message. For instance, a journalist in

Mexico City proudly announced in 1806 his intention to describe judicial punishments in detail as a means to achieve "*terror y escarmiento*," in imitation of contemporary European newspapers.[32]

A leading example of the symbolic power of harsh public punishment was *encubamiento*. In the late eighteenth century, nineteen-year-old Juliana Zambrano, a white woman who made her living as a weaver and seamstress in the northwestern Colombian town of Velez, was fetched by justice officials from Bogotá's public prison to face the death penalty. Zambrano had been jailed for her alleged participation more than three years earlier in the killing of her husband, Juan Rodríguez y Olarte. It was unclear whether, as she claimed, she helped her lover, twenty-five-year-old white day laborer (*jornalero*) Francisco Robles, stab Juan in the chest with a pocketknife after he surprised the adulterous pair in bed or, as a witness testified Robles had told him, she struck her husband several times with a hoe while Francisco held him from behind. However the murder transpired, the lovers cooperated in killing Juan and smuggling his corpse out of the house wrapped in a poncho under cover of night with the assistance of one of Juliana's minor children. They tied the corpse to a piece of wood, covered it with branches, and dumped it in a creek more than a league (*legua*) away from the house. At the conclusion of the criminal trial against the woman and her accomplice, the Bogotá Audiencia confirmed the death sentence for both defendants. Juliana's extraction from jail was the beginning of a somber ceremony leading to her execution.

Public scribe Gabriel Joseph de Villaseñor recorded in minute detail the circumstances surrounding Juliana's execution on February 19, 1773.[33] To begin, Juliana faced dragging (*arrastramiento*). The officials in attendance placed her on a straw mat (*estera*) tied to the tail of a horse, which dragged her ignominiously through the main streets of the city (*las calles públicas acostumbradas*), as the law prescribed for those who committed treacherous (*alevoso*) murders.[34] In addition to the official leading the horse, the public scribe certifying the events, the Augustinian monks praying for the woman from a distance (*de vista la auxiliaron*), curious passersby, and Juliana herself, a town crier (*pregonero*) accompanied the procession. He was charged with stopping at every intersection (*en cada esquina*) to announce the woman's crime and punishment, which he did in a loud voice as the law required to frighten all those who saw and heard the spectacle (*para escarmiento de los que vieren y oyeren*).[35]

After the procession reached the central square (*plaza mayor*), the executioner (*ejecutor de la justicia*) helped the terrified woman, her body by now probably quite bruised, climb the stairs leading to a wooden scaffold (*horca*). There she was hanged by the neck (*ahorcada naturalmente*), with the executioner either pulling on her legs or climbing on her shoulders—which method was used is not clear, but both were fairly common in deaths by hanging[36]—to accelerate her demise and save her a long and painful agony. A state official loudly called the woman's name up to three times, and when she failed to respond or make any movement, he pronounced her dead. By this time the plaza was packed with people (*a cuyo acto se halló mucho concurso de gentes*) avidly watching the morbid scene.

Hours later, after the public display was deemed sufficient, the woman's corpse was cut down and placed in a leather bag called a *cuba*. The sack was decorated with painted pictures of a monkey, a snake, a rooster, and a dog.[37] Although the evidence is missing, in Juliana's case, instead of being permanently consigned to the sea or a river as ancient law prescribed, the *cuba* was very likely subjected to a ritual submersion into the nearby San Francisco River. This was followed by retrieval and proper burial of the corpse by a religious brotherhood as in the Mexican incident described below. Such procedure had become standard practice in some Spanish regions by the eighteenth century.[38]

Juliana's lover, Francisco Robles, suffered a similar fate, the only difference being that during the procession preceding his hanging he was assisted not by Augustinian monks but rather Dominican and Franciscan friars. The local authorities had designated the members of these various orders, depending upon the defendant's gender, as the only ones authorized to assist condemned criminals under royal directives dating back to 1733. This seems to have been an attempt to avoid the havoc of too many monks from different religious orders competing to intervene as inmates were marched to their place of execution.[39]

New Granada was not the only region that practiced punishments such as dragging and *encubamiento*. In 1806 a journalist in New Spain published an article describing a recent execution in the capital. In an apparent effort to deter potential criminals, he offered rich detail about the last moments of twenty-two-year-old white tailor José María Jaso, executed for the stabbing death of his seventeen-year-old wife, María Guadalupe Montoya. The couple had been married for just one year, but José María claimed he wanted to be free of his financial obligations to his young wife. As was customary, prior to his execution he remained for three days in *capilla*, a special area of the jail designated for condemned inmates, who received visits from a chaplain and ate lavishly with the financial support of a charitable local nobleman, the Count of Medina. The morning of the execution, a priest helped José María dress in a special *ropón* (gown—white for noblemen, black for commoners). Before being blindfolded, he was allowed to kneel and pray briefly before a crucifix of the Christ of Mercy (*Cristo de la Misericordia*) brought especially to the jail for this purpose. Then, as in the earlier Colombian case, he was paraded through the city on a straw mat (*serón*) pulled by a horse.

The town crier presided over the well-staged procession, followed by four to six properly attired *comisarios* riding horses, numerous members (*caballeros*) of a religious brotherhood, and a few monks carrying candles and lamps.[40] Bringing up the rear were a judicial officer (*teniente de corte*) and the court scribe, both solemnly dressed and on horseback. Lines of royal soldiers marched alongside. The procession filed through the city streets to the Plaza de Mixcaleo, where soldiers on foot and horseback guarded the scaffold. The executioner helped the inmate climb a staircase to the right of the scaffold while a priest mounted a separate staircase to the left. In this particular case, José María was spared hanging in favor of garroting out of "consideration to his family," whose precise background or noble condition (required in theory for the application of *garrote*) are unclear. The priest performed a homily, and after the corpse was exhibited for several hours, authorities took it to a nearby creek and placed it inside a leather bag decorated with the images of a monkey, a rooster, a snake, and a dog. They dragged the bag briefly through the creek in a simulacrum of the original Roman ritual. Then the *comisarios*, *teniente*, and scribe charged with bringing the body back to the royal jail handed it over to the Brotherhood of Mercy. The brothers removed the gown, wrapped the corpse in a white sheet (*mortaja*), and placed it in a coffin, followed by a Christian burial.[41] Overall, the execution and ceremonial were quite a spectacle.

Michel Foucault commented insightfully on the equivalent spectacle of public punishments in ancien régime France, particularly deaths by quartering and hanging. He elaborated on their cultural and political meaning as acts of royal vengeance against the body of the condemned, noting that such exhibitions ultimately became contests between the king and an increasingly embittered populace.[42] In neighboring Spain and its overseas domains around the same time, punishment seemed a similarly body-centered, vengeful affair full of cultural and political symbolism, pomp, and public ceremony. However, there is little evidence of negative reactions or disturbances on the part of the common people. The public seems to have accepted that, as with crimes against God or the king (*crímenes de lesa magestad divina o humana*), the murder of one's spouse was an atrocious (*enormísimo*), qualified (*calificado*), grave (*agravado*) offense deserving harsher punishment than manslaughter or simple homicide.[43] This conception was not new, nor was it an invention of the absolutist Spanish monarchy or other contemporary European regimes.

As was profusely documented in famed jurist Juan de Solórzano Pereyra's little-known doctoral thesis on the subject (1605), Roman law considered individuals who killed their parents (parricides) so despicable that not even the earth was to be stained with their blood. Instead, the sentence for such criminals was to be placed alive into a ritual leather sack (*cuieus* or *culleus*), which was sealed and thrown into the water with the expectation that it would vanish forever, leaving no trace.[44] The *Lex Duodecim Tabularum* (Law of the Twelve Tables, ca. 450 BC) exacerbated the punishment by ordering the addition inside the sack of a monkey, a dog, a rooster, and a snake to torture, kill, and tear the body apart.[45] The *Lex Pompeia de parricidiis*, passed in the time of Coneus Pompeius (ca. 55–52 BC), extended the crime of parricide to the killing with *dolus malus* (bad deceit or evil criminal intent) of a brother, sister, uncle, aunt, or other relative, husbands and wives included. All murderers who fell into this category were punished *more majorum* (according to ancient custom) by being whipped till they bled, sewn up inside a sack with the aforementioned animals, and, if possible, thrown into the sea. This punishment seems to have endured well into the reign of Emperor Hadrian (AD 117–138), when parricides were thrown to wild beasts (*damnatio ad bestias*) or, in the time of jurist Paulus (mid-fourth century), burned alive.[46] The punishment of *encubamiento,* adopted as early as the medieval *Siete Partidas* in the Spanish kingdoms, derived from these ancient Roman practices.[47]

Encubamiento, originally preceded by flogging (*azotes*) and later, around the last quarter of the eighteenth century, dragging or *arrastramiento* as a means of public shame (*vergüenza pública*), became the standard punishment (*pena ordinaria*) for spousal murderers and other parricides under Spanish royal legislation.[48] The punishment subsequently spread to the Americas, and by the seventeenth century New Spain at least was imposing it with some regularity.[49] As the examples above illustrate, it was still in use in the late eighteenth and early nineteenth centuries in New Spain, New Granada, and, presumably, other Spanish American regions.[50]

According to available records, *encubamiento* occurred across the Spanish peninsula as well. As early as 1701, two brothers in Valencia accused of having killed one of their wives, who was seven months' pregnant at the time, received this sentence.[51] Near the close of the century, in 1783, Italian court dancer Domingo Rosateli was dragged (*arrastrado*), hanged (*ahorcado*), and subjected to *encubamiento* in Madrid for the stabbing death of his wife, Manuela Buendía, whom he claimed had treated him disrespectfully and insulted his honor by engaging in undisclosed romantic affairs with other men.[52] In the southern city of Cáceres in early 1786, the Granada Audiencia sentenced Francisco Fernández to a similar fate for the unspecified murder of his wife.[53] Thirty-eight-year-old Matías Piu, a tavern keeper (*bodegonero*) accused of stabbing his wife to death in Segovia, central Spain, met the same punishment in 1801.[54] In Galicia, in the peninsula's northwest, thirty-three-year-old carpenter Antonio Rodiño was sentenced to an equivalent punishment in 1803 for strangling his wife, María, so he could be free to live with his lover.[55] It is fair to assume that identical punishment took place elsewhere in the Spanish peninsula during the same time period and beyond.[56]

In several other executions, we have information about what was involved other than the full *encubamiento* ritual. In fact, a fair number of the individuals executed for having participated in the killing of their spouses or their lovers' spouses were hanged or, occasionally, shot without there being any evidence of subsequent *encubamiento*. For instance, the three individuals, all mulattos, sentenced to death in our case set for colonial Mexico, for crimes committed in 1780, 1809, and 1817, respectively, were executed by hanging without any additional ritual. Because of exceptional circumstances described in a previous chapter, two male Indians who helped a woman kill her husband at a remote mission north of Nueva Galicia (Guadalajara) were sentenced to death by hanging to serve as an example in their community (*servir de ejemplar a su nación*), but for lack of a hangman (*verdugo*) they were shot instead (*pasados por las armas*).[57] In colonial Colombia, a white man, a mulatto, a black slave, and a white or mestizo woman, all of whom killed or assisted in the killing of spouses in 1795, 1797, 1803 and 1805, respectively, were hanged without evidence of *encubamiento*.[58]

In Spain, some executions featured the *garrote* without any other accompanying ritual. In the Spanish peninsula, upon special review and order (*conmutación*) by high courts, the authorities could choose to impose the *garrote* instead of hanging as a sign of magnanimity.[59] As discussed earlier in this book, noblemen could expressly request this means of execution, and evidence exists of such petitions as early as the mid-eighteenth century.[60] Eventually, use of the *garrote,* widely believed to be more humane than the gallows, was extended to most women as well, sparing them the agony of death by hanging.[61] This happened in the case of thirty-two-year-old noblewoman María Vicenta Mendieta in the late 1790s. The Chancillería of Valladolid granted thirty-three-year-old María Lario a similar mercy at her execution for killing her husband, weaver Vicente Anguita, with the aid of a lover in the village of Medinaceli in November 1813.[62] By this time, Spain had outlawed hanging across the board and replaced it with the *garrote* for all defendants, whether noble or commoner, male or female. This trend, to which I will come back again at the end of this study, officially started during the early phase of the Napoleonic interregnum.[63]

Nothing special distinguishes the crimes that culminated in hanging, the firing squad, or the *garrote* from the rest of spousal murders to explain why *encubamiento* was omitted in those cases. Like other aspects of justice in the late colonial Spanish Atlantic, the choice of execution method seemed to have been capricious. The fact that *encubamiento* did not always occur in Spain and Spanish America could have been due to logistical difficulties or a perception among judicial officials that simply inflicting the death penalty was sufficient to deliver the legally mandated punishment and that hangings, in particular, instilled sufficient shame in criminals and fear in the rest of the population. Swifter forms of execution were unusual. For instance, death by firing squad (*armas*) was rather atypical and seems to have derived from exceptional logistical circumstances, while the *garrote* was not yet the norm, either. The fundamental reason for the decline of *encubamiento* was likely the growing concern in the late eighteenth century not so much over the death penalty itself but rather over the need to "humanize" it and other forms of punishment to reduce excessive or prolonged agony.[64] In any case, the trend is not consistent with Foucault's claims about the process occurring in France and elsewhere at around the same time. In the Spanish experience, the body remained a central target of punishment and public display a major component of its infliction. By modern standards, the punishment of criminals in the metropolis and its overseas territories continued to be characterized by harsh, vengeful, ritualistic, body-centered, and public (exhibitionist) displays.

Despite important changes in methods of punishment over time, criminals' bodies continued to be the object of gruesome and intimidating rituals. Some of the earliest evidence of such practices includes the Spanish Inquisition's infamous, terrifying trials (*autos de fe*) and punishments—burning at the stake, in particular—of individuals accused of religious heterodoxy, witchcraft, and crimes against family or sexual standards (bigamy, sodomy, and solicitation). These have been the subject of extensive academic attention and public fascination.[65] Widespread evidence also exists of executions, dismemberments, and exhibition of body parts (*cuartos*) of accused bandits, robbers, forgers, and other criminals in late eighteenth-century Spain and colonial Mexico, and probably elsewhere in the Spanish Atlantic. Even up until the early 1800s, Spanish archives contain abundant documentation of petitions by religious brotherhoods to royal authorities for permission to remove heads, hands, limbs, and other body parts from their places of public display for proper burial.[66] Further, for non-nobles at least, floggings remained common throughout the Spanish empire well into the late eighteenth century and beyond.[67] Spousal murderers were just one category in a long list of criminals who continued to be sentenced to horrifying, dishonorable, and public deaths.

The deeply symbolic spectacle of executions in Spain and its overseas territories found support in a series of laws and legal doctrines that viewed punishment not only as a way to mend wrongs and instill fear (*escarmiento*) but also as a means to put criminals to shame (*poner a la vergüenza*).[68] Such laws, inherited mainly from Roman practices, reflected the values of Church and Crown in their deep concern about the offenses that contemporaries considered most horrendous. In addition to spousal murder, these included sodomy, witchcraft, counterfeiting, smuggling, sedition, and brigandage. From a moral, religious, economic, or political point of view, these were loathsome, reprehensible behaviors that posed a threat to the kingdom's stability and the well-being of Catholic families and communities, and deserved painful and visible public vengeance. Despite this concern, however, subtle but significant changes continued to take place in the forms that this vengeance took.

In fact, the nature of punishment had begun to change, as a self-congratulatory contemporary put it, as a result of the "sweetness and piety" of the Spanish monarchy and Catholic religion, as well as cultural and humanitarian reasons (*la dulzura y piedad de nuestra religión, y de nuestro gobierno . . . [y] . . . la humanidad de nuestras costumbres, y . . . la cultura de nuestros tiempos*).[69] The evident transition from hanging to the *garrote* in the early nineteenth century reflected these merciful qualities. Even such practices as dragging and *encubamiento* underwent remarkable transformations in the eighteenth century: Instead of coming into direct contact with the ground, for instance, the body of the person being dragged was placed on mats (*esteras, serones,* and other *esparto*-based rugs) to cushion what would otherwise be excruciating pain; instead of being placed inside the leather bag alive, culprits were executed first; rather than dumped for good in the ocean or a river without proper burial, after a brief immersion corpses were quickly removed and offered Christian rites. Flogging fell into disuse during the eighteenth century in Spain (later in the overseas territories) as well. All of these changes spoke to deep concerns about the "civilization" of punishment and, more generally, the legitimacy of the monarchy administering it. Maintaining royal legitimacy also dictated attention to evidence and the crime's circumstances.

When the authorities had sufficient evidence to issue a final sentence, with or without any attempt at using torture, criminals faced not only "ordinary" punishment such as *encubamiento* but also "extraordinary" punishment. The latter occurred in exceptional exculpatory or mitigating circumstances (*excepciones*). Even if guilty, many defendants found good reasons to request and obtain a reduced sentence, especially to avoid the death penalty. Let us remember that the circumstances meriting such reductions varied, but the leading factors included drinking, insanity or rage, and deaths allegedly unrelated to the injuries inflicted by the defendant.

Following is a description of other ordinary punishments besides the death penalty and several extraordinary punishments generally imposed on spousal killers in our three regions between the 1750s and the 1820s. It shows the rarity of death sentences, addresses possible biases, describes the various forms of confinement, and again reveals the prevalence of pardons, especially in colonial regions.

PUNISHMENT, ETHNICITY, LEGAL CULTURE, AND ROYAL RITUALS IN NEW SPAIN

Punishment of spousal murderers varied and was somewhat inconsistent, in part because, as observed at the outset of this book, ancien régime laws were imprecise and involved considerable judicial discretion.[70] Going from the harshest to the mildest, only six of the Mexican cases examined ended in a death sentence, although in several of them it is not clear whether this verdict was ever carried out or was perhaps commuted later.[71] William Taylor, in any case, has already demonstrated the rarity of capital punishment in colonial Spanish America, even in cases of homicide. Execution, he notes, was normally reserved for instances with clear proof of assassination (murder for hire), premeditation, cruelty (*alevosia*), or treachery.[72] Legal manuals of the time treated *alevosia* and treachery as more or less equivalent and used them to describe cases in which the victim's death was "certain" rather than fought over (*peleada*). Examples included killing victims who were asleep, attacks from behind with a knife, or murders committed with a firearm or by poison.[73] For instance, the only example we have in our case set of Indians sentenced to death, discussed in the introductory chapter of this study, occurred near the Mission of San Antonio and involved a premeditated act of treachery by an Indian woman, Eulalia, and two male accomplices, including her lover, who strangled her husband while he slept. Later they said the victim had choked while chewing tobacco.[74]

In the rest of our cases, however, the defendant's ethnicity appears to have been a more compelling circumstance for capital punishment than premeditation, *alevosia*, or treachery. For instance, it is striking to find that three of only six defendants sentenced to death in late colonial Mexico were mulattos. In other words, in 50 percent of the few cases it was used, capital punishment fell on mulattos. Only one of these was a case seemingly aggravated by the fact that the victim was asleep. The other two were no different from several murders for which Indian defendants were sentenced to labor or short jail terms, or were eventually pardoned. Added to the fact that mulatto defendants committed only a few of the crimes in our case set—six of the eighty-seven homicides under examination—this means that 50 percent of killings by mulattos resulted in the death penalty, as opposed to 16.6 percent ((just two out of twelve defendants of those racial categories) by whites or mestizos and just 2.1 percent (just one out of forty-eight defendants in this racial group) by Indians. One of the longest prison terms on record also went to a mulatto woman, María Aguilar of Colima.[75]

The most common form of punishment for all defendants seems to have been incarceration or confinement of some kind, occurring in about 25 percent of the cases for which sufficient information is available.[76] If we add forced labor to this figure, total cases of confinement actually rise to more than 37 percent (see Table 7.1), more than one-third of known sentences. Considering the life expectancy at the time, around forty years, and the unhealthy conditions of colonial prisons, especially in major urban centers such as Mexico City or Guadalajara, jail sentences, which normally ranged from one to ten years, were harsh punishment indeed.[77] Prisons in large capital cities housed hundreds of inmates. In Mexico City, for instance, the royal prisons could provide bed, food, and shelter to between 200 and 300 people in the late eighteenth century.[78] Most jails were rough, dangerous, and unsanitary places. Inmates in Mexico City, Oaxaca, Puebla de los Angeles, and San Luis de Potosi complained that jailers inflicted cruel physical punishment, extorted money to allow visits from relatives, stole alms destined to alleviate the prisoners' lot, used the inmates as free labor for their personal and familial benefit, deprived them of food, and unjustifiably delayed their release.[79]

Women faced additional hardships in prison, especially the risk of being coerced into sex with their jailers. In San Luis de Potosi in 1778, spousal killer Maria Luisa Montante, who was under twenty years old, declared she was forced to have sex with several guards. She became pregnant more than once as a result.[80] There is also evidence that women sometimes used sex as a mechanism to negotiate their escape. Juana Salvadora Márquez, an Indian woman jailed in 1819 for killing her husband in the town of Colotlán, in northern Jalisco, had sex twice with her jailer, forty-year-old widower José María López, who eventually let her run away. She later denounced him.[81]

TABLE 7.1. *Punishments applied in spousal homicides in New Spain, 1747–1821, by gender and ethnicity*

Punishment	Total number	Percentage	Male (#)	Female (#)	Indian (#)	Mulatto (#)	White (#)
Death	6	7.9	6	—	1	3	2
6–10 years presidio	3	3.9	3	—	1	—	?
1–5 years presidio	4	5.2	4	—	—	1[a]	3
6–10 years jail (prison)	5	6.6	3	2	3	1	1
1–5 years jail (prison)	3	3.9	1	2	3	—	—
6–10 years *recogida*	4	5.2	—	4	?	1	?
1–5 years *recogida*	—	—	—	—	—	—	—
6–10 years labor	2	2.6	2	—	2	—	—
6 months to 5 years labor	8	10.5	8	—	6	?	?
6–10 years banishment	1	1.3	1	—	1	—	—
1–5 years banishment	2	2.6	2	—	2	—	—
Confinement in mental hospital	1	1.3	1	—	1	—	—
Pardon denied	9[b]	11.8	8	1	5	?	?
Pardon granted	23	30.2	19	4	14	?[c]	5
Acquitted	5	6.6	4	1	5	—	—
Undetermined	15[d]	16.5[e]	10	5	6	1[f]	1
Total	**91**						

SOURCES: AGN, Mexico City: Acordada, Californias, Criminales, General de Parte, Presidios y Cárceles; and Provincias Internas; AJO; AANG, Guadalajara, Criminales; AJP; Archivo Provincial de Zacatecas; Municipal Archive of Veracruz; *Diario de México* 176, March 25, 1806, 334–336; 1646, April 4, 1810, 373–374; Isabel Marín Tello, "Justicia penal y orden social en Michoacán en el siglo XVIII (1750-1810)," 217–218; Castro Gutiérrez, "Condición femenina y violencia," 6.

[a]An accomplice in a crime committed by a woman.

[b]Pardons were denied in most cases because the defendant was in hiding. This entry also suggests an unknown or pending jail sentence.

[c]At least two mestizos were pardoned.

[d]The total adds up to more than 87 because several pardons were granted after an initial sentence punishing the defendant, typically to a jail term.

[e]Percentages do not necessarily total 100 because some figures are rounded up.

[f]Two mestizos.

Besides circumstances such as mistreatment, lack of food, extortion, and sexual harassment, murderers sent to places of confinement ran the real risk of dying in jail. Several of the spousal murderers in our case sets passed away while awaiting trial or not long after sentencing. For instance, this happened to Indian Francisco Nicolas after about one year in a Cuernavaca jail for killing his wife, Maria Alexandra, in early 1816. Upon realizing he was ill, the local judge ordered that he be examined by a medical doctor, who certified that he suffered from dangerous diarrhea likely to end his life, even more so if he remained locked in the unsanitary local jail.[82] Presidio terms in remote or "ultramarine" military fortresses were also quite harsh. They were even rougher places and often required forced labor.[83] Luckily, penal servitude in *obrajes* (the Mexican textile industry) was uncommon by the time of the crimes under discussion, as was service in bakeries and butcher shops (*tocinerias*). In the past, prisoners were driven from place to place tied to a rope (*collera*) and forcibly "sold" for up to 180 pesos to reluctant owners for periods of from eight to ten years. Shop owners who refused to keep the prisoners were obliged to pay an equivalent fine.[84] Evidence of this practice during the time frame of this study is absent. Overall, our evidence of the specific conditions and dynamics of places of confinement is limited, and, for Spanish America at least, the subject of late colonial prisons and presidios still awaits further in-depth historical research.

The rest of the defendants in the Mexican case set met with relatively mild forms of chastisement. These included lighter forms of labor service: public works, especially the construction and repair of roads; working on a sugar hacienda, at a church, or in a hospital; tending boats on a lake; or, in the case of a native woman, assisting a presidio commander with domestic chores.[85] Banishment, sometimes imposed in addition to labor service, was a secondary form of punishment, as was confinement of women to *casas de recogidas,* correctional institutions for women who had gone astray. Several existed in Spain and the New World, including Guadalajara, Mexico, and Puebla. These establishments housed prostitutes, women undergoing divorce, and female criminals, even spousal killers. Confinement in them could be as harsh as in royal jails, and some inmates also died prior to completing their sentences there. For instance, spousal murderer María Julia died before completing her five-year-confinement in Guadalajara's *casa de recogidas.*[86]

Non-Spaniards, male and female alike, occasionally received between 100 and 200 lashes in addition to public works or jail terms. In San Luis de Potosí in the 1770s, spousal murderer Maria Luisa Montarte was sentenced to 200 lashes in addition to ten years in a *recogimiento*. Likewise, besides one year of public works, Oaxaca Indian José Mejia's sentence in 1810 also included flogging.[87]

Mercy was never lacking, however. As with the trial of Lorenzo Macapa, examined earlier in this study, close to one-third of the cases (23 out of 76) for which evidence of the final sentence is available resulted in pardons. Altogether, pardons, short terms of labor service, and banishment account for almost one-half of the cases (34 cases or 44.7 percent) for which sentencing data are available. And, of course, a few cases resulted in acquittals. At least by contemporary standards, therefore, a good number of spousal killers in colonial Mexico received very lenient treatment. As Table 7.2 suggests, the same pattern seems to hold true for other homicides as well.

TABLE 7.2. *Comparison of punishments applied in spousal and other homicides in New Spain*

	Spousal murders		General homicides					
	Mexico		Central Mexico		Mixteca Alta		Jalisco	
Punishment	Number	Percentage	Number	Percentage	Number	Percentage	Number	Percentage
Death	6	9.4	4	2.6	10	17.9	8	8.4
Labor service	10	15.6	49	32.2	13	23.2	36	37.9
Exile (banishment)	3	4.7	2	1.3	5	8.9	—	—
Pardon	23	35.9	56	36.8	1	—	42	44.2
Corporal punishment[a]	2	3.1	4	2.6	11	19.6	2	2.1
Fines	?	?	14	9.2	17	30.4	—	—
Other (jail/ confinement)	20	31.2	—	?	—	?	—	—

SOURCES: AGN, Mexico City: Acordada, Californias, Criminales, General de Parte, Presidios y Cárceles; and Provincias Internas; AJO; AANG, Guadalajara, Criminales; AJP; Archivo Provincial de Zacatecas; Municipal Archive of Veracruz; *Diario de México* 176, March 25, 1806, 334–336; 1646, April 4, 1810, 373–374; Isabel Marín Tello, "Justicia penal y orden social en Michoacán en el siglo XVIII (1750–1810)," 217–218; Castro Gutiérrez, "Condición femenina y violencia," 6; Taylor, *Drinking, Homicide, and Rebellion,* 98; idem, "Amigos de sombrero," 103.

[a]Lashes.

Legal biases in favor of men probably accounted for the light treatment of at least some male offenders accused of having killed their spouses.[88] Twenty-three out of sixty-one males for whom information is available, or 30.2 percent of our case set, received acquittals or pardons. However, considering the widespread use of this device for all types of homicides (4 women of 14, 28.5 percent of female criminals we have sufficient information for, also received pardon), the Mexican cases appear to suggest other, more significant reasons than gender behind sentencing patterns: namely, ethnicity, legal culture, and royal rituals, already addressed.

As noted above with regard to mulattos, ethnicity was without question a key factor in determining punishment. One might imagine harshness across the board for ethnic subalterns, in keeping with some of the findings of historical research into colonial ethnic relations and the law.[89] As Douglas Cope, among others, has demonstrated, anticipating Frederick Cooper's claims of the centrality of a "politics of difference" under colonial relations, "the distinction between Spaniard and Indian, conqueror and conquered, formed the basis of the colonial regime."[90] Even the natives' access to the courts and the paternalistic judicial system was a means to consolidate and legitimate Spanish hegemonic rule over Indian communities.[91] Other scholars have also suggested that, besides constituting a mechanism to legitimate the monarch and the colonial regime, legal paternalism was crucial for patriarchal domination and contributed to the general decline in the legal status of native women.[92]

As we already know, however, ethnic relations were quite fluid in practice, and some paternalistic practices actually favored the natives. Some historians have even praised the ultimate fairness of the paternalistic colonial legal culture and Indians' active participation in it.[93] Unlike mulattos, who fared much worse than others, Indian criminals generally received benign treatment. For them, ethnicity was not a hindrance but a factor in their favor, a major source of royal benevolence. Although a fair number of whites—five out of the eleven for whom we have information—also received pardons, in absolute terms Indians were unquestionably the main beneficiaries (60.1 percent—see Table 7.1). Had other Indian defendants not gone into hiding or failed to obtain the forgiveness of the victim's family, making them ineligible for judicial pardon, the percentage of pardons would have been even higher.

The fact that, as discussed elsewhere in this book, Indians were part of the broader Roman and canon law category of "privileged" legal subjects (*miserabiles personae*) and considered wretched in different regards seems to account for the judges' inclination to show leniency. This may be why twenty-two natives, half of the Indians for whom data is available, were pardoned, acquitted, or just sentenced to exile. Seven more received less than five years of labor service. Only one was sentenced to death, and just six more (12.5 percent of defendants from this ethnic group) received more or less harsh prison terms (see Table 7.1).

We have also discussed the importance of two other factors contributing to leniency for the natives. First was the regular occurrence of royal celebrations. The Spanish royals celebrated special dates and events by granting generous amnesties. Almost one-third of the cases examined in the New Spain case set ended in pardons enacted to commemorate special occasions, such as a royal wedding or birth, the ascent of a new monarch to the throne, or a significant legal or military event. These kinds of royal graces were decreed almost twenty times during the period of our study, from the late 1740s to about 1821.[94] Royal pardons, as the statistics suggest, were relatively generous toward the crimes under examination. Other chapters discuss cultural and legal features of this institution as well as notable exceptions. Second, contemporary scientific notions concerning the immediate causes of death also contributed to the exculpation of individuals who would be held responsible for murder under modern standards. As noted elsewhere, any significant lapse of time between the aggression and death was sufficient to raise the possibility that, rather than violence, the injured person's failure to seek adequate treatment (a charge typically leveled at Indians, who pursued native remedies rather than formal medical treatment) or intervening factors such as "*alunamiento*" (exposure to the moon), fevers, infections, or other unknown complications, were the real causes of death. In these cases, the aggressor could not be charged.[95] Following are a few additional comments concerning instances in which, instead of earning the defendant benign treatment, ethnicity could be a reason for harshness, as it was for blacks in Mexico and elsewhere.

MULATTOS, BLACK SLAVES, AND THE LAW

We already know that Christianity in general, and in particular the sacrament of marriage, represented an effective mechanism of social control in the Iberian kingdom. From early on, despite misgivings that it might increase their expectations of imminent freedom, the Spanish Crown considered Christian matrimony an ideal way to contain the rebellious behavior of persons of African descent in the New World.[96] Eventually, marriage petitions became a regular phenomenon, and thousands of black slaves born in Africa and their New World descendants, black and mulatto alike, married in Mexico and elsewhere.[97] Another common mechanism of control was subjecting blacks to ecclesiastical jurisdiction in cases of cohabitation, abandonment of their spouses, and other domestic conflicts. Several of them were jailed, sentenced to public humiliation, and otherwise punished for such offenses.[98] In any case, some of the marriages had soured beyond all remedy, and at least a few ended fatally. In such instances, some in this social group, particularly mulattos, seem to have received especially harsh treatment.

Although nothing in the letter of the law specified that mulattos should be treated differently, perhaps because in slave societies "autonomous free blacks embodied a threat to the social order," they were clearly punished more harshly than other defendants in cases of spousal murder.[99] Let us remember that even though they committed few of the homicides in the Mexican case set—just 6 of 87, or 6.9 percent—a full 50 percent of the mulattoes found guilty were sentenced to death. This was in stark contrast to the low percentage of whites or mestizos and Indians.

Capital punishment of mulattoes who murdered their spouses or concubines accounted for half of all instances in which this penalty was used in the late colonial Mexico case set. Moreover, only one of these free mulatto defendants, forty-eight-year-old farmer Miguel Manzano, was found guilty of the aggravating circumstance of killing his Indian lover's husband, Felipe Cruz, also an Indian, while he slept one night in 1817. Killing defenseless victims was, as we know, a factor commonly cited to justify imposition of the death penalty.[100] However, the other two cases closely resembled several murders for which Indian defendants were sentenced to lesser punishments or even pardoned.

In one of them, which took place in Puebla in 1780, José Bueno, a mulatto coach driver, stabbed his wife, Antonia, to death. Despite a lack of witnesses, the defendant's track record of habitual drinking and domestic disputes suggested that his crime was the culmination of a pattern of behavior. Because his whereabouts were unknown, he was tried in absentia. The defendant's contumacy and the fact that his drinking was not random but habitual may have contributed to the harsh sentence.[101] In the other case, a mining worker and artisan by the name of Tomás Aquino Ramírez stabbed his concubine, María Hilaria, upon finding her in the company of another man. The woman had also refused to follow orders from the defendant to stand up and follow him. The events occurred in Colima in 1809 while a group of peddlers awaited clearance at a customs checkpoint.[102]

The death sentence, normally used only in exceptional cases, appears to have been the judges' punishment of choice for mulatto spousal murderers. In addition, María Aguilar of Colima, a free mulatto woman who helped her lover kill her husband, Antonio, with a machete around 1812 in western Mexico, received quite a long prison term—six years.[103] Law and legal doctrine generally carried considerable weight, but it seems clear that in instances such as these, judicial practice often was informed more by racial prejudice than by specific doctrinal legal criteria.

The law was not evenhanded when it came to black slaves, either. To begin with, they lacked freedom, a fundamental attribute of human beings under natural law. This obviously restricted their mobility and generally gave their masters great control over their lives. Furthermore, under old legal provisions that lasted into the early nineteenth century, slaves were legally banned from entering into various types of civil contracts, particularly those involving the sale or exchange of jewels, gold, silver, or even clothing.[104]

As several scholars have demonstrated, however, "Spanish law and custom granted the slave a moral and juridical personality, as well as certain rights and protections not found in other slave systems."[105] For instance, the fact that slaves could and did marry and start families meant that, in aspects concerning their family lives, they had a great deal to say even in courts of justice. Besides, marriage itself enriched their human experience, affording opportunity for cohabitation, sexual exchange, and parenthood. Abundant evidence also shows that slaves took full advantage of the Church to protect their conjugal rights[106] and appealed to the law and the courts to promote their vital interests in general, even gain freedom.[107]

Further evidence exists of slaves' independent standing before law and justice. As they did in cases of others alleged to be legally incompetent, the courts actually accepted slaves' testimony during the investigation of crimes and for vouchsafing a defendant's character. Finally, it was illegal for anyone, even masters, to murder a slave.[108] In turn, slaves could appear in court and stand trial for crimes against their masters or others, including, of course, such offenses as spousal murder.[109]

According to the available records, however, cases of spousal murder involving slaves were relatively exceptional. Of the dozens of murders under consideration, only two included defendants who were slaves, both in Colombia (1791 and 1803). One slave worked on a hacienda in Tocaima, a small town in central Colombia, and the other in Cúcuta, a modest community near New Granada's northeastern border with the Captaincy of Venezuela. In both instances, the slave couple's own children brought the crime to public attention. The immediate cause of the first case was a dispute in which the wife tried to stop her husband from assigning work to their children, but the couple had already argued repeatedly over her alleged adultery with several other men. In fact, during the fatal argument the wife actually told her husband that the children were not his to boss around! Enraged, he killed her with a machete. No clear motive emerged for the other case, in which the husband beat his wife to death.[110]

The procedures followed in these cases were not unusual, except that the justice official in charge designated a defender of slaves (*defensor de esclavos*) to represent them. Like the *defensor de indios,* this officer was charged with representing the defendants' interests and advocating on their behalf. This suggests that, similar to Indians, slaves were to a certain extent included in the category of *miserabiles personae,* disadvantaged people in need of special paternalistic protection.[111] In at least one of the cases under study, the master relinquished his property rights over the slave so as not to restrict the punishment the Crown could impose. Francisco de la Bastida, the slave master, stated that he "handed over said slave, surrendering it to the King our lord so that he could decide his fate. . . ." (*"hago entrega de dicho esclavo, cediéndolo al Rey nuestro señor para que este disponga de él"*).[112]

Ultimately, the punishment met by both culprits was not out of the ordinary given the circumstances of the two incidents. One of the slaves was not even sentenced to death, as requested by the prosecutor, out of consideration of his rights as a patriarch. The court accepted his rage at his wife's "insolence" and "bad temper" as an extenuating factor. Instead of death, he received eight years of labor in the Cartagena public works, a harsh but not necessarily extraordinary penalty, particularly for slaves already subjected to strenuous labor conditions.[113] The other slave fled and was never found; after being tried in absentia (*en rebeldia*), he was sentenced to lashes followed by death by hanging because of the fact that the murder appeared to have been planned (*alevoso*) and the victim was defenseless.[114] Hangings and other forms of execution, in any case, gradually felt into disrepute and, as the colonial Colombian case discussed next illustrates, were somewhat exceptional in late colonial times.

PUNISHMENT IN NEW GRANADA

As Table 7.3 indicates, most of the accused in New Granada, about two-thirds, received prison (*presidio*) terms (4.6 percent received life terms, 41.8 percent received six to ten years, and 11.6 percent received less than five years); 11 percent more received terms of from one to ten years in jail (*prisión*), a milder form of internment. Except for life in prison, the rest of the sentences to confinement may appear strikingly mild by today's standards. However, with life expectancy around age forty at the time, six to ten years in an unsanitary, dangerous prison may have been tantamount to a life sentence in some cases.

In two rare cases, defendants in New Granada received a life sentence. Both instances also included "service to his majesty" through hard labor without any compensation, except food (*a ración y sin sueldo*). In the more than 200 cases this book deals with, these are the only two instances I could identify involving lifers. No similar punishments are recorded for spousal murderers in Mexico or Spain during the period of this study.

The first case was thirty-two-year-old mestizo dressmaker Antonio Nieto in the little town of Ubate, in central New Granada. In 1760, after a dispute with his brother-in-law over a game of dice, he stabbed to death his wife, Maria Rocha, when she intervened to protect her brother. Upon committing his crime, the man next stabbed his brother-in-law in the eye and then escaped on horseback. He was later apprehended and during his trial confessed not only to killing his wife but also to murdering a man a few years earlier with a pocketknife. The *audiencia* decided he was vicious and should spend his life term at the Cartagena works (*fabricas*).[115] The second case involved twenty-year-old white farmer Simpliciano Vega, who stabbed to death his wife, Dominga, after she surprised him and his lover near a river and hurled a rock at her rival. Days later, Dominga was attacked and killed. Authorities suspected the pair, especially since Dominga's body presented wounds from two separate weapons, a pocketknife and a regular knife. The lovers had dumped her corpse into a nearby river to hide their crime. This occurred in the central province

TABLE 7.3. *Punishments applied in cases of spousal homicide in colonial Colombia, 1750–1814, by gender and ethnicity*

Punishment	Total number[a]	Percentage	Male (#)	Female (#)	Indian (#)	Mestizo (#)	Mulatto/ *Zambo* (#)	Black (#)	White (#)
Death	6	13.9	4[b]	2	—	—	1	1	4
Life in presidio	2	4.6	2	—	—	1	—	—	1
6–10 years presidio	18	41.8	15	1	6	2	1	1	—
1–5 years presidio	5	11.6	5	—	1	2	—	—	—
6–10 years jail (prison)	4	9.3	—	3	—	—	1	—	—
1–5 years jail (prison)	1	2.3	—	1	—	—	—	—	1
6–10 years *recogida*	1	2.3	—	1	—	—	—	—	—
1–5 years *recogida*	—	—	—	—	—	—	—	—	—
6–10 years labor	—	—	—	—	—	—	—	—	—
6 months to 5 years labor	1	2.3	—	1	—	—	—	—	—
6–10 years banishment	—	—	—	—	—	—	—	—	—
1–5 years banishment	—	—	—	—	—	—	—	—	—
Confinement in mental hospital	—	—	—	—	—	—	—	—	—
Pardon denied	2	4.6	—	—	—	—	—	—	—
Pardon granted	3	6.9	2	1	1	—	—	—	—
Acquitted	?								
Undetermined	17	28.3							
Total	60								

SOURCES: AGN, Colonia, Juicios Criminales; Sosa Abella, *Labradores, tejedores y ladrones*, 60, 146–147; Luna Rivillas, "Documentos para el estudio de la criminalidad sexual en la provincia y gobernación de Antioquia," 554–564.

[a]The total adds up to more than 54 cases in the case set, for the table includes the punishment accorded accomplices in these crimes.

[b]Includes at least one woman's accomplice.

of Tunja in 1766. The spouses had a long history of domestic disputes. Simpliciano regularly mistreated his wife, who often sought shelter at her father's house, and he had long-standing relations with the other woman. He was originally sentenced to life in Cartagena, but the *audiencia* later decided to send him to a Havana fortress instead.[116]

Although both murders were committed with prohibited weapons, only the second case was the seemingly premeditated or treacherous murder of a defenseless victim, the gravest possible circumstance. Unlike the first case, it was not preceded by a fight and could hardly have been construed as accidental. In any case, it is clear that neither of the defendants in the two cases was a *miserabilis persona,* nor could either of them claim to have acted under the influence of alcohol, both typical excuses for a reduced sentence. Finally, we should point out that both incidents occurred early in the period of this study, in the 1760s, at a time when progressive enlightened ideas were just beginning to make an impact. This may partially explain why the punishment imposed in these two instances was so severe relative to the majority of cases under examination, except of course the few instances where death was applied. Death sentences, as we have noted, were also infrequent.

In fact, only a few New Granadan spousal murder defendants (six of the total, 13.9 percent of those for whom enough sentencing information is available) received a death sentence. In relative terms, though, they represented more than twice the percentage of Mexicans who received a similar punishment. Like those receiving harsh prison sentences, the majority (four) facing this punishment were white, in addition to one black slave and a free mulatto. Whereas in Mexico all of those sentenced to death were men, in New Granada men accounted for just two-thirds of the total (four of six). Also in relative terms, a few more New Granadan women (20 percent of criminals of the same sex for whom information on sentencing is available, as opposed to 14.2 percent of men) received the death penalty than their counterparts in Mexico. This may be a function of fragmentary records or because society considered female crimes of this nature to be more execrable or dangerous than those committed by men. As a prosecutor put it in 1805, "there is no worse enemy than the [female] domestic one . . . and men are seriously in danger when they are hated by their wives."[117] Other officials, including the one cited below, stressed the need for the death penalty to frighten and dissuade other women from committing such crimes. Despite these comments, however, the higher courts had ample opportunity to reduce defendants' sentences for both males and females alike.

Once local judges issued their sentences, the cases went for review before the *real audiencia,* the viceroyalty's high court in Santafé de Bogotá. It was not uncommon for the *audiencia* to be lenient and reduce the typically harsher punishment imposed by local mayors. In fact, the appeals court reversed four additional death sentences, substituting eight-to-ten-year prison terms without any clear explanation.[118] This certainly had to be construed as evidence of magnanimity on the part of the king's highest justice officials. Magnanimity remained, after all, an essential and arbitrary component of the criminal process.

As in Mexico and elsewhere in the Spanish kingdom, the celebration of special festive events could benefit some criminals with blank pardons from a generous and charitable Crown. Nevertheless, pardons seem to have been much less frequent in late colonial Colombia than in Mexico or Spain around the same time. Whereas in Mexico more than 30 percent of the accused were eventually pardoned, in Colombia the proportion was four times less: only two males and one woman in our case set, or 6.9 percent of the criminals whose sentences are known.[119] Several more requested a similar royal grace but were denied the benefit.[120] It is unclear why colonial authorities in Mexico were more generous with pardons, but most likely the explanation is again related to paternalistic attitudes toward the large Indian community in that region. Colonial Colombia, a largely mestizo society, probably elicited much less leniency.

Although a significant portion of jail terms for both males and females was within the two- to ten-year time frame, strict sentencing standards seem to have been lacking in New Granada, as they were in Mexico. Only on a couple of occasions did local officials, most of whom were not legal experts, cite the applicable laws to explain the parameters they followed in trying the case and imposing specific punishments. Even on these occasions, legal references tended to be vague and sentences probably followed customary practices, consistent with the image of a highly discretionary judicial practice.[121]

As implied above, fragmentary evidence shows a possible gender bias among the officials responsible for judicial decisions. For example, a prosecutor justifying his recommendation of death by hanging for a wife who murdered her husband insisted that the punishment would set an example, scaring other women (*escarmiento a las demás mujeres*) into curtailing their hidden enmity toward their husbands.[122] Biases against female defendants may be detected in several other instances, as well. Three male offenders sentenced to death had their sentences reduced to jail terms, compared to only one of three women in this situation. Besides, unlike the male offender, who was sentenced to hanging for stabbing his wife to death in a vicious, cold-blooded, and seemingly unjustifiable attack, one of the women whose death sentence was confirmed seems to have acted in self-defense, a consideration that officials accepted in several similar cases as an extenuating factor.[123] Moreover, given the lack of mitigating circumstances in at least two of the cases involving males, it is hard to understand why their death sentences were changed to jail terms.[124]

The evidence is far from conclusive, however, and one could point to cases in which males were in fact treated even more harshly than women. Only men, for instance, received life in prison. In fact, the impact of not only masculinity, but also whiteness or nobility, was not always beneficial and could be counterintuitive. The records of punishment for spousal murderers in Spain make this contradiction evident. The Spanish experience also illustrates the increasing humanization of even the death penalty over time, an issue also discussed at the end of this work.

PUNISHMENT AND SOCIAL HIERARCHIES IN SPAIN

In contrast to New Spain and New Granada, confinement in prisons, jails, or *recogimientos* was not the dominant form of punishment for spousal murderers in the Iberian Peninsula. Only thirteen people, about one-quarter (25.4 percent) of those for whom sentencing information is available, received this penalty (see Table 7.4). Although, as in the colonies, some people managed to escape before or during trial proceedings, the unfortunates who eventually suffered this penalty would have had to enter rather crowded facilities. For instance, the royal jails in Madrid held hundreds of inmates. As many as 277 prisoners were crowded into the Casa y Corte's jail by 1795, 66 of them females, with 240–260 more in the city jail (*Carcel de la Villa*). In turn, the two female jails (*galeras*) housed about 175 inmates in the 1760s.[125] Places such as these were insalubrious and unsafe.[126] In addition, almost half of those facing internment were sent to yet harsher penal fortresses (*presidios*) in Africa and, occasionally, the Philippines.[127] It is no wonder that several died not only in these but in local jails as well before the end of their prison terms. For example, spousal murderer Melchor Hernandez died of a fever in 1783 while under confinement in the Valladolid Royal Jail less than two years into his sentence, as did Antonia Velasco in Talavera de la Reina, western Castile, who succumbed to an epidemic in 1804, after three years of an eight-year jail term for the violent murder of her husband.[128]

TABLE 7.4. *Punishments of all criminals in Granada, Spain, 1799–1805*

Punishment	Number	Percentage
Death	25	0.9
Galleys, arsenals, prisons	609	23.4
Military service	263	10.1
Female jail and confinement in *hospicio*	94	3.6
Firing or suspension from public job	24	0.9
Fines	771	29.6
Warning/admonishment	728	28
Pardon (*indulto*)	84	3.2
Total	**2,598**	

SOURCE: ARCG, Libro de Providencias Definitivas en Causas Criminales, 324.

In Spain, however, the death penalty seems to have been more prevalent than imprisonment as punishment for spousal murderers. As Table 7.5 shows, fifteen spouse killers, equivalent to almost one-third of the Spanish defendants (29.4 percent) whose punishment is known, met the harshest possible sentence. Although evidence is fragmentary and may be a function of irregular data, as in the case of New Granada, women (6 out of the 14 that sentencing information is available for, or 42.8 percent) were apparently about twice more likely to be sentenced to death than were men (9 out of 37, or 24.3 percent). More important, and despite its decline over time, this penalty was generally more common in Iberia than in other places in the late eighteenth century.

The death penalty occurred more frequently in the Iberian Peninsula than seems to have been the case in either the colonies or some neighboring European regions. As described above, just 8 percent of spousal murderers in colonial Mexico for whom sentencing information is available

TABLE 7.5. *Punishments applied in spousal homicides in Spain, 1771–1824, by gender and social status*

Punishment	Number	Percentage	Male (#)	Female (#)	Noble (#)	Commoner (#)
Death	15	29.4	9	6	2	13
6–10 years presidio	6	11.8	6	—	1	5
1–5 years presidio	2	3.9	2	—	—	2
6–10 years jail (prison)	1	2	1	—	—	1
1–5 years jail (prison)	—	—	—	—	—	—
5–10 years *galera*	2	3.9	—	2	—	2
6–10 years *recogida*	1	2	—	1	—	1
1–5 years *recogida*	—	—	—	—	—	—
6–10 years labor	—	—	—	—	—	—
6 months to 5 years labor	1	2	1	—	—	1
6–10 years military service	1	2	1	—	—	1
6 months–5 years military service	1	2	1	—	—	1
6–10 years banishment	1	2	—	1	—	1
1–5 years banishment	—	—	—	—	—	—
Confinement to recover health	2	3.9	2	—	—	2
Fine	1	2	1	—	—	1
Pardon granted	5	9.8	5	—	—	5
Pardon request pending	2	3.9	2	—	—	2
Acquitted	10	19.6	6	4	—	10
Undetermined	19	27.1	15	4	—	19
Total	70[a]		**52**	**18**	3	67

SOURCES: ARCV, Pleitos Criminales and Sala de Vizcaya; AHN, Madrid, Consejos Suprimidos; ARG, La Coruña; AGI; ARCG, Libro de Providencias Definitivas; AHPC, Cordoba; AHPC, Cáceres; AGS, Gracia y Justicia; Mantecón, *La muerte de Antonia Isabel Sánchez*, 84; Morgado, *Derecho de asilo y delincuencia en la diócesis de Cádiz*, 124; "Acusación Fiscal contra Marcelo J . . . , reo confeso de parricidio por la muerte violenta dada a su muger María G . . . ; pronunciada el día 23 de Abril de 1798 en la sala segunda de Alcaldes de Casa y Corte," in Meléndez Valdés, *Discursos Forenses*, 46–70.

[a]Includes five accomplices.

faced death. In colonial Colombia, the figure was around 13.9 percent. In spite of growing humanitarian sensibility, therefore, metropolitan criminals were perhaps almost two to four times more likely to be put to death for killing their spouses than were criminals in overseas Spanish possessions. In continental Europe, in places like Amsterdam, for which reliable, comprehensive data exist, the death penalty in general had already become less common, at least since the mid-seventeenth century.[129] Spain was not part of this trend at that time. Single regions such as Valencia witnessed hundreds of executions in the 1600s.[130] Partial information for Granada and Seville also indicates close to 100 instances in each during just a portion of that century.[131]

Despite its rather wide application for spousal murderers, by the eighteenth century statistics for large places like Madrid suggest a general decline in the death penalty. Between 1755 and 1789, a lapse of thirty-four years, Madrid and its environs witnessed just over a dozen executions.[132] Other specialized studies have claimed as many as ninety-eight executions, about two to three each year, between 1751 and 1790.[133] In either case, judging by what we know about the situation in Valencia, Granada, and Seville in earlier centuries, the number of death sentences in the kingdom's capital seems considerably lower than before. Similar declines were occurring in other Spanish regions.

Few death sentences were issued in Granada, Extremadura, and elsewhere in the late eighteenth century. In Granada, from 1799 to 1805, death occurred in just 25 cases out of more than 2,500 crimes at the turn of the nineteenth century, less than 1 percent of the total (see Table 7.4). In Extremadura between 1792 and 1816, a period four times as long, there were but 21 executions.[134] Therefore, the trend for spousal murderers ran contrary to the general decline in the death penalty.

In contrast to the frequency to which they were sentenced to death and, to a lesser extent, confinement, only about 10 percent of spousal murderers in Spain received royal pardons.[135] In colonial Colombia, the percentage of pardons was slightly lower (6.9 percent) than in the peninsula, but the contrast with colonial Mexico is remarkable. About one-third (30.2 percent) of spousal killers in Mexico received pardons, more than three times the proportion of pardons granted in Spain. Further, in both Colombia and Mexico women appear among the beneficiaries, while in Spain pardons were for the benefit of an all-male group.

Contrary to the meager number of pardons, however, acquittals were probably more numerous in Spain than in Mexico (information for New Granada is missing). Whereas in colonial Mexico five out of seventy-six cases (6.5 percent) for which information is available ended this way, in Spain the records show ten acquittals out of a total of fifty-one cases, a proportion (19.6 percent) three times greater. It is hard to explain this contrast, but it probably relates to unwarranted prosecution of accidental deaths in Iberia, more rigorous and evenhanded investigations, or a combination of the two. Excessive leniency by judges does not seem to have been the cause; except for scattered royal pardons, sanctuary, and legally admissibly extenuating circumstances, the criminal justice system was fairly rigid, and few of its sentences were under the five-year confinement mark.

CONCLUSION

Body-centered, painful, and visible punishment, full of ritual, remained an important component of power and justice in the late colonial Spanish Atlantic. However, the specific modalities of retribution (still the main function of punishment) varied across regions. Spain seemed more attached to the death penalty for spousal murderers, whereas the colonies relied more on internment. The colonies were, in turn, more prone to forgiveness in the form of pardon, whereas Spain favored plain acquittals instead. Still, punishment remained vengeful and public on both sides of the Atlantic, and many of its characteristics were contradictory or, better put, counterintuitive.

In many cases, similar to what we saw with regard to honor, the prosecution and punishment of spousal murderers run counter to certain academic assumptions. Throughout this study we have observed patterns in the intensely hierarchical nature of Spanish criminal legislation and judicial procedure that established important differences between, among others, metropolitan and colonial subjects, nobles and commoners, whites and nonwhites, men and women. Judging by the standards observed in sentences for which we have more or less detailed information, however, these hierarchies did not always translate into favorable treatment for dominant as opposed to subaltern sectors.

Except for possible disparities in the treatment of males and females concerning the death penalty or pardons, defendants accused of murdering their spouses in the Spanish Atlantic were subject to the same general fate and treatment, whether harsh or benign, irrespective of their social condition, in particular their metropolitan or noble character. Further, metropolitan subjects accused of spousal murder in general met much harsher sentences and less leniency than their colonial counterparts, even subaltern Indians. Although the same cannot be said about blacks, for Indians, ethnicity and "misery" were in fact sources of leniency rather than severity.

In addition, out of three criminals of *hidalgo* status in Spain, two were condemned to death; the third, Juan Francisco Escudero, had his sentence reduced to a harsh ten-year presidio term, but only thanks to the protection of church sanctuary rather than his superior social origins.

In sum, metropolitans more so than colonials, nobles more than commoners, and whites more than Indians received the harshest possible penalties, including death and long presidio terms. Still, punishment continued to be mixed in with clemency. Over the years, as happened with torture and the means to inflict death, it softened even further. The final chapter of this book will address the developmental nature of some of these trends and their deepening as a result of the liberal transition caused by independence.

CHAPTER EIGHT

Transition to Independence

Humanized Justice and the Reinvention of Hegemony and Coercion in the Spanish Atlantic

It is not to live without laws that you have conquered liberty, but so that laws, drafted with your approval, be put into place instead of men's arbitrariness and caprice. (*No es para vivir sin ley para lo que habéis conquistado vuestra libertad, sino para que la ley, hecha con vuestra aprobación, se ponga en lugar de la arbitrariedad y los caprichos de los hombres.*)

—"Conclusion," Constitution of Cundinamarca, New Granada, April, 1811

As our discussion so far has noted, the mechanisms historically in place to address lawbreaking in the late colonial Spanish Atlantic included generous access to local and higher courts of justice, availability of widely known criminal rules and procedures, some means of secular or ecclesiastical protection and forgiveness, and an increasing trend toward more humane corporal punishment. Despite the discretionary and somewhat arbitrary nature of sentencing at the time and the socially unequal nature of the legal system, all of these factors assisted Crown and Church in building and maintaining not only some semblance of social and familial order but also hegemonic rule over society.

The disintegration of the Spanish Empire in the early nineteenth century caused adjustments to and, in some cases, a radical rearrangement of hegemonic mechanisms for dealing with social conflict, crime, and punishment. This affected the trial and resolution of marital disputes, spousal murders, and related crimes. Coercion, another key aspect of social control and criminal law, underwent some changes during the transition as well.

The discussion in this chapter takes legislation and spousal murders as a vantage point to address the timing and nature of the formal lightening or "humanization" of punishment for criminals that allegedly took place in the Spanish Atlantic around this time. We can trace this trend to the early nineteenth century, the period when, as a result of a major crisis in Iberia, regions such as Mexico, Colombia, and several other portions of Central and South America gained their independence from Spain and proceeded to carry out various liberal reforms. This phenomenon also took place in Spain itself under the leadership of Joseph Napoleon (1808–1813) and the Cortes de Cádiz (1810–1814).

New legal measures enacted during the Independence era and through the 1820s and 1830s in Spain, Mexico, and Colombia also allow us to ascertain the nature and extent of changes and continuities in substantive criminal law, criminal procedures, and punishment for spousal murder and related crimes—in particular, adultery and battery—as a result of the disintegration of the Spanish empire in America. Such legal narratives and texts are as valid a "social fact" as any other to gauge some of the period's key historical changes.[1] They allow us to examine changing cultural perceptions and new constructs of repression, crime, gender, and sexuality with the advent of "modernity." However, this work endorses a developmental or long-term approach, requiring us to go back in time at least briefly to detect incremental changes in the way the Spanish monarchy tackled crime and punishment, up until the undoubtedly momentous legal reforms of the 1810s and 1820s.

THE LONG TRANSFORMATION OF COERCION AND FEAR

The political economy of punishment seems to have been enigmatically altered in the late eighteenth century in France and, presumably, other European societies, too. Punishment allegedly ceased to be a body-centered and flamboyant enterprise, becoming instead increasingly centered on the transformation of minds through pedagogy, careful time management, and discipline, all applied with greater discretion than ever before to the chastisement of criminals. Revenge also gave way to a measure of "humanity," a concept which that most influential French thinker Foucault used with apparent cynicism, as it implied the rather abrupt and disingenuous discovery at the end of the ancien régime of the "man" behind the "criminal."[2] In the Spanish Atlantic, however, this was a more complex process whereby punishment appears to have softened over many decades prior to the actual crisis of the Spanish empire. The legal changes following the collapse of the empire are undeniable, but so also is their long lineage.

Analysis of early nineteenth-century cases and legislation makes it immediately apparent that the transition to constitutional rule and independence indeed marked the crystallization and formalization of a civilizing and liberal program for addressing criminal matters. Still, the agenda was not utterly new, but had been simmering for a long time. Important changes had already entered customary law and judicial practice; in fact, among this book's findings is the de facto, often unintended, humanization/civilization of criminal justice and punishment in the Spanish empire over the course of the eighteenth century and much earlier. This softening seems to have appeased the monarchy's Christian moral conscience while also strengthening its legitimacy. Humanization was not all an outcome of the Enlightenment, nor was the process always forward in motion.

The most important work on the subject of criminal law in eighteenth-century Spain, Francisco Tomás y Valiente's splendid *Derecho penal de la monarquía absoluta* (1969), hints at the long-term humanization of Spanish law and justice in the eighteenth century. Spanish legal historian Tomás y Valiente ultimately claims, though, that punishment according to "reason" really took place somewhat later, caused partly by a series of new legal reforms introduced from 1809 to 1822.[3]

The first of such reforms was an October 19, 1809, decree issued by Joseph Napoleon that ended death by hanging, replacing it with the garrote. It was followed by the Cortes of Cádiz and its collection of liberal reforms around 1810–1814. These norms, discussed later in this chapter, included decrees enacted on April 22, 1811, and January 24, 1812, banning torture and hanging, respectively. Also on the list is Article 303 of the Constitution of Cádiz, promulgated by the Cortes (parliament) in March 1812, enshrining the ban on torture into Spanish constitutional law.[4] An additional decree issued by the Cortes on September 8, 1813, put an end to flogging anywhere within the Spanish empire.

Another major legal reform that Tomás y Valiente lists took place in 1822, when the Spanish Cortes enacted a modern criminal code for the newly liberalized Spanish empire. Among other liberal provisions, Article 38 of the new code reinstated the elimination of death by hanging (a practice revived under King Ferdinand VII after his restoration in 1814), again replacing it with the garrote. Tomás y Valiente omits specific reference to the elimination of torture by the Napoleon-inspired Constitution of Bayona (widely known in English as the Bayonne Statute) as early as mid-1808, a little earlier than *Derecho penal de la monarquía absoluta* suggests, but from a formal standpoint the Spanish author is absolutely correct about the general timing of Enlightenment-based punitive reforms in Spain. However, many practical traces of such measures can be found in years past.

Judging by the experiences of at least a few spousal murderers, for instance, the reality of torture and punishment, as was illustrated in the previous chapter, had changed much earlier at the local and regional levels all over the Spanish empire. Death by hanging had also declined and was replaced by the garrote much earlier than decrees and laws of the 1808–1822 period suggest. Changes in these and other dimensions of crime and punishment were not merely the result of formal legal reforms, and neither did they take place overnight. Rather than an abrupt change resulting from the age of "reason" and revolution, the civilization of punishment was a developmental process that occurred over many decades (centuries!) in the Spanish Atlantic, more in the nature of the process that Pieter Spierenburg and Antonio M. Hespanha found to have occurred in various regions of Europe.[5] Even if the laws remained the same, the actual judicial practices embraced throughout the empire had changed in meaningful ways.

Humanized Punishment

What this book terms the "humanization" of punishment and criminal justice in the Spanish Atlantic, which others would prefer to call "civilization," means, in particular, the gradual end of a method for gathering evidence in place for hundreds of years—*tormento* (judicial torture). It also included informal practical restrictions on corporal punishment and the death penalty itself.[6] One must therefore look back several decades before the Enlightenment and Independence to reveal the roots of these important transformations.[7] Although some reforms were not enshrined in legislation until the early nineteenth century, the humanization of punitive practices in Spain and overseas occurred silently and by accretion over many years, way before the arrival of enlightened thinkers and rulers.

Many European countries, including England, France, Italy, Russia, and Sweden, credit the trend toward humanization of criminal procedures, evidence gathering, and punishment to the work of outspoken intellectuals and reformers. Important influences included the Frenchmen Baron de Montesquieu (1689–1755), Guilleme Le Trosne (1728–1780), and François-Marie Arouet, better known as Voltaire (1694–1778); Italy's Cessare Bonesana Marquis of Beccaria (1738–1794); the Englishmen William Eden (1745–1814), Samuel Romilly (1757–1818), and Jeremy Bentham (1748–1832); and enlightened rulers such as Russian Empress Catherine the Great (1729–1796) and Swedish King Gustavus III (1746–1792). Each of them argued in favor of or actually contributed to modernizing and softening criminal law and punitive practices, mainly during the second half of the eighteenth century and the early nineteenth century.

These reformers' influence resulted in more "precise" criminal statutes pioneered by the Tuscan and Austrian criminal codes of 1786 and 1787, respectively, and reflected in other criminal code projects such as the one Pascoal de Melo proposed in Portugal in late 1786.[8] The new codes generally proclaimed that there was "no crime without a law" and aspired to greater clarity in the definition of crime and punishment. Their goal was to reduce judicial arbitrariness and abuse, infusing the treatment of wrongdoers with greater respect and legal guarantees, and ameliorating gruesome ("inhuman") physical pain.[9]

In Spain, too, by the second half of the eighteenth century, collective sentiment found the public spectacle of bodily suffering increasingly unacceptable.[10] By the mid-eighteenth century, some legal experts started to challenge traditional punitive practices (dismemberment, burning, mutilation, etc.) as gruesome or "horrifying additions" (*aditamentos espantosos*).[11] Other intellectuals and statesmen demanded economic and criminal (procedural and punitive) modernity in the realm in accordance with new conceptions of emotions, behavioral styles, and personal rights.[12] Various authors called for an end to painful methods of gathering evidence and a systematic application of more-efficient (faster!) means of execution.

Those opposed to torture included several of the thinkers listed in the previous chapter, among them Juan Meléndez Valdés, Alfonso María de Acevedo, Manuel de Roda y Arrieta, Gaspar Melchor de Jovellanos, and Manuel de Lardizábal y Uribe. Also in agreement were the statesman José Moñino y Redondo, Conde de Floridablanca (1728–1808); law and theology professor Antonio Xavier Pérez y López (1736–1792); and jurist and magistrate Juan Sempere y Guarinos (1754–1830). The same claims were echoed in some of the legal academies, especially the Real Academia de Derecho Español y Público and the Real Academia de Jurisprudencia Práctica.[13] More and more, they viewed the reduction of physical pain for criminals as a mark of Christian piety and civilization.

In the Spanish Atlantic, however, many meaningful changes in punitive methods and practices traced back several centuries. As far back as the thirteenth century, King Alphonse X's *Siete Partidas* prohibited judges from applying branding, burning, or mutilation to a prisoner's face or eyes "because man's face was made by God in his own image" and thus ought not to be damaged. Though it did not explain the reason why, the same medieval legal code presumably found it excessively cruel and also prohibited the death of prisoners by stoning, crucifixion, or pushing them off a tower, bridge, or cliff (a punishment generically known as *despeñamiento*).[14]

Early modern rulers implemented several more changes. In 1532, for instance, King Charles I agreed to the request of the Cortes de Segovia to modify the practice of killing criminals by shooting arrows into their body, which was "an inhuman thing" (*cosa inhumana*). Prior to being pierced by arrows, the king decreed, such criminals should be suffocated or drowned first to spare them pain.[15] A 1561 decree by King Phillip II contained a pragmatic and utilitarian order that "ordinary" punishments (the most severe, even death) be forgotten and instead all criminals sent to work in a galley (*galera*), which became a dominant form of punishment in early modern Spain until its initial elimination in the mid-eighteenth century.[16]

Witness accounts also confirm that since at least the sixteenth century, parricides and spouse killers sentenced to *encubamiento* could not be placed inside the bag alive but had to be first killed by suffocation, hanging, or the garrote, a Roman method allegedly used secretly in early modern Spain for the killing of knights and once again in use in Madrid.[17] These steps made their death more honorable and humane. Unlike the other measures cited above, humanization of *encubamiento* was never enshrined in law, but it took place in practice nonetheless. Other humane innovations were adopted in a similar de facto or customary fashion.

Several of these changes resulted, as can be imagined, not from the pressure or designs of enlightened advocates of reform but rather from long-standing Christian sensibilities, the challenges of the day-to-day administration of justice, and, in particular, the king's spontaneous "humanity."[18] Broader "humanitarian" considerations entered the picture gradually, especially in the late colonial period, when middle- and upper-class sensibilities and moral outrage at the spectacle of distasteful bodily suffering were at a peak.[19]

Dominant practices for several decades suggest increasing social and moral disapproval of the prospect of painful punishment. The monarchy, never deaf to the dictates of religious dogma and popular feeling, seems to have taken the lead in making this charitable inclination a reality. As legal author Alvares Posadilla put it in the 1790s, "the humanity of Spanish monarchs wished to tolerate that all punishments [dismemberment, mutilation, burning, encubamiento] the law imposes to those sentenced to death, be executed on corpses. . . ."[20] This determined, for example, that only the bodies of executed criminals, not live human beings, could be burned, dismembered, or subjected to *encubamiento*.

The specific dates these various humanized practices started are not easy to pin down, but some certainly went back to the sixteenth century. Since that time, at least, society seemed to consider the infliction of unnecessary pain on a living human being to be contrary to Christian mores and thus problematic. Evidence is available from the mid-sixteenth century indicating that Spanish and Mexican criminals were first killed before being burned.[21] By the mid-eighteenth century, burning had long ceased to be an accepted means of execution, constituting instead a post-mortem ritual to denote the seriousness of certain crimes. Even this practice would come to an end before the arrival of enlightened reforms.

Therefore, every form of inhumane or painful punishment was now expected to follow rather than precede death. The public abhorred even these more-humane practices, however, and they acquired many loopholes or symbolic equivalents as time went on. By the 1760s, for instance, the king often commuted the burning of (dead) criminals, even those found guilty of counterfeiting or sodomy, crimes deemed especially despicable at the time.[22] If the corpses of executed criminals were burned, religious brotherhoods demanded that such displays be quite brief. In 1769 one brotherhood assuredly argued that "it was not necessary for the fire to entirely consume the corpse but it is enough to expose it briefly to the flames" ("*no es necesario que el fuego consuma enteramente el cadaver sino que basta ponerle entre las llamas*").[23] In fact, although occasional "burnings" in the humanized sense were recorded into the 1770s, the practice may have been largely discontinued as early as the late seventeenth century.[24]

Another important example is dismemberment. Perhaps the most scandalous remnant of the ancien régime's catalogue of punishments in the Spanish Atlantic, dismemberment continued well into the nineteenth century. In the early 1800s, for instance, judicial authorities ordered the exhibition of criminals' body parts in the metropolis for five months or longer![25] Dismemberment also occurred during late colonial rebellions and the wars of independence, when the king's armies displayed the limbs and heads of executed rebels to warn the public of the price of insurrection.[26] It receded in Spain only after the introduction of new criminal laws in the 1820s and 1830s, and in the Spanish American republics from the 1830s onward. As in the case of burning, however, dismemberment had been practiced only on corpses, not live human beings, since perhaps as far back as the seventeenth century. The practice was further sanitized or humanized by allowing Catholic brotherhoods to collect promptly the remnants of recently executed criminals: a hand here, a leg there, a couple of heads farther away. In fact, religious brotherhoods were more and more proactive and assertive in requesting permission to remove and bury body parts in the second half of the eighteenth century.[27]

The law progressively began to spare ancien régime criminals various forms of physical pain before dying as well, over the course of several decades and across the social board.[28] Many of the new, more "gentle" procedures did not corresponded strictly to the formal legislation in place. A charitable organization argued, in fact, that notwithstanding legal prescriptions, religious brotherhoods had afforded Christian burials to spousal murderers and other *encubados* after a brief immersion of their corpses in a water stream since at least the early eighteenth century, likely even much earlier, owing to the "piety of our glorious kings."[29] Referring to the possible burning of criminals as long as they were already dead, members of the Alcaldes de Casa y Corte also claimed that they were not aware when this practice had started or of a specific legal mandate that dictated it, but were convinced that by the 1760s this was the standard practice ("*[no]se halla más orden que la práctica*").[30]

In the context of such cultural shifts, judicial authorities in the Iberian Peninsula gradually stopped ordering judicial torture, dragging, hanging, and related punishments (branding, mutilation, and flogging), or introduced subtle but meaningful modifications to make them morally palatable to those who had to order, implement, or administer them (local justice officials, some appeals courts, executioners). By the time Spanish reformers entered the scene and proposed changes to royal displays of repression, many of these painful practices had actually already changed considerably in their day-to-day implementation or fallen entirely into disuse (*desuso*). Portugal seems to have mirrored these trends.[31] Change, even if not reflected in formal legislation, was thus an ongoing practical reality in Spain and elsewhere before the crisis and collapse of the ancien régime.

In contrast, several other medieval practices continued long into this period. For example, cases of flogging were recorded in the metropolis in 1792, 1802, and 1804, although this penalty also became the subject of reforms in the eighteenth century. As with other punishments, the first step was to exclude nobles from its scope, restricting its application to the common people (*la gente del pueblo*). Restrictions on flogging women also took place, in part to prevent onlookers from ogling their naked torsos.[32] To discourage its use, some justice officials even attempted to make flogging logistically costly or unpractical by requesting that an expert official (*verdugo*) be brought in from afar to administer the punishment properly.[33] It is no wonder that the practice declined over time.[34] However, flogging remained common in Spain's overseas territories, where it was a traditional penalty for nonwhites, especially the native population. But it too experienced some restrictions and, like judicial torture and the rest, was surrounded by disrepute.[35]

A Kinder Death Penalty

By 1782, therefore, when enlightened magistrate Manuel de Lardizábal y Uribe wrote and published his *Discurso sobre las penas* bemoaning judicial torture in Spain, this and other gruesome practices were already outmoded in the Iberian Peninsula. Lardizábal y Uribe himself hinted at this in various passages of his book and explicitly argued that "many of our old criminal laws have lost their force, are outmoded and in total disuse . . ." ("*nuestras antiguas leyes penales fueron perdiendo insensiblemente su vigor hasta haber llegado a quedar enteramente antiquadas* [*sic*] *y sin uso alguno* . . .").[36] He even gave a number of specific examples alluding to "general custom," practices contrary to laws still in place but in accordance with "humanity" and the "spirit of the times"—namely, a reluctance to burn criminals alive, pull out their eyes or teeth, or cut off their tongues or ears.[37] Torture was another case in point.[38] The same went for other painful procedures, including the death penalty itself. Although applied more often to spousal killers than to other murderers, as the previous chapter established, death as a punishment did not just decline almost all over Iberia, but the methods of inflicting it also appear to have been transformed in a humanizing direction.[39]

However, the transformation of the death penalty was rather more complex than the reduction of bodily pain in general. This was because, historically, opposition to capital punishment had been negligible. Even many reformers in the second half of the eighteenth century were not really opposed to it per se but just to the painful way of implementing it. Unlike his Italian role model and inspiration Beccaria, for instance, Lardizábal y Uribe and other leading Spanish Atlantic reformers were not against putting criminals to death. Although calling for great "circumspection" in its use, Lardizábal y Uribe, in fact, deemed the death penalty a necessary evil.[40] He and others merely advocated the need to carry it out in a more gentle and civilized way. In the meantime, as in other parts of Europe, the number of executions in Spain in the second half of the eighteenth century experienced a relative decline but remained nevertheless significant, even more so in the case of spousal murderers, as discussed previously.[41] Despite its lessening appeal, hanging remained the most common method.

For more than two centuries (the 1600s and 1700s), hanging was the dominant means of execution for Spaniards who killed their spouses and others. Of the 885 people executed in seventeenth-century Valencia, 802 died that way.[42] Granada also hanged dozens of criminals around the time.[43] Also in the 1600s, however, beheading often replaced hanging for those who could demonstrate nobility.[44] Ending as it did with the effusion of blood, and being carried with a sword, noble weapon par excellence, it was a most fitting culmination for a life of nobility, and it was swift, sparing its distinguished victims unnecessary agony. The only people eligible for this arguably more dignified and humane penalty had to belong at least to the lower nobility, have a decent occupation, and ideally be part of a family that had served the king.[45] The same was the case for individuals who pursued the garrote in the eighteenth century as an alternative to hanging, still the dominant method for inflicting death on criminals.

Death by hanging continued to occur in the eighteenth century all over Spain, especially against brigands. In the second half of the eighteenth century, most criminals executed in Madrid met their death at the gallows.[46] The method was also being used in Granada in the 1780s and sometimes involved several people at once, even as many as four in a single day.[47] Hangings of smugglers, assassins, and brigands—sometimes as many as twenty-five at once!—continued in places like Valladolid as well into the late 1780s.[48] To be sure, given the decline of capital punishment in general, the scale of its application was lower than in previous centuries, and it declined a bit further as a result of the growing attractiveness of the garrote.[49]

By the mid-eighteenth century and certainly in the times of Lardizábal y Uribe, many critics considered hanging to be a terribly inhumane method of killing. Increasingly, officials called in a *verdugo* (executioner) to climb or "ride" (*cabalgar*) on the person's shoulders to accelerate his or her death. The occupation was thus quite an unpopular one, and candidates were hard to find, providing an incentive for the transition to speedier means of execution such as garrote, the iron collar used to strangle or break the victim's neck discussed in the previous chapter.[50]

In addition to the knights rumored to be eligible for execution by the garrote in the sixteenth century, evidence exists that many ordinary criminals died this way, too.[51] There is also evidence of its use throughout the seventeenth century to execute several spousal murderers prior to their *encubamiento*.[52] By the mid-eighteenth century, though, the garrote appears to have become socially selective, gaining even wider acceptability among the upper classes. This was apparently the result of a February 1734 decree by King Philip V mandating its use to execute nobles accused of robbery in Madrid and its environs. Ordinary people, we can assume, came to have no alternative but hanging.[53] Thus, the garrote seems to have succeeded beheading as a subsidiary but increasingly dominant method of execution for all *hijosdalgo* (lower nobles) and other nobles, irrespective of the crime sending them to their death.[54]

This method as we already know was preferred for its ability to inflict death more quickly and without the agony typical of hanging. Although accessible in Madrid around the 1750s, outside the capital it was not commonly available until decades later. Even in Madrid, in the third quarter of the eighteenth century execution by garrote was still restricted to a few select occupational groups (expert craftsmen, professionals, and soldiers) and the nobility. Remember that such was the case of spousal murderer María Vicenta Mendieta and her lover, who were able to demonstrate nobility or a respectable occupation and apply for commutation from hanging to garrote.[55] Exceptions to the nobility rule were not entirely lacking, however, and eventually the punishment came to be disseminated more widely than was supposed to have occurred.

By the 1760s, and certainly by 1806, the Sala de Alcaldes already boasted of its generosity in prescribing the garrote for criminals sentenced to die, even those of non-noble ancestry or social distinction.[56] Toward the late eighteenth century, therefore, as humanitarianism and enlightened ideas took yet stronger hold, even persons explicitly lacking evidence of nobility started to benefit increasingly from the garrote.[57] The Napoleonic wars would expand its reach even more.

This efficient mechanism at last became the official means of execution in some portions of Spain in October 1809, under Napoleonic rule. Still, hangings continued in the form of summary and rural executions during the ongoing war in the Peninsula.[58] Although the authorities were intent on modernizing the death penalty to ensure it was applied as quickly (*pueda hacerse más pronta*) and painlessly as possible, only one garrote existed in Madrid at the time. The Minister of Justice especially encouraged any improvement to the available instrument to accomplish the purpose of efficient killings.[59] After several decrees, the Cortes de Cádiz at last officially abolished hanging all over the Spanish empire on January 24, 1812. The Cádiz Constitution itself, issued less than two months later, remained silent on the matter, but by the 1820s and 1830s the garrote had definitely become the only acceptable "modern" method for carrying out the death penalty in liberal Spain and the Spanish American republics, the culmination of a lengthy and intriguing process in need of further investigation.[60]

Ironically, the return of the garrote might not just have humanized but also perpetuated the death penalty in the Iberian Peninsula for a long time. After all, with it death could now be accomplished efficiently and without as much pain as before. "Gentler" executions by garrote continued in Spain for more than a century (actually until the Franco era!) as a display of *vindicta pública* and *escarmiento* for, among other offenses, the crime of murdering one's spouse.[61] But while good Christian consciences were appeased, punishment, contrary to Foucault's assertions, remained body-centered and rather ostentatious, too.

The spectacle of punishment did not cease entirely; in fact, as various cases described in previous chapters illustrate, executions in the 1760s could be quite theatrical. Even by the 1790s and early 1800s, criminals continued to be exhibited publicly, at least for a short while, to instill general fear in the population.[62] Over time, an increasingly squeamish public began to criticize the spectacle of corpses left dangling from scaffolds. In the 1780s, for instance, insistent petitions requested the expedited removal of such corpses without the required license from Madrid's Sala de Alcaldes, which still, through the late 1790s, typically ordered that the body be displayed for at least half a day.[63] Such examples confirm the fact that pressure from individuals or private groups was able to effect a variety of intriguing changes in punitive practices for decades, even centuries, without the need for explicit legal reforms. Several applied specifically to the treatment of spousal killers.

To sum up the expression of all of the above concerning the execution of spousal killers, according to the testimony of legal authors Gregorio López and Francisco Pradilla, since the early sixteenth century justice official ordered the execution of such killers and other parricides prior to their being put into the leather sack.[64] Painting animals on a box or the leather bag itself, rather than introducing them alive as in traditional *encubamientos,* was already accepted practice no later than the final decades of the seventeenth century. Briefly pulling a bagged corpse through the water for immediate retrieval and burial by a charitable brotherhood, instead of dumping a living person into the water without the right to Catholic burial, was also a common practice by the 1750s, and perhaps much earlier. Dragging a spousal killer through the streets on a straw mat rather than directly across the ground was also the norm overseas by the 1760s and in Spain by the 1780s, perhaps considerably earlier.[65] One legal expert alluded matter-of-factly to these various facets in the late eighteenth century while referring to general changes in the practice of *encubamiento:*

> Nowadays this mode of execution has been commuted to hanging or *garrote* and, later, one complies with the required rituals with the corpse, taking it to the side of the river with a hide on top, or inside a leather bag or *cuba,* on which the animals specified by law are painted . . . because in their **humanity** the Spanish monarchs have decided to accept that many of the penalties imposed by law **be applied to corpses,** except some that may not be uncomfortable as they are currently carried out, as is the case with those who are dragged [over a mat]. [emphasis in boldface added][66]

The various de facto changes in the implementation of punishment since at least the sixteenth century were probably part of the secular process of "conscience formation" and civilization that Spierenburg has documented in several of his works.[67] They also corresponded to the monarchy's practical response and adjustment to a number of day-to-day imperatives and demands. Several clearly involved concern over brutal procedures and despicable pain contrary to Christian principles and sensitivity. The Enlightenment unquestionably brought other types of pressure to bear, condemning painful practices as contrary to "reason," except this time practical adaptations were deemed insufficient. New laws to replace outdated ones would now express the "general will" of the "nation" toward such delicate subjects. In the meantime, though, the military campaigns of the time caused chaos and increased not only public but also domestic tensions.

INDEPENDENCE AND DOMESTIC CONFLICTS

Among the most significant politico–military developments marking the transition to Spanish American independence were the Napoleonic invasion of the Iberian Peninsula in October 1807 and May 1808, and the forced abdications of Kings Charles IV (March 19, 1808) and Ferdinand VII (May 6, 1808), whom the French replaced on the throne with Napoleon's brother, Joseph. With the French capture of the Spanish throne, factionalism and armed struggle broke out as early as 1808 in Spain and by 1809 in Spanish America. These turbulent developments affected at least some of the protagonists and circumstances of family conflicts in this period.

In several instances the revolutionary armies taking shape overseas intervened in either the liberation or capture of criminals, even those involved in domestic violence. In turn, some individuals charged with spousal murder seized the opportunity to petition for a reduction of their sentences. In the midst of the wars for independence, many cited loyalty to the Crown or the patriots as an exculpatory circumstance. In addition, the transitional regimes and new governments issued a wave of pardons to celebrate milestones of the resistance against the French enemy and independence itself, recalling the monarchy's long-standing use of forgiveness to mark royal occasions. Ironically, positions for or against the insurgency and men's absences from home for long periods of soldiering were opportunities for gossip, adultery, and, sometimes, domestic disputes and battery. Several cases in our Mexican set serve as examples of these various trends. Not surprisingly, many of them originated on the western Mexican coast (future states of Colima, Michoacán, and Guerrero), a hotbed of revolutionary upheaval.

Rebel armies marching through western Mexican towns opened the local jails, releasing a range of criminals, including men accused of murdering their wives or lovers. For instance, this happened to twenty-six-year-old mulatto mining worker and artisan Tomás Aquino Ramirez, detained in April 1809 for allegedly stabbing to death his Indian partner, Maria Hilaria, upon finding her in the company of another man. In mid-November 1810, after he had spent more than eighteen months in the royal jail of Colima, the insurgent armies freed him along with the rest of the inmates. It is unclear whether he joined the rebels, but it is apparent that he benefited from the impending political and military chaos to remain at large, perhaps for good. Almost a decade later, in early 1820, the judicial authorities were still trying to determine his whereabouts.[68] In other cases, rebel actions actually led to imprisonment, and release from jail could, therefore, be a function of loyalty to the king.

Loyalty to the monarchy and suffering at the hands of rebels (*bandidos*) is precisely what José Andrés Fernández claimed in August 1811, in a written petition for his freedom addressed to Mexico City's "Security Committee." On a September night in 1805 in the town of Tlatenango, jurisdiction of Guadalajara, Fernández had killed his wife, María Ignacia Flórez, and injured her lover, José Antonio Botello, a mestizo/Indian (*coyote*), upon finding them together in his house. After a short detention, he had escaped from jail and refused to cooperate with the judicial authorities who declared him in contumacy (*ausente* or "*en rebeldia*"). He managed to live as an outsider (*forastero*) in Mexico City for several years, thinking justice had "forgotten about him," but some people marching with the rebel armies recognized him and denounced his case to their commanders. A colonel in the rebel army ordered Fernández's detention around December 1810. With the Spanish authorities back in control in August 1811, he requested clemency and forgiveness, claiming he had been loyal to the monarchy and deserved to be covered by the recent pardon.[69]

Apart from contributing to jail escapes or formal releases from prison and, conversely, to imprisonment as well, conflicts between rebels and royal armies also provided additional fodder for domestic tensions and disputes, as several cases in our set show. In June 1812, on a rural ranch in Colima, a free mulatto woman, María Aguilar, and her mulatto lover, Antonio Ureña, were accused of killing Antonio Salas, María's husband. Ureña frequented the couple's home and addressed the head of the household as "cousin." On the night in question, the men argued when Ureña showed up drunk and asked María to serve him dinner. Salas, who was already in bed, became incensed. After mocking Ureña's arrogance (*garbo*), he called him a "*grandísimo carajo encallejado*" ("great damned follower of Calleja"), a reference to Felix María Calleja, the general who headed the royal army that fought Mexico's insurgents and went on to become viceroy (1813–1816). In return, Ureña accused Salas of support for the insurgency. A fight ensued, and Salas attacked Ureña with a club.

Ureña in turn pulled out a knife and seriously wounded Salas, who suffered cuts to various parts of his body, including his head, hands, and back. He eventually died, and on the same night as the incident the lovers escaped with the couple's three young children. The woman was captured a few days after the crime, in early July, but Ureña continued to evade capture. Apparently a committed royalist after all, he was killed in late 1813 by the patriot faction while still on the run for the murder of his lover's husband. María remained in jail until mid-1818, when, acting on the advice of officials who visited the jail, the *audiencia* decided to release her. Even after the news of Ureña's death, the *audiencia* continued to call for his capture anywhere he could be found.[70] If he had lived, he would have had two grounds to ask for indulgence: the fact that he was drunk at the time the crime was committed and, most important, his loyalty to the Crown.

Loyalty and the circumstances of the war for independence, especially long absences by men fighting in it, were also central in a case tried in Chihuahua in 1817 involving a white local man (*español*) by the name of Hermenegildo Peña, a thirty-five-year-old native of Nuevo Santander in what is today the state of Tamaulipas, northeast of Mexico City. In jail for killing his wife, Peña claimed during his confession that he did not have any occupation (*oficio*) because he had spent his entire life "serving the king." One of the reasons for Peña's rage against his wife was a rumor that she was having an affair with a local man named Ortega, a close friend of the household. Ortega's wife spread the rumor and suggested that the affair had begun during the long period Peña was absent from the town fighting in the king's army against the Mexican insurgents. Several friends, including at least one soldier who had served with him in the Segunda Compañia Volante, certified Peña's service to the royal cause and testified to his good character and conduct.[71] The case was still pending in 1819, when new witnesses corroborated Peña's loyal services to the king and asked to have him included in the recent royal pardon to celebrate Ferdinand VII's 1817 wedding, his second in what would turn out to be a rather long list of marriages.[72]

Also during the transition to independence, at least one spousal killer in Mexico appears to have been jailed for publicly praising the Virgin of Guadalupe, a symbol of the insurgents. During his deposition for the 1815 murder of his wife, Paulino López, a colorful character, admitted to having been jailed no fewer than twelve or thirteen times before. He claimed to be a leather worker (*picador de botas*), a native of Coahuila residing in Colima. His numerous jail stints were a mixed bag, including brief stays for violating the town's curfew, being caught in the nearby port after hours, having illicit relations with a single woman, and fighting with his wife. In some of these altercations, he was charged with cutting off her hair, punching her, flogging her with a leather belt, and beating her because of allegedly suspicious signals from another man. In one instance, López was also jailed for refusing to be reunited with his wife. On the occasion he hailed the Virgin of Guadalupe, he spent several days in jail until he could demonstrate his allegiance to the king's cause (*justificó su adicción al partido del rey*). Once free, however, he promptly invoked the name of the Virgin again, saying later he wanted only to exalt the virtues of the mother of Jesus! Most recently, he had been jailed for killing his wife with a spear after accusing her of misbehaving and being a publicly known whore.[73] It is unclear whether the changing political fortune of the insurgents led to his release at some point, but others certainly did benefit formally from the insurgents' ultimate rise to power.

In one final case, independence actually became a motive for official pardon. A pair of Indian lovers, Mariano Casillas and María Antonia Corona, was accused of poisoning the woman's blind husband, José Román Capilla, in October 1819. Capilla had previously reported the love affair to the authorities, and the defendants served time in jail as punishment. About three months after the Spanish Crown recognized Mexican independence under then-Emperor Agustin de Iturbide, on August 24, 1821, the provisional government committee (*Junta Provisional Gubernativa del Imperio Mexicano*) included the two lovers in a pardon to mark the declaration of independence and inauguration of the new government ("*con los plausibles motivos de la declaración de su independencia y de la instalación del gobierno supremo*").[74]

Similar to the celebration of royal coronations of old, the new regimes issued ample pardons (*indultos generales*) to mark the declaration of independence. However, future republican governments had fewer opportunities for pardons than did royals marking not only their enthronement but also numerous birthdays and weddings. Graces would be more sporadic now, but the long-standing practice of pardoning criminals would not disappear altogether under the new postcolonial regimes or the forcibly "liberalized" Spanish monarchy.

The text of the pardon issued in Spain in mid-1820 to mark the restoration of the Cádiz constitution is telling of the new reality. Its purpose was to "inscribe in memory the restoration of the Constitution of the monarchy" on the "glorious" (*venturoso*) day (July 9, 1820) when King Ferdinand VII swore before the "national Congress" that he would obey it.[75] All of the deserving inmates, even spousal murderers, in the kingdom's prisons, including those in ultramarine provinces, received pardons. [76] In Spain, therefore, some former royal graces coexisted with new constitutional rituals. Both in the reformed Spanish monarchy and the new Spanish American republics, pardons continued to be instrumental to the consolidation of hegemony, just as they had been since at least the sixteenth century.

In sum, independence caused chaos and disruption not just at the public level but also within Mexican—and, presumably, New Granadan—households.[77] The upheaval unquestionably contributed to erode stability, peace, and order, which is to say the hegemonic rule of the ancien régime's secular and ecclesiastical powers. Transitional governments strategically deployed pardons and other legal measures aimed at humanizing punishment in an attempt to restore tranquility and social control. As tends to happen even during the most turbulent periods in human history, however, these changes were not entirely new.

TRANSITION TO THE NEW LEGALITY OF INDEPENDENCE

How radically the handling of familial conflicts, criminal justice, and punishment changed during the transition to independence remains an open question. Criminal justice in the new era would be informed by Enlightenment ideas and liberal criteria. This involved restructuring of the court system to separate it from other government activities, observance of the principle of legality and equal justice, a more precise definition of crime and proportional punishment, and greater respect for due process and the constitutional rights of defendants and other citizens. Despite formal compliance with some of these provisions, however, the dominant comparative historiography postulates that during early postcolonial times, many former colonies exhibited considerable continuities with respect to the absolutist past.

On the positive side, some authors observe the persistence of colonial legislation, access to courts of justice, and the continuing importance of regular jail visitations (*visitas de carcel*) to monitor the condition of jails and inmates and the status and progress of their criminal investigations.[78] But negative factors seem to have outweighed these considerations: Not only do several works note the generally slow pace of change in the judicial system, but they also point to specific problems such as the interference of executive authorities in judicial matters, conflicts of jurisdiction among judicial and law enforcement institutions, the excessive power of constables, and lack of material resources, to mention but a few issues.[79] In the case of familial conflicts, notwithstanding women's continuing ability and readiness to use law and the judicial system or naked force to combat male abuses or enjoy the company of lovers, the persistence of patriarchy is another concern on the list of problematic features linking colonial and postcolonial legal systems, societies, and histories.[80]

Even though political collapse was the result of a deep crisis of imperial domination that unleashed revolutionary events, the available historical research thus makes clear that neither spousal relations nor dealings with crime and punishment in the postcolonial era started from tabula rasa. Elements of both colonial hegemony and coercion passed into the criminal systems of the new nation-states emerging in the Iberian Peninsula and the Americas in the early nineteenth century. Some greater or lesser degree of access to justice, procedural know-how, and predictability, and a measure of leniency, continued to aid hegemonic rule and domination under the new regimes, despite "revolutionary" renaming of and adjustment to institutions and procedures as the circumstances required. Punishment and fear of the old type continued as well under "modern" denominations and guises or with liberal adjustments.

The French troops occupying a large portion of the Iberian Peninsula did not leave it for another six years, until January 1814. This occurred a few months after the French king himself had abdicated the Spanish throne once his armies lost a major battle against the British, main supporters of the Spanish resistance. During his five-year rule (until mid-1813) over a portion of the peninsula, Joseph Bonaparte had attempted to modify the legal landscape and, with it, the world of justice and punishment. His regime, as we know, had been quick to formalize the abolition of judicial torture in the regrettably obscure Constitution of Bayonne, enacted on July 6, 1808, for enforcement in Spain, and the abolition of death by hanging in October 1809.[81] However, most histories dismiss the Bayonne charter and related decrees as spurious and ineffective in view of both practical difficulties during the ongoing war and developments at the Cortes of Cádiz (1810–1814), where the Spanish resistance pushed forward a major institutional overhauling of the monarchy to turn it into a legitimate constitutional regime.[82] With the French besieged by the Spanish guerrillas and overshadowed by the Cortes, the Napoleonic constitution and legislation did not take root.

While Napoleon tried to rule part of Spain, the Spanish resistance held parallel legislative meetings at the eventful Cortes Extraordinarias de Cádiz. Thanks in part to British naval protection, the numerous delegates to the Cortes, including many from Spanish America, met in the Atlantic port city from about September 1810 to September 1813, a gathering followed without interruption by an additional meeting of the Cortes Ordinarias lasting until May 1814. The Cádiz Constitution and several related decrees resulting from the Cortes formally transformed the ancien régime into a new, liberal-leaning constitutional monarchy.

This time it was not just obsolescence (*desuso*) but, first, a decree (April 22, 1811) and, later, a superior constitutional mandate that eliminated torture, a brutal mechanism for obtaining evidence.[83] Torture had continued to be used well into the 1760s and, though more and more outmoded, formally remained a part of the ancien régime's criminal law until the promulgation of the new norm. However, perhaps the major innovation of the transition to a constitutional regime was the January 24, 1812, decree abolishing hanging, a punishment "repugnant to humanity and the generous character of the nation."[84] Instead, the Cortes ordered generalized use of the garrote, meant as we have noted to accelerate (and thereby humanize) execution.

Like the Bayonne charter, the Cortes did not abolish the death penalty as such but rather changed the conduct of criminal procedures, designating new judicial authorities, requiring observance of due process guarantees, and softening executions. The Cádiz charter contained a true bill of rights for those charged with crimes, all explicitly and precisely spelled out in several of its articles addressing the independence of judges, the restriction of arbitrary arrests and confiscations, the need for written notification of the motives behind the arrest, and the end of secrecy, especially the early disclosure of all adverse testimonies supporting detentions.[85] These changes had, for example, an impact on the way domestic disputes would be settled, now by a larger number of locally elected chief constitutional mayors (*alcaldes constitucionales*). In turn, overseas territories, with a few notable exceptions, organized revolutionary committees and held constitutional conventions of their own.

Various provincial constitutional charters in Spain's former overseas possessions joined the "humanizing" trend in the first half of the 1810s. Constitutional changes in New Granada (early 1811 to the early 1820s) and New Spain (1812–1814 and the early 1820s), as well as other legal developments (criminal codes, for instance), led to formal transformation of the administration of criminal justice and punishment. Like the Cádiz model, all of these overseas charters and codes sanctioned a new understanding of punishment more in accordance with "civilization" and the "times."

Under the constitution enacted in Cádiz in early 1812 by the leadership of the Spanish resistance, the Spanish king, outmaneuvered by the Cortes during his absence, lost considerable power. His majesty became bound by the law and detached from judicial and legislative functions. The king and his political delegates, as well as the Cortes, ceased to have any jurisdiction over judicial cases.[86] Justice officials became, at least formally if not in practice, an autonomous entity independent from other public powers. The Cádiz Constitution also determined that a *Tribunal*

Supremo de Justicia would now review criminal conflicts at the former *audiencia* level.[87] Spain and some overseas territories, in particular Cuba, Puerto Rico, and Mexico, observed this provision.

For example, Mexico swore in the Constitution of Cádiz on September 30, 1812. The charter remained in place in the land of the Aztecs until about December 1814, by which time Iberia had restored the old regime. Its implementation, in any case, had an impact on the investigation of criminal cases in various ways. Later in 1812, for instance, Mexico's jurisdictions were rearranged into an *audiencia territorial* composed of twelve justices and three sections, or *salas*, two civil and one criminal.[88] Several cases it tried and some decided by the viceroy around that time cited institutional reforms enacted by the Spanish Cortes (1810 and 1813). At the level of townships, locally elected *alcaldes constitucionales* handled many cases instead of *alcaldes ordinarios* or *corregidores*. The new officials were present in a larger number of villages that were now entitled to elect a constitutional city council or *ayuntamiento constitucional* (the right of any village with a population of more than 1,000, according to Article 310 of the Constitution). These elected local officials seem to have handled more than just cases of "injury or light offenses," as originally expected.[89] More important, the transitional legal regime seems to have required superior (executive) intervention to clarify jurisdictions.

In October 1813, for instance, the viceroy of New Spain—the victorious royalist general Félix María Calleja—employed the new legislation in a case involving the murder of an Indian woman by her spouse, Sebastian Osorio, in the Indian jurisdiction of San Juan de Tianquismanalco, southwest of Puebla de los Ángeles. The viceroy recognized the local constitutional chief mayor, Sebastián Menez, as judicial authority in the first instance (*juzgado constitutional de 1a nominación*), all in accordance with the new constitutional order the Cortes de Cádiz had established ("*en quien residen las facultades amplias que nos concedió la soberanía y en su augusto nombre el supremo congreso de las cortes generales y extraordinarias*"). Menez and the town's city council (*ayuntamiento constitucional*) shared local authority with the guidance of a legal advisor (*asesor letrado*).[90] The indigenous community of San Juan de Tianquismanalco had already received a positive response from the local tribunal concerning the legality of proceedings in the case around August 1813. The viceregal mandate confirmed the authority of the chief constitutional mayor over the case as well as over the delegate judge (*sub-delegado*) of the neighboring town of Atlixco, who received orders not to obstruct (*embarazar*) the *alcalde*'s handling of the case under any pretext, even outstanding judicial fees (*costas*). The viceroy also instructed the native community to obey its *alcalde*.[91] The new constitutional order emerging from Cádiz thus had immediate legal implications.[92]

In New Granada, the impact of the Cádiz constitution was restricted to royalist regions (Pasto, Santa Marta, Riohacha, and Panamá) in 1813–1814. Its revival in the 1820s was partial as well, covering mostly the same areas where sectors in favor of the monarchy resisted the patriotic regime until around 1821–1823.[93] In the meantime, the rest of the provinces enacted a number of regional constitutions of their own in the 1810s. These paralleled or followed Cádiz's lead in abolishing torture and observing due process guarantees. They also preserved the death penalty. To cite just a few examples, at about the same time the decision was adopted in Cádiz, in April 1811, the royalist Constitution of Cundinamarca, New Granada's central province, abolished torture and required a judicial order for jailing suspects.[94] The republican Constitution of Tunja, issued in December 1811, outlawed judicial torture and limited confiscations to no more than one-fifth of a person's estate.[95]

The republican Constitution of Cundinamarca of 1812 also outlawed judicial torture, considering it an unacceptable practice.[96] The fairly liberal charter issued in Cartagena on June 14, 1812, abolished torture (Art. 29) and introduced due process.[97] The constitution issued in the province of Mariquita on March 3, 1815 included due process;[98] limited shackles, chains (*cepos, grillos, cadenas*), and similar restraints;[99] and decreed that all punishment be proportional and "useful."[100] The constitution issued in Antioquia on July 10, 1815, introduced due process.[101] Most important, it too abolished judicial torture.[102] These liberal provisions logically caused some disruption.

The complex liberal legal regimes in place in large portions of New Granada during the 1810s clearly caused some delay and confusion in the processing of pending criminal cases. For instance, local officials in the city of Medellín sentenced seventeen-year-old spousal murderer Rosalia Piedrahita to a ten-year-prison term in October 1818. The expectation was that during her confinement she would wear shackles and spend her time helping clean the jail, serving as cook, and performing other tasks "according to her sex" (*oficios propios de su sexo*).[103] In December 1818 the case went for consultation before the Bogotá *audiencia*, but with the tribunal exiled in Panama as a result of the ongoing revolution, the case had to wait until early 1820. By this time, the new regime had established a High Court of Justice (*Alta Corte de Justicia*) in Bogotá for the Free Provinces of Cundinamarca. The court's seemingly strict republican justices, invoking Spanish royal legislation, replaced the woman's original punishment with the death sentence. Their only liberal gesture was to order that she not be hanged but shot (*fusilada*) instead.[104] Upon receiving the new order, though, Medellín's justice officials seemed reluctant to comply and cited various excuses to delay the execution, arguing, for example, that the court had not legally designated soldiers as the executioners. The local military in fact sent the required rifles and ammunition but refused to lend their men to carry out the sentence. Another excuse was that the woman was claiming to be pregnant.[105] Before her pregnancy could be verified, however, the woman, perhaps with help from local jailers, escaped. By late 1823, authorities were still trying to determine her whereabouts.[106]

During the Spanish liberal interregnum (1820–1823) and following Spanish American independence, Mexico and New Granada eventually adopted national constitutions, as Spain had done at Cádiz in 1812 (and again in 1820). Republican constitutions enacted in Colombia and Mexico, in 1821 and 1824 respectively, followed similar enlightened trends as the Spanish and provincial constitutions mentioned above. For instance, Colombia's 1821 constitution eliminated torture (*apremio*)[107] and introduced a host of due process guarantees,[108] but at the same time preserved the death penalty. Mexico's 1824 charter also abolished judicial torture,[109] embraced due process, and, in keeping with the dominant mentality, tacitly accepted executions to dissuade (*escarmentar*) criminals.[110] Although all of them upheld the death penalty, the constitutions laid the foundation for a series of "modern" criminal codes enacted throughout the Spanish Atlantic in the following decades.

THE POST-REVOLUTIONARY ERA AND LIBERAL CRIMINAL CODES

New criminal codes in Spain, Mexico, and Colombia during the 1820s and 1830s contained still more changes. Overall, the new legislation formalized humanitarian reforms such as the abolition of torture, hanging, and dismemberment, but in an indication of the uneven pace and nature of change, at least one put an end to long-standing charitable canon law traditions such as Church sanctuary, thus marking the dominance of secular trends. Yet they also showed evident traces of continuing legal patriarchy.

Following the liberal military rebellion in 1820 that forced King Ferdinand VII to reactivate the Cádiz Constitution, Spain adopted a new criminal code. It was not entirely a product of the liberal revolution; in fact, Ferdinand himself had promoted the idea of a new code in late 1819. In a royal decree the king urged his advisory council to issue a new compendium of criminal laws that could contribute to determine penalties for the chastisement of criminals and ways to instill fear (*escarmiento*) in the populace with more "precision and clarity." The monarch also asked that the "severity" of punishment, some of it coming from the time of the *Partidas* (the thirteenth century!), be reduced and adjusted to match the "civilization and customs" of the day.[111] Eventually, instead of the king's advisors, a committee of mainly progressive deputies appointed by the Spanish Cortes designed the code, and the king reluctantly approved it in mid-1822.[112] It was a long (816 articles!), comprehensive, and neatly written volume modeled in part on Napoleon's 1810 criminal code but also influenced by a variety of enlightened authors, including Beccaria, Bentham, and Filangieri.[113]

Mexico's first federal criminal code would take many years to see the light of day.[114] In the meantime, several regional codes took a more "modern" approach to criminal matters (the *Código Penal para el Estado de Veracruz,* 1835, and, much later, the *Código Penal para el Distrito Federal y Territorio de Baja California*, 1871). New Granada issued the first code of the revolutionary period in 1837, not long after the first regional Mexican code. The section below examines these statutes to see whether they included any novelties in matters such as domestic disputes, Church asylum, exculpatory factors, and the penalties for injuring or killing one's spouse. Laws on the books are not always enforced, but as suggested above they are powerful discourses and "social facts" worthy of attention by historians searching for an understanding of past mentalities concerning a variety of things, in our case "modern" (and "scientific") approaches to crime, punishment, social control in general, and gender relations as well.[115]

Starting chronologically, the 1822 Spanish code allowed husbands to use admonishments and "moderate" domestic punishment to discipline their wives, a description vague enough that, similar to guidelines in colonial days, it undoubtedly left plenty of room for justifying domestic abuse in the decades ahead.[116] Another option was for husbands to bring their wives before the local mayor so that the public official could admonish them. This was considered appropriate punishment for wives who left home without their husband's permission, indulged in "excess," or "noticeably" disobeyed the male head of household.[117] The code, further endorsing patriarchal rule, diminished the responsibility of husbands who committed acts of domestic violence by "exceeding" their right to punish their dependents, wives included.[118] At the same time, the law authorized justice officials to arrest irresponsible husbands (*relajados*) or those who unjustifiably mistreated their wives, who were to be placed *en una casa de corrección* for no more than one year.[119]

The code punished female adultery with up to ten years in jail (husbands were charged with determining the exact length of the sentence). Unfaithful wives lost all of their rights to the domestic patrimony (*todos los derechos en la sociedad conyugal*). Male accomplices were also subject to up to ten years of confinement and were then to be exiled from the husband's town for as long as the husband lived.[120] However, husbands who had consented to their wives' extramarital affairs were unable to accuse them later of adultery. The same stipulation held true if they abandoned their wives without justification or kept a concubine within their household.[121]

Unlike earlier statutes, the 1822 code did not consider "voluntary" inebriation an exculpatory circumstance or a reason to diminish punishment.[122] Involuntary inebriation was a different matter, for after all crime was understood to be conduct committed "freely, willingly and with malice" (*libre, voluntaria y con malicia*).[123]

As for the maximum punishment, the code condemned those who killed spouses to the same sentences prescribed for assassins (those who committed murder for hire, with treachery, poison, explosives, torture, or to hide a crime). The sentence was infamy and death.[124] For those spared the death penalty, infamy meant the loss of citizenship rights as well as the right to serve in a public job or judicial commission (*curador, tutor, perito, albacea, arbitro*), the army, or the militia.[125] Husbands who killed wives or lovers they caught *in flagrante* were not completely off the hook, as they had been in the past. They could now be sentenced to between six months to two years in prison and banishment from the place of the crime for between two to six years.[126] Those who killed wives they had caught not actually having intercourse but engaging in "preparatory" or otherwise "dishonest" acts could be sentenced to between one and four years in jail and banished for between four and eight years.[127]

The code maintained the death penalty but ordered for it to be carried out exclusively by garrote, bringing hanging to an end once more as under the Cortes of Cádiz.[128] The statute outlawed dismemberment and introduced a number of due process regulations.[129] Those sentenced to death were to be notified of the impending execution at least 48 hours in advance, with a nine-day stay allowed for persons of high rank to settle their domestic affairs.[130] The code prescribed kind and merciful treatment for death row inmates and ample opportunity to meet with relatives. It required executions to be public with posters announcing the place and time, normally around noon.[131] However, to maintain decorum the code suspended the practice of carrying out executions on weekends, national holidays, or other festive occasions.[132]

This may have been a sign of diminished interest in the public character of executions, but it did not mark the end of all visible symbolism and ceremony. The condemned were to be accompanied to their place of execution by no more than two priests, a scribe, royal guards dressed in mourning clothes (*enlutados*), and the required security escort,[133] with a town crier who announced the criminal's name, the nature of the crime, and the sentence to be carried out every two to three hundred steps along the way.[134] While quite a crowd, this was still a more sober group than the throngs that had accompanied executions in the peninsula and the overseas territories prior to the transition to independence.

Most condemned prisoners were dressed in black tunics and hats, but parricides, including spousal killers, wore all white. They carried iron chains around their necks, the ends of which were held by the executioner following behind.[135] Signboards on their chests and backs indicated their offenses. Typically, condemned murderers proceeded to the place of execution on a mule, with their hands tied behind their backs; those sentenced to "infamy," however, including parricides, were sent on a *jumento* (donkey) with bare, shaved heads.[136] The place of execution was no longer a central square but usually a spot at the outskirts of town, where a simple wooden scaffold was erected. It was painted black without any decoration except for a banner announcing the condemned's crime, and the expectation was that it would be large enough to give the audience a good view (*proporcionado para muchos espectadores*).[137] The law ordered the corpse to be exhibited until sunset inside an open casket.[138] The body would then be returned to the deceased's relatives or friends, or removed for burial. The condemned also had the option to donate their bodies to anatomical science (*para alguna operación anatómica que convenga*).[139]

Monarchs continued to have exclusive privilege to pardon death sentences but now had to consult with the Council of State, a new body established by the Cádiz Constitution to advise the king on a host of sensitive matters.[140] The code dedicated an entire chapter to such pardons.[141] It extended the tradition of granting general pardons on the occasion of coronations, royal weddings, royal births, or peace treaties and continued to allow for individual pardons. Two other circumstances could lead to the suspension of the death penalty: a royal order delaying punishment until the king could decide a pending request for *indulto*[142] and presentation of new evidence or the retraction of key witness testimony.[143] In the case of jail sentences there were further restrictions, for the most the king could do was to reduce the prison term by one year.[144]

If the wars of independence had not occurred, this short-lived code[145] would most likely have been applied in all of Spain's overseas territories. As it was, only Cuba, Puerto Rico, and the Philippines implemented it. Colombia and Mexico enacted codes of their own, influenced by the new criminal legislation coming out of both Spain and France.

In 1835 the state of Veracruz enacted Mexico's first criminal code, a 759-article statute, more than a decade after Independence. Its second part had an entire title addressing crimes against "morality, honesty and public decency" (Tit. VI, arts. 472 to 511) with a section on "disputes and scandals within marriage" (Section VI, arts. 508 to 511).[146] It authorized husbands to use admonishment and moderate domestic punishment ("*amonestaciones y moderados castigos domésticos*"), whatever that meant, to correct their wives' disobedience, unauthorized absence from the household, or evil inclinations ("*mala inclinación*").[147] The code contained gender-neutral rules listing penalties for spouses who abandoned the household, incurred "excesses" against their partner, exhibited "derelict" (*relajado*) behavior, or caused a "scandal." Initially, some of these behaviors received judicial warning, but recidivists could go to jail for up to six months.[148] If committed against women, the crime was more serious or "aggravated," and judges had the discretion to impose harsher penalties.[149]

A separate part of the code had a title on "crimes against persons" (3rd part, Title 1), one of whose sections addressed "unrestrained conducts" including adultery.[150] The code punished adultery only when committed by wives, who could be jailed from four to ten years.[151] Only husbands could denounce this crime, but they lost this privilege after two years or if they abandoned their wife, agreed to her misbehavior, knowingly cohabited with her afterward, or were unfaithful themselves.[152] In case of a husband's infidelity, wives could request either the dissolution of the family property, the restitution of their dowry, their personal property and any profits obtained during marriage, and sanction of the other woman, or petition the judge to intervene to ensure the marriage's future peace.[153]

Like the Mexican Constitution of 1824, the 1835 code preserved the death penalty but rejected hanging in favor of the garrote or firing squad.[154] It mandated death sentences for those who committed spousal and premeditated murders;[155] however, another article considered those who killed in self-defense or during a moment of "jealousy-induced rage sufficient to perturb one's reason" ("*en un momento de ira ocasionado por los celos y capaz de perturbar la razón*") to have diminished responsibility for their actions. In these cases the sentence could be as low as two years in prison.[156] Excuses that had not been valid in colonial times were now acceptable. The same was true of those whose crimes occurred because of "love" or during a violent outburst of rage ("*arrebato violento de ira*").[157] Male defendants most likely took full advantage of such loopholes. The code also exempted from punishment those who killed unfaithful spouses and their lovers to defend their honor, or who committed any crime during their sleep, as a result of mental insanity or delirium, or because of involuntary lack of reason.[158] Voluntary inebriation did not now serve as an excuse, nor did it help to diminish one's punishment.[159]

The Veracruz statute required that death row inmates be notified of their execution 72 hours in advance and, much like the Spanish code, ordered that they be treated kindly, receive spiritual and material comfort, and be allowed unlimited visits from parents, children, other relatives, and friends.[160] Pregnant women could not be executed until 40 days after their delivery.[161] All executions were to be conducted in a public place between 11 a.m. and noon, except on Sundays, holidays, or days of public rejoicing (*regocijo*).[162] Those marching to their deaths could not address the crowd (*hacer arenga ni discurso a la concurrencia*). Spousal murderers and other parricides were led barefoot with their hands tied behind their back and their faces covered with a black cloth (*crespón*). They could not be buried alongside the "rest of the citizens," an additional token of their infamy[163] reminiscent of ancient prescriptions excluding spousal murderers from appropriate burial.[164]

Colombia passed its first postcolonial criminal code, even more extensive than the Spanish one (918 articles!), in 1837.[165] Its framers allegedly used Napoleon's 1810 criminal code and the Spanish code of 1822 as models. Like the Spanish code, it understood crime to be "willing and malicious" violation of the law.[166] In matters pertaining to domestic conflicts, the code stipulated that men who battered their wives got off with official admonishment the first time but could be jailed for up to one year for subsequent offenses, a more strict punishment than the colonial one.[167] However, women who abandoned their households, refused to live with their husbands, or engaged in unspecified domestic "excess" (*excesos contra el orden doméstico*) could face their husbands' "friendly admonitions" (*amigables amonestaciones*) or judicial warning (*apercibimiento*).[168] Recidivist wives could spend up to one year in confinement (*en casa de reclusion*).[169] Husbands who abandoned their wives without any justification could be incarcerated for anywhere from two months to one year.[170] When both parties were at fault, domestic scandals could earn each of them up to a year in prison.[171] Public and "scandalous" concubinage received a punishment of six to eighteen months in jail, with married men not legitimately separated from their wives equally as liable as the women.[172]

Women who committed adultery continued to receive serious penalties. The 1837 code sentenced married women who cheated on their husbands to the loss of all of their marital assets (*derechos de la sociedad marital*). Like the Spanish code, it punished female adultery with up to ten years in jail, the exact duration to be determined by the offended husband.[173] Male accomplices suffered the same prison term and were then exiled at least six leagues away from the town for as long as the husband lived, unless the husband agreed otherwise.[174] As in the Spanish statute, husbands could not accuse their wives of adultery if they had consented to the women's affairs, abandoned them without justification, kept a concubine within their own household, or otherwise consented to or condoned the wife's crime.[175] Finally, contrary to the forgiveness they enjoyed in colonial times, husbands who killed adulterous wives and/or lovers they surprised having sex (*acto carnal*) received lighter punishment: six months to two years in prison,[176] as was the case in Spain.

As for other extenuating circumstances, those who were drunk (*embriaguez absoluta*) at the time of their crime were exempt from punishment as long as the ingestion of alcohol was not planned as part of the crime but instead was "involuntary."[177] Spouses (most likely males!) also received reduced punishment when their aggression was product of "provocation," the "exaltation" of the moment, or a "sudden and unexpected outburst of passion,"[178] an important modern category in the criminological discourse that likely opened a major loophole unavailable in times past. Men in particular could claim to have killed their wives in a moment of overwhelming rage or "passion," a concept that did not exist in ancien régime law and that would be further refined by the psychological discourses of the last quarter of the nineteenth century. First-time offenders could also hope to receive a reduced sentence, as did criminals who voluntarily turned themselves in to the authorities.[179]

Like the Spanish code, the Colombian statute outlawed judicial torture and dismemberment,[180] but incorporated the declaration of infamy (*declaración expresa de infamia*), a punishment consisting of the loss of all rights of citizenship and the inability to serve in the army, the militia, or public job or perform any legal or judicial function (as a witness, arbitrator, tutor or curator, or member of a jury).[181] Culprits sentenced to this penalty faced public shame (*vergüenza pública*).[182] They were paraded through the streets on a donkey with their hands tied and accompanied by a town crier who announced their crime to the populace, first at the jailhouse gates and again at the place of punishment, usually a public square. There, authorities tied the unlucky culprit to a pole with a big sign giving his or her name, place of origin, and the nature of the crime. The person would be exhibited there for two hours, enduring the jeers of fellow citizens, and then brought back to jail.[183] This meant that public shame remained a central objective of punishment in postcolonial times.

The code still prescribed death for parricides, but wives and husbands were no longer included in this category.[184] Death was warranted for spousal killers only if their crimes were clearly premeditated or committed for pay; committed in a treacherous manner; committed using poison, fire, explosives, or torture; or committed as a means to incur or cover up another crime (perhaps extramarital liaisons or concubinage).[185] Even then, the death penalty was lifted if death occurred more than 60 days after the aggression, a clear limit meant to avoid colonial-era disputes about responsibility for delayed deaths. In such cases, authorities charged the defendants with serious injury but not murder.[186] In all other cases, the crime carried a sentence of two to ten years in prison if it was a result of the victim's provocation[187] or four to ten years if no provocation could be ascertained.[188]

In practice, besides, husbands could rarely be accused of premeditation. A crime could not be said to be premeditated if it was a product of insult, "provocation, offense or aggression, violence, mistreatment, injury or dishonor."[189] Husbands could easily cite such circumstances to diminish their responsibility, and as wives were legally subordinated to them, judges found it easy to treat male culprits more leniently. Legal patriarchy thus remained in place both directly and indirectly.

The code, as mentioned, retained the death penalty. In keeping with new liberal principles, though, execution was now carried out by garrote[190] in the public squares of provincial capitals or main towns.[191] As in the recent Spanish code, the expectation was for scaffolds to be sober structures devoid of decoration and draped in black (*cadalso o tablado sencillo, pintado o forrado de negro*).[192] Large signs announced the name of the person being executed, his or her place of birth and residence, and the nature of the crime.[193] Again in keeping with the Spanish code, executions of death row inmates could not take place on Sundays, on holidays, or during Holy Week.[194] They went to the scaffold wearing a black robe and hood (*gorro*), with their hands tied in front and the executioner holding the rope.[195] Spousal murderers had to march barefoot to the place of execution and wear a torn white tunic stained with blood (*ensangrentada y desgarrada*). They would have their hands tied behind their backs and a chain around their necks.[196]

Death row inmates came to their execution accompanied by several priests (*ministros de la religion*), the justice officer presiding over the execution, the scribe, royal guards in mourning clothes, and an armed escort.[197] The code prescribed a detailed ceremonial for the march itself. When the culprit left the jail, the town crier would issue a cry (*pregón*) stating: "In the name of the Republic and by the authority of the law, X.X., a native of X, neighbor of X, and sentenced for the crime of X., has been sentenced to death, as is about to occur. Whoever raises his voice asking for leniency, or whoever tries to disrupt or suspend the execution, will be held guilty of the crime of sedition."[198] From this moment on through the time of execution, all of the city's churches had to toll their bells as if calling to Mass (*tocar a plegaria*).[199] Upon arriving at the place of execution, the town crier would repeat the announcement. Following the death, a priest had to say a brief prayer over the corpse, which was to remain on exhibit for precisely two hours. Finally, relatives received the body for "appropriate" burial or donated it for medical purposes.[200] However, the Colombian code treated spousal murderers differently than Spanish law; in the newly independent republic, burial of these offenders took place in remote locations (*sitios retirados*), away from public cemeteries and without any marker whatsoever (*sin permitirse poner señal que denote el lugar de la sepultura*).[201] While rather more lenient, at least symbolically this provision recalls the Roman dumping of *encubados* in the ocean, a river, or a lake to make them disappear from memory and deny them a proper Christian burial.[202]

Finally, a major novelty of Colombia's 1837 code was the end of sanctuary in Catholic churches and related places. The republican government no longer tolerated this practice, bringing to an end a long-standing tradition of Spanish criminal law.[203] The ban reflected secular liberal trends that aimed to restrict the privileges of the Catholic Church.

In sum, the modern Spanish Atlantic territories continued to impose the death penalty for the most serious crimes, and executions occurred in the first half of the nineteenth century both in the peninsula and overseas. Post–Independence legal systems punished the murder of one's spouse or one's parents, in the most extreme cases, with death by garrote, a declaration of infamy, and transportation to a faraway and undetermined place of burial. In the most benign cases, husbands who caught their wives *in flagrante* could receive as little as two to ten years in prison or, in Colombia, just six months. Those who could claim to have been drunk or provoked into a blinding rage or passion could receive further reductions, or no punishment at all.

CONCLUSION

The transition to constitutional rule and independence brought with it the formalization of humanitarian and liberal trends in criminal law. However, several liberal innovations (the end of torture, dragging, and hanging) had already taken place in the practical day-to-day running of Spanish Atlantic criminal justice decades before, sometimes over the course of more than a century. Practical legal manuals in use by the legal and judicial communities on both sides of the Atlantic mentioned some of these trends, reflecting their rather traditional nature. The manuals were also suggestive of the widespread "humanitarian" consensus over the general handling of criminal proceedings and the repression of criminals. They, incidentally, contributed as well to make law and justice somewhat more accessible to literate sectors of society and, as much as leniency, for centuries served as a direct and indirect means for the building of consensus, legitimacy, obedience, and, ultimately, hegemony.

Political and legal changes from 1808 to the early 1820s gradually brought an end to long-standing legal institutions, in particular the *encubamiento* ritual inflicted on spousal murderers for centuries. Other ancient judicial traditions, in particular Church sanctuary, also disappeared in the new American republics. However, an extensive list of old and new excuses and extenuating circumstances remained available to spousal killers—especially husbands—seeking reduced punishment. This ultimately meant that despite the significant liberal trends at work during the transition, legal patriarchy remained deeply embedded in criminal legislation.

Conclusion

This study addresses familial relations and conflicts in the late colonial Spanish Atlantic and the way law and the judicial system dealt with them. One of its major themes concerns what could be termed the "female condition"—the situation of women living in familial milieus under the relative control of patriarchs (*pater familiae*) whose power over the household was generally sanctioned by the dominant legal regime. In a fairly vague way, the law even accepted a patriarch's "moderate" violence (*derecho de castigo discreto o moderado*) as a legitimate last resort for correcting misbehavior and obtaining obedience from household subordinates, wives included. Another theme in the book is the "colonial condition," in particular the status of "wretched" indigenous subjects living under the control of the Spanish monarchy, whose legal system presided over their familial and all other social interactions and exchanges, imposing what Frederick Cooper aptly termed a "politics of difference."[1] The law deemed the natives vulnerable (*miserabiles personae*) and deserving of benevolent treatment, even in instances when they committed grave felonies such as spousal murder. Still another theme involves not a condition but a social trait: honor and its role in the lives of men, women, and their families, all governed by socially crafted male-centered views of gender and sexuality, constructs to which honor was closely tied. The law upheld, in particular, the right of private vengeance for male heads of a household the honor of which was compromised by the sexually inappropriate behavior of female members.

Therefore, throughout the volume the discussion touches on perceptions, social practices, and legal norms concerning how to treat "gender others" (wives) who may have challenged or even assaulted the patriarch presiding over their household or, more frequently, suffered under his attacks. "Ethnic others" are a subject of analysis as well, especially the perceptions, practices, and norms for treating Indians who transgressed basic expectations of the marriage pact and, more generally, the social compact. Finally, the work also addresses perceptions, practices, and rules for virtueless and dishonorable "others," and appropriate responses to their actions in an allegedly honor-bound society. All of these ideas, practices, and discourses, in one way or another, refer to socially and culturally built, and legally sanctioned, hierarchies essential to the development and maintenance of social control and hegemony, a particular form of domination largely based on consent.[2] Various other sublevels (notions of humane or civilized punishment; views on nobility, drinking, rage, mental sanity, death, and forgiveness; and the nature and meaning of legal procedures and evidence) have also merited discussion along the way. They include not just legal practices and discourses but also intertwined religious, ethical, medical, and political considerations, with marriage and gender relations and conflicts at the core.

The tensions behind spousal homicides generally involved daily negotiation by men and women of their reciprocal expectations of the privileges and duties of married life. For instance, husbands claimed the right to "obedience" (in, among others, vigilance of household and family assets, child rearing, meals, and a spouse's time management and whereabouts); immediate and full observance of other patriarchal expectations (including satisfaction of their sexual demands, fidelity and female virtue more generally, a woman's relative seclusion and public restraint, silence or deferential answers to complaints, and even the observance of dress codes); and, otherwise, "appropriate correction" of insolent and disobedient dependents, including wives.

Wives in turn reserved the right to receive a fair share of the household income for child rearing, cooking, home supplies, and laundry; to be privy to information about their partner's whereabouts and disbursement of household resources; to retain their husband's sexual fidelity and exclusivity; and to uphold appropriate public appearances concerning the household hierarchy and, in particular, a wife's relative power in it. In sum, marital harmony in the period of our study hinged upon a number of concepts and expectations (obedience, loyalty, deference and respect, reservation, accountability, trustworthiness, temperance, social image), unspoken at times but central to the way that couples behaved (or misbehaved) on a daily basis.

As was established, verbal and physical conflicts among spouses followed disagreements about what each of them understood to be their respective rights and obligations as husbands and wives. Disputes derived, in particular, from unsatisfied patriarchal expectations, perceived lack of control, and general abuses (involving drinking, the right to correct and punish, the freedom to come and go, and so forth). Importantly, a fair amount of familial stress involved not just women's alleged "disobedience" and "insolence" but also their determination to reach out, gain greater freedom, and, especially, join men to whom they were sentimentally or sexually attached. Thus, women's unstoppable search for freedom, affection, and sexual satisfaction contributed to conflicts as well.

Therefore, confirming a trend documented in the historiography over the past decade, perhaps the most revealing finding in the area of gender is precisely the fact that women contested patriarchy on a daily basis and did not passively accept the limitations of marriage, even their restriction to domestic spaces. Disputes with husbands over public encounters (in their own homes, the homes of friends and relatives, taverns, marketplaces, popular festivals and celebrations, churches, and the street) with tenants, relatives, customers, partygoers, peers, parishioners, or passersby, whether acquaintances or strangers, could lead to heated arguments, physical fights, battering, even murder. Irrefutably, women's extramarital affairs and attempts to run away with lovers were the cause of many spousal murders. So it is no wonder that when they killed, women were more likely to target their spouses than other men they knew or total strangers.

Curiously, although husbands who felt disrespected often reacted violently to a wife's disobedience and insolence, betrayed husbands were not the most abundant subgroup among spousal killers. Rather than exercising their right to private vengeance, many cuckolded husbands seem to have preferred denouncing their wayward wives and taking them before justice officials, letting law and justice follow their course. Therefore, two findings of this book—adulterous women's propensity to kill their husbands and husbands' preference for royal justice over revenge—call into question conventional wisdom on the operation of the culture of honor in the Spanish Atlantic, in particular the perception of the betrayed husband frequently killing to avenge his honor. Other paradigms, especially those concerning colonial oppression of ethnically subaltern sectors of society, also require some qualification in light of evidence uncovered here.

In the case of subaltern ethnic groups, in particular members of indigenous communities, this research suggests that as with any other patriarchs, natives regularly asserted their authority in their household even by means of force. Nevertheless, in consideration of their "wretchedness," the civil and ecclesiastical legal systems addressed them as minors and treated them quite gently. Because of long-standing doctrines of Roman, canon, and feudal law, adapted to the realities of the New World, both the Crown and the Church opted to treat native criminals with great leniency. Strictly speaking, not to deny compassion's significance to legitimate royal power or other ulterior motives behind it, in this particular instance Cooper's politics of difference had a great deal more to do here with Western jurisprudence's tackling of civil and ecclesiastical jurisdiction over cases involving certain categories of vulnerable people than with a blank and dismissive colonialism.[3] This is why Indian offenders benefited greatly from the king's and the Church's clemency. In contrast, mixed-race individuals, especially mulattos, could expect to face much harsher outcomes in courts of law, as did whites. Even white noblemen met tougher sentences than Indians who committed similar crimes. This practice did not contradict the dominant legislation or legal culture but, perhaps as an expression of what Douglas Hay cynically called "the law's incorruptible impartiality," was actually their product.[4] Further, legal doctrines and the legal system overall had considerable weight in the determination not only of the judicial outcome of individual cases but also in overall appropriate social behavior and obedience by all royal subjects, which is to say, in the consolidation of hegemony and the persistence of imperial rule both in the metropolis and overseas.

This book looks at various reasons behind social obedience and the endurance of empire, for which the conflicts and crimes under consideration provide us valuable clues. The three-centuries-long domination of the Spanish monarchy and its major partner, the Catholic Church, over all kinds of social groups in a sizable transatlantic empire based itself, so it seems, on a complex combination of carrots and sticks, in the form of positive and negative legal and judicial incentives. Imperial subjects' behavior sprang from a variety of cultural mechanisms eliciting their willing acquiescence. Force and coercion leading to fearful compliance with political and social norms and expectations were equally important factors.

To be sure, criminals such as the ones whose behavior we have examined broke the law in major ways and sabotaged the marital and social pact. In other words, they did not obey after all! However, curiously enough, lawbreakers did not entirely refuse to let law and justice follow their course or fulfill their basic mission to aid social control and ensure social order. While some criminals opted for contumacy and surrendered only under duress, law and justice administration did not cease to operate just because of these few outliers. Society at large was held together with the assistance of enduring norms and institutional mechanisms of conflict resolution, largely keeping generalized disobedience and private vengeance at bay. Informal social control mattered, too.

As Spanish historian Tomás Mantecón argues, "infrajustice," or mutual social regulation, self-containment or self-disciplining that helped inhibit the escalation of conflicts in family structures (except for in a relatively small number of cases), accounted for a large share of social control and obedience in Spain and its domains.[5] Legislation and judicial enforcement were no less significant, however, and they followed certain parameters. Legal writers, judicial officials, and litigants generally were aware of and observed rules, regulations, and procedures, including rules of evidence and criminal proceedings. Lawbreakers and those who assisted in their defense also appear to have been somewhat familiar with the rules and practices of the judicial game. Some of these rules, and familiarity with them on their part, benefited many criminals. The best cases in point are perhaps sanctuary or the pursuit of royal pardon. As was noted above, however, the rules did not just favor criminals but also played a significant role in strengthening the legitimacy and consolidating the power and hegemony of both the monarchy and the Catholic Church.[6]

The capacity of the monarchy and its colonial delegates to command collective obedience ("mobilize consensus") is intriguing and worth learning more about. It stemmed from factors such as the daily contact by even ordinary people with laws, regulations, and restrictions of one kind or another, including those addressing familial tensions, and interaction with local judges, courts, and "legal offices" (*alcaldes* or *corregidores, escribanos, notarios*) and justice-related personnel of all sorts, not only notaries and scribes but also *curadores, tutores, depositarios,* lawyers and legal staffers, and village and local authorities ranging from local mayors and constables (*alguaciles*) to *corregidores,* governors, *audiencia* and high court justices (*oidores*), and viceroys. Also important was collective awareness of the negative consequences of disobedience, including confiscations and confinement, flogging, dragging through the streets, or even hanging. In sum, many people in the late colonial Spanish Atlantic seemed to have had sufficient awareness or even a good understanding of institutions, authorities, boundaries, and sanctions, as well as which were to be feared and obeyed and which could be used for one's own benefit.

The various historical actors appear to have well understood the means to leverage a better outcome in cases of domestic and other troubles by emphasizing one's ethnicity (to claim the more lenient treatment reserved for indigenous subjects), gender, drunkenness, excessive love, passion, or rage, and the rights of disobeyed, insulted, or dishonored husbands or of abused wives. Defendants also took advantage of Church asylum and royal pardons issued on such occasions as the accession of new monarchs, the birth of royal infants, or weddings and other celebrations at court. The possibility of forgiveness was a major element in the political economy of obedience. Even as spousal murderers and other criminals feared royal justice and *vindicta pública,* they knew that on special occasions (e.g., an imminent royal birth) they could benefit from the king's clemency and "love" or the Church's self-serving "charitable" intervention and assistance. These mechanisms were built not only into the collective mentality but also into the legal system.

The centrality of law and justice as discourses and practices shaping the state's day-to-day interaction with even its most despicable violators is thus evident. So is the fact that such peoples shaped law and justice at least in limited ways. The law, legal principles, legal culture, and judicial practices informed behavior and made apparent the lack of institutions we now take for granted: due process, equality before the law, and other liberal concepts. But to win their case or to obtain reduced sentences by claiming exceptional circumstances, women, Indians, commoners, and others also had means to influence legal and judicial outcomes. In sum, criminal legislation and justice shaped and were shaped by exchanges among men and women; Spaniards, creoles, and nonwhites; noblemen and commoners; and ecclesiastical officials, civil officials, and lay participants in the administration of justice.

The point is that just as marital pacts turned lethal, the social pact and stability endured, and even criminals played along and seemed willing and ready to influence judicial proceedings and outcomes. Abundant evidence exists of voluntary acquiescence: Many criminals surrendered, most answered depositions and even confessed their crimes, and several worked through their legal counsel, filed petitions and legal motions, used judicial strategies, and embraced protective mechanisms (sanctuary, claims to wretchedness, arguments pertaining to drunkenness, rage, and so forth, petitions for amnesty, etc.) to improve their lot, and generally took part in the system. They did not withdraw from participation in institutional justice, nor did they question the legitimacy or authority of legal norms, justice officials, or procedures. Instead, they engaged them. At the end of the day, they submitted themselves to the methods and commands of royal and ecclesiastical justice.

Both in their own eyes and those of society at large, justice thus appeared to be sufficiently legitimate, even kind, and worth pursuing. It seemed effective, too. Further, it was not mysterious at all but followed familiar protocols. There were even books and manuals explaining its ways in practical down-to-earth formats that any curious, literate person could generally understand. To add further confidence, those in charge of the justice system were local officials generally known by their peers, communities, and neighbors. Justice was neither remote nor incomprehensible, and it was not always harsh. Perhaps because the day-to-day operation of justice and law enforcement was rather obvious and seemed somewhat "natural" to many at the time, it is important to bear in mind that the workings of law and justice are *not,* after all, "natural" phenomena. They are rather a social occurrence worthy of further reflection than it typically receives in historical research. Law and justice are a socially crafted factor essential to making sense of the way communities hold together, whether voluntarily or by force.

This work therefore pays attention to long-standing, habitual, somewhat predictable, and widely known legal procedures for improving access to criminal justice and dispute resolution. It observes the lessening of punishment in general and physical pain in particular owing to diverse extenuating circumstances and cultural restrains embodied in written or customary royal and ecclesiastical law or in judicial practice. It also highlights the secular or ecclesiastical protection and forgiveness of criminals enshrined in law and justice. These were all factors that society at large understood to be ordinary components of collective life. But force or coercion was critical as well.

With regard to domination by force, the book addresses examples of late colonial *vindicta pública:* the application of a variety of punishments to spousal murderers and other criminals from the 1750s to the early 1800s. Until the late colonial era, such punishments included the death penalty and could involve public spectacle. The application of these punishments, though, varied across the Atlantic, with death for spousal murderers being, for instance, more prevalent in the metropolis than the colonies. In any case, over many decades, although some harsh laws remained on the books, the death penalty declined in significance overall and punishment in general became softer in practice on both sides of the Atlantic. A less severe form of, say, customary law prevailed everywhere. Nevertheless, formal law did not change. Penalties remained severe in theory and likely to scare (*escarmentar*) both criminals and bystanders alike, sometimes contributing to compel them eventually to submit and obey.

Finally, the study closes with references to the post–Independence period, which allegedly brought with it some major changes to the political and legal systems in the Spanish Atlantic. The changes had Enlightenment ideas and liberalism as their main guides and took the form of constitutional government, more civilized punishment, codification of more precise criminal definitions and procedures, and greater guarantees for criminals facing judicial investigation and trial. Whereas some of these changes were true in theory, the reality was that even the most dramatic ones, including the end of torture, the reduction of gruesome corporal punishment and bodily pain, and the elimination of death by hanging had been preceded by de facto customary substitutes during the entire eighteenth century and even earlier.

Much as in other parts of Europe, changes in repression in Spain and its colonies were long term or developmental and uneven, rather than abrupt and neat. On both sides of the Independence divide, repression displayed hybrid characteristics. For example, the colonial project had a long history of embracing more-civilized attitudes toward punishment, while the republic, in turn, would cling to regressive punishments such as the death penalty or public shame for a long time to come.[7] Also, as liberal republics tried to curtail the interference of the Catholic Church in civil matters, some criminal codes ended long-standing institutions, in particular ecclesiastical sanctuary (*asilo*), that had benefited murderers and other criminals for centuries. Other related aspects (civil marriage and divorce, in particular) would contribute to transform family relations in the years to come, but family violence would endure and remains a major legal and cultural challenge to this day.

Appendixes

APPENDIX ONE: INVENTORY OF SEQUESTERED PROPERTIES OWNED BY PRUDENCIO ZURITA, GUADALAJARA, NEW SPAIN (MEXICO), AUGUST, 1815

English translation:

[A] house made up of a living room, one bedroom and a small yard. Two maguey fields, a donkey sold for 10 pesos to José María Bera, a road, a hoe, 4 empty leather bags for storing wine, a yellow dress and a blue one, a black silk dress, a San Migueleño cotton cot, a white piece of woolen fabric, a pair of silk stockings of the best class, two silver spoons, three porcelain cups from Guanajuato, two *salónica* plates, a mended china cup, three small cases with some documents in a frame of Nuestra Sra. de los Dolores, a painting of San Anthony of Padua over a metallic plate, two colored *zoacales,* a little silver box for holding religious relics, scissors in a case, an awl, a bricklayer's spoon, an old bridle, a halter and a couple of spurs, a black hat, half a *quartillo* of scrap metal, two knives, a black bandana, some pieces of steel and old iron, a pair of black suede pants with silver buttons owned by Gabino Mendoza (aka Monte en Mano) pawned for two pesos, 33 pesos and 3 *reales* placed in the hands of Ignacio Gómez (aka El Charqueño), who also received on deposit all of the properties seized, committing himself to keep them in good condition, receive rents from the maguey farm and not return to the owner anything without the express authorization of the judge in the case. . . .

Original Spanish version:

[C]asa compuesta de sala, recamara y patiecito. Dos maguellales, un burro que estaba vendido por 10 pesos a José María Bera, una barra, un azadon, 4 botas de vino vacias, un reboso amarillo y uno azul, un reboso de seda negro, un catre San Migueleño de algodón, un paño blanco unas medias de seda de primera, dos cucharas de plata, tres tazas de loza de Guanajuato, dos platos de salonica, uno de china pegado, tres petaquitas con unos papeles en un bastidor de Nuestra Señora de los Dolores, y una lamina de ojalata con San Antonio de Padua: dos zoacales de colores, una caja de relicario de plata, un bainero con una tijera, una lesna, una cuchara de albañil, un freno viejo, un cabestro y un par de espuelas un sombrero negro un medio quartillo de ojalata y dos belduques una badana

negra unos pedazos de acero y fierro viejo, una saqueta de istle, unos calzones de gamuza negra con botones de plata propios de Gabino Mendoza (alias "monte en mano") enpeñados en dos pesos, treinta y un pesos tres reales en poder de Ignacio Gomez (alias el Chargueño), quien recibio en deposito dichos bienes embargados obligandose en toda forma a su conservacion, rentas de la finca y no entregar cosa alguna sin orden del señor juez que conoce en esta causa. No firma por no saber.

SOURCE: Audiencia de Guadalajara, AANG, Criminales, 13-6-308, fols. 8–12. White (Spanish) salesman (*Viajero*) accused of murdering his wife, Guadalupe Sarmiento, in Santa María de los Lagos, Mexico, 1815.

APPENDIX TWO: EXAMPLE OF THE WORDING OF REQUESTS IN CASES TO BE CONSIDERED FOR GOOD FRIDAY PARDON (*PERDON DE VIERNES SANTO*) ISSUED BY MADRID'S HIGH COURT (*SALA DE ALCALDES DE CASA Y CORTE*)

English translation:

Sr. Don Luis del Valle Salazar. Cases for Good Friday Pardon. The King's Chamber has decided that this Sala de Alcaldes de Casa y Corte should forward two cases of criminals sentenced to death so the King may consider them for a Holy Friday Pardon, selected from among those cases where there is no party demanding punishment, and as long the case is not a treacherous murder, robbery, or any other ugly and heinous crime unworthy of royal pardon given its particular circumstances and the serious need for public vengeance regarding its punishment. Your Lord [VS] would please forward such cases to me as promptly as possible so that we may process them with sufficient time. May God Keep VS. Madrid, February 20, 1767. (*Signed*) Joseph Ignacio de Goyeneche

Original Spanish version:

Sr. Don Luis del Valle Salazar. Causas para Indulto de Viernes Santo. La Cámara ha acordado que esta Sala de Alcaldes de Casa y Corte, remita a mis manos dos causas de reos de muerte para los indultos de viernes santo, que sean de aquellas en que no haya parte que pida, ni intervenga asesinato, robo, u otro de aquellos delitos feos y enormes indignos de perdón por sus circunstancias y por la vindicta pública y se interesa ésta gravemente en el castigo cuyas causas dispondrá VS se remitan a mis manos con la brevedad posible para darlas con tiempo el correspondiente curso. Dios Guarde a VS Madrid, 20 de Febrero de 1767. Firma Joseph Ignacio de Goyeneche

SOURCE: AHN, Madrid, Consejos, libro 1355, año 1767.

APPENDIX THREE: CRIMINAL PROCEDURE ARTICLES. CADIZ CONSTITUTION, MARCH 1812

The following are some articles of the constitution pertaining to the proceedings in criminal cases. Emphasis in boldface is added.

Art. 242. The power to **apply the laws in civil and criminal cases belongs exclusively to the courts.**

Art. 243. **Neither the Cortes nor the King shall be able to exercise in any case judicial functions,** or to remove pending cases, or to order cases that have been closed to be opened.

Art. 244. Laws shall set out the **order and formalities of the procedure that shall be uniform in all courts,** and neither the Cortes nor the King shall be able to set them aside.

Art. 247. **No Spaniard may be tried in civil or criminal cases by any commission but only by a competent court previously established by law.**

Art. 253. If the King shall receive complaints against any magistrate and the complaint as formed appears grounded, he shall, hearing the Council of State, suspend him, immediately passing the complaint to the Supreme Tribunal of Justice so that it judges in accordance with law.

Art. 258. **Civil, criminal, and commercial codes shall be the same for all of the Monarchy,** without prejudicing variations that the Cortes shall make in particular circumstances.

Art. 263. It shall belong to **the high courts to hear all civil cases from lower judges of their jurisdiction in the second and third instances, and the same for criminal cases,** as provided by law, and also the cases of suspension and separation of lower judges from the territory, as provided by law, giving notice to the King.

Art. 275. In all towns, judges (*alcaldes*) shall be established, and **laws shall determine the extent of their powers, just as in judicial matters** (*lo contencioso*) as in economic matters.

Art. 286. Laws shall determine the administration of criminal justice so that **procedure is carried out quickly, and without error, with the end that crimes are promptly punished.**

Art. 287. **No Spaniard may be imprisoned without a preceding summary information of the deed deserving corporal punishment according to law, and without an order of the judge in writing** that notifies him as he is being imprisoned.

Art. 290. The arrested, **before being placed in prison, shall be presented to the judge, as long as there is nothing that obstructs it, so that he provides a declaration;** but if this is not able to take place, he shall be brought to the prison as a detained person, and the **judge shall receive the declaration within 24 hours.**

Art. 298. The **declaration of the arrested shall be without oath** so that no one must give information in criminal matters about his own acts.

Art. 293. If it is resolved that the arrested should be placed in prison, or that he remain there as a prisoner, a **judicial order of detention duly justified shall be issued,** and a copy shall be given to the jailer, so that he inserts it in the book of prisoners; without this requirement the jailer shall not admit any prisoner as such, under the most strict responsibility.

Art. 294. **Seizure of goods shall only be done** when the proceedings are for crimes that carry with time pecuniary responsibility, and **in proportion to the quantity that the responsibility may extend.**

Art. 296. At whatever moment of the trial that it appears **that corporal punishment may not be imposed on the prisoner, he shall be put in liberty,** paying bond.

Art. 297. **Prisons shall be arranged in a manner that serves to hold and not to disturb prisoners** so that the jailer shall have those the judge orders to be without communication in good and separate custody, but never in unhealthy or underground cells.

Art. 300. Within **24 hours the accused (*tratado como reo*) shall be shown the reasons for his imprisonment,** and the name of his accuser, if there is one.

Art. 301. On taking the confession of the accused, there **shall be read to him in their entirety all documents and declarations by witnesses, with their names;** and if by the documents and declarations they are not known, there shall be given enough notice to determine who they are.

Art. 302. **Upon taking the declaration of the accused, proceedings shall be public** in the manner and form determined by law.

Art. 303. **Torture or pressure (*apremios*) shall not be used.**

Art. 304. **Neither shall the punishment of confiscation of goods be imposed.**

Art. 306. The **house of any Spaniard may not be searched unless in cases determined by law** for the good order and security of the State.

SOURCE: Adapted from M. C. Mirow, *Florida's First Constitution: The Constitution of Cádiz* (Durham: Carolina Academic Press, 2012), 4–52.

Abbreviations Used in Notes and Bibliography

ACC	Archivo Central del Cauca (Popayán, Colombia)
AAE	Archivo Audiencia de Extremadura (Cáceres, Spain)
AANG	Archivo de la Audiencia de Nueva Galicia (Guadalajara, Mexico)
ADC	Archivo Diocesano de Cádiz (Cádiz, Spain)
AGI	Archivo General de Indias (Seville, Spain)
AGN	Colombia, Archivo General de la Nación (Bogotá, Colombia)
AGN	México, Archivo General de la Nación (México, D.F.)
AGS	Archivo General de Simancas (Simancas, Spain)
AHA	Archivo Histórico de Antioquia (Medellin, Colombia)
AHN	Archivo Histórico Nacional (Madrid, Spain)
AHPC	Archivo Histórico Provincial de Cáceres (Caceres, Spain)
AHPCo	Archivo Histórico Provincial de Córdoba (Córdoba, Spain)
AHPS	Archivo Histórico Provincial de Sevilla (Seville, Spain)
AJO	Archivo Judicial de Oaxaca (Oaxaca, Mexico)
AJP	Archivo Judicial de Puebla (Puebla, Mexico)
APR	Archivo del Palacio Real (Madrid, Spain)
APS	Archivo Provincial de Segovia (Segovia, Spain)
ARCG	Archivo de la Real Chancillería de Granada (Granada, Spain)
ARCV	Archivo de la Real Chancilleria de Valladolid (Valladolid, Spain)
ARG	Archivo del Reino de Galicia (A Coruña, Spain)
ARV	Archivo del Reino de Valencia (Valencia, Spain)
BNC	Biblioteca Nacional de Colombia (Bogotá, Colombia)
BNE	Biblioteca Nacional de España (Madrid, Spain)
BRAH	Biblioteca de la Real Academia de Historia, Colección Mata Linares (Madrid, Spain)
BUS	Biblioteca Universidad de Sevilla (Seville, Spain)
HNM	Hemeroteca Nacional de México (México, D.F.)
MNA	Museo Nacional de Antropología, Subdirección de Documentación (Mexico, D.F.)

Notes

PREFACE

1. Pablo Neruda, "The Art of Poetry, No. 14." Interviewed by Rita Guibert, *Paris Review* (spring 1971), www.theparisreview.org/interviews/4091/the-art-of-poetry-no-14-pablo-neruda.

2. I thank my dear Florida International University colleague and fellow historian Bianca Premo for introducing me to the Neruda interview in which this passage appeared.

3. Michel Foucault, *Discipline and Punish: The Birth of the Prison* (New York: Pantheon, 1977).

4. Pieter Spierenburg, *The Spectacle of Suffering: Executions and the Evolution of Repression: From a Preindustrial Metropolis to the European Experience* (Cambridge: Cambridge University Press, 1984).

5. Ibid., viii.

6. Ibid., xix.

7. Ibid., xix–xx.

8. Francisco Tomás y Valiente, *El derecho penal de la monarquía absoluta (Siglos XVI, XVII y XVIII)* (Madrid: Editorial Técnos, 1992 [1969]).

9. Ibid., 23. *Estamental* refers to corporatist and deeply hierarchical societies made up of various unequal social estates or status groups.

10. "The triumph of reason took a long time to materialize. In criminal matters, the most important reforms, obviously based on Enlightenment ideology, would be implemented after the fall of the *anciene régime*." Tomás y Valiente, *El derecho penal*, 111.

INTRODUCTION

1. AGN, Mexico, Provincias Internas, 6, fols. 44–85. A *recogimiento* (*casa de recogida* or *arrepentidas*) housed women who had "perverted" themselves and offended God by committing crimes of "dishonesty or impurity." As in a monastery, the residents lived in community and typically supported themselves through sewing, embroidering, and the making of sweets. On the origin and operation of *casas de recogidas*, see María Dolores Pérez Baltasar, *Mujeres Marginadas: Las Casas*

de Recogidas en Madrid (Madrid: Gráficas Lormo, 1984); idem, "Orígenes de los recogimientos de mujeres," *Cuadernos de Historia Moderna y Contemporánea*, 6 (1985): 13–23; Josefina Muriel, *Los recogimientos de mujeres: Respuesta a una problemática social novohispana* (México: Universidad Nacional Autónoma de México, 1974); Barry Matthew Robinson, "La reclusión de mujeres rebeldes: el recogimiento en la Guerra de Independencia Mexicana, 1810–1819," *Fronteras de la Historia* 15:2 (2010): 225–244. On the complex historical meanings of *recogimiento,* see Nancy E. van Deusen, *Between the Sacred and the Worldly: The Institutional and Cultural Practice of Recogimiento in Colonial Lima* (Stanford: Stanford University Press, 2001).

2. Good examples are found in micro-histories (studies of the past on a very small scale—for example, of a single criminal incident or peasant village) addressing cases in eighteenth-century France, Spain, the United States, Italy, and the Netherlands, respectively: Benoît Garnot, *Un Crime Conjugal au XVIIIe Siècle: L'Affaire Boiveau* (Paris: Imago, 1993); Tomás Mantecón, *La muerte de Antonia Isabel Sánchez: Tiranía y escándalo en una sociedad del Norte español en el Antiguo Régimen* (Alcalá de Henares: Centro de Estudios Cervantinos, 1997); Deborah Navas, *Murdered by His Wife: An Absorbing Tale of Crime and Punishment in Eighteenth-Century Massachusetts* (Amherst: University of Massachusetts Press, 1999); Tommaso Astarita, *Village Justice: Community, Family and Popular Culture in Early Modern Italy* (Baltimore: Johns Hopkins University Press, 1999); and Pieter Spierenburg, *Written in Blood: Fatal Attraction in Enlightenment Amsterdam* (Columbus: Ohio University Press, 2004).

3. On the significance of colonial justice for the operation of the monarchy, see Sarah Chambers, "Citizens Before the Law: The Role of Courts in Postindependence State Building in Spanish America," in Miguel A. Centeno and Agustin E. Ferraro, eds., *State and Nation Making in Latin America and Spain: Republics of the Possible* (Cambridge: Cambridge University Press, 2013), 356–374; Tamar Herzog, *Upholding Justice: Society, State, and the Penal System in Quito (1650–1750)* (Ann Arbor: University of Michigan Press, 2004); and Brian Owensby, *Empire of Law and Indian Justice in Colonial Mexico* (Stanford: Stanford University Press, 2008). For the relatively comparable Portuguese case, see Antonio M. Hespanha, *La gracia del derecho: Economía de la cultura en la edad moderna* (Madrid: Centro de Estudios Constitucionales, 1993), 210–211.

4. Hegemony, a concept derived from the work of Marxist Italian philosopher Antonio Gramsci, can be understood as a dynamic and permanently in flux process of social and cultural domination by some over other individuals and social groups who willingly obey or consent, believing the situation to be natural, legitimate, inevitable, and even beneficial. Their beliefs and patterns of behavior are shaped in particular by religion, the legal system, the media, and education. See Antonio Gramsci, *Prison Notebooks* (New York: Columbia University Press, 1992), 233–238. For a dense account of the concept's nuances, character, intellectual development, and relevance to contemporary politics, see Ernesto Laclau and Chantal Mouffe, *Hegemony and Socialist Strategy* (London: Verso, 1986). For a reader-friendly general discussion of this notion, see John Charles Chasteen,

Born in Blood and Fire: A Concise History of Latin America (New York: Norton, 2011), 56–62.

5. Alamiro Avila Martel, *Esquema del derecho penal indiano* (Santiago: Universidad de Chile, 1941), 77–78.

6. I owe the use of this expression to the suggestion of Bianca Premo, whose comments on this introduction were of great benefit to me. For a historiographical essay on the complexities behind an Atlantic perspective, see Premo, "On Currents and Comparisons: Gender and the Atlantic 'Turn' in Spanish America," *History Compass* 8.3 (2010): 223–237.

7. Lawrence Stone, *Road to Divorce: England 1530–1987* (Oxford: Oxford University Press, 1990), 8–11.

8. Philippe Ariés, *Centuries of Childhood: A Social History of Family Life* (New York: Knopf, 1962); Georges Duby, *Love and Marriage in the Middle Ages* (Chicago: University of Chicago Press, 1996); Jean Louis Flandrin, *Familles: Parenté, maison, sexualité dans l'ancienne société* (Paris: Hachette, 1976); idem, *Sex in the Western World* (New York: Routledge, 1991); François Lebrun, *La vie conjugale sous l'Ancien Régime* (Paris: Armand Collin, 1985); Silvia M. Arrom, *The Women of Mexico City, 1790–1857* (Stanford: Stanford University Press, 1985); Richard Boyer, *Lives of the Bigamists: Marriage, Family and Community in Colonial Mexico* (Albuquerque: University of New Mexico Press, 1995); Ramón Gutiérrez, *When Jesus Came, the Corn Mothers Went Away: Marriage, Sexuality and Power in New Mexico, 1500–1846* (Stanford: Stanford University Press, 1991); Asunción Lavrín, ed., *Sexuality and Marriage in Colonial Latin America* (Lincoln: University of Nebraska Press, 1989); Patricia Seed, *To Love, Honor and Obey in Colonial Mexico* (Stanford: Stanford University Press, 1986); Susan Socolow, *The Women of Colonial Latin America* (Cambridge: Cambridge University Press, 2000); Ann Twinam, *Private Lives and Public Secrets* (Stanford: Stanford University Press, 1999); Carmen Castañeda, *Violación, estupro y sexualidad: Nueva Galicia, 1790–1821* (Guadalajara: Editorial Hexágono, 1989); Guiomar Dueñas, *Los hijos del pecado: Ilegitimidad y vida familiar en la Santafé de Bogotá colonial* (Bogotá: Editorial Universidad Nacional, 1997); Pilar Gonzalbo Aizpuru, *Familia y orden colonial* (México: El Colegio de México, 1998); Maria Emma Mannarelli, *Pecados públicos: La ilegitimidad en Lima, Siglo XVII* (Lima: Ediciones Flora Tirstán, 1993); María Beatriz Nizza da Silva, *Sistema de Casamento no Brasil Colonial* (São Paulo: Editora da Universidade de São Paulo, 1984); Sergio Ortega, *De la santidad a la perversión o de porque no se cumplía la ley de Dios en la sociedad novohispana* (México City: Grijalbo, 1986); Pablo Rodríguez, *Sentimientos y vida familiar en el Nuevo Reino de Granada* (Santafé de Bogotá: Editorial Ariel, 1997); Ronaldo Vainfas, org., *História e sexualidade no Brasil* (Rio de Janeiro: Graal, 1986); idem, *Trópico dos pecados* (Rio de Janeiro: Campus, 1989). For a more recent example, see Nicole Von Germeten, *Violent Delights, Violent Ends: Sex, Race, and Honor in Colonial Cartagena de Indias* (New Mexico: University of New Mexico Press, 2013).

9. See Victor M. Uribe-Uran, "Innocent Infants or Abusive Patriarchs? Spousal Homicides, the Punishment of Indians and the Law in Colonial Mexico,

1740s–1820s," *Journal of Latin American Studies* 38.4 (2006): 793–828; idem, "Colonial *Baracunatanas* and Their Nasty Men: Spousal Homicides and the Law in New Granada, 1750–1810," *Journal of Social History* 35.1 (2001): 43–72; and Richard Boyer, *Colonial Lives: Documents on Latin American History* (Oxford: Oxford University Press, 1999), 54–76, 185–200. See also Blanca Llanes Parra, "*El enemigo en casa: El parricidio y otras formas de violencia interpersonal doméstica en el Madrid de los Austrias (1580–1700),*" *Nuevo Mundo-Mundos Nuevos*, Coloquio 2008, 1–15, available at http://nuevomundo.revues.org/index24382.html; Scott K. Taylor, *Honor and Violence in Golden Age Spain* (New Haven: Yale University Press, 2008), 198; Lori Heise and Claudia Garcia-Moreno, "Violence by Intimate Partners," in Etienne G. Krug, Linda L. Dahlberg, James A. Mercy, Anthony B. Zwi, and Rafael Lozano, eds., *World Report on Violence and Health* (Geneva: World Health Organization, 2002), 87–113.

10. Catherine Komisaruk, *Labour and Love in Guatemala: The Eve of Independence* (Stanford: Stanford University Press, 2013), 196–206; Steve Stern, *The Secret History of Gender: Women, Men and Power in Late Colonial Mexico* (Chapel Hill: University of North Carolina Press, 1995), 57–59, 112; Heise and Garcia-Moreno, "Violence by Intimate Partners," 95.

11. Besides the ones already cited, some of the most significant monographs that address domestic conflicts and gender violence in the late colonial and early postcolonial periods include Raul A. Molina, *La familia porteña en los siglos XVII y XVIII: Historia de los divorcios en el período hispánico* (Buenos Aires: Fuentes Históricas y Genealógicas Argentinas, 1991); Eugenia Rodríguez Sáenz, *Hijas, novias y esposas: Familia, matrimonio y violencia en el Valle Central de Costa Rica* (Heredia: Editorial Universidad Nacional, 2000); Viviana Kluger, *Escenas de la vida conyugal: Los conflictos matrimoniales en la sociedad virreinal rioplatense* (Buenos Aires: Editorial Quorurm–UMSA, 2003), 245–246; José Luis Moreno, *Historia de la familia en el Río de la Plata* (Buenos Aires: Editorial Sudamericana, 2004), chapter 4; Arlene J. Díaz, *Female Citizens, Patriarchs, and the Law in Venezuela, 1786–1904* (Lincoln: University of Nebraska Press, 2004); Beatríz Patiño, *Criminalidad, ley penal y estructura social en la provincia de Antioquia, 1750–1820* (Medellín: IDEA, 1994), 375–377; Hermes Tovar Pinzón, *La batalla de los sentidos: Infidelidad, adulterio y concubinato a fines de la colonia* (Bogotá: Fondo Cultural Cafetero, 2004); Sarah Chambers, *From Subjects to Citizens: Honor, Gender, and Politics in Arequipa, Peru, 1780–1854* (University Park: Pennsylvania State University Press, 1999), 101–103; Ana María Alonso, *Thread of Blood: Colonialism, Revolution, and Gender on Mexico's Northern Frontier* (Tucson: University of Arizona Press, 1995), 213–230; Kimberley Gauderman, *Women's Lives in Colonial Quito: Gender, Law and Economy in Spanish America* (Albuquerque: University of New Mexico Press, 2003), chapter 3; and Chad Thomas Black, *The Limits of Gender Domination: Women, the Law and Political Crisis in Quito, 1765–1830* (Albuquerque: University of New Mexico Press, 2010), chapter 2.

12. This traditional explanation is summarized in J. A. Sharpe, "Domestic Homicide in Early Modern England," *Historical Journal* 24 (1981): 29–48, esp. 36.

13. For a pioneering work in this regard, see Arrom, *The Women of Mexico City,* chapter 4. Abundant evidence of women's public engagement and activities, economic and otherwise, can be found in Gauderman, *Women's Lives in Colonial Quito;* and Black, *The Limits of Gender Domination.* See also Susan Socolow, *The Women of Colonial Latin America* (Cambridge: Cambridge University Press, 2000).

14. See Arrom, *The Women of Mexico City,* chapter 4; Rodríguez Sáenz, *Hijas, novias y esposas,* chapter 2; Gauderman, *Women's Lives in Colonial Quito,* chapter 4; Pedro Pérez Herrero, "Evolución demográfica y estructura familiar en México 1750–1850," in Pilar Gonzalbo Aizpuru, ed., *Familias novohispanas: Siglos XVI al XIX* (México: El Colegio de México, 1991), 345–371, esp. 357–359; Carmen Castañeda, "La formación de la pareja y el matrimonio," in ibid., 73–90, esp. 81–82; Chambers, *From Subjects to Citizens,* 101–103; Susan Schroeder, Stephanie Wood, and Robert Haskett, eds., *Indian Women of Early Mexico* (Norman: University of Oklahoma Press, 1997), chapter 11; Komisaruk, *Labour and Love in Guatemala,* 9, 39–50, 54, 61–66, 114–129, 145–156, 187–192.

15. Hespanha, "De *Iustitia* a Disciplina," in idem, *La gracia del derecho,* 203–273, esp. 232. For comparative purposes, see Douglas Hay, "Property, Authority and the Criminal Law," in Douglas Hay et al., eds., *Albion's Fatal Tree: Crime and Society in Eighteenth-Century England* (New York: Pantheon, 1975), 17–63, esp. 40–49.

16. See María Teresa Mojica Rivadeneira, "El derecho masculino de castigo en la colonia," in René Salinas Mesa and María Teresa Mojica Rivadeneira, *Conductas ilícitas y derecho de castigo durante la colonia: Los casos de Chile y Colombia* (Bogotá: Universidad Externado de Colombia, 2005), 87–194. I thank Colombian historian Mabel López for this valuable reference.

17. Juan Javier Pescador, "Del dicho al hecho: Uxoricidios en el México central, 1769–1820," in Pilar Gozalbo Aizpuru and Cecilia Rabell Romero, eds., *Familia y vida privada en la historia de Iberoamerica: Seminario de historia de la familia* (México: Centro de Estudios Históricos del Colegio de México-Instituto de Investigaciones Sociales de la UNAM, 1996), 373–386. John Leddy Phelan also stresses the gap between law and practice in the classic essay "Authority and Flexibility in the Spanish Imperial Bureaucracy," *Administrative Science Quarterly* 5 (1960): 47–61. See also comments by Silvia Arrom, "New Directions in Mexican Legal History," *Americas* 50.4 (1994): 461–465.

18. See Alfonso García Valdecasas, *El hidalgo y el honor* (Madrid: Editorial Revista de Occidente, 1948), 198–214; Bartholomé Bennassar, *The Spanish Character: Attitudes and Mentalities from the Sixteenth to the Nineteenth Century,* translated and with a preface by Benjamin Keen (Berkeley: University of California Press, 1979), chapter VIII; J. G. Peristany, *Honour and Shame: The Values of Mediterranean Society* (Chicago: University of Chicago Press, 1966); J. G. Peristany and Julian Pitt-Rivers, eds., *Honour and Grace in Anthropology* (Cambridge: Cambridge University Press, 1992); Taylor, *Honor and Violence in Golden Age Spain.* An insightful analysis of the concept itself and its historiography can be found in Tomás A. Mantecón Movellán, "El honor Mediterráneo

desde la España moderna: Un traje nuevo del emperador?" *Cuadernos de Historia de España,* LXXXV–LXXXVI (2012): 435–458.

19. For a comparative volume on the colonial period, see Lyman Johnson and Sonya Lipsett-Rivera, eds., *The Faces of Honor: Sex, Shame and Violence in Colonial Latin America* (Albuquerque: University of New Mexico Press, 1999). See also Komisaruk, *Labour and Love in Guatemala,* 222–240. For the modern era, see Sueann Caulfield, Sarah C. Chambers, and Lara Putnam, eds., *Honor, Status, and Law in Modern Latin America* (Durham: Duke University Press, 2005). Several individual monographs touching on both male and female honor in Latin America are now available. For two recent ones on the period of our interest, see Lyman Johnson, *Workshop of Revolution: Plebeian Buenos Aires and the Atlantic World, 1776–1810* (Durham: Duke University Press, 2011), esp. chapter 2; Sonya Lipsett-Rivera, *Gender and the Negotiation of Daily Life in Mexico, 1750–1856* (Lincoln: University of Nebraska Press, 2012), 12–15 and chapters 6 and 8. See also Von Germeten, *Violent Delights, Violent Ends.*

20. Unquestionably, this was a relatively more fluid situation than was originally believed. See Twinam, *Private Lives and Public Secrets*; Komisaruk, *Labour and Love in Guatemala,* 222–240; Allyson M. Poska, *Women and Authority in Early Modern Spain: The Peasants of Galicia* (Oxford: Oxford University Press), esp. chapter 3; Von Germeten, *Violent Delights, Violent Ends.*

21. See Renato Barahona, *Sex Crimes, Honour, and the Law in Early Modern Spain: Vizcaya, 1528–1735* (Toronto: University of Toronto Press, 2003); Taylor, *Honor and Violence in Golden Age Spain;* Lyman Johnson and Sonia Lipsett-Rivera, eds., *The Faces of Honor;* Caulfield, Chambers, and Putnam, eds., *Honor, Status, and Law;* Johnson, *Workshop of Revolution,* 68; Pieter Spierenburg, *Violence and Punishment. Civilizing the Body Through Time* (Cambridge: Polity, 2013), esp. 3-7; idem, *A History of Murder: Personal Violence in Europe from the Middle Ages to the Present* (Cambridge: Polity, 2008), 7–10, 68–70, 108–110, 116.

22. This went several centuries back. See, for instance, Francisco Javier Sánchez-Cid, *La violencia contra la mujer en la Sevilla del Siglo de Oro* (1569–1626) (Sevilla: Universidad de Sevilla, 2011), 55–58. See also Pablo José Abascal Monedero, *La infidelidad y el adulterio en España (estudio histórico-legal)* (Cordoba: Servicio de Publicaciones Universidad de Cordoba, 2009), 71–129.

23. Mathew D. Stroud, *Fatal Union: A Pluralistic Approach to the Spanish Wife-Murder Comedias* (Lewisburg: Bucknell University Press, 1990); Marcelin Defourneaux, *Daily Life in Spain During the Golden Age* (Stanford: Stanford University Press, 1966), 146–148; Sánchez-Cid, *La violencia contra la mujer en la Sevilla del Siglo de Oro,* 67–80, 91–99.

24. Colonialism is marked by a "politics [and legality] of difference" that, albeit contested and porous, is imposed by alien occupiers on the peoples they nominally control. See Frederick Cooper, *Colonialism in Question: Theory, Knowledge, History* (Berkeley: University of California Press, 2005). Patriarchy is here understood as a historical system of political and social relations and cultural values whereby some men concentrate power, status, and authority in both public and private (household) spaces, deriving as a result sexual, economic, political, social, and cultural benefits. This does not mean that women lack any rights or are

under absolute subordination. See Elizabeth Dore, "One Step Forward, Two Steps Back: Gender and the State in the Long Nineteenth Century," in Elizabeth Dore and Maxine Molyneux, eds., *Hidden Histories of Gender and the State in Latin America* (Durham: Duke University Press), 3–32, esp. 11–12. For more-elaborate definitions, see Bianca Premo, *Children of the Father King: Youth, Authority, and Legal Minority in Colonial Lima* (Chapel Hill: University of North Carolina Press, 2005), 9–10; Stern, *The Secret History of Gender,* 21. For a feminist historical and theoretical critique distinguishing various modalities of feminism, see Carole Pateman, *The Sexual Contract* (Stanford: Stanford University Press, 1988), esp. 21–30 and chapter 2 overall. For controversial and rather selective works questioning the validity of this concept in colonial Spanish America, see Kimberley Gauderman, *Women's Lives in Colonial Quito;* and Black, *The Limits of Gender Domination.*

25. For a nuanced perspective on law as a means of domination, see Harold Berman, *Law and Revolution: The Formation of the Western Legal Tradition* (Cambridge, MA: Harvard University Press, 1983), 556.

26. See Carlos Aguirre and Ricardo Salvatore, "Introduction: Writing the History of Law, Crime and Punishment in Latin America," in Ricardo Salvatore, Carlos Aguirre, and Gilbert M. Joseph, eds., *Crime and Punishment in Latin America* (Durham: Duke University Press, 2001), 1–32; Mindie Lazarus-Black, *Everyday Harm: Domestic Violence, Court Rites and Cultures of Reconciliation* (Urbana: University of Illinois Press, 2007), 3, 159–176.

27. See, for instance, Rafael Altamira, *Historia del derecho español* (Madrid: Librería General de V. Suáres, 1903); idem, *Manual de investigación de la historia del derecho indiano* (México: Instituto Panamericano de Geografía e Historia, 1948); Ricardo Levene, *Historia del derecho argentino,* 5 vols. (Buenos Aires: Editorial Guillermo Fraksty Ltda., 1945); José María Ots Capdequí, *El estado español en las Indias* (México: Fondo de Cultura Económica, 1946); idem, *Historia del derecho español en América y del derecho indiano* (Madrid: Aguilar, 1969); Alfonso García Gallo, *Estudios de historia del derecho indiano* (Madrid: Instituto Nacional de Estudios Jurídicos, 1972); Silvio Zavala, *Las instituciones jurídicas en la conquista de América* (México: Editorial Porrúa, 1988).

28. See Hespanha, "De *Iustitia* a Disciplina," 207.

29. See, for instance, Steve J. Stern, *Peru's Indian Peoples and the Challenge of Spanish Conquest: Huamanga to 1640* (Madison: University of Wisconsin Press, 1993); Fernando de Trazegnies, *Ciriaco de Urtecho: Litigante por Amor* (Lima: Pontificia Universidad Católica, 1995); Susan Kellogg, *Law and the Transformation of Aztec Culture, 1500–1700* (Norman: University of Oklahoma Press, 1995); Sergio Serulnikov, *Subverting Colonial Authority: Challenges to Spanish Rule in Eighteenth-Century Southern Andes* (Durham: Duke University Press, 2003); Herman L. Bennett, *Africans in Colonial Mexico: Absolutism, Christianity, and Afro-Creole Consciousness, 1570–1640* (Bloomington: Indiana University Press, 2005); and Malick W. Ghachem, *The Old Regime and the Haitian Revolution* (Cambridge: Cambridge University Press, 2012).

30. See Twinam, *Public Lives and Private Secrets,* 232; and, for a later period, Tanja Christiansen, *Disobedience, Slander, Seduction and Assault: Women and Men in Cajamarca, Peru, 1862–1900* (Austin: University of Texas Press, 2004), 16–17.

31. See Woodrow Borah, *Justice by Insurance: The General Indian Court of Colonial Mexico and the Legal Aides of the Half Real* (Berkeley: University of California Press, 1983); Charles R. Cutter, *The Legal Culture of Northern New Spain, 1700–1810* (Albuquerque: University of New Mexico Press, 1995); and Owensby, *Empire of Law and Indian Justice.*

32. Premo, *Children of the Father King,* 6, 20.

33. Herzog, *Upholding Justice.*

34. Premo, *Children of the Father King,* 6.

35. See Hespanha, "De *Iustitia* a Disciplina," 204–205. Hespanha also insists on the powerful "intertextuality" of legal texts, a complex concept discussed later. See also Berman, *Law and Revolution,* especially its conclusion. On these texts' institutional nature and weight in economic development, see Jeremy Adelman, *Republic of Capital: Buenos Aires and the Legal Transformation of the Atlantic World* (Stanford: Stanford University Press, 1999).

36. For insightful comments on the customary nature of many laws and legal "rusticity" in general, see Antonio M. Hespanha, "Sabios y rústicos: La dulce violencia de la razón jurídica," in Hespanha, *La gracia del derecho,* 17–60. On the significance of custom for the formation of legal rules, see Berman. *Law and Revolution,* 555–556. See also Victor Tau Anzoategui, *El poder de la costumbre: Estudios sobre el derecho consuetudinario en América hispana hasta la emancipación* (Buenos Aires: Instituto de Investigaciones de Historia del Derecho, 2001).

37. It seems more accurate to say, though, as Berman insightfully established, that law is "custom transformed." Law tends to originate as "unsystematized . . . informal . . . relations within communities." The outgrowth of such customs turns into systematic legal rules of some kind. See Berman, *Law and Revolution,* 555–556.

38. See, for instance, Saliha Belmessous, ed., *Native Claims: Indigenous Law Against Empire, 1500–1920* (Oxford: Oxford University Press, 2011), 3–16.

39. Serulnikov believes that "mass violence and juridical strategies were inextricably entwined and cannot be understood in isolation." See Serulnikov, *Subverting Colonial Authority,* 138. See also Colin MacLachlan, *Spain's Empire in the New World: The Role of Ideas in Institutional and Social Change* (Berkeley: University of California Press, 1988), 124; and Hay, "Property, Authority and the Criminal Law."

40. Berman also stressed the multifaceted nature of Western law, which mixes dominant ideologies, protective mechanisms born out of custom, and canon law principles. Berman, *Law and Revolution,* 556–557.

41. Owensby, *Empire of Law*, 8. This is close to Herzog's view. See Herzog, *Upholding Justice,* passim.

42. Hespanha offers an insightful discussion of the power and force of "textual traditions" in "De *Iustitia* a Disciplina," 207–209, 232–234, 236, and 242.

43. For the genealogy and many nuances of the notion of autonomy of law and its fundamentally relational character, see Christopher Tomlins, "How Autonomous Is Law," *Annual Review of Law and Society* 3 (2007): 45–68.

44. Michael C. Scardaville, "Justice by Paperwork: A Day in the Life of a Court Scribe in Mexico City," *Journal of Social History* 36.4 (2003): 979–1007, esp. 984, 987. See also Owensby, *Empire of Law*, 207.

45. Richard Kagan, *Lawsuits and Litigants in Castile, 1500–1700* (Chapel Hill: University of North Carolina Press, 1981); Borah, *Justice by Insurance;* Stern, *Peru's Indian Peoples and the Challenge of Spanish Conquest;* Cutter, *The Legal Culture of Northern New Spain;* Herzog, *Upholding Justice.* On the comparable centrality of justice to the legitimacy of the Portuguese monarchy, see Hespanha, "De *Iustitia* a Disciplina," 206.

46. See note 29 above and also the outstanding work by Darío Dominino Crespo, *Escándalos y delitos de la gente plebe* (Córdoba, Argentina: Universidad Nacional de Córdoba, 2007); Seed, *To Love, Honor and Obey;* Malcolm Ebright, *Land Grants and Lawsuits in Northern New Mexico* (Albuquerque: University of New Mexico Press, 1994); Renzo Honores, "Estudios sobre la litigación y la litigiosidad colonial," *Revista de Historia del Derecho Privado*, Santiago, 2 (1999), 121–135; ibid., "A Legalistic Society: Lawyers, Procurators, and the Making of a Colonial Legal Culture in Lima and Potosi, 1550–1670" (Ph.D. dissertation, Department of History, Florida International University, 2007); Jeremy R. Mumford, "Litigation as Ethnography in Sixteenth-Century Peru: Polo de Ondergardo and the Mitimaes," *Hispanic American Historical Review* 88.1 (2008): 5–40; and Chambers, "Citizens Before the Law."

47. ARCG, Libro de Providencias Definitivas, 1799–1815, libro no. 324; ARG, Indice Topográfico Cronológico, sección 7, serie causas I—Años 1762–1835; Isabel Pérez Muñoz, "Conflictividad social y administración de justicia en el partido de Trujillo. 1791," in *Coloquios Históricos de Extremadura*, año 1993. Available at www.chde.org/index.php?option=com_content&view=article&id=703:conflictividad-social-y-administracion-de-justicia-en-el-partido-de-trujillo-1791&catid=43:1993&Itemid=60; Maria Luisa Candau Chacón, *Los delitos y las penas en el mundo eclesiástico sevillano del siglo XVIII* (Sevilla: Diputación Provincial, 1993); Tomas Mantecón, "La violencia marital en la corona de Castilla durante la edad moderna," in Antonio Yrigoyen López and Antonio L. Pérez Ortiz, eds., *Familia, transmisión y perpetuación (siglos XVI–XIX)* (Murcia: Universidad de Murcia, 2002), 19–55; María José de la Pascua Sánchez, "Violencia y Familia en la España del Antiguo Régimen," *Estudis: Revista de Historia Moderna* 28 (2002): 77–102; Barahona, *Sex Crimes, Honor, and the Law in Early Modern Spain;* MacLachlan, *Criminal Justice in Eighteenth Century Mexico;* Michael C. Scardaville, "Crime and the Urban Poor: Mexico City in the Late Colonial Period" (Ph.D. dissertation, University of Florida, 1977); William Taylor, *Drinking, Homicide, and Rebellion in Colonial Mexican Villages* (Stanford: Stanford University Press, 1979); Susan Socolow, "Women and Crime in Buenos Aires, 1757–1797," *Journal of Latin American Studies* 12.1 (1980): 39–54; François Giraud, "Viol et Société Coloniale: Le Case de la Nouvelle Espagne au XVIIIe Siècle," *Annals ESC* 41.3 (1986): 625–637; Teresa Lozano Armendares, *La criminalidad en la ciudad de México, 1800–1821* (Mexico City: Instituto de Investigaciones Históricas UNAM, 1987); Castañeda, *Violación, estupro y sexual-*

idad; Carlos Aguirre and Charles Walker, eds., *Bandoleros, abigeos y montoneros: Criminalidad y violencia en el Perú, siglos XVIII–XX* (Lima: IIAA, 1990); Lyman Johnson, ed., *The Problem of Order in Changing Societies: Essays on Crime and Policing in Argentina and Uruguay, 1750–1940* (Albuquerque: University of New Mexico Press, 1990), chapter 1; Guillermo Sosa Abella, *Labradores, tejedores y ladrones: Hurtos y homicidios en la provincia de Tunja, 1745–1810* (Bogotá: Instituto Colombiano de Cultura Hispánica, 1993); Leonardo Alberto Vega Umbasia, *Pecado y delito en la Colonia; bestialidad como una forma de contravención sexual (1740–1808)* (Bogotá: Instituto Colombiano de Cultura Hispánica, 1994); Patiño, *Criminalidad, ley penal y estructura social en la provincia de Antioquia;* Gabriel Haslip-Viera, *Crime and Punishment in Late Colonial Mexico City, 1692–1810* (Albuquerque: University of New Mexico Press, 1999); José Sánchez-Arcilla Bernal, "La administración de justicia inferior en la Ciudad de México a finales de la época colonial: La punición de la embriaguez en los libros de reos (1794–1798)," *Cuadernos de Historia del Derecho* 7 (2000): 309–453; Isabel Marin Tello, "Justicia penal y orden social en Michoacán en el siglo XVIII" (Ph.D. dissertation, Universidad de Sevilla, 2003); Catherine Komisaruk, "Rape Narratives, Rape Silences: Sexual Violence and Judicial Testimony in Colonial Guatemala," *Biography* 31.3 (2008): 369–339.

48. Valuable information can be found in Spierenburg, *A History of Murder.* The various works of Spanish historian Tomás A. Mantecón, cited throughout this study, are also obligatory references.

49. Taylor, *Drinking, Homicide, and Rebellion*; idem, "Amigos de sombrero: Patrones de homicidio en el centro rural de Jalisco, 1784–1820," in Antonio Escobar Ohmstede and Patricia Lagos Preisser, eds., *Indio, nación y comunidad en el México del siglo XIX* (Mexico City: Centro de Estudios Mexicanos y Centroamericanos, 1993), 63–103; Patiño, *Criminalidad, ley penal y estructura social,* 339–434; Eric Johnson, Ricardo Salvatore, and Pieter Spierenburg, eds., *Murder and Violence in Modern Latin America* (London: Wiley-Blackwell, 2013).

50. Pescador, "Del dicho al hecho"; Kevin Terraciano, "Crime and Culture in Colonial Mexico: The Case of the Mixtec Murder Note," *Ethnohistory* 45.4 (1998): 709–745; Uribe-Uran, "Colonial *Baracunatanas* and Their Nasty Men"; idem, "Innocent Infants or Abusive Patriarchs?" Spousal murders are also addressed in passing in Brian T. McCormack, "Conjugal Violence, Sex, Sin and Murder in the Mission Communities of Alta California," *Journal of the History of Sexuality* 16.3 (2007): 391–415; and Felipe Castro Gutiérrez, "Condición femenina y violencia conyugal entre los Purépechas durante la época colonial," *Mexican Studies* 14.1 (1998): 5–21. In the case of Spain, the most important research is the micro-history by Mantecón, *La muerte de Antonia Isabel Sánchez.* See also idem, "La violencia marital en la corona de Castilla durante la edad moderna," in Antonio Yrigoyen López and Antonio L. Pérez Ortiz, eds., *Familia, transmisión y perpetuación (siglos XVI–XIX)* (Murcia: Universidad de Murcia, 2002), 19–55, esp. 20, 44, 45; idem, "Hogares infernales: Una visión retrospectiva sobre la violencia doméstica en el mundo moderno," in Lorenzo Pinar, ed., *La familia en la historia* (Salamanca: Ediciones Universidad de Salamanca, 2009), 187–230; Llanes Parra, "El enemigo en casa," 2–15; Boyer, *Colonial Lives,*

54–76, 185–200. Some references can also be found in de la Pascua Sánchez, "Violencia y Familia en la España del Antiguo Régimen," 98.

51. See, for example, Dominino Crespo, *Escándalos y delitos*; Haslip-Viera, *Crime and Punishment;* Herzog, *La administración como un fenómeno social: La justicia penal de la ciudad de Quito (1650–1750)* (Madrid: Centro de Estudios Políticos y Constitucionales, 1995), 289; Patiño, *Criminalidad, ley penal y estructura social;* Johnson, *The Problem of Order in Changing Societies;* Lozano Armendares, *La criminalidad en la ciudad de México,* 35, 44; and Patricia Ann Aufderheide, "Order and Violence: Social Deviance and Social Control in Brazil, 1780–1840" (Ph.D. dissertation, University of Minnesota, 1976). See also MacLachlan, *Criminal Justice in Eighteenth-Century Mexico;* Taylor, *Drinking, Homicide, and Rebellion;* Alberto Flóres Galindo, *Aristocracia y plebe en Lima, 1760–1830 (Estructura de clases y sociedad colonial)* (Lima: Mosca Azul Editores, 1983), chapter 5; and Ivan Espinosa, *El sueño del ahorcado: Una experiencia subjetiva de la pena de muerte a finales de la colonia (Novita, siglo XVIII)* (Bogotá: Universidad de los Andes, 2008).

52. In colonial Mexico, cases of indebtedness and failure to pay tribute represented a significant percentage of crime. This does not seem to have been the case in New Granada. See Haslip-Viera, *Crime and Punishment,* 53, 54–55, 58–59; Zoila Gabriel de Domínguez, "Delito y sociedad en el Nuevo Reino de Granada período virreinal, 1740–1810," *Universitas Humanistica* 8–9 (1974–1975): 281–398, esp. 322–323. For Brazil, see Aufderheide, "Order and Violence," 372–379, 390.

53. See, for instance, Dominino Crespo, *Escándalos y delitos,* esp. chapters 4 and 5; Tomas A. Mantecón Movellán, *Conflictividad y disciplinamiento social en la Cantabria rural del Antiguo Régimen* (Santander: Universidad de Cantabria-Fundación Marcelo Botín, 1997), part 3; idem, "El peso de la infrajudicialidad en el control del crimen durante la edad moderna," in *Estudis: Revista de Historia Moderna* 28 (2002), 43–75; idem, "Social Control from Below: Popular Arbitration of Disputes in Old Regime Spain," in Herman Roodenburg and Pieter Spierenburg, *Social Control in Europe: Volume 1, 1500-1800* (Columbus: Ohio State University Press, 2004), 267–287; idem, "Disciplinamiento social, escenografías punitivas y cultura plebeya en el Antiguo Régimen," in Verónica Undurraga and Rafael Geune eds., *Formas de control y disciplinamiento: Chile, América y Europa, siglos XVI-XIX* (Santiago: Universidad Católica del Perú-Instituto Riva Agüero, 2014), 162–184; Benoit Garnot, "Justice, infrajustice, parajustice et extrajustice Dans la France d'Ancien Régime," *Crime, History and Societies* 4.1 (2000): 103–120. See also critical comments by Herzog, *Upholding Justice,* 11.

54. See Jill Lepore, "Rap Sheet: Why Is American History So Murderous?" *New Yorker,* November 9, 2009, 79–83, esp. 79. The problem, as we shall see, is not so much underreporting but the fact that records may have been destroyed over time.

55. For a readable and intriguing study of five deadly chemicals, including historical accounts of infamous poisoners and their victims, see John Emsley, *The Elements of Murder: A History of Poison* (New York: Oxford University Press, 2005).

56. See Taylor, *Drinking, Homicide, and Rebellion,* 75. On the importance of the category of "public" as opposed to "private" crimes during and after the ancien régime, see Hespanha, "De *Iustitia* a Disciplina," 246–248, 261–262. On public and private in colonial times in general, see Twinam, *Private Secrets, Public Lives;* Premo, *Children of the Father King,* 11. See note 72 below.

57. Haslip-Viera, *Crime and Punishment,* 51. A probably irregular sample of 474 crimes committed in Mexico City from 1800 to 1812 includes just 25 homicides, close to 5 percent of total crimes, or an average of just two per year. A larger, 4,352-arrest sample for 1798 Mexico City includes 13 homicides, a seemingly high number. See, respectively, Lozano Armendares, *La criminalidad en la ciudad de México,* 65; and Scardaville, "Crime and the Urban Poor," 38. For statistics on 1667–1816 Amsterdam, which had an average of close to 8 murders annually, see Pieter Spierenburg, "Facets of Violence: Homicide Trends and Cultural Meanings: Amsterdam, 1431–1816," *Journal of Social History* 27.4 (1994): 701–716, esp. 707.

58. Patiño, *Criminalidad, ley penal y estructura social,* 257, 534.

59. Angel Alloza, *La vara quebrada de la justicia: Un estudio histórico sobre la delincuencia madrileña entre los siglos XVI y XVIII* (Madrid: Catarata, 2000), 130–131.

60. The Galicia sample covers the years 1799–1805, whereas the sample for Granada is from 1803 to 1815.

61. 433 homicides occurred in a sample of 2,204 crimes, for a rate of 19.6 percent. See José-Miguel Palop Ramos, "Delitos y penas en la España del siglo XVIII," *Estudis: Revista de Historia Moderna* 22 (1996): 65–103, esp. 67.

62. Taylor, *Drinking, Homicide, and Rebellion,* 86

63. Crimes of "*uxoricidio*" listed in the judicial archives used for this work generally do not include murders involving common-law partners, concubines, and lovers.

64. Ten out of 43 homicides in the region from 1750 to 1812 are alleged to have involved spouses. See Patiño, *Criminalidad, ley penal y estructura social,* 376, 516. On late-colonial Antioquia society and economy, see Ann Twinam, *Miners, Merchants and Farmers in Colonial Colombia* (Austin: University of Texas Press, 1982).

65. AGN, Colonia, Juicios Criminales, indice.

66. In 1890s Chicago, spousal murders (dubbed "divorce by bullets") reached 13 percent of all homicides. See Jeffrey S. Adler, "'My Mother-in-Law Is to Blame, But I'll Walk on Her Neck Yet': Homicide in Late Nineteenth-Century Chicago," *Journal of Social History* 31.2 (1997): 253–276, esp. 259.

67. See Mantecón, "La violencia marital en la corona de Castilla durante la edad moderna," 20, 44–45.

68. One spousal murder per year, equivalent to around 3.01 of all homicides. This calculation comes from the sample of crimes listed in the Archivo del Reino de Galicia, Indice Topográfico Cronológico, sección 7, serie causas I—Años 1762–1835. An essay on similar crimes in seventeenth-century Madrid reports 64 spousal murders between 1580 and 1700 and estimates that they represented about 3.8 percent of total homicides in the region. See Llanes Parra, "El enemigo en casa," 3.

69. On the historiography of this era, see Victor M. Uribe-Uran, ed., *State and Society in Spanish America During the Age of Revolution* (Wilmington: Scholarly Resources, 2000).

70. The works on these various aspects are too abundant to cite. For a recent evaluation of some of the historiography and the reforms themselves, see John R. Fisher, "The Bourbon Reforms in Spanish America: A Semi-Autobiographical Evaluation," *Journal of Iberian and Latin American Research* 18.1 (2012): 1–14.

71. See Arrom, *The Women of Mexico City,* 95; and Dore, "One Step Forward, Two Steps Back," 10–14.

72. Victor M. Uribe-Uran, "The Birth of a Public Sphere in Latin America During the Age of Revolution," *Comparative Studies in Society and History* 42.2 (2000): 425–457, esp. 427–428; ibid., "The Great Transformation of Law and Legal Culture: 'The Public' and 'The Private' in the Transition from Empire to Nation in Mexico, Colombia, and Brazil, 1750–1850," in Joseph W. Esherick, Hasan Kayali and Eric Van Young, eds., *Empire to Nation: Historical Perspectives on the Making of the Modern World* (New York: Rowman & Littlefield, 2005), 68–105; Premo, *Children of the Father King,* 11; Alice Erh-Soon Tay and Eugene Kamenka, "Public Law–Private Law," in S. I. Benn and G. F. Gaus, eds., *Public and Private in Social Life* (New York: St. Martin's, 1983), 67–92. Some consider that this dichotomy was unproblematic in colonial times: Twinam, *Public Lives and Private Secrets;* Matthew Mirow, *Latin American Law: A History of Private Law and Institutions in Spanish America* (Austin: University of Texas Press, 2004).

73. See Victor M. Uribe-Uran, "Physical Violence Against Wives and the Law in the Spanish American World, 1820s–2000s," in Eric Johnson, Ricardo Salvatore, and Pieter Spierenburg, eds., *Murder and Violence in Modern Latin America,* 49–80.

74. On the "myth of women without rights" in colonial Spanish America, see Dore, "One Step Forward, Two Steps Back," 10–14.

75. A detailed discussion of the "public" nature of such crimes can be found in Juan Solorzano y Pereira, *Diligens & Accurata de Parricidi Crimine Disputatio* (1605), liber secundus, chapter XX.

76. For an influential work that stresses the strengthening of patriarchy in the late eighteenth century as a result of secularizing reforms restricting freedom to choose a marriage partner, see Seed, *To Love, Honor and Obey.* For alternative interpretations, see Gutierrez, *When Jesus Came, the Corn Mothers Went Away.*

77. This was a modality of punishment used since the dark ages and medieval times whereby red-hot irons, with a wooden handle on one end and a letter (typically a V, an F, or an S) on the other, were used to mark the body of those targeted for persecution, particularly vagabonds, gypsies, brawlers, and runaway slaves.

78. Foucault, *Discipline and Punish,* 8–12.

79. See the classical essay on comparative history by Marc Bloch, "Pour une Histoire Comparée Des Societes Europeennes," *Melanges Historiques*, vol. 1 (Paris: Ecole Pratique de Hautes Etudes, 1963), 16–40, translated into English as "Toward a Comparative History of European Societies," in Frederic C. Lane and Jelle C. Riemersma, eds., *Enterprise and Secular Change* (Homewood: R. D. Irwin, 1953), 494–521. See also Theda Skocpol and Margaret Somers, "The Uses of Comparative History in Macrosocial Inquiry," *Comparative Stud-*

ies in Society and History 22.2 (1980): 174–197; and Theda Skocpol, "Emerging Agendas and Recurrent Strategies in Historical Sociology," in Skocpol, ed., *Visions and Method in Historical Sociology* (Cambridge: Cambridge University Press, 1985), 356–391. For Latin America, see Magnus Morner, Julia Fawaz, and John D. French, "Comparative Approaches to Latin American History," *Latin American Research Review* 17.3 (1982): 55–89; and Victor M. Uribe-Uran and Luis J. Ortiz, eds., *Naciones, gentes y territorios: Ensayos de historia e historiografía comparada de América Latina y el Caribe* (Medellín: Universidad de Antioquia, 2000).

80. Several of the works cited thus far address Mexico, such as the ones by Maclachlan, Borah, Cutter, Kellogg, Owensby, Haslip-Viera, and Lozano Armendares.

81. For a valuable historiographical analysis, see Premo, "On Currents and Comparisons," and Phillip D. Morgan and Jack P. Greene, "Introduction: The Present State of Atlantic History," in Morgan and Greene, eds., *Atlantic History: A Critical Reappraisal* (Oxford: Oxford University Press, 2009), 3–33. For actual works, see, for instance, Jorge Cañizares Esguerra, *How to Write the History of the New World: Histories, Epistemologies and Identities in the Eighteenth-Century Atlantic World* (Stanford: Stanford University Press, 2001); Seymour Drescher, *Abolition: A History of Slavery and Antislavery* (Cambridge: Cambridge University Press, 2009); Christopher Schmidt-Nowara, *Empire and Antislavery: Spain, Cuba and Puerto Rico, 1833–1874* (Pittsburgh: University of Pittsburgh Press, 1999); Noble David Cook and Alexandra Parma Cook, *Good Faith and Truthful Ignorance: A Case of Transatlantic Bigamy* (Durham: Duke University Press, 1991); Wim Klooster, *Revolutions in the Atlantic World: A Comparative Perspective* (New York: NYU Press, 2009).

82. The Atlantic perspective on colonial and postcolonial days has been particularly enriched by the legal historical work of Lauren Benton, *Law and Colonial Cultures: Legal Regimes in World History, 1400–1900* (Cambridge: Cambridge University Press, 2002). See esp. chapter 1, "Legal Regimes and Colonial Cultures," 1–30. See also her study *A Search for Sovereignty: Law and Geography in European Empires, 1400–1900* (Cambridge: Cambridge University Press, 2010).

83. For valuable methodological comments on the use of judicial sources in modern France, largely applicable to the Spanish experience, see Benoît Garnot, Pascal Bastien, Hervé Piant, et al., *La Justice et l'Histoire: Sources Judiciaires à l'Époque Moderne (XVIe, XVIIe, XVIIIe Siècles)* (Rosny-sous-Bois: Bréal, 2006).

84. This was particularly the case of the records obtained at Simancas, but also several of the ones coming from Mexico.

85. For instance, two recent historical studies of crime in Michoacán during a similar period based on detailed local records from the capital of Morelia (formerly Valladolid) and the locality of Patzcuaro list only three cases of spousal murder. See Marin Tello, "Justicia penal y orden social en Michoacán," 217–218; and Castro Gutiérrez, "Condición femenina y violencia," 6. Another study of the region of Toluca lists only a single case for our period. See Deborah E. Kanter, "*Hijos del pueblo*: Family, Community, and Gender in Rural Mexico. The Toluca Valley Region, 1730–1830" (Ph.D. dissertation, University of Virginia, 1993), 176.

86. On the impact of *expurgos* on Spanish judicial archives, see Ma. Isabel Simó Rodríguez, "Fondos judiciales en los archivos históricos provinciales," *Boletín de la Asociación Nacional de Archiveros, Bibliotecarios, Arqueólogos y Documentalistas* XXXII, 1–2 (January–June, 1982): 27–41, esp. 35–36; idem, "El Archivo de la Real Audiencia de Extremadura: Doscientos años de Historia," *Historia, Instituciones, Documentos*, Separata Publicaciones de la Universidad de Sevilla, 25 (1998): 653–675, esp. 661–665. For examples of even recent *expurgos* of judicial archives, see www.recbib.es/noticia/el-mayor-expurgo-judicial-de-la-historia-de-espana-en-el-archivo-provincial-de-valencia. In some instances, judicial files were sold out as packing paper by the pound. See Angel González Palencia, ed., *Archivo Histórico Nacional. Consejo de Castilla. Sala de Alcaldes de Casa y Corte. Catálogo por Materias* (Madrid, 1925), xii.

87. The criminal records of the Balearic Islands' *audiencia,* in the city of Mallorca, were destroyed almost in their entirety in the mid-nineteenth century. The same is true of the Audiencia de Asturias in Oviedo, about half of which was destroyed in the mid-nineteenth century and most of the rest consumed by a fire in 1934. In the case of the Audiencia de Aragón in Zaragoza, it seems many of the criminal records were destroyed during the war of independence's second siege of Zaragoza in 1808. It is likely that several relevant cases could have been found in the archives of the three remaining *audiencias* (Aragón, Canary Islands, and Catalonia) that I was unable to consult. All criminal records in Spain's National Archive concerning crimes prior to 1700 were sold out as paper. See José María Zuaznavar y Francia, *Noticias para literatos acerca de los archivos públicos de la hoy extinguida Sala de Alcaldes de Casa y Corte* (San Sebastián: Ignacio Ramón Baroja, 1834), 4; Vicente Vignau y Ballester, "Discurso Del Sr. D. Vicente Vignau y Ballester," in Archivo Histórico Nacional, *Discursos leidos ante la real Academia de la Historia en la recepción Pública del Sr. Vicente Vignau y Ballester el día 18 de Junio de 1898* (Madrid: Tip. Viuda e Hijos de Tello, 1898), 5–38, esp. 24–29.

88. Spierenburg, *A History of Murder,* 2; Randolph Roth, *American Homicide* (Cambridge, MA: Belknap, 2009), xi. See also Manuel Eisner, "Modernization, Self-Control and Lethal Violence: The Long-Term Dynamics of European Homicide Rates in Theoretical Perspective," *British Journal of Criminology* 41 (2001): 618–638; Manuel Eisner, "Long-Term Historical Trends in Violent Crime," *Crime and Justice: A Review of Research*, 30 (2003): 83–142; Eric Monkkonen, "Homicide: Explaining American Exceptionalism," *American Historical Review* 111.1 (2006): 76–94; and Roger Lane, *Murder in America: A History* (Columbus: Ohio State University Press, 1997). Nothing even remotely comparable exists for Latin America, where the most influential historical study remains a work on colonial times written three decades ago: Taylor, *Drinking, Homicide, and Rebellion.* A recent anthology fills some gaps: Johnson, Salvatore, and Spierenburg, eds., *Murder and Violence in Modern Latin America.*

89. Roth, *American Homicide,* 27.

90. Spierenburg, *A History of Murder,* 3–6.

91. Norbert Elias, *The Civilizing Process: The History of Manners* (New York: Urizen, 1978).

92. Roth, *American Homicide,* 108.

93. Spierenburg does notice, though, that around the Middle Ages there were about 2 intimate homicides per 100,000, whereas in the nineteenth and twentieth centuries the total had gone down to 0.5 per 100,000. Spierenburg, *A History of Murder,* 133–134.

94. Jonathan Fletcher and other scholars have noted Elias's lack of attention to gender violence. See Fletcher, *Violence and Civilization: An Introduction to the Work of Norbert Elias* (Cambridge: Polity, 1997), 49–50. On reasons behind the increase in domestic violence in Spain during the period of this book, see de la Pascua Sánchez, "Violencia y Familia en la España del Antiguo Régimen," esp. 86. For Spanish America, see Uribe-Uran, "Physical Violence Against Wives and the Law in the Spanish American World, 1820s–2000s." See also Spierenburg, *A History of Murder,* 135.

95. Leslie Dossey, "Wife Beating and Manliness in Late Antiquity," *Past and Present* 199.1 (2008): 3-40; Orit Kamir, *Every Breath You Take: Stalking Narratives and the Law* (Ann Arbor: University of Michigan Press, 2001). For a concrete example, see Sarah B. Pomeroy's fascinating study *The Murder of Regilla: A Case of Domestic Violence in Antiquity* (Cambridge, MA: Harvard University Press, 2009).

96. UNFPA, *State of World Population,* 2005, chapter 7, "Gender-Based Violence: A Price Too High."

97. Heise and Garcia-Moreno, "Violence by Intimate Partners," 93.

98. U.S. Department of Justice, *Crime in the United States* (Washington, DC: Author, 1984).

99. David Adams, *Why Do They Kill: Men Who Murder Their Intimate Partners* (Nashville: University of Tennessee Press, 2007), 4.

100. "Governor Declares Domestic Violence Emergency," *Boston Herald,* June 6, 2008.

101. To cite just three recent examples in a UNICEF study, a 1994 survey of 2,315 women in Estonia found that 29 percent of women ages 18–24 feared domestic violence. The highest percentage, 52 percent, were women 65 or older. In Poland a 1993 survey by the Centre for the Examination of Public Opinion reported that 60 percent of divorced women said that their ex-husbands had struck them at least once; an additional 25 percent reported repeated violence. According to a detailed survey in Tajikistan, 23 percent of 550 women ages 18–40 reported physical abuse. UNICEF, "Domestic Violence Against Women and Girls," *Innocenti Digest* 6 (2000). See also International Helsinki Federation for Human Rights, *Women 2000: An Investigation into the Status of Women's Rights in Central and South-Eastern Europe and the Newly Independent States* (9 November 2000). For other cases, see L. A. Mcloskey, C. Williams, and U. Larsen, "Gender Inequality and Intimate Partner Violence Among Women in Moshi, Tanzania," *International Family Planning Perspectives* 31.3 (2005): 124–130; Dan K. Kaye et al., "The Social Construction and Context of Domestic Violence in Wakiso District, Uganda," *Culture, Health and Sexuality* 7.6 (2005): 625–635; Michael A. Koenig et al., "Prevalence, Patterns and Correlates of Domestic Violence in Rural Bangladesh: Individual and Community-Level Effects," *Demogra-*

phy 40.2 (2003): 269–288; Kathryn M. Yount and Jennifer S. Carrera, "Domestic Violence Against Married Women in Cambodia," *Social Forces* 85.1 (2006): 355–387; Sanja Copic, "Wife Abuse in the Countries of the Former Yugoslavia," *Feminist Review* 76 (2004): 46–64.

CHAPTER ONE

1. Daisy Ripodas Ardanas, *El matrimonio en Indias: Realidad social y regulación jurídica* (Buenos Aires: Fundación para la Educación, la Ciencia y la Cultura, 1977); Antonio Dougnac Rodríguez and Alejandro Guzmán Brito, *Esquema del derecho de familia indiano* (Santiago: Instituto de Historia del Derecho Juan de Solórzano y Pereyra, 2003).

2. Avila Martel, *Esquema del derecho penal indiano;* Tomás y Valiente, *El derecho penal;* José Luis de las Heras Santos, *La Justicia penal de los Austrias en la Corona de Castilla* (Salamanca: Ediciones de la Universidad de Salamanca, 1994).

3. In Spanish America, interpretations and regulations emanating from various councils held, among other places, in Mexico City and Lima enriched canon law, as did *constituciones sinodales* issued by local synods in places as relatively central as Cuba and as remote as Tucumán. See Ripodas Ardanas, *El matrimonio en Indias;* R. H. Helmholz, *The Spirit of Classical Canon Law* (Athens: University of Georgia Press, 1996), chapter 1; and James Muldoon, *Canon Law, the Expansion of Europe and World Order* (Aldershot, England: Ashgate, 1998).

4. Victor M. Uribe-Uran, *Vidas honorables: Abogados, familia, sociedad y política en Colombia, 1780–1850* (Bogotá: Banco de la República–EAFIT, 2008), chapter 4.

5. His words: "[El] *Sacramento del Matrimonio grande según San Pablo por la excelencia de su significación, nada menos que la unión de la naturaleza divina con la humana.*" AHN, Madrid, Consejos, Alcaldes de Casa y Corte, legajo 9344, no folio.

6. Manuel Silvestre Martinez, *Libreria de juezes, utilisima y universal para abogados, alcaldes mayores y ordinarios, corregidores e intendentes, juezes de residencia, y de visita, escribanos de toda España, receptores de Castilla, y Aragón, regidores, juntas de propios, contribución, pósitos, y demás individuos de Tribunales Ordinarios: añadida, e ilustrada en esta segunda impresión, con más de dos mil leyes reales, que autorizan su doctrina,* 7 vols. (Madrid: Imprenta de la Comisaria de Cruzada, 1764–1772), 1: 10.

7. See Charles J. Reid, Jr., *Power over the Body, Equality in the Family: Rights and Domestic Relations in Medieval Canon Law* (Grand Rapids: Eerdmans, 2004), esp. chapters 2 and 3; James A. Brundage, *Law, Sex, and Christian Society in Medieval Europe* (Chicago: University of Chicago Press, 1987), 92, 115, 122, 236, 254; Marie A. Kelleher, *The Measure of Woman: Law and Female Identity in the Crown of Aragon* (Philadelphia: University of Pennsylvania Press, 2010), 25–26; Domingo Cavallario, *Instituciones de derecho canónico* (Madrid: Imprenta de Gomez Fuentenebro, 1843); Adhemar Esmein, *Le marriage en droit*

canonique (New York: Burt Franklin, 1968); Seed, *To Love, Honor and Obey in Colonial Mexico;* Ripodas Ardanas, *El matrimonio en Indias.* See also Mabel López, "*Conyugicidios en la Nueva Granada: Una via de escape hacia la violencia contra la mujer en la colonia.*" Unpublished manuscript, 2006, 2–3; idem, "Las conyugicidas de la Nueva Granada: Transgresión de un viejo ideal de mujer," *Memoria y Sociedad* 10.20 (2006): 49–58, esp. 52.

8. Even before the fourteenth-century *Ordenamiento de Alcalá,* the Crown was understood to have *patronato* or supervision over the Church and was entitled, for instance, to authorize the election of bishops and archbishops. See book 1, tit. 17, "Novisima Recopilación," in *Los Códigos Españoles Concordados y anotados,* 12 vols. (Madrid: Imprenta de la Publicidad, 1847–1851), 7: 93.

9. Juan de Solorzano y Pereyra, *Política indiana,* 5 vols. (Madrid: Compañia Iberoamericana de Publicaciones, 1972), vol. 1, chapter 29; Paulino Castañeda, "La condición miserable del indio y sus privilegios," *Anuario de Estudios Americanos* 28 (1971): 245–335, esp. 263–275; Ripodas Ardanas, *El matrimonio en Indias.*

10. AGN, Mexico, Criminal, vol. 5, exp. 11, fol. 366.

11. Jonathan Bird, "For Better or Worse: Divorce and Annulment Lawsuits in Colonial Mexico (1544–1799)" (Ph.D. dissertation, Department of History, Duke University, 2013); Kluger, *Escenas de la vida conyugal;* Silvia Mallo, "Justicia, divorcio, alimentos y malos tratos en el Río de la Plata, 1766–1857," *Investigaciones y Ensayos* 42 (January–December 1992): 373–400; Dora Teresa Dávila Mendoza, "Hasta que la muerte nos separe (el divorcio eclesiástico en el arzobispado de México, 1702–1800)" (Ph.D. dissertation, Department of History, Colegio de México, 1998); María Teresa Pita Moreda, "Conflictos familiares y tribunales de justicia a finales de la colonia: Algunos casos novohispanos," in *Familia y vida privada en la historia de Iberoamérica,* ed. Pilar Gonzalbo Aizpuru and Cecilia Rabell Romero, 341–358; Juan Javier Pescador, "Entre la espada y el olvido: pleitos matrimoniales en el provisorato eclesiástico de México, siglo XVIII," in *La familia en el mundo iberoamericano,* ed. Pilar Gonzalbo Aizpuru and Cecilia Rabell (México: UNAM, 1998), 192–225, esp. 202–205; René Salinas Mesa, "Uniones ilegítimas y desuniones legítimas: El matrimonio y la formación de la pareja en el Chile colonial," in ibid., 173–192; Pilar Gonzalbo Aizpuru, "Violencia y discordia en las relaciones personales en la ciudad de México a fines del siglo XVIII," *Historia Mexicana* (October–December 2001): 233–259; Silvia Arrom, *La mujer mexicana ante el divorcio eclesiástico, 1800–1857* (México: Septentas, 1976).

12. See Edward Behrend-Martínez, *Unfit for Marriage: Impotent Spouses on Trial in the Basque Region of Spain, 1650–1750* (Reno: University of Nevada Press, 2007), 1–10; Bird, "For Better or Worse," 6–8 and chapter 2.

13. Thomas Sánchez, *Compendium Totius Tractatus de Sancto Matrimonij Sacramnento* (Hispali ex officina Franciscum de Lyra: vendese en casa de Antonio de Toro, 1623), 315v; Justo Donoso, *Instituciones de derecho canónico americano,* 3 vols. (Paris: Libreria de Rosa y Bouret, 1868), 2: 377–378. From as early as the thirteenth century, royal legislation also listed this prohibition. See law 19, tit. 2, partida 4, "Las Siete Partidas," in *Códigos españoles,* 3: 422.

14. AGN, Colombia, Criminales, vol. 167, fols. 292–326.

15. On the centrality of battery and adultery in the separation of Catholic marriages, and for a detailed description of procedures followed before ecclesiastical courts in late colonial Mexico, see Lourdes Villafuerte Garcia, Teresa Lozano Armendares, Sergio Ortega Noriega, and Rocio Ortega Soto, "La sevicia y el adulterio en las causas matrimoniales en el Provisorato de México a fines de la era colonial: Un estudio de la técnica procesal jurídica," *Estudios de Historia Novohispana* 38 (2008): 87–161, esp. 91.

16. See AGN, Mexico, Criminal, vol. 108, case 10, fols. 264–277, esp. fol. 273.

17. Francisco Antonio de Elizondo y Alvarez, *Practica universal forense de los tribunales de España y de las Indias,* 6th ed. (Madrid: Imprenta de Ramón Ruíz, 1796), 1: 351; ibid., 3: 359–361; ibid., 7: 161–185; Tomás Sánchez, *Moral jesuítica: O sea controversias del santo Sacramento del Matrimonio* (Madrid Imprenta Popular a cargo de Tomás Rey, 1887 [1623]); Jaime de Corella, *Practica del confesonario y explicacion de las 65 proposiciones condenad. por la Santidad de N.S.P. Inocencio XI: su materia, los casos más selectos de la Theologia Moral, su forma, vn dialogo entre el confesor y penitente* (Zaragoza: Por Domingo Gascon, Infancon, 1688).

18. In his words: "*si tal cual vez le falto la paciencia le suele dar una bofetada. . . .*" AGS, Gracia y Justicia, legajo 874, no folio.

19. His words: "*[recuerdo] haberle levantado la mano cosa de cinco ocasiones dandole en cada una de ella un solo lijero manazo por asuntos que nunca faltan entre casados.*" AANG, Guadalajara, Criminales, 131-1-978, fol. 8v.

20. AANG, Guadalajara, Criminales, 57-12-925, fols. 3–4.

21. For obvious cultural reasons, cases of physical abuse of husbands by their wives were considerably underreported. See Mantecón, "Hogares infernales: una visión retrospectiva sobre la violencia doméstica en el mundo moderno," 197.

22. Dávila Mendoza, "Hasta que la muerte nos separe," 236–237. See also Bird, "For Better or Worse," 9, 48–49.

23. See Marín Tello, "Justicia penal y orden social en Michoacán en el siglo XVIII," 217; AGN, Mexico, Criminal, vol. 2, case 2, fols. 31–69. See also a case from Segovia tried in 1801: ARCV, Criminales, caja 31, exp. 2, fols. 40v–43.

24. On adultery as an exclusively female crime, see lib. 8, tit. 20, *Recopilación de leyes de estos reinos,* 3 vols. (Madrid, 1723), 2: 347; Juan Alvarez Posadilla, *Practica Criminal por Principios o Modo y Forma de Instruir los Procesos Criminales de las Causas de Oficio de Justicia contra los abusos introducidos. Necesaria, no solo a todos los escribanos que tienen que actuar con jueces legos y Alcaldes ordinarios, sino también a los Letrados jóvenes para precaver abusos de tan fatales consecuencias, con otros puntos curiosos de policía y gobierno de los pueblos, que se tratan por incidencia Compuesta por el Licenciado Juan Alvarez Posadilla, Corregidor que ha sido de Distintas Poblaciones, Villas y Ciudades del Reyno,* 3 vols., 3a. edición (Madrid: En la Imprenta que fue de García, 1815 [1794]), 3: 186–191; Antonio de la Peña, *Orden de los juicios y penas criminales* [sixteenth century]. BNE, unpublished manuscript no. 6379, 116–118; Brundage, *Law, Sex, and Christian Society,* 511.

25. See Sanchez, *Compendium,* 3–6, 62–71; Brundage, *Law, Sex, and Christian Society,* 93, 241–248, passim; Elizondo, *Práctica universal forense,* 7: 162; Asunción Lavrin, "Sexuality in Colonial Mexico: A Church Dilemma," in Asuncion Lavrin, ed., *Sexuality and Marriage in Colonial Latin America* (Lincoln: University of Nebraska Press, 1989): 47–92, esp. 72–80; AANG, Guadalajara, Criminales, 15, 7, 345.

26. See Elizondo, *Práctica universal forense,* 7: 160–185.

27. Bird, "For Better or Worse," chapter 3.

28. Rene de la Pedraja, "La mujer criolla y mestiza en la sociedad colonial, 1700–1830," *Desarrollo y Sociedad* 13 (January 1984), 199–229, esp. 215–217; Rodríguez, *Sentimientos y vida familiar,* 237–253; Guiomar Dueñas, *Hijos del pecado,* 182–187; Maria Himelda Ramirez, *Las mujeres y la sociedad colonial de Santafe de Bogota, 1750–1810* (Bogotá: Instituto Colombiano de Antropología e Historia, 2000), 151–160; Behrend-Martínez, *Unfit for Marriage,* 113. See also Boyer, *Lives of the Bigamists.* On excommunication and other forms of censure, see Donoso, *Instituciones de derecho canónico,* 3: 356–389. On criminal cases against those who abandoned their spouses in eighteenth-century Madrid, see Christine Benavides, *Les Femmes Délinquantes à Madrid: Justice et Société en Espagne Au XVIIIe Siècle* (Toulouse: CRIC–Ophrys, 2000), 145–146. For the prevalence of "informal divorces" in colonial Guatemala, see Komisaruk, *Labor and Love in Guatemala,* chapter 5, esp. 192–196.

29. See AJO, vol. 14, case 43, fols. 1–48.

30. See AGN, Colombia, Colonia, Criminales, vol. 161, fol. 557.

31. Elizondo, *Práctica universal,* 3: 351. For the case of a woman killed by her husband and father-in-law after she denounced the former to the criminal section of Mexico's *audiencia,* see Francisco Sedano, *Noticias de México: Crónicas del siglo XVI al siglo XVIII,* 3 vols. (Mexico City: Secretaría de Obras y Servicios, 1974), 3: 93.

32. A detailed discussion of some of these can be found in Kelleher, *The Measure of Woman,* chapter 1, esp. 20–24.

33. See partida 2, tit. 21, ley 3, in "Siete Partidas," Marcelo Martínez Alcubilla, *Códigos Antigüos de España,* 2 vols. (Madrid: J. López Camacho Impresor, 1885), 1: 332: "*hidalguia . . . es nobleza que viene a los hombres por linaje, y por ello deben mucho guardar los que tienen derecho a ella, que no la dañen ni la menguen . . . casando con villana o el villano con hijodalga. Pero la mayor parte de la hidalguia ganan los hombres por la honra de los padres, pues cuando la madre sea villana y el padre hijodalgo, hijodalgo es el hijo que de ellos naciese, y por hijodalgo se puede contar, mas no por noble, mas si naciese de hijadalga y de villano, no tuvieron por derecho que fuese contado por hijodalgo.*"

34. Addressed to Castilians and originally published in 1771, by 1806 seven editions of it had been printed and circulated widely both throughout Spain and overseas. See Ignacio Jordan de Asso and Miguel de Manuel y Rodríguez, *Instituciones del derecho civil de Castilla que escribieron los doctores Asso y Manuel, enmendadas, ilustradas y añadidas conforme a la real orden de 5 de Octubre de 1802 por el Dr. Don Joaquín María Palacios,* 3 vols., 7a ed. (Madrid: Imprenta

de Don Tomás Albán, 1806 [1771]), vol. 1, libro 1, tit. 1 and 5. At the time of its seventh printing, however, the manual attributed limited value to the last of the distinctions, except when alluding to blacks who worked overseas (*en Indias*) in mines or were held in bondage there by particular people. See ibid., 35.

35. See Asso y del Rio and De Manuel, *Instituciones del derecho civil de Castilla,* 1: 66.

36. See "Siete Partidas," partida 7, tit. XVII, leys 1 and 2, in Martínez Alcubilla, *Códigos Antigüos,* 1: 645.

37. See "Siete Partidas," partida 7, tit. XVII, leys 13, 14, and 15, in Martínez Alcubilla, *Códigos Antigüos,* 1: 647.

38. "Siete Partidas," partida 7, tit. VIII, ley 12, Martínez Alcubilla, *Códigos Antigüos,* 1: 627.

39. For a comprehensive collection of all these laws, see Martínez Alcubilla, *Códigos Antigüos,* and *Códigos españoles,* 12 vols. Regarding the applicability of the different laws and their hierarchy, see laws 3–11, tit. 2, book 3, *Novisima Recopilación,* in ibid., 7: 263–265.

40. Martínez Alcubilla, *Códigos Antigüos,* 2: 1907.

41. These were compiled in various regional *cedularios.* See, for instance, the 1574 *cedulario* of Alonso de Zorita, *Leyes y ordenanzas reales de las Indias del Mar Océano, por las cuales primeramente se han de librar todos los pleitos civiles y criminales de aquellas partes, y lo que por ellos no estuviese determinado se han de librar por las leyes y ordenanzas de los Reinos de Castilla* (México: Ed. Miguel Angel Porrúa, 1985); or Diego de Encinas, *Cedulario Indiano,* 4 vols. (Madrid: Ediciones Cultura Hispánica, 1945–1946 [1596]). See Rafael Altamira, "Los cedularios como fuente histórica de la legislación indiana," *Revista de Historia de América* 19 (June 1945): 61–129.

42. Avila Martel, *Esquema del derecho penal indiano;* María del Refugio González, "Estudio introductorio," in Eusebio Bentura Beleña, *Recopilación sumaria,* 2 vols. (México: Universidad Nacional Autónoma de México, 1991), 1: vii–lix; Alfonso García Gallo, *Manual de historia del derecho español,* 2 vols., 5a. ed. (Madrid: Artes Gráficas Ediciones, 1973); idem, "Leyes, recopilaciones y códigos," in *Recopilación de leyes de los Reynos de las Indias: Estudios Histórico-Jurídicos,* ed. Francisco de Icaza Dufour (México: Miguel Angel Porrúa, 1987), 5–21; Solórzano y Pereyra, *Política indiana.*

43. de las Heras Santos, *La Justicia penal de los Austrias,* passim.

44. AHN, Madrid, Consejos, libro 1390, fols. 74–96. More on the *fábrica* and the *fuero* can be found in María Dolores Villaverde Sastre, "La real fábrica de paños y la ciudad de Guadalajara," *Wad-aL-Hayara: Revista de Estudios de Guadalajara* 8 (1981): 453–468, esp. 461–464.

45. AGN, Mexico, Californias, vol. 65, case 6, fols. 241–252v, and esp. fol. 252v.

46. Diego de Covarrubia Leyva, *Clementinae, Si Furiosus de Homicidio, Relectio* (Salamanticae: Excudebat Andreas a Portonarijs, SCM Typographus, 1560); and Antonio Gomezio, *Commentariorum Variarum que Resolutionum Iuris Civilis Communis & Regij,* 3 vols. (aedibus Dominci a Portonaris, C.M. Typographi,

1569); Gregorium López, *Index seu repertorium materiarum ac vtriusque iuris decisionum quae in singulis Septem partitarum glossis continentur* (Salmanticae: in aedibus Dominici â Portonarijs, 1576). See also Laurentius Mathaew Et Sanz, *Tractatus de Re Criminali* (Lugduni: Apud Fratres Anissonios, Ioann. Posuel & Claudium Ridaug, 1686).

47. See Ioannis Bernardi Diaz de Luco [Juan Bernardo Diaz de Lugo], *Practica criminalis canonica* (Medina del Campo: Apud Gillelmum de Millis, 1545); Egidio Bossi, *Practica et tractatus varii, seu quaestiones, Aegidii Bossii . . . criminalem materiam siue actionem fere omnem exacte continentes* (Per Sebastianum Henricpetri, 1578); Proseri Farinacii, *Praxis, et Theoricae Criminales,* 4 vols. (Lugduni: Sumptibus Iacobi Cardon, 1634 [1603]); Francesco Pitigiani, Ilarione Sacchetti, and CiottiGiovanni Battista, *Practica criminalis canonica* (apud Io. Baptistam Ciottum, 1621). See also the earliest known practical manual in Castilian, by Gabriel Monterroso y Alvarado, *Practica Civil y Criminal & Instruccion de Escribanos* (Valladolid: Francisco Fernandez de Cordova Impresor, 1566) (see Figure 1.1). An even earlier Castilian version of an important and widely quoted doctrinal text, an annotated code of laws, is Gregorio López, *Las Siete Partidas del Sabio Rey don Alonso el Nono nuevamente glosadas por el licenciado Gregorio López; con su Reportorio muy copioso, asi del Testo como de la Glosa* (Salamanca: por Andrea de Portonaris, 1555).

48. See Jerónimo Castillo de Bobadilla, *Política para corregidores y señores de vasallos en tiempo de paz y de guerra,* 2 vols. (Madrid: Por Luis Sánchez, 1597). Originally published in the late sixteenth century, it went through numerous editions and was still in use in the early nineteenth century. See also Victor M. Uribe-Urán, "Preparando 'mandarines': Apuntes sobre la historia de la ciencia administrativa en Nueva Granada durante la colonia y comienzos de la república, 1590–1850," *Innovar, Revista de Ciencias Administrativas y Sociales* 7 (Universidad Nacional de Colombia, Bogotá, January–June, 1996): 87–97. Another highly popular one was Juan de Hevia Bolaños, *Curia filipica, donde breve y compendioso se trata de los iucios, mayormente forenses, eclesiásticos y seculares, con lo sobre ellos hasta ahora dispuesto por derecho, resuelto por doctores antiguos y modernos y practicable. Util para los profesores de entrambos derechos, y fueros, y jueces, abogados, escribanos y procuradores, litigantes y otras personas* (Madrid: por la Viuda de Alonso Martin, 1627 [1605]).

49. See, for instance, Elizondo, *Práctica universal;* Martinez, *Libreria de juezes, utilisima y universal;* Alvarez Posadilla, *Practica criminal,* 3a. ed. See also Juan Muñoz, *Práctica de procuradores para seguir pleitos civiles y criminales* (Madrid: Emprenta del Lic ciado Castro, 1596), which was reprinted in 1642, 1659, 1723, and 1728; and Alonso de Villadiego Vascuñana's *Instrucción Política y Práctica Judicial* (Madrid: Luis Sanchez, 1612), eleven editions of which circulated between 1612 and 1788. For additional citations, see Tomás y Valiente, *El derecho penal,* esp. chapter 2.

50. See Teodoro Hampe Martínez, *Bibliotecas privadas del mundo colonial: La difusión de libros e ideas en el virreinato del Perú (Siglos XVI–XVII)* (Madrid: Iberoamericana, 1996), 154, 172, 235; Guillermo Furlong, *Bibliotecas argentinas durante la dominación hispánica* (Buenos Aires: Editorial Nuarpes, 1944), 28, 36,

39, 43, 56–80, 96–97. For the nineteenth century, see Javier Rodríguez Torres, "Libros jurídicos en la biblioteca de un obispo mejicano de los inicios del siglo XIX," *Revista Chilena de Historia del Derecho* 17 (1992): 113–134, esp. 121–124; Bernardino Bravo Lira, "El derecho indiano despues de la independencia en la América española," *Historia* 19 (1984): 5–52, esp. 7–19; and Jesús A. Martínez Martín, *Lectura y lectores en el Madrid del siglo XIX* (Madrid: Consejo Superior de Investigaciones Científicas, 1991), 95–106.

51. See AANG, Guadalajara, Criminales, 64, 7, 1023, fols. 1–5. See also similar situations discussed in Cutter, *The Legal Culture of Northern New Spain*, 4.

52. See AGN, Mexico, Criminales, 140, 6, 165–242; AGN, Mexico, Acordada, 28, 78; AGN, Mexico, Criminales, 118, 5, 160–183. See MacLachlan, *Criminal Justice in Eighteenth-Century Mexico.*

53. See Alloza, *La vara quebrada de la justicia,* chapters 1 and 2; de las Heras Santos, *La Justicia penal de los Austrias,* 65–87.

54. Eudosio Varon Vallejo and Angel González, "Introducción," in AHN, *Consejo de Castilla. Sala de Alcaldes de Casa y Corte. Catálogo por Materias* (Madrid, 1925), xv–xx; laws 1–17, tit. 27, book 4, and laws 1–5, tit. 28, book 4, "Novísima Recopilación," in *Los Códigos españoles,* 7: 492–505; Miguel Cayetano Sanz, *Modo y forma de instruir y substanciar las causas criminales* (Madrid: Imprenta de Don Joseph Doblado, 1790), 32.

55. Premo, *Children of the Father King.*

56. Hevia Bolanos, *Curia Filipica,* 76v–77. See also Asso y del Rio and De Manuel, *Instituciones del derecho civil de Castilla,* 264.

57. Partida 3, tit. 16, law 9, in "Siete Partidas," Martinez Alcubilla, *Códigos Antiguos,* 1: 413.

58. Hevia Bolaños, *Curia Filipica,* 77.

59. "[P]or los niños se descrubren los crimenes ocultos." See ARCV, Pleitos Criminales, caja 270, case 2, fol. 376.

60. See AANG, Guadalajara, vol. 1, case 16.

61. See AGN, Mexico, Criminales, vol. 8, fols. 301–357.

62. ARCV, Pleitos Criminales, caja 270, case 2.

63. ARCV, Pleitos Criminales, caja 270, case 2, fols. 134–136, 208–210.

64. "[D]erecho reprueba por testigos abiles aun en materias de menor gravedad." See ARCV, Pleitos Criminales, caja 270, case 2, fols. 152, 168, 178v, 188. For similar claims in an 1813 Guadalajara case, see AANG, Guadalajara, Criminales, 39, 12–925, fols. 7–10.

65. On this point, see Hevia Bolaños, *Curia Filipica,* 214v–215.

66. See "Siete Partidas," partida 3, tit. XVI, ley 8 and 13, in Martínez Alcubilla, *Códigos Antiguos,* 1: 413–414.

67. Solórzano y Pereira, *Política indiana,* 1: 425.

68. Cutter, *Legal Culture in Northern New Spain,* 118. See also Owensby, *Empire of Law and Indian Justice,* 193.

69. See AANG, Guadalajara, Criminales, 59-4-951, no folio. See also AGN, Mexico, Criminales, v. 29, exp. 6–7, fol. 99; AGN, Mexico, Criminales, v. 140, exp. 6, fol. 224v. See also Owensby, *Empire of Law and Indian Justice,* 193.

70. Only on occasion were they charged with neglect. See exceptional accusations of procrastination (*morosidad*) against an official who took over a decade to prosecute a case. AGN, Colombia, Colonia, Juicios Criminales, vol. 36, fols. 1–175.

71. Law 6, tit. 23, lib. 8, *Recopilación de las leyes de estos reynos*, 2: 287; Alvarez Posadilla, *Práctica criminal,* 1: 10; Eugenio de Tapia, *Febrero Novisimo o libreria de jueces, abogados y escribanos,* 10 vols. (Valencia: Imprenta de Idelfonso Monpié, 1830), 7: 123–124. On the difference between *delitos privados* and *delitos públicos,* see Castillo de Bobadilla, *Política para corregidores y señores de vasallos,* 2: 521–523; de Asso y del Río and de Manuel, *Instituciones del derecho civil de Castilla*, ccxxv–ccxlvii. For references to *vindicta pública,* see, for instance, AGN, Colombia, Criminales, Colonia, vol. 117, fol. 252, 255; ARCV, Pleitos Criminales, caja 270, case 2, fols. 198, 349.

72. See AGN, Colombia, Criminales, Colonia, vol. 194, fol. 771.

73. AANG, Guadalajara, Criminales, 11-4-199, no folio.

74. *Plena prueba* typically derived from at least two separate "legitimate" testimonies or the defendant's voluntary confession. See Joseph Marcos Gutiérrez, *Compendio de las Varias Resoluciones de Antonio Gómez* (Madrid: En la Imprenta de don Benito Cano, 1789), 77; Elizondo, *Práctica universal forense,* 4: 339–347.

75. AGN, Colombia, Negros y Esclavos, Santander, vol. 4, fol. 902v.

76. Other cases can be found in AGN, Colombia, Criminales, República, vol. 15, doc. 10, fols. 420v, 429; AGN, Colombia, Colonia, Negros y Esclavos, Santander, vol. 4, fol. 902v.

77. See AGN, Mexico, Criminal, vol. 35, exp. 16, fols. 377–378. See also AGN, Colombia, Criminales, República, vol. 7, fols. 747–893.

78. This was standard practice in cases of assault and homicide. See Vilanova y Mañez, *Materia criminal forense,* 3: 35; Juan Sala, *Ilustración del derecho real de España,* 5 vols. (México: Imprenta de Galván, 1833), 5: 18–19. See also Sanz, *Modo y forma de instruir y substanciar las causas,* 5–18.

79. See AGN, Colombia, Criminales, Colonia, vol. 44, fol. 42v; ARCV, Pleitos Criminales, caja 154, exp. 4, fols. 25–26. See also Sanz, *Modo y forma de instruir y substanciar las causas criminales,* 16; Gutiérrez, *Práctica criminal de España,* 1: 129.

80. ARCV, Pleitos Criminales, caja 154, exp. 4, fols. 25–26v.

81. See AGN, Colombia, Criminales, Colonia, vol. 194, fol. 783.

82. See Elizondo, *Práctica universal forense,* 4: 35; Alvarez Posadilla, *Práctica criminal,* 1: 212–213. For a full list of prohibited arms as of 1723, see laws V–XX, tit. XXIII, *Recopilación de las leyes de estos reinos* (Madrid: Imprenta de Juan de Ariztia, 1723), vol. 2: 351–353v. For a full list as of 1805, see tit. 19, tomo 5, *Novisima recopilación* (Madrid: n.e., 1805), vol. 3: 381–392.

83. See ARCV, Pleitos Criminales, caja 131, exp. 2, fols. 1–5; ibid., caja 202, exp. 2.

84. AANG, Guadalajara, Criminal, 33-9-351, no folio. For additional examples and commentaries, see AGN, Colombia, Criminales, Colonia, vol. 174, fol. 831. For comments, see Asso y del Rio and de Manuel, *Instituciones del derecho civil de Castilla,* 267.

85. AANG, Guadalajara, Criminal, 60-3-965, fols. 3–4.

86. By law, this confession had to be conscious and free ("*a sabiendas*" and "*de su grado*"). See *Las Siete Partidas*, laws 4–5, tit. 13, part. 13. See also Juan Meléndez Valdés, *Discursos Forenses de D. Juan Meléndez Valdés, fiscal que fue de la Sala de Alcaldes de Casa y Corte e Individuo de las Academia Española y de San Fernando, y de la de San Carlos de Valencia* (Madrid: En la Imprenta Real, 1821), 21, 27–28.

87. AANG, Guadalajara, Criminal, 11-4-199, no folio.

88. See AANG, Guadalajara, Criminal, 57-12-925, fols. 2–3.

89. He was moved from the jail in the little town of Furmiel to the one in Medinaceli. See ARCV, Pleitos Criminales, caja 245, exp. 2, fol. 28.

90. See AGN, Colombia, Criminales, Colonia, vol. 194, fol. 794.

91. According to a popular legal manual, the confiscation of a deceased female defendant's property (*mujer que causa la muerte de su marido*) was one of the few exceptions to the rule that criminal procedures against the dead were unwarranted. See Hevia Bolaños, *Curia filipica,* 185, 185v.

92. ARG, Causas, leg. 110, no. 34.

93. See ARCV, Pleitos Criminales, caja 428, case 1, fols. 41–59v.

94. AGN, Mexico, Criminales, 41, 7, fols. 127–139, 140–174.

95. ARCV, Pleitos Criminales, caja 154, 4, liquidation at the end of file.

96. See, for instance, AGN, Colombia, Colonia, Juicios Criminales, vol. 15, fol. 361; vol. 153, fol. 831.

97. See ARCV, Pleitos Criminales, caja 270, case 2, fols. 194–194v; Guadalajara, AANG, 131-1-1978, fols. 21v–24; Alvarez Posadilla, *Práctica criminal,* 2: 277.

98. See ARCV, Pleitos Criminales, caja 154, exp. 4, fols. 87-87v. Sometimes this proved difficult when regular appointees excused themselves on the grounds of health, imminent travel, and other impediments. See AGN, Colombia, Criminales, Colonia, vol. 174, fols. 797v–802; AANG, Guadalajara, Criminal, 8-14-201.

99. See AANG, Guadalajara, Criminal, 26-7-417, fols. 30v–33.

100. On the need for and importance of ratification, see Hevia Bolaños, *Curia Filipica,* 210–210v. For examples of ratifications, see ARCV, Pleitos Criminales, caja 270, case 2, fols. 236–254.

101. See, for instance, AGN, Colombia, Criminales, Colonia, vol. 174, fol. 831; ARCV, Pleitos Criminales, caja 270, case 2, fols. 204–204v, 210–210v, 217, 221–225; AANG, Guadalajara, Criminal, 131-1-1978, folios corresponding to proceedings of November 5, 1819; Asso y del Rio and de Manuel, *Instituciones del derecho civil de Castilla,* 267.

102. AGN, Colombia, Colonia, Criminales, vol. 194, fols. 791v–792.

103. "*[Q]ue aunque sean los testigos menores de 16 años, se pueden admitir para el tormento y las inhábiles, las cuales son buenas para la inquisición cuando los delitos son de difícil probanza. . . .*" See ARCV, Pleitos Criminales, caja 270, case 2, fols. 355–356, 368v–369.

104. Hevia Bolaños, *Curia Filipica,* 215.

105. See Gutiérrez, *Compendio de las Varias Resoluciones,* 13–14.

106. See, for instance, AGN, Colombia, Criminales, Colonia, vol. 194, fols. 889–889v.

107. See Abelardo Levaggi, "La fundamentación de las sentencias en el derecho Indiano," *Revista de Historia del Derecho* 6 (1978): 45–73.

108. See Alvares Posadilla, *Práctica criminal,* 2: 407. See also Marta Lorente, "El juez y la ley: La motivación de las sentencias (Castilla, 1489–España, 1855)," *Anuario de la Facultad de Derecho de la Universidad Autónoma de Madrid* 1 (1997): 97–142; Tomás y Valiente, *El derecho penal,* 200; Hespanha, "De *Iustitia* a Disciplina," 234–236.

109. See Hevia Bolaños, *Curia Filipica,* 211v–215v; Asso y del Rio and de Manuel, *Instituciones del derecho civil de Castilla,* lib. 3, tit. 7; ARCV, caja 270, exp. 2, fol. 350v.

110. For a representative example, see AGN, Colombia, Criminales, Colonia, vol. 194, fol. 892.

111. For additional details on the criminal investigation, see Hevia Bolaños, *Curia Filipica,* 157v–245; Alvarez Posadilla, *Práctica criminal,* 2: 300–431. See also María Paz Alonso, *El proceso penal en Castilla (siglos XIII–XVIII)* (Salamanca: Ediciones Universidad de Salamanca, 1982), passim; Cutter, *Legal Culture of Northern New Spain,* chapters 5 and 6.

112. See Victor M. Uribe-Uran, "'*Iglesia me llamo*': Church Asylum and the Law in Spain and Colonial Spanish America," *Comparative Studies in Society and History* 49.1 (2007): 446–472.

113. Hevia Bolaños, *Curia Filipica.*

CHAPTER TWO

1. Founded in 1774, this was one of 28 missions established in Baja California. See Jerry D. Moore and Mary J. Norton, "'I Solemnly Baptize': Religious Conversion and Native Demography in Northern Baja California," *Journal of California and Great Basin Anthropology* 14.2 (1992): 201–215.

2. See *Las Siete Partidas,* partida 7, title 8, laws I–XVI; *Fuero Real,* laws 1–2, title 17, book 4; *Ordenamiento de Alcala,* ley 2, title 22; *Recopilación de las Leyes de estos Reynos,* 3 vols. (Madrid, 1723), ley 15, title 23, book 8, 2: 351v.

3. The captains' key role is highlighted in Moore and Norton, "'I Solemnly Baptize,'" 209–210. A total of 557 natives converted in those years (72.3 percent of all gentile converts). Captain Macapa himself and his four young daughters were baptized in August 1775.

4. AGN, México, Californias, 72: 293–300.

5. On the politics of difference characteristic of imperial rule, see Burbank and Cooper, *Empires in World History,* 9–14.

6. See Helmholz, *The Spirit of Classical Canon Law,* chapter 5. See also Charles Henry Cunningham, *The Audiencia in the Spanish Colonies as Illustrated by the Audiencia in Manila, 1583–1800* (Berkeley: University of California Press, 1919), 1–31; and Borah, *Justice by Insurance,* 12–16, 80–81, 83.

7. Helmholz, *The Spirit of Classical Canon Law,* 128–129.

8. Berman, *Law and Revolution,* 556.

9. This is widely claimed to have been the case in Latin American societies. See, for instance, Carlos Aguirre and Ricardo Salvatore, "Writing the History

of Law, Crime and Punishment in Latin America," 15–17. For a classical article explaining the rationale behind the gap in colonial Spanish America, see Phelan, "Authority and Flexibility," 47–65. See also Arrom, "New Directions in Mexican Legal History," 461–465. Hespanha points to a similar gap between "law" and the decisions of judicial tribunals in Portugal in "De *Iustitia* a Disciplina," 225.

10. On comparable judicial discretion in eighteenth-century Portuguese criminal law, see Hespanha,"De *Iustitia* a Disciplina," esp. 234–235.

11. Insightfully discussed for the Portuguese case in ibid, 228–232.

12. Pescador, "Del dicho al hecho," 373–386.

13. A classic formulation of this dilemma can be found in Jean Bodin, *The Six Bookes of a Commonweale*, edited with an introduction by Kenneth Douglas McRae (Cambridge, 1962 [facsimile reprint of the 1606 English translation]).

14. On the complementary nature of royal paternalism and patriarchy, see Arrom, *The Women of Mexico City*, and Premo, *Children of the Father King*. For the view that there was an intrinsic contradiction between the king's patriarchal justice and the authority of heads of household (*pater familiae*), and the opinion that patriarchal customs and practices took precedence over written laws in the late colonial period, see Pescador, "Del dicho al hecho."

15. See Herzog, *Upholding Justice*, esp. chapter 1; Premo, *Children of the Father King*, 27.

16. On images of Amerindians through time, see William B. Taylor, "'. . . de corazón pequeño y animo apocado.' Conceptos de los curas párrocos sobre los Indios en la Nueva España del siglo XVIII," *Relaciones* 39 (Summer 1989): 5–67; Benjamin Keen, *La imagen Azteca en el pensamiento occidental* (Mexico City: Fondo de Cultura Económica, 1984), esp. chapters 5 and 7. On legal paternalism, see Charles R. Cutter, *The Protector de Indios in Late Colonial Mexico, 1659–1821* (Albuquerque: University of New Mexico Press, 1986); idem, *The Legal Culture of Northern New Spain;* Borah, *Justice by Insurance.*

17. For studies of periods close to the one addressed in this essay, see Dominino Crespo, *Escándalos y delitos;* Herzog, *La administración como un fenómeno social;* idem, *Upholding Justice*; Scardaville, "Crime and the Urban Poor"; Haslip-Viera, *Crime and Punishment in Late Colonial Mexico City;* Patiño, *Criminalidad, ley penal y estructura social en la provincia de Antioquia;* and MacLachlan, *Criminal Justice in Eighteenth-Century Mexico.*

18. Pescador, "Del dicho al hecho."

19. Uribe-Uran, "Colonial *Baracunatanas* and Their Nasty Men." See also Mabel López, "Conyugicidios en la Nueva Granada: Una vía de escape a la violencia contra la mujer," paper presented at the XVI Congreso de Historia de Colombia, Bogotá, 2008, esp. 2–3.

20. Stern, *The Secret History of Gender*, esp. chapters 3 and 4.

21. Kellogg, *Law and the Transformation of the Aztec Culture.* For evidence of Indian women's frequent use of the courts to confront their spouses from the mid-sixteenth century to the mid-eighteenth century, see, for instance, Lisa Mary Sousa, "Women and Crime in Colonial Oaxaca: Evidence of Complementarity in Mixtec and Zapotec Societies," in Schroeder et al., eds., *Indian Women of*

Early Mexico, 199–214; Marta Espejo-Ponce Hunt and Matthew Restall, "Work, Marriage, Status," in ibid. 231–252, esp. 237–239.

22. The one in Mexico was established in 1527. Guadalajara's was created in 1548. A third *audiencia* was established in Guatemala in 1543, but this work does not consider cases tried there.

23. Mexico City's 1793 population was 112,926, compared to 42,444 people in Philadelphia and just 31,131 in New York around the same time. See Friar Ilarione da Bergamo, Robert R. Miller, and William J. Orr, *Daily Life in Colonial Mexico: The Journey of Friar Ilarione da Bergamo, 1761–1768* (Norman: University of Oklahoma Press, 2000), 13; and Eric Van Young, *Hacienda and Market in Eighteenth-Century Mexico: The Rural Economy of the Guadalajara Region, 1675–1820* (Berkeley: University of California Press, 1981), 35.

24. The populations of major Mexican cities in 1793 were Mexico City, 112,926; Puebla, 52,717; Guanajuato, 32,098; Guadalajara, 28,250; Zacatecas, 24,495; and Antequera (Oaxaca), 19,069. See Van Young, *Hacienda and Market in Eighteenth-Century Mexico,* 35.

25. See Joseph de Galvez, "Informe sobre el estado de las provincias internas, 1780" AGI, Guadalajara, 253, esp. fols. 5v–6. See also Laura M. Shelton, *For Tranquility and Order: Family and Community on Mexico's Northern Frontier, 1800–1850* (Tucson: University of Arizona Press, 2010), chapter 1.

26. See Pilar Gonzalbo Aizpuru and Cecilia Rabell Romero, "La familia en México," in Pablo Rodriguez, ed., *La Familia en Iberoamerica, 1550–1980* (Bogotá: Universidad Externado de Colombia–Convenio Andrés Bello, 2004), 93–124, esp. 101, 104. The king even dedicated royal gifts to subsidizing dowries for poor and orphan girls. See "*Dotes para doncellas honestas, pobres y huerfanas, del caudal que se habia de invertir en fiestas por el nacimiento del infante. Noviembre 12 de 1771,*" AGI, Consulados, 53.

27. Robert McCaa, "Tratos nupciales: La constitución de uniones formales e informales en México, 1500–1900," in Pilar Gozalbo Aizpuru and Cecilia Rabell, coords., *Familia y vida privada en la historia de Iberoamérica: Seminario de Historia de la Familia* (Mexico: El Colegio de México–Univ. Nacional Autónoma de México, 1996), 21–57; idem, "Familias y género en México: Crítica metodológica y desafío investigativo para el fin del milenio," in Victor M. Uribe-Uran and Luis Javier Ortiz, eds., *Naciones, gentes y territorios,* 103–138; Cecilia Rabell Romero, "Trayectorias de vida familiar, raza y género en Oaxaca colonial," in Pilar Gozalbo Aizpuru and Cecilia Rabell, coords., *Familia y vida privada en la historia de Iberoamérica,* 75–118.

28. The previous composite descriptions are based on archival records cited throughout and in the writings of Ilarione Da Bergamo, *Daily Life in Colonial Mexico;* Jose Antonio Villaseñor y Sanchez, *Theatro Americano; Instrucciones y Memorias de los Virreyes Novohispanos,* 2 vols. (Mexico City: Editorial Porrúa, 1991); Taylor, *Drinking, Homicide, and Rebellion;* Douglas Cope, *The Limits of Racial Domination: Plebeian Society in Colonial Mexico, 1660–1720* (Madison: University of Wisconsin Press, 1999); Eric J. Van Young, *Hacienda and Market in Eighteenth-Century Mexico;* Pedro Viqueira Alban, *Propriety and Permissiveness*

in Bourbon Mexico (Wilmington: Scholarly Resources, 1999); Lipsett-Rivera, *Gender and the Negotiation of Daily Life;* Schroeder et al., *Indian Women of Early Mexico;* and Arnold J. Bauer, *Goods, Power, History: Latin America's Material Culture* (Cambridge: Cambridge University Press, 2001).

29. AJP, 1763, 3873, fol. 1.

30. AGN, Mexico, Criminales, vol. 41, exp. 3, fols. 46–52. See similar cases in AJO, 39, 1133, fols. 1–3.

31. AGN, Mexico, Criminales 8, fols. 309–311.

32. AANG, Guadalajara, 139, 10-2091, fols. 1–6.

33. Stern, *Secret History of Gender,* passim; Sonya Lipsett-Rivera, "La violencia dentro de las familias formal e informal," in Pilar Gonzalbo Aizpuru and Cecilia Rabell, eds., *Familia y vida privada en la historia de Iberoamérica,* 325–340; idem, "Marriage and Family Relations in Mexico During the Transition from Colony to Nation," in Victor M. Uribe-Uran, ed., *State and Society in Spanish America During the Age of Revolution,* 121–148; idem, *Gender and the Negotiation of Daily Life,* chapter 6; Pescador, "Del dicho al hecho"; Pilar Gonzalbo Aizpuru, "Violencia y discordia en las relaciones personales en la ciudad de México a fines del siglo XVIII," *Historia Mexicana* 51 (October–December, 2001): 233–259; Castro Gutiérrez, "Condición femenina y violencia conyugal entre los Purépechas"; Teresa Lozano Armendares, "Momentos de desamor en algunas parejas novohispanas," in Sergio Ortega Noriega et al., eds., *Amor y desamor: Vivencias de parejas en la sociedad novohispana* (Mexico City: Instituto Nacional de Antropología e Historia, 1992), 51–79.

34. See confessional and other religious manuals and catechisms cited by Pilar Gonzalbo Aizpuru, "Con amor y reverencia: Mujeres y familias en el México colonial," in *Jahrbuch für Geschichte Lateinamerikas* 35 (1998): 1–24; Richard Boyer, "Women, *la Mala Vida,* and the Politics of Marriage," in *Sexuality and Marriage in Colonial Latin America,* ed. Asunción Lavrín (Lincoln: University of Nebraska Press, 1989), 252–286, esp. 256; and Lipsett-Rivera, "Marriage and Family Relations," 131.

35. Tapia, *Febrero novísimo,* 7: 141–142. See López, "Conyugicidios en la Nueva Granada."

36. See ibid.; Vilanova y Mañez, *Materia criminal forense,* 1: 309; 3: 52.

37. See Bird, "For Better or Worse," 134; Pilar Gonzalbo Aizpuru and Cecilia Rabell Romero, "La familia en México," 105. On *sevicia*'s legal meaning, see Rípodaz Ardanas, *El matrimonio en Indias,* 383, 388; Maria Beatriz, *Sistema de Casamento no Brasil Colonial* (São Paulo: Editora da Universidade de São Paulo, 1984), 212, 219–223.

38. See "Real instrucción de Corregidores de 15 de Mayo de 1788," cited in Tapia, *Febrero novísimo,* 7: 142; Senen Vilanova y Mañez, *Materia criminal forense, ó, Tratado universal teórico y práctico, de los delitos y delinquentes en género y especie, para la segura y conforme expedicion de las causas de esta naturaleza: obra útil y precisa á jueces de todas clases, fiscales, abogados, asesores, escribanos, y demás que versan sus facultades en el foro,* 4 vols. (Madrid: En la Imprenta de Tomas Alban, 1807), 1: 309; and Pita Moreda, "Conflictos familiares

y tribunales de justicia a finales de la colonia: algunos casos novohispanos," 341–358.

39. See Arrom, *La mujer mexicana ante el divorcio eclesiastico;* Pescador, "Entre la espada y el olvido: Pleitos matrimoniales en el provisorato eclesiástico de México, siglo XVIII," 202.

40. AJO, Villalta, Penal, 14, fol. 4.

41. AGN, Mexico, Criminales, 8, fol. 329v.

42. Ibid., fol. 352v.

43. AGN, Mexico, Criminales, 8, fols. 354–355. On *parricidio,* see Joseph Berni, *Práctica criminal con notas de los delitos, sus penas, presunciones y circunstancias que los agravan y disminuyen* (Valencia: Simón Faure, Librero, 1769), 48; Alvarez Posadilla, *Práctica criminal* 3: 114–115; and Joseph Marcos Gutiérrez, *Práctica criminal de España,* 3 vols. (Madrid: En la oficina de don Benito García y Compañía, 1806 [1789]) 3: 43–44.

44. See Lipsett-Rivera, *Gender and the Negotiation of Daily Life,* chapter 4.

45. AANG, Guadalajara, 339–351.

46. The archives considered are the Archivo General de la Nación in Mexico City, the Judicial Archives of Puebla and Oaxaca, the Audiencia de Nueva Galicia archive in Guadalajara, the Provincial Archive of Zacatecas, and the city archive of Veracruz.

47. The cases occurred in the following places: Mexico City (7 cases), Pachuca (7), Oaxaca (6), Colima (5), Cuernavaca (5), Guadalajara (5), Xochimilco (4), Teposcolula (4), Puebla de los Ángeles (3), Tulancingo (3), Villa Alta (3), Oaxaca (3), Actopan (2), Real de Zacualpan (2), Valladolid (2), Atlitalaquia (1), Baja California Mission (1), Chihuahua (1), Coyoacán (1), Colotlan (1), Ixmiquilpan (1), Nueva Galicia (1), Nuevo Santander (1), San Bartolo (Patzcuaro) (1), Ozumba (1), Presidio de Loreto (1), Puebla (1), San Juan Teotihuacan (1), San Luis de Potosí (1), San Miguel Tulancingo (1), San Pedro, Guadalajara (1), Santa Ana La Joya, Guadalajara (1), Santa Fe, New Mexico (1), Santa Isabel, Guadalajara (1), Santa María Lagos, Guadalajara (1), Sombrerete (1), Taltenango, Guadalajara (1), Tetela del Río (1), Tizapan del Alto, Guadalajara (1), Valladolid, Morelia (1) and Villa Nombre de Dios, Guadalajara (1).

48. Taylor, *Drinking, Homicide, and Rebellion,* 77.

49. In Taylor's study, 176 (71 percent) of a total of 257 homicides for Central Mexico, 20 (36 percent) of 56 for the Mixteca Alta, and 86 (71.6 percent) of 120 for Central Jalisco occurred within the community. Between 15 percent and 30 percent of these occurred in the home of offender or victim, from 6 percent to 20 percent near a *pulquería,* and from 16 percent to 20 percent in the street. See Taylor, *Drinking, Homicide, and Rebellion,* 79; idem, "Amigos de sombrero," 88.

50. Uribe-Uran, "Colonial Baracunatanas," 52.

51. For additional comments on the use of poison and difficulty of detecting crimes committed with it, see Uribe-Uran, "Colonial Baracunatanas," 52, note 41; Spierenburg, *A History of Murder,* 128-130.

52. Cope, *The Limits of Racial Domination,* 49.

53. Uribe-Uran, "Colonial Baracunatanas"; Pescador, "Del dicho al hecho," 383; Haslip-Viera, *Crime and Punishment in Late Colonial Mexico City;* Patiño,

Criminalidad, ley penal y estructura social; Edward Hatton, "Domestic Assassins: Spousal and Intimate Homicide in Antebellum America" (Ph.D. dissertation, Temple University, 1997); Adler, "'My Mother-in-Law Is to Blame"; Stern, *The Secret History of Gender;* Taylor, "Amigos de sombrero"; Daniel A. Cohen, "Homicidal Compulsion and the Conditions of Freedom: The Social and Psychological Origins of Familicide in America's Early Republic," *Journal of Social History* 24.4 (1995): 725–764; Maeve E. Doggett, *Marriage, Wife-Beating and the Law in Victorian England* (New York: Columbia University Press, 1993); Pamela Haag, "The 'Ill-Use of a Wife': Patterns of Working Class Violence in Domestic and Public New York City, 1860–1880," *Journal of Social History* 25.3 (1992): 447–477; David Peterson, "Wife Beating: An American Tradition," *Journal of Interdisciplinary History* 13.1 (1992): 97–118; Kathryn Harvey, "Amazons and Victims: Resisting Wife-Abuse in Working Class Montréal, 1869–1879," *Journal of the Canadian Historical Association* 2 (1991): 131–148; Arturo Morgado-García, *Derecho de asilo y delincuencia en la Diócesis de Cádiz* (Cádiz: Diputación Provincial, 1991), esp. 81–85; Elizabeth Pleck, *Domestic Tyranny: The Making of Social Policy Against Family Violence from Colonial Times to the Present* (New York: Oxford University Press, 1987); J. A. Sharpe, "Domestic Homicide in Early Modern England," *Historical Journal* 24 (1981): 29–48.

54. "Memoria que el Virrey Carlos Francisco de Croix dejo a Don Fray Antonio Maria de Bucareli y Ursúa, 1-IX-1771," in *Instrucciones y Memorias de los Virreyes Novohispanos* (México: Editorial Porrúa, 1991) 2: 979–980.

55. See Arrom, *The Women of Mexico City, 1790–1857*, 234.

56. Lyman Johnson and Sonya Lipsett-Rivera, eds., *The Faces of Honor*, 179–200; Taylor, "Amigos de sombrero" and *Drinking, Homicide, and Rebellion;* Taylor, "Between Global Processes and Local Knowledge: An Inquiry into Early Latin American Social History, 1500–1900," in *Reliving the Past: The Worlds of Social History*, ed. Oliver Zunz (Chapel Hill: University of North Carolina Press, 1985), 115–190; Linda Gordon, *Heroes of Their Own Lives: The Politics and History of Family Violence, Boston, 1880–1960* (Champaign: University of Illinois Press, 1988); Borah, *Justice by Insurance.*

57. Uribe-Uran, "Colonial Baracunatanas," 50; Morgado-Garcia, *Derecho de asilo y delincuencia*, 85.

58. See note 53.

59. Scardaville, "Crime and the Urban Poor," 41; Haslip-Viera, *Crime and Punishment*, 55; Morgado-Garcia, *Derecho de asilo y delincuencia*, 77.

60. Uribe-Uran, "Colonial Baracunatanas."

61. Taylor, *Drinking, Homicide, and Rebellion*, 84–85.

62. Uribe-Uran, "Colonial Baracunatanas," passim.

63. Marta Espejo-Ponce Hunt and Matthew Restall, "Work, Marriage, Status," 239. See also Lipsett-Rivera, *Gender and the Negotiation of Daily Life*, passim.

64. Uribe-Uran, "Colonial Baracunatanas," 56–58. See Arrom, *The Women of Mexico*, chapter 4; Schroeder et al., *Indian Women of Early Mexico*. See also Socolow, *Women of Colonial Latin America*, passim. Several decades ago, prominent historians believed otherwise. See Taylor, *Drinking, Homicide, and Rebellion*, 88.

65. For the expression "*de color quebrado*" to allude to mixed-race individuals, see, respectively, reports from the Guadalajara Audiencia in July 1728 and an October 1785 letter by an estate administrator in AGI, Guadalajara 99, Cartas y Expedientes del Presidente y Oidores; AGI, Guadalajara 406, Expedientes a Instancia de Parte, 1790–1793.

66. Uribe-Uran, "Colonial Baracunatanas," 49.

67. Ibid.

68. For an insightful review of the literature on the history of gender, see Caulfield, "The History of Gender in the Historiography of Latin America." Some of the most recent and significant monographs on gender conflicts include Stern, *The Secret History of Gender;* Hunefeldt, *Liberalism in the Bedroom;* Molina, *La familia porteña en los siglos XVII y XVIII;* Rodríguez Saenz, *Hijas, novias y esposas;* and Kluger, *Escenas de la vida conyugal.* Various articles on divorce and marital disputes are cited below as appropriate.

69. See Castañeda, *Violación, estupro y sexualidad: Nueva Galicia;* and Ward Stavig, *Amor y violencia sexual: Valores indígenas en la sociedad conyugal* (Lima: Instituto de Estudios Peruanos, 1995). Several of the contributions published in the proceedings of the various Seminarios de Historia de las Mentalidades y Religión, held in Mexico, are also part of this literature, for example *El placer de pecar y el afán de normar* (México: Joaquín Mortiz/INAH, 1987) and *La memoria y el olvido* (México: INAH, 1985). See also Sergio Ortega, ed., *De la santidad a la perversión o de porque no se cumplía la ley de Dios en la sociedad novohispana* (México: Grijalbo, 1986); Ana María Atondo Rodríguez, *El amor venal y la condición femenina en el México colonial* (México: INAH, 1992); and Sueann Caulfield, *In Defense of Honor: Sexual Morality, Modernity, and Nation in Early Twentieth Century Brazil* (Durham: Duke University Press, 2000). Important for comparative purposes are the critical works of Pleck, *Domestic Tyranny;* and Laura Gowing, *Domestic Dangers: Women, Words and Sex in Early Modern London* (Oxford: Clarendon, 1996).

70. See Gowing, *Domestic Dangers*, 8.

71. Stern, *Secret History;* Hunefeldt, *Liberalism in the Bedroom;* Eugenia Rodríguez Saenz, "Civilizing Domestic Life in the Central Valley of Costa Rica, 1750–1850," in Elizabeth Dore and Maxine Molyneux, eds., *Hidden Histories of Gender and the State in Latin America* (Durham: Duke University Press, 2000), 85–107; Lipsett-Rivera, "Marriage and Family Relations"; Kanter, "Hijos del pueblo."

72. See AGI, Guadalajara, 400, Expedientes a Instancia de Parte, 1732–1753. Asuncion Lavrin provides other telling examples. See "Sexuality in Colonial Mexico: A Church Dilemma," in Lavrin ed., *Sexuality and Marriage,* 47–92, esp. 69.

73. See, among others, García Valdecasas, *El hidalgo y el honor,* 198–214; Albert S. Gérard, "The Loving Killers: The Rationale of Righteousness in Baroque Tragedy," *Comparative Literature Studies* 2 (1965): 209–232; Frank P. Casa, "Honor and the Wife-Killers of Calderón," *Bulletin of the Comediantes* 28 (1977): 27–31; Tomas A. Mantecón, "Honour and Social Discipline in Early Modern Spain," in Heinz Schilling, ed., *Institutionem, Instrumente und Akteure Sozialer Kontrolle und Disziplinierung im Frühneuzeitlichen Europa* (Frankfurt: Vittorio Klostermann, 1999), 203–223; and Stroud, *Fatal Union.*

74. See *Recopilación*, ley 3, title 20, book 8; Alvarez Posadilla, *Práctica criminal*, 3: 108–109, 180; Gutiérrez, *Práctica criminal*, 3: 42; Pescador, "Del dicho al hecho," 376; Arrom, *The Women of Mexico City*, 75–76.

75. AGN, Mexico, Criminales, 29, 13, 343–391.

76. AGN, Mexico, Criminales, 140, 6, 165–242.

77. AANG, Guadalajara, Criminales, 59, 4, 951.

78. See AGN, Mexico, Provincias Internas, 6, 44–85; AANG, Guadalajara, Criminales, 142, 11, 2146.

79. See AGN, Mexico, Criminales, 103, 1, 1–21.

80. Pita Moreda, "Conflictos familiares y tribunales de justicia a finales de la colonia"; Lavrin, "Sexuality in Colonial Mexico," 73–77; Pescador, "Entre la espada y el olvido"; Stern, *Secret History of Gender*. See also Lipsett-Rivera, "Violencia dentro de las familias formal e informal," 325–327.

81. This all fits the views on the synthetic definition of patriarchy proposed by, for instance, Boyer, "Women, *La Mala Vida*, and the Politics of Marriage," and Stern, *Secret History of Gender*, 21.

82. AANG, Criminales, 39, 12-925, fols. 5v, 27–29.

83. Dore, "One Step Forward, Two Steps Back," 11–12; Premo, *Children of the Father King*, 9–10; Stern, *Secret History of Gender*, 21.

84. AJO, 14, 243, fols. 1–48; AGN, Mexico, Criminales, 42, 15, fols. 426–519; AGN, Mexico, Criminales, 8, fols. 301–357; AGN, Mexico, Criminales, 35, 16, fols. 375–381; AGN, Mexico, Criminales, 46, 3, fols. 86–125; AANG, Guadalajara, Criminales, 57, 12-925; AGN, Mexico, Criminales, 108, 10, fols. 264–277; AANG, Criminales, 24, 9-531, fols. 7–7v.

85. Lipsett-Rivera, "Marriage and Family Relations," 122.

86. Linked to this complaint were allegations that husbands spent all of the family's cash on gambling, drinking, or mistresses. Ibid., 126.

87. Ibid., 131–135; idem, "Violencia dentro de las familias formal e informal"; Mojica Rivadeneira, "El derecho masculino de castigo en la colonia."

88. Taylor, *Drinking, Homicide, and Rebellion*, 96; Stern, *Secret History*, 50–51.

89. AGN, Mexico, Criminales, vol. 33, exp. 2., fols. 43–63, and vol. 113, exp. 2, fols. 51–52; AANG, Guadalajara, Criminales, 18, 8-308; AANG, Guadalajara, Criminales, 10, 1-238.

90. See Chapters 3 and 5 of this text.

91. See Chapter 7 of this text.

92. Kellogg, *Law and the Transformation of Aztec Culture*, chapter 3.

93. For the controversial nature of the Kellogg thesis, see various comments in Schroeder and associates, *Indian Women of Early Mexico*.

CHAPTER THREE

1. For a similar situation in the Portuguese realm, see Hespanha, "De *Iustitia* a Disciplina," 239–242.

2. This gap is also noticeable in Portugal. See Hespanha, "De *Iustitia* a Disciplina," 225.

3. In 1803 the authorities were considering the possibility of including the defendant in a recently issued royal pardon (*indulto*), but since the man was still at large, the pardon could not be granted. AGN, Mexico, Criminales, vol. 29, exp. 6–7, fols. 58–113.

4. Taylor, *Drinking, Homicide, and Rebellion,* 64.

5. "*[C]omo lo dice San Agustín, la embriaguez es 'madre de todos los delitos, materia y raíz y origen de todas las culpas y vicios, turbación de la cabeza, subversión del sentido, borrasca de la lengua, tempestad del cuerpo, naufragio de la castidad, perdida del tiempo, voluntaria locura, enfermedad ignominiosa, torpeza de las costumbres, deshonra de la vida, infamia de la honestidad, corruptela del alma, demonio blando, duro veneno, por el cual no solo comete el hombre innumerables pecados sino que el hombre se constituye todo pecado. . . .*'" See "Expediente sobre el pulque en Antequera de Oaxaca," AGI, Mexico, 872, esp. fols. 41v–42. See also Consejo de Indias, February 2, 1730, letter to the Audiencia de Guadalajara. In AGI, Guadalajara 79, Minutas, reales cédulas y reales provisiones.

6. Taylor, *Drinking, Homicide, and Rebellion,* chapter 2. See also Michael Scardaville, "Alcohol Abuse and Tavern Reform in Late Colonial Mexico City," *Hispanic American Historical Review* 60.4 (1980): 643–671.

7. Scardaville, "Alcohol Abuse and Tavern Reform."

8. Viqueira Albán, *Propriety and Permissiveness in Bourbon Mexico.*

9. As early as the sixteenth and seventeenth century, the Crown issued laws trying to limit consumption of *pulque* and wine. See lib. 6, tit. 1, leyes 36–37, *Recopilación de Leyes de los Reynos de las Indias,* 2: 197–198.

10. For earlier Church complaints, see "Expediente sobre el pulque en Antequera de Oaxaca," AGI, Mexico, 872, esp. fol. 55v. The subsequent desire for tithes is documented in "Pleito entre la Metropolitana de México y los dueños de Magueyes acerca de satisfacción del diezmo de este fruto, 1753," AGI, Mexico, 725.

11. See "Expediente sobre el estanco de aguardiente en el virreinato de Santafe promovido por el Colegio de los Jesuitas de Cartagena de Indias, vistos en el Consejo, 1750–1751." AGI, Santafe, 393.

12. Haslip Vieira, *Crime and Punishment,* 98.

13. Information is lacking for about 36 cases, or 45 percent of the total sample.

14. Taylor, *Drinking, Homicide, and Rebellion,* 96; idem, "Amigos de sombrero," 79.

15. Uribe-Uran, "Colonial Baracunatanas," 52. The Colombian and Spanish cases more closely resemble those of the Mixteca Alta, where, according to Taylor, alcohol-related homicides were much less frequent (13 percent) than in Central Mexico or Jalisco. See Taylor, *Drinking, Homicide, and Rebellion,* 63, 95–96; and "Amigos de sombrero," 79.

16. Taylor, *Drinking, Homicide, and Rebellion,* 95–96.

17. Stern, *Secret History,* 51. Taylor also shows that defendants frequently cited alcohol as the cause of their violent behavior, for drinking was a mitigating factor in sentencing. Taylor, *Drinking, Homicide, and Rebellion,* 64–65.

18. Taylor, *Drinking, Homicide, and Rebellion,* 64.

19. There is ample evidence of official concern over intoxicants. See, for instance, AGN, Colombia, Colonia, Aguardientes, Antioquia, vol. 1, fols. 331–334; AGN, Colombia, Colonia, Aguardientes, Boyacá, vol. 1, fols. 154–155. See also Taylor, *Drinking, Homicide, and Rebellion,* chapter 2; Scardaville, "Alcohol Abuse and Tavern Reform."

20. See Brundage, *Law, Sex, and Christian Society,* 301.

21. Gomezio, *Commentariorum Variarum que Resolutionum Iuris Civilis Communis & Regij,* 3: cap. 1, no. 73, 23.

22. Covarrubia Leiva, *Clementinae, Si Furiosus de Homicidio, Relectio,* 66–79.

23. His precise words were "*Qinta caussa minuendi est ebrietas. regula enim iuris est, + quod omne delictum quantumuis grave, & atrox durante ebrietate commissum non ordinaria poena, des extra ordinem, & mitius punitur, text.*" Farinacii, *Praxis, et Theoricae Criminalis,* 3: 154.

24. Law 5, tit. 8, partida 7, Siete Partidas, in *Códigos Españoles,* 4: 323; law 21, tit. 6, libro 7, *Recopilación de Leyes de los Reynos de las Indias,* 2: 373; AGN, Mexico, Criminales, 50, 16, fol. 413.

25. Elizondo y Álvarez, *Práctica universal forense,* 4: 362.

26. Ibid., 7: 174, 3: 362.

27. AGN, Mexico, Criminales, 29, 6–7, fols. 76, 92, 102.

28. See AGN, Mexico, Criminales, vol. 380, fols. 296–325, esp. fol. 311v.

29. See AGN, Colombia, Negros y Esclavos, Santander, vol. 4, fol. 951.

30. See AGN, Colombia, Criminales, Colonia, vol. 61, fols. 541–651.

31. AGN, Colombia, Criminales, República, vol. 7, fols. 747–893.

32. Elizondo y Álvarez, *Práctica universal forense,* 7: 174, 3: 362.

33. AGS, Gracia y Justicia, legajo 804.

34. ARG, legajo 87, no. 3.

35. Hevia Bolaños, *Curia Filípica,* 2: 211.

36. See AGN, Mexico, Criminales, vol. 33, fols. 43–63.

37. See ARG, Causas, legajo 159, no. 15.

38. For other examples, see ARG, Causas, legajo 118, no. 20. See also the 1814 case against Paulino López in Colima, Mexico. AANG, Guadalajara, Criminales, 10, 1–238.

39. See Gutiérrez, *Compendio de las Varias Resoluciones de Antonio Gómez,* 18.

40. AGN, Colombia, Colonia, Negros y Esclavos, Cundinamarca, vol. IV, fols. 261v–266.

41. See, for instance, the case against mulatto Tomás Aquino, who killed his lover, Maria Ilaria, in Colima, Mexico, in 1809: AANG, Guadalajara, Criminales, 100-9-1525, fols. 30–33. See also the case against Vicente Arroyo for murdering his wife, Maria Guadalupe, in Zacatecas in 1807: AANG, Guadalajara, Criminales, 139-10-2091, fol. 15v.

42. AHN, Madrid, Consejos Suprimidos, libro 1374, fols. 1288–1302.

43. ARG, Sección Causas, legajo 20, no. 34.

44. See, for instance, AHN, Colombia, Criminales, Colonia, vol. 194, fols. 864v–865.

45. Farinacci, *Praxis et Theoricae Criminalis,* 3: 129, 154.

46. See Vilanova y Mañez, *Materia criminal forense,* 3: 35.

47. See Uribe-Uran, "Physical Aggression Against Wives and the Law in Spanish America, 1780s–2000s."

48. AJO, 51, 1499, fols. 24, 27, 36. For similar cases, see AGN, Colombia, Caciques e Indios, vol. 70, fols. 557–607.

49. AGN, Colombia, Caciques e Indios, 9, fols. 343–373. For similar allegations of *alunamiento* in another case, see AGN, Colombia, Caciques e Indios, 70, fols. 582–585.

50. See, for instance, AGN, Colombia, Colonial, Criminales, vol. 158, fols. 586, 607.

51. Gutiérrez, *Compendio de las Varias Resoluciones de Antonio Gómez,* 38.

52. See a detailed discussion of rules of evidence applying to these cases in Gutiérrez, *Compendio de las Varias Resoluciones de Antonio Gómez,* 38.

53. On the contradictory relation between Spaniards and Indians since the sixteenth century, see, for instance, Laura A. Lewis, *Power, Witchcraft and Caste in Colonial Mexico* (Durham: Duke University Press, 2003), esp. 91. See also inconsistencies in the discourse on *limpieza de sangre* relative to native peoples in María-Elena Martínez, *Genealogical Fictions: Limpieza de Sangre, Religion, and Gender in Colonial Mexico* (Stanford: Stanford University Press, 2008), 7.

54. Taylor, "'De corazón pequeño y ánimo apocado,'" esp. 22.

55. The most authoritative discussion is by Castañeda, "La condición miserable del indio y sus privilegios." See also Carlos Sempat Assadourian, "Fray Bartolomé de las Casas, Obispo: La Condicion Miserable de las Naciones Indias y el derecho de la Iglesia (un escrito de 1545)," *Allpanchis* XII, 35–36 (1990): 29–104; Thomas Duve, "Algunas observaciones acerca del *modus operandi* y la prudencia del juez en el derecho canónico indiano," *Revista de Historia del Derecho* 35 (2007): 195–226; idem, "La condición juridica del Indio y su consideración como persona miserabilis en el derecho indiano," in Mario Losano, ed., *Un giudici e due leggi: Pluralismpo normativo e conflitti agrari in Sud-America* (Milano: Universitá degli Studi di Milano, 2004), 3–33; R. H. Helmholz, *The Spirit of Classical Canon Law,* chapter 5, esp. 122, 126; and Caroline Cunill, "El indio miserable: nacimiento de la teoría legal en la América colonial del siglo XVI," *Cuadernos Inter.c.a.mbio* 8.9 (2011): 229–248.

56. See Helmholz, *The Spirit of Classical Canon Law,* chapter 5, esp. 126–129; Cunningham, *The Audiencia in the Spanish Colonies,* 1–31; Borah, *Justice by Insurance,* 12–16, 80–81, 83; Owensby, *Empire of Law and Indian Justice,* 55–56.

57. Helmholz, *The Spirit of Classical Canon Law,* 128–129. On the possible timing of its usage, see Martinez, *Genealogical Fictions,* 103. However, this author is mistaken in referring to the status as "juridical-theological" (104). It was just juridical, but some of it derived from "canon" or ecclesiastical law.

58. See lib. 7, tit. 6, ley 21, and tit. 8, ley 10, *Recopilación de Leyes de los Reynos de las Indias,* 2: 373, 380–381; Solorzano y Pereira, *Politica indiana,* 1: 417–429; Helmholz, *The Spirit of Classical Canon Law,* 116–132; Borah, *Justice by Insurance,* 12–16, 80–81, 83; Cunningham, *The Audiencia in the Spanish Colonies,* 1–31; Owensby, *Empire of Law and Indian Justice,* 55.

59. Martínez, *Genealogical Fictions*, 103. See also Martha Norma Oliveros, "La construcción jurídica del regimen tutelar del Indio," *Revista del Instituto de Historia del Derecho Ricardo Levene* 18 (1967): 105–128; José María Díaz Consuelo, "El Ius Commune y los privilegios de los indigenas en la América española," *Revista de Historia del Derecho* 29 (2001): 267–306, esp. 277–284.

60. Solorzano y Pereyra, *Política indiana*, 1: 427. See also Laura A. Lewis, "The 'Weakness' of Women and the Feminization of the Indian," *Colonial Latin American Review* 5.1 (2006): 73–94.

61. A comprehensive list can be found in Ismael Sánchez Bella, Alberto de la Hera, and Carlos Díaz Rementeria, *Historia del derecho indiano* (Madrid: Mapfre, 1992), 59–60.

62. For a detailed discussion of the "minor" status of Indians, see Premo, *Children of the Father King*, 32–34.

63. AANG, Guadalajara, 26-7-417, fols. 30–30v.

64. See Sanz, *Modo de instruir y substanciar*, 22–24; Gutiérrez, *Compendio de las varias resoluciones*, 15–16. For examples of designation of *curadores*, see AGN, México, Criminales, 29, 6–7, fols. 68–68v, 84; 42, 15, fol. 492; 46, 3, fols. 99–99v, 107; 46, 14, fol. 366v; 50, 16, fols. 264v, 401. On *tutela* and *curaduria* in general, see Asso y del Rio and De Manuel, *Instituciones del derecho civil de Castilla*, 1: 8–34.

65. AANG, Gudalajara, Criminales, 36-8-573, fols. 36–40.

66. See AGN, Californias, vol. 65, case 6, fol. 46v, 248. For other examples, see AGN, Mexico, Criminales, 5, 11, fols. 368, 370; AGN, Mexico, Criminales, vol. 29, exp. 6–7, fols. 58–113. On the use of translators, see Owensby, *Empire of Law and Indian Justice*, 77, 170.

67. See Constantino Bayle, *El protector de Indios* (Sevilla: Escuela de Estudios Hispanoamericanos, 1945); Charles Cutter, *The Protector de Indios in Colonial New Mexico, 1659–1821* (Albuquerque: University of New Mexico Press, 1986); Assadourian, "Fray Bartolomé de las Casas, Obispo," 29–104; Carmen Ruigómez Gómez, *Una política indigenista de los Habsburgo: El Protector de Indios en el Perú* (Madrid: Ediciones de Cultura Hispánica, 1988); Diana Bonnett, *Los protectores de naturales en la Audiencia de Quito: Siglos XVII y XVIII* (Quito: FLACSO, 1992); Javier Ivan Saravia Salazar, "El fiscal protector de Indios en la Audiencia de Lima Siglo XVII: Espacios de poder y arbitrismo," *Nueva Crónica* 1 (January 2013): 1–22; *Recopilación de Indias*, lib. II, tit. v, ley 1; lib. II, tit. xviiii, ley 34–46. On parallels with Rome's *defensor civitates*, see Francisco Cuena Boy, "El defensor civitatis y el protector de indios: Breve ilustración de un paralelo," *Ius Fugit: Revista interdisciplinar de estudios histórico-jurídicos* 7 (1989): 178–196.

68. AGN, Mexico, Criminales, 5, 11, fols. 321, 363v. See lib. 6, tit. 6, laws 1–4, *Recopilación de Indias*, 2: 242–245. See also "Real cedula determinando que la elección y nombramiento de los protectores de indios corresponde al fiscal de la audiencia," *El Pardo*, March 11, 1781, Biblioteca de la Real Academia de Historia, Colección Mata Linares, doc. 7585, vol. CIX, fol. 256.

69. Borah, *Justice by Insurance*.

70. Martinez, *Genealogical Fictions*, 102.

71. Owensby, *Empire of Law and Indian Justice*, chapter 3, 88. See also Andrés González Lira, *El amparo colonial y el juicio de amparo mexicano* (Mexico: FCE, 1972).

72. Cutter, *The Protector de Indios;* Borah, *Justice by Insurance*, 97.

73. AGN, Mexico, Criminales, 50, 16, fol. 432.

74. For references to this *auto,* see AGN, Mexico, Criminales, 41, 7, fols. 127–139; and AGN, Mexico, Criminales, 29, 6–7, fol. 61. On confiscations or embargos as routine procedure, see Berni, *Práctica criminal,* 108–110. A representative example of an Indian whose properties were confiscated can be found in Mexico, AGN, Criminales, 41, 7, fols. 127–139, 140–174.

75. See lib. 7, tit. 6, ley 21, and tit. 8, ley 10, *Recopilación de Indias,* 2: 373, 380–381.

76. AGN, Mexico, Criminales, 50, 16, fol. 413v.

77. "*[S]u calidad es Indio, y estos infelices carecen de unos principios sólidos, de una completa razón, y están faltos de la instrucción necesaria por lo cual consiven* [*sic*] *y obran torpemente.*" AGN, Mexico, Criminales, 42, 15, fol. 493.

78. See AGN, Mexico, Criminales, 140, fols. 188, 226; AGN, Mexico, Californias, 72, fol. 298v; AJO, 51, 1499, fol. 24; AANG, Guadalajara, 26, 7, 417, fol. 33; AGN, Californias, 65, 6, 284, 95; AGN, Mexico, Criminales, 29, 6–7, fols. 75, 101; AGN, Mexico, Criminales, 42, 15, fol. 493; AGN, Mexico, Criminales 46, 14, fol. 372v; AGN, Mexico, Criminales, 63, 8, fols. 413v, 436. See also Owensby, *Empire of Law and Indian Justice,* 176.

79. "*[E]n guerra con sus vecinos, sus parientes y sus mujeres por más que las estimen, de donde viene el abuso entre las Indias quienes no creen que las quieran sus maridos cuando no las maltratan.*"AGN, Mexico, Criminales, 29, 7, fol. 100v.

80. See AANG, Guadalajara, Criminales, 26-7-417, fols. 27–28v.

81. "*[M]uchos lo han hecho [cometer suicidio], lo hace muy factible en el caso el carácter vengativo de estos naturales: cuantas veces no sucede que las indias por tener el torpe gusto de que castiguen a su marido se desoyan ellas mismas, se maltratan el rostro y causan otros daños para dar más crédito y verosimilitud a sus quejas. No hay cosa más común y en el caso no hay dificultad en creer que la Cayetana Justa previendo el perjuicio que con su muerte se seguiría a su marido, quisiese vengarse de este modo [suicidándose] de los azotes de mi parte.*" AGN, Mexico, Criminales, 46, 14, fol. 372v.

82. AGN, Mexico, Criminales, 46, 14, fol. 373.

83. See AANG, Guadalajara, Criminales, 142, 11-2146, fol. 16.

84. AGN, Mexico, Criminales, 50, 16, fols. 436v, 442v; 42, 15, fol. 496v; Cutter, *The Legal Culture of Northern New Spain,* 141.

85. AJO, 14, 243, 1–48; AGN, Mexico, Californias, 72, 293–300; AGN, Mexico, Criminales, 730, 1, 2–30; AGN, Mexico, Criminales, 118, 5, 160–183.

86. Foucault, *Discipline and Punish,* 53. See also Hay, "Property, Authority and the Criminal Law," 40–49. An authoritative discussion of theological and juridical dimensions of various modalities of pardon, its performance, and social function in early modern times can be found in Ottavia Niccoli, *Perdonare.*

Idee, Pratiche, Rituali in Italia tra Cinque e Seicento (Rome-Bari: Editori Laterza, 2007). I thank Tomás Mantecón for this valuable reference.

87. On the king's dual pursuit of fear and love, see Juan López de Cuellar, *Tratado jurídico-político: Práctica de indultos conforme a las leyes y ordenanzas reales de Castilla y Navarra, en que se ponderan los delitos por su gravedad, no comprehendidos y los expresamente exceptuados por las Reales Cédulas de Indultos* (Pamplona, Spain: Por Martín Gregorio de Zabala, impresor del reyno, 1690), 3.

88. Ibid., 96. See also Tomás A. Mantecón, "Criminals and Royal Pardon in Eighteenth Century Spain," *Cahiers de L'Institute d'Anthropologie Juridique* 3 (1999): 477–506, esp. 480; Avila Martel, *Esquema del derecho penal indiano*, 49–52.

89. On the intriguing origin and demise of the "healing touch," see Marc Bloch, *Les rois Thaumaturges: Étude sur le caractère surnaturel attribué à la puissance royale particulièrement en France et en Angleterre* (Paris: Armand Colin, 1961).

90. On the origin and evolution of pardons under the French monarchy, see F. L. Ganshof, "La 'Gratia' des Monarques francs," *Anuario de Estudios Medievales* 3.3 (Barcelona: 1966): 3–26. See also Natalie Zemon Davis, *Fiction in the Archives: Pardon Tales and Their Tellers in Sixteenth-Century France* (Stanford: Stanford University Press, 1987).

91. Concerning evidence of *indultos* since the thirteenth century and *perdones de Viernes Santo* as early as 1447, see, respectively, María Immaculada Rodríguez Flóres, *El perdón real en Castilla (Siglos XIII–XVIII)* (Salamanca: University de Salamanca, 1971), 48; and Ana Isabel Carrasco Manchado, *Isabel I de Castilla y la sombra de la ilegitimidad: Propaganda y representación en el conflicto sucesorio* (Madrid: Siex Ediciones, 2006), 348. For sixteenth- and seventeenth-century *indultos* in Spain, see López de Cuellar, *Tratado jurídico-político*, 4–5; and for these and subsequent centuries, see Tomás y Valiente, *El derecho penal*, 397–407; Rudy Chaulet, "La Violence en Castille au XVIIe Siècle à Travers les *Indultos de Viernes Santo* (1623–1699)," *Crime, Histoire & Sociétés* 1.2 (1997): 5–27; and Olivier Caporossi, "Les Madrilènes Face à la Violence: La Pratique du Pardon Privé Au XVIIe Siècle," *Hispania Sacra*, LX, 121 (2008): 231–266.

92. See Elizondo, *Práctica universal forense*, 5: 267; see also López de Cuellar, *Tratado jurídico-político*, 5.

93. See Alejandra Osorio, *Inventing Lima: Baroque Modernity in Peru's South Sea Metropolis* (New York: Palgrave-Macmillan, 2008); and Alejandro Cañeque, *The King's Living Image: The Culture and Politics of Viceregal Power in Colonial Mexico* (New York: Routledge, 2004).

94. See AGN, Mexico, Criminal, vol. 22, exp. 14, fols. 201–223; AGN, vol. 59, exp. 16, fols. 254–274; AGN, Colombia, Criminales, colonia, vol. 179, fols. 408–435; vol. 2, exp. 2, fols. 748–751.

95. "*[S]u Gobernador y Capitán General . . . pasando el estandarte a su mano, pedido silencio por los reyes de armas, prorrumpió dicho ilustrísimo señor*

presidente diciendo Nueva Galicia, Nueva Galicia, Nueva Galicia, por el Sr. Don Fernando Sexto, rey de Castilla y León y de las Indias, que Dios guarde muy felices! A que le correspondieron los integrísimos senadores y demás que ocupaban el teatro con el Amen, Amen, Viva Viva!, que multiplico todo el concurso y se dio carga cerrada por las compañías que estaban formadas en dicha plaza así del lucido comercio, como del gremio de sastres y naturales Indios de los tres pueblos de San Joseph, San Sebastián de Analco y San Juan de Mixcalzingo: tiraron fuentes de monedas de plata, así por parte del Alférez Mayor Real como de su padrino el Alcalde Ordinario de Primero Voto. Soltaron solemne repique las campanas en todas las iglesias de esta ciudad y pasado rato pidieron atención dichos reyes de armas y el Alférez Mayor Real con el estandarte empuñado hizo su aclamación diciendo en voz alta: Guadalajara, Guadalajara, Guadalajara, por el Sr. Don Fernando Sexto, nuestro Rey y señor natural que Dios Guarde muchos años. Viva, Viva! respondieron a una voz todos y se volvieron a repetir los repiques tiros de fusiles, flechas y monedas." See "Cartas y Expedientes de los Cabildos Seculares," AGI, Guadalajara, 112.

96. Ibid.

97. For such ceremonies in 1747 Mexico and 1794 Peru, see, for example, AGI, Guadalajara, 110; and AGI, Estado, 75, 5. For several later ones in Puerto Rico, described in rich detail, see AHN, Madrid, Ultramar, 8, exp. 19; AHN, Madrid, Ultramar, 2006, exp. 2; AHN, Madrid, Ultramar, 5064, exp. 18. See also Frances Ramos, *Identity, Ritual, and Power in Colonial Puebla* (Tucson: University of Arizona Press, 2012).

98. AGN, Mexico, Criminales, vol. 50, case 16, fols. 254–274.

99. See also AGS, Gracia y Justicia, leg. 875; AGN, Madrid, Reales Cédulas, vol. 119, exp. 29; vol. 119, exp. 92; vol. 123, esp. 71; vol. 126, exp. 62; vol. 127, exp. 11; vol. 132, exp. 178.

100. See copies of the decrees and references to same in APR, Madrid, Sección Histórica, caja 81.

101. Tedorora Gómez Herrero, *Diccionario-guía legislativo español: Comprende todas las disposiciones legales que se han publicado en el siglo XIX* (Madrid: Librería de Don Victoriano Suarez, 1902), vol. 2, pt. 2: 327.

102. AGS, Gracia y Justicia, legajo 875.

103. Gómez Herrero, *Diccionario-guía legislativo español,* vol. 2, pt. 2: 327.

104. AGN, Madrid, Reales Cedulas, vol. 163, exp. 235; vol. 164, exp. 113, fols. 208–209; vol. 165, fols. 167–168; vol. 165A, fols. 106–107.

105. López de Cuellar, *Tratado jurídico-político,* 6–7.

106. See AGN, Madrid, Reales Cedulas, vol. 203, exp. 234; vol. 204, exp. 174; vol. 206, exp. 307. See also APR, Madrid, Sección Histórica, Cuerpos Colegislativos, caja 37, exp. 16; caja 37, exp. 35.

107. "*Indulto general concedido por nuestro católico Monarca, a todos los individuos que sean capaces de él, con el plausible motivo del restablecimiento de nuestra sagrada constitución*" (Madrid: Imprenta de Arjona, 1820).

108. See January 1779 letter titled "Consideraciones acerca de la poca eficacia de los indultos," in APR, Madrid, Sección Histórica, caja 81.

109. AGS, Consejos, Gracia y Justicia, legajo 875.

110. López de Cuellar, *Tratado jurídico-político,* 6–9; Rodríguez Flóres, *El perdón real en Castilla,* 26, 54–58, 82–84, 92.

111. For the role of the Consejo y Cámara and the designation and opinions of its members dealing with pardons, see Antonio Martínez, *Colección de memorias y noticias del gobierno del Consejo* (Madrid: Oficina de Antonio Sanz, 1764), 522–526; APR, Madrid, Sección Histórica, Caja 81. See also Mantecón, "Criminals and Royal Pardon," 485.

112. On crimes typically excluded by royal pardons, see López de Cuellar, *Tratado jurídico-político,* 43–56, 161, 176. See also lib. 8, tit. 25, ley 1, *Recopilación de las Leyes de estos Reynos,* 2: 358v.

113. López de Cuellar, *Tratado jurídico-político,* 19–22.

114. In only a few cases not relevant to this study, the victim's remission was unnecessary. These involved duels (*desafíos*), occasional fights not producing major injuries, and the possession of illegal weapons. See López de Cuellar, *Tratado jurídico-político,* 21.

115. Ibid., 15.

116. On the need for forgiveness by the deceased's immediate relatives, see Francisco Tomás y Valiente, "El perdón de la parte ofendida en el derecho penal castellano (siglos XVI, XVII y XVIII)," *Anuario de Historia del Derecho Español* 31 (Madrid, 1962): 55–114; Rodríguez, *El perdón en Castilla,* 119–140; and Gómez, *Commentariorum Variarum,* 53–55. Noble David Cook and Alexandra Parma Cook have gathered a significant sample of such letters (*cartas de perdón y finiquito*) from sixteenth-century notarial archives in Seville, Spain, and will soon publish their findings. Among them is one issued in September 1603 involving Juan Chávez Vera, found guilty of killing his wife, Doña Isabel de Medina: AHPS, esc. no. 14448. For comparative purposes, see also Zemon Davies, *Fiction in the Archives.* These letters differed from *apartamientos* or private pardons discussed in Caporossi, "Les Madrilènes Face à la Violence," 231–266.

117. APR, Madrid, Sección Histórica, Indultos, caja 81.

118. See other historical and technical comments on these royal graces in López de Cuellar, *Tratado jurídico-político,* 19–25, passim; Elizondo, *Práctica universal forense,* 5: 267–285; and Gutiérrez, *Práctica criminal de España,* 1: 329–347.

119. Interestingly enough, as was also the case for Holy Friday pardons, alcohol played a role in almost half of the cases (11), a circumstance that probably eased concession of the grace.

120. See book 8, tit. 25, law 1, *Recopilación de las Leyes de estos Reynos,* 2: 358v.

121. See, for example, AGN, Mexico, Criminales, 22, 14, 201–223; 44, 12, 303–342; and 50, 16, 254–274.

122. "*[O]tro medio por Donde el rey nuestro señor dispensa los efectos de su real clemencia, pues sus ministros en su augusto nombre dan libertad a los que deben gozar de ella. . . .*" López de Cuellar, *Tratado jurídico-político,* 34–35. See also Alloza, *La vara quebrada de la justicia,* 93–95. Treatises on the subject

were already available in the eighteenth century. See Avila Martel, *Esquema del derecho penal indiano,* 45–47.

123. Ibid, 39.

124. López de Cuellar, *Tratado jurídico-político,* 34–35.

125. AGN, Madrid, Consejos, book 1395, fols. 1024–1027.

126. AGN, Mexico, Carceles y Presidios, vol. 28, exp. 93, fol. 258; vol. 28, exp. 94, fols. 259–259v.

CHAPTER FOUR

1. See "Mercedes concedidas con motivo de la exaltación al trono del Rey Don Carlos IV: Su entrada en Madrid, celebración de Cortes Generales y jura de Don Fernando Príncipe de Asturias," *Revista Hidalguía* LIII, 319 (2006): 835–874, esp. 845.

2. Spierenburg, *A History of Murder,* 8, 116, 120. See also Anton Blok, *Honor and Violence* (Cambridge: Polity, 2001), 173–209; Bennassar, *The Spanish Character,* 216.

3. See a discussion of these marriage-related notions in Patricia Seed, *To Love, Honor and Obey in Colonia Mexico.*

4. Tomás A. Mantecón emphasizes the centrality of honor and verbal crimes against it in a considerable portion of Spain in "The Patterns of Violence in Early Modern Spain," *Journal of the Historical Society* 7.2 (2007): 229–289, esp. 238, 241.

5. For a list of its members in the year 1797, see *Kalendario manual y guia de forasteros en Madrid para el año 1797* (Madrid: Biblioteca Nacional de España, 1797), 76–77.

6. On the history of this institution and its power, see Angel González Palencia, ed., *Archivo Historico Nacional. Consejo de Castilla. Sala de Alcaldes de Casa y Corte.* Catalogo por Materias (Madrid, 1925), xviii–xix. See also Alloza, *La vara quebrada de la justicia,* 31–46.

7. See Meléndez Valdés, *Discursos Forenses.*

8. AHN, Madrid, Consejos, Alcaldes de Casa y Corte, legajo 9344, no folio. See also "Acusación Fiscal contra Don Santiago de N. y Dona María Vicenta de F., reos del parricidio alevoso de Don Francisco del Castillo, Marido de la Dona María, pronunciadas el día 28 de Marzo de 1798 en la sala segunda de Alcaldes de Corte," in Meléndez Valdés, *Discursos Forenses,* 1–43.

9. AHN, Madrid, Consejos, Alcaldes de Casa y Corte, legajo 9344, no folio.

10. Ibid.

11. Meléndez Valdés, *Discursos Forenses,* 1–4; idem, "Discurso sobre los grandes frutos que debe sacar la provincia de Extremadura de su nueva Real Audiencia . . . 27 abril 1791," *Discursos Forenses,* 229–271, esp. 249–250; Georges Demerson, *Don Juan Meléndez Valdés y su tiempo (1754–1817),* 2 vols. (Madrid: Taurus, 1971), vol. 1, chapter 9.

12. On the meaning of *apremios* at the time, see José Luís Bermejo Cabrero, "Tormentos, apremios, cárceles y patibulos a finales del antiguo régimen," *Anuario de Historia del Derecho Español* 56 (1986): 683–727, esp. 685–696.

13. Manuel de Lardizábal y Uribe, *Discurso sobre las penas contrahido a las leyes criminales de España para facilitar su reforma* (Madrid: por Joachin Ibarra, 1782), esp. 115–136; Demerson, *Don Juan Meléndez Valdés y su tiempo,* vol. 1, chapter 9.

14. See, as an example, the views of University of Seville theology and law professor Pérez y López, *Principios del orden esencial,* 258–262.

15. The mockery of ignorant cuckolds was a standard theme of the picaresque narrative and continued to draw the attention of even enlightened Spaniards. See Bennassar, *The Spanish Character,* 216, 231.

16. The Sala de Alcaldes de Casa y Corte required the demonstration of "*hidalguia o empleo no bajo*" and for the sake of the "family's honor" commuted hanging and granted the garrote. See AGS, Gracia y Justicia, legajo 804.

17. In 1809, Napoleonic rule no longer required proof of nobility or decent occupation for execution by garrote. See AHN, Madrid, Consejos, Copia del Real Decreto Aboliendo la Pena de Horca y Acuerdos de la Sala con Motivo de la anterior disposición, 1809, fols. 863–875 (p. 406), libro 1400 (9). This trend actually started decades earlier. See AHN, Madrid, Consejos, book 1338, fols. 44–45, 121–123; AGN, Madrid, Consejos, legajo 9344, part. 2, doc. 15, "Causa contra Antonio Pérez por la muerte violenta que dió a Águeda Leal en 1806." Petitions of this sort had been common since at least the mid-eighteenth century, and the king usually granted them after hearing the opinion of the Alcaldes de Casa y Corte. See, for instance, the case of Manuel de Aionejar and Maria Beguillas in October 1753 for the killing of the woman's husband, the case of Juan Gonzalez Rivero for an undetermined crime in May 1760, and a 1765 petition by spousal murderer Catalina Diaz, AGS, Gracia y Justicia, legajo 804.

18. AGS, Gracia y Justicia, legajo 804; Bennassar, *The Spanish Character,* 230.

19. AHN, Madrid, Madrid, Consejos Suprimidos, legajo 9344, caso 8, no folio.

20. See "Leyes de las Siete Partidas," ley 12, titulo 8, partida 7.

21. Granting decoration with *blandones* was a special prerogative recorded in several instances as early as the 1750s. See AHN, Madrid, Consejos, libro 1338.

22. AHN, Madrid, Consejos Suprimidos, legajo 9344, caso 8; libro 1388, fols. 411–429; "Acusación Fiscal contra Don Santiago de N. y Doña María Vicenta de F. . .," 1–43.

23. Poska, *Women and Authority in Early Modern Spain,* 7–9 and chapter 3. See also Margarita Ortega López, "Protestas de las mujeres castellanas contra el orden patriarcal privado durante el siglo XVIII," *Cuadernos de Historia Moderna* 19 (1997): 65–89.

24. See AHN, Consejos, libro 1390, fols. 74–96.

25. The list of "historical regions" includes Andalusia, Aragon, Asturias, the Balearic and Canary Islands, Old and New Castile, Extremadura, Galicia, León, Murcia, Navarra, Valencia, and the Basque country. This is a loosely defined term used in authoritative pieces such as the informative demographic study by

Fausto Dopico and Robert Roland, "Demografía del censo de Floridablanca: Una aproximación," *Revista de Historia Económica* 3.8 (1990): 591–618.

26. Though long, the list is worth quoting. It includes Alava, Aragón, Asturias, Avila, the Balearic Islands (Mallorca, Menorca, Ibiza, and Formentera), Burgos, the Canary Islands, Catalonia, Córdoba, Cuenca, Extremadura, Galicia, Granada, Guadalajara, Guipúzcoa, Jaén, La Mancha, León, Madrid, Murcia, Navarra, Nuevas Poblaciones, Palencia, Salamanca, Segovia, Seville, Soria, Toledo, Toro, Valencia, Valladolid, Vizcaya, and Zamora. See January 10, 1810, "Convocatoria para las ciudades de voto en Cortes."

27. The 1749 *Ordenanza para el Restablecimiento e Instrucción de Intendentes de Provincia y Exercito* revived the figure of *intendente,* which had fallen into disuse after being introduced originally in 1718. The *intendente* was the highest authority in his jurisdiction and the exclusive judge on tax matters. His decisions were subject to appeal directly before the king. He also had control over all of the administrators and tax farmers in his territory, and over the accountant and provincial treasurer of the local treasure (*caja provincial*). Concerning justice administration, the *intendente* acted as *corregidor,* assisted by *alcaldes mayores.*

28. José María de Zuaznavar y Francia, "*Noticias para literatos acerca de los archivos públicos de la hoy extinguida Sala de Alcaldes de Casa y Corte.*" San Sebastian: Ignacio Ramon Barója, 1834. BNE, manuscript 1/3475, 4; AHN, Madrid, Consejos, libro 1390, fols. 74–96.

29. Aragon (Zaragoza), Asturias (Oviedo), Catalonia (Barcelona), the Canary Islands (Palma), Extremadura (Cáceres), Granada, Galicia (La Coruña), Mallorca (Palma de Mallorca), Seville, Valencia (Valencia), and Valladolid all had *reales audiencias.*

30. A detailed census compiled by Zenón de Somodevilla y Bengoechea, better known as the Marqués de la Ensenada (1702–1781), a dedicated, tax-hungry bureaucrat who served as King Ferdinand VI's minister of fiscal affairs (*hacienda*).

31. The Catastro del Marqués de la Ensenada, a valuable source of historical information, details, town by town, village by village, and location by location, the shape of local society at the time, the main crops cultivated, whether or not hospitals and jails were available, what kind of taxes were paid and to whom, etc.

32. See, for instance, Massimo Livi Bacci, "Fertility and Nuptiality Changes in Spain from the Late Eighteenth to the Early Twentieth Century: Part 1," *Population Studies* 22.1 (1968): 83–102. The most highly regarded of these counts is Floridablanca's 1780s census.

33. Livi Bacci, "Fertility and Nuptiality Changes in Spain," passim.

34. See, for instance, how difficult it was to travel from Austurias to neighboring Leon in 1760. AGS, Gracia y Justicia, legajo 861.

35. Antonio Dominguez Ortíz, *Sociedad y estado en el Siglo XVIII español* (Barcelona: Editorial Ariel, 1976), 202.

36. For a detailed province-by-province list of industrial establishments and workshops by 1770, see "Estado y noticia general de las fábricas de sedas, paños, bayetas, sombreros, curtidos y otros géneros," *Correo General de España* no. 1, February 2, 1769; no. 2, February 9, 1769; no. 3, February 16, 1769; no. 4, February 23, 1769; no. 5, March 2, 1770.

37. This is the place where one of our culprits, a rural landowner by the last name of Escudero García, met his future lover Teresa Ballesteros, likely during a trip with his herd of sheep in wintertime.

38. "Estado y noticia general de las fábricas. . . ."

39. That occurred with the murder by a *fabrica* smelter, Andres Corral, of his wife, Juliana Nogues, also an employee, in December 1799. AHN, Madrid, Consejos, libro 1390, fols. 74–96. More on the *fabrica* and the *fuero* can be found in María Dolores Villaverde Sastre, "La real fábrica de paños y la ciudad de Guadalajara," *Wad-aL-Hayara: Revista de Estudios de Guadalajara* 8 (1981): 453–468, esp. 461–464.

40. On the treatment of gypsies, see Alloza, *La vara quebrada de la justicia,* 233–238. On the meaning and evolution of *limpieza de sangre* (absence of Jewish and heretical traces), see Martínez, *Genealogical Fictions.*

41. The data in this section come from the Floridablanca Census, published by Spain's National Statistics Institute (INE), www.ine.es/censo2001/florida.htm.

42. Some are developed in Bennassar, *The Spanish Character.*

43. Ibid., 213; Taylor, *Honor and Violence in Golden Age Spain,* chapters 2 and 3.

44. Mantecón, *Conflictividad y disciplinamiento social,* 34–64.

45. AHN, Madrid, Consejos, libro 2793, "Inventario general de las Causas criminales que se Hallan en el Archivo de la Sala," Sres. Alcaldes de Casa y Corte de S.M. fecho por su mandato. Tomo 11. Incluye desde el año 1770 hasta el de 1789. AHN Madrid, Consejos, libro 2793; Alloza, *La vara quebrada de la justicia,* 111–115, 124, 148, 190.

46. This coincides in general terms with other research on late eighteenth-century Spanish crime. For instance, of more than 2,200 crimes in the entire kingdom, 35.6 percent were crimes against life and physical integrity, 31.5 percent against property, 19.5 percent against public order, and 6.8 percent against public morality. See José-Miguel Palop Ramos, "Delitos y penas en la España del siglo XVIII," *Estudis: Revista de Historia Moderna* 22 (1996): 65–103, esp. 67. Approximately the same percentages applied for cases pending trial in 1791 in Trujillo, Extremadura. In a sample of 176 criminal cases, close to 40 percent were crimes of violence (including slander), about 28 percent crimes against property, around 8 percent sexual crimes, and about 8 percent more escapes from prison and the illegal carrying of weapons. See Isabel Pérez Muñoz, "Conflictividad social y administración de justicia en el partido de Trujillo: 1791," in *Coloquios Históricos de Extremadura,* 1993 (www.chde.org/index.php?option=com_content&view=article&id=703:conflictividad-social-y-administracion-de-justicia-en-el-partido-de-trujillo-1791&catid=43:1993&Itemid=60). However, a different pattern can be observed in a sample from the Canary Islands in 1786: Of 81 crimes, 26 percent were cases of homicide or injury, 22 percent crimes against property, 9 percent assorted crimes, and an unusually high 41 percent crimes against "dominant sexual morality." See Jose-Miguel Palop Ramos, "Notas sobre la criminalidad en Canarias a finales del siglo XVIII," in *Seminario de Humanidades Agustín Millares Carlo: Homenaje de Bethencourt Massieu,* 3 vols. (Las Palmas: Ediciones del Cabildo Insular de Canaria, 1995), 3: 1–10. For the claim that crimes against

property increased while crimes against physical integrity, in particular homicide, decreased in the eighteenth century, see Tomás A. Mantecón, "The Patterns of Violence in Early Modern Spain," *Journal of the Historical Society* 7.2 (2007): 229–264. See also Alloza, *La vara quebrada de la justicia,* 149, 156.

47. See Tomás Mantecón, "La violencia marital en la corona de Castilla durante la edad moderna," in *Familia, transmisión y perpetuación (siglos XVI–XIX)*, ed. Antonio Yrigoyen López and Antonio L. Pérez Ortiz (Murcia: Universidad de Murcia, 2002), 19–55, esp. 20, 44, 45.

48. This calculation comes from the sample of crimes listed in the ARG, Indice Topográfico Cronológico, sección 7, serie causas I—años 1762–1835. An essay on similar crimes in seventeenth-century Madrid reports 64 spousal murders between 1580 and 1700, an estimated 3.8 percent of total homicides in the region. See Llanes Parra, "El enemigo en casa," 3.

49. This corresponds to an increase in crimes of physical, homicide, and verbal aggression in Cantabria and Galicia during the critical years of the crisis of the ancien regime and in the context of the war of independence. See Mantecón, "Civilizacion y brutalización," 115–117.

50. The research for this book, as explained in the introduction, comprised the historical archives of Valladolid, Seville, Galicia, Granada, Extremadura, and Valencia, more than half of the royal *audiencias* in existence at the end of the eighteenth century. Criminal records for our period in the Kingdom of Aragon's Real Audiencia de Zaragoza seem to have been destroyed during the war of independence's second siege of Zaragoza in 1808. Records for the Balearic Islands Audiencia, in the city of Mallorca, were also almost entirely destroyed in an undetermined way. As for the Audiencia of Asturias in Oviedo, about half the records were destroyed in the mid-nineteenth century, and most of the rest were consumed by a fire in 1934. The National Archive records corresponding to Madrid's Alcaldes de Casa y Corte, charged with investigating crimes in the kingdom's capital; the records of the Gracia y Justicia Section of the Archivo General de Simancas, which contain evidence of royal pardons granted to various criminals during Holy Week; and the information on local crime in provincial archives in Cádiz, Córdoba, and Segovia served as supplementary evidence. Finally, criminal archives suffered major losses throughout Spain as a result of cleaning or *expurgos* authorized by the government to free up space in overcrowded provincial archives and also in the national one in Madrid, where all criminal cases prior to 1700 were sold as paper. Zuaznavar y Francia, *Noticias para literatos,* 4, 6; Simó Rodríguez, "Fondos judiciales en los archivos históricos provinciales," 35; idem, "El Archivo de la Real Audiencia de Extremadura," 661–665; Vicente Vignau y Ballester, "Discurso Del Sr. D. Vicente Vignau y Ballester," en Archivo Histórico Nacional, *Discursos leidos ante la real Academia de la Historia en la recepción Pública del Sr. Vicente Vignau y Ballester el día 18 de Junio de 1898* (Madrid: Tip. Viuda e Hijos de Tello, 1898), 5–38, esp. 24–29.

51. For representative cases of distinguished aristocrats accused of abusing their spouses physically and psychologically, see the 1795 "confidential" (*reservada*) dispute between the Countess of Robledon and her husband (AGS, Gracia y Justicia,

legajo 863) and the 1805 accusations against the Count of Campogiro for allegedly trying to poison his wife and brother-in-law (AGN, Madrid, Consejos, libro 1395, fols. 522–539).

52. ARG, Sección Causas, legajo 5, no. 23.

53. Ibid., legajo 18, no. 10.

54. See AHPC, Cáceres, Sección Criminal, caja 608, exp. 189, against José García for mistreating his wife, Celestina Perdices, in the town of Azuaga, 1799; caja 668, exp. 54, against José María Dávila for mistreating his wife in the town of Arroyomolinos, 1799. For other examples, see caja 608, exp. 250, against Manuel Prim for mistreating his wife, Antonia Rozo, Trujillo, 1799; caja 605, exp. 145, against Joaquin Fernández for mistreating his wife, Claudia López, Guadalupe, 1799; caja 668, exp. 34, against Pedro Silva for mistreating his wife, María del Carmen Rodríguez, San Lorenzo, 1799; and caja 603, exp. 113, against José Parra for mistreating his wife, Francisca J. Castellanos, Villa de Brosas, 1816.

55. Several examples for the years 1751 and 1752 are in the ARV, Sección Alcalde Mayor Criminal, Alcalde Ordinario, cajas 6/9, 6/96, 6/100, 7/113, and 8/138.

56. For instance, in April 1752 a couple had various clashes (*diferentes quimeras*) over reports that the husband, a man named Manuel Prats Micuceo, was having an affair with another man's wife. ARV, Sección Alcalde Mayor Criminal, Alcalde Ordinario, caja 8/124.

57. ARCV, Pleitos Criminales, caja 131, exp. 2. For a similar case of a wife killing her husband, see ARCV, Pleitos Criminales, caja 5, exp. 6. For cases of domestic aggression in Cantabria for which Valladolid served as an appeals court, see Mantecón, *Conflictividad y disciplinamiento social,* 63–64.

58. The *botero* manufactured leather containers to store wine, vinegar, and oil.

59. Yanguas belonged to the province of Soria in Spain's Castile and León region. In the 1780s, the *intendencia* of Soria was larger than the current province of Soria, whose borders were set in 1833.

60. AGS, "Catastro de Ensenada, Respuestas Generales, Villa de Yanguas and Lugar de Vizmános," books 584 and 606, fols. 92–93.

61. On the history of sanctuary for criminals, see Uribe-Uran, "'*Iglesia me llamo,*'" 446–472.

62. See Pérez Baltasar, "Origenes de los recogimientos de mujeres," 13–23; idem, *Mujeres Marginadas.*

63. ARCV, Pleitos Criminales, caja 270, exp. 2.

64. AHN, Madrid, Consejos Suprimidos, libro 1374, fols. 1288–1302. A similar claim can be found in cases tried in colonial Colombia. See, for instance, AHN, Colombia, Criminales, Colonia, vol. 194, fols. 864v–865.

65. ARCV, Causas Criminales, caja 202, exp. 2.

66. Ibid., caja 245, exp. 2.

67. ARG, Sección Causas, legajo 187, no. 3.

68. Ibid., legajo 322, no. 6.

69. This "seems to have been more prevalent in literature than in reality." See Poska, *Women and Authority in Early Modern Spain,* 7.

70. A recent invitation to debunk the honor–shame myth is found in Poska, *Women and Authority,* 7–9.

71. Defourneaux, *Daily Life in Spain During the Golden Age,* 146–148; Bennassar, *The Spanish Character,* 180.

72. Ibid., 196.

73. Ibid., 198.

74. Taylor, *Honor and Violence,* esp. chapter 6. Related works have also focused on the deflowering of women as the most dominant manifestation of crimes against honor. See Barahona, *Sex Crimes, Honour and the Law in Early Modern Spain.*

75. As an example, in Galicia there were more cases in which a husband denounced his wife's adultery than killed her. Several examples from 1801, 1806, and 1819 can be found in ARG, Causas, legajo 15, no. 33; legajo 34, no. 13; legajo 118, no. 40; legajo 157, no. 62. For additional examples, see AGN, Madrid, Consejos, libro 2793, fols. 373–374v.

76. See the classical work by Stroud, *Fatal Union: A Pluralistic Approach to the Spanish Wife-Murder Comedias.* A more recent rendering can be found in Taylor, *Honor and Violence in Golden Age Spain,* esp. chapter 6; and Poska, *Women and Authority,* 7–9.

77. Bennassar, *The Spanish Character,* 180.

78. Ibid., 213. See also Mantecón, *Conflictividad y disciplinamiento social,* 68–83.

79. Bennassar, *The Spanish Character,* 214–216, 223–231. On the origins and evolution of honor as a social value, see also Defourneaux, *Daily Life in Spain,* 32–36; and García Valdescasas, *El hidalgo y el honor.* On honor, nobility, and trade, see as well William J. Callahan, *Honor, Commerce and Industry in Eighteenth Century Spain* (Boston: Baker Library, Harvard Graduate School, 1972). For comparisons of honor and gender in Spanish America, see Seed, *To Love, Honor, and Obey,* esp. chapters 6 and 9; Ann Twinam, "Honor, Sexuality and Illegitimacy in Colonial Spanish America," in *Sexuality and Marriage in Colonial Latin America,* ed. Asunción Lavrin (Lincoln: University of Nebraska Press, 1989), 118–155; Gutiérrez, *When Jesus Came, the Corn Mothers Went Away,* chapters 5–8; Stern, *The Secret History of Gender,* 13–17; and Lyman Johnson and Sonya Lipsett-Rivera, eds., *The Faces of Honor,* passim.

80. Bennassar, *The Spanish Character,* 233–234; see also Spierenburg, *A History of Murder,* 8, 116, 120. Abundant examples of such situations in the sixteenth century can be found in Iñaki Bazán, "La pena de muerte en la Corona de Castilla en la Edad Media," *Clio & Crimen* 4 (2007): 306–352, esp. 311–315.

81. Poska, *Women and Authority in Early Modern Spain,* 7.

82. Bennassar, *The Spanish Character,* 235.

83. For widespread behaviors contrary to the alleged honor code in Spanish America, see Twinam, *Private Secrets, Public Lives.*

84. See ADC, leg. 1841, exp. 3; and ARG, Sección Causas, legajo 246, no. 1.

CHAPTER FIVE

1. See Ernst H. Kantorowicz, *The King's Two Bodies: A Study in Medieval Political Theology* (Princeton: Princeton University Press, 1997 [1957]); Kenneth Pennington, *The King and the Law, 1200-1600: Sovereignty and Rights in the Western Legal Tradition* (Berkeley: University of California Press, 1993); Berman, *Law and Revolution;* Giorgio Agamben, *The Kingdom and the Glory: For a Theological Genealogy of Economy and Government* (Stanford: Stanford University Press, 2011).

2. In the kingdoms of Aragon and Valencia, sodomy was under the jurisdiction of the Holy Inquisition. In Castile it was investigated by the royal courts. See Alloza, *La vara quebrada de la justicia,* 193.

3. Rodríguez Flóres, *El perdón real en Castilla;* Roberto J. González Zalacain, "El perdón real en Castilla: Una fuente privilegiada para el estudio de la criminalidad y la conflictividad social a fines de la Edad Media," *Clio & Crimen* 8 (2011): 289–352, esp. 309; idem, *El perdón real en Castilla a fines de la Edad Media: El ejemplo de la Cornisa Cantábrica* (Bilbao: Servicio Editorial de la Universidad del País Vasco UPV/EHU, 2013).

4. After Maria left her home, totally beaten up, Peña went back to check if she had died, in which case he would seek refuge at a nearby church ("*y en tal caso refugiarse en la iglesia*"). See AANG, Guadalajara, Criminales, 131, 1, 978, fols. 6–6v.

5. For an extensive comparative article that is the source of portions of this chapter, see Uribe-Uran, "'*Iglesia me llamo*': Church Asylum and the Law in Spain and Colonial Spanish America," 446–472.

6. Examples of the utterance can be found in literary and judicial narratives. See, for instance, the seventeenth-century Spanish novel by Diego Duque de Estrada, *Comentarios del desengañado de si mismo, vida del mismo autor,* edited and with an introduction and notes by Henry Ettinghausen (Madrid: Clásicos Castalia, 1982 [c. 1640s.]), 156–161. Several judicial cases in early eighteenth-century Cádiz are cited in the excellent case study by Morgado García, *Derecho de asilo y delincuencia en la diocesis de Cádiz,* 33, 38. Colonial Mexican judicial cases from the late eighteenth century also include frequent references to *asilo;* see AGI, Guadalajara, 158; AGI, Guadalajara, 402.

7. Hevia Bolaños, *Curia Philipica,* III parte, par. 12, "*retraídos.*"

8. MNA, Mexico, Subdirección de Documentación, Serie Oaxaca, reel 14, no folio.

9. Fernando González de Socueba, *Instrucción Manual para la más breve expedición de los casos prácticos y disputas de inmunidad local: Noticia histórica de su origen, progresos y estado* (Sevilla: Imprenta del Doctor Don Gerónymo de Castilla, 1766), 92–95; Pierre Timbal-Duclaux de Martin, *Le droit d'asile* (Paris: Librairie du Recueil Sirey, 1939), 150–151.

10. For a religious perspective, see López de Cuellar, *Tratado jurídico-político.* For a well-documented, contemporary practical manual and history written from a royalist perspective, see González de Socueba, *Instrucción Manual.*

11. In 1864, asserting that it formed part of the *ius divinum,* one of Pope Pius IX's Syllabus of Errors condemned the view that ecclesiastical immunity was civil

in origin. See R. H. Helmholz, "The Law of Sanctuary," in idem, *The Ius Commune in England* (Oxford: Oxford University Press, 2001), 16–80, esp. 18.

12. Among the Greeks and especially the Romans, temples, altars, and statues of the emperor were places of refuge. When Christianity became the state religion, the emperor extended the right of sanctuary to churches. Authoritative discussions of the origin of asylum among the Hebrews and in Greece and Rome can be found in Timbal-Duclaux de Martin, *Le droit d'asile,* part 1; Ken J. Rigsby, *Asylia: Territorial Inviolability in the Hellenistic World* (Berkeley: University of California Press, 1996); Charles de Beaurepaire, "Essai sur l'asile Religieux dans l'Empire Romain et la Monarchie Francaise," *Bibliotheque de l'Ecole de Chartes* 14 (1853): 351–375; 15 (1853): 151–175, 341–359; Anne Ducloux, "L'Eglise, l'asile et l'aide aux condamne´s d'apres la constitution du 27 juillet 398," in *Revue d'Histoire du Droit Français et Etranger* 69 (1991): 141–176; Norman Maclaren Trenholme, "The Right of Sanctuary in England: A Study in Institutional History," *University of Missouri Studies* 1.5 (1903): 1–106, esp. 4–9; Luis Redonet y López-Doriga, "Nacimiento del derecho de asilo," *Discursos Leídos ante la Real Academia de la Historia* (Madrid: Imprenta Viuda e Hijos de Jaime Rates, 1928), 10–88; and Gab. Le Bas, "Asile," *Dictionnaire d'histoire et de Géographie Ecclésiastiques,* vol. 4 (1912), 1036–1048. Anne Ducloux discusses asylum's origin in Christian churches in *Ad ecclesiam Confugere: Naissance du droit d'asile dans les eglises (IVe- milieu du Ve. S.)* (Paris: De Boccard, 1994), 5–25, passim. For a discussion of some of the Roman laws on the subject, see Timbal Duclaux de Martin, *Le droit d'asile,* 77, 119, 135; Michel Fixot and Elisabeth Zadora-Rio, "Introduction: La topographie des lieux d'asile dans les campagnes médiévales," in *L'Eglise, le terroir,* eds. Fixot and Zadora-Rios (Paris: Editions du CNRS, 1989), 11.

13. See L. R. Misserey, "Asile en Occident," *Dictionnaire de Droit Canonique* 1 (1935): 1089–1104, esp. 1090.

14. For its presence in King Gundemaro's 610 law and in seventh-century church councils, see the well-documented study by Rafael Olaechea, "Anotaciones sobre la inmunidad local en el siglo XVIII español," *Miscelanea Comillas* 46 (July–December 1966): 296–381, esp. 324.

15. Ruth J. Macrides, "Killing, Asylum and the Law in Bizantium," *Speculum* 63 (1988): 509–538. See also E. Herman, "Asile Dans l'Eglise Oriental," in *Dictionnaire de Droit Canonique* 1 (1935): 1084–1089.

16. On local *fueros,* see Rafael Serra Ruíz, *El derecho de asilo en los castillos fronterizos de la reconquista* (Murcia, Spain: Patronato de Cultura, 1965), 29–46, passim.

17. See laws 1–4, title 1, book 10, Fuero Juzgo, in *Códigos españoles,* 1: 179.

18. See laws 7–8, title 5, book 1, and law 15, title 20, book 3, Fuero Real, both in *Códigos españoles* 1: 353–401.

19. AGN, Mexico, Californias, vol. 65, case 2, fol. 251.

20. See laws 1–5, title 11, partida 1, in *Códigos españoles* 2: 210–215; José María Ortuño Sánchez Pedreño, "El derecho de asilo en iglesias y sus cementerios

en la legislación de Partidas," *Glossae: Revista de Historia del Derecho Europeo* 5–6 (1993–1994): 187–193.

21. Law 6, title 2, book 1, *Ordenanzas Reales de Castilla por las cuales primeramente se han de librar todos los pleitos civiles y criminales* (Toledo: En casa de Juan de Ayala, 1549), ii. See also Socueba, *Instrucción Manual,* 97–100.

22. See Uribe-Uran, "'*Iglesia me llamo,*'" 454–457.

23. Laws 1–3, title 2, book 1, *Recopilación de leyes de estos reynos* 1: 5.

24. See Morgado García, *Derecho de asilo y delincuencia en la diócesis de Cádiz,* 62–65.

25. Gonzalo Fernández de Oviedo, *Historia General y Natural de las Indias,* 5 vols. (Madrid: Biblioteca de Autores Españoles, 1959) 3: 277 [corresponds to book 9, second part, chapter 17, of the original edition].

26. This provision was later incorporated into the *Recopilación de las Leyes de Indias.* See title 5, book 1. See, for instance, another incident tried in Mariquita, central New Granada, in 1603: AGN, Colombia, Criminales, 25, D. 15.

27. Catalina de Erauso, *Lieutenant Nun: Memoir of a Basque Transvestite in the New World.* Trans. Michele Stepto and Gabriel Stepto (Boston: Beacon, 1996), 3, 11, 14–15, 22–25, 45–47, 55–57.

28. For a detailed analysis, see Elizabeth Howard West, "The Right of Asylum in New Mexico in the Seventeenth and Eighteenth Centuries," *Hispanic American Historical Review* 8.3 (1928): 357–391, esp. 362.

29. See all the laws in title 5, book 1, *Recopilación de las Leyes de Indias;* Tomás de Aquino García y García, *El derecho de asilo en Indias* (Madrid: Editorial Reus, 1930), 35–40.

30. AGN, Mexico, Californias, vol. 675, case 6, fols. 241–301; ibid., vol. 65, case 8, fols. 335–370; AGN, Provincias Internas, vol. 6, fols. 44–85. See also West, "The Right of Asylum in New Mexico."

31. See Gómez, *Commentariorum Variarum que Resolutionum Iuris Civilis Communis & Regij,* 3: chapter 10, 73–75, esp. 73v; Covarrubias Leiva, *Variarum ex Iure Pontificio, Regio, & Caesareo Resolutionum,* book II, chapter 20, 156v–64, esp. 164.

32. ARCV, Spain, caja 245, exp. 2, fols. 76, 86, 199.

33. Castillo de Bobadilla, *Política para corregidores y señores de vasallos,* 1: 422–423, book 2, chapter 14, no. 93.

34. Hevia Bolaños, *Curia Philipica,* III parte, par. 12, "retraídos."

35. Doctrinal commentaries continued to be published between the sixteenth and eighteenth centuries. See, for instance, Antonio de Aguilar Mendivil, *Manifestación jurídica sobre el derecho de inmunidad y sagrado de las iglesias y monasterios* (Murcia, Spain: 1688).

36. González de Socueba, *Instrucción manual,* 4–5, 101–103, passim.

37. AGS, Gracia y Justicia, legajo 804; AGN, Madrid, Consejos, libro 2793, fol. 16.

38. Elizondo, *Práctica universal forense,* 1: 260–285.

39. On various attempts at reform, see Uribe-Uran, "'*Iglesia me llamo,*'" 467–469.

40. AGI, Guadalajara, 402; AGI, Guadalajara, 158.

41. AGI, Panama, 196.

42. For examples from the eighteenth century, see AGI, Panama, 196; AGI, Guadalajara, 100; AGI, Guadalajara, 158, fols. 3–203; AGI, Guadalajara, 402; AGI, Guadalajara, 404; AGI, Mexico, 682; BRAH, Madrid, Colección Benito de la Mata Linares, 1672, fols. 115–116, 203–371.

43. See, for instance, AGI, Guadalajara, 402 and 404; AGN, Mexico, Criminal, vol. 2, 33, 112; AGN, Mexico, Californias, vol. 65, cases 6 and 8; AJO, vols. 31 and 32, cases 937 and 951; AGN, Colombia, Criminales, Colonia, vols. 43, fols. 996–1000; vol. 44, fols. 1–262; vol. 95, fols. 380–499.

44. AGI, Indiferente, 3025.

45. Under the law, escaped prisoners were not eligible for asylum, but the evidence suggests that they sometimes received this benefit anyway. See AGN, Mexico, Criminal, vol. 2, case 2, fols. 31–69; ARCV, box 270, case 2. On the exclusion of these cases, see Miguel Cayetano Sánz, *Modo y forma de instruir y substanciar las causas criminales* (Madrid: Imprenta de Don Joseph Doblado, 1790), 32–44. Elizondo, among others, suggested that all *parricidas,* spousal murderers included, were excluded from asylum, yet in practice they were not. Some contemporary prosecutors shared his opinion. See Elizondo, *Práctica universal forense,* 1: 284; Mexico, AGN, Criminal, 8, fols. 354–355.

46. AGI, Guadalajara, 402.

47. Ibid.

48. For a review of picaresque novels and asylum, see Uribe-Uran, "'*Iglesia me llamo,*'" 454–457.

49. AGI, Indiferente, 3025.

50. "Memoria que el Virrey Carlos Francisco de Croix dejo a Don Fray Antonio María de Bucareli y Ursua, 1-IX-1771," in *Instrucciones y memorias de los virreyes novohispanos* (México: Editorial Porrúa, 1991) 2: 954–1008, esp. 960–961.

51. AGI, Guadalajara, 402.

52. For the story and character of this tribunal, see MacLachlan, *Criminal Justice in Eighteenth-Century Mexico.*

53. These and other cases are discussed in a bulky volume of criminal and administrative records: AGI, Guadalajara, 402.

54. Ibid.

55. Ibid.

56. Ibid., 404.

57. Ibid, 402.

58. Ibid.

59. For a detailed study of the *fuerza* procedure in eighteenth-century Spain, see María Teresa Bouzada Gil, *La vía de fuerza: La práctica en la Real Audiencia del Reino de Galicia. Siglos XVII–XVIII* (Santiago de Compostela, Spain: Xunta de Galicia, 2001).

60. Documents of the time sometimes omitted mention of ethnicity when mestizos were involved. A fair number—around 25 percent—of colonial Mexican subjects fell into this category by this time.

61. "*Que hará una junta de tantos perbersos* [*sic*]*? Cuál será su estudio y sus maquinaciones, las lecciones que mutuamente se den, el aliento que se infundan?*" AGI, Guadalajara, 402.

62. Baltasar Ladrón de Guevara, *fiscal* of Mexico's Real Audiencia, and the Mexican bishop both reported these and other solutions in January and March 1778. The measures were embraced the following month. See AGI, Guadalajara, 402.

63. AGI, Indiferente, 3025.

64. The long list of papal decrees includes Benedict XIII, "*Ex quo divina,*" June 8, 1725; Clement XII, "*In suprema justitiæ,*" January 29, 1734; Benedict XIV, "*Officii nostri ratio,*" March 1750; and Clement XIV, "*Ad perpetuam rei memoriam,*" Sept. 12, 1772. Copies of some of these can be found in AGI, Indiferente, 3025; BRAH, Madrid, Colección Benito de la Mata Linares, 1761, fols. 607–617. References also include asylum-related measures enacted by, among others, the Cuban Synod (i.e., constitution 7, tit. 14, book 3) and the Fourth Concilio Provincial Mexicano (book 3, title 22). See AGI, Indiferente, 3025; and titles 5 and 9, libro 1, *Recopilación de las Leyes de Indias.*

65. See laws 4 and 5, title 4, book 1, Novísima Recopilación, in *Códigos españoles* 7: 18–19.

66. See royal *cédulas* issued in October 1750, April 1764, July 1768, October 1770, November 1773, and March 1787. AGI, Indiferente, 3025; AGI, Guadalajara, 402–403. See also AGI, Filipinas, 335, L. 17, 2, 60–63; various other royal decrees concerning asylum for soldiers and the military; and laws 7–11, title 4, book 1, Novísima Recopilación, in *Códigos españoles* 7: 22–24.

67. See AGI, Guadalajara, 402.

68. AGN, Mexico, Californias, vol. 65, case 8, fol. 353.

69. See royal *cédula* issued in San Lorenzo on November 11, 1800, in law 6, title 4, book 1, Novísima Recopilación, in *Códigos españoles* 7: 21–22. For the 1787 regulations and the 1797 reminder, see BRAG, Madrid, Coleccción Benito de la Mata Linares, 1768, fols. 353–356; 1773, fols. 394–399.

70. *Diario de México,* no. 176, Tuesday, March 25, 1806, 336.

71. ARCV, box 245, case 2, fols. 84, 86v, 89, 91v, 194, 198v–199, 202v, 204v, 207v.

72. See the royal *cédula* issued in Aranjuez on March 13, 1807, in BRAH, Colección Benito de la Mata Linares, 1768, fols. 353–356; 1777, fols. 277–279.

73. Gutiérrez, *Compendio de las varias resoluciones de Antonio,* chapter X, 69–70.

74. The list included the following: "*los que cometen los ladrones públicos, salteadores de caminos, los que talan los campos, los que cometieren homicidios o mutilaciones de miembros en las Iglesias o sus cementerios, y los que hicieren alguna muerte a traición, los asesinos, los reos de heregía o lesa Magestad, los que cometieren el homicidio de caso pensado o deliberado, los falsificadores de letras apostólicas, los superiores y empleados en los Montes de Piedad u otros fondos públicos o Bancos, que cometieren hurtos o falsedad, los monederos falsos, o los que cercenan moneda de oro o plata, los que fingiendose Ministros de Justicia se entran en casas ajenas y cometen en ella robos con muerte o mutilación de miem-*

bro, los que conspiran contra los Reynos con contra el estado, el fallido y alzado en sus bienes, pero no el que sin alzarse se acoge; los que hubiesen contribuido al homicidio alevoso con mandato o consejo, inducción, auxilio cooperativo, u otro favor y ayuda, aunque sean menores de 25 años, como sean mayores de 20, los indiciados y procesados, o en rebeldía llamados por edictos y pregones, y condenados por causa de homicidio, aunque sea hecho en pendencia con armas, o instrumentos proporcionados por su naturaleza para matar, como no sea el homicidio casual o en propia defensa." See Alvarez Posadilla, *Práctica,* 1: 307.

75. Sánz, *Modo y forma de instruir y sustanciar las causas criminales,* 32–45.

76. Elizondo, *Práctica universal forense* 1: 284–89. For examples of desperate requests in this sense, see AGI, Guadalajara, 100.

77. Reference to Easter pardons can be found in López de Cuellar, *Tratado jurídico-político,* 9. On the designation of Easter as the *día de indulgencias,* see Rodríguez Flóres, *El perdón real en Castilla,* 46–47.

78. Partida 7, title XXXII, law 1, in Martinez Alcubilla, *Códigos Antiguos,* 1: 661.

79. *Cortes de los Antiguos Reynos de León y Castilla,* 4 vols. (Madrid: Imprenta de Rivadeneyra, 1866), 3: 528–529.

80. Taylor, *Honor and Violence in Golden Age Spain,* 14.

81. AGS, legajo 874.

82. See González Zalacain, "El perdón real en Castilla: Una fuente privilegiada para el estudio de la criminalidad," esp. 309; idem, *El perdón real en Castilla a fines de la Edad Media: El ejemplo de la Cornisa Cantábrica* (Servicio Editorial de la Universidad del País Vasco UPV/EHU, 2013).

83. See Taylor, *Honor and Violence in Golden Age Spain,* 15, note 32.

84. See Rudy Chaulet, "La Violence en Castille au XVIIe Siècle à Travers les *Indultos de Viernes Santo* (1623–1699)," *Crime, Histoire & Sociétés* 1.2 (1997): 5–27, esp. 12.

85. The *cárcel de corte* housed those whose crimes had taken place in Madrid and about 81 localities under its jurisdiction. See González Palencia, ed., *Archivo Histórico Nacional. Consejo de Castilla: Sala de Alcaldes de Casa y Corte,* xx; Alloza, *La vara quebrada de la justicia,* 38–46, 268.

86. For evidence of remission of cases and royal notification to the various *audiencias* about the outcome of *perdones de Viernes Santo,* see AHN, Madrid, Consejos, Sala de Alcaldes de Casa y Corte, leg. 5742, assorted folios.

87. "*[N]o haya parte que pida, ni intervenga asesinato, robo, u otro de aquellos delitos feos y enormes indignos de perdón por sus circunstancias y por la vindicta pública y se interesa está gravemente en el castigo cuyas causas. . . .*" AHN, Madrid, Consejos, libro 1355.

88. AGS, legajo, 874.

89. Ibid.

90. Ibid.

91. AGN, Madrid, Consejos, Sala de Alcaldes de Casa y Corte, leg. 5742.

92. For several *Viernes Santo* pardons in the period of our interest, see also AGN, Consejos, Alcaldes de Casa y Corte, libros 5687–5767. For numerous

documents concerning "Perdones de Viernes Santo" during earlier centuries, see AGS, legajos 804, 808, and 874.

93. AGS, Gracia y Justicia, legajos 804, 808, and 874.

94. AGS, Gracia y Justicia, legajo 804. Evidence of additional denials can be found in AHN, Madrid, Consejos, book 1384, fols. 422–431; book 1394, fol. 644.

95. See Pieter Spierenburg, "The Green, Green Grass of Home: Reflections on Capital Punishment and the Penal System in Europe and America from a Long-Term Perspective," in idem, *Violence and Punishment,* 104–126, esp. 105–111. Evidence from early modern Rome can be found in Tomás Mantecón, "The Pope's Sword: Early Modern Capital Punishment, Homicide and Cultures of Suffering—Rome in the European Context," in Olli Matikainen and Satu Lidman, eds., *Morality, Crime and Social Control in Europe 1500–1900* (Helsinki: Finnish Literature Society, 2014), 259–297.

96. Daniel Sueiro, *Los verdugos españoles: Historia y actualidad del garrote vil* (Madrid: Alfaguara, 1971), 271.

97. Pedro de León, *Compendio de algunas experiencias en los ministerios [de que usa] la Compañia de Jesús. . . .* 2 vols. (Granada: Colegio de la Compañia de Jesús, 1619), vol. 1, appendix (www.cervantesvirtual.com/obra/compendio-de-algunas-experiencias-de-industrias-en-los-ministerios-de-que-usa-la-compania-de-jesus-con-que-practicamente-se-muestra-con-algunos-acontecimientos-y-documentos-el-buen-acierto-en-ellos-tomo-primero-ano-de-1619). Accessed October, 21, 2013.

98. *Diario de Mexico,* II, January–March, 1806, no. 177, March 27, 1806, 343.

99. Ibid., March 26, 1806, 338–339; no. 178, March 27, 1806, 343–344.

100. AGN, Colombia, Criminales, vol. 45, fols. 783–859; AHN, Madrid, Consejos, libro 1388, fols. 418–425.

101. AGS, Gracia y Justicia, legajo 804.

102. AHN, Consejos, books 1352, 1355, 1364, 1369, 1381, 1382, 1397. See also AHN, Madrid, Index 2783–93, Inventarios de causas criminales—1542–1789, passim.

CHAPTER SIX

1. The *bunde* was an Afro-Colombian rhythm popular along the country's Pacific Coast. From there it spread to the interior, including areas in northern Antioquia populated by miners and journeymen of African descent. It was typically played at night in streets, public squares, and backyards and was popular among blacks, Indians, mestizos, mulattoes, and *zambos*. The Catholic clergy disliked the lascivious nature of *bunde*'s lyrics, the "indecent" bodily movements of dancers, and the disorderly mix of men and women of all races, who usually failed to attend church the day after the dances. See Victor Manuel Patiño, *Historia de la cultura material en la America Equinoccial,* vol. IV: *Vestidos, Adornos y Vida Social* (Bogotá: Instituto Caro y Cuervo, 1992), 332–333; Adolfo González Henríquez,

"La música del Caribe Colombiano durante la Independencia y comienzos de la república," *Historia Crítica* 4 (July–December 1990): 85–112.

2. On the Mojana's agricultural, ranching, trading, and mining economy and material life, see Orian Jiménez Meneses and Edgardo Pérez Morales, *La Mojana medio ambiente y vida material en perspectiva histórica* (Medellin, Colombia: Universidad de Antioquia, 2007).

3. "*una tunica o saya burda y oscura que denote la gravedad de su delito . . .,*" AGN, Colombia, Criminales, vol. 194, fol. 889.

4. In 1777 a good portion of today's Venezuela joined Caracas and separated definitively from the Viceroyalty of New Granada, receiving independent legal status as a Captaincy General. The area received its own *audiencia* ten years later. Ecuador remained within New Granada but behaved quite independently, and several of its regions were eventually transferred back to Peru before the end of the colonial period.

5. The major implication of this for the current study is that at the local level, cases of domestic violence and spousal homicide continued to be handled by *alcaldes ordinarios* or *corregidores* rather than by *intendancies* and their *subdelegados,* as was the case in Mexico.

6. In 1779 the population of major Colombian cities was as follows: Santafe de Bogotá, 15,723; Antioquia City, 19,318 (data for year 1788 from Twinam [1982], 18); Medellín, 16,750 (data for year 1788 from Twinam [1982], 18); Popayán, 13,623; Cartagena, 13,630; Buga, 12,417; Pasto, 11,113; and Cali, 10,298. See contemporary census data reproduced in Tovar Pinzon et al., *Convocatoria al poder del número,* 290–291, 308, 484; "Padrón General del Nuevo Reyno de Granada in 1778," in Pérez Ayala, *Antonio Caballero y Góngora: Virrey y Arzobispo.*

7. *Zambos* were individuals of mixed African and Amerindian ancestry.

8. This section's composite descriptions are based on archival records cited throughout and in the writings of Francisco Silvestre, *Descripcion del reyno de Santa Fé de Bogota;* idem, *Relacion de la Provincia de Antioquia;* German Colmenares, ed., *Relaciones e informes de los gobernantes de la Nueva Granada;* Allan J. McFarlane, *Colombia Before Independence;* David Bushnell, *The Making of Modern Colombia;* Frank R. Safford, *The Ideal of the Practical;* Allan J. Kuethe, *Military Reform and Society in New Granada;* Ann Twinam, *Miners, Merchants and Farmers in Colonial Colombia;* Kris Lane, *Colour of Paradise: Colombian Emeralds in the Age of Gunpowder Empires;* Jaime Jaramillo Uribe, *Ensayos de historia social colombiana;* and Pablo Rodriguez, *Sentimientos y vida familiar en el Nuevo Reino de Granada.*

9. Fragmented records indicate that at least 12 spouses involved in judicial disputes complained of abandonment between 1750 and 1810. See AGN, Colombia, Colonia, Criminales, vol. 67, fols. 556–589; vol. 87, fols. 141–161, 162–164; vol. 113, fols. 472–480, 815–826; vol. 120, fols. 719–745, 836–845; vol. 154, fols. 398–431; vol. 173, fols. 875–918; vol. 178, fols. 1–168; vol. 201, fols. 517–581. See also René de la Pedraja, "La mujer criolla y mestiza en la sociedad colonial, 1700–1830," *Desarrollo y Sociedad* 13 (January 1984): 199–229, esp. 215–217; Rodríguez, *Sentimientos y vida familiar,* 237–253; Guiomar Dueñas,

Hijos del pecado, 182–187; María Himelda Ramírez, *Las mujeres y la sociedad colonial de Santafe de Bogotá, 1750–1810* (Bogotá: Instituto Colombiano de Antopología e Historia, 2000), 151–160.

10. See, among others, AGN, Colombia, Colonia, Criminales, vol. 9, fols. 1055–1065; vol. 11, fols. 170–176; vol. 12, fols. 444–446; vol. 15, fols. 969–1001; vol. 22, fols. 652–667; and vol. 209, fols. 836–883.

11. AGN, Colombia, Colonia, Criminales, vol. 132, fols. 626–689.

12. Ibid., vol. 20, fols. 975–1033.

13. Ibid., vol. 199, fols. 727–758. Cases in which the couple's children were injured while trying to protect their mothers from abuse were also common. See, for instance, AGN, Colombia, Colonia, Criminales, 15, fols. 969–1014.

14. AGN, Colombia, Colonia, Criminales, vol. 9, fols. 368–401.

15. López, "Conyugicidios en la Nueva Granada," passim.

16. AGN, Colombia, Colonia, Criminales, vol. 36, fols. 1–175.

17. Ibid., vol. 163, fols. 452–477.

18. Ibid., vol. 117, fols. 226–303.

19. Ibid., vol. 32, fols. 420–450.

20. Notice that there are no records at all for the decade 1770–1779 and very few for 1760–1769 and 1780–1789. An average of 8 to 10 murders of this type may have occurred per decade, in which case the total for the period under study may have been as high as 70.

21. Only three cases (5.8% of the total) seem to have occurred in major urban centers—two in Santa Fé and one in Medellín.

22. This and other facts pertaining to the regional distribution of the cases remain unexplained and are likely due to lopsided record keeping. The high proportion of cases in Antioquia relative to this region's population is another issue requiring further study. On the demographic makeup of New Granada's regions, see McFarlane, *Colombia Before Independence,* 353–363. Patiño provides quantitative information on Antioquia in *Criminalidad, ley penal y estructura social en la provincia de Antioquia,* 376, 516. For total crime figures in New Granada, I relied on a databased I created based on Colombia's Archivo General de la Nación, Colonia, Juicios Criminales, Indice.

23. A sample of 48 crimes committed in this region between 1591 and 1792 shows two cases of spousal homicide (one in 1591, another in 1629), suggesting the likelihood of further instances in the late colonial period. It is possible the criminal records are to be found in the neighboring archive of the Quito Audiencia. See ACC, Catálogo General, Judicial, Criminal, vol. 4, fols. 627, 631. See also Germán Colmenares, *Historia económica y social de Colombia, II: Popayán: una sociedad esclavista, 1680–1800* (Bogotá, 1979); idem, *Cali: Terratenientes, mineros y comerciantes, Siglo XVIII* (Cali, 1983).

24. For the coal-throwing attack by 48-year-old day laborer Eugenio Verdugo against his wife, María, see AGN, Colombia, Colonia, Criminales, vol. 172, fol. 940. Farmer and weaver Juan F. Ortíz, 57, admitted that he *refregó* (stirred) the sexual organs of his wife, Silvestra Nempaque, causing her mortal injury: AGN, Colombia, Colonia, Criminales, vol. 97, fols. 778, 784.

25. AGN, Colonia, Juicios Criminales, vol. 167, fols. 292–326; vol. 36, fols. 622–768. Spanish legal treatises dedicated extensive space to discussing homicide by poison. See Vilanova y Mañez, *Materia criminal forense,* 3: 41–45. On poison, arsenic in particular, as a common means of murder in the nineteenth century, see Randa Helfield, "Female Poisoners of the Nineteenth-Century: A Study of Gender Bias in the Application of the Law," *Osgoode Hall Law Journal* 28.1 (1990): 53–101. For nineteenth-century France, see A. Lacassagne, "Notes statistiques sur l'empoisonnement criminel en France," *Archives d'Anthropologie Criminelles et des Sciences Penales* l (1886): 260–264.

26. This confirms the findings of Rodríguez, *Sentimientos y vida familiar,* 231.

27. See McFarlane, *Colombia Before Independence,* 54–57.

28. Rodríguez, *Sentimientos y vida familiar,* 77.

29. Scardaville, "Crime and the Urban Poor," 41; Haslip-Viera, *Crime and Punishment,* 55; Taylor, "Amigos de sombrero," 72–73.

30. Haslip-Viera, *Crime and Punishment,* 56.

31. For the mestizo character of late colonial New Granada, see Haslip-Viera, *Crime and Punishment,* 34.

32. Specialized research on crimes committed by Indians in the province of Tunja uncovered six cases of spousal homicide between 1740 and 1810. When added to the data, this information would mean that 8 of 34 spousal homicides were committed by Indians. See Sosa Abella, *Labradores, tejedores y ladrones,* 60, 146–147.

33. For the African component of New Granada's 1778–1780 population, see McFarlane, *Colombia Before Independence,* 353. He gives no specific statistics for mulattos and *zambos.* For crimes committed by mulattos, see AGN, Colonia, Juicios Criminales, vol. 98, fols. 899–1001; vol. 117, fols. 266–303. For a *zambo* murderer, see vol. 204, fols. 488–613.

34. AGN, Colombia, Colonia, Criminales, vol. 163, fols. 452–477.

35. Ibid., vol. 61, fols. 549–552.

36. Ibid., vol. 3, fols. 423–424.

37. Ibid., vol. 97, fols. 778–784.

38. AGN, Colombia, Colonia, Juicios Criminales, vol. 204, fols. 488–613.

39. Taylor, *Drinking, Homicide, and Rebellion,* 94–95; idem, "Amigos de sombrero," 78–80; Lozano Armendares, *La criminalidad en la ciudad de México,* 67; Scardaville, "Crime and the Urban Poor," 40.

40. For example, recent research shows that spousal homicides in late nineteenth-century Chicago were the culmination of long-festering disputes and abuses. See Adler, "My Mother-in-Law Is to Blame," 259; see also Pleck, *Domestic Tyranny,* 222–223.

41. A portion of the 436 recorded cases of *lesiones personales* (bodily injuries). AGN, Colonial, Juicios Criminales. Patiño provides evidence of increase in *maltrato* cases in the late colonial period in *Criminalidad, ley penal y estructura social,* 265.

42. Mallo, "Justicia, divorcio, alimentos y malos tratos en el Río de la Plata," 373–400; Socolow, "Women and Crime. Buenos Aires, 1757–97," 4–6; Eugenia Rodríguez Saenz, "'*Ya me es insoportable mi matrimonio.*' El maltrato de las

esposas en el Valle Central de Costa Rica (1750–1850)," *Ciencias Sociales* 68 (June 1995): 73–93; idem, "Civilizing Domestic Life in the Central Valley of Costa Rica, 1750–1850," in *Hidden Histories of Gender and the State in Latin America,* ed. Elizabeth Dore and Maxine Molyneux, 85–107; Pescador, "Entre la espada y el olvido," 202–205; Stavig, *Amor y violencia sexual: Valores indígenas en la sociedad colonial,* 77–87; Stern, *Secret History of Gender,* passim.

43. AGN, Colombia, Colonia, Criminales, vol. 172, fols. 936–972.

44. Ibid., vol. 15, fols. 360–393.

45. Ibid., vol. 60, fols. 775–895.

46. Ibid., vol. 207, fols. 448–492.

47. Ibid., vol. 97, fols. 776–831.

48. AHA, Criminales, caja B–101, legajo 1800–1810, doc. 2, fol. 16v. See also Mojica Rivadeneira, "El derecho masculino de castigo."

49. AGN, Colombia, Colonia, Criminales, vol. 97, fols. 776–831.

50. Ibid.

51. Ibid., vol. 181, fol. 489.

52. Ibid., vol. 169, fols. 955–986.

53. Ibid., vol. 41, fols. 673–765.

54. Ibid., vol. 204, fols. 488–613.

55. Ibid., vol. 3, fols. 423–424; vol. 61, fols. 549–552.

56. Ibid., vol. 117, fols. 226–303.

57. AGN, Colombia, Colonia, Criminales, vol. 117, fols. 226–303.

58. AHA, Criminales, caja B–101, legajo 1800–1810, doc. 2, f. 2–4, 9–10, 16v; Patiño, *Criminalidad, ley penal y estructura social en Antioquia,* 376.

59. Stern, *The Secret History of Gender,* chapter 4.

60. See Patiño, *Criminalidad, ley penal y estructura social,* 380, 405; López, "Conyugicidios en la Nueva Granada," 6.

61. AGN, Colombia, Colonia, Criminales, vol. 181, fol. 489.

62. Ibid., vol. 170, fols. 922–974. In 1684 Mixtec Indian Pedro de Caravantes killed his wife, María de Montiel, after accusing her of adultery. Similar cases likely occurred throughout colonial Spanish America. See Terraciano, "Crime and Culture in Colonial Mexico."

63. AGN, Colombia, Colonia, Criminales, vol. 153, fols. 831–880.

64. Ibid., vol. 165, fols. 300–352.

65. Ibid., vol. 204, fols. 488–613.

66. Nizza da Silva, *Sistema de Casamento no Brasil Colonial,* 194–195; Rodríguez, *Sentimientos y vida familiar,* 233–237; Johnson and Sonya Lipsett-Rivera, eds., *The Faces of Honor,* 179–200; Socolow, "Women and Crime," 13.

67. Historical works are cited in the case study on Spain. As for literary evidence, see, to mention but a few works, Taylor, *Honor and Violence in Golden Age Spain,* chapter 6; García Valdecasas, *El hidalgo y el honor,* 198–214; Albert S. Gérard, "The Loving Killers: The Rationale of Righteousness in Baroque Tragedy," *Comparative Literature Studies* 2 (1965): 209–232; Frank P. Casa, "Honor and the Wife-Killers of Calderón," *Bulletin of the Comediantes* 28 (1977): 27–31; and Stroud, *Fatal Union: A Pluralistic Approach of the Spanish Wife-Murder Comedias.*

68. AGN, Colombia, Colonia, Criminales, vol. 167, fols. 292–326.
69. Ibid., vol. 153, fols. 122–267.
70. Ibid., vol. 61, fols. 541–651; vol. 32, fols. 420–450.
71. Ibid., vol. 194, fols. 736–910.
72. Ibid., vol. 43, fols. 996–1001; vol. 44, fols. 1–262.
73. Ibid., vol. 98, fols. 899–1001.
74. Ibid., vol. 95, fols. 380–499.
75. Ibid., vol. 64, fols. 164–344.
76. Socolow, "Women and Crime," 4.
77. Haslip-Viera, *Crime and Punishment,* 56.
78. Aufderheide, "Order and Violence," 216. Statistical tables offered later seem to indicate that female arrests were as high as 16 percent of the total, still a modest figure. See also pages 375, 380.
79. Author's database containing more than 2,600 crimes derived from AGN, Colonia, Juicios Criminales, Indice.
80. J. M. Beattie, "The Criminality of Women in Eighteenth-Century England," *Journal of Social History* 8 (Summer 1975): 80–116, esp. 85.
81. Lozano Armendares, *La criminalidad en la ciudad de México,* 127.
82. AGN, Colombia, Colonia, Criminales, Indice. Out of a total of 374 homicides, women appear to have been involved in just 30, half of the time with male accomplices. Men alone committed more than 332.
83. James Buchanan Given, *Society and Homicide in Thirteenth Century England* (Stanford: Stanford University Press, 1977), 56–61.
84. Sharpe, "Domestic Homicide," 36.
85. Harwing L. Voss and John R. Hepburn, "Patterns in Criminal Homicide in Chicago," *Journal of Criminal Law and Criminology* 59.4 (1969): 499–508, esp. 506; Marvin E. Wolfgang, *Patterns of Criminal Homicide* (New York: Science Editions, 1966), 209.
86. Comparable evidence exists for England and the United States. Women committed 33 percent of spousal murders in selected English counties from 1202 to 1276 and 34 percent in the period from 1300 to 1348; in Essex they were responsible for 33.3 percent in the 1560–1709 period; in Essex, Hertfordshire, and Sussex, they were responsible for 26 percent from 1559 to 1625. In Philadelphia, women were charged with 14.2 percent of spousal homicides committed between 1839 and 1901, and 47.2 percent between 1948 and 1952. From 1963 to 1982, U.S. women were charged with 38 percent to 48 percent of these murders. See Pleck, *Domestic Tyranny,* 223–224.
87. For a clear summary of such views, see Sharpe, "Domestic Homicide," 36.
88. For similar allegations of excessive female public life in late colonial Argentina, see Mallo and Silvia, "Justicia, divorcio, alimentos y malos tratos," esp. 381.
89. AGN, Colonia, Juicios Criminales, vol. 181, fols. 476–562; vol. 61, fols. 541–651; vol. 60, fols. 775–895; vol. 172, fols. 936–972; vol. 169, fols. 955–986; vol. 15, fols. 360–393; vol. 32, fols. 420–450.
90. AGN, Colonia, Juicios Criminales, vol. 117, fols. 226–303; vol. 36, fols. 1–175; vol. 41, fols. 673–765; vol. 153, fols. 122–267. A few of the fugitives

managed to evade justice for several years. See, for instance, the case of María T. Saavedra and her lover, Matías, who spent three years in hiding (ibid., vol. 108, fols. 950–951). It took four years to apprehend 32-year-old tailor Antonio Nieto (ibid., vol. 16, fols. 755–831). Almost 15 years passed before weaver María Quintero was questioned about her crime (ibid., vol. 36, fols. 8–9).

91. For buried bodies, see AGN, Colombia, Colonia, Juicios Criminales, vol. 98, fols. 899–1001; vol. 167, fols. 292–326; vol. 194, fols. 736–910. For corpses thrown into rivers and creeks, see vol. 169, fols. 650–729; vol. 161, fols. 557–604; vol. 108, fols. 914–966.

92. AGN, Colombia, Colonia, Juicios Criminales, vol. 172, fol. 969.

93. Ibid., vol. 167, fol. 293; vol. 169, fol. 964.

94. Ibid., vol. 181, fol. 489.

95. Socolow, "Women and Crime," 4; idem, *The Women of Colonial Latin America,* 148.

96. Arrom, *The Women of Mexico City,* 46–48, presents pioneering findings in this regard. See also subsequent confirmation in Socolow, *Women of Colonial Latin America,* 65, 113–115, 126; Marta Espejo-Ponce Hunt and Matthew Restall, "Work, Marriage, Status," 237–239; and Gauderman, *Women's Lives in Colonial Quito,* passim.

97. For an early formulation of the public/domestic analytic dichotomy to explain women's subordination, see Michelle Zimbalist Rosaldo, "Woman, Culture and Society: A Theoretical Overview," in *Woman, Culture, and Society,* ed. Michelle Zimbalist Rosaldo and Louise Lamphere (Stanford: Stanford University Press, 1974), 17–43; Anna Yeatman, "Gender and the Differentiation of Social Life into Public and Domestic Domains," *Social Analysis* 15 (August 1984), 32–49. For a historical discussion of the early cultural transformation of domesticity, see Glenna Matthews, "*Just a Housewife*": *The Rise and Fall of Domesticity in America* (New York: Oxford University Press, 1987), esp. chapters 1–3. See also critiques and recent evaluations of the public/domestic split in Joan B. Landes, "The Public and the Private Sphere: A Feminist Reconsideration," in *Feminists Read Habermas: Gendering the Subject of Discourse,* ed. Johanna Meehan (New York: Routledge, 1995), 91–116; and Alejandro Lugo and Bill Mauer, "The Legacy of Michelle Rosaldo: Politics and Gender in Modern Societies," in *Gender Matters: Rereading Michelle Z. Rosaldo,* eds. Alejandro Lugo and Bill Mauer (Ann Arbor: University of Michigan Press, 2000), 16–34. I thank my colleague Lara Kriegel for discussing with me some of the issues raised in this literature.

98. See Viqueira Alban, *Propriety and Permissiveness;* William H. Beezley, Cheryl English Martin, and William E. French, eds., *Rituals of Rule, Rituals of Resistance: Public Celebrations and Popular Culture in Mexico* (Wilmington: Scholarly Resources, 1994); Linda A. Curcio-Nagy, *The Great Festivals of Colonial Mexico City: Performing Power and Identity* (Albuquerque: University of New Mexico Press, 2004), 63.

99. See numerous instances of this situation in Stern, *The Secret History of Gender.*

CHAPTER SEVEN

1. Foucault, *Discipline and Punish.*

2. Ibid., 74, 82, 90, 101–103.

3. The historical reasons why the Roman canon law evidentiary system created the need for the use of torture are discussed in John H. Langbein, *Torture and the Law of Proof: Europe and England in the Anciene Régime* (Chicago: University of Chicago Press, 1977).

4. Gutiérrez, *Compendio de las varias resoluciones de Antonio Gómez,* 86. See also the 1806 edition of Asso y del Rio and de Manuel, *Instituciones del derecho civil de Castilla,* 2: 341–342.

5. See AGN, Colombia, Colonia, Criminales, vol. 64, fols. 983–989.

6. Ibid., vol. 144, fols. 403–485.

7. See Lardizábal y Uribe, *Discurso sobre las penas,* 115–136.

8. See ARCV, caja 270, exp. 2, fols. 350v, 358v.

9. For examples of critical references, see Hevia Bolaños, *Curia Filipica,* esp. 263–265; and Vicente Vizcaino Pérez, *Código y práctica criminal arreglado a las leyes de España* (Madrid: Imprenta de la Viuda de Ibarra, 1797), 356–360.

10. References to these older forms of torture continued to appear in nineteenth-century legal manuals. See Asso y del Rio and de Manuel, *Instituciones del derecho civil de Castilla,* 2: 342. For a description of other traditional methods, see Tomás y Valiente, *La tortura en España,* 114–118.

11. See laws 1–9, tit. 30, partida 7, "Las Siete Partidas," in *Códigos españoles* 4: 459–464; Alvarez Posadilla, *Práctica criminal,* 2: 361–380; Elizondo y Alvarez, *Práctica universal forense,* 4: 372–373; Gutiérrez, *Compendio de las Varias Resoluciones de Antonio Gómez,* 13–14, 85–99; Asso y del Rio and de Manuel, *Instituciones del derecho civil de Castilla,* 2: 341–344. Earlier treatises invariably dealt with torture in greater detail. See, for instance, Antonio Quevedo y Hoyos, *Libro de indicio y tormentos* (Madrid: Imp. Francisco Martínez, 1632); Hevia Bolaños, *Curia filípica,* 213v–217v; Monterroso y Alvarado, *Práctica Civil y Criminal,* 50–52. See also Tomás y Valiente, *La tortura en España,* and idem, *La tortura judicial en España* (Barcelona: Crítica, 2000).

12. See Gutiérrez, *Compendio de las Varias Resoluciones de Antonio Gómez,* 94.

13. See the case of soldier Gerónimo de Gola, who killed a fellow soldier and confessed his crime under torture in 1763, even though soldiers were supposedly exempt from such duress. AGS, Gracia y Justicia, legajo 874; Gutiérrez, *Compendio de las Varias Resoluciones de Antonio Gómez,* 86. There is evidence of several more cases during the late eighteenth century, including five reported in Granada in the decade after 1767. See Lucienne Domergue and Antonio Risco, *L'Alcade et Le Malandrin: Justice et Société en Espagne Au XVIIIe Siècle* (Toulouse: CRIC et Ophrys, 2001), chapter IV, esp. 181–182.

14. Madrid, AGN, Consejos, libro 1388, fol. 414. On *apremios,* see Bermejo Cabrero, "Tormentos, apremios, cárceles y patibulos," 685–696.

15. Renowned legal historian Francisco Tomás y Valiente holds that torture fell into disuse in Spain between 1774 and 1804. See Tomás y Valiente, *La tortura*

judicial en España, 133. An authoritative wider history of judicial torture is in Piero Fiorelli, *La tortura guidiziaria nel Diritto comume,* 2 vols. (Rome: Giuffré, 1953–1954).

16. The main defender was clergyman Pedro de Castro, *Defensa de la tortura y leyes patrias que la establecieron e impugnación del tratado que escribió contra ella el Doctor D. Alfonso de Acevedo* (1778). This work was endorsed by the lawyers' guild. See also comments on support for torture in the banned 1778 work *Disertaciones prácticas criminales* by Mariano Colón, in Domergue and Risco, *L'Alcade et Le Malandrin,* chapter IV.

17. See Cesare Beccaria, *Dei delitti e delle pene,* 6th ed. (Harlem: Chez Molini Librairie, 1766 [1764]), esp. chapter 16. Considered a founding text of classical criminology, this work was translated into Spanish as early as 1774 under the title *De los delitos y de las penas.*

18. Author of *De reorum absolutione objecta crimina negatium apud equuleum ac de hujus usu eliminando praesertim ab ecclessiasticis tribunalibus, Matriti* (1770). [*Ensayo acerca de la tortura o cuestión del tormento; de la absolución de los reos que niegan en el potro los delitos que se les imputan, y de la abolición del uso de la tortura principalmente en los tribunales eclesiásticos.* Spanish translation, Madrid, 1817]. See a summary of his arguments in Tomás y Valiente, *La tortura judicial en España,* 127–130.

19. Gaspar Melchor de Jovellanos, *El delincuente honrado* (1773).

20. This author considered torture to be "painful, useless, indecent and horrible. . . ." "Discurso sobre los grandes frutos que debe sacar la provincia de Extremadura de su nueva Real Audiencia . . . 27 abril 1791"; Meléndez Valdés, *Discursos Forenses,* 229–271, esp. 249–250. See also Ángel Rodríguez Sánchez, "Treinta de mayo de 1790: La Real Audiencia de Extremadura (1790–1990)," *Revista del Poder Judicial,* número especial XVI: Bicentenario de la Audiencia Territorial de Cáceres (1990): 39–50.

21. J. P. Forner, *Discurso sobre la tortura* (Barcelona: Critica, 1990 [1792]).

22. See Juan Sempere y Guarinos, *Ensayo de una biblioteca española de los mejores escritores del reinado de Carlos III,* 6 vols. (Madrid: Imprenta Real, 1785–1789), 3: 166.

23. Antonio Risco, *La Real Academia de Santa Barbara de Madrid 1730–1808* (Toulouse: Université de Toulouse–Le Mirails, 1979), appendix 1; Domergue and Risco, *L'Alcade et Le Malandrin,* chapter IV, 188.

24. Lardizábal y Uribe, *Discurso sobre las penas,* 244–245, 251, 252–255.

25. For the changes in the law of evidence linked to the decline in "blood sanctions," see Langbein, *Torture and the Law of Proof: Europe,* 43–44.

26. The most important work in this regard is by the Spanish historian Mantecón, *Conflictividad y disciplinamiento social.* See also idem, "Social Control from Below"; idem, "Disciplinamiento social, escenografías punitivas y cultura plebeya en el Antiguo Régimen." See as well the insightful work by Dominino Crespo, *Escándalos y delitos,* esp. chapters 4–6.

27. The nature of private vengeance in Spain, particularly through dueling, is nicely discussed in Tomás y Valiente, *El derecho penal,* 46–80.

28. See Iñaki Bazán, "La pena de muerte en la Corona de Castilla en la Edad Media," *Clio & Crimen* 4 (2007): 306–352, esp. 310, 313.

29. See, for instance, an 1815 case tried in Guadalajara whose opening statement is "*para escarmentar al delincuente y que su delito no quede sin castigo se dicta auto cabeza ordenando investigación de los hechos.*" AANG, Guadalajara, 24-9-531. For reference to the need for "*escarmiento público,*" see also the proceedings of a similar crime in 1817, AANG, Guadalajara, 131-1-1978, fols. 58–61; and the case in Cajitlan, Colima, tried in 1820, AANG, Guadalajara, 142–11–2146, fol. 63v. On punishment as a means to instill terror, see Elizondo y Alvarez, *Práctica universal forense,* 5: 80. See also Pedro Trinidad Fernandez, *La defensa de la sociedad: Carcel y delincuencia en España (Siglos XVIII–XX)* (Madrid: Alianza Editorial, 1991), chapters 1 and 2, esp. 20–26. A suggestive alternative interpretation viewing punishment not as deterrence but rather as a means of collective redemption or healing of the collective wound caused by the criminal is offered by Paul Friedland, "Beyond Deterrence: Cadavers, Effigies, Animals and the Logic of Executions in Premodern France," *Historical Reflections* 29.2 (2003): 295–317. I thank Tomás A. Mantecón for this valuable reference.

30. "*[T]odos los que lo oyeren e vieren tomen exemplo e apercibimiento para guardarse que no yerren por miedo de las penas. . .,*" partida 7, tit. 31, law 1, in Martinez Alcubilla, *Codigos Antiguos,* 2: 659.

31. In 1792, justice officials in Guadalajara, Spain, ruled that lashings should be applied on a Tuesday because "*es día de mercado y concurren las gentes de los pueblos inmediatos de donde son naturales los reos y ser más probable por esta razón el fruto del escarmiento.*" See AGN, Madrid, Consejos, libro 1382, fol. 452v.

32. See *Diario de México,* no. 176, Tuesday, March 25, 1806, 324.

33. AGN, Colombia, Criminales, vol. 45, fols. 783–859.

34. See Gutierrez, *Compendio de las Varias Resoluciones de Antonio Gómez,* 30–31.

35. See law 11, tit. 31, partida 7, Siete Partidas, *Codigos españoles,* 4: 327.

36. For evidence of such procedures, see AGI, Ultramar, 47.

37. See law 12, title 8, partida 7, Siete Partidas, in *Códigos españoles,* 4: 327; Jose Vicente Orti y Mayo, *Diario de lo sucedido en la Ciudad de Valencia desde el 3 de octubre de 1700 hasta el 1 de septiembre de 1715* (Biblioteca Histórica, Universidad de Valencia, Manuscrito, 282v); Joseph Berni Catala, *Apuntamientos sobre las leyes de partida 6 y 7* (Valencia: Por los Herederos de Gerónimo Conejos, 1759), 30.

38. See "Homicidio" in Joseph Berni Catala, *Instituta española que facilita el estudio de la Juris-Prudencia Real: Para el uso de los principiantes juristas* (Biblioteca Histórica, Universidad de Valencia, Manuscrito); idem, *Apuntamientos,* 30; and Orti y Mayo, *Diario de lo sucedido,* 283.

39. See a copy of such an order in BRAH, Madrid, Colección Benito de la Mata Linares, 1758, fol. 61.

40. *Diario de México,* no. 116, Friday, January 24, 1806, 95. The article mocked the elegance of the state officials participating on horseback, comparing them to godparents attending a wedding or people dressed for a bullfight.

41. "Ejecución de Justicia," *Diario de México,* no. 176, Tuesday, March 25, 1806, 336–337; no. 177, Wednesday, March 26, 1806, 338–339; no. 336, Monday, September 1, 1806, 2. See an additional description by a royal official in *Diario de México,* no. 343, September 8, 1806, 34–35.

42. Foucault, *Discipline and Punish,* esp. chapters 1 and 2.

43. The category of aggravated homicide included at least five other variants (use of poison, treachery, murder for hire, duels, and "homicide against oneself," or suicide). See Gomezio, *Commentariorum Variarum,* 3: 33–38; Gutiérrez, *Compendio de las varias resoluciones de Antonio Gómez,* 30–33. On the distinction between simple and "qualified" homicides, see Gutiérrez, *Práctica criminal de España,* 3: 41–43.

44. For the original Latin version, currently being translated into Spanish, annotated, and edited by the author and Andrés Rodríguez Cumplido, see Juan de Solórzano y Pereyra, *Diligens & accurate de parricidii crimini disputatio* (Salamanticae: Excudebat Artus Taberniel, 1605) [*Disertación sobre el crimen del parricidio diligente y cuidadosamente (elaborada), comprendida en dos libros, de los cuales el primero explica exactamente las penas constituidas para este crimen; el segundo trata con no menor cuidado de quienes son sometidos a ellas*]. On spousal killings, see especially book 2, chapter 13.

45. For various explanations of the practical and symbolic meaning of each animal, see Iñaki Bazán, "La pena de muerte en la Corona de Castilla en la Edad Media," 306–352, esp. 325–327. See also Enzo Nardi, *L'Otre Dei Parricidi e le Bestie Incluse* (Milano: Dott A. Giuffre Editore, 1980), esp. chapters 18–19; Hans Von Hentig, *La pena: Formas primitivas y conexiones culturales* (Madrid: Espasa Calpes, 1967), 339–340.

46. See Gutiérrez, *Práctica criminal de España,* 3: 43; D. G. Kyle, *Spectacles of Death in Ancient Rome* (London: Routledge, 1998); Manuel Torres Aguilar, *El parricidio: Del pasado al presente de un delito* (Madrid: Editorial Revista de Derecho Privado, 1991), esp. 38–64. On the Roman antecedents, see Nardi, *L'Otre Dei Parricidi e le Bestie Incluse,* passim.

47. Earlier, law 16, title 5 of the *Fuero Juzgo* provided for the death penalty to be executed in a way similar to the crime it was meant to punish. Title 17, book 4 of the *Fuero Real de España* prescribed death by *arrastramiento* for any treacherous homicide. Title 22 of the *Ordenamiento de Alcalá* established harsher penalties only for homicides not resulting from fights. *Códigos españoles* 1: 157, 415, 457.

48. Law 12, tit. 31, partida 7, Siete Partidas, in *Códigos españoles,* 4: 327. By the 1780s, *azotes* were already rather uncommon. See Gutiérrez, *Compendio de las varias resoluciones,* 3: 30, note 3.

49. For references to the *encubamientos* of individuals accused of spousal murder in late seventeenth-century Mexico, see Antonio de Robles, *Diario de sucesos notables (1665–1703),* 3 vols. (México: Editorial Porrúa, 1946), 1: 72, 102, 147.

50. See AGN, Colombia, Criminales, Colonia, vol. 45, fols. 783–859. For an 1814 case where, rather than in a *cuba,* the defendant was placed in a wooden box with the animals painted on it, see AGN, Colombia, Criminales, República,

vol. 7, fols. 748–793. For a case in 1768 Quito, see Ann Twinam, "Drinking, Gambling and Death on a Colonial Hacienda," in Boyer and Spurling, eds., *Colonial Lives,* 185–200.

51. Vicente Orti y Mayo, *Diario de lo sucedido en la Ciudad de Valencia,* 282v.

52. AGN, Madrid, Consejos Superiores, legajo 1371, fols. 484–517; AGS, Gracia y Justicia, legajo 804.

53. See AHPC, Sección Criminal, caja 80, exp. 10.

54. The man was sentenced to death by hanging and encubamiento: "*metido en un cuero y pintados los cuatro animales de un perro, una víbora, una mona y un gallo en la forma ordinaria.*" ARCV, caja 31, exp. 2, fols. 113–113v.

55. ARG, Real Audiencia, Causas, legajo 20, No. 34.

56. In Extremadura, for instance, there is evidence of *encubamiento* executions as late as 1837. See Angel Rodríguez Sánchez, *Morir en Extremadura: La muerte en la horca a finales del antiguo régimen (1792–1909)* (Caceres: Diputación Provincial, 1980), 60.

57. Two other death sentences, one against an Indian woman and the other against a white man, were ultimately commuted to prison terms. See AGN, Mexico, Criminales, vol. 380, exp. 17; AANG, Guadalajara, vol. 100, 9–1525; vol. 142, 11–2146. For the execution of the two Indians, see AGN, Mexico, Provincias Internas, vol. 6, fols. 44–85. For the commuted sentences, see AANG, Guadalajara, vol. 40, 11–632; vol. 26, 7–417.

58. See AGN, Colombia, Criminales, Colonia, vol. 181, fols. 467–562; vol. 64, fols. 164–344; AGN, Colombia, Negros y Esclavos, vol. 4, fols. 901–960. See AGN, Colombia, Criminales, Colonia, vol. 61, fols. 541–651.

59. See evidence of decisions taken in 1751 in AGN, Madrid, Consejos, libro 1338, fols. 44–45, 121–123.

60. See one such request by Joseph Joaquin Fullus Ybarrota in 1772: AGS, Gracia y Justicia, legajo 804.

61. Discussions about sparing women from hanging began around 1765. See AHN, Madrid, Consejos, libro 1352, fols. 222–224.

62. See AGN, Madrid, Consejos, Alcaldes de Casa y Corte, legajo 9344, case 8; ARCV, Pleitos Criminales, caja 245, exp. 2.

63. AGN, Madrid, Consejos, libro 1400, fols. 863–875.

64. See Beccaria, *Dei delitti e delle pene;* Lardizábal y Uribe, *Discurso sobre las penas,* esp. chapter 5, 81–91; Foucault, *Discipline and Punish,* chapter 2.

65. See, for instance, E. William Monter, *Frontiers of Heresy: The Spanish Inquisition from the Basque Lands to Sicily* (Cambridge: Cambridge University Press, 1990); Francisco Garau, *La fé triunfante: Los grandes Autos de Fé celebrados en Mallorca en 1691* (Mallorca: Miquel Font Editor, 1999); Martin A. Cohen, *The Martyr Luis de Carvajal: A Secret Jew in Sixteenth-Century Mexico* (Albuquerque: University of New Mexico Press, 2002); Rene Millar Carvacho, *Misticismo e Inquisición en el virreinato peruano: Los procesos a los alumbrados de Santiago de Chile 1710–1736* (Santiago: Ediciones Universidad Católica de Chile, 2000); Solange Alberro, *La actividad del Santo Oficio de la Inquisición en Nueva España, 1571–1700* (Mexico City: Instituto Nacional de Antropología e

Historia, Departamento de Investigaciones Históricas, Seminario de Historia de las Mentalidades y Religión en el México Colonial, 1981); idem, *Inquisición y sociedad en México, 1571–1700* (Mexico City: Fondo de Cultura Económica, 1988); Javier Villa-Florez, *Dangerous Speech: A Social History of Blasphemy in Colonial Mexico* (Tucson: University of Arizona Press, 2006).

66. See AGN, Madrid, Consejos, libro 1352, fols. 345–347; libro 1355, fols. 387–389; libro 1361, fols. 536–541; libro 1364, fol. 208; libro 1369, fols. 349–353; libro 1372–1373, fol. 462; libro 1374, fol. 208; libro 1381, fols. 257–258; libro 1382, fols. 222–224; libro 1387, fols. 724–737; libro 1397; AGN, Madrid, Consejos, Alcaldes de Casa y Corte, legajo 9344, part 1, no. 11. See also Rodríguez Sánchez, *Morir en Extremadura;* and Bermejo Cabrero, "Tormentos, apremios, cárceles y patíbulos a finales del Antiguo Régimen," 683–727.

67. For news of regular hangings, dismemberments, and floggings in seventeenth-century Mexico, see Robles, *Diario de sucesos notables,* passim. See news of similar executions in the eighteenth century also in AGI, Guadalajara, 158. In the case of Spain, abundant evidence exists in AHN, Madrid, Consejos, libro 1382, fols. 222–223v, 277, 452; libro 1355; libro 1361; libro 1364; libro 1369; legajo 9344.

68. Laws 1, 4, and 11, tit. 31, partida 7, Siete Partidas, in *Códigos españoles,* 4: 465–467, 473.

69. See *El Diario de México,* no. 177, Wednesday, March 26, 1806, 339.

70. See Hespanha, "De *Iustitia* a Disciplina," 234–235; Herzog, *Upholding Justice.*

71. Evidence indicates that in Guadalajara a sentence of death by hanging was later commuted to a five-year jail term. AANG, Guadalajara, Criminales, 26, 7–417.

72. Taylor, *Drinking, Homicide, and Rebellion,* 98–99. Evidence of hangings in seventeenth-century Mexico City can be found in the comments of a contemporary observer: Antonio de Robles, *Diario de sucesos notables (1665–1703),* passim.

73. See Gomezio, *Commentariorum Variarum que Resolutionum Iuris Civilis Communis & Regij,* 3: 35–38; Alvarez Posadilla, *Practica criminal,* 3: 132–133; Gutiérrez, *Práctica criminal de España,* 3: 45; Rodríguez Flóres, *El perdón real en Castilla,*102–105; law 15, title 23, book 8, *Recopilación de las Leyes de estos Reynos,* 2: 351v. See also the mention of the *alevoso* killing of someone lured out of his house under the guise of friendship listed in the 1764 *Libro de los principales rudimientos tocantes a todos juicios, criminal, civil y ejecutivo,* cited by Taylor, *Drinking, Homicide, and Rebellion,* 99.

74. The two males were executed, and the woman was confined in a *casa de recogidas* for six years. See AGN, Provincias Internas, 6, 44–85.

75. AAGN, Criminales, 11, 4, 199.

76. This differs markedly from the judicial treatment of accused insurgents, a majority of whom were sentenced to hard labor. See Eric Van Young, *The Other Rebellion: Popular Violence, Ideology and the Mexican Struggle for Independence, 1810–1821* (Stanford University Press, 2011), 55.

77. Taylor, *Drinking, Homicide, and Rebellion,* 102.

78. Mexico City's Carcel de Corte housed 219 people (195 men and 24 women) in 1790. The Acordada housed 302 more (286 men and 16 women). See "Estado General de la Población de Mexico Capital de esta Nueva España. no. 1, año de 1790," AGI, Estado, 20, no. 63.

79. AGN, Mexico, Presidios y Carceles, vol. 14, exp. 8, fols. 290–301; vol. 18, exp. 6, fols. 161–171; vol. 21, exp. 15, fols. 89–171; vol. 22, exp. 8, fols. 144–158; vol. 22, exp. 10, fols. 185–195.

80. AGN, Criminales, vol. 444, 4, fols. 132–141.

81. AANG, Guadalajara, Criminales, 21-7-345, fols. 8–10.

82. AGN, Mexico, Criminales, vol. 203, 11, 433–446, esp. fol. 441v. For other examples in Spain and Colombia, respectively, see ARCV, caja 428, no. 1; AGN, Colombia, Criminales, Colonia, vol. 64, 93, 983–989; vol. 169, fols. 650–729.

83. Mexican Indians usually served their presidio sentences in Veracruz. See Ruth Pike, "Penal Servitude in the Spanish Empire: Presidio Labor in the Eighteenth Century," *Hispanic American Historical Review* 58.1 (1958): 21–40, esp. 35.

84. On the significance of convict labor of this type, see Richard Greenleaf, "The Obraje in the Late Mexican Colony," *Americas* 23 (January 1967): 227–250; and Samuel Kagan, "Penal Servitude in New Spain: The Colonial Textile Industry" (Ph.D. dissertation, City University of New York, 1976), esp. chapters 5–7. On *collera*s and service in bakeries and butcheries, see "Memoria que el Virrey Carlos Francisco de Croix dejo . . . 1771," 966.

85. See AJO, vol. 51, case 1499, fols. 1–34; vol. 37, case 1076, fols. 1–2; vol. 14, case 243, fols. 1–48; AANG, Guadalajara, Criminales, 33-9-531; AGN, Mexico, Californias, vol. 65, case 6, fols. 241–301.

86. See AANG, Guadalajara, 36, 8, 573, fols. 28–31, 92. On the harsh conditions in the San Luis de Potosí *casa de recogidas,* see AGN, Mexico, Carceles y Presidios, vol. 22, exp. 10, fols. 185–195. See Muriel, *Los recogimientos de mujeres.*

87. AGN, Mexico, Criminales, vol. 444, case 4, fols. 132–141; AJO, vol. 51, case 1499, fols. 1–34.

88. Uribe, "Colonial Baracunatanas."

89. From this abundant literature the monographs most relevant to this study are Cope, *The Limits of Racial Domination;* Kellogg, *Law and the Transformation of the Aztec Culture;* and Cutter, *The Legal Culture of Northern New Spain.* However, an important recent work finds little correlation between the punishment of Mexican insurgents and their ethnicity. See Van Young, *The Other Rebellion,* 63–64.

90. Cope, *The Limits of Racial Domination,* 3.

91. See Stern, *Peru's Indian Peoples and the Challenge of Spanish Conquest.*

92. On the decline of the status of Indian women in the seventeenth century, see Kellogg, *Law and the Transformation of Aztec Culture,* chapter 3.

93. See Cutter, *Legal Culture in Northern New Spain,* passim; Borah, *Justice by Insurance;* Owensby, *Empire of Law and Indian Justice.*

94. See AGN, Criminales, 22, 14, 201–223; AANG, Guadalajara, Criminales, 67, 4, 1092; AANG, Guadalajara, Criminales, 131, 1, 1978. See comments

on these royal graces in Elizondo, *Práctica universal forense,* 5: 267–285; and Gutiérrez, *Práctica criminal de España,* 1: 329–347. Pardons also played a central role in Portuguese law at the time. See Hespanha, "De *Iustitia* a Disciplina," 229–233.

95. See, for instance, AJO, 51, 1499, 1–34; AGN, Mexico, Criminal, 140, 6, 165–242.

96. See Herman L. Bennett, *Africans in Colonial Mexico: Absolutism, Christianity and Afro-Creole Consciousness, 1570–1640* (Bloomington: Indiana University Press, 2006), esp. chapter 2; idem, *Colonial Blackness: A History of Afro-Mexico* (Bloomington: Indiana University Press, 2009), chapters 1–2, esp. 30–33, 61–64.

97. On numerous black marriages, see Bennett, *Africans in Colonial Mexico,* chapter 4; idem, *Colonial Blackness*, chapters 2 and 7. See also Patrick J. Carroll, *Blacks in Colonial Veracruz: Race, Ethnicity, and Regional Development* (Austin: University of Texas Press, 1991), 120–124; Alejandro García de la Fuente, "Los matrimonios de esclavos en la Habana, 1585–1645," *Ibero-Amerikanisches Archiv* 16.4 (1990): 507–528; L. W. Bergard, *The Comparative History of Slavery in Brazil, Cuba and the United States* (New York: Cambridge University Press, 2007), 165–177; and Alejandro Garcia de la Fuente and Ariela Gross, "Comparative Studies of Law, Slavery and Race in the Americas," University of Southern California Gould School of Law, *Legal Studies Research Paper Series* 10.2 (2010), esp. 11–14.

98. Those involved in witchcraft, heresy, or bigamy were in turn subject to the jurisdiction of the Holy Inquisition from its inception in New Spain during the early 1570s. Bennett, *Africans in Colonial Mexico,* chapter 3; idem, *Colonial Blackness,* chapter 1. Many blacks were also prosecuted for blasphemy in colonial Mexico. See Javier Villa-Flores, "'To Lose One's Soul': Blasphemy and Slavery in New Spain, 1596–1669," *Hispanic American Historical Review* 82.3 (2002): 435–468.

99. See Bennett, *Colonial Blackness,* 48.

100. AANG, Guadalajara, Criminales, 142, 11, 2146, fols. 9v–10v.

101. See AGN, Mexico, Criminales, vol. 380, case 17, fols. 296–325.

102. AANG, Guadalajara, Criminales, 100, 9, 1525.

103. Ibid., 11, 4, 199.

104. See lib. 10, tit. 1, law 16 of the Novisima Recopilación in *Códigos Antiguos de España,* 2: 1711.

105. See Jane Landers, *Black Society in Spanish Florida* (Urbana: University of Illinois Press, 1999), 139. See also Hans W. Baade, "The Law of Slavery in Spanish Louisiana, 1769–1803," in *Louisiana's Legal Heritage,* ed. Edward F. Haas (Pensacola: Perdido Bay, 1983), 43–86; Alejandro García de la Fuente, "Slave Law and Claims-Making in Cuba: The Tannenbaum Debate Revisited," *Law and History Review* 22.2 (2004): 339–369; and Bennett, *Africans in Colonial Mexico,* chapter 2.

106. Bennett, *Africans in Colonial Mexico,* 148, 151.

107. This literature is insightfully discussed in De la Fuente and Gross, "Comparative Studies of Law, Slavery and Race in the Americas," 7–11. For some re-

cent examples, see Sherwin K. Bryant, "Enslaved Rebels, Fugitives and Litigants: The Resistance Continuum in Colonial Mexico," *Colonial Latin American Review* 13.1 (2004): 7–46: Lyman Johnson, "'A Lack of Legitimate Obedience and Respect': Slaves and their Masters in the Courts of Buenos Aires," *Hispanic American Historical Review* 87.4 (2007): 631–657; Rebeca Scott, "'She . . . Refuses to Deliver up Herself as the Slave of Your Petitioner': Emigrés, Enslavement and the 1808 Louisiana Digest of Civil Laws," *Tulane European and Civil Law Forum* 24 (2009): 115–136; and the terrific essay by Bianca Premo, "An Equity Against the Law: Slave Rights and Creole Jurisprudence in Spanish America," *Slavery and Abolition* 32.4 (2011): 495–517; Komisaruk, *Labor and Love in Guatemala*, 71–107; Ghachem, *The Old Regime and the Haitian Revolution*.

108. Although masters were sometimes absolved of killing or abusing their slaves, at least some cases were reopened when they reached Spain. See, for instance, an 1805 case against a New Granada state official in AGI, Santafe, 548.

109. For a valuable summary of the slave provisions in Spanish medieval law, see David Brion Davis, *The Problem of Slavery in Western Culture* (Ithaca: Cornell University Press, 1966), 102–106.

110. See AGN, Colombia, Colonia, Negros y Esclavos, Cundinamarca, vol. 4, fols. 240–287; AGN, Colombia, Negros y Esclavos, Santander, vol. 4, fols. 901–960.

111. On this status in the case of slaves, see Premo, *Children of the Father King*, esp. chapters 1 and 7; Johnson, "'A Lack of Legitimate Obedience and Respect,'" 631; Magdalena Díaz Hernández, "La identidad de los esclavos negros como miserables en Nueva España: Discursos y acciones (siglos XVI–XVIII), in Aurelia Martín Casares, ed., *Esclavitudes Hispánicas (Siglos XV–XXI): Horizontes socioculturales* (Granada: Universidad de Granada, 2014), 41–57.

112. AGN, Colombia, Colonia, Negros y Esclavos, Cundinamarca, vol. 4, fol. 246. The slave master in the other case had died, and his will (*testamentaria*) was pending execution. See AGN, Colombia, Negros y Esclavos, Santander, vol. 4, fol. 902.

113. AGN, Colombia, Colonia, Negros y Esclavos, Cundinamarca, vol. 4, fol. 287.

114. AGN, Colombia, Negros y Esclavos, Santander, vol. 4, fol. 951.

115. AGN, Colombia, Colonia, Criminales, vol. 16, fols. 755–831.

116. Ibid., vol. 161, fols. 557–604.

117. "*no hay peor enemigo que el doméstico . . . ni mas expuesto está el marido que cuando su mujer lo aborrece. . . .*" AHN, Colombia, Criminales, Colonia, vol. 61, fol. 536.

118. See, for instance, the cases of Indian Jacinto González, whose death sentence for stabbing his wife to death was reduced to 10 years in prison, and farmer Emigdio Pabón and *zambo* rower Tomás A. Sierra, who were sentenced to death by hanging for similar crimes but on appeal had their sentences reduced to 8 and 10 years in prison, respectively. Weaver Maria del Carmen Martinez's death sentence was also commuted, and she received eight years in the local jail. AGN, Colonia, Juicios Criminales, vol. 170, fols. 922–974; vol. 41, fols. 673–765; vol. 204, fols. 488–613; vol. 61, fol. 629. On death sentences, in particular

hanging, as a threat more than a reality, see Espinosa, *El sueño del ahorcado,* 119–121.

119. Such was the case of María T. Saavedra and her lover. The two were caught after their escape and spent two years in jail but were later amnestied by a royal decree (*indulto*) issued in 1760. After one year in jail for killing his wife, Marcos Hernandez received a royal pardon in 1802. After more than six years in jail for a similar crime, Indian Cayetano Salvador was pardoned in 1808. AHN, Colombia, Criminales, Colonia, vol. 108, fol. 951; vol. 2, case 2, fols. 748–751; vol. 178, fols. 408–435.

120. AGN, Colombia, Criminal, Colonia, vol. 61, fols. 541–651; AGN, Colombia, Criminal, Republica, vol. 15, case 10, fols. 415–494.

121. See, for instance, AGN, Colonia, Juicios Criminales, vol. 117, fol. 298; Levaggi, "La fundamentación de las sentencias en el derecho indiano," 45–73; Lorente, "El juez y la ley: La motivación de las sentencias," 97–142; Tomás y Valiente, *El derecho penal,* 200; Hespanha, "De *Iustitia* a Disciplina," 234–236.

122. AHA, Criminales, caja B-101, legajo 1800–1810, doc. 2, f.6v.

123. Weaver María del C. Martínez and white male hat maker Martín Ruíz received no leniency. Their death sentences were confirmed in 1799 and 1800, respectively. AGN, Colonia, Juicios Criminales, vol. 61, fol. 550; vol. 181, fol. 51. The other woman whose death sentence was abrogated owed the reduction in punishment to a plea of self-defense. AGN, Colonia, Juicios Criminales, vol. 117, fol. 298.

124. See AGN, Colonia, Juicios Criminales, vol. 41, fol. 763; vol. 204, fol. 606.

125. See Christine Benavides, *Les Femmes Délinquantes à Madrid: Justice et Société en Espagne Au XVIIIe Siècle* (Toulouse: CRIC–Ophrys, 2000), chapter VII, 174; Trinidad Fernandez, *La defensa de la sociedad,* chapters 1–2. Evidence of frequent escapes from jail is abundant in our records. See also academic comments in Espinosa, *El sueño del ahorcado,* 130-131.

126. Trinidad Fernández, *La defensa de la sociedad,* 26–28; Rafael Salillas, *Evolución Penitenciaria en España,* 2 vols. (Madrid: Imprenta Clásica Española, 1913), 1: 88, 118; Pedro Fraile, *Un espacio para castigar: La carcel y la ciencia penitenciaria en España (siglos XVIII–XIX)* (Barcelona: Ediciones Serbal, 1987), 103–104.

127. See ARCV, Pleitos Criminales, caja 202, no. 2; caja 270, case 2; ARG, legajo 110, no. 34; legajo 246, no. 1; AHN, Madrid, Consejos, libro 1394, fols. 644, 1303–1323.

128. See ARCV, Causas Criminales, caja 428, case 1, fol. 74; caja 202, case 2.

129. In the second half of the eighteenth century, for instance, the death penalty was rare in Amsterdam. See Spierenburg, *The Spectacle of Suffering;* idem, *The Broken Spell: A Cultural and Anthropological History of Preindustrial Europe* (New Brunswick: Rutgers University Press, 1991), 229; Tomás Mantecón, "La economía del castigo y el perdón en los tiempos de Cervantes," *Revista de Historia Económica* 23.S1 (2005): 69–97, esp. 75; idem, "The Pope's Sword," 287.

130. See Pablo Pérez García and Jorge A. Catalá Sanz, "La pena capital en la Valencia del XVII," *Estudis* 24 (1998): 203–245, esp. 212; Alloza, *La vara quebrada de la justicia*, 261–263.

131. Angel Rodríguez Sánchez, "La soga y el fuego: La pena de muerte en la España de los siglos XVI y XVII," *Cuadernos de Historia Moderna*, 15 (1994): 13–39, esp. 26–31, 34–36.

132. They included one execution by *garrote* in June 1756, three hangings between June 1758 and December 1759, three more hangings in 1765, and just one each year in 1766, 1769, 1770, 1775, 1783, and 1790. For these and other statistics of executions in the second half of the eighteenth century in Madrid, see AHN, Madrid, Consejos, legajo 9344, no. 11. Alternatively, see Ruth Pike, "Penal Practices in Early Modern Spain," *Criminal Justice History* V (1984): 45–55, esp. 47; and Alloza, *La vara quebrada de la justicia,* 255.

133. Alloza, *La vara quebrada de la justicia*, 263; Ruth Pike, "Capital Punishment in Eighteenth-Century Spain," *Histoire Sociale–Social History* 18.36 (1985): 375–386, esp. 378–380.

134. See Rodríguez Sánchez, *Morir en Extremadura*, 36.

135. Tomás Antonio Mantecón Movellán, "Los criminales ante la concesión del indulto en la España del Siglo XVIII," *Prohistoria: Historia, políticas de la historia* 5 (2001): 55–82; Alloza, *La vara quebrada de la justicia,* 263.

CHAPTER EIGHT

1. For legal texts as "social facts," see Hespanha, "De *Iustitia* a Disciplina," 205.

2. Foucault, *Discipline and Punish,* 74–103, esp. 74–75.

3. Tomás y Valiente, *El derecho penal,* 111, 365–68, 376, 384.

4. *Colección de los decretos y ordenes que han expedido las Cortes Generales y Extraordinarias desde su instalación en 24 de Septiembre de 1810 hasta igual fecha de 1811* (Madrid: Imprenta Nacional, 1813), 1: 124–125; *Colección de los decretos y ordenes que han expedido las Cortes Generales y Extraordinarias desde 24 de Septiembre de 1811 hasta 24 de Mayo de 1812* (Madrid: Imprenta Nacional, 1820), 2: 64.

5. Spierenburg, *The Spectacle of Suffering,* viii; Hespanha, "De *Iustitia* a Disciplina," 228–229. Spierenburg's subsequent work became less critical of Foucault. See "Punishment, Power and History: Foucault and Elias," in idem, *Violence and Punishment*, 75–91.

6. In several of his works, Spierenburg, a follower of Norbet Elias, prefers to see these developments as part and parcel of a broader secular process of "civilization." See Spierenburg, *A History of Murder*, 7–10, 68–70, 108–110, 116; idem, *Violence and Punishment,* 3–7.

7. On the introduction of humanism (and also "utility") as a means to express social responsibilities on the part of jurists, see Hespanha, "De *Iustitia* a Disciplina," 208.

8. On several of these issues, see Leon Radzinowicz, *A History of English Criminal Law and Its Administration from 1750,* 5 vols. (London: Stevens and Sons, 1948), 1: chapter 10, 301–354; Tomás y Valiente, *El derecho penal,* 85–110, 353. See also Charles Secondat Baron de Montesquieu, David Wallace,

et al., *Montesquieu's Science of Politics: Essays on the Spirit of Laws* (New York: Rowman and Littlefield, 2001), 333, note 64; Hespanha, "De *Iustitia* a Disciplina," 203–209, 246–248.

9. See, for instance, Michael Ignatieff, *A Just Measure of Pain: The Penitentiary in the Industrial Revolution, 1750–1850* (New York: Columbia University Press, 1978); Piers Beirne, ed., *The Origins and Growth of Criminology: Essays on Intellectual History, 1760–1945* (Hants: Darmouth, 1994); Philip Jenkins, "Varieties of Enlightenment Criminology: Beccaria, Godwin, de Sade," *British Journal of Criminology* 24.2 (1984): 112–130; Radzinowics, *A History of English Criminal Law,* vol. 1.

10. Tomás Mantecón, "Civilización y brutalización del crimen en una España de Ilustración," in Manuel-Reyes García Hurtado, ed., *La vida cotidiana en la España del siglo* XVIII (Madrid: Sílex, 2009), 95–124; Trinidad Fernández, *La defensa de la sociedad,* chapter 2; Spierenburg, *A History of Murder,* 8; Foucault, *Discipline and Punish,* 73–103.

11. The views of a contemporary reformer are graphic and telling. See Antonio X. Pérez y López, *Principios del orden esencial de la naturaleza, establecidos por fundamento y por prueba de la religión* (Madrid: Imprenta Real, 1785), 258. On the civilization of punishment in Spain since the early eighteenth century, see Tomás A. Mantecón, "Recits de Punition et de Pardon Dans la Castille Moderne," in Benoit Garnot, dir., *Normes juridiques et pratiques judiciaires du Moyene Age a l'epoque contemporaine* (Dijon: Editions Universitaires de Dijon, 2007), 377–384, esp. 378; see also his essay "Civilización y Brutalización."

12. Several more reformers are listed and discussed in Domergue and Risco, *L'alcalde et le Malandrin,* esp. chapters 1 and 4. See also Trinidad Fernández, *La defensa de la sociedad,* chapter 2.

13. For some of their views and works, see Domergue and Risco, *L'alcalde et le Malandrin,* chapter 4; and Risco, *La Real Academia de Santa Barbara de Madrid 1730–1808,* appendix 1.

14. See partida 7, tit. XXXI, law 6, in Martínez Alcubilla, *Códigos Antiguos,* 2: 660. See also de las Heras Santos, *La justicia penal de los Austrias,* 299.

15. See lib. 8, tit. 13, law 46, "Nueva Recopilación." See also Eugenio Cuello Calón, "Contribución al estudio de la historia de la pena de muerte en España," *Anuario de derecho penal y ciencias penales* 10 (1957): 9–40, esp. 11; Tomás y Valiente, *El derecho penal,* 385; Bazán, "La pena de muerte en la Corona de Castilla," 322.

16. Pérez y López, *Principios del orden esencial de la naturaleza,* 258–262, esp. 259. Sentencing to *galeras* was, in any case, harsh and greatly feared until its abolition from 1748 until 1784, and again in 1803. See Trinidad Fernández, *La defensa de la sociedad,* 24; I. A. A. Thomson, "A Map of Crime in Sixteenth-Century Spain," *Economic History Review* XXI (2nd series) (1968): 244–267; Ismael Almazán, "Penas corporales y disciplina social en la justicia catalana de los siglos XVI y XVII," *Pedralbes* 12 (1992): 127–148, esp. 135; Juan Antonio Alejandre, "La función penitenciaria de las galeras," *Historia* 16, Extra VII (1978): 47–54; Ruth Pike, *Penal Servitude in Early Modern Spain* (Wisconsin: University

of Wisconsin Press, 1983); de las Heras Santos, *La justicia penal de los Austrias,* 304–316; Alloza, *La vara quebrada de la justicia,* 251, 256–259. On criticisms of corporal punishment since the seventeenth century, see Mantecón, "La economía del castigo," 79. On possible utilitarian logic as the reason behind what others interpret as humanitarianism, see Trinidad Fernández, *La defensa de la sociedad,* chapter 2.

17. See Castillo de Bobadilla's *Politica para corregidores,* 2: 19, 25; Francisco de la Pradilla Barnuevo, *Tratado y suma de todas las leyes penales, canónicas y civiles de estos reynos . . .* (Pamplona: Nicolas de Afsiayn, 1622), 22; Cuello Calón, "Contribución al estudio de la historia de la pena de muerte en España," 15.

18. Alvarez Posadilla, *Práctica Criminal,* 3: fol. 123.

19. Hespanha, "De *Iustitia* a Disciplina," 208. For the moral condemnation of inflicting pain linked to the debate over slavery in the eighteenth century and beyond, see Margaret Abruzzo, *Polemical Pain: Slavery, Cruelty, and the Rise of Humanitarianism* (Baltimore: Johns Hopkins University Press, 2011).

20. "*[L]a humanidad de los Monarcas españoles ha querido tolerar el que todas las penas que las leyes imponen a los reos que han de ser ajusticiados se executen en los cadáveres. . . .*" See Alvarez Posadilla, *Práctica Criminal,* 3: fol. 123.

21. See Sueiro, *Los verdugos españoles,* 269–271.

22. AHN, Madrid, Consejos, book 1352, fols. 371–377; Cuello Calón, "Contribución al estudio de la historia de la pena de muerte en España," 12, 14.

23. AGS, Gracia y Justicia, legajo 804.

24. AHN, Madrid, Consejos, book 1352, fols. 371–377; Lardizábal y Uribe, *Discurso sobre las penas,* 186.

25. See a March 1792 request for the removal of a hand that had been on display since October of the previous year. AHN, Consejos, book 1382, vol. 222.

26. John L. Phelan, *The People and the King: The Comunero Revolution in Colombia, 1781* (Madison: University of Wisconsin Press, 1978). See also the work of Sara Ortelli, *Trama de una guerra conveniente,* on wars against the Apaches in northern New Spain, cited in Mantecón, "The Pope's Sword," 266, note 14. On independence, see Victor M. Uribe-Uran, "Abogados, independencia y muerte en la Nueva Granada, 1813–1819," in Pablo Rodríguez, ed., *Historia que no cesa: La independencia de Colombia, 1780–1830* (Bogotá: Universidad del Rosario, 2010), 133–148.

27. AHN, Consejos, books 1352, 1355, 1364, 1369, 1381, 1382, 1397. See also AHN, Madrid, Index 2783–93. Inventarios de causas criminales—1542–1789, passim.

28. See Alloza, *La vara quebrada de la justicia,* 265–266; Pike, "Penal Practices," 47.

29. AGS, Gracia y Justicia, legajo 804. The Spanish National Historical Archive also contains pleas that women should not be subject to hanging as early as the 1760s, a concession that would become a reality only decades later as a result of an incident in the Caribbean. AHN, Madrid, Consejos, libro 1352, fols. 222–224. See also Mantecón, "Civilización y Brutalización," 124; Alloza, *La vara quebrada de la justicia,* 251.

30. AGS, Gracia y Justicia, legajo 804, no folio.

31. For *desuso* of harsh penalties such as flogging (*azotes*) or the amputation of limbs, and for the "seldom applied" death penalty in Portugal until the middle of the eighteenth century, see Hespanha, "De *Iustitia* a Disciplina," 225–227.

32. AHN, Madrid, Consejos, libro 1382, fols. 278–279v; Lardizábal y Uribe, *Discurso sobre las penas,* 196.

33. AHN, Madrid, Consejos, libro 1382, fols. 452–455; libro 1394, fol. 704; AHN, Madrid, "Inventarios de causas criminales—1542–1789," fols. 210–217; AHN, Madrid, Index 2783-93, "Inventarios de causas criminales—1542–1789," 406; *Gaceta de Madrid,* no. 1, January 2, 1787, 143; Tomás y Valiente, *El derecho penal,* 367. On saving nobles from flogging, see AHN, Madrid, Consejos, Legajo 9344.

34. Lardizábal y Uribe, *Discurso sobre las penas,* 193–194.

35. For a case in Mexico as late as 1819, see AANG, Criminales, 131-1-1978, fols. 58–61.

36. Lardizábal y Uribe, *Discurso sobre las penas,* 15.

37. Ibid., 186–187, 191.

38. Logistical difficulties (lack of appropriate instruments) or little zeal and willingness to comply on the part of local justice officials and *audiencias,* both in the peninsula and overseas, rendered it uncommon. See examples cited in the previous chapter and Tomás y Valiente, *El derecho penal,* 173. See also Langbein, *Torture and the Law of Proof,* 45–70.

39. General statistics for Navarre, Seville, Aragón, the Canary Islands, and Asturias suggest a mere 3 percent of death sentences in the eighteenth century. See Palop Ramos, "Delitos y penas en la España del siglo XVIII," 101. Other research on Navarre seems inconsistent. See Pedro Oliver Olmo, "Pena de muerte y proceso de criminalización (Navarra, siglos XVII–XX)," in *Historia Contemporánea* 26 (2003): 269–292; idem, "Genealogia de la 'corrigenda': Mujeres encarceladas en Pamplona (Siglos XVI–XIX)," *Huarte de San Juan: Geografia e Historia* 5 (1998): 7–42, esp. 13.

40. Lardizábal y Uribe, *Discurso sobre las penas,* 166, 185.

41. For the better-documented Portuguese case as an example, see Hespanha, "De *Iustitia* a Disciplina," 215–228.

42. See Pérez García and Catalá Sanz, "La pena capital en la Valencia del XVII," 212.

43. See Rodríguez Sánchez, "La soga y el fuego," 28–29.

44. Of those executed in seventeenth-century Valencia, 25 were beheaded. See Pérez García and Catalá Sanz, "La pena capital en la Valencia del XVII," 212. Granada had 10 similar cases among about 100 death sentences. See Rodríguez Sánchez, "La soga y el fuego," 28–29. See also Ruth Pike, "Capital Punishment in Eighteenth-Century Spain," *Histoire Social–Social History* 18.36 (November 1985): 375–386, esp. 382; Cuello Calón, "Contribución al estudio de la historia de la pena de muerte en España," 12. On beheadings of noblemen in early modern Rome, see Mantecón, "The Pope's Sword," 283.

45. Pérez García and Catalá Sanz, "La pena capital en la Valencia del XVII," 212; Pike, "Capital Punishment in Eighteenth-Century Spain," 382–383; de las

Heras Santos, *La Justicia penal de los Austrias,* 318. On the significance of the sword for the decapitation of noblemen, see Spierenburg, "The Green, Green Grass of Home," 113.

46. AHN, Madrid, Consejos, libro 1355; legajo 9344, part. 1, doc. 11. See also Tomás y Valiente, *El derecho penal,* 367; Alloza, *La vara quebrada de la justicia,* 263; Pike, "Capital Punishment in Eighteenth-Century Spain," esp. 378–380.

47. *Gaceta de Madrid,* no. 1, January 2, 1787, 143.

48. Ibid., no. 1, January 2, 1787, 143; no. 32, April 22, 1783, 360–361.

49. See Rodríguez Sánchez, *Morir en Extremadura,* 36; Ruth Pike, "Capital Punishment in Eighteenth-Century Spain," 380.

50. Lardizábal y Uribe, *Discurso sobre las penas,* 188.

51. Evidence of its secret use to kill knights appears in Castillo de Bobadilla's *Política para corregidores,* 2: 19, 25. For its use in dealing with ordinary criminals, see Sueiro, *Los verdugos españoles,* 268–272.

52. Sueiro, *Los verdugos españoles,* 273–278. However, an authoritative work points out that in the seventeenth century even professional executioners did not know how to use the garrote properly. See Tomás y Valiente, *El derecho penal,* 385.

53. See Sueiro, *Los verdugos españoles,* 279.

54. See de las Heras Santos, *La Justicia penal de los Austrias,* 318. For evidence that the garrote was being applied to *hidalgos* and those with "*empleo no bajo*" in 1753, 1764, and 1772, see AGS, Gracia y Justicia, legajo 804; AHN, Madrid, Consejos, libro 1338. See also Tomás y Valiente, *El derecho penal,* 383.

55. See Chapter 4. See also AGS, Gracia y Justicia, legajo 804, documents, October 2, 1753, and May 23, 1760; AHN, Madrid, Consejos, libros 1338, 1380.

56. See AHN, Madrid, Consejos, libro 1338, fols. 44–45, 121–123; AGN, Madrid, Consejos, legajo 9344, part. 2, doc. 15, "Causa contra Antonio Pérez por la muerte violenta que dió a Águeda Leal en 1806."

57. In 1806 this happened explicitly, for instance, to artisan Antonio Perez. AHN, Madrid, Consejos, legajo 9344, doc. 15. Once it was used more frequently, Spanish authorities had to inventory the availability of garrotes and the need for repair of the few existing ones. See AHN, Madrid, Consejos, libro 1401, fols. 351–358. This also seems to have occurred overseas. "Ejecución de Justicia," *El Diario de México,* no. 176, Tuesday, March 25, 1806, 336–337; no. 177, Wednesday, March 26, 1806, 338–339; no. 336, Monday, September 1, 1806, 2.

58. On the continuation of hanging under Napoleon, see José María Puyol Montero, "La abolición de la pena de horca en España," *Cuadernos de Historia del Derecho* 4 (1997): 91–140, esp. 107.

59. "*Expediente para averiguar el estado de la pena de garrote, sus instrumentos, utensilios, y lo que sea necesario para su ejecución y en poder de quien se halla para proceder a su reconocimiento, 1810,*" AHN, Consejos, libro 1401, fols. 351–398, esp. fols. 353, 358, 364.

60. Ample evidence exists in the archives on "Perdones de Viernes Santo," AGS, Gracia y Justicia, legajos 5557–5569. See also Ruth Pike, "Capital Punishment in Eighteenth-Century Spain"; Tomas y Valiente, *El derecho penal,* 385; Pike, "Penal Practices," 51. The very few garrote executions occurring in

Extremadura between 1792 and 1816 presumably also benefited nobles. See Rodríguez Sánchez, *Morir en Extremadura,* 37. To celebrate his wife's birthday, King Ferdinand VII—in a decree dated April 24, 1832—forever (*para siempre*) abolished death by hanging in the Spanish domains and ordered the use of garrote thereafter.

61. At the time of Franco, and until its abolition by the 1978 Constitution, at least one-third of the sentences ordering it came from military courts. See a fascinating chronicle of numerous executions and those in charge of implementing them in Sueiro, *Los verdugos españoles.*

62. See AGN, Madrid, Consejos, libro 1352, fols. 345–347; libro 1355, fols. 387–389; libro 1361, fols. 536–541; libro 1364, fol. 208; libro 1369, fols. 349–353; libro 1372–1373, fol. 462; libro 1374, fol. 208; libro 1381, fols. 257–258; libro 1382, fols. 222–224; libro 1387, fols. 724–737; libro 1397; AGN, Madrid, Consejos, Alcaldes de Casa y Corte, legajo 9344, part 1, no. 11.

63. AHN, Madrid, Consejos, libro 1387, fols. 724–737.

64. Bazán, "La pena de muerte en la Corona de Castilla," 327; Francisco de la Pradilla Barnuevo, *Tratado y suma de todas las leyes penales, canónicas y civiles* (Pamplona: por Nicolas de Afsiayn, 1622), 22.

65. See AAE, Cáceres, Criminales, caja 680, exp.10.

66. "*Hoy en día esta pena ha sido conmutada en la de horca o garrote y después en el cadáver se executa* [*sic*] *la formalidad de ellas, metiéndole en el río a la orilla, con un cuero encima, o dentro de un cuero o cuba, en donde están pintados los animales que la ley señala . . . porque la humanidad de los Monarcas españoles ha querido tolerar el que todas las penas que las leyes imponen a los reos que han de ser ajusticiados se executen en los cadáveres, a excepción de algunas que no les incomodan en el modo que hoy se executan, como sucede en la de los arrastrados.*" See Alvarez Posadilla, *Práctica Criminal* [1794], 3: fol. 123.

67. Spierenburg, *The Spectacle of Suffering;* idem, *A History of Murder;* idem, *Violence and Punishment.*

68. AANG, Criminales, 100-9-1525, fols. 47v, 99v.

69. AANG, Guadalajara, Criminales, 90-15-1409, 1805–1811, fols. 45–48.

70. Ibid., 8-14-201.

71. Ibid., 131-1-1978, fol. 20.

72. Ibid., 131-1-1978, fols. 47–50.

73. Ibid., 10-1-238. López was eventually declared insane with the certification of medical expert witnesses.

74. Ibid., 59-4-951.

75. By early 1823, Spain was undergoing a civil war, and King Ferdinand VII once more abolished all legal acts enacted by the "so-called constitutional government." José Antón Oneca, "Historia del Código Penal de 1822," *Anuario de Derecho Penal y Ciencias Penales* 17.2 (1965): 263–278.

76. "*Yndulto General concedido por Nuestro Católico Monarca a todos los individuos que sean capaces de el, con el plausible motivo del restablecimiento de nuestra Sagrada Constitución y apertura del Congreso Nacional,*" Madrid, Imprenta de Arjona, 1820. Biblioteca Real Academia de Jurisprudencia, Madrid, 1-17083.

77. For an excellent narrative of a love triangle involving participants in New Granada's independence, see Aida Martínez Carreño, *Extravios: El mundo de los criollos ilustrados* (Bogotá: Colcultura, 1995).

78. See, for example, Chambers, "Citizens Before the Law"; Linda Arnold, "Vulgar and Elegant: Politics and Procedure in Early National Mexico," *Americas* 50.4 (1994): 481–500.

79. See Chambers, "Citizens Before the Law," 357, 373; Sergio García Avila and Eduardo Miranda Arrieta, *Desorden social y criminalidad en Michoacán, 1825–1850* (Morelia: Supremo Tribunal de Justicia del Estado de Michoacan de Ocampo, 1994), 63, 91–92; Jaime Hernández Díaz, *Orden y desorden social en Michoacán: El derecho penal en la primera República Federal, 1824–1835* (Morelia: Universidad Michoacana de San Nicolás de Hidalgo, 1999), chapters 3–4; Teresa Lozano Armendares, *La criminalidad en la ciudad de México, 1820–1821* (México: UNAM, 1987), chapter 4; Alexander Montoya Prada, "La transición del orden jurídico: Entre la colonia y la República en los procesos criminales en Querétaro (1830–1849)," *Signos Históricos* 26 (July–December 2011): 16–42, esp. 24; Osvaldo Barreneche, *Crime and the Administration of Justice in Buenos Aires* (Lincoln: University of Nebraska Press, 2006), 48–67; idem, "Jueces, policía y la administración de justicia criminal en Buenos Aires, 1810–1850," in Sandra Gayol and Gabriel Kessler, eds., *Violencias, justicias y delitos en la Argentina* (Manantial: Universidad Nacional de General Sarmiento, 2002), 207–225, esp. 209; Patiño, *Criminalidad, ley penal y estructura social;* Francisco Roberto Barbosa Delgado, *Justicia: Rupturas y continuidades. El aparato judicial en el proceso de configuración del Estado-Nación en Colombia, 1821–1853* (Bogotá: Pontificia Universidad Javeriana, 2007), 149–152, chapter 3. Even authors who have claimed that the courts remained strong and effective after independence acknowledge their lack of adherence to legal rules and guidelines. See, for instance, Ruben Zahler, "Honor, Corruption and Legitimacy: Liberal Projects in the Early Venezuelan Republic, 1821–1850" (Ph.D. dissertation, University of Chicago, 2005, 224–233); idem, "Liberal Justice: Judicial Reform in Venezuela's Courts, 1786–1850," *Hispanic American Historical Review* 88.1 (2008): 489–522, esp. 490; idem, "Complaining Like a Liberal: Redefining Law, Justice, and Official Misconduct in Venezuela, 1790–1850," *Americas* 65.3 (2009): 351–374, esp. 352, 364.

80. Arlene J. Diaz, *Female Citizens, Patriarchs and the Law in Venezuela, 1786–1904* (Lincoln: University of Nebraska Press, 2004); Sarah Chambers, "To the Company of a Man Like My Husband No Law Can Compel Me: The Limits of Sanctions Against Wife-Beating in Arequipa, Peru, 1780–1850," *Journal of Women's History* 11.1 (1999): 31–52. Patriarchy involved not only rights but also critical obligations such as the need to support one's wife and children. See Chambers, "Citizens Before the Law," 360–361, 364, 372–373; idem, "The Paternal Obligation to Provide: Political Familialism in Early Nineteenth-Century Chile," *American Historical Review* 117.4 (2012): 1123–1148.

81. AHN, Madrid, Consejos, libro 1400, fols. 863–875.

82. There is evidence that hanging continued to be used as a means of execution because of the exigencies of war during the reign of Napoleon. See Puyol Montero, "La abolición de la pena de horca en España," 107.

83. Constitution of Cádiz, article 303.

84. *Colección de los decretos y ordenes que han expedido las Cortes Generales y Extraordinarias desde 24 de Septiembre de 1811 hasta 24 de Mayo de 1812*, 2: 64.

85. See especially articles 242–244, 247, 253, 287, 293, 296–297, 300–303, and 306.

86. See Constitution of Cádiz, article 243. However, article 257 states that all justice was delivered in the name of the king: "*La justicia se administrará en nombre del Rey, y las ejecutorias y provisiones de los tribunales superiores se encabezarán también en su nombre.*"

87. Constitution of Cádiz, articles 259–261.

88. Linda Arnold, "La Audiencia de Mexico durante la fase gaditana, 1812–1815 y 1820–1821," in *Memoria del II Congreso de Historia del Derecho Mexicano* (Mexico: UNAM, 1981), 361–375, esp. 366. See also idem, *La Suprema Corte de Justicia: Sus orígenes y primeros años, 1808–1847* (Mexico: Suprema Corte de Justicia de la Nación, 1986).

89. Arnold, "La Audiencia de México," 366.

90. I owe this primary information to Professor José María del Portillo Valdés, who gathered it as part of his research on constitutional historical topics. He generously shared it with me, for which I am most grateful. Control over the criminal file in dispute alternated between the Subdelegado of Atlisco, Francisco Crallo, and the indigenous community of Tiasquismalnalco. The proceedings had been pending since at least May 1813. See the case against Sebastián Osorio for injuries to his wife, Juana María. AHN, Mexico, Indiferente, Civil, Virreinal, exp. 18, fol. 1; año 1813, caja 4037; exp. 83, 1813, caja 5513; AHN, Mexico, Indiferente Virreinal, Subdelegados, exp. 37, año 1813, caja 2993.

91. See Arnold, "La Audiencia de México," 361–375.

92. For a comparative study of the practical impact of the Constitution de Cádiz in several regions of Spanish America, see Bonilla, ed., *La Constitución de 1812 en Hispanoamérica y España* (Bogotá: Editorial Universidad Nacional de Colombia–Alcaldia Mayor de Bogotá, 2012).

93. See Victor M. Uribe-Uran, "Cádiz contra las Provincias: Constitución, revolución y reacción en Nueva Granada, 1811–1821," *Boletín de Historia y Antigüedades* 97.849 (2010): 295–319; idem, "La Constitución de Cádiz en la Nueva Granada, teoría y realidad, 1812–1821," in Bonilla, ed., *La Constitución de 1812 en Hispanoamérica y España*, 273–303.

94. Constitución de Cundinamarca (1811), articles 35 and 37.

95. Constitución de Tunja (1811), section XII.

96. Constitución de Cundinamarca (1812), section IV, article 1.

97. Constitución de Cartagena (1812), Judicial Powers, articles 6–7, 17, 20–22.

98. Constitución de Mariquita (1815), articles 13, 16–21.

99. Ibid., article 9.

100. Ibid., article 22.

101. Constitución de Antioquia (1815), Section 1: Rights of Man: articles 7, 9, 10, 11.

102. See Constitución de Antioquia (1815), Section III, Judicial Powers, article 1. Manuel Antonio Pombo and José Joaquín Guerra, *Constituciones de Colombia,* 3 vols. (Bogotá: Fondo de Promoción de la Cultura Banco Popular, 1986), vol. 1.

103. AGN, Colombia, República, Criminales, legajo 19, fols. 868–970, esp. fol. 869.

104. Ibid., fol. 870.

105. Ibid., fols. 890, 907.

106. Ibid., fols. 910, 970.

107. Constitución de Colombia (1821), article 167.

108. Ibid., articles 156–177.

109. Constitución de Mexico (1824), article 149.

110. Ibid., articles 146–156.

111. Antón Oneca, "Historia del Código Penal de 1822," 263–278.

112. One of the committee's most influential members was liberal Extremaduran jurist and former Cortes of Cádiz deputy José María Calatrava. Another illustrious member was historian, jurist, and liberal priest Francisco Martinez Marina. See Antón Oneca, "Historia del Código Penal de 1822," 268–269, 274–275.

113. Antón Oneca, "Historia del Código Penal de 1822," 270–271.

114. It was the *Código para el Distrito y Territories Federales,* enacted in 1871. See Martín Gabriel Barrón Crúz, coord., *Cinco ordenamientos penales del siglo XIX* (México: Instituto Nacional de Ciencias Penales, 2010), 10–17.

115. Hespanha, "De *Iustitia* a Disciplina," 204.

116. The code's expression was "*amonestaciones y moderados castigos domésticos.*" See Código penal español, articles 561 and 569.

117. Ibid., article 561.

118. Ibid., article 670.

119. Ibid., article 571.

120. Ibid., article 683.

121. Ibid., article 684.

122. Ibid., article 26.

123. The 1822 code's definition of crime as "free, willing and malicious conduct" was relatively similar to the one in the medieval *Siete Partidas* ("*yerro que los hombres hacen a sabienda con mala intención*"). Antón Oneca, "Historia del Código Penal de 1822," 272–273.

124. Código penal español, articles 609 and 612.

125. Ibid., article 74.

126. Ibid., article 619.

127. Ibid., article 619.

128. Ibid., article 38.

129. Ibid., articles 28 and 31.

130. Ibid., article 31.

131. Ibid., article 39.

132. Ibid., article 39.

133. Ibid., article 41.

134. Ibid., article 42.

135. Ibid., article 40.
136. Ibid., article 40.
137. Ibid., articles 37 and 39.
138. Ibid., article 46.
139. Ibid., article 46.
140. Ibid., article 35.
141. Ibid., chapter X, articles 156–170.
142. Ibid., article 166.
143. Ibid., article 35.
144. Ibid., article 169.
145. The code went into effect in January 1823 and remained in place for only a couple more months. By early 1823, Spain was undergoing a civil war, and King Ferdinand VII once more abolished all legal acts enacted by the "so-called constitutional government." Antón Oneca, "Historia del Código Penal de 1822," 274–275.
146. The text in its entirety can be found in Martín Gabriel Barrón Cruz, *Cinco ordenamientos penales del siglo XIX* (México: INACIPE, 2010), 65–187.
147. Código Penal para el Estado de Veracrúz, articles 500 and 508.
148. Ibid., articles 508–511.
149. Ibid., article 119, no. 7.
150. Ibid., Section V, *delitos de incontinencia.*
151. Ibid., article 636.
152. Ibid., articles 176 and 639.
153. Ibid., article 641.
154. Ibid., section II, articles 2–15.
155. Ibid., articles 543, 548, 550.
156. Ibid., articles 550 and 552.
157. Ibid., article 120.
158. Ibid., article 557, no. 5; article 580.
159. Ibid., article 116.
160. Ibid., article 6.
161. Ibid., article 3.
162. Ibid., article 10.
163. Ibid., article 15.
164. See also Enrique Díaz Aranda and Olga Islas de González Mariscal, *Pena de muerte* (Mexico City: UNAM–Instituto Nacional de Ciencias Penales, 2003), 18–22.
165. See its text in *Recopilación de Leyes de la Nueva Granada. Formada y publicada . . ., por Lino de Pombo* (Bogotá: Imprenta de Zoilo Salazar, 1845), 174–227.
166. Código Penal de la Nueva Granada, article 1.
167. Ibid., article 470.
168. Ibid., article 468.
169. Ibid., article 469.
170. Ibid., article 471.
171. Ibid., article 472.

172. Ibid., article 464.
173. Ibid., article 729.
174. Ibid., article 730.
175. Ibid., article 731.
176. Ibid., article 623.
177. Ibid., article 107.
178. Ibid., article 120.
179. Ibid., article 120.
180. Ibid., article 18.
181. Ibid., article 58.
182. Ibid., article 19.
183. Ibid., article 51.
184. "*Son parricidas los que matan a su padre o madre, a su abuelo, u otro ascendiente en línea recta . . .*," Código Penal de la Nueva Granada, article 61.
185. Ibid., article 610.
186. Ibid., article 646.
187. Ibid., article 618.
188. Ibid., article 605.
189. Ibid., article 606, no. 1.
190. Ibid., article 32.
191. Ibid., articles 27, 33.
192. Ibid., article 33.
193. Ibid., article 33.
194. Ibid., article 30.
195. Ibid., article 34.
196. Ibid., article 34.
197. Ibid., article 34.
198. Ibid., article 35.
199. Ibid., article 36.
200. Ibid., article 37.
201. Ibid., article 38.
202. Ibid., article 37.
203. Ibid., article 94.

CONCLUSION

1. Unlike nation-states that foster the homogeneity of the various populations within their borders, empires tend to make explicit the differences among those they rule and openly embrace the need to govern different peoples differently. See Cooper, *Colonialism in Question;* Frederick Cooper and Jane Burbank, *Empires in World History* (Princeton: Princeton University Press, 2010), 9–14.

2. Except in a brief passage of the introduction, this book does not explicitly broach the notion of hegemony, a concept that some Latin Americanists have explored creatively in important works. See, for instance, Steve J. Stern, *Peru's Indian Peoples;* Florencia Mallon, *Peasant and Nation.*

3. On the analogous significance of mercy to legitimate power in eighteenth-century England, see insightful comments by Hay, "Property, Authority and the Criminal Law," 40–49.

4. The occasional punishment of the powerful was a central part of legal ideology, making the law an effective means of domination. Hay, "Property, Authority and the Criminal Law," 38–39, 48.

5. Mantecón, *Conflicto y disciplinamiento social;* idem, "El peso de la infrajudicialidad en el control del crimen durante la edad moderna"; idem, "Social Control from Below"; idem, "Disciplinamiento social, escenografías punitivas y cultura plebeya en el Antiguo Régimen." See also Dominino Crespo, *Escandalos y delitos de la gente plebe.*

6. The sharpest discussion of this circumstance, using the English example, continues to be by Hay, "Property, Authority and the Criminal Law," 40–49

7. This resembles what Diana Paton found in the case of postabolitionist ("modern") Jamaica. See Diana Paton, *No Bond but the Law: Punishment, Race and Gender in Jamaican State Formation, 1780–1870* (Durham: Duke University Press, 2004).

Glossary

Alcalde del crimen Subordinate justice active in the resolution of criminal cases within one of the high courts of justice (*audiencias* or *chancillerias*) of the Spanish monarchy.

Alcaldes de Casa y Corte Justices of a special high tribunal charged with the investigations of crimes committed in the city of Madrid, capital of the Kingdom of Castille, and its surrounding areas (*rastro*).

Alunamiento Exposure to the moon, popularly believed to cause or aggravate illnesses and even lead to one's death.

Amacio Permanent common law partner. Expression used in New Spain (Mexico).

Apremios Physical or psychological pressure used to extract a criminal's confession or a witness's information about a crime, less intense in nature than torture and commonly used until the early nineteenth century.

Asesor letrado Lawyer consulted by lay judges in order to reach major decisions in judicial cases, in particular issuing the final sentence.

Asilo Institution whereby criminals sought sanctuary in a Catholic church or holy place (e.g., hermitage, convent, monastery, cemetery, or the parish priest's home adjacent to the church). The main benefit derived from it was one's immunity from the death penalty or from serious physical punishment, in particular mutilation. This expression also applied to the place of sanctuary itself.

Audiencia High court of appeals in the Spanish monarchy. There were several (around eleven by the late eighteenth century) in Spain itself and at least one in each colonial region overseas. Each was typically divided into a criminal section and a civil section.

Auto Any preliminary judicial decisions in criminal proceedings.

Ayuntamientos Local city councils, also referred to as *cabildos*. Typically, they were staffed by prominent neighbors elected by their also elite peers.

Blandones Mourning candles placed around one's coffin.

Branding A modality of punishment used since the dark ages and medieval times whereby red-hot irons, with a wooden handle on one end and a letter (typically a *V* for vagabond, an *F* for fighter, or an *S* for runaway slave) on the other, were used to mark the body of those targeted for persecution, particularly vagabonds, gypsies, brawlers, and runaway slaves.

Bunde Afro-Colombian rhythm popular along Colombia's Pacific coast. From there it spread to the interior, including areas in northern Antioquia populated by miners and journeymen of African descent. It was typically played at night in streets, public squares, and backyards, and was popular among blacks, Indians, mestizos, mulattoes, and *zambos*. The Catholic clergy disliked the lascivious nature of *bunde*'s lyrics, the "indecent" bodily movements of dancers, and the disorderly mix of men and women of all races, who usually failed to attend church the day after the dances.

Canon law Body of law enacted by the Catholic clergy (the pope, meetings of cardinals and bishops, individual cardinal and bishops, etc.) to regulate and sanction the behavior of ecclesiastical authorities and parishioners, in particular the observance of the holy sacraments and doctrine.

Casta(s) The mixed-race segment of the population. Expression was used both as an adjective and as a noun.

Castigo extraordinario Reduced punishment in consideration of the circumstances of the crime or social condition of the criminal. In the case of spousal murder, it could include the execution of a criminal by more-humane means or exemption from the death penalty altogether.

Castigo ordinario Punishment normally imposed on the person responsible of crime. In the case of spousal murder, it formally consisted of the death penalty by *encubamiento*.

Caución juratoria Security bond required to ensure compliance with a decision by a civil or an ecclesiastical court.

Censura Ecclesiastical sanction in response to the violation of a canon law precept. It mainly consisted of excommunication.

Chancilleria The highest-ranking appeals court in the Spanish peninsula. There were only two at the end of the late eighteenth century: one in Valladolid and another one in Granada.

Chicha Corn beer, a common inebriant among working-class groups in the Andean region.

Contumacia Resistance to answer a judicial summons and appear before court. A judicial declaration that it had occurred was typically issued after several summons were delivered and went unanswered. The formal declaration was needed to proceed with the judicial investigation.

Conyugicidio Generic expression used to refer to the murder of one's spouse.

Corregidores Highest executive and judicial officials in a region comprising typically an important city and several adjacent towns. In Spain these officials tended to be trained in the law. In the colonial territories, several were laymen. As opposed to local mayors, they were not elected but designated by the king or the local viceroy.

Cortes Spanish parliament. The most significant for the purpose of this study was the one meeting in Cádiz between 1810 and 1814. It produced the Cádiz Constitution of 1812 and a number of liberal decrees.

Cuerpo del delito Main body of evidence to demonstrate the commission of a crime. In the case of a murder, it was a corpse; in the case of theft, it was the stolen goods.

Curador Person appointed to represent the interests of a minor (all Indians included) in a criminal case.

Débito [conjugal] A wife's obligation to deliver sex to her husband upon request.

Delito privado A crime that could be investigated and prosecuted only upon the request of the victim. Adultery was in this category.

Delito público A crime whose investigation and prosecution could be conducted ex officio by the judicial authorities without the need of a formal request (*querella*) from the victim or other parties. This included murder and other serious offenses.

Denuncia Notice brought to the authorities that a crime had been committed.

Depósito Placement of a woman under the care of an institution or individual to ensure her protection and good behavior during the investigation of a legal dispute involving her. In many instances it occurred upon the request of husbands. It was considered a means to safeguard women's honesty and good name or protect their physical integrity.

Derecho Indiano Body of law developed to regulate colonial affairs involving aboriginal communities. Tended to include not only legislation enacted in Spain itself but also a number of casuistic decisions and orders issued in the overseas colonial territories by a variety of authorities, in particular viceroys and the various appeals courts (*audiencias*).

Destierro Banishment from one's area of residence. Punishment imposed on those committing certain crimes, even spousal murder.

Dispensas Ecclesiastical exemptions or waivers issued in order to, for instance, make it possible for people to marry under circumstances (e.g., without the required banns) or with individuals (e.g., close kin) otherwise prohibited by canon law.

Divorcio Bodily separation of spouses that did not allow them to contract a new marriage.

Encubamiento Punishment applied since Roman times to those who murdered their spouses or close kin. Adopted by Spanish law, it originally included the introduction of the living criminal in a leather sack along with a number of dangerous animals (e.g., a monkey, a rooster, a snake, and a dog), after which the sack was sealed and dumped for good in an ocean or a river, thus denying the aggressor proper Christian burial. As time went on, the actual practice included the execution of the criminal prior to his or her placement in the sack, the painting of animals on the outside of the sack rather than the use of real beasts, and the brief immersion of the sack in a stream followed by its prompt rescue by a religious brotherhood charged with burying it properly.

Escribanos Public scribes charged with drafting and keeping legal records, even criminal files. They bore witness to the truthfulness of legal transactions and were in charge of issuing certified copies (*testimonios*) of proceedings. Important cities could have several of them in place.

Estado llano Commoners in the Spanish Peninsula.

Estamentos Social groupings hierarchically arranged in consideration of their importance. Typically, they included the nobility, the clergy, the military, and the commoners.

Estupro Extraction of sexual favors under false pretenses or promise of marriage.

Excepciones Legal explanations presented in both criminal and civil cases to excuse one's behavior.

Fandango A popular celebration typically held at a private home and involving music and dancing.

Fiscalde lo criminal Prosecuting attorney in criminal cases.

Fueros Exemptions from ordinary legislation or judicial treatment. These legal privileges could cover entire communities or towns, or particular individuals, especially clergymen and the military.

Furia Rage. In cases involving physical aggression, it was typically invoked to excuse one's criminal behavior.

Galera It had two possible meanings. First of all, it was a ship operated by prisoners who typically served as rowers. Alternatively, it was the name given to jails exclusively for female inmates.

Gañan Peon or landless agricultural worker.

Garrote Instrument used to execute a person by strangulation. It typically consisted of a chair with a pole that had affixed an iron collar to secure the prisoner's neck. The collar was tightened gradually with a screw until the person choked to death while his or her vertebrae were crushed. It was used since medieval times and became in late colonial times the preferred mechanisms for the execution of noble people.

Gentil Non-Christian. Generally applied to Indians who had not yet converted to Catholicism.

Hidalgo Lower nobleman in the Spanish peninsula.

Honra One's social worth, closely dependent upon one's gender. In the case of men, it involved manliness, bravery, and services to the monarch. In the case of women, it involved sexual virtue, timidity, seclusion, and dedication to the care of one's household.

Indicios Judicial clues. Several were required to constitute full proof of a crime.

Indulto Royal forgiveness. There were general ones (*indultos generales*) and individual ones (*indultos particulares*). The monarch typically issued them to celebrate joyous occasions (his coronation, a royal wedding, the birth of a royal infant).

Inmunidad Attribute of those covered by sanctuary. It typically included the exemption from the death penalty and bodily mutilation.

Instrucción manual Hands-on or practical legal manual.

Justicias mayores Local justice officials.

Labradores Farmers or land tillers.

Lesiones Physical or bodily injury.

Limpieza de sangre Absence of nonwhite or non-Catholic ancestry.

Lutos Colors and decorations used to symbolize the mourning of the death of close kin.

Malos tratos Physical aggression against one's spouse.

Miserabiles personae (pl.)/Miserabilis persona (sing.) A Roman and canon law category to address wretched people or a wretched individual. Those covered by it were entitled to preferential legal treatment in consideration of their vulnerability. Ecclesiastical judges had priority over the handling of their cases. The category typically included widows, the physically disabled, and, in the Spanish colonies, Indians.

Neófitos Those persons newly baptized and inducted into the Catholic faith.

Nulidades Procedural or substantial defects that could lead to the nullification of civil contracts and judicial proceedings.

Obrajero Worker in a textile workshop (*obraje*).

Pardo Mixed-race individual, particularly a mulatto (resulting from the mixing of a white and a black person).

Parricidio/Parricida Generic way to refer in earlier colonial times to the crime of killing close kin, even one's spouse.

Pater familiae Male head of a household.

Perdon de viernes santo Pardon granted by the king to murderers on the occasion of Good Friday.

Plena prueba Full proof of a fact, typically consisting of the testimony of two direct credible witnesses or an assortment of compelling clues.

Práctica criminal Practical legal manual addressed to practicing attorneys, judicial officials, scribes, and bureaucrats.

Práctico Legal or medical expert trained empirically, not at a university.

Presidio Military fort in frontier areas of the empire, typically near a Catholic mission.

Privilegios Legal prerogatives, in particular immunity (*fuero*).

Probanzas Proofs or evidence.

Procuradores Solicitors. They were legal experts without formal legal training but knowledgeable of the practice of law and able to file petitions before courts of justice on behalf of litigants.

Pulque/pulquerías/pulquero Fermented alcoholic drink derived from agave/places where it was sold/artisan who had expertise in the extraction and fermentation of the drink.

Querella Legal notice, denunciation, or complaint.

Ratificación A witness's reiteration of his or her testimony before a court of justice.

Rebeldia Contumacy (resistance to answer a legal summons and appear in court).

Recogida A woman locked in a *recogimiento*.

Recogimiento An institution (also called a *casa de recogida* or *arrepentidas*) that housed women who had "perverted" themselves and offended God by committing crimes of "dishonesty or impurity." As in a monastery, the residents lived in community and typically supported themselves through sewing, embroidering, and the making of sweets.

Reconvención Judicial admonition used as a minor sanction in criminal cases.

Recurso de fuerza Judicial appeal before royal courts against decisions by the ecclesiastical judges, especially the granting of sanctuary, deemed to be in violation of civil (royal) law. Sometimes, legal records just refer to "*fuerza*" or "*hacer fuerza*."

Retraído Someone (typically a criminal) who was being sheltered at a place of sanctuary.

Secuestro Judicial seizure of a criminal's properties during the course of proceedings.

Sentencia Final decision or verdict in a judicial case.

Sentencia ejecutoriada A judge's final decision that has already gone through all possible appeals and been confirmed.

Sentencia interlocutoria Temporary or partial judicial ruling during criminal proceedings.

Sevicia Cruelty or savagery. Commonly used to refer to intense battering.

Solimán Mercury-based poisonous compound found in Spanish pharmacies.

Sumario Initial phase of a criminal investigation, prior to the discovery of evidence.

Tachar/Tachas Legal challenge to the validity of judicial evidence or judicial procedure.

Testimonio Oral testimony. Expression was also used to refer to copies of judicial proceedings.

Tormento Judicial torture, a legally acceptable means to obtain evidence in criminal investigations until the end of colonial times.

Traslado Notification to the parties of any decision during judicial proceedings. The main purpose was to give the opportunity to challenge the decision.

Vindicta pública Punishment administered by the monarchy's judicial system. The expression was meant to symbolize that criminals were no longer subject to private vengeance but to royal justice.

Zambo Racial term used in colonial Spanish America to designate a person of mixed African and Amerindian ancestry.

Bibliography

NEWSPAPERS

Correo General de España, 1769–1771
El Diario de México, 1805–1810

PRIMARY SOURCES

Acevedo, Alfonso María de, *De reorum absolutione objecta crimina negatium apud equuleum ac de hujus usu eliminando praesertim ab ecclessiasticis tribunalibus, Matriti* (1770). [*Ensayo acerca de la tortura o cuestión del tormento; de la absolución de los reos que niegan en el potro los delitos que se les imputan, y de la abolición del uso de la tortura principalmente en los tribunales eclesiásticos.* Spanish translation, Madrid, 1817].

Aguilar Mendivil, Antonio de, *Manifestación jurídica sobre el derecho de inmunidad y sagrado de las iglesias y monasterios* (Murcia, Spain: 1688).

Alvarez Posadilla, Juan, *Práctica criminal por principios o modo y forma de instruir los procesos criminales de las causas de oficio de justicia contra los abusos introducidos*, 3 vols. (Madrid: En la imprenta que fue de García, 1815 [1794]).

Archivo de la Real Chancillería de Granada (ARCG), *Libro de Providencias Definitivas, 1799–1815*, libro 324.

Archivo del Reino de Galicia (ARG), *Indice Topográfico Cronológico*. Sección 7. Serie Causas I—Años 1762–1835.

Asso y del Río, Ignacio Jordán de, and Miguel de Manuel y Rodríguez, *Instituciones del derecho civil de Castilla que escribieron los doctores Asso y Manuel, enmendadas, ilustradas y añadidas conforme a la real orden de 5 de Octubre de 1802 por el Dr. Don Joaquín María Palacios*. 7a ed. 3 vols. (Madrid: Imprenta de Don Tomás Albán, 1806 [1771]).

Barrón Cruz, Martín Gabriel, *Cinco ordenamientos penales del siglo XIX* (México: INACIPE, 2010).

Beccaria, Cesare, *Dei delitti e delle pene*, 6th ed. (Harlem: Chez Molini Librairie, 1766 [1764]).

Berni Catala, Joseph, *Apuntamientos sobre las leyes de partida 6 y 7* (Valencia: Por los Herederos de Gerónimo Conejos, 1759).

———, *Instituta española que facilita el estudio de la Juris-Prudencia Real. Para el uso de los principiantes juristas*, Biblioteca Histórica, Universidad de Valencia, Manuscrito.

———, *Práctica criminal con notas de los delitos, sus penas, presunciones y circunstancias que los agravan y disminuyen* (Valencia: Simón Faure, Librero, 1769).

Bodin, Jean, *The Six Bookes of a Commonweale*, edited with an introduction by Kenneth Douglas McRae (Cambridge, 1962; a facsimile reprint of the English translation of 1606).

Bossi, Egidio, *Practica et tractatus varii, seu quaestiones, Aegidii Bossii . . . criminalem materiam siue actionem fere omnem exacte continentes* (Basileae: Per Sebastianum Henricpetri, 1578).

Castillo de Bobadilla, Jerónimo, *Política para corregidores y señores de vasallos en tiempos de paz y de guerra*, 2 vols. (Madrid: Por Luis Sánchez, 1597).

———, *Política para corregidores y señores de vasallos en tiempos de paz y de guerra* (Madrid: Edición facsímil, Instituto de Estudios de Administración Local, 1978).

Castro, Pedro de, *Defensa de la tortura y leyes patrias que la establecieron e impugnación del tratado que escribió contra ella el Doctor D. Alfonso de Acevedo* (Madrid: M. Escribano, 1778).

Cavallario, Domingo, *Instituciones de derecho canónico* (Madrid: Imprenta de Gómez Fuentenebro, 1843).

[Los] *Códigos españoles concordados y anotados*, 12 vols. (Madrid: Imprenta de la Publicidad, a cargo de M. Rivadeneyra, 1847–1851).

Colección de los decretos y ordenes que han expedido las Cortes Generales y Extraordinarias desde su instalación en 24 de Septiembre de 1810 hasta igual fecha de 1811 (Madrid: Imprenta Nacional, 1813).

Colección de los decretos y ordenes que han expedido las Cortes Generales y Extraordinarias desde 24 de Septiembre de 1811 hasta 24 de Mayo de 1812 (Madrid: Imprenta Nacional, 1820).

Colmenares, German ed., *Relaciones e informes de los gobernantes de la Nueva Granada*, 3 vols. (Bogotá: Fondo de Promoción de la Cultura del Banco Popular, 1989).

Corella, Jaime de, *Practica del confesonario y explicación de las 65 proposiciones condenad. por la Santidad de N.S.P. Inocencio XI: su materia, los casos más selectos de la Theologia Moral, su forma, vn dialogo entre el confesor y penitente* (Zaragoza: Por Domingo Gascon, Infancon, 1688).

Covarrubia Leiva, Diego, *Clementinae, Si Furiosus de Homicidio, Relectio* (Salamanticae: Excudebat Andreas a Portonarijs, SCM Typographus, 1560).

———, *Variarum ex Iure Pontificio, Regio & Caesareo Resolutionum* (Salamanca: Andreas a Portonarijs, 1552),

Davis, Natalie Zemon, *Fiction in the Archives: Pardon Tales and Their Tellers in Sixteenth-Century France* (Stanford: Stanford University Press, 1987).

Diario de viaje que por orden de la sagrada congregación de propaganda fie hizo a la America Septentrional en el siglo XVIII el Padre Fray Francisco de Ajofrin, Capuchino, 2 vols. (Madrid: Maestre, 1958–1959).

Diaz de Luco, Ioannis Bernardi [Juan Bernardo Diaz de Lugo], *Practica criminalis canonica* (Medina del Campo: Apud Gillelmum de Millis, 1545).

Donoso, Justo, *Instituciones de derecho canónico americano*, 3 vols. (Paris: Libreria de Rosa y Bouret, 1868).

Duque de Estrada, Diego, *Comentarios del desengañado de si mismo, vida del mismo autor*. Edited and with an introduction and notes by Henry Ettinghausen (Madrid: Clásicos Castalia, 1982 [c. 1640s.]).

Elizondo y Alvarez, Francisco, *Practica universal forense de los tribunales de España y de las Indias*, 8 vols. (Madrid: Por D. Joachin Ibarra Impresor de Camara de S.M., 1785 [1770]).

Elizondo y Alvarez, Francisco Antonio de, *Practica universal forense de los tribunales de España y de las Indias*, 6th edition (Madrid: Imprenta de Ramón Ruíz, 1796).

Encinas, Diego de, *Cedulario Indiano*, 4 vols. (Madrid: Ediciones Cultura Hispánica, 1945–1946 [1596]).

Erauso, Catalina de, *Lieutenant Nun: Memoir of a Basque Transvestite in the New World*. Trans. by Michele Stepto and Gabriel Stepto, foreword by Marjorie Garber (Boston: Beacon, 1996).

Farinacii, Prosperi, *Praxis, et Theoricae Criminales*. Editio Ultima (Lugduni: Sumptibus Iacobi Cardon, 1634 [1612]).

Fernández de Oviedo, Gonzalo, *Historia General y Natural de las Indias*, 5 vols. (Madrid: Biblioteca de Autores Españoles, 1959).

Floridablanca Census, published by Spain's National Statistics Institute (INE), www.ine.es/censo2001/florida.htm.

Forner, J. P., *Discurso sobre la tortura* (Barcelona: Critica, 1990 [1792]).

Gomezio, Antonio [Antonio Gomez], *Commentariorum Variarum que Resolutionum Iuris Civilis Communis & Regij*, 3 vols. (Salamanca: C.M. Tipography, 1569).

Gonzalez de Socueba, Fernando, *Instruccion Manual para la más breve expedición de los casos prácticos y disputas de immunidad local. Noticia histórica de su origen, progresos y estado. A la inteligencia de las más modernas constituciones pontificias* (Sevilla: Imprenta del Doctor Don Geronymo de Castilla, 1766).

Gutiérrez, Joseph Marcos, *Compendio de las varias resoluciones de Antonio Gómez, en que se contiene todo lo sustancial de éstas, y se ponen muchas notas de las más útiles e importantes de Atillón y Suárez con otras diversas no menos necesarias. . .* (Madrid: En la Imprenta de Don Benito Cano, 1789).

———, *Práctica criminal de España*, 3 vols. (Madrid: En la oficina de don Benito García y Compañía, 1806 [1789]).

Hevia Bolaños, Juan de, *Curia filipica, donde breve y compendioso se trata de los iucios, mayormente forenses, eclesiásticos y seculares, con lo sobre ellos hasta ahora dispuesto por derecho, resuelto por doctores antiguos y modernos y practicable* (Madrid: por la Viuda de Alonso Martin, 1627 [1605]).

Humboldt, Alejandro, *Ensayo político sobre el reino de la Nueva España* (Mexico: Editorial Porrúa, 1966 [1822]).

Ilarione da Bergamo, Fray, Robert R. Miller, and William J. Orr, *Daily Life in Colonial Mexico: The Journey of Friar Ilarione da Bergamo, 1761–1768* (Norman: University of Oklahoma Press, 2000).

"Indulto general concedido por nuestro católico Monarca, a todos los individuos que sean capaces de él, con el plausible motivo del restablecimiento de nuestra sagrada constitución" (Madrid: Imprenta de Arjona, 1820).

Jovellanos, Gaspar Melchor de, *El delincuente honrado: Comedia en prosa* (1773), www.rinconcastellano.com/biblio/ilustracion/jovellanos_dh.html#.

Kalendario manual y guia de forasteros en Madrid para el año 1797 (Madrid, 1797). BNE.

Lardizábal y Uribe, Manuel de, *Discurso sobre las penas contrahido a las leyes criminales de España para facilitar su reforma* (Madrid: por Joachin Ibarra, 1782).

León, Pedro de, *Compendio de algunas experiencias en los ministerios [de que usa] la Compañia de Jesús. . . .* 2 vols. (Granada: Colegio de la Compañia de Jesús, 1619).

Llamas y Molina, Sancho de, *Comentario crítico-jurídico-literal a las ochenta y tres Leyes del Toro*, 3 vols. (Madrid: Imprenta de Repullés, 1827).

López, Gregorium [Gregorio López], *Index seu repertorium materiarum ac vtriusque iuris decisionum quae in singulis Septem partitarum glossis continentur* (Salmanticae: in aedibus Dominici â Portonarijs, 1576).

———, *Las Siete Partidas del Sabio Rey don Alonso el Nono nuevamente glosadas por el licenciado Gregorio Lopez . . . con su Reportorio muy copioso, asi del Testo como de la Glosa* (Salamanca: por Andrea de Portonaris, 1555).

López de Cuellar, Juan, *Tratado jurídico-político de indultos conforme a las leyes y ordenanzas reales de Castilla y Navarra en que se ponderan los delitos por su gravedad, no comprendidos los expresamente exceptuados por las reales cedulas de indultos* (Pamplona: Por Martin Gregorio de Zabala, Impresor del Reyno, 1690).

Martínez, Antonio, *Colección de memorias y noticias del gobierno del Consejo* (Madrid: Oficina de Antonio Sanz, 1764).

Martínez, Manuel Silvestre, *Librería de juezes, utilísima y universal para abogados, alcaldes mayores y ordinarios, corregidores e intendentes, juezes de residencia, y de visita, escribanos de toda España, receptores de Castilla, y Aragón, Regidores, juntas de propios, contribución, pósitos, y demás individuos de Tribunales Ordinarios: añadida, e ilustrada en esta segunda impresión, con mas de dos mil leyes reales, que autorizan su doctrina*, 7 vols. (Madrid: Imprenta de la Comisaria de Cruzada, 1764–1772).

Martínez Alcubilla, Marcelo, ed., *Códigos Antiguos de España*, 2 vols. (Madrid: J. López Camacho Impresor, 1895).

Mathaew Et Sanz, Laurentius D. D., *Tractatus de Re Criminali* (Lugduni: Apud Fratres Anissonios, Ioann. Posuel & Claudium Ridaug, 1686).

Meléndez Valdés, Juan, *Discursos Forenses de D. Juan Meléndez Valdés, fiscal que fue de la Sala de Alcaldes de Casa y Corte e Individuo de las Academia*

Española y de San Fernando, y de la de San Carlos de Valencia (Madrid: En la Imprenta Real, 1821).

"Memoria que el Virrey Carlos Francisco de Croix dejo a Don Fray Antonio María de Bucareli y Ursua, 1–IX–1771," in *Instrucciones y memorias de los virreyes novohispanos* (Mexico City: Editorial Porrúa, 1991) 2: 954–1008.

"Mercedes concedidas con motivo de la exaltación al trono del Rey Don Carlos IV: Su entrada en Madrid, celebración de Cortes Generales y jura de Don Fernando Príncipe de Asturias," *Revista Hidalguía* LIII.319 (2006): 835–874.

Monterroso y Alvarado, Gabriel, *Practica Civil y Criminal & Instrucción de Escribanos dividida en nueve tratados: Agora de nuevo enmendada y añadida, en esta segunda impresión, en muchas cosas a ella necesarias. especialmente en el quinto tratado* (Valladolid, por Francisco Fernández de Cordova, Impresor se SRM., 1566).

Montesquieu, Charles Secondat Baron de, and David Wallace et al., *Montesquieu's Science of Politics: Essays on the Spirit of Laws* (New York: Rowman and Littlefield, 2001).

Muñoz, Juan, *Práctica de procuradores para seguir pleitos civiles y criminales* (Madrid: Emprenta del Licëciado Castro, 1596).

Novísima Recopilación de las Leyes de España. Dividida en XII Libros. En que se reforma la Recopilación Publicada por el Señor Felipe II en el año de 1567, reimpresa últimamente en el de 1775: Y se incorporan las pragmáticas, cedulas, decretos, órdenes y resoluciones reales, y otras providencias no recopiladas, y expedidas hasta el año de 1804. Mandada a formar por el Señor Don Carlos IV (Madrid: n.e., 1805).

Ordenanzas Reales de Castilla por las cuales primeramente se han de librar todos los pleytos civiles y criminales. En los que por ellas no se hallare determinados se han de librar por las otras leyes y fueros recibidos. Nuevamente corregidas y muchos vicios y faltas que por el discurso del tiempo tenían lo cual muy fácilmente podrán ver y conocer (Toledo: Casa de Juan de Ayala, 1549).

Orti y Mayo, Jose Vicente, *Diario de lo sucedido en la Ciudad de Valencia desde el 3 de octubre de 1700 hasta el 1 de septiembre de 1715*. Biblioteca Histórica, Universidad de Valencia, Manuscrito.

"Padrón general del Virreinato del Nuevo Reino de Granada, 1778–1781," in José Manuel Pérez Ayala, *Antonio Caballero y Góngora: Virrey y arzobispo de Santafé, 1723–1796* (Bogotá: Imprenta Municipal, 1946).

Peña, Antonio de la, *Orden de los juicios y penas criminales* [sixteenth century], BNE, unpublished manuscript 6379.

Pérez y López, Antonio X., *Principios del orden esencial de la naturaleza, establecidos por fundamento y por prueba de la religión* (Madrid: Imprenta Real, 1785).

Pitigiani, Francesco, Ilarione Sacchetti, and Giovanni Battista Ciotti, *Practica criminalis canonica* (apud Io. Baptistam Ciottum, 1621).

Pombo, Manuel Antonio, and José Joaquín Guerra, *Constituciones de Colombia*, 3 vols. (Bogotá: Fondo de Promocion de la Cultura Banco Popular, 1986).

Pradilla Barnuevo, Franciso de la, *Tratado y suma de todas las leyes penales, canónicas y civiles de estos reynos* . . . (Pamplona: Nicolas de Afsiayn, 1622).

Quevedo y Hoyos, Antonio, *Libro de indicio y tormentos* (Madrid: Imp. Francisco Martínez, 1632).

Recopilación de las Leyes de estos Reynos hechas por Mandado de la Mag. Catholica del Rey Don Phelipe Quinto. 4 vols. (Madrid: Imprenta de Juan de Ariztia, 1723).

Recopilación de Leyes de la Nueva Granada: Formada y publicada . . ., por Lino de Pombo (Bogotá: Imprenta de Zoilo Salazar, 1845).

Robles, Antonio de, *Diario de sucesos notables (1665–1703)*, 3 vols. (México: Editorial Porrúa, 1946).

Rodríguez de San Miguel, Juan N., *Pandectas Hispano-Megicanas*, 2 vols. (México: Librería de J. F. Rosa, 1852).

Sala, Juan, *Ilustración del derecho real de España*, 5 vols. (México: Imprenta de Galván, 1833).

———, *Sala Mexicano, o sea Ilustración al Derecho Real de España . . . ilustrada con noticias oportunas sobre el derecho romano, y las leyes y principios que actualmente rigen en la república mexicana*, 4 vols. (México: Libreria del Portal de Mercaderes, 1845).

Sánchez, Thomas, *Compendium Totius Tractatus de Sancto Matrimonij Sacramnento* (Hispali ex officina Franciscum de Lyra: vendese en casa de Antonio de Toro, 1623).

———, *Moral jesuítica: O sea controversias del santo Sacramento del Matrimonio* (Madrid Imprenta Popular a cargo de Tomás Rey, 1887 [1623]).

Sanz, Miguel Cayetano, *Modo y forma de instruir y substanciar las causas criminales* (Madrid: Imprenta de Don Joseph Doblado, 1790).

Sedano, Francisco, *Noticias de México: Crónicas del siglo XVI al siglo XVIII*. 3 vols. (México: Secretaría de Obras y Servicios, 1974).

Sempere y Guarinos, Juan, *Ensayo de una biblioteca española de los mejores escritores del reinado de Carlos III*, 6 vols. (Madrid: Imprenta Real, 1785–1789).

Silvestre, Francisco, *Descripción del Reyno de Santa Fé de Bogotá escrita en 1789 por Don Francisco Silvestre, Secretario que Fue del Virreinato y antiguo Gobernador de la Provincia de Antioquia. Copia del Original que se encuentra en Sevilla. Por Ricardo Pereira* (Bogotá: Prensas del Ministerio de Educación Nacional, 1950 [1887]).

———, *Relación de la Provincia de Antioquia* (Medellín: Secretaria de Educación y Cultura de Antioquia, 1988).

Solorzano y Pereira, Juan, *Diligens & Accurata de Parricidi Crimine Disputatio* (Salamanticae: Vs. TABERNIEL Antuerpianos,1605).

———, *Política indiana*, 5 vols. (Madrid: Compañía Iberoamericana de Publicaciones, 1972).

Tapia, Eugenio de, *Febrero Novísimo o librería de jueces, abogados y escribanos*, 10 vols. (Valencia: Imprenta de Idelfonso Monpié, 1830).

Tovar Pinzón, Hermes, Jorge A. Tovar Mora, Camilo E. Tovar Mora, et al., *Convocatoria al poder del número: Censos y estadísticas de la Nueva Granada, 1750–1830* (Bogotá: Archivo General de la Nación, 1994).

Vignau y Ballester, Vicente, "*Discurso Del Sr. D. Vicente Vignau y Ballester*," en Archivo Histórico Nacional, *Discursos leidos ante la real Academia de la*

Historia en la recepción Pública del Sr. Vicente Vignau y Ballester el día 18 de Junio de 1898 (Madrid: Tip. Viuda e Hijos de Tello, 1898), 5–38.

Vilanova y Mañez, Senén, *Materia criminal forense, ó, Tratado universal teórico y práctico, de los delitos y delinquentes en género y especie, para la segura y conforme expedición de las causas de esta naturaleza: obra útil y precisa á jueces de todas clases, fiscales, abogados, asesores, escribanos, y demás que versan sus facultades en el foro,* 4 vols. (Madrid: En la Imprenta de Tomas Albán, 1807).

Villadiego Vascuñana, Alonso de, *Instrucción Política y Práctica Judicial* (Madrid: Luis Sanchez, 1612).

Villaseñor y Sánchez, José Antonio, *Theatro Americano: Instrucciones y Memorias de los Virreyes Novohispanos,* 2 vols. (México: Editorial Porrúa, 1991).

Vizcaino Pérez, Vicente, *Código y práctica criminal arreglado a las leyes de España* (Madrid: Imprenta de la Viuda de Ibarra, 1797).

Zorita, Alonso de, *Leyes y ordenanzas reales de las Indias del Mar Océano, por las cuales primeramente se han de librar todos los pleitos civiles y criminales de aquellas partes, y lo que por ellos no estuviese determinado se han de librar por las leyes y ordenanzas de los Reinos de Castilla* (México: Ed. Miguel Angel Porrúa, 1985).

Zuaznavar y Francia, José María de, *Noticias para literatos acerca de los archivos públicos de la hoy extinguida Sala de Alcaldes de Casa y Corte* (San Sebastián: Ignacio Ramón Baroja, 1834).

SECONDARY SOURCES

Abascal Monedero, Pablo José, *La infidelidad y el adulterio en España (estudio histórico-legal)* (Córdoba: Servicio de Publicaciones Universidad de Córdoba, 2009).

Abruzzo, Margaret, *Polemical Pain: Slavery, Cruelty, and the Rise of Humanitarianism* (Baltimore: Johns Hopkins University Press, 2011).

Adams, David, *Why Do They Kill: Men Who Murder Their Intimate Partners* (Nashville: University of Tennessee Press, 2007).

Adelman, Jeremy, *Republic of Capital: Buenos Aires and the Legal Transformation of the Atlantic World* (Stanford: Stanford University Press, 1999).

Adler, Jeffrey S., "'My Mother-in-Law Is to Blame, But I'll Walk on Her Neck Yet': Homicide in Late Nineteenth-Century Chicago," *Journal of Social History* 31.2 (1997): 253–276.

Agamben, Giorgio, *The Kingdom and the Glory: For a Theological Genealogy of Economy and Government* (Stanford: Stanford University Press, 2011).

Aguirre, Carlos, Gilbert M. Joseph, and Ricardo Salvatore, eds., *Crime and Punishment in Latin America* (Durham: Duke University Press, 2001).

Aguirre, Carlos, and Charles Walker, eds., *Bandoleros, abigeos y montoneros: Criminalidad y violencia en el Perú, siglos XVIII–XX* (Lima: IIAA, 1990).

Alberro, Solange, *La actividad del Santo Oficio de la Inquisición en Nueva España, 1571–1700* (México: Instituto Nacional de Antropología e Historia,

Departamento de Investigaciones Históricas, Seminario de Historia de las Mentalidades y Religión en el México Colonial, 1981).
———, *Inquisición y sociedad en México, 1571–1700* (México: Fondo de Cultura Económica, 1988).
Alejandre, Juan Antonio, "La función penitenciaria de las galeras," *Historia* 16, Extra VII (1978): 47–54.
Alloza, Angel, *La vara quebrada de la justicia: Un estudio histórico sobre la delincuencia madrileña entre los siglos XVII y XVIII* (Madrid: Catarata, 2000).
Almazán, Ismael, "Penas corporales y disciplina social en la justicia catalana de los siglos XVI y XVII," *Pedralbes* 12 (1992): 127–148.
Alonso, Ana María, *Thread of Blood: Colonialism, Revolution, and Gender on Mexico's Northern Frontier* (Tucson: University of Arizona Press, 1995).
Altamira, Rafael, "Los cedularios como fuente histórica de la legislación indiana," *Revista de Historia de América* 19 (June 1945): 61–129.
———, *Historia del derecho español* (Madrid: Librería General de V. Suáres, 1903).
———, *Manual de investigación de la historia del derecho indiano* (México: Instituto Panamericano de Geografía e Historia, 1948).
Amado, Jorge, *Gabriela, Clove and Cinnamon* (New York: Avon, 1988).
Antón Oneca, José, "Historia del Código Penal de 1822," *Anuario de Derecho Penal y Ciencias Penales* 17.2 (1965): 263–278.
Ariés, Philippe, *Centuries of Childhood: A Social History of Family Life* (New York: Knopf, 1962).
Arnold, Linda, "La Audiencia de Mexico durante la fase gaditana 1812–1815, 1820–1823," *Memoria del II congreso de historia del derecho mexicano* (México: UNAM, 1981), 361–375.
———, *La Suprema Corte de Justicia: Sus orígenes y primeros años, 1808–1847* (México: Suprema Corte de Justicia de la Nación, 1986).
———, "Vulgar and Elegant: Politics and Procedure in Early National Mexico," *Americas* 50.4 (1994): 481–500.
Arrom, Silvia M., *La mujer mexicana ante el divorcio eclesiástico, 1800–1857* (México: Septentas, 1976).
———, "New Directions in Mexican Legal History," *Americas* 50.4 (1994): 461–465.
_____ *The Women of Mexico City, 1790–1857* (Stanford: Stanford University Press, 1985).
Assadourian, Carlos Sempat, "Fray Bartolomé de las Casas, Obispo: La Condicion Miserable de las Naciones Indias y el derecho de la Iglesia (un escrito de 1545)," *Allpanchis* XII.35–36 (1990): 29–104.
Astarita, Tommaso, *Village Justice: Community, Family and Popular Culture in Early Modern Italy* (Baltimore: Johns Hopkins University Press, 1999).
Atondo Rodríguez, Ana María, *El amor venal y la condición femenina en el México colonial* (México: INAH, 1992).
Avila Martel, Alamiro, *Esquema del derecho penal indiano* (Santiago: Universidad de Chile, 1941).

Baade, Hans W., "The Law of Slavery in Spanish Louisiana, 1769–1803," in Edward F. Haas, ed., *Louisiana's Legal Heritage* (Pensacola: Perdido Bay, 1983), 43–86.

Barahona, Renato, *Sex Crimes, Honour, and the Law in Early Modern Spain: Vizcaya, 1528–1735* (Toronto: University of Toronto Press, 2003).

Barbosa Delgado, Francisco Roberto, *Justicia: Rupturas y continuidades. El aparato judicial en el proceso de configuración del Estado-Nación en Colombia, 1821–1853* (Bogotá: Pontificia Universidad Javeriana, 2007).

Barreneche, Osvaldo, *Crime and the Administration of Justice in Buenos Aires* (Lincoln: University of Nebraska Press, 2006).

———,"Jueces, policia y la administración de justicia criminal en Buenos Aires, 1810–1850," in Sandra Gayol and Gabriel Kessler, comps., *Violencias, justicias y delitos en la Argentina* (Manantial: Universidad Nacional de General Sarmiento, 2002), 207–225.

Bauer, Arnold J., *Goods, Power, History: Latin America's Material Culture* (Cambridge: Cambridge University Press, 2001).

Bayle, Constantino, *El protector de Indios* (Sevilla: Escuela de Estudios Hispanoamericanos, 1945).

Bazán, Iñaki, "La pena de muerte en la Corona de Castilla en la Edad Media," *Clio & Crimen* 4 (2007): 306–352.

Beattie, J. M., "The Criminality of Women in Eighteenth-Century England," *Journal of Social History* 8 (Summer 1975): 80–116.

Beaurepaire, Charles de, "Essai sur l'asile Religieux dans l'Empire Romain et la Monarchie Francaise," *Bibliotheque de l'Ecole de Chartes* 14 (1853): 351–375; 15 (1853): 151–175, 341–359.

Beezley, William H., Cheryl English Martin, and William E. French, eds., *Rituals of Rule, Rituals of Resistance: Public Celebrations and Popular Culture in Mexico* (Wilmington: Scholarly Resources, 1994).

Behrend-Martínez, Edward, *Unfit for Marriage: Impotent Spouses on Trial in the Basque Region of Spain, 1650–1750* (Reno: University of Nevada Press, 2007).

Beirne, Piers, ed., *The Origins and Growth of Criminology: Essays on Intellectual History, 1760–1945* (Hants: Darmouth, 1994).

Belmessous, Saliha, ed., *Native Claims: Indigenous Law Against Empire, 1500–1920* (Oxford: Oxford University Press, 2011).

Benavides, Christine, *Les Femmes Délinquantes à Madrid: Justice et Société en Espagne Au XVIIIe Siècle* (Toulouse: CRIC–Ophrys, 2000).

Bennassar, Bartolomé, *The Spanish Character: Attitudes and Mentalities from the Sixteenth to the Nineteenth Century,* translated and with a preface by Benjamin Keen (Berkeley: University of California Press, 1979).

Bennett, Herman L., *Africans in Colonial Mexico: Absolutism, Christianity and Afro-Creole Consciousness, 1570–1640* (Bloomington: Indiana University Press, 2006).

———, *Colonial Blackness: A History of Afro-Mexico* (Bloomington: Indiana University Press, 2009).

Benton, Lauren, *Law and Colonial Cultures: Legal Regimes in World History, 1400–1900* (Cambridge: Cambridge University Press, 2002).

———, *A Search for Sovereignty: Law and Geography in European Empires, 1400–1900* (Cambridge: Cambridge University Press, 2010).

Bergard, L. W., *The Comparative History of Slavery in Brazil, Cuba and the United States* (New York: Cambridge University Press, 2007).

Berman, Harold, *Law and Revolution: The Formation of the Western Legal Tradition* (Cambridge, MA: Harvard University Press, 1983).

Bermejo Cabrero, José Luís, "Tormentos, apremios, cárceles y patíbulos a finales del Antiguo Régimen," *Anuario de Historia del Derecho Español* 56 (1986): 683–727.

Black, Chad Thomas, *The Limits of Gender Domination: Women, the Law and Political Crisis in Quito, 1765–1830* (Albuquerque: University of New Mexico Press, 2010).

Bloch, Marc, "Pour une Histoire Comparée Des Societes Europeennes," *Melanges Historiques*, vol. 1 (Paris: Ecole Pratique de Hautes Etudes, 1963), 16–40. Translated into English as "Toward a Comparative History of European Societies," in Frederic C. Lane and Jelle C. Riemersma, eds., *Enterprise and Secular Change* (Homewood: Irwin, 1953), 494–521.

———, *Les rois Thaumaturges: Étude sur le caractère surnaturel attribué à la puissance royale particulièrement en France et en Angleterre* (Paris: Armand Colin, 1961).

Blok, Anton, *Honor and Violence* (Cambridge: Polity, 2001).

Bonnett, Diana, *Los protectores de naturales en la Audiencia de Quito: Siglos XVII y XVIII* (Quito: FLACSO, 1992).

Borah, Woodrow, *Justice by Insurance: The General Indian Court of Colonial Mexico and the Legal Aides of the Half Real* (Berkeley: University of California Press, 1983).

Bouzada Gil, María Teresa, *La vía de fuerza: La práctica en la Real Audiencia del Reino de Galicia. Siglos XVII–XVIII* (Santiago de Compostela: Xunta de Galicia, 2001).

Boyer, Richard, *Lives of the Bigamists: Marriage, Family and Community in Colonial Mexico* (Albuquerque: University of New Mexico Press, 1995).

———, "Women, la Mala Vida, and the Politics of Marriage," in Asunción Lavrín, ed., *Sexuality and Marriage in Colonial Latin America* (Lincoln: University of Nebraska Press, 1989), 252–286.

Boyer, Richard, and Geoffrery Spurling, eds., *Colonial Lives: Documents on Latin American History* (Oxford: Oxford University Press, 1999).

Bravo Lira, Bernardino, "El derecho indiano despues de la independencia en la América española," *Historia* 19 (1984): 5–52.

Brundage, James A., *Law, Sex, and Christian Society in Medieval Europe* (Chicago: University of Chicago Press, 1987).

Bushnell, David, *The Making of Modern Colombia: A Nation in Spite of Itself* (Berkeley: University of California Press, 1993).

Callahan, William J., *Honor, Commerce and Industry in Eighteenth Century Spain* (Boston: Baker Library, Harvard Graduate School, 1972).

Candau Chacón, Maria Luisa, *Los delitos y las penas en el mundo eclesiástico sevillano del siglo XVIII* (Seville: Diputación Provincial, 1993).
Cañeque, Alejandro, *The King's Living Image: The Culture and Politics of Viceregal Power in Colonial Mexico* (New York: Routledge, 2004).
Cañizares Esguerra, Jorge, *How to Write the History of the New World: Histories, Epistemologies and Identities in the Eighteenth-Century Atlantic World* (Stanford: Stanford University Press, 2001).
Caporossi, Olivier, "Les Madrilènes Face à la Violence: La Pratique du Pardon Privé Au XVIIe Siècle," *Hispania Sacra* LX, 121 (2008): 231–266.
Carrasco Manchado, Ana Isabel, *Isabel I de Castilla y la sombra de la ilegitimidad: Propaganda y representación en el conflicto sucesorio* (Madrid: Silex Ediciones, 2006).
Carroll, Patrick J., *Blacks in Colonial Veracruz: Race, Ethnicity, and Regional Development* (Austin: University of Texas Press, 1991).
Casa, Frank P., "Honor and the Wife-Killers of Calderón," *Bulletin of the Comediantes* 28 (1977): 27–31.
Castañeda, Carmen, "La formación de la pareja y el matrimonio," in Pilar Gonzalbo Aizpuru, *Familias novohispanas: Siglos XVI al XIX* (México: El Colegio de México, 1991), 73–90.
———, *Violación, estupro y sexualidad: Nueva Galicia, 1790–1821* (Guadalajara: Editorial Hexágono, 1989).
Castañeda, Paulino, "La condición miserable del indio y sus privilegios," *Anuario de Estudios Americanos* 28 (1971): 245–335.
Castro Gutiérrez, Felipe, "Condición femenina y violencia conyugal entre los Purépechas durante la época colonial," *Mexican Studies* 14.1 (1998): 5–21.
Caulfield, Sueann, "The History of Gender in the Historiography of Latin America," *Hispanic American Historical Review* 81.3–4 (2001): 449–490.
———, *In Defense of Honor: Sexual Morality, Modernity, and Nation in Early Twentieth Century Brazil* (Durham: Duke University Press, 2000).
Caulfield, Sueann, Sarah C. Chambers, and Lara Putnam, eds., *Honor, Status, and Law in Modern Latin America* (Durham: Duke University Press, 2005).
Chambers, Sarah, "Citizens Before the Law: The Role of Postindependence State Building in Spanish America," in Miguel A. Centeno and Agustin E. Ferraro, eds., *State and Nation Making in Latin America and Spain: Republics of the Possible* (Cambridge: Cambridge University Press, 2013): 356–374.
———, *From Subjects to Citizens: Honor, Gender, and Politics in Arequipa, Peru, 1780–1854* (University Park: Pennsylvania State University Press, 1999).
———, "The Paternal Obligation to Provide: Political Familialism in Early Nineteenth-Century Chile" *American Historical Review* 117.4 (2012): 1123–1148.
———, "To the Company of a Man Like My Huband No Law Can Compel Me: The Limits of Sanctions Against Wife-Beating in Arequipa, Peru, 1780–1850," *Journal of Women's History* 11.1 (1999): 31–52.
Chasteen, John Charles, *Born in Blood and Fire: A Concise History of Latin America* (New York: Norton, 2011).
Chaulet, Rudy, "La Violence en Castille au XVIIe Siècle à Travers les *Indultos de Viernes Santo* (1623–1699)," *Crime, Histoire & Sociétés* 1.2 (1997): 5–27.

Christiansen, Tanja, *Disobedience, Slander, Seduction and Assault: Women and Men in Cajamarca, Peru, 1862–1900* (Austin: University of Texas Press, 2004).

Cohen, Daniel A., "Homicidal Compulsion and the Conditions of Freedom: The Social and Psychological Origins of Familicide in America's Early Republic," *Journal of Social History* 24.4 (1995): 725–764.

Cohen, Martin A., *The Martyr Luis de Carvajal: A Secret Jew in Sixteenth-Century Mexico* (Albuquerque: University of New Mexico Press, 2002).

Colmenares, Germán, *Cali: Terratenientes, mineros y comerciantes, Siglo XVIII* (Bogotá: Banco Popular, 1983).

———, *Historia económica y social de Colombia, II: Popayán: una sociedad esclavista, 1680–1800* (Bogotá: Tercer Mundo Ed., 1979).

Cook, Noble David, and Alexandra Parma Cook, *Good Faith and Truthful Ignorance: A Case of Transatlantic Bigamy* (Durham: Duke University Press, 1991).

Cooper, Frederick, *Colonialism in Question: Theory, Knowledge, History* (Berkeley: University of California Press, 2005).

Cooper, Frederick, and Jane Burbank, *Empires in World History* (Princeton: Princeton University Press, 2010).

Cope, Douglas, *The Limits of Racial Domination: Plebeian Society in Colonial Mexico, 1660–1720* (Madison: University of Wisconsin Press, 1999).

Copic, Sanja, "Wife Abuse in the Countries of the Former Yugoslavia," *Feminist Review* 76 (2004): 46–64.

Cuello Calón, Eugenio, "Contribución al estudio de la historia de la pena de muerte en España," *Anuario de derecho penal y ciencias penales* 10 (1957): 9–40.

Cuena Boy, Francisco, "El defensor civitatis y el protector de indios: Breve ilustración de un paralelo," *Ius Fugit: Revista interdisciplinar de estudios histórico-jurídicos* 7 (1989): 178–196.

Cunill, Caroline, "El indio miserable: Nacimiento de la teoría legal en la América colonial del siglo XVI," *Cuadernos Inter.c.a.mbio* 8.9 (2011): 229–248.

Cunningham, Charles H., *The Audiencia in the Spanish Colonies as Illustrated by the Audiencia of Manila (1583–1800)* (Berkeley: University of California Press, 1919).

Curcio-Nagy, Linda A., *The Great Festivals of Colonial Mexico City: Performing Power and Identity* (Albuquerque: University of New Mexico Press, 2004).

Cutter, Charles R., *The Legal Culture of Northern New Spain, 1700–1810* (Albuquerque: University of New Mexico Press, 1995).

———, *The Protector de Indios in Late Colonial Mexico, 1659–1821* (Albuquerque: University of New Mexico Press, 1986).

Davis, David Brion, *The Problem of Slavery in Western Culture* (Ithaca: Cornell University Press, 1966).

Davis, Natalie Zemon, *Fiction in the Archives: Pardon Tales and Their Tellers in Sixteenth-Century France* (Stanford: Stanford University Press, 1987).

de la Pascua Sánchez, María José, "Violencia y Familia en la España del Antiguo Régimen," *Estudis: Revista de Historia Moderna* 28 (2002): 77–102.

de Trazegnies, Fernando, *Ciriaco de Urtecho: Litigante por Amor* (Lima: Pontificia Universidad Católica, 1995).

Defourneaux, Marcelin, *Daily Life in Spain During the Golden Age* (Stanford: Stanford University Press, 1966).

Demerson, Georges, *Don Juan Meléndez Valdés y su tiempo (1754–1817)*, 2 vols. (Madrid: Taurus, 1971).

Díaz, Arlene J., *Female Citizens, Patriarchs, and the Law in Venezuela, 1786–1904* (Lincoln: University of Nebraska Press, 2004).

Díaz Aranda, Enrique, and Olga Islas de González Mariscal, *Pena de muerte* (México: UNAM-Instituto Nacional de Ciencias Penales, 2003).

Díaz Consuelo, José María, "El Ius Commune y los privilegios de los indigenas en la América española," *Revista de Historia del Derecho* 29 (2001): 267–306.

Díaz Hernández, Magdalena, "La identidad de los esclavos negros como miserables en Nueva España: Discursos y acciones (siglos XVI–XVIII), in Aurelia Martín Casares, ed., *Esclavitudes Hispánicas (Siglos XV–XXI): Horizontes socioculturales* (Granada: Universidad de Granada, 2014), 41–57.

Doggett, Maeve E., *Marriage, Wife-Beating and the Law in Victorian England* (New York: Columbia University Press, 1993).

Domergue, Lucienne, and Antonio Risco, *L'Alcade et Le Malandrin: Justice et Société en Espagne Au XVIIIe Siècle* (Toulouse: CRIC et Ophrys, 2001).

Domínguez Ortíz, Antonio, *Sociedad y estado en el Siglo XVIII español* (Barcelona: Editorial Ariel, 1976).

Dominino Crespo, Darío, *Escándalos y delitos de la* gente plebe (Córdoba: Universidad Nacional de Córdoba, 2007).

Dopico, Fausto, and Robert Roland, "Demografía del censo de Floridablanca: Una aproximación," *Revista de Historia Económica* 3.8 (1990): 591–618.

Dore, Elizabeth, "One Step Forward, Two Steps Back: Gender and the State in the Long Nineteenth Century," in Elizabeth Dore and Maxine Molyneux, eds., *Hidden Histories of Gender and the State in Latin America* (Durham: Duke University Press), 3–32.

Dossey, Leslie, "Wife Beating and Manliness in Late Antiquity," *Past and Present* 199.1 (2008): 3–40.

Dougnac Rodríguez, Antonio, and Alejandro Guzmán Brito, *Esquema del derecho de familia indiano* (Santiago: Instituto de Historia del Derecho Juan de Solórzano y Pereyra, 2003).

Drescher, Seymour, *Abolition: A History of Slavery and Antislavery* (Cambridge: Cambridge University Press, 2009).

Duby, Georges, *Love and Marriage in the Middle Ages* (Chicago: University of Chicago Press, 1996).

Ducloux, Anne, *Ad ecclesiam Confugere: Naissance du droit d'asile dans les eglises (IVe- milieu du Ve. S.)* (Paris: De Boccard, 1994): 5–25.

———, "L'Eglise, l'asile et l'aide aux condamnes d'apres la constitution du 27 juillet 398," in *Revue d'Histoire du Droit Franc¸ais et Etranger* 69 (1991): 141–176.

Dueñas, Guiomar, *Hijos del pecado: Ilegitimidad y vida familiar en la Santafé de Bogotá colonial* (Bogotá: Editorial Universidad Nacional, 1997).

Duve, Thomas, "Algunas observaciones acerca del modus operandi y la prudencia del juez en el derecho canónico indiano," *Revista de Historia del Derecho* 35 (2007): 195–226.

———, "La condición juridical del Indio y su consideración como persona miserabilis en el derecho indiano, " in Mario Losano, ed., *Un giudici e due leggi: Pluralismpo normativo e conflitti agrari in Sud-America* (Milano: Universitá degli Studi di Milano, 2004), 3–33.

Ebright, Malcolm, *Land Grants and Lawsuits in Northern New Mexico* (Albuquerque: University of New Mexico Press, 1994).

Eisner, Manuel, "Long-Term Historical Trends in Violent Crime," *Crime and Justice: A Review of Research* 30 (2003): 83–142.

———, "Modernization, Self-Control and Lethal Violence: The Long-Term Dynamics of European Homicide Rates in Theoretical Perspective," *British Journal of Criminology* 41 (2001): 618–638.

Elias, Norbert, *The Civilizing Process: The History of Manners* (New York: Urizen, 1978).

Emsley, John, *The Elements of Murder: A History of Poison* (New York: Oxford University Press, 2005).

Esmein, Adhemar, *Le marriage en droit canonique* (New York: Franklin, 1968).

Espejo-Ponce Hunt, Marta, and Matthew Restall, "Work, Marriage, Status," in Schroeder et al., *Indian Women of Early Mexico*, 231–252.

Espinosa, Ivan, *El sueño del ahorcado: Una experiencia subjetiva de la pena de muerte a finales de la colonia (Novita, siglo XVIII)* (Bogotá: Universidad de los Andes, 2008).

Fiorelli, Piero, *La tortura guidiziaria nel Diritto comume*, 2 vols. (Rome: Giuffré, 1953–1954).

Fisher, John R., "The Bourbon Reforms in Spanish America: A Semi-Autobiographical Re-evaluation," *Journal of Iberian and Latin American Research* 18.1 (2012): 1–14.

Fixot, Michel, and Elisabeth Zadora-Rio, "Introduction: La topographie des lieux d'asile dans les campagnes médiévales," in *L'Eglise, le terroir,* eds. Fixot and Zadora-Rio (Paris: Editions du CNRS, 1989).

Flandrin, Jean Louis, *Familles: Parenté, maison, sexualité dans l'ancienne société* (Paris: Hachette, 1976).

———, *Sex in the Western World* (New York: Routledge, 1991).

Fletcher, Jonathan, *Violence and Civilization. An Introduction to the Work of Norbert Elias* (Cambridge: Polity, 1997).

Flóres Galindo, Alberto, *Aristocracia y plebe en Lima, 1760–1830 (Estructura de clases y sociedad colonial)* (Lima: Mosca Azul Editores, 1983).

Foucault, Michel, *Discipline and Punish: The Birth of the Prison* (New York: Pantheon, 1977).

———, *Microfísica del poder* (Madrid: Ediciones de la Piqueta, 1979).

Fraile, Pedro, *Un espacio para castigar: La cárcel y la ciencia penitenciaria en España (Siglos XVIII–XIX)* (Barcelona: Ediciones Serbal, 1987).

Friedland, Paul, "Beyond Deterrence: Cadavers, Effigies, Animals and the Logic of Executions in Premodern France," *Historical Reflections* 29.2 (2003): 295–317.

Furlong, Guillermo, *Bibliotecas argentinas durante la dominación hispánica* (Buenos Aires: Editorial Nuarpes, 1944).

Gabriel de Domínguez, Zoila, "Delito y sociedad en el Nuevo Reino de Granada período virreinal, 1740–1810," *Universitas Humanistica* 8–9 (1974–75): 281–398.

Ganshof, F. L., "La 'Gratia' des Monarques francs," *Anuario de Estudios Medievales* 3.3 (1966): 3–26.

Garau, Francisco, *La fé triunfante: Los grandes Autos de Fé celebrados en Mallorca en 1691* (Mallorca: Miquel Font Editor, 1999).

García Avila, Sergio, and Eduardo Miranda Arrieta, *Desorden social y criminalidad en Michoacan, 1825–1850* (Morelia: Supremo Tribunal de Justicia del Estado de Michoacan de Ocampo, 1994).

García de la Fuente, Alejandro, "Los matrimonios de esclavos en la Habana, 1585–1645," *Ibero-Amerikanisches Archiv* 16.4 (1990): 507–528.

———, "Slave Law and Claims-Making in Cuba: The Tannenbaum Debate Revisited," *Law and History Review* 22.2 (2004): 339–369.

Garcia de la Fuente, Alejandro, and Ariela Gross, "Comparative Studies of Law, Slavery and Race in the Americas," University of Southern California Gould School of Law, *Legal Studies Research Paper Series* 10–2 (2010).

García Gallo, Alfonso, *Estudios de historia del derecho indiano* (Madrid: Instituto Nacional de Estudios Jurídicos, 1972).

———, "Leyes, recopilaciones y códigos," in Francisco de Icaza Dufour, ed., *Recopilación de leyes de los Reynos de las Indias: Estudios Histórico-Jurídicos* (México: Miguel Angel Porrúa, 1987), 5–21.

———, *Manual de historia del derecho español*. 5a. ed. 2 vols. (Madrid: Artes Gráficas Ediciones, 1973).

García y García, Tomás de Aquino, *El derecho de asilo en Indias* (Madrid: Editorial Reus, 1930).

García Valdecasas, Alfonso, *El hidalgo y el honor* (Madrid: Editorial Revista de Occidente, 1948).

Garnot, Benoît, *Un Crime Conjugal au XVIIIe Siècle: L'Affaire Boiveau* (Paris: Imago, 1993).

———, "Justice, infrajustice, parajustice et extrajustice dans la France d'Ancien Régime," *Crime, History and Societies* 4.1 (2000): 103–120.

Garnot, Benoît, Pascal Bastien, Hervé Piant, et al., *La Justice et l'Histoire: Sources Judiciaires à l'Époque Moderne (XVIe, XVIIe, XVIIIe Siècles)* (Rosny-sous-Bois: Bréal, 2006).

Gauderman, Kimberly, *Women's Lives in Colonial Quito* (Austin: University of Texas Press, 2003).

Geertz, Clifford, *The Interpretation of Cultures: Selected Essays* (New York: Basic, 1973).

Gérard, Albert S., "The Loving Killers: The Rationale of Righteousness in Baroque Tragedy," *Comparative Literature Studies* 2 (1965): 209–232.

Ghachem, Malick W., *The Old Regime and the Haitian Revolution* (Cambridge: Cambridge University Press, 2012).

Giraud, François, "Viol et Société Coloniale: Le Case de la Nouvelle Espagne au XVIIIe Siècle," *Annals ESC* 41.3 (1986): 625–637.

Given, James Buchanan, *Society and Homicide in Thirteenth Century England* (Stanford: Stanford University Press, 1977).

Gómez Herrero, Tedorora, *Diccionario-guía legislativo español: Comprende todas las disposiciones legales que se han publicado en el siglo XIX*, 4 vols. (Madrid: Librería de Don Victoriano Suarez, 1902).

Gonzalbo Aizpuru, Pilar, "Con amor y reverencia: Mujeres y familias en el México colonial," in *Jahrbuch für Geschichte Lateinamerikas* 35 (1998): 1–24.

———, *Familia y orden colonial* (México: El Colegio de México, 1998).

———, "Violencia y discordia en las relaciones personales en la ciudad de México a fines del siglo XVIII," *Historia Mexicana* 51 (October–December, 2001): 233–259.

Gonzalbo Aizpuru, Pilar, and Cecilia Rabell, coords., *Familia y vida privada en la historia de Iberoamérica* (México: El Colegio de México-UNAM, 1996).

Gonzalbo Aizpuru, Pilar, and Cecilia Rabell Romero, "La familia en México," in Pablo Rodriguez, ed., *La Familia en Iberoamerica, 1550–1980* (Bogotá: Universidad Externado de Colombia-Convenio Andrés Bello, 2004), 93–124.

González, Angel, "Introducción," in Archivo Histórico Nacional, *Consejo de Castilla: Sala de Alcaldes de Casa y Corte. Catálogo por Materias* (Madrid, 1925), xv–xx.

González, María del Refugio, "Estudio introductorio," in Eusebio Bentura Beleña, *Recopilación sumaria*, 2 vols. (México: Universidad Nacional Autónoma de México, 1991) 1: vii–lix.

González Henríquez, Adolfo, "La música del Caribe Colombiano durante la Independencia y comienzos de la república," *Historia Crítica* 4 (July–December 1990): 85–112.

González Lira, Andrés, *El amparo colonial y el juicio de amparo mexicano* (México: FCE, 1972).

González Palencia, Angel, ed., *Archivo Histórico Nacional. Consejo de Castilla: Sala de Alcaldes de Casa y Corte*. Catálogo por Materias (Madrid, 1925).

González Zalacain, Roberto J., "El perdón real en Castilla: Una fuente privilegiada para el estudio de la criminalidad y la conflictividad social a fines de la Edad Media," *Clio & Crimen* 8 (2011): 289–352.

———, *El perdón real en Castilla a fines de la Edad Media: El ejemplo de la Cornisa Cantábrica* (Bilbao: Servicio Editorial de la Universidad del País Vasco UPV/EHU, 2013).

Gordon, Linda, *Heroes of Their Own Lives: The Politics and History of Family Violence. Boston, 1880–1960* (Champaign: University of Illinois Press, 1988).

"Governor Declares Domestic Violence Emergency," *Boston Herald*, Friday, June 6, 2008.

Gowing, Laura, *Domestic Dangers, Women, Words and Sex in Early Modern London* (Oxford: Clarendon, 1996).

Gramsci, Antonio, *Prison Notebooks* (New York: Columbia University Press, 1992).

Greenleaf, Richard, "The Obraje in the Late Mexican Colony," *Americas* 23 (January 1967): 227–250.

Gutierrez, Ramón, *When Jesus Came, the Corn Mothers Went Away: Marriage, Sexuality and Power in New Mexico, 1500–1846* (Stanford: Stanford University Press, 1991).

Haag, Pamela, "The 'Ill-Use of a Wife': Patterns of Working Class Violence in Domestic and Public New York City, 1860–1880," *Journal of Social History* 25.3 (1992): 447–477.

Hampe Martínez, Teodoro, *Bibliotecas privadas del mundo colonial: La difusión de libros e ideas en el virreinato del Perú (Siglos XVI–XVII)* (Madrid: Iberoamericana, 1996).

Harvey, Kathryn, "Amazons and Victims: Resisting Wife-Abuse in Working Class Montréal, 1869–1879," *Journal of the Canadian Historical Association* 2 (1991): 131–148.

Haslip-Viera, Gabriel, *Crime and Punishment in Late Colonial Mexico City, 1692–1810* (Albuquerque: University of New Mexico Press, 1999).

Hay, Douglas, "Property, Authority and the Criminal Law," in Douglas Hay et al., eds., *Albion's Fatal Tree: Crime and Society in Eighteenth-Century England* (New York: Pantheon, 1975), 17–63, esp. 40–49.

Heise, Lori, and Claudia Garcia-Moreno, "Violence by Intimate Partners," in Etienne G. Krug, Linda L. Dahlberg, James A. Mercy, Anthony B. Zwi, and Rafael Lozano, eds., *World Report on Violence and Health* (Geneva: World Health Organization, 2002), 87–113.

Helfield, Randa, "Female Poisoners of the Nineteenth-Century: A Study of Gender Bias in the Application of the Law," *Osgoode Hall Law Journal* 28.1 (1990): 53–101.

Helmholz, R. H., "The Law of Sanctuary," in *The Ius Commune in England* (Oxford: Oxford University Press, 2001), 16–80.

———, *The Spirit of Classical Canon Law* (Athens: University of Georgia Press, 1996).

Helsinki Federation for Human Rights, *Women 2000: An Investigation into the Status of Women's Rights in Central and South-Eastern Europe and the Newly Independent States* 436 (2000).

Heras Santos, José Luis de las, *La Justicia penal de los Austrias en la Corona de Castilla* (Salamanca: Ediciones de la Universidad de Salamanca, 1994).

Herman, E., "Asile Dans l'Eglise Oriental," in *Dictionnaire de Droit Canonique* 1 (1935): 1084–1089.

Hernández Díaz, Jaime, *Orden y desorden social en Michoacán: El derecho penal en la primera República Federal, 1824–1835* (Morelia: Universidad Michoacana de San Nicolas de Hidalgo, 1999).

Herzog, Tamar, *La administración como un fenómeno social: La justicia penal de la ciudad de Quito (1650–1750)* (Madrid: Centro de Estudios Constitucionales, 1995).

———, *Upholding Justice: Society, State, and the Penal System in Quito (1650–1750)* (Ann Arbor: University of Michigan Press, 2004).

Hespanha, Antonio M., *La gracia del derecho: Economía de la cultura en la edad moderna* (Madrid: Centro de Estudios Constitucionales, 1993).

———, "De *Iustitia* a Disciplina," in *La gracia del derecho*, 203–273.

Honores, Renzo, "Estudios sobre la litigación y la litigiosidad colonial," *Revista de Historia del Derecho Privado* 2 (1999): 121–135.

Hunefeldt, Christine, *Liberalism in the Bedroom: Quarreling Spouses in Nineteenth-Century Lima* (University Park: Pennsylvania State University Press, 2000).

Ignatieff, Michael, *A Just Measure of Pain: The Penitentiary in the Industrial Revolution, 1750–1850* (New York: Columbia University Press, 1978).

International Helsinki Federation for Human Rights, *Women 2000: An Investigation into the Status of Women's Rights in Central and South-Eastern Europe and the Newly Independent States* 436 (2000).

Jaramillo Uribe, Jaime, *Ensayos Sobre historia social colombiana* (Bogotá: Universidad Nacional de Colombia, 1968).

Jenkins, Philip, "Varieties of Enlightenment Criminology: Beccaria, Godwin, de Sade," *British Journal of Criminology* 24.2 (1984): 112–130.

Jiménez Meneses, Orian, and Edgardo Pérez Morales, *La Mojana medio ambiente y vida material en perspectiva histórica* (Medellin: Universidad de Antioquia, 2007).

Jimeno, Myriam, *Crimen pasional. Contribución a una antropología de las emociones* (Bogotá: Universidad Nacional de Colombia, 2002).

Johnson, Eric, Ricardo Salvatore, and Pieter Spierenburg, eds., *Murder and Violence in Modern Latin America* (London: Wiley-Blackwell, 2013).

Johnson, Lyman, "'A Lack of Legitimate Obedience and Respect': Slaves and their Masters in the Courts of Buenos Aires," *Hispanic American Historical Review* 87.4 (2007): 631–657.

———, ed., *The Problem of Order in Changing Societies: Essays on Crime and Policing in Argentina and Uruguay, 1750–1940* (Albuquerque: University of New Mexico Press, 1990).

———, *Workshop of Revolution: Plebeian Buenos Aires and the Atlantic World, 1776–1810* (Durham: Duke University Press, 2011).

Johnson, Lyman, and Sonya Lipsett-Rivera, eds., *The Faces of Honor: Sex, Shame and Violence in Colonial Latin America* (Albuquerque: University of New Mexico Press, 1999).

Kagan, Richard, *Lawsuits and Litigants in Castile, 1500–1700* (Chapel Hill: University of North Carolina Press, 1981).

Kamas, Juraj, *The Separation of the Spouses with the Bond Remaining: Historical and Canonical Study with Pastoral Applications* (Rome: Gregorian University Press, 1997).

Kamir, Orit, *Every Breath You Take: Stalking Narratives and the Law* (Ann Arbor: University of Michigan Press, 2001).

Kantorowicz, Ernst H., *The King's Two Bodies: A Study in Medieval Political Theology* (Princeton: Princeton University Press, 1997 [1957]).

Kaye, Dan K., et al., "The Social Construction and Context of Domestic Violence in Wakiso District, Uganda," *Culture, Health and Sexuality* 7.6 (2005): 625–635.

Keen, Benjamin, *La imagen Azteca en el pensamiento occidental* (México: Fondo de Cultura Económica, 1984).
Kelleher, Marie A., *The Measure of Woman: Law and Female Identity in the Crown of Aragon* (Philadelphia: University of Pennsylvania Press, 2010).
Kellogg, Susan, *Law and the Transformation of Aztec Culture, 1500–1700* (Norman: University of Oklahoma Press, 1995).
Klooster, Wim, *Revolutions in the Atlantic World: A Comparative Perspective* (New York: NYU Press, 2009).
Kluger, Viviana, *Escenas de la vida conyugal: Los conflictos matrimoniales en la sociedad virreinal rioplatense* (Buenos Aires: Editorial Quorurm-UMSA, 2003).
Koenig, Michael A., et al., "Prevalence, Patterns and Correlates of Domestic Violence in Rural Bangladesh: Individual and Community-Level Effects," *Demography* 40.2 (2003): 269–288.
Komisaruk, Catherine, *Labor and Love in Guatemala: The Eve of Independence* (Stanford: Stanford University Press, 2013).
———, "Rape Narratives, Rape Silences: Sexual Violence and Judicial Testimony in Colonial Guatemala," *Biography* 31.3 (2008): 369–396.
Kuethe, Allan J., *Military Reform and Society in New Granada, 1773–1808* (Gainesville: University Presses of Florida, 1978).
Kyle, D. G., *Spectacles of Death in Ancient Rome* (London: Routledge, 1998).
Lacassagne, Al, "Notes statistiques sur l'empoisonnement criminale en France," *Archives d'Anthropologie Criminelles et des Sciences Penales* 1 (1886): 260–264.
Laclau, Ernesto, and Chantal Mouffe, *Hegemony and Socialist Strategy* (London: Verso, 1986).
Landers, Jane, *Black Society in Spanish Florida* (Urbana: University of Illinois Press, 1999).
Landes, Joan B., "The Public and the Private Sphere: A Feminist Reconsideration," in Johanna Meehan, ed., *Feminists Read Habermas: Gendering the Subject of Discourse* (New York: Routledge, 1995), 91–116.
Lane, Kris, *Colour of Paradise: Colombian Emeralds in the Age of Gunpowder Empires* (New Haven: Yale University Press, 2010).
Lane, Roger, *Murder in America: A History* (Columbus: Ohio State University Press, 1997).
Langbein, John H., *Torture and the Law of Proof: Europe and England in the Anciene Régime* (Chicago: University of Chicago Press, 1977).
Lanza, Ramón, *La población y el crecimiento económico de Cantabria en el Antiguo Régimen* (Madrid: UNAM-Universidad de Cantabria, 1991).
Lavrín, Asunción, ed., *Sexuality and Marriage in Colonial Latin America* (Lincoln: University of Nebraska Press, 1989).
———, "Sexuality in Colonial Mexico: A Church Dilemma," in Lavrin, ed., *Sexuality and Marriage in Colonial Latin America*: 47–92.
Lazarus-Black, Mindie, *Everyday Harm: Domestic Violence, Court Rites and Cultures of Reconciliation* (Urbana: University of Illinois Press, 2007).
Le Bas, Gab., "Asile," *Dictionnaire d'histoire et de Ge´ographie Ecclésiastiques*, vol. 4 (1912): 1036–1048.
Lebrun, François, *La vie conjugale sous l'Ancien Régime* (Paris: Armand Collin, 1985).

Lepore, Jill, "Rap Sheet: Why Is American History So Murderous?" *New Yorker*, November 9, 2009, 79–83.

Levaggi, Abelardo, "La fundamentación de las sentencias en el derecho indiano," *Revista de Historia del Derecho* 6 (1978): 45–73.

Levene, Ricardo, *Historia del derecho argentino*, 5 vols. (Buenos Aires: Editorial Guillermo Fraksty Ltda., 1945).

Lewis, Laura A., *Power, Witchcraft and Caste in Colonial Mexico* (Durham: Duke University Press, 2003).

———, "The 'Weakness' of Women and the Feminization of the Indian," *Colonial Latin American Review* 5.1 (2006): 73–94.

Lipsett-Rivera, Sonya, *Gender and the Negotiation of Daily Life in Mexico, 1750–1856* (Lincoln: University of Nebraska Press, 2012).

———, "Honor, familia y violencia en México," in Pilar Gonzalbo Aispuru and Verónica Zárate Toscano, coords., *Gozos y sufrimientos en la historia de México* (México: El Colegio and Instituto de Investigaciones Históricas José María Luis Mora, 2007), 185–199.

———, "Marriage and Family Relations in Mexico During the Transition from Colony to Nation," in Victor M. Uribe-Uran, ed., *State and Society in Spanish America During the Age of Revolution* (Wilmington: Scholarly Resources, 2001), 121–148.

———, "La violencia dentro de las familias formal e informal," in Pilar Gonzalbo Aizpuru and Cecilia Rabell, coords., *Familia y vida privada en la historia de Iberoamérica*, 325–340.

Livi Bacci, Massimo, "Fertility and Nuptiality: Changes in Spain from the Late 18th to the Early Twentieth Century, Part 2," *Population Studies* 22.2 (1968): 211–234.

Llanes Parra, Blanca, "El enemigo en casa: El parricidio y otras formas de violencia interpersonal doméstica en el Madrid de los Austrias (1580–1700)," *Nuevo Mundo-Mundos Nuevos*, Coloquio 2008, 1–15, http://nuevomundo.revues.org/index24382.html.

López, Mabel, "Las conyugicidas de la Nueva Granada: Transgresión de un viejo ideal de mujer," *Memoria y Sociedad* 10.20 (2006): 49–58.

———, "Conyugicidios en la Nueva Granada: Una vía de escape a la violencia contra la mujer," paper presented at the XVI Congreso de Historia de Colombia, Bogotá, 2008.

Lorente, Marta, "El juez y la ley: La motivación de las sentencias (Castilla, 1489–España, 1855)," *Anuario de la Facultad de Derecho de la Universidad Autónoma de Madrid* 1 (1997): 97–142.

Lozano Armendares, Teresa, *La criminalidad en la ciudad de México, 1800–1821* (México: Instituto de Investigaciones Históricas UNAM, 1987).

———, "Momentos de desamor en algunas parejas novohispanas," in Sergio Ortega Noriega et al., eds., *Amor y desamor: Vivencias de parejas en la sociedad novohispana* (México: Instituto Nacional de Antropologia e Historia, 1992), 51–79.

Lugo, Alejandro, and Bill Mauer, "The Legacy of Michelle Rosaldo: Politics and Gender in Modern Societies," in *Gender Matters: Rereading Michelle Z.*

Rosaldo, ed. Alejandro Lugo and Bill Mauer (Ann Arbor: University of Michigan Press, 2000), 16–34.

MacLachlan, Colin M., *Criminal Justice in Eighteenth Century Mexico: A Study of the Tribunal of the Acordada* (Berkeley: University of California Press, 1974).

Macrides, Ruth J., "Killing, Asylum and the Law in Bizantium," *Speculum* 63 (1988): 509–538.

Mallo, Silvia C., "Justicia, divorcio, alimentos y malos tratos en el Río de la Plata," *Investigaciones y ensayos* 42 (January–December 1992): 373–400.

Mallon, Florencia R., *Peasant and Nation. The Making of Postcolonial Mexico and Peru* (Berkeley: University of California Press, 1995).

Mannarelli, Maria Emma, *Pecados públicos: La ilegitimidad en Lima, Siglo XVII* (Lima: Ediciones Flora Tirstán, 1993).

Mantecón, Tomás, "Civilización y brutalización del crimen en una España de Ilustración," in Manuel-Reyes García Hurtado, ed., *La vida cotidiana en la España del siglo* XVIII (Madrid: Sílex, 2009), 95–124.

———, *Conflictividad y disciplinamiento social en la Cantabria del Antiguo Régimen* (Santander: Universidad de Cantabria-Fundación Marcelino Botín, 1997).

———, "Los criminales ante la concesión del indulto en la España del Siglo XVIII," *Prohistoria: historia, políticas de la historia* 5 (2001): 55–82.

———, "Criminals and Royal Pardon in the 18th Century Spain," *Cahiers de L'Institute d'Anthropologie Juridique* 3 (1999): 477–506.

———,"Disciplinamiento social, escenografías punitivas y cultura plebeya en el Antiguo Régimen," in Verónica Undurraga and Rafael Geune, eds., *Formas de control y disciplinamiento: Chile, América y Europa, siglos XVI-XIX* (Santiago: Universidad Católica del Perú-Instituto Riva Agüero, 2014), 162–184.

———, "La economía del castigo y el perdón en los tiempos de Cervantes," *Revista de Historia Económica* 23.S1 (2005): 69–97.

———, "El honor Mediterráneo desde la España moderna: Un traje nuevo del emperador?" *Cuadernos de Historia de España* LXXXV–LXXXVI (2012): 435–458.

———, "Hogares infernales: Una visión retrospectiva sobre la violencia doméstica en el mundo moderno," in Lorenzo Pinar, ed., *La familia en la historia* (Salamanca: Ediciones Universidad de Salamanca, 2009), 187–230.

———, "Honour and Social Discipline in Early Modern Spain," in Heinz Schilling, ed., *Institutionem, Instrumente und Akteure Sozialer Kontrolle und Disziplinierung im Frühneuzeitlichen Europa* (Frankfurt: Vittorio Klostermann, 1999), 203–223.

———, *La muerte de Antonia Isabel Sánchez: Tiranía y escándalo en una sociedad del Norte español en el Antiguo Régimen* (Alcalá de Henares: Centro de Estudios Cervantinos, 1997).

———, "The Patterns of Violence in Early Modern Spain," *Journal of the Historical Society* 7.2 (2007): 229–264.

———, "El peso de la infrajudicialidad en el control del crimen durante la edad moderna," *Estudis: Revista de Historia Moderna* 28 (2002): 43–75.

———, "Recits de Punition et de Pardon Dans la Castille Moderne," in Benoît Garnot (dir.), *Normes juridiques et pratiques judiciaires du Moyene Age a l'epoque contemporaine* (Dijon: Editions Universitaires de Dijon, 2007), 377–384.

———, Social Control from Below: Popular Arbitration of Disputes in Old Regime Spain," in Herman Roodenburg and Pieter Spierenburg, eds., *Social Control in Europe. Vol. 1, 1500–1800* (Columbus: Ohio State University Press, 2004), 267–287.

———, "La violencia marital en la corona de Castilla durante la edad moderna," in Antonio Yrigoyen López and Antonio L. Pérez Ortiz, eds., *Familia, transmisión y perpetuación (siglos XVI–XIX)* (Murcia: Universidad de Murcia, 2002), 19–55.

Martínez, María-Elena, *Genealogical Fictions: Limpieza de Sangre, Religion, and Gender in Colonial Mexico* (Stanford: Stanford University Press, 2008).

Martínez Carreño, Aida, *Extravios: El mundo de los criollos ilustrados* (Bogotá: Colcultura, 1995).

Martínez Martín, Jesús A., *Lectura y lectores en el Madrid del siglo XIX* (Madrid: Consejo Superior de Investigaciones Científicas, 1991).

Matthews, Glenna, "*Just a Housewife*": *The Rise and Fall of Domesticity in America* (New York: Oxford University Press, 1987).

McCaa, Robert, "Familias y género en México: Crítica metodológica y desafío investigativo para el fin del milenio," in Victor M. Uribe-Uran and Luis Javier Ortiz, eds., *Naciones, gentes y territorios: Ensayos de historia e historiografía comparada de América Latina y el Caribe* (Medellín: Universidad de Antioquia, 2000), 103–138.

———, "Tratos nupciales: La constitución de uniones formales e informales en México, 1500–1900," in Pilar Gozalbo Aizpuru and Cecilia Rabell, coords., *Familia y vida privada en la historia de Iberoamérica: Seminario de Historia de la Familia* (México: El Colegio de México-University Nacional Autónoma de México, 1996), 21–57.

McCloskey, Laura Ann, Corrine Williams, and Ulla Larsen, "Gender Inequality and Intimate Partner Violence Among Women in Moshi, Tanzania," *International Family Planning Perspectives* 31.3 (2005): 124–130.

McCormack, Brian T., "Conjugal Violence, Sex, Sin and Murder in the Mission Communities of Alta California," *Journal of the History of Sexuality* 16.3 (2007): 391–415.

McFarlane, Anthony, *Colombia Before Independence: Economy, Society, and Politics Under Bourbon Rule* (Cambridge: Cambridge University Press, 1993).

Milanich, Nara, *Children of Fate: Childhood, Class, and the State in Chile, 1850–1930* (Durham: Duke University Press, 2009).

Millar Carvacho, Rene, *Misticismo e Inquisición en el virreinato peruano: Los procesos a los alumbrados de Santiago de Chile 1710–1736* (Santiago: Ediciones Universidad Católica de Chile, 2000).

Mirow, Matthew, *Florida's First Constitution: The Constitution of Cádiz* (Durham: Carolina Academic Press, 2012).

———, *Latin American Law: A History of Private Law and Institutions in Spanish America* (Austin: University of Texas Press, 2004).

Misserey, L. R., "Asile en Occident," *Dictionnaire de Droit Canonique* 1 (1935): 1089–1104.

Mojica Rivadeneira, María Teresa, "El derecho masculino de castigo en la colonia," in René Salinas Mesa and María Teresa Mojica Rivadeneira, *Conductas ilícitas y derecho de castigo durante la colonia: Los casos de Chile y Colombia* (Bogotá: Universidad Externado de Colombia, 2005), 87–194.

Molina, Raul A., *La familia porteña en los siglos XVII y XVIII: Historia de los divorcios en el período hispánico* (Buenos Aires: Fuentes Históricas y Genealógicas Argentinas, 1991).

Monkkonen, Eric, "Homicide: Explaining American Exceptionalism," *American Historical Review* 111.1 (2006): 76–94.

Monter, E. William, *Frontiers of Heresy: The Spanish Inquisition from the Basque Lands to Sicily* (Cambridge: Cambridge University Press, 1990).

Montoya Prada, Alexander, "La transición del orden jurídico: Entre la colonia y la República en los procesos criminales en Queretaro (1830–1849)," *Signos Históricos* 26 (July–December, 2011): 16–42.

Moore, Jerry D., and Mary J. Norton, "'I Solemnly Baptize': Religious Conversion and Native Demography in Northern Baja California," *Journal of California and Great Basin Anthropology* 14.2 (1992): 201–215.

Moreno, José Luis, *Historia de la familia en el Río de la Plata* (Buenos Aires: Editorial Sudamericana, 2004).

Morgado-García, Arturo, *Derecho de asilo y delincuencia en la Diócesis de Cádiz* (Cádiz: Diputación Provincial, 1991).

Morgan, Phillip D., and Jack P. Greene, "Introduction: The Present State of Atlantic History," in Phillip D. Morgan and Jack P. Greene, eds., *Atlantic History: A Critical Reappraisal* (Oxford: Oxford University Press, 2009), 3–33.

Morner, Magnus, Julia Fawaz, and John D. French, "Comparative Approaches to Latin American History," *Latin American Research Review* 17.3 (1982): 55–89.

Muldoon, James, *Canon Law, the Expansion of Europe and World Order* (Aldershot: Ashgate, 1998).

Mumford, Jeremy R., "Litigation as Ethnography in Sixteenth-Century Peru: Polo de Ondergardo and the Mitimaes," *Hispanic American Historical Review* 88.1 (2008): 5–40.

Muriel, Josefina, *Los recogimientos de mujeres: Respuesta a una problemática social novohispana* (Mexico: Universidad Nacional Autónoma de México, 1974).

Nardi, Enzo, *L'Otre Dei Parricidi e le Bestie Incluse* (Milano: Dott A. Giuffré Editore, 1980).

Navas, Deborah, *Murdered by His Wife: An Absorbing Tale of Crime and Punishment in Eighteenth-Century Massachusetts* (Amherst: University of Massachusetts Press, 1999).

Niccoli, Ottavia, *Perdonare. Idee, Pratiche, Rituali in Italia tra Cinque e Seicento* (Rome-Bari: Editori Laterza, 2007).

Nizza da Silva, Maria Beatriz, *Sistema de Casamento no Brasil Colonial* (São Paulo: Editora da Universidade de São Paulo, 1984).

Obregón, Liliana, "Between Civilization and Barbarism: Creole Interventions in International Law," *Third World Quarterly* 25.7 (2006): 815–832.

Olaechea, Rafael, "Anotaciones sobre la inmunidad local en el siglo XVIII español," *Miscelanea Comillas* 46 (July–December 1966): 296–381.

Oliver Olmo, Pedro, "Genealogia de la 'corrigenda': Mujeres encarceladas en Pamplona (Siglos XVI–XIX)," *Huarte de San Juan: Geografia e Historia* 5 (1998): 7–42.

———, "Pena de muerte y proceso de criminalización (Navarra, siglos XVII–XX)," *Historia Contemporánea* 26 (2003): 269–292.

Oliveros, Martha Norma, "La construcción jurídica del regimen tutelar del Indio," *Revista del Instituto de Historia del Derecho Ricardo Levene* 18 (1967): 105–128.

Ortega, Sergio, ed., *De la santidad a la perversión o de porque no se cumplía la ley de Dios en la sociedad novohispana* (México: Grijalbo, 1986).

Ortega López, Margarita, "Protestas de las mujeres castellanas contra el orden patriarcal privado durante el siglo XVIII," *Cuadernos de Historia Moderna* 19 (1997): 65–89.

Ortuño Sánchez Pedreño, José María, "El derecho de asilo en iglesias y sus cementerios en la legislación de Partidas," *Glossae: Revista de Historia del Derecho Europeo* 5–6 (1993–1994): 187–193.

Osorio, Alejandra, *Inventing Lima: Baroque Modernity in Peru's South Sea Metropolis* (New York: Palgrave-Macmillan, 2008).

Ots Capdequí, José María, *El estado español en las Indias* (México: Fondo de Cultura Económica, 1946).

———, *Historia del derecho español en América y del derecho indiano* (Madrid: Aguilar, 1969).

Owensby, Brian, *Empire of Law and Indian Justice in Colonial Mexico* (Stanford: Stanford University Press, 2008).

Palop Ramos, José-Miguel, "Delitos y penas en la España del siglo XVIII," *Estudis: Revista de Historia Moderna*, 22 (1996): 65–103.

———, "Notas sobre la criminalidad en Canarias a finales del siglo XVIII," in *Seminario de Humanidades Agustín Millares Carlo: Homenaje de Bethencourt Massieu*, 3 vols. (Las Palmas: Ediciones del Cabildo Insular de Canaria, 1995), 3: 1–10.

Pateman, Carole, *The Sexual Contract* (Stanford: Stanford University Press, 1988).

Patiño, Beatríz, *Criminalidad, ley penal y estructura social en la provincia de Antioquia, 1750–1820* (Medellín: IDEA, 1994).

Patiño, Victor Manuel, *Historia de la cultura material en la América Equinoccial*, Vol. IV: *Vestidos, Adornos y Vida Social* (Bogotá: Instituto Caro y Cuervo, 1992).

Paton, Diana, *No Bond but the Law: Punishment, Race and Gender in Jamaican State Formation, 1780–1870* (Durham: Duke University Press, 2004).

Paz Alonso, María, *El proceso penal en Castilla (siglos XIII–XVIII)* (Salamanca: Ediciones Universidad de Salamanca, 1982).
Pedraja, René de la, "La mujer criolla y mestiza en la sociedad colonial, 1700–1830," *Desarrollo y Sociedad* 13 (January 1984): 199–229.
Pennington, Kenneth, *The King and the Law, 1200–1600: Sovereignty and Rights in the Western Legal Tradition* (Berkeley: University of California Press, 1993).
Pérez Baltasar, María Dolores, *Mujeres Marginadas: Las Casas de Recogidas en Madrid* (Madrid: Gráficas Lormo, 1984).
———, "Orígenes de los recogimientos de mujeres," *Cuadernos de Historia Moderna y Contemporánea* 6 (1985): 13–23.
Pérez García, Pablo, and Jorge A. Catalá Sanz, "La pena capital en la Valencia del XVII," *Estudis* 24 (1998): 203–245.
Pérez Herrero, Pedro, "Evolución demográfica y estructura familiar en México 1750–1850," in Pilar Gonzalbo Aizpuru, *Familias novohispanas: Siglos XVI al XIX* (México: El Colegio de México, 1991), 345–371.
Pérez Muñoz, Isabel, "Conflictividad social y administración de justicia en el partido de Trujillo: 1791," in *Coloquios Históricos de Extremadura*, 1993, www.chde.org/index.php?option=com_content&view=article&id=703:conflictividad-social-y-administracion-de-justicia-en-el-partido-de-trujillo-1791&catid=43:1993&Itemid=60.
Peristany, J. G., *Honour and Shame: The Values of Mediterranean Society* (Chicago: University of Chicago Press, 1966).
Peristany, J. G., and Julian Pitt-Rivers, eds., *Honour and Grace in Anthropology* (Cambridge: Cambridge University Press, 1992).
Pescador, Juan Javier, "Del dicho al hecho: Uxoricidios en el México central, 1769–1820," in Pilar Gozalbo Aizpuru and Cecilia Rabell Romero, eds., *Familia y vida privada en la historia de Iberoamerica: Seminario de historia de la familia* (México: Centro de Estudios Históricos del Colegio de México-Instituto de Investigaciones Sociales de la UNAM, 1996), 373–386.
———, "Entre la espada y el olvido: Pleitos matrimoniales en el provisorato eclesiástico de México, siglo XVIII," in Pilar Gonzalbo Aizpuru and Cecilia Rabell, eds., *La familia en el mundo iberoamericano* (México: UNAM, 1998), 192–225.
Peterson, David, "Wife Beating: An American Tradition," *Journal of Interdisciplinary History* 13.1 (1992): 97–118.
Phelan, John Leddy, "Authority and Flexibility in the Spanish Imperial Bureaucracy," *Administrative Science Quarterly* 5 (1960): 47–61.
———, *The People and the King: The Comunero Revolution in Colombia, 1781* (Madison: University of Wisconsin Press, 1978).
Pike, Ruth, "Capital Punishment in Eighteenth-Century Spain," *Histoire Sociale—Social History* 18.36 (1985): 375–386.
———, "Penal Practices in Early Modern Spain," *Criminal Justice History* 5 (1984): 45–55.
———, *Penal Servitude in Early Modern Spain* (Wisconsin: University of Wisconsin Press, 1983).

———, "Penal Servitude in the Spanish Empire: Presidio Labor in the Eighteenth Century," *Hispanic American Historical Review* 58.1 (1985): 21–40.

Pita Moreda, María Teresa, "Conflictos familiares y tribunales de justicia a finales de la colonia: Algunos casos novohispanos," in Pilar Gonzalbo Aizpuru and Cecilia Rabell Romero, eds., *Familia y vida privada en la historia de Iberoamérica,* 341–358.

Pleck, Elizabeth, *Domestic Tyranny: The Making of Social Policy Against Family Violence from Colonial Times to the Present* (New York: Oxford University Press, 1987).

Pomeroy, Sarah B., *The Murder of Regilla: A Case of Domestic Violence in Antiquity* (Cambridge, MA: Harvard University Press, 2009).

Poska, Allyson M., *Women and Authority in Early Modern Spain: The Peasants of Galicia* (Oxford: Oxford University Press).

Premo, Bianca, *Children of the Father King: Youth, Authority and Legal Minority in Colonial Lima* (Chapel Hill: University of North Carolina Press, 2005).

———, "An Equity Against the Law: Slave Rights and Creole Jurisprudence in Spanish America," *Slavery and Abolition* 32.4 (2011): 495–517.

———, "On Currents and Comparisons: Gender and the Atlantic 'Turn' in Spanish America," *History Compass* 8.3 (2010): 223–237.

Puyol Montero, José María, "La abolición de la pena de horca en España," *Cuadernos de Historia del Derecho* 4 (1997): 91–140.

Rabell Romero, Cecilia, "Trayectorias de vida familiar, raza y género en Oaxaca colonial," in Pilar Gozalbo Aizpuru and Cecilia Rabell, coords., *Familia y vida privada en la historia de Iberoamérica*, 75–118.

Radzinowicz, Leon, *A History of English Criminal Law and Its Administration from 1750*, 5 vols. (London: Stevens, 1948).

Ramírez, María Himelda, *Las mujeres y la sociedad colonial de Santafé de Bogotá, 1750–1810* (Bogotá: Instituto Colombiano de Antopología e Historia, 2000).

Ramos, Frances, *Identity, Ritual, and Power in Colonial Puebla* (Tucson: University of Arizona Press, 2012).

Redonet y López-Doriga, Luis, "Nacimiento del derecho de asilo," *Discursos Leídos ante la Real Academia de la Historia* (Madrid: Imprenta Viuda e Hijos de Jaime Rates, 1928), 10–88.

Reid, Charles J., *Power over the Body, Equality in the Family: Rights and Domestic Relations in Medieval Canon Law* (Grand Rapids: Eerdmans, 2004).

Rigsby, Ken J., *Asylia: Territorial Inviolability in the Hellenistic World* (Berkeley: University of California Press, 1996).

Rípodaz Ardanas, Daisy, *El matrimonio en Indias: Realidad social y regulación jurídica* (Buenos Aires: Fundación para la Educación, la Ciencia y la Cultura, 1977).

Risco, Antonio, *La Real Academia de Santa Barbara de Madrid 1730–1808* (Toulouse: Université de Toulouse-Le Mirails, 1979).

Robinson, Barry Matthew, "La reclusión de mujeres rebeldes: El recogimiento en la Guerra de Independencia Mexicana, 1810–1819," *Fronteras de la Historia* 15.2 (2010): 225–244.

Rodriguez, Pablo, *Sentimientos y vida familiar en el Nuevo Reino de Granada* (Santafé de Bogotá: Editorial Ariel, 1997).

Rodríguez Flóres, María Imaculada, *El perdón real en Castilla (Siglos XIII–XVIII)* (Salamanca: Universidad de Salamanca, 1971).

Rodríguez Sáenz, Eugenia, "Civilizing Domestic Life in the Central Valley of Costa Rica, 1750–1850," in Elizabeth Dore and Maxine Molyneux, eds., *Hidden Histories of Gender and the State in Latin America*, 85–107.

———, *Hijas, novias y esposas: Familia, matrimonio y violencia en el Valle Central de Costa Rica* (Heredia: Editorial Universidad Nacional, 2000).

———, "'*Ya me es insoportable mi matrimonio*': El maltrato de las esposas en el Valle Central de Costa Rica (1750–1850)," *Ciencias Sociales* 68 (June 1995): 73–93.

Rodríguez Sánchez, Ángel, *Morir en Extremadura: La muerte en la horca a finales del antiguo régimen* (Cáceres: Institución Cultural El Brocense, 1980).

———, "La soga y el fuego: La pena de muerte en la España de los siglos XVI y XVII," *Cuadernos de Historia Moderna* 15 (1994): 13–39.

———, "Treinta de mayo de 1790: La Real Audiencia de Extremadura (1790–1990)," *Revista del Poder Judicial*. Número especial XVI: Bicentenario de la Audiencia Territorial de Cáceres (1990): 39–50.

Rodríguez Torres, Javier, "Libros jurídicos en la biblioteca de un obispo mejicano de los inicios del siglo XIX," *Revista Chilena de Historia del Derecho* 17 (1992): 113–134.

Rosaldo, Michelle Zimbalist, "Woman, Culture and Society: A Theoretical Overview," in Michelle Zimbalist Rosaldo and Louise Lamphere, eds., *Woman, Culture, and Society* (Stanford: Stanford University Press, 1974).

Roth, Randolph, *American Homicide* (Cambridge, MA: Belknap, 2009).

Ruggiero, Kristin, "Houses of Deposit and the Exclusion of Women in Turn-of-the-Century Argentina," in Carolyn Strange and Alison Bashford, eds., *Isolation: Places and Practices of Exclusion* (London: Routledge, 2003), 119–132.

———, "Wives on 'Deposit': Internment and the Preservation of Husbands' Honor in Late Nineteenth-Century Buenos Aires," *Journal of Family History* 17.3 (1992): 253–270.

Ruigómez Gómez, Carmen, *Una política indigenista de los Habsburgo: El Protector de Indios en el Perú* (Madrid: Ediciones de Cultura Hispánica, 1988).

Safford, Frank R., *The Ideal of the Practical: Colombia's Struggle to Form a Technical Elite* (Austin: University of Texas Press, 1976).

Salillas Rafael, *Evolución Penitenciaria en España*, 2 vols. (Madrid: Imprenta Clásica Española, 1913).

Salinas Mesa, René, "Uniones ilegítimas y desuniones legítimas: El matrimonio y la formación de la pareja en el Chile colonial," in Pilar Gonzalbo Aizpuru and Cecilia Rabell, eds., *La familia en el mundo iberoamericano* (México: UNAM, 1998), 173–192.

Sánchez-Arcilla Bernal, José, "La administración de justicia inferior en la Ciudad de México a finales de la época colonial: La punición de la embriaguez en los libros de reos (1794–1798)," *Cuadernos de Historia del Derecho* 7 (2000): 309–453.

Sánchez Bella, Ismael, Alberto de la Hera, and Carlos Díaz Rementeria, *Historia del derecho indiano* (Madrid: Mapfre, 1992).

Sánchez-Cid, Francisco Javier, *La violencia contra la mujer en la Sevilla del Siglo de Oro* (1569–1626) (Sevilla: Universidad de Sevilla, 2011).

Saravia Salazar, Javier Ivan, "El fiscal protector de Indios en la Audiencia de Lima Siglo XVII: Espacios de poder y arbitrismo," *Nueva Crónica* 1 (January 2013): 1–22.

Scardaville, Michael C., "Alcohol Abuse and Tavern Reform in Late Colonial Mexico City," *Hispanic American Historical Review* 60.4 (1980): 643–671.

———, "Justice by Paperwork: A Day in the Life of a Court Scribe in Mexico City," *Journal of Social History* 36.4 (2003): 979–1007.

Schmidt Nowara, Christopher, *Empire and Antislavery: Spain, Cuba and Puerto Rico, 1833–1874* (Pittsburgh: University of Pittsburgh Press, 1999).

Schroeder, Susan, Stephanie Wood, and Robert Haskett, eds., *Indian Women of Early Mexico* (Norman: University of Oklahoma Press, 1997).

Scott, Rebeca, "'She . . . Refuses to Deliver Up Herself as the Slave of Your Petitioner': Emigrés, Enslavement and the 1808 Louisiana Digest of Civil Laws," *Tulane European and Civil Law Forum* 24 (2009): 115–136.

Seed, Patricia, *To Love, Honor and Obey in Colonial Mexico* (Stanford: Stanford University Press, 1986).

Seminarios de Historia de las Mentalidades y Religión, *La memoria y el olvido* (México: INAH, 1985).

———, *El placer de pecar y el afán de normar* (México: Joaquín Mortiz/INAH, 1987).

Serra Ruíz, Rafael, *Honor, honra e injuria en el derecho medieval español* (Murcia: Sucesores de Nogués, 1969).

Serulnikov, Sergio, *Subverting Colonial Authority: Challenges to Spanish Rule in Eighteenth-Century Southern Andes* (Durham: Duke University Press, 2003).

Sharpe, J. A., "Domestic Homicide in Early Modern England," *Historical Journal* 24 (1981): 29–48.

Shelton, Laura M., *For Tranquility and Order: Family and Community on Mexico's Northern Frontier, 1800–1850* (Tucson: University of Arizona Press, 2010).

Simó Rodríguez, Ma. Isabel, "El Archivo de la Real Audiencia de Extremadura, Doscientos años de Historia," *Historia, Instituciones, Documentos* 25 (1998): 653–675.

———, "Fondos judiciales en los archivos históricos provinciales," *Boletín de la Asociación Nacional de Archiveros, Bibliotecarios, Arqueólogos y Documentalistas* 32.1–2 (1982): 27–41.

Skocpol, Theda, "Emerging Agendas and Recurrent Strategies in Historical Sociology," in Skocpol, ed., *Visions and Method in Historical Sociology* (Cambridge: Cambridge University Press, 1985), 356–339.

Skocpol, Theda, and Margaret Somers, "The Uses of Comparative History in Macrosocial Inquiry, *Comparative Studies in Society and History* 22.2 (1980): 174–197.

Socolow, Susan, "Women and Crime in Buenos Aires, 1757–1797," *Journal of Latin American Studies* 12.1 (1980): 39–54.

———, *The Women of Colonial Latin America* (Cambridge: Cambridge University Press, 2000).

Sosa Abella, Guillermo, *Labradores, tejedores y ladrones: Hurtos y homicidios en la provincia de Tunja, 1745–1810* (Bogotá: Instituto Colombiano de Cultura Hispánica, 1993).

Sousa, Lisa Mary, "Women and Crime in Colonial Oaxaca: Evidence of Complementarity in Mixtec and Zapotec Societies," in Schroeder et al., *Indian Women of Early Mexico*, 199–214.

Spierenburg, Pieter, "Facets of Violence: Homicide Trends and Cultural Meanings: Amsterdam, 1431–1816," *Journal of Social History* 27.4 (1994): 701–716.

———, *A History of Murder: Personal Violence in Europe from the Middle Ages to the Present* (Cambridge: Polity, 2008).

———, *The Spectacle of Suffering: Executions and the Evolution of Repression: From a Preindustrial Metropolis to the European Experience* (Cambridge: Cambridge University Press, 1984).

———, *Violence and Punishment: Civilizing the Body Through Time* (Cambridge: Polity, 2013).

———, *Written in Blood: Fatal Attraction in Enlightenment Amsterdam* (Columbus: Ohio State University Press, 2004).

Stavig, Ward, *Amor y violencia sexual: Valores indígenas en la sociedad conyugal* (Lima: Instituto de Estudios Peruanos, 1995).

Stern, Steve, *Peru's Indian Peoples and the Challenge of Spanish Conquest: Huamanga to 1640* (Madison: University of Wisconsin Press, 1993).

———, *The Secret History of Gender: Women, Men and Power in Late Colonial Mexico* (Chapel Hill: University of North Carolina Press, 1995).

Stone, Lawrence, *Road to Divorce: England 1530–1987* (Oxford: Oxford University Press, 1990).

Stroud, Mathew D., *Fatal Union: A Pluralistic Approach to the Spanish Wife-Murder Comedias* (Lewisburg: Bucknell University Press, 1990).

Sueiro, Daniel, *Los verdugos españoles: Historia y actualidad del garrote vil* (Madrid: Alfaguara, 1971).

Tau Anzoategui, Victor, *El poder de la costumbre: Estudios sobre el derecho consuetudinario en América hispana hasta la emancipación* (Buenos Aires: Instituto de Investigaciones de Historia del Derecho, 2001).

Tay, Alice Erh-Soon, and Eugene Kamenka, "Public Law-Private Law," in S. I. Benn and G. F. Gaus, *Public and Private in Social Life* (New York: St. Martin's, 1983), 67–92.

Taylor, Scott K., *Honor and Violence in Golden Age Spain* (New Haven: Yale University Press, 2008).

Taylor, William, "Amigos de sombrero: Patrones de homicidio en el centro rural de Jalisco, 1784–1820," in Antonio Escobar Ohmstede and Patricia Lagos Preisser, eds., *Indio, nación y comunidad en el México del siglo XIX* (México: Centro de Estudios Mexicanos y Centroamericanos, 1993), 63–103.

———, "Between Global Processes and Local Knowledge: An Inquiry into Early Latin American Social History, 1500–1900," in Oliver Zunz, ed., *Reliving the*

Past: The Worlds of Social History (Chapel Hill: University of North Carolina Press, 1985), 115–190.

———, "'. . . de corazón pequeño y animo apocado.' Conceptos de los curas párrocos sobre los Indios en la Nueva España del siglo XVIII," *Relaciones* 39 (Summer 1989): 5–67.

———, *Drinking, Homicide and Rebellion in Colonial Mexican Villages* (Stanford: Stanford University Press, 1979).

Terraciano, Kevin, "Crime and Culture in Colonial Mexico: The Case of the Mixtec Murder Note," *Ethnohistory* 45.4 (1998): 709–745.

Thomson, I. A. A., "A Map of Crime in Sixteenth-Century Spain," *Economic History Review* XXI (2nd series) (1968): 244–267.

Timbal-Duclaux de Martin, Pierre, *Le droit d'asile* (Paris: Librairie du Recueil Sirey, 1939).

Tomás y Valiente, Francisco, *El derecho penal de la monarquía absoluta (Siglos XVI, XVII y XVIII)* (Madrid: Editorial Técnos, 1992 [1969]).

———, "El perdón de la parte ofendida en el derecho penal castellano (siglos XVI, XVII y XVIII)," *Anuario de Historia del Derecho Español* 31 (1962): 55–114.

———, *La tortura en España: Estudios históricos* (Barcelona: Ariel, 1973).

———, *La tortura judicial en España* (Barcelona: Crítica, 2000).

Tomlins, Christopher, "How Autonomous Is Law," *Annual Review of Law and Society* 3 (2007): 45–68.

Tovar Pinzón, Hermes, *La batalla de los sentidos: Infidelidad, adulterio y concubinato a fines de la colonia* (Bogotá: Fondo Cultural Cafetero, 2004).

Torres Aguilar, Manuel, *El parricidio: Del pasado al presente de un delito* (Madrid: Editorial Revista de Derecho Privado, 1991).

Trenholme, Norman Maclaren, "The Right of Sanctuary in England. A Study in Institutional History," *University of Missouri Studies* 1.5 (1903): 1–106.

Trinidad Fernandez, Pedro, *La defensa de la sociedad: Carcel y delincuencia en España (Siglos XVIII–XX)* (Madrid: Alianza Editorial, 1991).

Twinam, Ann, "Drinking, Gambling and Death on a Colonial Hacienda," in Boyer and Spurling, eds., *Colonial Lives*, 185–200.

———, "Honor, Sexuality and Illegitimacy in Colonial Spanish America," in Asunción Lavrin, ed., *Sexuality and Marriage in Colonial Latin America* (Lincoln: University of Nebraska Press, 1989), 118–155.

———, *Miners, Merchants and Farmers in Colonial Colombia* (Austin: University of Texas Press, 1982).

———, *Private Lives and Public Secrets* (Stanford: Stanford University Press, 1999).

UNFPA, *State of World Population*, 2005.

UNICEF, "Domestic Violence Against Women and Girls," *Innocenti Digest* 6 (June 2000): 1–29.

Uribe-Uran, Victor M., "Abogados, independencia y muerte en la Nueva Granada, 1813–1819," in Pablo Rodríguez, ed., *Historia que no cesa: La independencia de Colombia, 1780–1830* (Bogotá: Universidad del Rosario, 2010), 133–148.

———, "The Birth of a Public Sphere in Latin America During the Age of Revolution," *Comparative Studies in Society and History* 42.2 (2000): 425–457.

———, "Cádiz contra las Provincias: Constitución, revolución y reacción en Nueva Granada, 1811–1821," *Boletín de Historia y Antigüedades* 97.849 (2010): 295–319.

———, "Colonial *Baracunatanas* and Their Nasty Men: Spousal Homicides and the Law in New Granada, 1750–1810," *Journal of Social History* 35.1 (2001): 43–72.

———, "La Constitución de Cádiz en la Nueva Granada, teoría y realidad, 1812–1821," in Heraclio Bonilla, ed., *La Constitución de 1812 en Hispanoamérica y España* (Bogotá: Editorial Universidad Nacional de Colombia-Alcaldia Mayor de Bogotá, 2012), 273–303.

———, "The Great Transformation of Law and Legal Culture: 'The Public' and 'The Private' in the Transition from Empire to Nation in Mexico, Colombia, and Brazil, 1750–1850," in Joseph W. Esherick, Hasan Kayali, and Eric Van Young, eds., *Empire to Nation: Historical Perspectives on the Making of the Modern World* (New York: Rowman and Littlefield, 2005), 68–105.

———, "'*Iglesia me llamo*': Church Asylum and the Law in Spain and Colonial Spanish America," *Comparative Studies in Society and History* 49.1 (2007): 446–472.

———, "Innocent Infants or Abusive Patriarchs? Spousal Homicides, the Punishment of Indians and the Law in Colonial Mexico, 1740s–1820s," *Journal of Latin American Studies* 38.4 (2006): 793–828.

———, "Physical Aggression Against Wives and the Law in Spanish America, 1780s–2000s," in Eric Johnson, Ricardo Salvatore, and Pieter Spierenburg, eds., *Murder and Violence in Modern Latin America* (London: Wiley-Blackwell, 2013).

———, "Preparando 'mandarines': Apuntes sobre la historia de la ciencia administrativa en Nueva Granada durante la colonia y comienzos de la república, 1590–1850," *Innovar: Revista de Ciencias Administrativas y Sociales* 7 (January–June 1996): 87–97.

———, ed., *State and Society in Spanish America During the Age of Revolution* (Wilmington: Scholarly Resources, 2000).

———, *Vidas honorables: Abogados, familia, sociedad y política en Colombia, 1780–1850* (Bogotá: Banco de la República-EAFIT, 2008).

Uribe-Uran, Victor, and Luis J. Ortiz, eds., *Naciones, gentes y territorios: Ensayos de historia e historiografía comparada de América Latina y el Caribe* (Medellín: Universidad de Antioquia, 2000).

U.S. Department of Justice, *Crime in the United States* (Washington, DC: Author, 1984).

Vainfas, Ronaldo, org., *História e sexualidade no Brasil* (Rio de Janeiro: Graal, 1986).

———, *Trópico dos pecados* (Rio de Janeiro: Campus, 1989).

Van Deusen, Nancy E., *Between the Sacred and the Worldly: The Institutional and Cultural Practice of Recogimiento in Colonial Lima* (Stanford: Stanford University Press, 2001).

Van Young, Eric, *Hacienda and Market in Eighteenth-Century Mexico: The Rural Economy of the Guadalajara Region, 1675–1820* (Berkeley: University of California Press, 1981).

———, *The Other Rebellion: Popular Violence, Ideology and the Mexican Struggle for Independence, 1810–1821* (Stanford: Stanford University Press, 2011).

Van Young, Eric, Joseph W. Esherick, and Hasan Kayali, eds., *Empire to Nation: Historical Perspectives on the Making of the Modern World* (New York: Rowman and Littlefield, 2005).

Varon Vallejo, Eudosio, and Angel González, "Introducción," in Archivo Histórico Nacional, *Consejo de Castilla. Sala de Alcaldes de Casa y Corte. Catálogo por Materias* (Madrid, 1925), xv–xx.

Vega Umbasia, Leonardo Alberto, *Pecado y delito en la Colonia: Bestialidad como una forma de contravención sexual (1740–1808)* (Bogotá: Instituto Colombiano de Cultura Hispánica, 1994).

Villa-Florez, Javier, *Dangerous Speech: A Social History of Blasphemy in Colonial Mexico* (Tucson: University of Arizona Press, 2006).

———, "'To Lose One's Soul': Blasphemy and Slavery in New Spain, 1596–1669," *Hispanic American Historical Review* 82.3 (2002): 435–468.

Villafuerte García, Lourdes, Teresa Lozano Armendares, Sergio Ortega Noriega, and Rocio Ortega Soto, "La sevicia y el adulterio en las causas matrimoniales en el provisorato de México a fines de la era colonial: Un estudio de la técnica procesal jurídica, " *Estudios de Historia Novohispana* 38 (2008): 87–161.

Villaverde Sastre, María Dolores, "La real fábrica de paños y la ciudad de Guadalajara," *Wad-aL-Hayara: Revista e Estudios de Guadalajara* 8 (1981): 453–468.

Viqueira, Alban Pedro, *Propriety and Permissiveness in Bourbon Mexico* (Wilmington: Scholarly Resources, 1999).

Von Germeten, Nicole, *Violent Delights, Violent Ends: Sex, Race, and Honor in Colonial Cartagena de Indias* (Albuquerque: University of New Mexico Press, 2013).

Von Hentig, Hans, *La pena: Formas primitivas y conexiones culturales* (Madrid: Espasa Calpe, 1967).

Voss, Harwing L., and John R. Hepburn, "Patterns in Criminal Homicide in Chicago," *Journal of Criminal Law and Criminology* 59.4 (1969): 499–508.

West, Elizabeth Howard, "The Right of Asylum in New Mexico in the Seventeenth and Eighteenth Centuries," *Hispanic American Historical Review* 8.3 (1928): 357–391.

Wolfgang, Marvin E., *Patterns of Criminal Homicide* (New York: Science Editions Paperback, 1966).

Yeatman, Anna, "Gender and the Differentiation of Social Life into Public and Domestic Domains," *Social Analysis* 15 (August 1984): 32–49.

Yount, Kathryn M., and Jennifer S. Carrera, "Domestic Violence Against Married Women in Cambodia," *Social Forces* 85.1 (2006): 355–387.

Zahler, Ruben, "Complaining Like a Liberal: Redefining Law, Justice, and Official Misconduct in Venezuela, 1790–1850," *Americas* 65.3 (2009): 351–374.

———, "Liberal Justice: Judicial Reform in Venezuela's Courts, 1786–1850," *Hispanic American Historical Review* 88.1 (2008): 489–522.

Zavala, Silvio, *Las instituciones jurídicas en la conquista de América* (México: Editorial Porrúa, 1988).

DOCTORAL DISSERTATIONS AND THESES

Aufderheide, Patricia Ann, "Order and Violence: Social Deviance and Social Control in Brazil, 1780–1840," University of Minnesota, 1976.

Bird, Jonathan, "For Better or Worse: Divorce and Annulment Lawsuits in Colonial Mexico (1544–1799)," Department of History, Duke University, 2013.

Dávila Mendoza, Dora Teresa, "Hasta que la muerte nos separe (el divorcio eclesiástico en el arzobispado de México, 1702–1800)," Department of History, Colegio de México, 1998.

Hatton, Edward, "Domestic Assassins: Spousal and Intimate Homicide in Antebellum America," Temple University, 1997.

Honores, Renzo, "A Legalistic Society: Lawyers, Procurators, and the Making of a Colonial Legal Culture in Lima and Potosi, 1550–1670," Florida International University, 2007.

Kagan, Samuel, "Penal Servitude in New Spain: The Colonial Textile Industry," City University of New York, 1976.

Kanter, Deborah E., "*Hijos del pueblo:* Family, Community, and Gender in Rural Mexico. The Toluca Valley Region, 1730–1830," University of Virginia, 1993.

Luna Rivillas, Gloria, "Documentos para el estudio de la criminalidad sexual en la provincia y gobernación de Antioquia (Siglos 17 y 18)," Universidad Nacional de Colombia, Medellín, 1988. B.A. thesis.

Marin Tello, Isabel, "Justicia penal y orden social en Michoacán en el siglo XVIII," Universidad de Sevilla, 2003.

Scardaville, Michael C., "Crime and the Urban Poor: Mexico City in the Late Colonial Period," University of Florida, 1977.

Zahler, Ruben, "Honor, Corruption and Legitimacy: Liberal Projects in the Early Venezuelan Republic, 1821–1850," University of Chicago, 2005.

Index

MIX
Papier | Fördert gute Waldnutzung
FSC® C083411

Kolibri 360 GmbH
Ferdinand-Jühlke-Straße 7
99095 Erfurt, Deutschland
produktsicherheit@kolibri360.de